Differentiating the Financial Statements

Fundamental Accounting Principles uses a colour scheme to help students differentiate between the four key financial statements.

Finlay Interiors
Income Statement
For Month Ended January 31, 2011

⟵ Income Statement

Revenues:		
Consulting revenue	$ 3,800	
Rental revenue	300	
Total revenues		$ 4,100
Operating expenses:		
Rent expense	$ 1,000	
Salaries expense		
Total operating expenses		
Net income		

Statement of Owner's Equity

Finlay Interiors
Statement of Owner's Equity
For Month Ended January 31, 2011

Carol Finlay, capital, January 1		$ -0-
Add: Investments by owner	$10,000	
Net income	2,400	12,400
Total		$12,400
		600
		$11,800

Finlay Interiors
Balance Sheet
January 31, 2011

Asset		Liabilities	
Cash	$ 8,400	Accounts payable	$ 200
Supplies	3,600	Notes payable	6,000
Furniture	6,000	Total liabilities	$ 6,200
		Owner's Equity	
		Carol Finlay, capital	11,800
		Total liabilities and	
Total assets	$18,00(		

⟵ Balance Sheet

Finlay Interiors
Cash Flow Statement
For Month Ended January 31, 2011

Cash Flow Statement ⟶

Cash flows from operating activities		
Cash received from clients	$ 4,100	
Cash paid for supplies	(3,400)	
Cash paid for rent	(1,000)	
Cash paid to employee	(700)	
Net cash used by operating activities		$ (1,000)
Cash flows from investing activities		-0-
Cash flows from financing activities		
Investment by owner	$10,000	
Withdrawal by owner	(600)	
Net cash provided by financing activities		9,400
Net increase in cash		$ 8,400
Cash balance, January 1		-0-
Cash balance, January 31		$ 8,400

VOLUME

②

Fundamental Accounting Principles

TWELFTH CANADIAN EDITION

Kermit D. Larson
University of Texas – Austin

Tilly Jensen
Northern Alberta Institute of Technology

McGraw-Hill Ryerson

Toronto   Montréal   Boston   Burr Ridge, IL   Dubuque, IA   Madison, WI
New York   San Francisco   St. Louis   Bangkok   Bogotá   Caracas
Kuala Lumpur   Lisbon   London   Madrid   Mexico City   Milan
New Delhi   Seoul   Singapore   Sydney   Taipei

Fundamental Accounting Principles
Volume 2
Twelfth Canadian Edition

ISBN-13: 978-0-07-095171-6
ISBN-10: 0-07-095171-3

1 2 3 4 5 6 7 8 9 10   TCP   0 9 8 7

Printed and bound in Canada

Care has been taken to trace ownership of copyright material contained in this text; however, the publisher will welcome any information that enables them to rectify any reference or credit for subsequent editions.

Editorial Director: Joanna Cotton
Publisher: Nicole Lukach
Sponsoring Editor: Rhondda McNabb
Marketing Manager: Joy Armitage Taylor
Senior Developmental Editor: Suzanne Simpson Millar
Developmental Editor: Marcia Luke
Senior Editorial Associate: Christine Lomas
Senior Supervising Editor: Margaret Henderson
Copy Editor: Laurel Sparrow
Senior Production Coordinator: Andrée Davis
Cover Design: Liz Harasymczuk Design
Cover Image: © David Cutler/images.com—The Stock Illustration Source
Interior Design: Liz Harasymczuk Design
Page Layout: Bookman Typesetting Company
Printer: Transcontinental Interglobe Printing

Library and Archives Canada Cataloguing in Publication

Larson, Kermit D.
    Fundamental accounting principles / Kermit D. Larson, Tilly Jensen. — 12th Canadian ed.

Vol. 3 has authors: Kermit D. Larson, Suresh Kalagnanam.
Includes bibliographical references and index.
ISBN-13: 978-0-07-095171-6 (v. 1)
ISBN-13: 978-0-07-095172-3 (v. 2)
ISBN-13: 978-0-07-095173-0 (v. 3)
ISBN-10: 0-07-095171-3 (v. 1)
ISBN-10: 0-07-095172-1 (v. 2)
ISBN-10: 0-07-095173-X (v. 3)

    1. Accounting—Textbooks.   I. Jensen, Tilly   II. Kalagnanam, Suresh Subbarao   III. Title.

HF5635.L343 2007   657   C2006-904838-X

About the Authors

Kermit D. Larson, University of Texas – Austin

Kermit D. Larson is the Arthur Andersen & Co. Alumni Professor of Accounting Emeritus at the University of Texas at Austin. He served as chairman of the University of Texas, Department of Accounting and was visiting associate professor at Tulane University. His scholarly articles have been published in a variety of journals, including *The Accounting Review*, *Journal of Accountancy*, and *Abacus*. He is the author of several books, including *Financial Accounting* and *Fundamentals of Financial and Managerial Accounting*, both published by Irwin/McGraw-Hill.

Professor Larson is a member of the American Accounting Association, the Texas Society of CPAs, and the American Institute of CPAs. His positions with the AAA have included vice-president, southwest regional service president, and chairperson of several committees, including the Committee of Concepts and Standards. He was a member of the committee that planned the first AAA doctoral consortium and served as its director.

Tilly Jensen, Northern Alberta Institute of Technology

Tilly Jensen graduated from the University of Alberta with a Bachelor of Commerce degree and later attained the designation of Certified Management Accountant. She worked in private industry for a number of years before making teaching her full-time career. Tilly is an accounting instructor at the Northern Alberta Institute of Technology (NAIT) in Edmonton, Alberta. In addition, Tilly is an academic coordinator with Athabasca University, Canada's open, online university. She obtained her M.Ed. at the University of Sheffield in Britain while travelling abroad and is currently engaged in doctoral studies at the University of Calgary (via distance) focusing on how educational technologies can be used to enhance critical thinking. Tilly spent four years in the Middle East teaching at Dubai Men's College of the Higher Colleges of Technology in the United Arab Emirates. While overseas, she also taught financial accounting to students enrolled in the Chartered Institute of Management Accountants (CIMA) program, a British professional accounting designation. During her recent sabbatical, Tilly taught accounting in China to ESL students at Shenyang Ligong University. She authored LIFA—Lyryx Interactive Financial Accounting—a dynamic, leading-edge, Web-based teaching and learning tool produced by Lyryx. Tilly has also authored material for CGA-Canada. In addition to her professional interests, Tilly places a priority on time spent with her family and friends.

Brief Contents

Contents

To the Instructors—Facilitators of Student Success

As instructors, you and I know that the responsibility for student success lies ultimately with the student. Our role is to create an environment that fosters learning: we can present and demonstrate concepts in a variety of ways and then help students apply those concepts to new situations; we can be there (face-to-face or online) to respond to their questions with questions that help them find the answer; and we can direct students to a variety of tools to enhance their success. To help with our role, we need quality tools to facilitate student success both in and out of the classroom. *Fundamental Accounting Principles* is still the core tool to achieve that end, and the Twelfth Canadian Edition—in response to instructor requests—has made three major changes that explicitly focus on students and their success.

First, the **Student Success *Cycle*—Read–Do–Check–Apply**—has been incorporated throughout the textbook. It is denoted by the symbol shown at left, and reminds students that to achieve success, they must **read** the textbook, **do** the exercises and problems to practise concepts, **check** their work (taking appropriate remedial action), and **apply** knowledge to demonstrate learning in contrast to memorization.

Second, the **Student Success *Cycle*** is linked to the new online **Student Success Centre** at www.mcgrawhill.ca/studentsuccess/FAP, where a detailed learning guide is provided to help students master introductory accounting concepts. Student success at the post-secondary level is not measured by how much knowledge a student has acquired but rather by how well a student can ***use*** or ***apply*** knowledge . . . a concept also known as critical thinking! If students compartmentalize knowledge, they are challenged when they have to engage in the activities of application, analysis, synthesis, or evaluation—the higher-level competencies. We can help students develop higher-level skills by introducing them to a model for critical thinking. Instructors typically give students formulas to perform calculations such as amortization and interest; why not provide them with a formula for thinking as well?!

And that leads to the third innovation: on the inside cover of this textbook is an outline of a basic model for teaching/learning critical thinking skills. To foster the development of critical thinking proficiency, analysis-type questions have been added to many exercises and problems in the Twelfth Canadian Edition. In addition, a new problem series—Critical Thinking Mini Cases—has been introduced.

Education is a continuous journey and by giving students a model and tools for both successful learning and critical thinking, the Twelfth Canadian Edition of *Fundamental Accounting Principles* is, once again, the standard-setter in the study of accounting. However, it is only because of the contributions of dedicated accounting instructors across Canada that this textbook is able to continually improve. I am truly privileged to have had the opportunity to work with so many of you in this regard; you have my sincerest appreciation. I would also like to thank and acknowledge Phil Paradis of NAIT, who planted the seed for a student success and critical thinking focus.

Take care,

Tilly Jensen

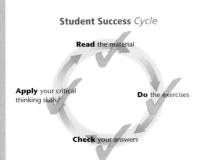

Student Success *Cycle*

Read the material

Apply your critical thinking skills

Do the exercises

Check your answers

To the Students—A Guide For Your Success

Your primary goal in this course should be to learn the basics about financial accounting in order to understand and use financial statements and related information effectively in decision making. These skills are essential, whether you are going to be a business owner, a marketing specialist, or a financial planner, or occupy some other business role.

Student success means different things to many different people. For the purpose of this accounting course, we will define a successful student as having two qualities:

1. Active in the learning process, and
2. Able to apply critical thinking skills.

To learn anything, you must acquire knowledge. For example, I can learn about playing golf by reading a book. But once I finish the book, will I be able to play golf? It is very unlikely. I will need to practise. After a couple of hours spent swinging a golf club at a driving range and realizing that my progress is limited, I might do some more reading, get some instruction, watch a video, and keep on practising. I will continue to apply my growing knowledge of golf, and over time I will begin to improve.

To learn accounting, you would follow the same process. Begin by reading this textbook. Will you understand accounting after simply reading? It is very unlikely. You will need to practise the concepts by doing the exercises and problems. Then, check your work. Are you on track? If not, do some more reading, get some instruction, use another tool to help you learn the material, but above all, be sure you master the material and apply your knowledge before continuing to new concepts.

The process just described—**read** the material, **do** the exercises, **check** your answers, and **apply** your critical thinking skills—can be summarized as: **Read–Do–Check–Apply**, or the **Student Success *Cycle***. You will see this symbol—the circular icon shown at right—throughout the textbook; it is a reminder to check your progress and to go to the online **Student Success Centre** at www.mcgrawhill.ca/studentsuccess/FAP for additional study tools.

Once you have acquired knowledge in a specific area and mastered it through practice, you are ready for the next step of the learning process: critical thinking. Critical thinking involves the higher-level competencies of application, analysis, synthesis, and evaluation. To make business decisions, you need to ***use*** the knowledge acquired in many subject areas (including accounting, economics, statistics, and so on): critical thinking is the application of knowledge across topics and across disciplines. The inside front cover provides a model to help you improve your critical thinking skill development so that once you ***acquire*** knowledge, you are able to ***apply*** it using analysis, synthesis, and/or evaluation.

This textbook was designed to help you learn efficiently and effectively. If you follow the **Student Success *Cycle*** and use it in conjunction with other tools available on the online **Student Success Centre**, you will be successful in learning accounting.

Good luck with your studies,

Tilly Jensen

Tilly Jensen

Inside the Chapters

As educators, instructors strive to create an environment that fosters learning and to provide students with the tools they need to succeed. The Eleventh Canadian Edition upheld the high standards the market expects from *Fundamental Accounting Principles*. With this Twelfth Canadian Edition we have introduced innovative student-centred pedagogy and incorporated a higher-level competency—critical thinking skills—throughout the text.

All the pedagogical tools are carefully designed for ease of use and understanding, helping the instructor teach and giving the students what they need to succeed.

New Student-Centred Pedagogy

Student Success *Cycle*

Read the material

Do the exercises

Check your answers

Apply your critical thinking skills

Student Success *Cycle*

Student success at the post-secondary level is not measured by how much knowledge a student has acquired, but rather by how well a student can *use* knowledge. The Student Success Cycle, illustrated by a circular icon (shown at left), reinforces decision-making skills by highlighting key steps toward understanding and critically evaluating the information the student has just read. **Read, Do, Check, Apply**—this reinforces active learning (as opposed to passive learning). Displayed on each chapter-opening page (as well as with Checkpoint questions, Demonstration Problems, and end-of-chapter material), the Student Success Cycle is also linked to the Student Success Centre (www.mcgrawhill.ca/studentsuccess/FAP) (See page xxiv for more information).

Critical Thinking Challenge

An essential element of critical thinking is the ability to ask questions while reading (or listening or speaking). These exercises are designed to help students develop the skills related to questioning. Suggested answers are posted on the online Student Success Centre.

CHAPTER 2

Financial Statements and Accounting Transactions

Fiction Drives the Bottom Line!

In the electronic entertainment world, BioWare has attracted a lot of attention. BioWare Corp. is a Canadian company well-known throughout the world for its development of market-leading role-playing games like Baldur's Gate, Neverwinter Nights, Star Wars: Knights of the Old Republic, and Jade Empire.

BioWare has also attracted a lot of attention in the business world by recording outstanding revenue growth in an industry plagued by unique challenges and fierce competition—with an increase in revenue of more than 988% since 1997. That information comes from financial statements that report on the realities of BioWare's operations.

Joint CEOs Greg Zeschuk and Ray Muzyka learned in BioWare's early years how important it was to understand financial statements: banks and financial institutions require strong balance sheets to justify providing capital for growth; income statements provide a mechanism for tracking performance over time; and financial projections of both income statements and balance sheets provide a blueprint for future planning. Greg and Ray also use financial statements as a factor in assessing potential business partners for development and publishing opportunities. Obtaining additional business training enhanced Ray and Greg's appreciation for the subtleties of accounting and financial projections critical to BioWare's success.

Student Success *Cycle*

Read the material

Do the exercises

Check your answers

Apply your critical thinking skills

CRITICAL THINKING CHALLENGE

If BioWare were obtaining a bank loan, what kind of financial information might the bank be interested in? If BioWare were successful in obtaining a loan from the bank, should this transaction be shown on BioWare's financial statements or as part of the owners' personal financial statements?

Checkpoint

Previously called Flashback, this series of questions within the chapter reinforces the immediately preceding material. These questions allow the student to "Do" problem material referencing what they have just learned, and answers at the end of each chapter will then allow them to "Check" their work. Additional Quick Study questions (available at the end of each chapter) are identified for the student to "Do," with answers available online to "Check."

---

1. What are the four major financial statements?
2. Describe revenues and expenses.
3. Explain assets, liabilities and equity.
4. What are three differences in financial statements for different forms of organization?

Do: QS 2-1

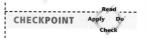

CHECKPOINT

Analysis Component

An analysis component has been added to each mid- and end-of-chapter demonstration problem, taking students beyond the numbers and promoting critical thinking. Several exercises, problems, and Focus on Financial Statements questions also include an analysis component to provide opportunities for students to practise these skills.

Retained Student-Centred Pedagogy

Real-World Focus

Like previous editions, the Twelfth Canadian Edition includes strong ties to the real world of accounting, be it through detailed interviews with businesspeople for the chapter-opening vignettes, examples of ethical standards and treatments, or annual reports for end-of-chapter material. This integration with real-world companies helps engage students while they read.

Learning Objectives

Learning Objectives have long been a standard in the Larson textbook. By giving students a head start on what the following material encompasses, the text readies them for the work ahead. These Learning Objectives are fully integrated into the online Student Success Centre, allowing the students to actively focus on one objective at a time.

Did You Know?

Social responsibility continues to be important for students to learn early in their accounting courses. Through the Did You Know? feature, accounting's role in ethics and social responsibility is described by both reporting and assessing its impact. Relating theory to a real-life situation piques interest and reinforces active learning.

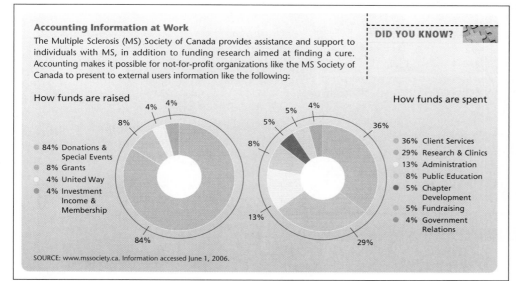

Accounting Information at Work

DID YOU KNOW?

The Multiple Sclerosis (MS) Society of Canada provides assistance and support to individuals with MS, in addition to funding research aimed at finding a cure. Accounting makes it possible for not-for-profit organizations like the MS Society of Canada to present to external users information like the following:

How funds are raised

- 84% Donations & Special Events
- 8% Grants
- 4% United Way
- 4% Investment Income & Membership

How funds are spent

- 36% Client Services
- 29% Research & Clinics
- 13% Administration
- 8% Public Education
- 5% Chapter Development
- 5% Fundraising
- 4% Government Relations

SOURCE: www.mssociety.ca. Information accessed June 1, 2006.

THE LARSON ADVANTAGE

Judgement Call

This feature requires students to make accounting and business decisions by using role-playing to show the interaction of judgement, awareness, and the impact of decisions made. Guidance answers are available at the end of each chapter.

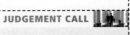

JUDGEMENT CALL

Answer—p. 17

Entrepreneur
You and a friend have developed a new design for mountain bikes that improves speed and performance by a remarkable 25% to 40%. You are planning to form a small business to manufacture and market these bikes. You and your friend are concerned about potential lawsuits from individuals who may become injured because of using the speed feature of the bikes with reckless abandon. What form of organization do you set up?

Extend Your Knowledge

Supplementary material has been developed to explore some topics in more detail than the textbook can allow. When available, the Student Success Centre icon is displayed in the margin, alerting students to visit www.mcgrawhill.ca/studentsuccess/FAP if they choose to delve deeper into the material.

Extend Your Knowledge

SSC

2-4

Cost Principle

All transactions are recorded based on the actual cash amount received or paid. In the absence of cash, the cash equivalent amount of the exchange is recorded.[5]
  Example: If Finlay Interiors purchased used furniture for $5,000 cash, it is recorded in the accounting records at $5,000. It makes no difference if Carol Finlay thinks that the value of the furniture is $7,000.

Annual Reports

Features and assignments that highlight companies such as WestJet (a company that provides services) and Danier (a merchandiser) show accounting in a modern and global context. As students go directly to the financial statements of real companies, they remain engaged in the active learning process. Portions of these annual reports are reproduced at the end of both Volumes 1 and 2.

End-of-Chapter Material

Fundamental Accounting Principles sets the standard for quantity and quality of end-of-chapter material.

Summary

LO1 | **Identify and explain the content and reporting aims of financial statements.** The major financial statements are: income statement (shows a company's profitability determined as revenues less expenses equals net income or loss), statement of owner's equity (explains how owner's equity changes from the beginning to the end of a period), balance sheet (reports on a company's financial position, including assets, liabilities, and owner's equity), and cash flow statement (identifying all cash inflows and outflows for the period). The differences in financial statements across forms of business organization are: 1. The name of the equity section of the balance sheet: owner's equity for a sole proprietorship, partners' equity for a partnership, and shareholders' equity for a corporation; 2. Distributions of assets to the owner(s) are called

continues to operate. The monetary unit principle assumes that transactions can be captured in money terms and that the monetary unit is stable over time. The revenue recognition principle means that revenue is recognized when earned, assets received from selling products and services do not have to be in cash, and revenue recognized is measured by cash received plus the cash equivalent (market) value of other assets received.

LO3 | **Explain and interpret the accounting equation.** Investing activities are funded by an organization's financing activities. An organization's assets (investments) must equal its financing (from liabilities and from equity). This basic relation gives us the accounting equation: Assets = Liabilities + Owner's Equity.

---

guidance answer to **JUDGEMENT CALL**

Supplier

We can use the balance sheet, or accounting equation, to help us identify risky customers to whom we would not want to extend credit. The accounting equation can be written as: Assets − Liabilities = Owner's Equity. A balance sheet provides us with amounts for each of these

key components. The lower the owner's equity, the less likely you should be to extend credit. A low owner's equity means that there is little value in the business on which other creditors do not already have claims. Note that any decision to grant credit would normally include an examination of the complete financial statements.

---

guidance answers to **CHECKPOINT** Read / Apply / Do / Check

1. The four major financial statements are: income statement, statement of owner's equity, balance sheet, and cash flow statement.

2. Revenues are the value of assets received in exchange for products or services provided to customers as part of a business's main operations. Expenses are costs incurred or the using up of assets that result from providing products or services to customers. Expenses also can arise from increases in liabilities.

case, the business has received the cash from the customer without providing the product. Therefore, the business has not realized a revenue but instead has incurred a liability; it owes the customer the product.

8. A transaction that involves changing the form of one asset for another asset would *not* affect any liability and equity accounts. (2) offers an example.

Glossary

Accounting equation A description of the relationship between a company's assets, liabilities, and equity; expressed as Assets = Liabilities + Owner's Equity; also called the *balance sheet equation.* (p. 33)

Account payable A liability created by buying goods or services on credit. (p. 29)

Account receivable An asset created by selling products or services on credit. (p. 29)

Assets Properties or economic resources owned by the business; more precisely, resources with an ability to provide future benefits to the business. (p. 29)

Economic consideration Something of value (e.g., products, services, money, and rights to collect money). (p. 34)

Equity The owner's claim on the assets of a business; more precisely, the assets of an entity that remain after deducting its liabilities; also called *net assets.* (p. 30)

Expenses Costs incurred or the using up of assets as a result of the major or central operations of a business. (p. 27)

Event See *business events.* (p. 34)

Financial statements The most important products of accounting; include the income statement, statement of owner's equity, balance sheet, and cash flow statement.

Problem Material

Demonstration Problems

These problems reinforce the chapter material and further bolster the Student Success Cycle.

demonstration problem

Read · Apply · Do · Check

Rupert Jones works in a public accounting firm. The management of ShadowTech Company invites Jones to prepare a 'bid' to review ShadowTech's financial statements. In discussing the review's fee, ShadowTech's management suggests a fee range where the fee amount depends on the reported profit of ShadowTech. The higher its profit, the higher the review fee paid to Jones's firm.

Required

1. Identify the parties potentially affected by this situation.
2. What are the ethical factors in this situation?
3. Would you recommend that Jones accept this review fee arrangement? Why?
4. Describe some of the factors guiding your recommendation.

Questions

These short-answer questions reinforce the chapter content by Learning Objective.

Questions

1. What tasks are performed with the work sheet?
2. Why are the debit and credit entries in the Adjustments columns of the work sheet identified with letters?
3. What two purposes are accomplished by recording closing entries?
10. What is a company's operating cycle?
11. How is an unearned revenue classified on the balance sheet?
12. What classes of assets and liabilities are shown on a typical classified balance sheet?

Quick Study

These single-topic exercises give the students a quick test of each key element in the chapter and are referenced to Learning Objectives. Answers to these items are available on the online Student Success Centre.

Quick Study

In preparing a work sheet, indicate the financial statement debit column to which a normal balance of each of the following accounts should be extended. Use *IS* for the Income Statement Debit column and *BS* for the Balance Sheet or Statement of Owner's Equity Debit column.

1. Equipment
2. Owner, withdrawals
3. Insurance expense
4. Prepaid insurance
5. Accounts receivable
6. Amortization expense, equipment

QS 5-1
Applying a work sheet
LO¹

Exercises

Exercises provide students with an additional opportunity to reinforce basic chapter concepts by Learning Objective.

Exercises

These accounts are from the Adjusted Trial Balance columns in a company's 10-column work sheet. In the blank space beside each account, write the letter of the appropriate financial statement column to which a normal account balance should be extended.
a. Debit column for the income statement.
b. Credit column for the income statement.
c. Debit column for the balance sheet and statement of owner's equity.
d. Credit column for the balance sheet and statement of owner's equity.

_____ 1. Roberta Jefferson, withdrawals
_____ 2. Interest earned
_____ 3. Accumulated amortization, machinery
_____ 9. Cash
_____ 10. Office supplies
_____ 11. Roberta Jefferson, capital

Exercise 5-1
Extending adjusted account balances on a work sheet
LO¹

Problems

Problems typically incorporate two or more concepts. As well, there are two groups of problems: A problems and Alternate or B problems. B problems mirror the A problems to help improve understanding through repetition.

Problems

The Stilton Company has the following inventory and credit purchases during the fiscal year ended December 31, 2011.

Beginning	500 units	@	$90/unit
Feb. 10	250 units	@	$84/unit
Aug. 21	130 units	@	$100/unit

Problem 7-1A
Alternative cost flows—perpetual
LO²

Ethics Challenge

You are a cashier at a retail convenience store. When you were hired, the owner explained to you the policy of immediately ringing up each sale. Recently, lunch hour traffic has increased dramatically and the manager asks you to take customers' cash and make change without ringing up sales to avoid delays. The manager says she will add up cash and ring up sales equal to the cash amount after lunch. She says that in this way the register will always be accurate when the owner arrives at 3:00 p.m.

EC 3-1

Required
1. Identify the advantages and disadvantages of the manager's suggestion.
2. Identify the ethical dilemma and evaluate at least two courses of action you might consider and why.

Ethics Challenge

Each chapter includes at least one Ethics Challenge to reinforce critical thinking skills for the students and open up discussion about various ethical topics.

Focus on Financial Statements

Travis McAllister operates a surveying company. For the first few months of the company's life (through April), the accounting records were maintained by an outside bookkeeping service. According to those records, McAllister's owner's equity balance was $75,000 as of April 30. To save on expenses, McAllister decided to keep the records himself. He managed to record May's transactions properly, but was a bit rusty when the time came to prepare the financial statements. His first versions of the balance sheet and income statement follow. McAllister is bothered that the company apparently operated at a loss during the month, even though he was very busy.

FFS 3-1

Focus on Financial Statements

Each chapter includes a technical and analytical question that incorporates into the financial statements all major topics covered up to that point. New to the Twelfth Canadian Edition are additional Focus on Financial Statements questions, available online at the Student Success Centre.

Critical Thinking Mini Case

You have worked with XYZ Contractors as the marketing manager for a number of years. Each of your salespeople must submit a monthly report detailing money they spent while conducting business on behalf of XYZ Contractors. Each item on the monthly report must be coded as to the effect on assets, liabilities, and equity. As marketing manager, one of your duties is to review the monthly reports. One salesperson's report for September shows the following:

Date	Description of Transaction	Amount of Transaction	Effect on Assets	Effect on Liabilities	Effect on Equity
Aug. 28	Sold 80 units of product to a customer for cash	$150,000	Increased Cash	No effect	Increased Revenues
Sept. 10	Purchased new desk for office to be paid in October	$1,500	No effect	Increased Accounts Payable	Increased Office Expense
Sept. 2–30	Took clients for lunch and paid cash	$680	Decreased Cash		Increased Owner Investments
Oct. 5	Paid for September cell phone usage	$130	Decreased Cash		Increased Expenses

Required
Using the elements of critical thinking described on the inside front cover, respond.

Critical Thinking Mini Cases

New to the Twelfth Canadian Edition, the Mini Cases give students the opportunity to apply critical thinking skills to concepts learned in the chapter, thus further reinforcing the "Apply" step of the Student Success Cycle.

END-OF-CHAPTER MATERIAL

The Accounting Standard

We listened! In addition to obtaining individual reviewer comments, we held focus groups in cities throughout Canada to hear the issues and concerns instructors like you have about the materials you use to teach introductory financial accounting. We were the first textbook to go to these lengths for market research, and we do more every year. We think you'll like what you see.

Throughout the Text

Preface

– Added the Critical Thinking Model and the Student Success Cycle to the Preface

Chapters Overall

– Edited and updated the chapters in general
– Added Critical Thinking Challenge questions, a new feature following the opening vignette, to help students learn to ask/answer questions while reading, speaking, or listening
– Renamed the Flashback feature as Checkpoint to correspond to the Student Success Cycle emphasis and critical thinking initiative
– Added an Analysis Component to the Demonstration Problem and Mid-Chapter Demonstration Problem

End-of-Chapter

– Linked the Quick Study questions to the Checkpoints within the body of the chapter, and provided solutions online to encourage students to "Do" and "Check" while they "Read"
– Added a new Critical Thinking Mini Case to each chapter
– Added an index of the Extend Your Knowledge items to the back of the textbook
– Deleted the Leon's annual report from the end of the textbook and replaced it with that of Danier Leather, a different merchandiser

Chapter 12

– Added new Quick Study questions/Exercises
– Regarding amortization of intangible assets, changed credit to 'Accumulated Amortization, Intangible' versus 'Intangible' to agree to *Handbook* change
– Regarding exchange of capital assets, deleted appendix as it is no longer required given *Handbook* changes; updated discussion of exchanges within chapter to reflect changes in the *Handbook* effective January 2006

Chapter 13

– Added new Quick Study questions/Exercises
– Added Extend Your Knowledge 13-2 – Examples, by region, of journal entries including PST/GST (Duplicate of Extend Your Knowledge 6-1)

Chapter 14

– Added new Quick Study questions/Exercises
– Provided a new Mid-Chapter Demonstration Problem

Chapter 15

– Expanded the illustration of the closing entries for a corporation in the textbook and added a more detailed description/illustration online as Extend Your Knowledge 15.2
– Added new Quick Study questions/Exercises

Chapter 16

– Added new Quick Study questions/Exercises
– Based on reviewer requests, reordered Learning Objectives and split former Learning Objective 2 into two Learning Objectives

Chapter 17

– Moved retirement of bonds to before the Mid-Chapter Demonstration Problem per reviewer request
– Added new Quick Study questions/Exercises
– Created two new Extend Your Knowledge items based on reviewer requests

Chapter 18

– Created new Mid-Chapter Demonstration Problem and Demonstration Problem to correspond to changes in the *CICA Handbook*
– Made major revisions to the chapter to correspond to changes in the *CICA Handbook*
– Learning Objective 5 in the textbook briefly describes accounting and reporting available-for-sale investments,

which is expanded upon on the Web site as Extend Your Knowledge 18-1 for those wishing the details. Because of OCI issues, this topic was determined to be far beyond the intro level and therefore inappropriate to include within the textbook
- Added new Quick Study questions/Exercises
- Moved former Appendix 18A – Consolidations to the Web site as Extend Your Knowledge 18-2
- Moved former LO8 – Foreign Exchange Transactions to the appendix

Chapter 19
- Added new Quick Study questions/Exercises
- Moved the indirect method from the appendix to the chapter and the direct method from the chapter to the appendix

- Created new Mid-Chapter Demonstration Problem and end-of-chapter Demonstration Problem for indirect method, including analysis component to both
- The direct method is in the appendix but includes a demonstration problem with analysis component
- Reformatted appendix questions so that they immediately follow the question being referred to
- Combined former LO4 and 5 into Learning Objective 4
- New Extend Your Knowledge – Using T-accounts to prepare a cash flow statement per reviewer request

Chapter 20
- Added new Quick Study questions/Exercises
- Added Accounts Payable Turnover Ratio to ratios

Technology Solutions to Help You Succeed

Fundamental Accounting Principles offers a wealth of resources unmatched in educational publishing

Student Success Centre   www.mcgrawhill.ca/studentsuccess/FAP

Reinforcing its commitment to student success, the Larson/Jensen Online Learning Centre has been completely redesigned and redeveloped with the student in mind.

Complementing the pedagogy of the text, the Student Success Cycle is now fully integrated into this online resource. Students can review each Learning Objective and following the steps of the Student Success Cycle, work through self-study quizzes and critical thinking exercises for each learning outcome. Or, they can start at the chapter level and, if challenged by a particular concept while completing the quizzes, focus on this specific Learning Objective using the Student Success Cycle as a guide.

The Centre continues to offer self-study quizzes, a searchable glossary, crossword puzzles to practise key terms for each chapter, Excel Templates for select problems in the text, and additional resources including "Extend Your Knowledge" modules and video segments.

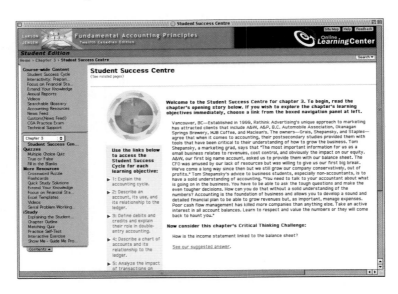

Studying on the Go

Students can study on the go with McGraw-Hill's course content for the Apple iPod.

Our innovative approach allows students to download audio and video presentations directly into their iPod and take learning materials with them wherever they go. Whether it's in the car, on the train, or waiting between classes—it's easy to get a quick refresher on key course content and makes review and study time as easy as putting on headphones!

Visit the Student Success Centre to download these resources.

Online Assessment

Lyryx Interactive Financial Accounting (LIFA) is a Web-based assessment tool that has captured the attention of post-secondary schools across the country. By reflecting the classroom environment, LIFA significantly benefits both instructors and students.

Each chapter is broken down into several **Lessons**, condensed versions of the material in the text.

Each Lesson is supported by a self-correcting **Exploration** that allows the students to practise the Lesson's concept. Because these Explorations are algorithmically generated, the students can try them as often as they want and get a different question each time.

Once the students master the Exploration, the instructor can set up a homework assignment, or **Lab**. These Labs are algorithmically generated and automatically graded, so students get instant feedback. Grades are instantly recorded into a Gradebook that the students and the instructor can view. Less of the instructor's time is spent on marking, *and* students get built-in feedback!

LIFA motivates students in two ways: (1) it is tied to assessment, and (2) Labs can be tried as many times as the students wish, with only the best grade being recorded. Instructors know that if students are doing their accounting homework, they will enjoy success. Recent research has shown that when Labs are tied to assessment, even if they are worth only a small percentage of the total grade for the course, students WILL do their homework—*and more than once!*

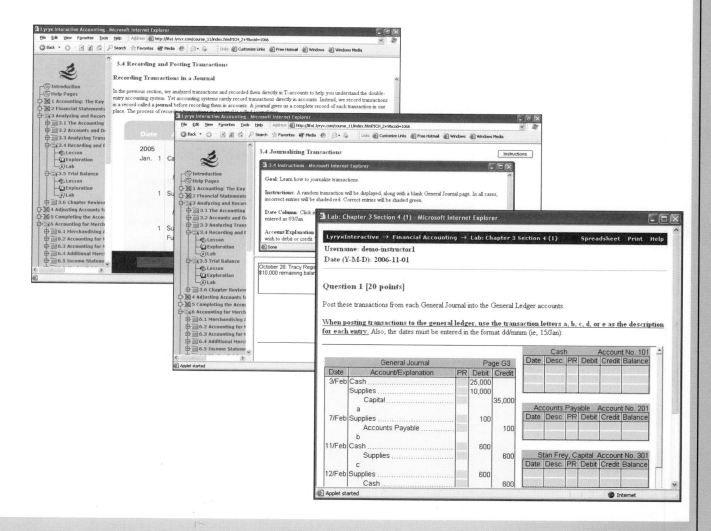

Supplements for the Students

*i*Study

[*i*study]

*i*Interact *i*Learn *i*Succeed

Available 24/7: providing instant feedback when you want, how you want, and where you want. This online *i*Study space was developed to help you master concepts and achieve better grades with all the learning tools you've come to expect, including chapter summaries, quiz questions, and additional problems. *i*Study also offers new "Show Me, Guide Me" tutorial problems, numerous animations, and even an interactive, fun game called *TetrAccounting*. *i*Study offers the best, most convenient way to interact, learn, and succeed.

   *i*Study can be purchased through the online Student Success Centre or by purchasing a PIN code card through the campus bookstore. Instructors: Please contact your *i*Learning Sales Specialist for more information on how to make *i*Study part of your student's success.

Working Papers

Available for purchase by students, Working Papers for Volumes 1 and 2 match the end-of-chapter assignment material. They include papers that can be used to solve all of the Quick Study questions, Exercises, and Problems. Each chapter also contains papers for both the A and B problem sets.

Excel Templates

Selected end-of-chapter exercises and problems, marked in the text with an icon, can be solved using these Excel templates located on the Student Success Centre.

Excel Exercise 2-12

Given Data:

a.	Cash invested by owner	$ 2,500
b.	Office supplies purchased on credit	$ 200
c.	Cash received for work done for a client	$ 600
d.	Government grant applied for	$ 10,000
e.	Salary paid to assistant	$ 1,500
f.	Work completed for a customer on credit	$ 1,250

Answer:

			Assets		=	Liabilities
			Accounts			
	Cash	+	Receivable	+	Office Supplies	=	Accounts Payable
a.	$ -0-		$ -0-		$ -0-		$ -0-
b.	-0-		-0-		-0-		-0-
Bal.							
c.	-0-		-0-		-0-		-0-
Bal.							
d.	-0-		-0-		-0-		-0-
Bal.							
e.	-0-		-0-		-0-		-0-
Bal.							
f.	-0-		-0-		-0-		-0-
Bal.		+		+		=	

Supplements for the Instructor

Instructor's CD-ROM (ICD)

This CD-ROM contains materials for managing an active learning environment—all in one place!

Solutions Manual

Fundamental Accounting Principles continues to set the standard for accuracy of its problem material. The Solutions Manual has been technically checked for accuracy by six different instructors during its development. The Solutions Manual, available in both Microsoft Word and PDF format on the ICD, includes solutions for all end-of-chapter material.

Instructor's Manual

The Instructor's Manual cross-references assignment materials by Learning Objective and also provides a convenient chapter outline.

Computerized Test Bank

The Test Bank has been extensively revised and technically checked for accuracy both to reflect the changes in the Twelfth Canadian Edition and to improve the quality. Grouped according to Learning Objective and difficulty level, the questions in the Computerized Test Bank include true/false, multiple choice, matching, short essay, and problem material. (Note: the Test Bank is available in Rich Text Format on the ICD for ease of printing.)

PowerPoint® Presentations

These presentation slides have been extensively redesigned for this edition and are fully integrated with the text in effort to better illustrate chapter concepts.

Image Bank

All exhibits and tables displayed in the text are available for your use, whether for creating transparencies or handouts, or customizing your own PowerPoint presentations.

Excel Template Solutions

Solutions to the problems using Excel templates are available.

Online Learning Centre—Instructor's Area

Instructor Centre

Instructors can access downloadable supplements including the Instructor's Manual, Solutions Manual, Microsoft® Powerpoint slides, Image Bank, and Microsoft® Excel® template solutions.

Support for the Instructor

Superior Service

Service takes on a whole new meaning with McGraw-Hill Ryerson. More than just bringing you the textbook, we have consistently raised the bar in terms of innovation and educational research. These investments in learning and the education community have helped us understand the needs of students and educators across the country, thus allowing us to foster the growth of truly innovative, integrated learning solutions.

Integrated Learning Sales Specialist

Your Integrated Learning Sales Specialist is a McGraw-Hill Ryerson representative who has the experience, product knowledge, training, and support to help you assess and integrate all of the *Fundamental Accounting Principles* supplements, technology, assessment, course management, and services into your course for optimum teaching and learning performance. Whether it is using our Test Bank software, helping your students improve their grades, or putting your entire course online, your *i*Learning Sales Specialist is there to help you do it. Contact your local *i*Learning Sales Specialist today to learn how to maximize all of McGraw-Hill Ryerson's resources.

Course Management

PageOut is the McGraw-Hill Ryerson Web site development software, which is available free of charge to all adopters. This tool is designed to help faculty create an online course, complete with assignments, quizzes, Web links and more—all in just a few minutes. Visit www.mhhe.com/pageout for more information.

In addition, content cartridges are available for both **WebCT** and **Blackboard** course management systems. These platforms provide instructors with user-friendly, flexible teaching tools. Contact your local McGraw-Hill Ryerson *i*Learning Sales Specialist for details.

*i*Learning Services Program

McGraw-Hill Ryerson offers a unique *i*Services package designed for Canadian faculty. Our mission is to equip providers of higher education with superior tools and resources required for excellence in teaching. For additional information, visit www.mcgrawhill.ca/highereducation/iservices.

Teaching, Technology, and Learning Conference Series

The educational environment has changed tremendously in recent years, and McGraw-Hill Ryerson continues to be committed to helping you acquire the skills you need to succeed in this new milieu. Our innovative Teaching, Technology, and Learning Conference Series brings faculty together from across Canada with 3M Teaching Excellence award winners to share teaching and learning best practices in a collaborative and stimulating environment. Preconference workshops on general topics, such as teaching large classes and technology integration, are also offered. We will also work with you at your own institution to customize workshops that best suit the needs of your school's faculty.

Developing a Market-Driven Text

The success of this text is the result of an exhaustive process, which has gone beyond the scope of a single edition. Hundreds of instructors and educators across the country have been involved in giving their feedback to help develop the most successful accounting fundamentals text in the country. We owe thanks to all of those who took the time to evaluate this textbook and its supplemental products.

Twelfth Canadian Edition reviewers

Glenn Arnold	Northern Alberta Institute of Technology	Doug Leatherdale	Georgian College
Jerry Aubin	Algonquin College	Cynthia Lone	Red River College
Les Barnhouse	Athabasca University	Bonnie Martel	Niagara College
Warren Beck	St. Clair College	Debbie Musil	Kwantlen University College
Maria Belanger	Algonquin College	Penny Parker	Fanshawe College
Mark Binder	Red River College	George Pelzer	Northern Alberta Institute of Technology
Dave Bopara	CDI College	Guy Penney	College of the North Atlantic
David Burrell	Okanagan University College	Joe Pidutti	Durham College
Robert A. Coke	Durham College	Traven Reed	Canadore College
Robert Despatie	York University—Glendon College	Lou Richards	Southern Alberta Institute of Technology
Randy Dickson	Red Deer College		
Denise Dodson	Nova Scotia Community College	Doug Ringrose	Grant MacEwan College
Carolyn Doni	Cambrian College	David Sale	Kwantlen University College
George Fisher	Simon Fraser/UBC/CGA	Gabriela Schneider	Northern Alberta Institute of Technology
David Fleming	George Brown College		
Amanda Flint	Trinity Western University	Donald R. Smith	Georgian College
Jeremy Frape	Humber College	Helen Stavaris	Dawson College
Donna Grace	Sheridan Institute of Technology and Advanced Learning	Nancy Tait	Sir Sandford Fleming College
		Denise Terry	SIAST—Palliser Campus
Diana Grant	Nova Scotia Community College	Ron Thornbury	Seneca College
Elizabeth Hicks	Douglas College	Rod Tilley	Mount St. Vincent University
John Holliday	Northern Alberta Institute of Technology	John Varga	George Brown College
		Jeannine Wall	Red River College
Paul Hurley	Durham College	Richard Wright	Fanshawe College
Gerri Joosse	Lethbridge College	Patricia Zima	Mohawk College
Nadine Lancaster	British Columbia Institute of Technology		

Eleventh Edition reviewers

Cecile Ashman	Algonquin College	Suzanne Coombs	Kwantlen University College
Les Barnhouse	Athabasca University	William Cormier	St Francis Xavier University
Keith Barrett	Humber College	John Currie	Humber College
Maria Belanger	Algonquin College	John Daye	New Brunswick Community College
Gary Biggs	Grant MacEwan College		
Mark Binder	Red River College	Randy Dickson	Red Deer Community College
Dave Bopara	Toronto School of Business	Chaman Doma	Centennial College
Rick Boyack	Southern Alberta Institute of Technology	Carolyn Doni	Cambrian College
		Dave Eliason	Southern Alberta Institute of Technology
Walt Burton	Okanagan University College		
Cheryl Christoff	Toronto School of Business	Sheila Elworthy	Camosun College
Alice Cleveland	Nova Scotia Community College	Albert Ferris	University of Prince Edward Island
Louise Connors	Nova Scotia Community College	David Fleming	George Brown College
Joan Conrod	Dalhousie University	Amanda Flint	Trinity Western University

Jeremy Frape	*Humber College*	Bonnie Martel	*Niagara College*
Henry Funk	*Red River College*	Dani Moss	*Durham College*
Jack Halliday	*Northern Alberta Institute of Technology*	Jan Nyholdt	*Southern Alberta Institute of Technology*
Ern Harley	*Sheridan Institute of Technology and Advanced Learning*	Penny Parker	*Fanshawe College*
		Clifton Philpott	*Kwantlen University College*
Elizabeth Hicks	*Douglas College*	Joe Pidutti	*Durham College*
Michael Hockenstein	*Vanier College*	Sharon Ramstad	*Grant MacEwan College*
Sue Hogan	*Capilano College*	Traven Reed	*Canadore College*
Pat Humphreys	*Medicine Hat College*	Clara Reid	*Lethbridge Community College*
Stephanie Ibach	*Northern Alberta Institute of Technology*	Doug Ringrose	*Grant MacEwan College*
		David Sale	*Kwantlen University College*
Connie Johl	*Douglas College*	Giuseppina Salvaggio	*Dawson College*
Geraldine Joosse	*Lethbridge Community College*	Michael Sirtonski	*Assiniboine College*
Barbara Jordan	*Cambrian College*	Melbourne Sparks	*Lambton College*
Jane Kaake-Nemeth	*Durham College*	Greg Streich	*DeVry Institute of Technology (Calgary)*
Dave Kennedy	*Lethbridge Community College*		
Val Kinnear	*Mount Royal College*	Selina Tang	*Douglas College*
Laurette Korman	*Kwantlen University College*	Marie Templeton	*Southern Alberta Institute of Technology*
Rafik Kurji	*Mount Royal College*		
Douglas Leatherdale	*Georgian College*	John Varga	*George Brown College*
Michael Lee	*Humber College*	John Vermeer	*Humber College*
Cynthia Lone	*Red River College*	Jeannine Wall	*Red River College*
Marie Madill-Payne	*George Brown College*	Brenda Warner	*Conestoga College*
Michael Malkoun	*St. Clair College*	Dennis Wilson	*Centennial College*
Patricia Margeson	*New Brunswick Community College*	Richard Wright	*Fanshawe College*
		Brian Zwicker	*Grant MacEwan College*

CHAPTER 12

Capital Assets and Goodwill

Black Gold!

In 1967, Suncor Energy made history by producing the first commercial barrel of synthetic crude oil in its Athabasca oil sands development, one of the largest petroleum reserves in the world . . . and it is located near Fort McMurray, Alberta. Suncor's more than $16 billion of property, plant and equipment at December 31, 2005, consisted of plant, mine and mobile equipment, pipeline, properties, and other facilities and equipment. Accumulated amortization on this date totalled $3.5 billion so that the net property, plant and equipment appearing on the December 31, 2005, balance sheet was about $13 billion. This amount represented a staggering 84% of Suncor's total assets. Suncor uses straight-line amortization and the various assets have estimated useful lives ranging from 3 to 40 years. Sales for 2005 topped $11 billion, demonstrating that Suncor uses its assets to generate revenues effectively.

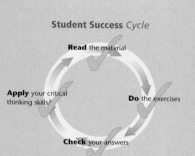

Student Success *Cycle*

Read the material

Apply your critical thinking skills

Do the exercises

Check your answers

CRITICAL THINKING CHALLENGE

If Suncor changed its amortization method from straight-line to double-declining balance, what effect would this have on the income statement and balance sheet?

www.suncor.com

learning objectives

LO1 Describe capital assets and apply the cost principle to calculate their cost.

LO2 Explain, record, and calculate amortization using the methods of straight-line, units-of-production, and double-declining-balance.

LO3 Explain and calculate amortization for partial years.

LO4 Explain and calculate revised amortization.

LO5 Account for asset disposal through discarding, selling, or exchanging an asset.

LO6 Account for natural resources and their amortization.

LO7 Account for intangible capital assets and their amortization.

LO8 Account for goodwill.

chapter preview

This chapter focuses on non-current assets used in the operation of a company: *capital assets* and *goodwill*.[1] Recall from Chapter 5 that property, plant, and equipment and intangible assets other than goodwill are referred to collectively as *capital assets*.[2] Capital assets represent a major investment for most companies and make up a large portion of assets on the balance sheet. They also affect the income statement because their costs are charged to amortization expense, often one of the largest expenses on the income statement. This chapter will describe the purchase and use of these assets. We also explain what distinguishes capital assets from other types of assets, how to determine their cost, how to allocate their costs to periods benefiting from their use, and how to record their disposal.

Capital Assets

LO1 Describe capital assets and apply the cost principle to calculate their cost.

Capital assets are assets used in the operations of a company and have a useful life of more than one accounting period. Capital assets are divided into two groups:

1. Tangible capital assets known as property, plant, and equipment[3] and
2. Intangible capital assets (which excludes goodwill).[4]

Property, plant, and equipment (PPE), sometimes referred to as **fixed assets**, includes land, buildings, equipment, machinery, leasehold improvements, and natural resources. For instance, WestJet's $1,803,497,000 of capital assets as at December 31, 2005, includes aircraft, property and equipment, buildings, leasehold improvements, and other capital assets as detailed in Note 2 of the financial statements located in Appendix I at the end of the text. **Intangible assets** lack physical substance and include patents, copyrights, leaseholds, and trademarks. Goodwill is also an intangible asset but it is shown on the balance sheet separately from capital assets.

For many companies, capital assets make up the single largest asset category on the balance sheet. For example, on its January 28, 2006, balance sheet, Reitmans (Canada) Limited shows total assets of $523,233,000 with capital assets comprising $206,184,000 of this amount. TransCanada Pipelines Limited showed $20,038 million of property, plant, and equipment at December 31, 2005, representing 83% of total assets. The Hudson's Bay Company uses the term *fixed assets* on its January 31, 2006, balance sheet to describe its $1,111,606,000 of property, plant, and equipment; total assets on this date were $3,769,301,000.

Capital assets are set apart from other assets by two important features:

1. *They are used in business operations to help generate revenue.* This makes them different from *inventory*, for instance, which is an asset that is *not used* in operations but rather held for the purpose of resale. A company that purchases a computer for the purpose of selling it reports the computer on the balance sheet as inventory. But if the same company purchases this computer for use in operations, it is classified as a capital asset.

---

[1] Section 3060 of the *CICA Handbook*, "Capital Assets," was superseded (displaced) effective December 31, 2002.
[2] *CICA Handbook*, Section 3061, "Property, Plant and Equipment," par. .04.
[3] *CICA Handbook*, Section 3061, "Property, Plant and Equipment."
[4] *CICA Handbook*, Section 3062, "Goodwill and Other Intangible Assets."

2. *Capital assets have useful lives extending over more than one accounting period.* This makes capital assets different from *current assets* such as *supplies* that are usually consumed soon after they are placed in use. The cost of current assets is assigned to a single period when they are used.

Accounting for capital assets reflects these two important features. We must measure capital assets (balance sheet focus) and match their cost to periods benefiting from their use (income statement focus).

Exhibit 12.1 shows the three main accounting issues with capital assets. They are:

1. Calculating and accounting for the initial and subsequent costs of capital assets

2. Allocating the costs of capital assets against revenues for the periods they benefit

3. Recording the disposal of capital assets.

This chapter focuses on the decisions and factors surrounding these three important issues.

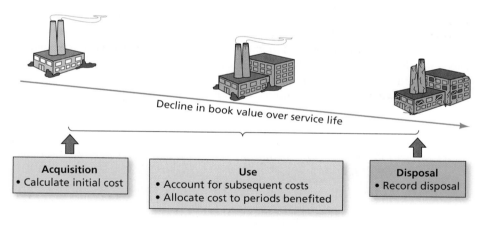

Exhibit 12.1

Issues in Accounting for Capital Assets

Cost of Capital Assets

Consistent with the *cost principle* P. 32, capital assets are recorded at **cost**, which includes all normal and reasonable expenditures necessary to get the asset in place and ready for its intended use.[5] The cost of a factory machine, for instance, includes its invoice price, less any cash discount for early payment, plus freight, unpacking, assembling costs, and non-refundable sales taxes (PST). The cost of a capital asset also includes the necessary costs of installing and testing a machine before placing it in use. Examples are the costs of building a base or foundation for a machine, of providing electrical hook-ups, and of adjusting the machine before using it in operations. These are all examples of *capital expenditures*. **Capital expenditures** are

---

[5] *CICA Handbook*, Section 3061, "Property, plant and equipment," par. .05.

costs of capital assets that provide material benefits extending beyond the current period. They are debited to capital asset accounts and reported on the balance sheet.

When expenditures regarding capital assets are *not* considered a normal part of getting the asset ready for its intended use, they are charged to another account. For example, if a machine is damaged during unpacking, the **repairs** are recorded as an expense. Also, a traffic fine paid for moving heavy machinery on city streets without a proper permit is an expense and *not* part of the machinery's cost. These are **revenue expenditures**: costs that maintain an asset but do not materially increase the asset's life or productive capabilities. They are recorded as expenses and deducted from revenues in the current period's income statement. Consistent with this rule, Air Canada reports:

> Maintenance and repair costs are charged to operating expenses as incurred. Significant modification costs are capitalized and amortized over the remaining service lives of the assets.
>
> Source: Air Canada

Subsequent Expenditures

When a capital asset is acquired and put into service, additional or *subsequent* expenditures often are incurred after the acquisition to operate, maintain, repair, and improve it. In recording these subsequent expenditures, we must decide whether they are to be accounted for as a *capital* or *revenue* expenditure. Exhibit 12.2 can be used to determine if a subsequent expenditure is capital or revenue in nature. Subsequent expenditures that would be capitalized or debited to the related capital asset account are sometimes referred to as **betterments**. Examples include roofing replacement, plant expansion, and major overhauls of machinery and equipment. Examples of subsequent expenditures that would be

Exhibit 12.2

Is It a Capital or Revenue Expenditure?

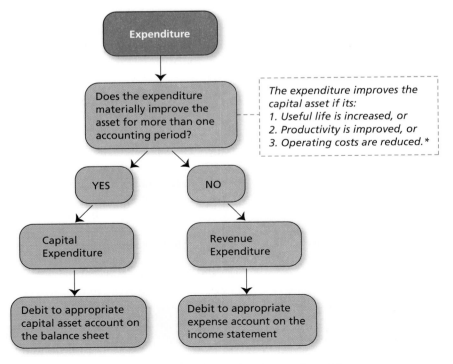

CICA Handbook, Section 3061, "Property, plant and equipment," par. 26.

classified as revenue expenditures and recorded as an expense on the income statement are supplies, fuel, lubricants and electric power. For example, the installation of a new battery in a car is a revenue expenditure and is recorded as an expense. Revenue expenditures like the purchase of the battery do not materially improve the capital asset but rather *maintain* it, keeping it in good working order over its estimated useful life. However, putting a new engine in a car *is* an improvement because the useful life of the car is extended. Therefore, the new engine is recorded as a capital expenditure. A betterment does not always increase an asset's useful life. An example is replacing manual controls on a machine with automatic controls to reduce labour costs. This machine will still wear out just as fast as it would with manual controls but because the automatic controls improve the machine's efficiency in terms of labour cost savings, it is a capital expenditure.

Financial statements P. 26 are affected for several years as a result of the choice between recording costs as revenue expenditures or as capital expenditures. Therefore, managers must be careful when classifying costs.

Capital Asset Subledger

For accounts payable and accounts receivable, we discussed and illustrated the benefits in maintaining both a control account in the General Ledger and a corresponding subledger. In the case of accounts receivable, the subledger recorded the detailed transactions by customer. Many companies also keep a subledger for capital assets. The Capital Asset Subledger details information such as cost, residual value, estimated useful life, date of purchase, amortization P. 136, serial number, and other relevant data for each capital asset or group of capital assets. This information is useful in recording amortization but is also a valuable form of internal control P. 10 over capital assets. The subledger can be used to verify recorded capital assets against a physical count.

Low Cost Asset Purchases

Maintaining individual capital asset records can be expensive, even in the most advanced system. For that reason, many companies do not keep detailed records for assets costing less than some minimum amount such as $100. Instead, these low cost capital assets are treated as revenue expenditures. This means their costs are directly charged to an expense account at the time of purchase. This practice is acceptable under the *materiality principle* P. 337. Treating immaterial capital expenditures as revenue expenditures is unlikely to mislead users of financial statements. As an example, in a recent annual report Coca-Cola disclosed that it only capitalizes *major* or material betterments:

> Additions and major replacements or betterments are added to the assets at cost. Maintenance and repair costs and minor replacements are charged to expense when incurred.
>
> Source: Coca-Cola

Mechanic

You are a mechanic who recently opened your own auto service centre. Because of a cash shortage, you are preparing financial statements in the hope of getting a short-term loan from the bank. A friend of yours suggests that you treat as many expenses as possible as capital expenditures. What are the effects on financial statements of treating expenses as capital expenditures? What do you think of your friend's proposal?

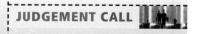

JUDGEMENT CALL

Answer—p. 620

CHECKPOINT

1. What is included in the cost of a capital asset?

2. Explain the difference between revenue expenditures and capital expenditures and how they are recorded.

3. What is a betterment? How is a betterment recorded?

Do: QS 12-1, QS 12-2

In the remainder of this section we explain how to determine the capital costs for each of five types of tangible capital assets: land (property), land improvements, buildings (plant), leasehold improvements, and machinery and equipment. Natural resources, also a tangible capital asset, are discussed in a separate section.

Land

When land is purchased for a building site, its cost includes the total amount paid for the land, including any real estate commissions, fees for insuring the title, legal fees, and any accrued property taxes paid by the purchaser. Payments for surveying, clearing, grading, draining, and landscaping[6] are also included in the cost of land. Other costs of land include assessments by the local government, whether incurred at the time of purchase or later, for items such as roadways, sewers, and sidewalks. These assessments are included because they permanently add to the land's value.

Land purchased as a building site sometimes includes a building or other obstructions that must be removed. In such cases, the total purchase price is charged to the Land account along with the cost of removing the building, less any amounts recovered through sale of salvaged materials. To illustrate, assume a company bought land for a retail store for $170,000. This land contains an old service garage that is removed at a net cost of $15,000 ($20,000 in costs less $5,000 proceeds from salvaged materials). Additional closing costs totalled $10,000, and consisted of brokerage fees ($8,000), legal fees ($1,500), and title costs ($500). The cost of this land is $195,000, calculated as:

Net cash price of land	$ 170,000
Net cost of garage removal	15,000
Closing costs	10,000
Cost of Land	**$195,000**

Land Improvements

Because land has an unlimited life and is not consumed when used, it is not subject to amortization. But **land improvements** such as parking lot surfaces, driveways, fences, and lighting systems have limited useful lives. While these costs increase the usefulness of the land, they are charged to a separate capital asset account called Land Improvements so their costs can be allocated to the periods they benefit.

Buildings

A Building account is charged for the costs of purchasing or constructing a building when it is used in operations. When purchased, the costs of a building usually include its purchase price, brokerage fees, taxes, title fees, and legal costs. Its costs

---

[6] Landscaping is included in the cost of land if it is considered permanent in nature. Landscaping costs with a finite life of greater than one accounting period are included in Land Improvements.

also include all expenditures to make it ready for its intended use, such as repairs or renovations that include wiring, lighting, flooring, and wall coverings.

When a building, or any capital asset, is constructed by a company for its own use, its cost includes materials and labour plus a reasonable amount of amortization on machinery, heat, lighting, and power used to construct the asset. Cost of construction also includes design fees, building permits, and interest and insurance during construction. But interest and insurance costs incurred *after* the asset is placed in use are operating expenses.

Leasehold Improvements

Property is rented under a contract called a **lease**. The property's owner grants the lease and is called the **lessor**. The one who secures the right to possess and use the property is called the **lessee**. Long-term leases sometimes require the lessee to pay for alterations or improvements to the leased property—such as partitions, painting, and storefronts—called **leasehold improvements**. Leasehold improvements become part of the property and revert to the lessor at the end of the lease. These costs are debited to a *Leasehold Improvements* account and amortized over the life of the lease or the life of the improvements, whichever is shorter. In its notes to the financial statements found in Appendix I of the text, WestJet reports leasehold improvements at December 31, 2005, of $6,302,000, at cost, amortized using the straight-line method over the term of the lease.

Machinery and Equipment

The cost of machinery and equipment consists of all costs normal and necessary to purchase it and prepare it for its intended use. It includes the purchase price, less discounts, plus non-refundable sales taxes, transportation charges, insurance while in transit, and the installing, assembling, and testing of machinery and equipment.

Lump-Sum Asset Purchase

A **lump-sum purchase**, also called a **basket purchase**, is the purchase of capital assets in a group with a single transaction for a lump-sum price. When this occurs, we allocate the cost of the purchase among the different types of assets acquired based on their *relative market values*. Their market values P. 137 can be estimated by appraisal or by using the tax-assessed valuations of the assets. To illustrate, Cola Company paid $630,000 cash to acquire land appraised at $210,000, land improvements appraised at $70,000, and a building appraised at $420,000. The $630,000 cost was allocated on the basis of appraised values as shown in Exhibit 12.3:

	Appraised Value	Percent of Total		Apportioned Cost	
Land	$210,000	30	($210,000/$700,000)	$189,000	($630,000 × 30%)
Land improvements.....	70,000	10	($70,000/$700,000)	63,000	($630,000 × 10%)
Building	420,000	60	($420,000/$700,000)	378,000	($630,000 × 60%)
Totals	$700,000	100		$630,000	

Alternatively, the calculation can be done by dividing the total cost by the total appraised value ($630,000/$700,000 = 0.90 or 90%) and applying the 90% to the individual appraised values as follows:

Land	$210,000	×	90% =	$189,000
Land improvements..........	70,000	×	90% =	63,000
Building............................	420,000	×	90% =	378,000

Exhibit 12.3

Calculating Costs in a Lump-Sum Purchase

4. Identify the account charged for each of the following expenditures: (a) purchase price of a vacant lot, (b) cost of paving that vacant lot.

5. What amount is recorded as the cost of a new machine given the following items related to its purchase: gross purchase price, $700,000; sales tax, $49,000; purchase discount taken, $21,000; freight to move machine to plant, $3,500; assembly costs, $3,000; cost of foundation for machine, $2,500; cost of spare parts used in maintaining the machine, $4,200?

Do: QS 12-3

Amortization

LO2 | Explain, record, and calculate amortization using the methods of straight-line, units-of-production, and double-declining-balance.

Because capital assets (except for land) wear out or decline in usefulness as they are used, an expense must be recorded. **Amortization**[7] is the process of matching (or allocating) the cost of the capital asset over the time that the asset is used. The cost of capital assets should be amortized over their useful lives in a rational and systematic manner.[8]

To illustrate, assume a delivery van is purchased for $40,000 on January 1, 2011. It is estimated that the van will help generate $30,000 in revenues each year for four years. At the end of the four-year period, it is estimated that the van will be worthless. We could record the $40,000 as an expense in the year it was purchased as illustrated in Exhibit 12.4. However, income is distorted because we have not matched the expense of the delivery van over the four years that it is creating revenue. The treatment in Exhibit 12.4 is therefore not in conformance with GAAP.

Exhibit 12.4

Cost of the Delivery Van Recorded as an Expense in Year of Purchase

	2011	2012	2013	2014
Revenues..........................	$30,000	$30,000	$30,000	$30,000
Expense	40,000	-0-	-0-	-0-
Income (Loss)...................	($10,000)	$30,000	$30,000	$30,000

Estimated four-year life of the delivery van.

If instead we apply the matching principle and allocate the cost of the delivery van against the periods it generates revenue, we achieve a more accurate reflection of performance across time, as Exhibit 12.5 illustrates.

Exhibit 12.5

Cost of the Delivery Van Matched Against Revenues Generated Over Its Four-Year Useful Life

	2011	2012	2013	2014
Revenues..........................	$30,000	$30,000	$30,000	$30,000
Expense	10,000*	10,000*	10,000*	10,000*
Income (Loss)...................	$20,000	$20,000	$20,000	$20,000

Estimated four-year life of the delivery van.

*$40,000 ÷ 4 years = $10,000 per year.

---

[7] In many countries, such as the United States, the term **depreciation** is used to describe the allocation of the cost of a tangible asset over its useful life; *amortization* is used to describe the allocation of the cost of an intangible asset; and **depletion** is used to describe the allocation of the cost of a natural resource over its useful life. The *CICA Handbook*, Section 3061, "Property, plant and equipment," par. 29, indicates that amortization may also be termed *depreciation* or *depletion*.

[8] *CICA Handbook*, Section 3061, "Property, plant and equipment," par. .28.

This allocation of the delivery van's cost is *amortization*.

Note that amortization is a process of cost allocation, not asset valuation. *Amortization does not measure the decline in the van's market value each period.* Nor does it measure the physical deterioration of the van. Amortization is a process of allocating a capital asset's cost to expense over its useful life, nothing more. Because amortization reflects the cost of using a capital asset, we do not begin recording amortization charges until the asset is actually put into use.

Reporting Amortization on Assets

Both the cost and accumulated amortization of capital assets are reported on the balance sheet. Alcan reports the following on its December 31, 2005, balance sheet:

(in million of US $)	2005	2004
Property, plant and equipment, net (Note 20)		
Cost (excluding construction work in progress)	$16,990	$21,595
Construction work in progress	1,604	1,177
Less: Accumulated amortization	7,561	9,478
	$11,033	$13,294

Many companies show capital assets on one line at the net amount of cost less *accumulated amortization*. When this is done, the amount of accumulated amortization P. 136 is disclosed in a footnote. Flint Energy Services Ltd., for instance, reports $180,021,000 as the net amount of its property, plant and equipment on its December 31, 2005, balance sheet. To satisfy the *full disclosure principle*[9] P. 348, it also describes its amortization methods in Note 1(f) and the following net book values of individual capital assets in Note 7.

7. Property, Plant and Equipment	(thousands of Canadian dollars)		
December 31, 2005	Cost	Accumulated Amortization	Net Book Value
Land	$ 10,575	$ —	$ 10,575
Buildings and improvements.............................	41,955	11,098	30,857
Construction and automotive equipment...........	214,873	99,018	115,855
Office furniture and equipment.........................	31,363	14,316	17,047
Construction and automotive equipment under construction..	5,687	—	5,687
	$304,453	$124,432	$180,021

Reporting both the cost and accumulated amortization of capital assets helps balance sheet readers compare the assets of different companies. For example, a company holding assets costing $50,000 and accumulated amortization of $40,000 is likely in a different situation than a company with new assets costing $10,000. The **book value** (original cost of the capital asset less its accumulated amortization) is the same in both cases, but the first company may have more productive capacity available and likely is facing the need to replace older assets.

We emphasize that amortization is a process of cost allocation. Capital assets are reported on a balance sheet at their book values, not at market values. This emphasis on costs rather than market values is based on the *going concern principle* P. 32. This

---

[9] *CICA Handbook*, Section 3061, "Property, plant and equipment," par. .38.

principle states that, unless there is evidence to the contrary, we assume that a company will continue in business. This implies that capital assets are held and used long enough to recover their cost through the sale of products and services. Market values of capital assets are not reported in the financial statements since capital assets are not intended to be sold until they are no longer useful. Instead, assets are reported on a balance sheet at cost less accumulated amortization. This is the remaining portion of the cost that is expected to benefit future periods.

Factors in Calculating Amortization

Three factors are relevant in determining amortization. They are:

1. Cost,   **2.** Residual value, and   **3.** Useful (service) life.

1. Cost

The *cost* of a capital asset, as described earlier in this chapter, consists of all necessary and reasonable expenditures to acquire it and to prepare the asset for its intended use.

2. Residual Value

Residual value, also called *salvage value*, is an estimate of the amount we expect to receive from selling the asset or trading it in at the end of its useful life or benefit period.[10] The total amount of amortization to be expensed over an asset's benefit period equals the asset's cost minus its estimated residual value. For example, the cost and estimated residual value of the delivery van in Exhibit 12.5 were $40,000 and $0 respectively. Therefore, the total amount of amortization to be expensed over the van's useful life is $40,000 (= $40,000 − $0). If we expect an asset to be traded in on a new asset, its residual value is the expected trade-in value.

3. Useful (Service) Life

The **useful life** of an asset is the length of time it is productively used in a company's operations. Useful life, also called **service life**, is not necessarily as long as the asset's total productive life. As an example, the productive life of a computer may be four years. Yet some companies trade in old computers for new ones every two years. In this case, these computers have a two-year useful life. This means the cost of these computers (less their expected trade-in value) is charged to amortization expense over a two-year period.

Several variables often make the useful life of an asset hard to predict, such as wear and tear from use in operations, *inadequacy*, and *obsolescence*. **Inadequacy** refers to the condition where the capacity of a company's capital assets is too small to meet the company's productive demands. **Obsolescence** refers to a condition where, because of new inventions and improvements, a capital asset is no longer useful in producing goods or services with a competitive advantage. A company usually disposes of an obsolete asset before it wears out. Obsolescence, like inadequacy, is hard to predict.

To predict the useful life of a new asset, a company uses its past experience or, when it has no experience with a type of asset, it relies on the experience of others or on engineering studies and judgement.

---

[10] *CICA Handbook*, Section 3061, "Property, plant and equipment," par. 12.

The life expectancy of capital assets is often in the eye of the beholder. Take Imperial Oil and Suncor Energy, for instance. Both compete in the oil industry, yet their refineries' life expectancies are quite different. Imperial amortizes its refineries over 25 years, but Suncor amortizes its refineries over an average of 32 years. Such differences can dramatically impact their financial statement numbers.

Amortization Methods

There are many *amortization methods* for allocating a capital asset's cost over the accounting periods in its useful life. We explain three methods in this section:

1. Straight-line, the most frequently used method of amortization,
2. Units-of-production, and
3. Double-declining-balance, an accelerated method.

The calculations in this section use information from an athletic shoe manufacturer. In particular, we look at equipment used for inspecting shoes before packaging. This equipment is used by manufacturers such as Beta, Converse, Reebok, Adidas, and L.A. Gear, and its data for amortization are shown in Exhibit 12.6.

Cost	$10,000
Estimated residual value	1,000
Cost to be amortized............................	$ 9,000
Estimated useful life:	
Accounting periods...........................	5 years
Units inspected	36,000 shoes

Exhibit 12.6

Data for Shoe-Inspection Equipment

Straight-Line Method

Straight-line amortization P. 136 charges the same amount to expense for each period of the asset's useful life. A two-step process is used to calculate expense.

1. First calculate the *cost to be amortized* over the asset's life by subtracting the asset's residual value from its total cost.
2. Second, divide the cost to be amortized by the asset's useful life.

Total cost to be amortized
= Cost − Residual

The formula and calculation for straight-line amortization of the inspection equipment just described is shown in Exhibit 12.7.

$$\frac{\text{Cost} - \text{Estimated residual value}}{\text{Estimated useful life in years}} = \frac{\$10,000 - \$1,000}{5 \text{ years}} = \$1,800 \text{ per year}$$

Exhibit 12.7

Straight-Line Amortization Formula

If this equipment is purchased on January 1, 2011, and used throughout its predicted useful life of five years, the straight-line method allocates an equal amount of amortization to each of the years 2011 through 2015. We make the following adjusting entry P. 134 at the end of each of these five years to record straight-line amortization of this equipment:

Dec.	31	Amortization Expense......................................	1,800	
		Accumulated Amortization, Equipment...		1,800
		To record annual amortization over its five-year useful life.		

The $1,800 Amortization Expense appears on the income statement among operating expenses. This entry credits Accumulated Amortization, a contra account P. 137 to the Equipment account in the balance sheet.

The net balance sheet amounts are the asset's book values for each of those years and are calculated as the asset's original cost less its accumulated amortization. At the end of year two, its book value is $6,400 and is reported in the capital asset section of the balance sheet as shown in Exhibit 12.8:

$$\text{Book value} = \text{Cost} - \text{Accumulated amortization}$$

Exhibit 12.8

Balance Sheet Presentation After Two Years of Amortization

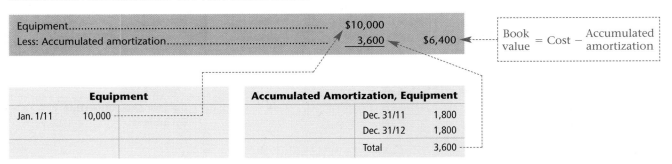

Equipment...	$10,000	
Less: Accumulated amortization...................................	3,600	$6,400

$$\text{Book value} = \text{Cost} - \text{Accumulated amortization}$$

Equipment				Accumulated Amortization, Equipment		
Jan. 1/11	10,000				Dec. 31/11	1,800
					Dec. 31/12	1,800
					Total	3,600

Instead of listing the cost less accumulated amortization, many balance sheets show capital assets *net* of accumulated amortization. The *net* means *after* accumulated amortization has been subtracted from the cost of the asset. Recall that cost less accumulated amortization is *book value*. Exhibit 12.9 shows this alternative form of presentation for the equipment of Exhibit 12.8 (cost of $10,000 less accumulated amortization of $3,600).

Exhibit 12.9

Alternative Balance Sheet Presentation

Equipment (net)...	$6,400

The graphs in Exhibit 12.10 show: (1) why this method is called straight-line amortization, and (2) the decline in book value by $1,800 amortization each year.

Exhibit 12.10

Financial Statement Effects of Straight-Line Amortization

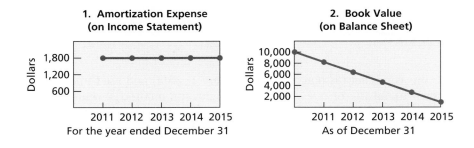

1. **Amortization Expense (on Income Statement)** — For the year ended December 31

2. **Book Value (on Balance Sheet)** — As of December 31

The straight-line amortization *rate* is calculated as 100% divided by the number of periods in the asset's useful life. In the case of our inspection equipment, this rate is 20% (100% ÷ 5 years). We use this rate and other information on the equipment to calculate the machine's *straight-line amortization schedule* shown in Exhibit 12.11.

| | Amortization for the Period | | | End of Period | |
Period	Cost to be Amortized	Amortization Rate	Amortization Expense	Accumulated Amortization	Book Value
	—	—	—	—	10,000*
2011	$9,000**	20%	$1,800	$1,800	8,200
2012	9,000	20	1,800	3,600	6,400
2013	9,000	20	1,800	5,400	4,600
2014	9,000	20	1,800	7,200	2,800
2015	9,000	20	1,800	9,000	1,000

Exhibit 12.11

Straight-Line Amortization Schedule

*Cost on January 1, 2011
**$10,000 − $1,000

Note three items in this schedule:

1. Amortization expense is the same each period.
2. Accumulated amortization is the sum of current and prior periods' amortization expense.
3. Book value declines each period until it equals residual value at the end of its useful life.

Straight-line is by far the most frequently applied amortization method in financial reporting.

Units-of-Production Method

If capital assets are used about the same amount in each accounting period, the straight-line method produces a reasonable matching of expenses with revenues. Yet the use of some capital assets varies greatly from one accounting period to the next. A builder, for instance, may use a piece of construction equipment for a month and then not use it again for several months.

When use of equipment varies from period to period, the units-of-production amortization method can provide a better matching of expenses with revenues than straight-line amortization. **Units-of-production amortization** charges a varying amount to expense for each period of an asset's useful life depending on its usage.

A two-step process is used to calculate units-of-production amortization:

1. Calculate the amortization per unit by subtracting the asset's residual value from its total cost, and then dividing by the total number of units expected to be produced during its useful life. Units of production can be expressed in units of product or in any other unit of measure such as hours used or kilometres driven. This gives us the amount of amortization per unit of service provided by the asset.
2. Calculate amortization expense for the period by multiplying the units used in the period by the amortization per unit.

Exhibit 12.12 shows the formula and calculation for units-of-production amortization for the inspection equipment described in Exhibit 12.6 (assume 7,000 shoes inspected in 2011).

Exhibit 12.12

Units-of-Production Amortization Formula

Step 1:

$$\text{Amortization per unit} = \frac{\text{Cost} - \text{Estimated residual value}}{\text{Total estimated units of production}} = \frac{\$10,000 - \$1,000}{36,000 \text{ units}}$$

$$= \$0.25 \text{ per shoe}$$

Step 2:

$$\text{Amortization expense} = \text{Amortization per unit} \times \text{Units used in period}$$
$$0.25 \text{ per shoe} \times 7,000 \text{ shoes} = \mathbf{\$1,750}$$

Using the production estimates for the equipment, we calculate the *units-of-production amortization schedule* shown in Exhibit 12.13. If the equipment inspects 7,000 shoes in 2011, its first year, amortization for 2011 is $1,750 (7,000 shoes at $0.25 per shoe). If the equipment inspects 8,000 shoes in 2012, amortization for 2012 is 8,000 shoes times $0.25 per shoe, or $2,000.

Exhibit 12.13

Units-of-Production Amortization Schedule

| | Amortization for the Period | | | End of Period | |
Period	Number of Units	Amortization per Unit	Amortization Expense	Accumulated Amortization	Book Value
	—	—	—	—	$10,000*
2011	7,000	$0.25	$1,750	$1,750	8,250
2012	8,000	0.25	2,000	3,750	6,250
2013	9,000	0.25	2,250	6,000	4,000
2014	7,000	0.25	1,750	7,750	2,250
2015	6,000**	0.25	1,250***	9,000	1,000

*Cost on January 1, 2011
**6,000 units were actually inspected, but the maximum number of units on which amortization can be calculated in 2015 is 5,000 [36,000 total estimated units less 31,000 units amortized to date (7,000 + 8,000 + 9,000 + 7,000)]. Recall that an asset must not be amortized below its residual value.
***5,000 × 0.25 = 1,250

Note that amortization expense depends on unit output, that accumulated amortization is the sum of current and prior periods' amortization expense, and book value declines each period until it equals residual value at the end of the asset's useful life.

The units-of-production amortization method is not as frequently applied as straight-line. Suncor Energy Inc. uses units-of-production and reported in its December 31, 2005, annual report:

Acquisition costs of proved properties are depleted using the unit-of-production method based on proved reserves.

Source: Suncor Energy Inc.

Declining-Balance Method

An **accelerated amortization method** yields larger amortization expenses in the early years of an asset's life and smaller charges in later years. While several accelerated methods are used in financial reporting, the most common is the

declining-balance method of amortization, which uses an amortization rate of up to twice the straight-line rate and applies it to the asset's beginning-of-period book value. Because book value *declines* each period, the amount of amortization also declines each period.

The **double-declining-balance method (DDB)** is applied in two steps:[11]

1. Calculate the double-declining-balance rate (= 2 ÷ Estimated years of useful life), and
2. Calculate amortization expense by multiplying the rate by the asset's beginning-of-period book value.

Note that residual value is not used in these calculations.

Returning to the shoe inspection equipment, we can apply the double-declining-balance method to calculate its amortization expense. Exhibit 12.14 shows this formula and its first-year calculation for the inspection equipment. The abbreviated two-step process is:

1. 2 divided by the estimated useful life of 5 years to get a declining-balance rate of 0.40 or 40% per year, and
2. Calculate annual amortization expense as the declining-balance rate multiplied by the book value at the beginning of each period (see Exhibit 12.15).

Step 1:
Double-declining-balance rate = 2 ÷ Estimated useful life = 2 ÷ 5 years = 0.40 or 40%

Step 2:
Amortization expense = Double-declining-balance rate × Beginning period book value
= 40% × $10,000 = **$4,000**

Exhibit 12.14

Double-Declining-Balance Amortization Formula

Maximum accumulated amortization*
= Cost − Residual
OR
(another way to describe the same thing)
Minimum book value*
= Residual value
regardless of method

The *double-declining-balance amortization schedule* is shown in Exhibit 12.15. The schedule follows the formula except in the year 2015, when amortization expense is $296. The $296 is calculated by subtracting the $1,000 residual value from the $1,296 book value at the beginning of the fifth year. This is done because an asset is never amortized below its residual value. If we had used the $518.40 (40% × $1,296) for amortization expense in 2015, then ending book value would equal $777.60, which is less than the $1,000 residual value.

---

[11] The double-declining-balance method is also described as being *twice the straight-line rate* because it can be alternatively applied as follows to get the same results:
1. Calculate the asset's straight-line amortization rate (100% ÷ Estimated useful life in years),
2. Double it, and
3. Calculate amortization expense by multiplying this rate by the asset's beginning-of-period book value.

Exhibit 12.15

Double-Declining-Balance
Amortization Schedule

	Amortization for the Period			End of Period	
Period	Beginning-of-Period Book Value	Amortization Rate	Amortization Expense	Accumulated Amortization	Book Value
	—	—	—	—	10,000*
2011	$10,000	40%	$4,000	$4,000	6,000
2012	6,000	40	2,400	6,400	3,600
2013	3,600	40	1,440	7,840	2,160
2014	2,160	40	864	8,704	1,296
2015	1,296	40	296**	9,000**	1,000

*Cost on January 1, 2011
**Year 2015 amortization is $1,296 − $1,000 = $296. This is because maximum accumulated amortization
  equals cost minus residual (or book value cannot be less than residual value).

Comparing Amortization Methods

Exhibit 12.16 shows amortization expense for the shoe-inspection equipment
under each of the three amortization methods.

Exhibit 12.16

Amortization Methods Compared

Period	Straight-Line	Units-of-Production	Double-Declining-Balance
2011	$ 1,800	$ 1,750	$ 4,000
2012	1,800	2,000	2,400
2013	1,800	2,250	1,440
2014	1,800	1,750	864
2015	1,800	1,250	296
	$9,000	$9,000	$9,000

While the amount of amortization expense per period is different for different
methods, *total* amortization expense is the same ($9,000) for the machine's useful
life. Each method starts with a total cost of $10,000 and ends with a residual value
of $1,000. The difference is the *pattern* in amortization expense over the useful life.
This pattern is graphically represented in Exhibit 12.17. The book value of the asset
when using straight-line is always greater than book value from using double-
declining-balance, except at the beginning and end of an asset's useful life. Also,
the straight-line method yields a steady pattern of amortization expense, while
units-of-production does not because it depends on the number of units produced.
But all of these methods are acceptable as they allocate cost in a rational and
systematic manner.[12]

Exhibit 12.17

Graphic Comparison of
Amortization Methods

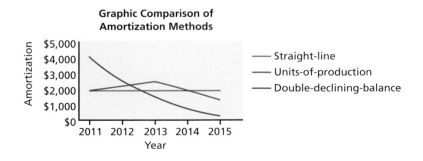

Graphic Comparison of
Amortization Methods

[12] Ibid.

CHECKPOINT   Read · Apply · Do · Check

6. On January 1, 2011, a company pays $77,000 to purchase office furniture with a residual value of zero. The furniture's useful life is somewhere between 7 and 10 years. What is the 2011 straight-line amortization on the furniture using: (a) a 7-year useful life, and (b) a 10-year useful life?

7. What is the meaning of the term *amortization* in accounting?

8. A company purchases a new machine for $96,000 on January 1, 2011. Its predicted useful life is five years or 100,000 units of product, and its residual value is $8,000. During 2011, 10,000 units of product are produced. Calculate the book value of this machine on December 31, 2011, assuming: (a) straight-line amortization, and (b) units-of-production amortization.

Do: QS 12-4, QS 12-5, QS 12-6, QS 12-7

Amortization for Income Tax Reporting

The rules a company follows for financial accounting P. 8 purposes are usually different from the rules it follows for income tax accounting purposes. Financial accounting aims to report useful information on financial performance and position, whereas income tax accounting reflects government objectives in raising revenues. Differences between these two bases are normal and expected. Amortization is a common example of one of the differences.

The *Income Tax Act* requires that companies use a declining-balance method for calculating the maximum *capital cost allowance* that may be claimed in any period. **Capital cost allowance (CCA)** is the term used to describe amortization for tax purposes. CCA reduces taxable income in the early years of an asset's life because amortization is greatest in the early years. The company's goal here is to postpone its tax payments. The *Income Tax Act* permits the use of CCA to encourage capital investment. The money a company saves in taxes in the early years means a company has the resources to earn additional profit. The *Income Tax Act* specifies the rates for various groups of assets. For example, a rate of 20% would be used for general machinery and equipment, and a rate of 4% for most buildings. Provincial Acts are also involved in setting capital cost allowances as a means of encouraging investment in various provincial jurisdictions. Further discussion of the details of tax reporting for capital assets is deferred to a more advanced course.

Partial-Year Amortization

Assets are purchased and disposed of at various times during a period. When an asset is purchased (or disposed of) at a time other than the beginning or end of an accounting period, amortization is recorded for part of a year. This is to make sure that the year of purchase or the year of disposal is charged with its share of the asset's amortization. There are different ways to account for the amortization for partial years. We are going to look at two methods:

LO³ Explain and calculate amortization for partial years.

1. Nearest whole month, and   2. Half-year rule.

Nearest Whole Month

When calculating amortization for partial years to the nearest whole month, amortization for a month is calculated if the asset was in use for more than half of that month. To illustrate, let's return to the shoe-inspection equipment. Assume this equipment is purchased and placed in service on April 8, 2011, and the annual accounting period ends on December 31. This equipment costs $10,000, has a useful life of five years, and a residual value of $1,000. Because this equipment is purchased and used for more than half of April plus all of May through December in 2011, the amount of amortization reported is based on nine months (if the purchase date had been April 28, the amortization would have been calculated for eight months since the asset was not in use for more than half of April). Amortization is not calculated by taking into account specific days of use because this would imply that amortization is precise, when in fact it is based on estimates of the useful life and residual values. Using straight-line amortization, we calculate nine months' amortization of $1,350 as follows:

$$\frac{\text{Cost} - \text{Estimated residual value}}{\text{Estimated useful life in years}} = \frac{\text{Amortization}}{\text{per year}} \times \frac{\text{Fraction}}{\text{of year}} \quad \frac{\$10,000 - \$1,000}{5 \text{ years}} = \$1,800/\text{year} \times \frac{9}{12} = \mathbf{\$1,350}$$

A similar calculation is necessary when disposal of an asset occurs during a year. As an example, let's suppose the equipment described above is sold on June 4, 2015. Amortization for 2015 is recorded for the period January 1 through June 4, or five months. Because the asset was held for less than half of June, amortization is not calculated for June. This partial year's amortization, calculated to the nearest whole month, is:

$$\frac{\$10,000 - \$1,000}{5 \text{ years}} = \$1,800/\text{year} \times \frac{5}{12} = \mathbf{\$750}$$

Exhibit 12.18 demonstrates the calculations for a partial year's amortization to the nearest month for the units-of-production and double-declining-balance methods. *Notice that the amortization expense calculation for units-of-production is not affected by the partial year.* This is because the units-of-production method is a function of use, not of time.

Exhibit 12.18

Partial Year's Amortization Calculated to Nearest Month Under the Units-of-Production and Double-Declining-Balance Methods

Date of Purchase	Units-of-Production	Double-Declining-Balance
April 8, 2011	$\dfrac{\$10,000 - \$1,000}{36,000 \text{ units}}$	Rate $= \dfrac{2}{5} = 0.40$ or 40%
		40% × $10,000
	$= \$0.25/\text{unit} \times 7,000 \text{ units} = \mathbf{\$1,750}$	$= \$4,000/\text{year} \times \dfrac{9}{12} = \mathbf{\$3,000}$

Half-Year Convention

For companies that have a large number of capital asset expenditures year after year, tracking when individual assets were put into use and then calculating amortization to the nearest month can be a costly process. Because this kind of accuracy would not necessarily increase the usefulness of information related to amortization, the *materiality principle* P. 337 allows us the flexibility to use a method more appropriate for the situation, such as the *half-year convention*. When calculating amortization for partial years using the **half-year convention**, six months' amortization is recorded for the partial period regardless of when during the period the asset was acquired or disposed of. Exhibit 12.19 illustrates the application of the half-year convention assuming the shoe-inspection equipment was purchased and put into use on April 8, 2011.

Exhibit 12.19

Partial Year's Amortization Calculated Using the Half-Year Convention Under the Straight-Line, Units-of-Production, and Double-Declining-Balance Methods

Date of Purchase	Straight-Line	Units-of-Production	Double-Declining-Balance
April 8, 2011	$\dfrac{\$10,000 - \$1,000}{5 \text{ years}}$	$\dfrac{\$10,000 - \$1,000}{36,000 \text{ units}}$	Rate $= \dfrac{2}{5} = 0.40$ or 40% 40% × \$10,000
	$= \$1,800/\text{year} \times \dfrac{6}{12} = \textbf{\$900}$	$= \$0.25/\text{unit} \times 7,000 \text{ units} = \textbf{\$1,750}$	$= \$4,000/\text{year} \times \dfrac{6}{12} = \textbf{\$2,000}$

Notice again that the calculation of units-of-production is not affected by partial years.

9. Why is amortization for a partial year not calculated to the nearest day?

Do: QS 12-8, QS 12-9, QS 12-10

CHECKPOINT   Read Apply Do Check

Revising Amortization Rates

Amortization is based on the original cost of an asset, estimated residual value, and estimated useful life. If the cost of the asset changes because of a betterment or if the estimates for residual value and/or useful life are adjusted, *revised amortization* for current and future periods must be calculated. For example, Shell Canada announced on January 17, 2005, that its fourth-quarter earnings were reduced by $10 million after revising amortization of the Scotford heavy-oil upgrader's useful life from 40 years to 30.

LO4 Explain and calculate revised amortization.

Revising Amortization Rates When There is a Change in the Estimated Residual Value and/or Estimated Useful Life

Because amortization is based on predictions of residual value and useful life, amortization expense is an estimate. If our estimate of an asset's useful life and/or residual value changes, we use the new estimate(s) to calculate **revised amortization** for current and future periods. This means we revise the amortization expense calculation by spreading the cost that has not yet been amortized over the remaining useful life. This approach is used for all amortization methods.

Let's return to our shoe-inspection equipment using straight-line amortization. At the beginning of this asset's third year, its book value is $6,400, calculated as:

Cost	$10,000
Less: Two years' accumulated amortization	3,600
Book value	$ 6,400

At the beginning of its third year, the predicted number of years remaining in its useful life changes from three to four years and its estimate of residual value changes from $1,000 to $400. Amortization for each of the equipment's four remaining years is calculated as shown in Exhibit 12.20.

$$\frac{\text{Remaining book value} - \text{Revised residual value}}{\text{Revised remaining useful life}} = \frac{\$6,400 - \$400}{4 \text{ years}} = \textbf{\$1,500 per year}$$

Exhibit 12.20

Calculating Revised Amortization Rates

This means $1,500 of amortization expense is recorded for the equipment at the end of the third through sixth years of its remaining useful life.

Since this asset was amortized at the rate of $1,800 per year for the first two years, it is tempting to conclude that amortization expense was overstated in these first two years. But these expenses reflected the best information available at that time.

Revising estimates of the useful life or residual value of an asset is referred to as a **change in an accounting estimate**. A change in an accounting estimate results from "the exercise of judgement and reappraisal as new events occur, as more experience is acquired, or as additional information is obtained."[13] A change in an accounting estimate is given prospective treatment. This means that it is reflected in current and future financial statements, and not in prior statements.[14]

Revising Amortization Rates When There is a Betterment

We also calculate revised amortization if the cost of the asset changes because of a betterment, such as the installation of a new engine. Revised amortization would be calculated from the date of the betterment. Study Part 3 of the Mid-Chapter Demonstration Problem, which illustrates the calculations for this type of situation.

CHECKPOINT

10. In early January 2011, a company acquires equipment at a cost of $3,800. The company estimates this equipment to have a useful life of three years and a residual value of $200. Early in 2013, the company changes its estimate to a total four-year useful life and zero residual value. Using straight-line amortization, what is amortization expense on this equipment for the year ended December 31, 2013?

Do: QS 12-11, QS 12-12

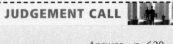

JUDGEMENT CALL

Answer—p. 620

Controller

You are the controller for Fascar Company. Fascar has struggled financially for more than two years, and there are no signs of improvement. Fascar's operations require major investments in equipment, and amortization is a large item in calculating income. Fascar's industry normally requires frequent replacements of equipment, and equipment is typically amortized over three years. Your company's president recently instructed you to revise estimated useful lives of equipment from three to six years and to use a six-year life on all new equipment. You suspect this instruction is motivated by a desire to improve reported income. What actions do you take?

---

[13] *CICA Handbook*, Section 1506, "Accounting Changes," par. .22.
[14] Ibid. par. .25.

mid-chapter demonstration problem

Read
Apply   Do
Check

Part 1

Exeter Consulting purchased equipment for cash of $160,000 on September 3, 2011. The estimated life of the equipment is 10 years but due to technological advances, Exeter expects to replace the equipment in five years. The residual value is estimated to be $40,000. Exeter's year-end is December 31.

Required

Complete a schedule similar to the following for each year of the asset's estimated useful life using the (a) straight-line, and (b) double-declining-balance methods (round calculations to the nearest whole dollar).

	2011	2012	2013	2014	2015	2016
Cost						
Less: Accumulated amortization						
Book value						
Amortization expense......................						

Analysis component:

Which amortization method, straight-line or double-declining-balance, will give the highest total net income over the asset's useful life? Explain your answer.

Part 2

Exeter Consulting purchased a vehicle for $30,000 on August 21, 2011. The company planned to use it for 100,000 kilometres or about three years and then trade it in for $10,000. The actual kilometres driven were:

2011	10,250
2012	33,700
2013	37,980
2014	19,710

Required

Complete a schedule similar to that required in Part 1 using the units-of-production method.

Part 3

On January 4, 2011, Exeter purchased a machine for $48,120 and it was estimated to have a useful life of six years and a residual value of $15,000. On October 4, 2013, the motor in the machine was replaced at a total cost of $7,685. It was determined that with the new motor, the total useful life of the machine should be revised to eight years and the residual value would increase by $2,000.

Required

Record amortization expense on the machine for the year ended December 31, 2013.

solution to *Mid-Chapter Demonstration Problem* _____

Part 1

a. Straight-line

	2011	2012	2013	2014	2015	2016
Cost..................................	160,000	160,000	160,000	160,000	160,000	160,000
Less: Accumulated amortization	8,000[1]	32,000[2]	56,000	80,000	104,000	120,000
Book value......................	152,000	128,000	104,000	80,000	56,000	40,000
Amortization expense	8,000[1]	24,000[3]	24,000	24,000	24,000	16,000[4]

^{1} $(160,000 - 40,000)/5 = 24,000/\text{year} \times \dfrac{4}{12} = 8,000$
^{2} $8,000 + 24,000 = 32,000$
^{3} $(160,000 - 40,000)/5 = 24,000/\text{year}$
^{4} $(160,000 - 40,000)/5 = 24,000/\text{year} \times \dfrac{8}{12} = 16,000$

b. Double-declining-balance

	2011	2012	2013	2014	2015	2016
Cost..................................	160,000	160,000	160,000	160,000	160,000	160,000
Less: Accumulated amortization	21,333	76,800[2]	110,080	120,000	120,000	120,000
Book value......................	138,667	83,200	49,920	40,000	40,000	40,000
Amortization expense	21,333[1]	55,467[3]	33,280[4]	9,920[5]	-0-	-0-

^{1} $40\% \times 160,000 = 64,000 \times \dfrac{4}{12} = 21,333$
^{2} $21,333 + 55,467 = 76,800$
^{3} $40\% \times 138,667 = 55,467$
^{4} $40\% \times 83,200 = 33,280$
^{5} $40\% \times 49,920 = 19,968$. However, this exceeds the maximum accumulated amortization allowed of 120,000 (cost less residual of $160,000 - 40,000$). Therefore, the maximum amortization expense is 9,920 (= 120,000 maximum allowable accumulated amortization less 110,080 accumulated amortization to date).

Analysis component:

Because both methods will have a total amortization expense of $120,000 over the life of the asset, total net income over the asset's useful life will be identical regardless of amortization method used.

Part 2

	2011	2012	2013	2014
Cost..	30,000	30,000	30,000	30,000
Less: Accumulated amortization.........................	2,050	8,790[2]	16,386	20,000
Book value...	27,950	21,210	13,614	10,000
Amortization expense	2,050[1]	6,740[3]	7,596[4]	3,614[5]

^{1} $(30,000 - 10,000)/100,000 = \$0.20/\text{km}$; $10,250 \text{ km} \times \$0.20/\text{km} = \$2,050$
^{2} $\$2,050 + \$6,740 = \$8,790$
^{3} $33,700 \text{ km} \times \$0.20/\text{km} = \$6,740$
^{4} $37,980 \text{ km} \times \$0.20/\text{km} = \$7,596$
^{5} $19,710 \text{ km} \times \$0.20/\text{km} = \$3,942$. However, this would exceed the maximum allowed accumulated amortization of $20,000 (= \$30,000 - \$10,000$). Therefore, amortization expense is limited to $3,614 (= \$20,000 - 16,386$).

Part 3

2013			
Dec. 31	Amortization Expense, Equipment.................	5,265[5]	
	Accumulated Amortization, Equipment...		5,265
	To record revised amortization.		

Calculations:

1. Revised amortization =

$$\frac{(\$48,120 + \$7,685) - \$15,180^2 - (\$15,000 + \$2,000)}{8 - 2\frac{9}{12} = 5.25 \text{ years}} = \$4,500/\text{year} \times \frac{3}{12} = \$1,125 \text{ for}$$
Oct. 4/13 to Dec. 31/13

2. Accumulated amortization at October 4, 2013 =
$5,520^3$ (2011) + $5,520 (2012) + $4,140^4$ (Jan. 1/13 to Oct. 4/13) = $15,180

3. ($48,120 − $15,000)/6 = $5,520/year

4. $5,520/year $\times \frac{9}{12}$ = $4,140 for Jan. 1/13 to Oct. 4/13

5.

$4,140^4$	+	$1,125^1$	=	$5,265
for Jan. 1/13 to Oct. 4/13		for Oct. 4/13 to Dec. 31/13		total for 2013

Disposals of Capital Assets

Assets are disposed of for several reasons. Many assets eventually wear out or become obsolete. Other assets are sold because of changing business plans. Sometimes an asset is discarded or sold because it is damaged by fire or accident. Regardless of the cause, disposals of capital assets occur in one of three ways: discarding, sale, or exchange. The accounting for disposals of capital assets is described in Exhibit 12.21.

LO5 Account for asset disposal through discarding, selling, or exchanging an asset.

1. Record amortization expense up to the date of disposal. This updates the accumulated amortization account.
2.* Remove the balances of the disposed asset and related accumulated amortization accounts. *Why? If the asset is gone, all accounts related to the asset (the asset account and its related accumulated amortization) must be taken off the books as well.*
3.* Record any cash (and other assets) received or paid in the disposal.
4.* Compare the asset's book value with the net amount received or paid at disposal and record any resulting gain or loss.

*Steps 2, 3, and 4 are recorded in one journal entry.

Exhibit 12.21

Accounting for Disposals of Capital Assets

Discarding Capital Assets

A capital asset is *discarded* when it is no longer useful to the company and it has no market value. To illustrate, assume a machine costing $9,000 with accumulated amortization of $9,000 is discarded on June 5. When accumulated amortization equals the asset's cost, the asset is fully amortized and the entry to record the discarding of this asset is:

June	5	Accumulated Amortization, Machinery...........	9,000	
		Machinery...		9,000
		To record the discarding of fully		
		amortized machinery.		

This entry reflects all four steps of Exhibit 12.21. Step 1 is not needed since the machine is fully amortized. Step 2 is shown in the debit to *Accumulated Amortization* and credit to *Machinery*. Since no cash is involved, Step 3 is irrelevant. Since book value is zero and no cash is involved, no gain or loss is recorded in Step 4.

How do we account for discarding an asset that is not fully amortized or whose amortization is not up to date? Consider equipment costing $8,000 with accumulated amortization of $6,000 on December 31, 2011. This equipment is being amortized using the straight-line method over eight years with zero residual value. On July 1, 2012, it is discarded. Step 1 is to bring amortization expense up to date:

July	1	Amortization Expense, Equipment..................	500	
		Accumulated Amortization, Equipment...		500
		To record six months' amortization;		
		Jan. 1/12 to July 1/12; $1,000 \times \dfrac{6}{12}.$		

The July 1 balance in the Accumulated Amortization, Equipment account after posting this entry is:

Accumulated Amortization, Equipment					Acct. No. 168
Date	Explanation	PR	Debit	Credit	Balance
2011 Dec. 31	Balance	✔			6,000
2012 July 1		G8		500	6,500

The second and final entry reflects Steps 2 to 4 of Exhibit 12.21.

2012 July	1	Accumulated Amortization, Equipment	6,500	
		Loss on Disposal of Equipment	1,500	
		Equipment		8,000
		To record the discarding of machinery		
		having a $1,500 book value.		

The loss is calculated by comparing the equipment's book value of $1,500 (= $8,000 − $6,500) with the zero net cash proceeds. The loss on disposal is reported in the *Other Revenues and Expenses* section of the income statement.

Gain (loss)
    on   Cash   Book
disposal* = proceeds − value

* A gain occurs when proceeds are greater than book value; a loss occurs when proceeds are less than book value.

Selling Capital Assets

To illustrate the accounting for selling assets, we consider SportsWorld's April 1, 2012, sale of its delivery equipment costing $16,000 with accumulated amortization of $12,000 on December 31, 2011. Annual amortization on this equipment is $4,000 calculated using straight-line amortization. The entry (Step 1) to record amortization expense and update accumulated amortization to April 1 is:

2012			
April 1	Amortization Expense, Equipment..................	1,000	
	Accumulated Amortization, Equipment...		1,000
	To record three months' amortization;		
	Jan. 1/12 to April 1/12; $4,000 \times \dfrac{3}{12}$.		

The April 1 balance in the Accumulated Amortization, Equipment account after posting this entry is:

	Accumulated Amortization, Equipment					Acct. No. 168
Date	Explanation	PR	Debit	Credit		Balance
2011 Dec. 31	Balance	✔				12,000
2012 Apr. 1		G11		1,000		13,000

The second entry to reflect Steps 2 to 4 of Exhibit 12.21 depends on the amount received in the sale. We consider three different possibilities:

			Book Value = $16,000 − $13,000 = $3,000			
	Sale at Book Value		**Sale Above Book Value (Cash Proceeds = $7,000)**		**Sale Below Book Value (Cash Proceeds = $2,500)**	
2012						
Apr. 1	Cash.. 3,000		Cash 7,000		Cash 2,500	
	Accum. Amort., Equip 13,000		Accum. Amort., Equip............. 13,000		Accum. Amort., Equip............. 13,000	
	Equipment 16,000		Gain on Disposal of Equip... 4,000		Loss on Disposal of Equip......... 500	
	To record the sale of equipment for $3,000.		Equipment...................... 16,000		Equipment...................... 16,000	
			To record the sale of equipment for $7,000.		*To record the sale of equipment for $2,500.*	

Exchanging Capital Assets

Many assets such as machinery, automobiles, and office equipment are disposed of by exchanging them for new assets. The acquisition of a new asset by exchanging a used asset is called a trade-in. The exchange is viewed as both a sale of the old asset and a purchase of a new asset. Both the cost and related accumulated amortization of the old asset must be removed from the books. The cost of the new asset will be recorded as the fair value of the asset(s) given up unless the fair value of the asset(s) received is more reliable. Any gains or losses realized on the exchange are also recorded.[15]

---

[15] Effective January, 2006, Section 3831 supersedes Section 3830 such that the former '10% rule' is no longer in effect regarding non-monetary exchanges. When fair values are not available, the new asset is recorded at the book value of the asset given up with any losses recognized immediately; gains are not recognized. The application of the latter is beyond the scope of this textbook and will therefore be left for discussion in a more advanced course.

In a typical exchange of capital assets, a trade-in allowance is received on the old asset and the balance is paid in cash. Often, the trade-in allowance offered ***does not*** reflect the fair value of the asset being traded-in. For example, if you are buying a new car and trading in your old vehicle, the trade-in value being offered by the seller is very likely inflated to make you think you are benefiting.

To illustrate, assume that on January 2, 2011, Crandell Company exchanges an automobile with a fair value of $19,000 for a trailer that has a list price of $41,000. The original cost of the automobile was $30,000 and related accumulated amortization was $12,000 up to the date of the exchange, resulting in a book value of $18,000 (= $30,000 − $12,000). Crandell received a trade-in-allowance of $20,000 and paid the $21,000 balance in cash. The entry to record this transaction is as follows:

	2011			
Jan.	2	Trailer..	40,000	
		Accumulated Amortization, Automobile.........	12,000	
		Automobile..		30,000
		Cash		21,000
		Gain on Asset Exchange		1,000
		To record exchange of automobile and		
		cash for trailer.		

Notice that the trailer received by Crandell was recorded at $40,000, the fair value of the assets given up. This was calculated as the $19,000 fair value of the automobile used as a trade-in plus the cash paid of $21,000. The difference between the assets received by Crandell ($40,000) and the *book value* of the assets given up ($18,000 + $21,000) represents the gain on the exchange ($1,000).

If the value of the asset(s) received is less than the book value of the assets given up, a loss would be recognized on the exchange. For example, if in the previous example the fair value of the automobile was $16,000 instead of $19,000, the exchange would have been recorded as follows:

	2011			
Jan.	2	Trailer..	37,000	
		Accumulated Amortization, Automobile.........	12,000	
		Loss on Asset Exchange.................................	2,000	
		Automobile..		30,000
		Cash		21,000
		To record exchange of automobile and		
		cash for trailer.		

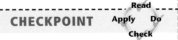

CHECKPOINT   Read   Apply   Do   Check

11. A company acquires equipment on January 10, 2011, at a cost of $42,000. Straight-line amortization is used assuming a five-year life and $7,000 residual value. On June 27, 2012, the company sells this equipment for $32,000. Prepare the entry or entries for June 27, 2012.

12. A company trades an old truck for a new tractor. The original cost of the old truck is $30,000, and its accumulated amortization at the time of the trade is $23,400. The new tractor has a list price of $45,000. Prepare entries to record the trade under two different assumptions where the company receives: (a) a $3,000 trade-in allowance, or (b) a $7,000 trade-in allowance. Assume that the trade-in allowance equals the fair value of the old truck.

Do: QS 12-13, QS 12-14, QS 12-15

Natural Resources

Natural resources are tangible capital assets that are physically consumed when used, and include items such as standing timber, mineral deposits, and oil and gas fields. Because they are consumed when used, they are often called *wasting assets*. The natural state of these assets represents inventories of raw materials that will be converted into a product by cutting, mining, or pumping. But until that conversion takes place, they are non-current assets and reported in a balance sheet using titles such as Timberlands, Mineral deposits, or Oil reserves. These natural resources are reported under capital assets or as a separate category. Suncor Energy Inc. reports its natural resources under the balance sheet title *Capital assets*. In the related note to the financial statements, Suncor reports separate amounts for *Oil Sands* and *Exploration and Production Properties*.

LO6 Account for natural resources and their amortization.

Acquisition Cost and Amortization

Natural resources are initially recorded at cost. Cost includes all expenditures necessary to acquire the resource and prepare it for its intended use. Amortization is the process of allocating the cost of natural resources to periods when they are consumed, known as the resource's *useful life*. Natural resources are reported on the balance sheet at cost less *accumulated amortization*. The amount these assets are amortized each year by cutting, mining, or pumping is usually based on units extracted or depleted. This is similar to units-of-production amortization. Imperial Oil uses this approach to amortize the costs of discovering and operating its oil wells.

To illustrate amortization of natural resources, let's consider a mineral deposit with an estimated 500,000 tonnes of available ore. It is purchased for $500,000 and we expect zero residual value. The amortization charge is calculated in Exhibit 12.22, assuming 85,000 tonnes of ore are extracted during the period.

Step 1:

$$\text{Amortization per unit} = \frac{\text{Cost} - \text{Residual value}}{\text{Total units of capacity}} = \frac{\$500,000 - \$0}{500,000 \text{ tonnes}} = \$1 \text{ per tonne}$$

Step 2:

Amortization expense = Amortization per unit × Units extracted in period
$$= \$1 \times 85,000 = \$85,000$$

Exhibit 12.22

Amortization Formula and Calculations

Amortization expense is recorded as:

Dec.	31	Amortization Expense, Mineral Deposit	85,000	
		Accumulated Amortization,		
		Mineral Deposit		85,000
		To record amortization of the		
		mineral deposit.		

The balance sheet at the end of this first year reports the deposit as shown in Exhibit 12.23.

Balance Sheet Presentation of Natural Resorurces		
Mineral deposit	$500,000	
Less: Accumulated amortization	85,000	$415,000

Exhibit 12.23

Balance Sheet Presentation of Natural Resources

Because the 85,000 tonnes of mined ore are sold in the year, the entire $85,000 amortization charge is reported on the income statement. But if some of the ore remains unsold at year-end, the amortization cost related to the unsold ore is carried forward on the balance sheet and reported as Unsold Ore Inventory, which is a current asset.

Recall that natural resource assets are tangible capital assets and are therefore shown on the balance sheet as part of property, plant, and equipment.[16]

Capital Assets Used in Extracting Resources

The conversion of natural resources by mining, cutting, or pumping usually requires machinery, equipment, and buildings. When the usefulness of these assets is directly related to the amortization of the natural resource, amortization is calculated using the units-of-production method in proportion to the natural resource's amortization charges. For example, if a machine is permanently installed in a mine and one-eighth of the mine's ore is mined and sold in the year, then one-eighth of the machine's cost (less salvage value) is charged to amortization expense. The same procedure is applied if the machine is abandoned once the resources are fully extracted. But if this machine will be moved to another site when extraction is complete, then it is amortized over its useful life.

CHECKPOINT

13. Give an example of a natural resource.

14. A mining company pays $650,000 for an ore deposit. The deposit is estimated to have 325,000 tonnes of ore that will be fully mined over the next 10 years. During the current year, 91,000 tonnes are mined, processed, and sold. What is the current year's amortization expense?

Do: QS 12-16

Intangible Assets

LO7 | Account for intangible capital assets and their amortization.

Intangible capital assets are rights, privileges, and competitive advantages to the owner of capital assets that have no physical substance and are used in operations. Examples are patents, copyrights, leaseholds, and trademarks. *Goodwill is an intangible asset but it is not a capital asset; it is shown separately on the balance sheet.* Lack of physical substance is not sufficient for an asset to be an intangible. Accounts receivable, for instance, lack physical substance but are not used in operations to produce products or services. Assets without physical substance that are not used in operations are reported as either current assets or investments.

Accounting for Intangible Capital Assets

Accounting for intangible capital assets is similar to that for all other capital assets. An intangible capital asset is recorded at cost when purchased. Its cost must be systematically allocated to expense over its estimated useful life through the process of amortization.[17] The amortization period for other intangible assets is based on legal, regulatory, contractual, competitive, economic, or other factors that might limit its useful life.[18] Disposal of an intangible capital asset involves removing its

---

[16] *CICA Handbook*, Section "Property, plant and equipment," par. .08 and .11.
[17] Section 3062 of the *CICA Handbook*, "Goodwill and other intangible assets," discusses special circumstances when amortization is not applied to intangible capital assets. For simplicity in this introductory course, we will assume that all intangible capital assets are amortized.
[18] *CICA Handbook*, section 3062, "Goodwill and other intangible assets," par. .15.

book value, recording any asset received, and recognizing any gain or loss for the difference.

Intangible capital assets are amortized in a similar manner to other capital assets except that only the straight-line method is used *unless* the company can show that another method is preferable for matching purposes.

Intangible capital assets are shown on the balance sheet separately from property, plant, and equipment. For example, Alcan Inc.'s December 31, 2005, balance sheet shows the following:

(in millions of US$)	2005	2004
Intangible assets, net of accumulated amortization of $233 in 2005 and $172 in 2004 (Note 9).....................................	$1,013	$1,230

Patents

The federal government grants patents to encourage the invention of new machines, mechanical devices, and production processes. A **patent** is an exclusive right granted to its owner to manufacture and sell a patented machine or device, or to use a process, for 20 years. When patent rights are purchased, the cost of acquiring the rights is debited to an account called *Patents*. If the owner successfully engages in lawsuits to defend a patent, the cost of lawsuits is debited to the Patents account. The costs of research and development leading to a new patent are expensed when incurred.[19]

While a patent gives its owner exclusive rights to it for 20 years, its cost is amortized over the shorter of its legal life of 20 years or estimated useful life. If we purchase a patent costing $25,000 with a useful life of 10 years, the following entries are made to record the acquisition of the patent and the annual adjusting entry over the 10-year period to amortize one-tenth of its cost:

Jan.	2	Patents...	25,000	
		Cash		25,000
		To record purchase of patents.		
Dec.	31	Amortization Expense, Patents	2,500	
		Accumulated Amortization, Patents[20]		2,500
		To write off patent cost over its 10-year useful life.		

The debit of $2,500 to Amortization Expense, Patents appears on the income statement as a cost of the product or service provided under the protection of the patent. This entry credits the Accumulated Amortization, Patents account, but crediting the Patents account rather than using a contra account is also done in practice.

Copyrights

A copyright is granted by the federal government or by international agreement. A **copyright** gives its owner the exclusive right to publish and sell a musical, literary, or artistic work during the life of the creator plus 50 years. Yet the useful life of most copyrights is much shorter. The costs of a copyright are amortized over its useful life. The only identifiable cost of many copyrights is the fee paid to the Copyright Office and if immaterial, the cost is charged directly to an expense account; if material, such as the cost of purchasing the copyrights to songs by the

[19] *CICA Handbook*, section 3450, "Research and Development," par. .16 & .18.
[20] *CICA Handbook*, Section 3062, "Goodwill and other intangible assets", par. 51(b) suggests that the disclosure of intangible assets subject to amortization should include the gross carrying amount and accumulated amortization.

Beatles, they are capitalized and periodically amortized by debiting an account called *Amortization Expense, Copyrights.*

Trademarks and Trade Names

Companies often adopt unique symbols or select unique names and brands in marketing their products. A **trademark** or *trade name* is a symbol, name, phrase, or jingle identified with a company, product, or service. Examples are Speedy Muffler, Tim Hortons, Second Cup, Coca-Cola, and Honda. Ownership and exclusive right to use a trademark or trade name are often established by showing that one company used it before another. But ownership is best established by registering a trademark or trade name with the government's Patent Office. The cost of developing, maintaining, or enhancing the value of a trademark or trade name by means such as advertising is charged to expense when incurred. But if a trademark or trade name is purchased, its cost is debited to an asset account and amortized.

Leaseholds

A **leasehold** refers to the rights granted to the lessee to use a specific asset by the lessor in the lease. A leasehold is an intangible asset for the lessee if a long-term lease requires the lessee to pay a bonus in advance.[21] The resulting debit to a Leasehold account is amortized over the term of the lease by debiting Rent Expense and crediting Leaseholds.

Accounting for Goodwill

LO8 | Account for goodwill.

Goodwill,[22] an intangible asset, is the amount by which the price paid for a company exceeds the fair market value of this company's net assets (assets minus liabilities) if purchased separately. This usually implies that the company has certain valuable attributes not measured among its net assets. These can include superior management, skilled workforce, superior supplier and customer relations, quality products or services, excellent location, or other competitive advantages. Goodwill is a major part of many company purchases. For instance, Danier Leather shows goodwill on its June 25, 2005, balance sheet of $342,000.

GAAP do not permit firms to record internally generated goodwill. Permission to do so could lead to abuse and values arrived at would lack objectivity. The purchase transaction provides objective evidence that goodwill exists. The purchase of a business is recorded by debiting the assets acquired and crediting the liabilities assumed at fair market values. Cash is credited for the purchase price of the business acquired and goodwill is debited for the amount that the purchase price exceeds the fair value of the net assets. To illustrate, assume that on January 2, 2011, Canadian Tire acquired Best Tools for $8,000,000. The market value of Best Tools' assets was $7,000,000 and its liabilities were valued at $2,000,000. Goodwill is calculated at $3,000,000 as follows:

Purchase price to acquire Best Tools		$ 8,000,000
Total market value of Best Tools' assets..................................	$7,000,000	
Less: Liabilities assumed..	2,000,000	
Net assets purchased..		5,000,000
Goodwill		**$3,000,000**

---

[21] Some long-term leases give the lessee essentially the same rights as a purchaser and result in tangible assets and liabilities reported by the lessee. The details of this advanced topic are left to an intermediate accounting course.

[22] The excess of the cost of the purchase price over the net of the amounts assigned to assets acquired and liabilities assumed should be reflected as goodwill. (CICA 1581 par. 40).

Canadian Tire's entry to record the purchase is:

2011			
Jan. 2	Assets (shown individually)............................	7,000,000	
	Goodwill	3,000,000	
	Liabilities (shown individually)..............		2,000,000
	Cash		8,000,000
	To record purchase of Best Tools and to record goodwill equal to the excess of the purchase price over the net assets.		

Goodwill is not amortized. Instead, goodwill is decreased only if its value has been determined by management to be impaired.[23] **Impairment of goodwill** results when the current value of goodwill (fair value of the organization less the fair value of its net assets) is less than the carrying value of goodwill.

The entry to record the impairment is:

Loss on impairment of goodwill	XX	◄----------------- Reported on the
Goodwill	XX	income statement

Causes of impairment might include ongoing past or potential cash flow losses or negative changes in variables supporting original calculations of goodwill. Testing for impairment should be done at least annually.

Goodwill write-offs decrease income on the income statement and also decrease assets and equity on the balance sheet. Corel, BCE Inc., and Celistica are examples of Canadian companies that recently each recorded multimillion-dollar write-offs of goodwill. In the multibillion U.S. dollar range of goodwill write-offs are Nortel with $15 billion, JDS Uniphase at $50 billion, and AOL with $100 billion.

DID YOU KNOW?

---

15. On January 6, 2011, a company pays $120,000 for a patent with a 20-year legal life to produce a toy that is expected to be marketable for about three years. Prepare entries to record its acquisition and the December 31, 2011, adjustment.

Do: QS 12-17

CHECKPOINT   Read   Apply   Do   Check

Summary

LO1 | **Describe capital assets and apply the cost principle to calculate their cost.** Capital assets (1) are used in the operations of a company, and (2) have a useful life of more than one accounting period. There are three main accounting issues with capital assets: (1) calculating and accounting for their initial and subsequent costs, (2) allocating their costs to the periods they benefit, and (3) recording their disposal. Capital assets are recorded at cost when purchased. Cost includes all normal and reasonable expenditures necessary to get the asset in place and ready for its intended use. Revenue expenditures expire in the current period and are debited to expense accounts. Capital expenditures benefit future periods and are debited to asset accounts. The cost of a lump-sum purchase is allocated among its individual assets based on their relative market values.

---

[23] *CICA Handbook* paragraphs 3062.22, 3062.23, and 3062.25.

LO2 | **Explain, record, and calculate amortization using the methods of straight-line, units-of-production, and double-declining-balance.** Amortization is the process of allocating to expense the cost of a capital asset over the accounting periods benefiting from use of the capital asset. Amortization does not measure the decline in a capital asset's market value, nor does it measure the asset's physical deterioration. Three factors determine amortization: cost, residual value, and useful life. Residual value is an estimate of the asset's value at the end of its benefit period. Useful (service) life is the length of time an asset is productively used in operations. The straight-line method of amortization divides the cost less residual value by the number of periods in the asset's useful life to determine amortization expense for each period. The units-of-production method divides the cost less residual value by the estimated number of units the asset will produce to determine the amortization per unit. The double-declining-balance (DDB) method multiplies the asset's book value by a rate that is double the straight-line rate. The amount of amortization expense per period is usually different for different methods but total amortization expense is the same. The difference is in the pattern in amortization expense over the asset's useful life. The straight-line method yields a steady pattern of amortization expense, while units-of-production does not because it depends on the number of units produced. DDB is an accelerated amortization method.

LO3 | **Explain and calculate amortization for partial years.** When capital assets are bought and sold throughout the year, amortization can be calculated either to the nearest whole month **or** by applying the half-year convention.

LO4 | **Explain and calculate revised amortization.** Amortization is revised when material changes occur in the estimated residual value and/or useful life and/or there is a betterment. Revised amortization is calculated by spreading the **remaining** cost to be amortized over the remaining useful life of the asset.

LO5 | **Account for asset disposal through discarding, selling, or exchanging an asset.** When a capital asset is discarded, sold, or exchanged, its cost and accumulated amortization are removed from the accounts. Any cash proceeds from discarding or selling an asset are recorded and compared to the asset's book value to determine a gain or loss. When assets are exchanged, the new asset is recorded at its fair value, and any gain or loss on disposal is recognized.

LO6 | **Account for natural resources and their amortization.** The cost of a natural resource is recorded in an asset account and amortization is recorded by allocating its cost to expense normally using the units-of-production method. Amortization is credited to an Accumulated Amortization account.

LO7 | **Account for intangible capital assets and their amortization.** An intangible capital asset is recorded at the cost incurred to purchase the asset. Amortization is normally recorded using the straight-line method. Intangible capital assets include patents, copyrights, leaseholds, franchises, and trademarks. Goodwill is an intangible asset but is *not* an intangible capital asset.

LO8 | **Account for goodwill.** Goodwill is an intangible asset. It is the amount by which the price paid for a company exceeds the fair market value of the purchased company's net assets. Goodwill is not amortized but is instead decreased if its value has been impaired.

---

guidance answers to | **JUDGEMENT CALL**

Mechanic

Treating an expense as a capital expenditure results in lower reported expenses and higher income. This is because, unlike an expense, a capital expenditure is not expensed immediately. Instead, the cost of a capital expenditure is spread out over the asset's life. Treating an expense as a capital expenditure also means asset and equity totals are reported at a larger amount. This continues until the asset is fully amortized. Your friend is probably trying to help, but the suggestion hints at unethical behaviour. You must remember that only an expenditure benefiting future periods is a capital expenditure. If an item is truly an "expense" not benefiting future periods, then it must not be treated as a capital expenditure.

Controller

Before you conclude that this instruction is unethical, you might tell the president of your concern that the longer estimate doesn't seem realistic in light of past experience with three-year replacements. You might ask if the change implies a new replacement plan. Depending on the president's response, such a conversation might eliminate your concern. It is possible the president's decision to change estimated useful life reflects an honest and reasonable prediction of the future. Since the company is struggling financially, the president may have concluded that the normal pattern of replacing assets every three years can't continue. Perhaps the strategy is to avoid costs of frequent replacements and stretch use of the equipment a few years longer until financial conditions improve. Even if you doubt the company will be able to use the equipment for six years, you should consider the possibility that the president has a more complete understanding of the situation and honestly believes a six-year life is a good estimate.

On the downside, you may be correct in suspecting that the president is acting unethically. If you conclude the president's decision is unethical, you might confront the president with your opinion that it is unethical to change the prediction just to increase income. This is a personally risky course of action and you may want to remind the president of her own ethical responsibility. Another possibility is to wait and see if the auditor will insist on not changing the estimate. You should always insist the statements be based on reasonable estimates.

---

guidance answers to : CHECKPOINT   Read / Apply / Do / Check

1. Consistent with the cost principle, capital assets are recorded at cost, which includes all normal and reasonable expenditures needed to get the asset ready for use.

2. A revenue expenditure benefits only the current period and should be charged to expense of the current period. A capital expenditure has a benefit that extends beyond the end of the current period and should be charged to an asset.

3. A betterment involves enhancing an existing capital asset, usually by replacing part of the asset with an improved or superior part. A betterment should be debited to the improved asset's account.

4. (a) Land

   (b) Land Improvements

5. $700,000 + $49,000 − $21,000 + $3,500 + $3,000 + $2,500 = $737,000$

6. (a) Straight-line with 7-year life: ($77,000/7) = $11,000

   (b) Straight-line with 10-year life: ($77,000/10) = $7,700

7. Amortization is a process of allocating and charging the cost of capital assets to the accounting periods that benefit from the assets' use.

8. (a) Book value using straight-line amortization:
   $96,000 − [($96,000 − $8,000)/5] = $78,400

   (b) Book value using units of production:
   $96,000 − [($96,000 − $8,000) × (10,000/100,000)] = $87,200

9. Amortization is based on an estimated useful life so to calculate it to the nearest day would imply a degree of accuracy that is not possible and not required.

10. ($3,800 − $200)/3 = $1,200

    $1,200 × 2 = $2,400

    ($3,800 − $2,400)/2 = $700

11.

Jan. 27	Amortization Expense..............	3,500	
	Accum. Amortization		3,500
27	Cash	32,000	
	Accum. Amortization	10,500	
	Gain on Sale of Equip..........		500
	Equipment..........................		42,000

12. (a)

Mar. 3	Tractor (new)	45,000	
	Loss on Trade-In.......................	3,600	
	Accum. Amortization (old)	23,400	
	Truck (old)		30,000
	Cash		42,000

(b)

Mar. 3	Tractor (new)	45,000	
	Accum. Amortization (old)	23,400	
	Truck (old)		30,000
	Cash		38,000
	Gain on Trade-In..................		400

13. Examples of natural resources are timberlands, mineral deposits and oil reserves.

14. $650,000 × (91,000/325,000) = $182,000$

15.

Jan. 6	Patents.....................................	120,000	
	Cash		120,000
Dec. 31	Amortization Expense...............	40,000	
	Accumulated Amortization, Patents..............................		40,000
	[Amortization calculation: $120,000/3 = $40,000]		

Read
Apply   Do
Check

demonstration problem

QLT Services purchased a machine on March 2, 2011, for $62,000 cash. It had an estimated useful life of five years and a residual value of $14,000. On February 25, 2014, the machine was disposed of. QLT's year-end is December 31, and it calculates amortization to the nearest whole month.

Required

1. Prepare the entry to record the disposal under each of the following independent assumptions:

   a. The machine was sold for $26,000 cash.

   b. The machine was sold for $33,200 cash.

   c. The machine was sold for $34,180 cash.

   d. The old machine was exchanged for tools with a market value of $88,000. A trade-in allowance of $25,000 was offered on the old machine and the balance was paid in cash. Assume the trade-in allowance was equal to the fair value of the old machine.

Additional company transactions to account for dealing with capital assets:

2. On January 4, 2014, the company purchases with cash a patent for $100,000. The company estimates the useful life of the patent to be 10 years. Journalize the patent acquisition and amortization for the year.

3. On October 17, 2014, the company makes its final addition to property and equipment with the acquisition of an ore deposit for $600,000 cash. Access roads and shafts are added for an additional cost of $80,000 cash. Residual value of the mine is estimated to be $20,000. The company estimates 330,000 tonnes of available ore. Only 10,000 tonnes of ore are mined and sold before the end of the year. Journalize the mine's acquisition and first year's amortization.

Analysis component:

Regarding the purchase of the mine in Part 3, why wasn't the $80,000 paid for the roads and shafts debited to an expense account instead of to a capital asset account?

Planning the Solution

- Remember that all amortization must be recorded before removing a disposed asset from the books. Calculate and record the amortization expense for 2011 through to 2014 using the straight-line method calculated to the nearest whole month. Record the gain/loss on the disposal as well as the removal of the asset and its related accumulated amortization from the books.

- Record the patent as an intangible asset for its purchase price. Use straight-line amortization over the years of useful life to calculate amortization expense.

- Record the ore deposit as a natural resource asset including all additional costs to ready the mine for use. Calculate amortization per tonne using the units-of-production amortization formula. Multiply the amortization amount per tonne by the number of tonnes mined since the acquisition to calculate the appropriate amortization expense for the current year.

solution to *Demonstration Problem*

1a.

2014				
Feb.	25	Amortization Expense, Machine	1,600	
		Accumulated Amortization, Machine.....		1,600
		To update amortization to date of sale.		
	25	Accumulated Amortization, Machine[1]	28,800	
		Cash..	26,000	
		Loss on Disposal[2]..	7,200	
		Machine..		62,000
		To record sale of machine.		

1b.

Feb.	25	Amortization Expense, Machine	1,600	
		Accumulated Amortization, Machine.....		1,600
		To update amortization to date of sale.		
	25	Accumulated Amortization, Machine..............	28,800	
		Cash..	33,200	
		Machine..		62,000
		To record sale of machine.		

1c.

Feb.	25	Amortization Expense, Machine	1,600	
		Accumulated Amortization, Machine.....		1,600
		To update amortization to date of sale.		
	25	Accumulated Amortization, Machine..............	28,800	
		Cash..	34,180	
		Machine..		62,000
		Gain on Disposal[3]................................		980
		To record sale of machine.		

1d.

Feb.	25	Amortization Expense, Machine	1,600	
		Accumulated Amortization, Machine.....		1,600
		To update amortization to date of exchange.		
	25	Accumulated Amortization, Machine..............	28,800	
		Tools[4]	88,000	
		Loss on Disposal[5]..	8,200	
		Machine..		62,000
		Cash		63,000
		To record exchange of machine.		

[1] 2011: $(62,000 - 14,000)/5 \times 10/12 = 8,000$
2012: $(62,000 - 14,000)/5 \qquad\ = 9,600$
2013: $\qquad\qquad\qquad\qquad\qquad = 9,600$
2014: $(62,000 - 14,000)/5 \times 2/12 = \underline{1,600}$
Accumulated Amortization $\qquad\quad \underline{\underline{28,800}}$

[2] Gain (loss) $\;= $ Proceeds $-$ Book value
$\qquad\qquad\quad = 26,000 - (62,000 - 28,800) = \underline{\underline{(7,200)}}$

[3] Gain (loss) $\;= 34,180 - (62,000 - 28,800) = \underline{\underline{\ 980\ }}$

[4] Tools $\qquad\; = $ Fair value of assets given up
$\qquad\qquad\quad = 25,000 + 63,000 = \underline{\underline{88,000}}$

[5] Gain (loss) $\;= 88,000 - [63,000 + (62,000 - 28,800)] = \underline{\underline{(8,200)}}$

2.

2014			
Jan. 4	Patent	100,000	
	Cash		100,000
	To record patent acquisition.		
Dec. 31	Amortization Expense, Patent.........................	10,000	
	Accumulated Amortization, Patent........		10,000
	To record amortization expense		
	($100,000/10 years = $10,000).		

3.

2014			
Oct. 17	Ore Deposit...	680,000	
	Cash		680,000
	To record ore deposit aquisition and		
	related costs.		
Dec. 31	Amortization Expense, Ore Deposit	20,000	
	Accumulated Amortization,		
	Ore Deposit		20,000
	To record amortization expense		
	[($680,000 − $20,000)/ 330,000 tonnes		
	available] = $2.00 per tonne;		
	10,000 tonnes mined and sold × $2.00		
	= $20,000 amortization.		

Analysis component:

The $80,000 paid for the roads and shafts was debited to a capital asset account in accordance with the matching principle, which requires that the $80,000 be allocated over the tonnes of ore produced by the mine. If the $80,000 were expensed in 2014, the year it was paid, expenses in 2014 would be overstated because the $80,000 was not used entirely during one year; the roads and mining shafts, to which the $80,000 relates, will be used as the mine produces ore.

Glossary

Accelerated amortization method   An amortization method that produces larger amortization charges during the early years of an asset's life and smaller charges in the later years. (p. 602)

Amortization   A process of systematically allocating the cost of a capital asset to expense over its estimated useful life. (p. 596)

Basket purchase   See *lump-sum purchase*. (p. 595)

Betterment   An expenditure to make a capital asset more efficient or productive and/or extend the useful life of a capital asset beyond original expectations; also called an improvement. Betterments are debited to a capital asset account. (p. 592)

Book value   The original cost of a capital asset less its accumulated amortization. (p. 597)

Capital assets   Tangible and intangible assets (excluding goodwill) used in the operations of a company that have a useful life of more than one accounting period. (p. 590)

Capital cost allowance (CCA)   The system of amortization required by federal income tax law for federal income tax purposes. (p. 606)

Capital expenditures   Costs of capital assets that provide material benefits extending beyond the current period. They are debited to capital asset accounts and reported on the balance sheet. (p. 591)

Change in an accounting estimate   A change in a calculated amount used in the financial statements that results from new information or subsequent developments and from better insight or improved judgement. (p. 608)

Copyright   A right granted by the federal government or by international agreement giving the owner the exclusive privilege to publish and sell musical, literary, or artistic work during the life of the creator plus 50 years. (p. 617)

Cost   Includes all normal and reasonable expenditures necessary to get a capital asset in place and ready for its intended use. (p. 591)

Declining-balance amortization   An amortization method in which a capital asset's amortization charge for the period is determined by applying a constant amortization rate (up to twice the straight-line rate) each year to the asset's book value at the beginning of the year. (p. 603)

Depletion   The process of allocating the cost of natural resources to the periods in which they are consumed. Another term for *amortization* of natural resources. (p. 596)

Depreciation   An American term used to describe amortization. See *amortization*. (p. 596)

Double-declining-balance amortization   An amortization method in which amortization is determined at twice the straight-line rate. (p. 603)

Fixed assets   See *property, plant, and equipment*. (p. 590)

Goodwill   The amount by which the value of a company exceeds the fair market value of the company's net assets if purchased separately; goodwill is an intangible asset; it is *not* a capital asset; goodwill is *not* amortized but is instead subject to an annual impairment test. (p. 618)

Half-year convention   A method of calculating amortization for partial periods. Six months' amortization is taken for the partial period regardless of when the asset was acquired or disposed of. (p. 606)

Impairment of goodwill   Results when the current value of goodwill is less than its carrying value. (p. 619)

Inadequacy   A condition in which the capacity of the company's capital assets is too small to meet the company's productive demands. (p. 598)

Intangible assets   Rights, privileges, and competitive advantages to the owner of assets used in operations that have a useful life of more than one accounting period but have no physical substance; examples include patents, copyrights, leaseholds, franchises, and trademarks. Goodwill is an intangible asset. (p. 590)

Intangible capital assets   Intangible assets that include patents, copyrights, leaseholds, franchises, and trademarks. Goodwill is an intangible asset but it is *not* a capital asset. (p. 616)

Land improvements   Assets that increase the usefulness of land but that have a limited useful life and are subject to amortization. (p. 594)

Lease   A contract allowing property rental. (p. 595)

Leasehold   A name for the rights granted to the lessee by the lessor in a lease. (p. 618)

Leasehold improvement   An asset resulting from a lessee paying for alterations or improvements to the leased property. (p. 595)

Lessee   The party to a lease that secures the right to possess and use the property. (p. 595)

Lessor   The party to a lease that grants to another the right to possess and use property. (p. 595)

Lump-sum purchase   Purchase of capital assets in a group with a single transaction for a lump-sum price. The cost of the purchase must be allocated to individual asset accounts; also called a *basket purchase*. (p. 595)

Natural resources   Assets that are physically consumed when used; examples include timber, mineral deposits, and oil and gas fields; also called wasting assets. (p. 615)

Obsolescence   A condition in which, because of new inventions and improvements, a capital asset can no longer be used to produce goods or services with a competitive advantage. (p. 598)

Patent   An exclusive right granted to its owner by the federal government to manufacture and sell a machine or device, or to use a process, for 20 years. (p. 617)

PPE   A common abbreviation for *property, plant, and equipment*. (p. 590)

Property, plant, and equipment   Tangible capital assets used in the operations of a company that have a useful life of more than one accounting period; often abbreviated as *PPE*; sometimes referred to as fixed assets. (p. 590)

Repairs Expenditures made to keep a capital asset in normal, good operating condition; treated as a revenue expenditure. (p. 592)

Residual value Management's estimate of the amount that will be recovered at the end of a capital asset's useful life through a sale or as a trade-in allowance on the purchase of a new asset; also called salvage value. (p. 598)

Revenue expenditure An expenditure that should appear on the current income statement as an expense and be deducted from the period's revenues because it does not provide a material benefit in future periods. (p. 592)

Revised amortization Recalculated amortization because of a change in cost, residual value, or useful life. (p. 607)

Service life See *useful life*. (p. 598)

Straight-line amortization A method that allocates an equal portion of the total amortization for a capital asset (cost minus residual) to each accounting period in its useful life. (p. 599)

Trademark A symbol, name, phrase, or jingle identified with a company, product, or service. Also referred to as a trade name. (p. 618)

Units-of-production amortization A method that charges a varying amount to expense for each period of an asset's useful life depending on its usage; expense is calculated by taking the cost of the asset less its residual value and dividing by the total number of units expected to be produced during its useful life. (p. 601)

Useful life The estimated length of time in which a capital asset will be productively used in the operations of the business; also called *service life*. (p. 598)

For more study tools, quizzes, and problem material,
visit the **Student Success** *Centre* at
www.mcgrawhill.ca/studentsuccess/FAP

Questions

1. What characteristics of a capital asset make it different from other assets?
2. What is the balance sheet classification of land held for future expansion? Why is the land not classified as a capital asset?
3. In general, what is included in the cost of a capital asset?
4. What is the difference between land and land improvements?
5. Does the balance of the Accumulated Amortization, Machinery account represent funds accumulated to replace the machinery when it wears out?
6. What is the difference between an ordinary repair and a betterment and how should they be recorded?
7. What accounting principle justifies charging the $75 cost of a capital asset immediately to an expense account?
8. Refer to the balance sheet for WestJet in Appendix I. On what basis are aircraft amortized:  straight-line, units-of-production, or double-declining-balance?
9. What are some of the events that might lead to the disposal of a capital asset?
10. What is the name for the process of allocating the cost of natural resources to expense as the natural resources are used?
11. What are the characteristics of an intangible capital asset?
12. Is the declining-balance method an acceptable means of calculating amortization of natural resources?
13. What general procedures are followed in accounting for intangible capital assets?
14. When does a business have goodwill?
15. A company bought an established business and paid for goodwill. If the company plans to incur substantial advertising and promotional costs each year to maintain the value of the goodwill, must the company also amortize the goodwill?

Quick Study

QS 12-1
Cost of capital assets
LO¹

Sydney Lanes installed automatic scorekeeping equipment. The electrical work required to prepare for the installation was $18,000. The invoice price of the equipment was $180,000. Additional costs were $3,000 for delivery and $600 for insurance during transportation. During the installation, a component of the equipment was damaged because it was carelessly left on a lane and hit by the automatic lane cleaning machine during a daily maintenance run. The cost of repairing the component was $2,250. What is the cost of the automatic scorekeeping equipment?

QS 12-2
Revenue and capital expenditures
LO¹

1. Classify the following expenditures as revenue (R) or capital expenditures (C):
   a. The monthly replacement cost of filters on an air conditioning system, $120.
   b. The cost of replacing a compressor for a meat packing firm's refrigeration system that extends the estimated life of the system by four years, $40,000.

c. The cost of annual tune-ups for delivery trucks, $200.

d. The cost of $175,000 for an addition of a new wing on an office building.

2. Prepare the journal entry to record each of the above (assume all transactions occurred on March 15, 2011, and were for cash).

On April 14, 2011, Lestok Company purchased land and a building for a total price of $540,000, paying cash of $85,000 and borrowing the balance from the bank. The bank appraised the land at $320,000 and the building at $180,000. Complete the following table and prepare the entry to record the purchase.

QS 12-3
Lump sum purchase
LO¹

Capital Asset	(a) Appraised Values	(b) Ratio of Individual Appraised Value to Total Appraised Value (a) ÷ Total Appraised Value	(c) Cost Allocation (b) × Total Actual Cost
Land			
Building			
Totals			

TechCom has provided the following selected account information, in alphabetical order, from its adjusted trial balance at October 31, 2011 (assume normal balances):

QS 12-4
Balance sheet presentation
LO²

Accounts receivable..	$16,400
Accumulated amortization, equipment	3,800
Accumulated amortization, patent	3,100
Accumulated amortization, vehicles	13,800
Allowance for doubtful accounts	800
Cash	9,000
Equipment	25,000
Land	48,000
Patent	20,100
Vehicles..	62,000

Prepare the asset section of the classified balance sheet at October 31, 2011.

On January 2, 2011, Crossfire acquired sound equipment for concert performances at a cost of $55,900. The rock band estimated that it would use this equipment for four years, and then sell the equipment for $1,900. Calculate amortization for each year of the sound equipment's estimated life using the straight-line method. Crossfire's year-end is December 31.

QS 12-5
Calculating amortization—
straight-line
LO²

Delta Company purchased a photocopier costing $45,000 on January 1, 2011. The equipment is expected to produce a total of 4,000,000 copies over its productive life. Its residual value at the end of its useful life is estimated to be $5,000. The equipment actually produced: 650,000 copies in 2011; 798,000 copies in 2012; 424,000 copies in 2013; 935,000 copies in 2014; and 1,193,000 copies in 2015. Calculate amortization for 2011 through to 2015 using the units-of-production method. Delta's year-end is December 31.

QS 12-6
Calculating amortization—
units-of-production
LO²

Wimberly Holdings acquired a delivery truck on January 1, 2011, for $86,000. It is expected to last five years and then sell for about $16,000. Calculate amortization for each year of the truck's life using the double-declining-balance method. Wimberly's year-end is December 31.

QS 12-7
Calculating amortization—
double-declining balance
LO²

QS 12-8
Calculating amortization—
partial periods
LO2, 3

Equipment with an estimated life of 10 years and no expected residual value was purchased on account for $60,000 on March 6, 2011. Assuming a year-end of December 31, calculate amortization for 2011 and 2012 using the straight-line method:
a. to the nearest whole month.　　　　　**b.** using the half-year convention.

QS 12-9
Double-declining balance—
partial periods
LO2, 3

Refer to the information in QS 12-8. Assume the equipment is amortized using the double-declining balance method. Calculate amortization for 2011 and 2012:
a. to the nearest whole month, and　　　**b.** using the half-year convention.

QS 12-10
Units-of-production—partial
periods
LO2, 3

AbeCo borrowed $75,000 from the bank to purchase a machine that was estimated to produce 120,000 units of product; its expected residual value is $15,000. During 2011 and 2012, the machine produced 20,000 and 28,000 units, respectively. Calculate amortization for 2011 and 2012 assuming the units-of-production method is used:
a. to the nearest whole month, and　　　**b.** using the half-year convention.

QS 12-11
Revised amortization—change
in useful life and residual value
LO4

On January 1, 2011, Kaldex Company purchased for $35,720 equipment with an estimated useful life of eight years and an estimated residual value at the end of its life of $4,200. Early in January of 2014, it was determined that the total estimated useful life on the equipment should be 10 years with a revised estimated residual value of $1,570. Kaldex uses the straight-line method to calculate amortization and its year-end is December 31. Calculate revised amortization for 2014.

QS 12-12
Revised amortization—betterment
LO4

On January 1, 2011, Pyongyang Servicing purchased for $25,000 machinery with an estimated useful life of four years and an estimated residual value of $5,000. On January 2, 2014, a new motor costing $12,000 was installed in the machinery, which extended its useful life to eight years with no change in the residual value. Pyongyang uses the straight-line method to calculate amortization and its year-end is December 31. Record the amortization for the year ended December 31, 2014.

QS 12-13
Disposal of capital assets
LO5

Dorsier Company showed the following adjusted account balances on September 30, 2011:

Equipment	$ 56,000
Accumulated amortization, equipment	39,000
Machinery	109,000
Accumulated amortization, machinery	96,000
Delivery truck	48,000
Accumulated amortization, delivery truck	33,000
Furniture	26,000
Accumulated amortization, furniture	21,000

Prepare the entries to record the following on October 1, 2011:
a. equipment was sold for cash of $17,000.
b. machinery was sold for cash of $27,000.
c. delivery truck was sold for cash of $11,000.
d. furniture was given to a charity.

QS 12-14
Exchanging an asset
LO5

Dean Carpet Stores owned an automobile with a $15,000 cost that had $13,500 accumulated amortization as of December 31, 2011. Its fair value on this date was $3,000. On the same day, Dean exchanged this auto for a computer with a list price of $5,800. Dean was required to pay an additional $2,750 cash. Prepare the entry to record this transaction for Dean.

QS 12-15
Exchanging an asset
LO5

On March 1, 2011, Wallace Company purchased a new machine with a suggested retail price of $123,000. The new machine was to replace an old machine that originally cost $90,000 and had $36,000 of accumulated amortization at the time of the exchange. The retailer was offering Wallace a trade-in allowance of $60,000. Record the exchange assuming the fair value of the old machine was (a) $57,000, or (b) $48,000.

Sudbury Industries acquired a mine on May 4, 2011, at a cost of $1,300,000 cash. On the same day, the company had to pay an additional $200,000 cash to access the mine. The mine is estimated to hold 500,000 tonnes of ore and the estimated value of the land after the ore is removed is $150,000.
a. Prepare the entry to record the acquisition.
b. Prepare the year-end adjusting entry at December 31, assuming that 90,000 tonnes of ore were mined in 2011.

QS 12-16
Natural resources and amortization
LO6

On January 4, 2011, Amber's Boutique paid cash of $95,000 for a ten-year franchise. Prepare the entry to record the purchase of the franchise and the adjusting entry at December 31, 2011.

QS 12-17
Intangible assets and amortization
LO7

Exercises

Santiago Co. purchased a machine for $11,500, terms 2/10, n/60, FOB shipping point. The seller prepaid the freight charges, $260, adding the amount to the invoice and bringing its total to $11,760. The machine required a special steel mounting and power connections costing $795, and another $375 was paid to assemble the machine and get it into operation. In moving the machine onto its steel mounting, it was dropped and damaged. The repairs cost $190. Later, $30 of raw materials were consumed in adjusting the machine so that it would produce a satisfactory product. The adjustments were normal for this type of machine and were not the result of the damage. However, the items produced while the adjustments were being made were not saleable. Prepare a calculation to show the cost of this machine for accounting purposes. (Assume Santiago pays for the purchase within the discount period.)

Exercise 12-1
Cost of a capital asset
LO1

Check figure:
Total acquisition costs = $12,730

After planning to build a new plant, Weber Manufacturing purchased a large lot on which a small building was located. The negotiated purchase price for this real estate was $1,000,000 for the lot plus $480,000 for the building. The company paid $138,000 to have the old building torn down and $204,000 for levelling the lot. Finally, it paid $2,880,000 in construction costs, which included the cost of a new building plus $342,000 for lighting and paving a parking lot next to the building. Present a single journal entry to record the costs incurred by Weber, all of which were paid in cash (assume a date of March 10, 2011, for your entry).

Exercise 12-2
Recording costs of real estate
LO1

Check figure:
Dr Land $1,822,000

On April 12, 2011, Horizon Company paid cash of $368,250 for real estate plus $19,600 cash in closing costs. The real estate included: land appraised at $166,320; land improvements appraised at $55,440; and a building appraised at $174,240. Prepare a calculation similar to QS 12-3 showing the allocation of the total cost among the three purchased assets and present the journal entry to record the purchase.

Exercise 12-3
Lump-sum purchase
LO1

Check figure:
Dr Land $162,897

On January 1, 2011, Advitech purchased land, a building, equipment, and tools for a total price of $3,600,000, paying cash of $920,000 and borrowing the balance from the bank. The bank appraiser valued the assets as follows: $960,000 for the land; $1,120,000 for the building; $832,000 for the equipment; and $288,000 for the tools. Prepare the entry to record the purchase.

Exercise 12-4
Lump-sum purchase
LO1

Check figure:
Dr Tools $324,000

On January 1, 2011, Petcetera purchased a used truck for $25,000. A new motor had to be installed to get the truck in good working order; the costs were $9,000 for the motor and $4,500 for the labour. The truck was also painted for $3,500. It was ready for use by January 4. A six-month insurance policy costing $2,400 was purchased to cover the vehicle. The driver filled it with $120 of gas before taking it on its first trip. It is estimated that the truck has a five-year useful life and a residual value of $5,000. Petcetera uses the straight-line method to amortize all of its vehicles. Record amortization at year-end, December 31, 2011.

Exercise 12-5
Cost of capital asset, straight-line amortization
LO1, 2

Exercise 12-6
Alternative amortization methods—straight-line, double-declining-balance, and units-of-production

LO²

Check figures:
b. 2013: $9,150
c. 2014: $19,780

On January 2, 2011, Douglas Consulting installed a computerized machine in its factory at a cost of $84,600. The machine's useful life was estimated at four years or a total of 181,500 units with a $12,000 trade-in value. Douglas's year-end is December 31. Calculate amortization for each year of the machine's estimated useful life under each of the following methods:

a. straight-line
b. double-declining-balance
c. units-of-production, assuming actual units produced were:

2011	38,300	2013	52,600
2012	41,150	2014	56,000

Exercise 12-7
Calculating amortization

LO²

Check figure:
b. $47,680

JavaJoe's purchased a truck on January 1, 2011, for $119,200 cash. Its estimated useful life is five years or 240,000 kilometres with an estimated residual value of $23,200.

Required
Calculate amortization expense for the year ended December 31, 2011, using each of the following methods:

a. straight-line
b. double-declining balance
c. units-of-production (assume 38,000 kilometres were actually driven in 2011).

Analysis component:
Which method will produce the highest net income for JavaJoe's in 2011?

Exercise 12-8
Alternative amortization methods

LO²

On January 3, 2011, Wallace Servicing purchased computer equipment for $250,500. The equipment will be used in research and development activities for five years or a total of 8,500 hours and then sold for about $38,000. Prepare a schedule with headings as shown below. Calculate amortization and book values for each year of the equipment's life for each method of amortization. Wallace's year-end is December 31.

	Straight-Line		Double-Declining-Balance		Units-of-Production*	
Year	Amortization Expense	Book Value at December 31	Amortization Expense	Book Value at December 31	Amortization Expense	Book Value at December 31

*Assume actual usage in hours of:

2011	1,350	2014	2,980
2012	1,780	2015	2,700
2013	2,400		

Check figures:
Amort. exp. 2013:
Straight-line, $42,500;
DDB, $36,072;
Units, $60,000

Analysis component:
Which method will result in the greatest:
a. total assets being reported on the balance sheet in 2011? in 2014?
b. operating expenses being reported on the income statement in 2011? in 2014?

Exercise 12-9
Lump-sum purchase, double-declining-balance

LO¹, ²

Check figures:
2012 amortization:
Land, $0;
Building, $153,600;
Equipment, $43,200;
Tools, $13,333

On January 1, 2011, Albacore purchased land, building, equipment, and tools for a total of $1,800,000. An appraisal identified the fair values to be $500,000 (land), $800,000 (building), $150,000 (equipment), and $50,000 (tools). The estimated useful life and residual value of the building was 10 years and $500,000; for the equipment, five years and $30,000; and for the tools, three years and $5,000. Calculate amortization for 2011 and 2012 using the double-declining-balance method. Albacore's year-end is December 31.

Analysis component:
Explain amortization as it applies to land.

At December 31, 2010, Dover Industries' balance sheet showed total capital assets of $970,000 and total accumulated amortization of $271,980 as detailed in the Capital Asset Subledger below. Dover Industries calculates amortization to the nearest whole month.

Exercise 12-10
Calculating amortization
LO²

| | | **Cost Information** | | | | **Amortization** | | |
| | Date of Purchase | Amortization[1] Method | Cost[2] | Residual | Life | Balance of Accum. Amort. Dec. 31, 2010 | Amortization Expense for 2011 | Balance of Accum. Amort. Dec. 31, 2011 |
Description								
Building	May 2, 2005	S/L	$650,000	$250,000	10 yr.	$226,667		
Land	May 2, 2005	N/A	240,000	N/A	N/A	-0-		
Truck	Jan. 25, 2008	DDB	80,000	10,000	8 yr.	45,313		

[1] S/L—Straight-Line; DDB—Double-Declining-Balance; N/A—not applicable
[2] There have been no disposals or betterments since the date of purchase.

Required
Complete the schedule by calculating amortization expense for 2011 for each asset and then determining the balance of accumulated amortization at December 31, 2011 (round to the nearest whole dollar).

Check figure:
Amortization expense, truck: $8,672

Analysis component:
Why has amortization not been calculated on the land?

Refer to Exercise 12-10. Assume that the only other assets at December 31, 2010, were total current assets of $338,000. Prepare the asset section of Dover Industries' classified balance sheet at December 31, 2010.

Exercise 12-11
Balance sheet presentation
LO²

Check figure:
Total assets = $1,036,020

Rock Energy recently paid $313,600 for equipment that will last five years and have a residual value of $70,000. By using the machine in its operations for five years, the company expects to earn $114,000 annually, after deducting all expenses except amortization. Complete the schedule below assuming each of (a) straight-line amortization and (b) double-declining-balance amortization.

Exercise 12-12
Income statement effects of alternative amortization methods
LO²

Check figure:
b. Amortization expense
Year 3: $42,896

	Year 1	Year 2	Year 3	Year 4	Year 5	5-Year Totals
Income before amortization........						
Amortization expense						
Net income						

Analysis component:
If Rock Energy wants the Year 1 balance sheet to show the highest value possible for the equipment, which amortization method will it choose? Explain

On January 3, 2011, Golden Electrical paid $106,000 for equipment with an estimated useful life of four years or 160,000 units and a residual value of $34,000. Complete the following schedule for each year of the equipment's life, assuming Golden's year-end is December 31.

Exercise 12-13
Alternative amortization methods
LO²

| | **Straight-Line** | | | **Double-Declining-Balance** | | | **Units-of-Production*** | | |
Year	Amort. Expense	Accum. Amort.	Book Value, Dec. 31	Amort. Expense	Accum. Amort.	Book Value, Dec. 31	Amort. Expense	Accum. Amort.	Book Value, Dec. 31

*Assume actual units produced of:

2011	51,000	2013	52,000
2012	46,000	2014	39,000

Analysis component:
Which method will result in the greatest:
a. total equity being reported on the balance sheet in 2011? in 2014?
b. net income being reported on the income statement in 2011? in 2014?

Check figures:
Amort. exp. 2014:
Straight-line, $18,000;
DDB, $0;
Units, $4,950

Exercise 12-14
Partial period amortization—
nearest month
LO3

Check figures:
Straight-line 2012: $18,000
Units 2012: $36,180

Genstar bought a truck on September 10, 2011, for $130,000. It was determined that the truck would be used for six years or 200,000 km and then sold for about $22,000. Complete the schedule below by calculating annual amortization to the nearest whole month for 2011, 2012, and 2013. Genstar's year-end is December 31.

	Amortization	
Year	Straight-Line	Units-of-Production*

*Assume actual units produced of:

2011	31,000	2013	52,000
2012	67,000		

Analysis component:
If amortization is not recorded, what is the effect on the income statement and balance sheet?

Exercise 12-15
Partial period amortization—
half-year convention
LO3

Check figures:
Straight-line 2013, $10,000;
DDB 2013, $9,600

International Imports purchased on October 1, 2011, $50,000 of furniture that was put into service on November 10, 2011. The furniture will be used for five years and then donated to a charity. Complete the schedule below by calculating annual amortization for 2011, 2012, and 2013 applying the half-year convention for partial periods. The year-end is December 31.

	Amortization	
Year	Straight-Line	Double-Declining-Balance

Analysis component:
What effect would it have on the financial statements if the furniture had been debited to an expense account when purchased instead of being recorded as a capital asset?

Exercise 12-16
Alternative amortization methods—
partial year's amortization
LO3

Check figure:
a. 2012 $45,000
b. 2012 $70,000

On April 1, 2011, Zarcon Gasfitting Co. purchased a trencher for $250,000. The machine was expected to last five years and have a residual value of $25,000.

Required
Calculate amortization expense for 2011 and 2012 to the nearest month, using (a) the straight-line method, and (b) the double-declining-balance method. Zarcon has a December 31 year-end.

Exercise 12-17
Revising amortization rates—
change in useful life and
residual value
LO4

Check figure:
2. $6,800

The Royal Glenora Club used straight-line amortization for a used Zamboni* that cost $43,500, under the assumption it would have a four-year life and a $5,000 trade-in value. After two years, The Royal Glenora determined that the Zamboni still had three more years of remaining useful life, after which it would have an estimated $3,850 trade-in value.

Required
1. Calculate the Zamboni's book value at the end of its second year.
2. Calculate the amount of amortization to be charged during each of the remaining years in the Zamboni's revised useful life.

*"Zamboni" is a trademark name for an ice resurfacing machine.

On April 3, 2011, Finnbar Equipment purchased a machine for $178,000. It was assumed that the machine would have a five-year life and a $38,000 trade-in value. Early in January of 2014, it was determined that the machine would have a seven-year useful life and the trade-in value would be $20,000. Finnbar uses the straight-line method to the nearest month for calculating amortization.

Required
Record amortization at December 31, 2014, Finnbar's year-end. Round to the nearest whole dollar.

Exercise 12-18
Revising amortization rates—change in useful life and residual value
LO4

Check figure:
Revised amortization = $19,059

The Jinks O'Neill Company owns a building that appeared on its balance sheet at December 31, 2011, at its original $561,000 cost less $420,750 accumulated amortization. The building has been amortized on a straight-line basis under the assumption that it would have a 20-year life and no residual value. On January 11, 2012, major structural repairs were completed on the building at a cost of $67,200. The repairs did not increase the building's capacity, but they did extend its expected life for seven years beyond the 20 years originally estimated.

Required
a. Determine the building's age as of December 31, 2011.
b. Give the entry to record the repairs on January 11, 2012, which were paid for with cash.
c. Determine the book value of the building after the repairs were recorded.
d. Give the entry to record the amortization at December 31, 2012. Round to the nearest whole dollar.

Exercise 12-19
Revising amortization rates—betterment
LO1, 4

Check figure:
c. $207,450

Teem Company purchased equipment costing $214,000 on March 3, 2011, under the assumption it would have a five-year life and a $34,000 trade-in value. On February 20, 2015, a major overhaul on the equipment required the installation of a new motor. The total cost of the installation was $56,000 and the useful life was adjusted to a total of seven years and a $30,000 trade-in value. Teem uses the straight-line method to the nearest month for calculating amortization.

Required
1. Record the installation of the new motor on February 20, 2015 (Teem paid cash).
2. Record amortization for the years 2011, 2012, 2013, and 2014.
3. Record amortization at December 31, 2015, Teem's year-end. Round to the nearest whole dollar.

Exercise 12-20
Revising amortization rates—betterment
LO1, 3, 4

Check figure:
3. Amortization for 2015 = $32,667

Gildan Activewear sold a van on March 1, 2011. The accounts showed adjusted balances on February 28, 2011, as follows:

Van	$38,500
Accumulated Amortization, Van	21,850

Required
Record the sale of the van assuming the cash proceeds were:
a. $16,650   b. $18,400   c. $13,000   d. $0 (the van was scrapped).

Exercise 12-21
Disposal of capital assets
LO5

Check figures:
b. Gain $1,750
c. Loss $3,650

Ferris Co. purchased and installed a machine on January 1, 2011, at a total cost of $185,500. Straight-line amortization was taken each year for four years, based on the assumption of a seven-year life and no residual value. The machine was disposed of on July 1, 2015, during its fifth year of service. Ferris's year-end is December 31.

Required
Present the entries to record the partial year's amortization on July 1, 2015, and to record the disposal under each of the following unrelated assumptions:
a. The machine was sold for $70,000 cash.
b. Ferris received an insurance settlement of $60,000 resulting from the total destruction of the machine in a fire.

Exercise 12-22
Partial year's amortization; disposal of capital asset
LO3, 5

Check figures:
a. Gain $3,750
b. Loss $6,250

Exercise 12-23
Exchanging capital assets
LO5

Check figure:
b. Loss $29,000

On October 6, 2011, Greenbelt Construction traded in an old tractor for a new truck, receiving a $56,000 trade-in allowance and paying the remaining $164,000 in cash. The old tractor cost $190,000, and straight-line amortization of $105,000 had been recorded as of October 6, 2011. Assume the fair value of the old tractor was equal to the trade-in allowance.

Required
a. What was the book value of the old tractor?
b. What is the gain or loss on the exchange?
c. What amount should be debited to the new Truck account?
d. Record the exchange.

Exercise 12-24
Exchanging capital assets
LO5

Check figures:
a. Gain = $2,000
b. Loss = $1,000

On November 3, 2011, Tillemanns Company exchanged a capital asset with a fair value of $87,000 for another capital asset that had a list price of $190,000. The original cost of the old capital asset was $150,000 and related accumulated amortization was $65,000 up to the date of the exchange. Tillemanns received a trade-in-allowance of $100,000 and paid the balance in cash.

Required
a. Record the exchange.
b. Assume that the fair value of the old asset was $84,000 instead of $87,000. Record the exchange.

Analysis component:
What is the dollar value that will be used to amortize the new capital asset? Explain which GAAP helped you answer the question correctly.

Exercise 12-25
Recording capital asset disposal or exchange
LO5

Check figures:
a. Loss $6,250
b. Gain $1,250
c. Loss $2,750
d. Gain $11,250

On January 2, 2011, Suzuki Service Co. disposed of a machine that cost $84,000 and had been amortized $45,250. Present the journal entries to record the disposal under each of the following unrelated assumptions:
a. The machine was sold for $32,500 cash.
b. The machine was traded in on new tools having a $117,000 cash price. A $40,000 trade-in allowance was received, and the balance was paid in cash.
c. The machine plus $68,000 was exchanged for a cube van having a fair value of $104,000.
d. The machine was traded for vacant land adjacent to the shop to be used as a parking lot. The land had a fair value of $75,000, and Suzuki paid $25,000 cash in addition to giving the seller the machine.

Exercise 12-26
Amortization of natural resources
LO6

Check figure:
Amortization Expense,
Ore Deposit $398,310
Machinery $18,744

On April 2, 2011, Northern Mining Co. paid $3,633,750 for an ore deposit containing 1,425,000 tonnes. The company also installed machinery in the mine that cost $171,000, had an estimated seven-year life with no residual value, and was capable of removing all the ore in six years. The machine will be abandoned when the ore is completely mined. Northern began operations on May 1, 2011, and mined and sold 156,200 tonnes of ore during the remaining eight months of the year. Give the December 31, 2011, entries to record the amortization of the ore deposit and the amortization of the mining machinery.

Exercise 12-27
Amortization of intangible assets
LO7

Check figure:
Amortization Expense,
Copyright $9,860

The Minuet Gallery purchased the copyright on a watercolour painting for $118,320 on January 1, 2011. The copyright legally protects its owner for 19 more years. However, Minuet Gallery plans to market and sell prints of the original for the next 12 years. Prepare journal entries to record the purchase of the copyright and the annual amortization of the copyright on December 31, 2011.

Corey Boyd has devoted years to developing a profitable business that earns an attractive return. Boyd is now considering the possibility of selling the business to you and has calculated that a fair selling price is $720,000. You agree to pay this price. The following information is available:

Exercise 12-28
Recording goodwill
LO8

Account	Account Balance December 31, 2011	Fair Value
Current assets	$249,000	$236,000
Land	38,000	294,000
Building	52,000	69,000
Accumulated amortization, building	46,000	
Equipment..	152,000	42,000
Accumulated amortization, equipment	73,000	
Total liabilities	132,500	132,500

Required
1. Prepare the entry to record your purchase of the business on January 1, 2012, assuming you paid cash of $100,000 and borrowed the balance.
2. Assume that on December 31, 2014, management performed an impairment test on the goodwill calculated in Part 1. What is the appropriate entry if the fair value of the company was determined to be $520,000 and the net identifiable assets had a current fair value of $468,500?

Check figure:
1. Goodwill $211,500

Problems

On March 31, 2011, Beechy Investments paid $5,600,000 for a tract of land and two buildings on it. The plan was to demolish Building 1 and build a new store in its place. Building 2 was to be used as a company office and was appraised at a value of $1,282,600. A lighted parking lot near Building 2 had improvements (Land Improvements 1) valued at $816,200. Without considering the buildings or improvements, the tract of land was estimated to have a value of $3,731,200. Beechy incurred the following additional costs:

Problem 12-1A
Real estate costs
LO1

Cost to demolish Building 1	$ 845,200
Cost of additional landscaping	334,400
Cost to construct new building (Building 3)	4,038,000
Cost of new land improvements near Building 2 (Land Improvements 2)..........	316,000

Required
1. Prepare a schedule having the following column headings: Land, Building 2, Building 3 Land Improvements 1, and Land Improvements 2. Allocate the costs incurred by Beechy to the appropriate columns and total each column.
2. Prepare a single journal entry dated March 31, 2011, to record all the incurred costs, assuming they were paid in cash on that date.

Check figure:
2. Land $4,763,600

Problem 12-2A
Balance sheet presentation
LO²

The adjusted balances at December 31, 2011, for Nymark Services are shown in alphabetical order below:

	2011	2010		2011	2010
Accounts payable	71,000	12,000	Office supplies	3,000	2,900
Accumulated amortization, equipment	91,000	81,000	Operating expenses	976,000	714,000
Accumulated amortization, franchise	24,000	14,000	Patent	20,000	20,000
Accumulated amortization, patent	5,000	3,000	Prepaid rent	50,000	60,000
Accumulated amortization, tools	56,000	53,000	Reg Nymark, capital*	227,900	77,900
Accumulated amortization, vehicles	136,000	122,000	Reg Nymark, withdrawals	40,000	48,000
Cash	15,000	36,000	Salaries payable	41,000	33,000
Equipment	200,000	125,000	Service revenue	900,000	942,000
Franchise	52,000	52,000	Tools	179,900	126,000
Notes payable, due in 2020	300,000	162,000	Vehicles	316,000	316,000

*The owner, Reg Nymark, made no additional investments during the year.

Check figures:
2010 Total assets = $464,900
2011 Total assets = $523,900

Required
Prepare a comparative classified balance sheet at December 31, 2011.

Analysis component:
Are Nymark's assets financed mainly by debt or equity in 2010? in 2011? Is the change in how assets were financed from 2010 to 2011 favourable or unfavourable? Explain.

Problem 12-3A
Calculating amortization—
partial periods
LO², 3

Check figure:
DDB 2013: $92,000

Malaspina Touring Company runs boat tours along the west coast of British Columbia. It purchased on March 5, 2011, for cash of $690,000, a cruising boat with a useful life of 10 years or 13,250 hours with a residual value of $160,000. The company's year-end is December 31.

Required
Calculate amortization expense for the fiscal years 2011, 2012, and 2013 by completing a schedule with the following headings (round to the nearest whole dollar):

	Amortization Method[1]:		
Year	Straight-Line	Double-Declining-Balance	Units-of-Production[2]

[1] Amortization is calculated to the nearest month.
[2] Assume actual hours of service were: 2011, 720; 2012, 1,780; 2013, 1,535.

Analysis component:
If you could ignore the matching principle, how could you record the purchase of the boat? What impact would this have on the financial statements in the short and long term?

Problem 12-4A
Calculating amortization—
partial periods
LO², 3

Check figure:
DDB 2013: $99,360

Refer to the information in Problem 12-3A. Redo the question assuming that amortization for partial periods is calculated using the half-year convention.

On July 1, 2011, Dofasco Company purchased for $450,000 equipment having an estimated useful life of eight years with an estimated residual value of $75,000. Amortization is taken for the portion of the year the asset is used. The company has a December 31 year-end.

Required
Complete the following schedules (round calculations to the nearest whole dollar):

	2011	2012	2013
1. Double-declining-balance method			
Equipment	_____	_____	_____
Less: Accumulated amortization	_____	_____	_____
Year-end book value..	_____	_____	_____
Amortization expense for the year......................	_____	_____	_____
2. Straight-line method			
Equipment	_____	_____	_____
Less: Accumulated amortization	_____	_____	_____
Year-end book value..	_____	_____	_____
Amortization expense for the year......................	_____	_____	_____

Problem 12-5A
Calculating amortization—partial periods
LO2, 3

Check figures:
1. 2013 Amortization expense $73,828
2. 2013 Amortization expense $46,875

Avis Company
Partial Balance Sheet
April 30, 2011

Property, plant, and equipment:

Land..		$1,300,000
Building[1]	$1,950,000	
Less: Accumulated amortization	1,430,000	520,000
Equipment[2]	1,500,000	
Less: Accumulated amortization	636,000	864,000
Total property, plant, and equipment.............................		$2,684,000

[1] The building was purchased on May 3, 2000, and is amortized to the nearest whole month using the straight-line method. Amortization is based on a 15-year life after which it will be demolished and replaced with a new one.

[2] The equipment was purchased on November 3, 2008, and is amortized to the nearest whole month using the double-declining-balance method. The total estimated useful life is 10 years with a residual value of $500,000.

Problem 12-6A
Calculating amortization
LO2

Check figures:
1. Dr. Amortization Expense, Building $130,000
1. Dr. Amortization Expense, Equipment $172,800
2. Total PPE = $2,381,200

Required
1. Calculate **and** record amortization for the year just ended April 30, 2012, for both the building and equipment.
2. Prepare the property, plant, and equipment section of the balance sheet at April 30, 2012.

Cally Construction recently negotiated a lump-sum purchase of several assets from a company that was going out of business. The purchase was completed on March 1, 2011, at a total cash price of $1,575,000 and included a building, land, certain land improvements, and 12 vehicles. The estimated market values of the assets were: building, $816,000; land, $578,000; land improvements, $85,000; and vehicles, $221,000. The company's fiscal year ends on December 31.

Required
1. Prepare a schedule to allocate the lump-sum purchase price to the separate assets that were purchased. Also present the journal entry to record the purchase.
2. Calculate the 2011 amortization expense on the building using the straight-line method to the nearest whole month, assuming a 15-year life and a $51,300 residual value.
3. Calculate the 2011 amortization expense on the land improvements assuming a five-year life and double-declining-balance amortization calculated to the nearest whole month.

Problem 12-7A
Capital asset costs; partial year's amortization; alternative methods
LO1, 2, 3

Check figures:
2. $39,150
3. $26,250

Analysis component:
Assume the assets purchased on March 1, 2011, were not put into service until May 23, 2011. Would this affect your answers in parts 2 and 3 above? Explain.

Problem 12-8A
Alternative amortization methods; partial year's amortization
LO2, 3

Check figures:
2011 SL = $31,667
2013 DDB = $87,500
2015 Units = $74,720

A machine that cost $420,000, with a four-year life and an estimated $40,000 residual value, was installed in Magnotta Company's factory on September 1, 2011. The factory manager estimated that the machine would produce 475,000 units of product during its life. It actually produced the following units: 2011, 21,400; 2012, 122,400; 2013, 119,600; 2014, 118,200; and 2015, 102,000. Magnotta's year-end is December 31.

Required
Prepare a form with the following column headings:

Year	Straight-Line	Units-of-Production	Double-Declining-Balance

Show the amortization for each year and the total amortization for the machine under each amortization method calculated to the nearest whole month. Round to the nearest whole dollar.

Problem 12-9A
Calculating amortization; partial year's amortization
LO2, 3

At December 31, 2011, Espo Servicing's balance sheet showed capital asset information as detailed in the schedule below. Espo calculates amortization to the nearest whole month.

	Cost Information					Amortization		
Description	Purchase	Date of Method	Amortization Cost[1]	Residual	Life	Balance of Accum. Amort. Dec. 31, 2011	Amortization Expense for 2012	Balance of Accum. Amort. Dec. 31, 2012
Office Equip.	March 27/08	Straight-line	$104,000	$28,000	10 yr.			
Machinery	June 4/08	Double-declining-balance	$550,000	$92,000	6 yr.			
Truck	Nov. 13/11	Units-of-production	$226,000	$52,000	250,000 km[2]			

[1] There have been no disposals or betterments since the date of purchase.
[2] Actual kilometres driven were: 2011, 14,000; 2012, 68,000.

Check figures:
Amort. Expense:
Office equip. $7,600;
Machinery $39,276;
Truck $47,328

Required
Complete the schedule (round only your final answers).

Problem 12-10A
Partial year's amortization; revising amortization rates
LO1, 2, 4

BMI Company completed the following transactions involving delivery trucks:

	2011	
Mar.	26	Paid cash for a new delivery truck, $38,830 plus $2,330 provincial sales tax. The truck was estimated to have a five-year life and a $6,000 trade-in value.
Dec.	31	Recorded straight-line amortization on the truck to the nearest whole month.
	2012	
Dec.	31	Recorded straight-line amortization on the truck to the nearest whole month. However, due to new information obtained early in January, the original estimated useful life of the truck was changed from five years to four years, and the original estimated trade-in value was increased to $7,000.

Check figure:
Dec. 31/12 Amort. Exp. $8,888

Required
Prepare journal entries to record the transactions.

The December 31, 2011, adjusted trial balance of WeldCo showed the following information:

Machinery	$696,000
Accumulated amortization, machinery[1]	308,000
Office furniture	112,000
Accumulated amortization, office furniture[2]	62,000

[1] Remaining useful life four years; estimated residual $80,000
[2] Remaining useful life five years; estimated residual $14,000.

On July 7, 2012, a highly specialized component costing $104,000 was installed on the machinery to increase its productivity significantly. The useful life of the machinery did not change but the residual value was adjusted to $120,000. At the beginning of 2012, it was determined that the estimated life of the office furniture should be reduced by two years and the residual value decreased by $8,000. WeldCo calculates amortization using the straight-line method to the nearest month.

Required
Prepare the entries to record amortization on the machinery and office furniture for the year ended December 31, 2012 (round calculations to the nearest whole dollar).

Problem 12-11A
Revising amortization rates
LO[4]

Check figures:
Amort. Exp., Machinery $86,143;
Amort. Exp., Office Furn. $14,667

Wall Construction showed the following adjusted balances in selected capital asset accounts at January 1, 2011:

Machinery	$750,000
Accumulated amortization, machinery[1]	340,000
Truck	120,000
Accumulated amortization, truck[2]	40,000

[1] Remaining useful life eight years; estimated residual $110,000
[2] Remaining useful life four years; estimated residual $30,000

The following transactions occurred during 2011 and 2012 regarding the above assets:

2011
Jan. 1 Purchased a new motor for the truck; $30,000 on account; terms 2/10, n/30. Labour costs to install the motor were $15,000; assume cash.
30 Paid for the January 1 purchase.
June 15 The annual maintenance was performed on the machinery at a cost of $12,000 cash.
Dec. 31 Recorded straight-line amortization on the machinery and truck.
2012
Feb. 10 New tires were purchased for the truck; the tires cost a total of $3,000 and the installation costs were $800; paid cash.
Oct. 15 Determined that a new truck would be purchased at the end of 2013 and the current one sold; no change in estimated residual value.
Dec. 31 Recorded straight-line amortization on the machinery and truck.

Problem 12-12A
Revenue and capital expenditures; revising amortization rates
LO[1, 2, 4]

Required
Record the amortization expense at December 31, 2011, and December 31, 2012, for both the machinery and the truck.

Check figures:
Machinery: Dec. 31/12 = $37,500
Truck: Dec. 31/12 = $23,750

Analysis component:
Assume that Wall Construction had $500,000 of revenue expenditures and debited these to various capital asset accounts. What is the effect on the income statement and balance sheet? Identify which GAAP are being violated and why.

Problem 12-13A
Revenue and capital expenditures; partial year's amortization; revising amortization rates

LO1, 2, 3, 4

Anzak Air Services completed these transactions involving the purchase and operation of a used small aircraft:

	2011	
July	1	Paid $510,000 cash for a used small aircraft, plus $30,800 in provincial sales tax and $5,000 for transportation charges. The aircraft was estimated to have a four-year life and a $69,000 residual value.
Oct	2	Paid $7,320 to install air conditioning in the aircraft. This increased the estimated residual value of the aircraft by $2,220.
Dec.	31	Recorded straight-line amortization on the aircraft (to nearest whole month).
	2012	
Feb.	17	Paid $1,840 to repair the aircraft after some minor damage in the storage area.
June	30	Paid $9,000 to overhaul the aircraft's engine. As a result, the estimated useful life of the aircraft was increased by two years.
Dec.	31	Recorded straight-line amortization on the aircraft (to nearest whole month).

Check figures:
Dec. 31/11 Amort. Exp.,
Aircraft $59,940;
Dec. 31/12 Amort. Exp.,
Aircraft $97,348

Required
Prepare journal entries to record the transactions.

Problem 12-14A
Partial period amortization; disposal of capital assets

LO2, 3, 5

MicroWare showed the following selected capital asset balances on December 31, 2011:

Land	$496,000
Building	658,000
Accumulated amortization, building[1]	492,000
Equipment	214,000
Accumulated amortization, equipment[2]	93,000

[1] Remaining estimated useful life is eight years with a residual value of $100,000; amortized using the straight-line method to the nearest whole month.
[2] Total estimated useful life is 10 years with a residual value of $20,000; amortized using the double-declining-balance method to the nearest whole month.

Check figures:
1. Gain $84,188
2. Loss $29,833

Required
Prepare the entries for each of the following (round final calculations to the nearest whole dollar).
1. The land and building were sold on September 27, 2012, for $740,000 cash.
2. The equipment was sold on November 2, 2012, for $71,000 cash.

Problem 12-15A
Disposal of capital assets

LO1, 2, 3, 5

Thomasville Furniture purchased a used machine for $83,500 on January 2, 2011. It was repaired the next day at a cost of $3,420 and installed on a new platform that cost $1,080. The company predicted that the machine would be used for six years and would then have a $14,800 residual value. Amortization was to be charged on a straight-line basis to the nearest whole month. A full year's amortization was recorded on December 31, 2011. On September 30, 2016, it was retired.

Check figures:
2. Dec. 31/11 $12,200
3a. Loss $2,850
3b. Gain $1,650
3c. Gain $550

Required
1. Prepare journal entries to record the purchase of the machine, the cost of repairing it, and the installation. Assume that cash was paid.
2. Prepare entries to record amortization on the machine on December 31 of its first year and on September 30 in the year of its disposal (round calculations to the nearest whole dollar).
3. Prepare entries to record the retirement of the machine under each of the following unrelated assumptions:
   a. It was sold for $15,000.
   b. It was sold for $19,500.
   c. It was destroyed in a fire and the insurance company paid $18,400 in full settlement of the loss claim.

In 2011, Rhondda Company completed the following transactions involving delivery trucks:

July 5 Traded in an old truck and paid $25,600 in cash for furniture. The accounting records on July 5 showed the cost of the old truck at $36,000 and related accumulated amortization of $6,000. The furniture was estimated to have a six-year life and a $6,268 trade-in value. The invoice for the exchange showed these items:

Price of the furniture	$45,100
Trade-in allowance (equal to fair value of truck)	(19,500)
Total paid in cash	$25,600

Dec. 31 Recorded straight-line amortization on the furniture (to nearest whole month).

Required
Prepare journal entries to record the transactions.

Antigonish Co. completed the following transactions involving machinery:

Machine No. 15-50 was purchased for cash on April 1, 2011, at an installed cost of $105,800. Its useful life was estimated to be six years with an $8,600 trade-in value. Straight-line amortization was recorded for the machine at the ends of 2011, 2012, and 2013. On March 29, 2014, it was traded for Machine No. 17-95, with an installed cash price of $124,000. A trade-in allowance of $60,420 was received for Machine No. 15-50, and the balance was paid in cash.

Machine No. 17-95's life was predicted to be four years with a trade-in value of $16,400. Double-declining-balance amortization on this machine was recorded each December 31. On October 2, 2015, it was traded for Machine No. BT-311, which had an installed cash price of $1,074,000. A trade-in allowance of $40,000 was received for Machine No. 17-95, and the balance was paid in cash.

It was estimated that Machine No. BT-311 would produce 200,000 units of product during its five-year useful life, after which it would have a $70,000 trade-in value. Units-of-production amortization was recorded for the machine for 2015, a period in which it produced 31,000 units of product. Between January 1, 2016, and August 21, 2018, the machine produced 108,000 more units. On August 21, 2018, it was sold for $162,400.

Required
Prepare journal entries to record:
a. The amortization expense recorded to the nearest whole month on the first December 31 of each machine's life.
b. The purchase/exchange/disposal of each machine. Assume any trade-in values are equal to the asset's fair value.

On February 20, 2011, Red River Industries Ltd. paid $4,640,000 for land estimated to contain 11.6 million tonnes of recoverable ore of a valuable mineral. It installed machinery costing $696,000, which had a 12-year life and no residual value, and was capable of exhausting the ore deposit in nine years. The machinery was paid for on May 24, 2011, six days before mining operations began. The company removed 744,000 tonnes of ore during the first seven months of operations.

Required
Prepare entries to record:
a. The purchase of the land
b. The installation of the machinery
c. The first seven months' amortization on the mine under the assumption that the land will be valueless after the ore is mined
d. The first seven months' amortization on the machinery, which will be abandoned after the ore is fully mined.

Problem 12-16A
Partial year's amortization; exchanging capital assets
LO2, 3, 5

Check figures:
July 5/11: Loss $10,500
Dec. 31/11: Amort. Exp. $3,236

Problem 12-17A
Partial year's amortization; alternative methods; exchange/ disposal of capital assets
LO2, 3, 5

Check figures:
a. Machine 15-50: $12,150;
   Machine 17-95: $46,500;
   Machine BT-311: $155,620

Problem 12-18A
Natural resources
LO6

Check figures:
c. $297,600
d. $44,640

Problem 12-19A
Intangible assets
LO⁷

Check figure:
b. $20,000

On October 1, 2011, Bayster purchased for $240,000 the copyright to publish the music composed by a local Celtic group. Bayster expects the music to be sold over the next three years.

Required
Prepare entries to record:
a. The purchase of the copyright, and
b. The amortization for the year ended December 31, 2011, calculated to the nearest whole month.

Alternate Problems

Problem 12-1B
Real estate costs
LO¹

In 2011, WebSpeed Technologies paid $1,350,000 for a tract of land on which two buildings were located. The plan was to demolish Building A and build a new factory (Building C) in its place. Building B was to be used as a company office and was appraised at a value of $472,770. A lighted parking lot near Building B had improvements valued at $125,145. Without considering the buildings or improvements, the tract of land was estimated to have a value of $792,585.

WebSpeed incurred the following additional costs:

Cost to demolish Building A	$ 117,000
Cost to landscape new building site	172,500
Cost to construct new building (Building C)	1,356,000
Cost of new land improvements (Land Improvements C)	101,250

Check figure:
2. Dr. Land $1,059,000

Required
1. Prepare a schedule having the following column headings: Land, Building B, Building C, Land Improvements B, and Land Improvements C. Allocate the costs incurred by WebSpeed to the appropriate columns and total each column.
2. Prepare a single journal entry dated June 1 to record all the incurred costs, assuming they were paid in cash on that date.

Problem 12-2B
Balance sheet presentation
LO²

The adjusted balances at September 30, 2011, for Aidan Consulting are shown in alphabetical order below:

	2011	2010		2011	2010
Accounts payable	3,000	1,750	Consulting fees earned	300,000	346,000
Accounts receivable	1,000	2,400	Copyright	4,000	4,000
Accumulated amortization, building	30,000	28,000	Land	38,000	38,000
Accumulated amortization, copyright	600	300	Machinery	164,000	64,000
Accumulated amortization, machinery	50,000	46,000	Notes payable, due October 2016	127,900	31,000
Aidan Cummings, capital	125,600	150,140	Operating expenses	310,000	347,540
Aidan Cummings, withdrawals	40,000	23,000	Prepaid insurance	0	850
Building	125,000	125,000	Unearned fees	46,000	3,100
Cash	500	1,500			

The owner, Aidan Cummings, made a $75,000 additional investment during the year ended September 30, 2011.

Check figures:
2010 Total assets = $161,450
2011 Total assets = $251,900

Required
Prepare a comparative classified balance sheet at September 30, 2011.

Analysis component:
How were Aidan's assets mainly financed in 2010? In 2011? Has the change in how assets were financed from 2010 to 2011 *strengthened* the balance sheet? (To strengthen the balance sheet is to decrease the percentage of assets that are financed by debt as opposed to equity.)

Tundra Tours runs tundra buggy expeditions in northern Manitoba for tourists to catch a glimpse of the abundant caribou, polar bears, and other wildlife. Tundra purchased a tundra buggy on October 19, 2011, for cash of $145,000. Its estimated useful life is five years or 100,000 kilometres with a residual value estimated at $25,000. Tundra Tours' year-end is December 31.

Problem 12-3B
Calculating amortization; partial periods
LO2, 3

Check figure:
DDB 2013: $32,480

Required

Calculate amortization expense for each fiscal year of the asset's useful life by completing a schedule with the following headings *(round calculations to the nearest whole dollar)*:

	Amortization Method¹:		
Year	**Straight-Line**	**Double-Declining-Balance**	**Units-of-Production²**

¹ Amortization is calculated to the nearest month.
² Assume actual kilometres of use were: 2011, 5,800; 2012, 19,400; 2013, 22,850; 2014, 25,700; 2015, 19,980; 2016, 14,600.

Refer to the information in Problem 12-3B. Redo the question assuming that amortization for partial periods is calculated using the half-year convention.

Problem 12-4B
Calculating amortization; partial periods
LO2, 3

Check figure:
DDB 2013: $27,840

On April 2, 2011, CryptoLogic Company purchased for $420,000 machinery having an estimated useful life of 10 years with an estimated residual value of $40,000. The company's year-end is December 31. Amortization is calculated using the half-year rule.

Problem 12-5B
Calculating amortization; partial periods
LO2, 3

Check figures:
1. 2013 Amortization expense $60,480
2. 2013 Amortization expense $38,000

Required

Complete the following schedules:

	2011	2012	2013
1. Double-declining-balance method			
Machinery..			
Less: Accumulated amortization			
Year-end book value......................................			
Amortization expense for the year..................			
2. Straight-line method			
Machinery..			
Less: Accumulated amortization			
Year-end book value......................................			
Amortization expense for the year..................			

Problem 12-6B

Calculating amortization

LO²

Ace Mechanical
Partial Balance Sheet
December 31, 2011

Property, plant, and equipment:

Delivery van¹	$125,000	
Less: Accumulated amortization	82,500	$ 42,500
Machinery²	320,000	
Less: Accumulated amortization	256,667	63,333
Total property, plant, and equipment		$105,833

¹ The delivery van was purchased on January 1, 2006, and is amortized to the nearest whole month using the straight-line method. Its total estimated useful life is eight years with a $15,000 residual value.

² The machinery was purchased on August 1, 2009, and is amortized to the nearest whole month using the double-declining-balance method. The useful life is estimated to be four years with a residual value of $9,000.

Check figures:
1. Dr. Amortization Expense, Van $13,750;
1. Dr. Amortization Expense, Machinery $31,667
2. Total PPE = $60,416

Required
1. Calculate and record amortization for the year just ended December 31, 2012, for both the delivery van and machinery (round calculations to the nearest whole dollar).
2. Prepare the capital asset section of the balance sheet at December 31, 2012.

Problem 12-7B

Capital asset costs; partial year's amortization; alternative methods

LO¹, ², ³

Willo Company recently negotiated a lump-sum purchase of several assets from a contractor who was planning to change locations. The purchase was completed on September 30, 2011, at a total cash price of $870,000, and included a building, land, certain land improvements, and a heavy general purpose truck. The estimated market values of the assets were: building, $552,750; land, $331,650; land improvements, $100,500; and truck, $20,100. The company's fiscal year ends on December 31.

Check figures:
2. $7,350
3. $5,438

Required
1. Prepare a schedule to allocate the lump-sum purchase price to the separate assets that were purchased. Also present the journal entry to record the purchase.
2. Calculate the 2011 amortization expense on the building using the straight-line method to the nearest whole month, assuming a 15-year life and a $37,500 residual value.
3. Calculate the 2011 amortization expense on the land improvements assuming an eight-year life and double-declining-balance amortization to the nearest whole month (round calculations to the nearest whole dollar).

Problem 12-8B

Alternative amortization methods; partial year's amortization

LO², ³

On May 2, 2011, Gibbons Co. purchased and installed a new machine that cost $195,000, with a five-year life and an estimated $27,300 residual value. Management estimated that the machine would produce 120,000 units of product during its life. Actual production of units was as follows:

2011	16,800
2012	26,400
2013	24,000
2014	22,800
2015	19,000
2016	22,100

Check figures:
2011 SL = $22,360
2016 Units = $15,100
2013 DDB = $34,320

Required
Prepare a schedule with the following column headings.

Year	Straight-Line	Units-of-Production	Double-Declining-Balance

Show the amortization for each year (calculated to the nearest whole month) and the total amortization for the machine under each amortization method. For units-of-production, round the amortization charge per unit to two decimal places. Gibbons Co.'s year-end is December 31.

At April 30, 2011, East Coast Helicopter's year-end, the balance sheet showed capital asset information as detailed in the schedule below. East Coast Helicopter calculates amortization for partial periods using the half-year convention.

Problem 12-9B
Calculating amortization;
partial year's amortization
LO2, 3

			Cost Information			Amortization		
Description	Purchase	Date of Method	Amortization[1] Cost[1]	Residual	Life	Balance of Accum. Amort. Apr. 30, 2011	Amortization Expense for 2012	Balance of Accum. Amort. Apr. 30, 2012
Hangar	Oct. 3/08	Straight-line	$ 52,000	$ 14,000	20 yr.			
Helicopter	Oct. 28/08	Units-of-Production	$540,000	$180,000	10,000 flying hours[2]			
Tools	Nov. 3/08	Double-declining-balance	$ 64,000	$ 15,000	5 yr.			

[1] There have been no disposals or betterments since the date of purchase.
[2] Actual flying hours were (for years ended April 30): 2009, 94; 2010, 1,015; 2011, 928; 2012, 1,059.

Required
Complete the schedule.

Whitty Company completed the following transactions involving the purchase of delivery equipment.

Problem 12-10B
Partial year's amortization;
revising amortization rates
LO1, 2, 4

2011
June   26   Paid cash for a new truck, $34,200 plus $1,710 in provincial sales taxes. The truck was estimated to have a four-year life and a $9,000 residual value.
July   5   Paid $1,890 for special racks installed on the truck. The racks did not increase the truck's estimated trade-in value but did improve the truck's usefulness.
Dec.   31   Recorded straight-line amortization on the truck to the nearest whole month.
2012
Jan.   5   It was determined that the estimated useful life of the truck should be revised to a total of six years and the residual value changed to $5,050.
Mar.   15   Paid $330 for repairs to the truck's fender damaged when the driver backed into a loading dock.
Dec.   31   Recorded straight-line amortization on the truck to the nearest whole month.

Required
Prepare journal entries to record the transactions.

The December 31, 2011, adjusted trial balance of Cascades Company showed the following information:

Problem 12-11B
Revising amortization rates
LO4

Building...	$229,000
Accumulated amortization, building[1]	112,000
Equipment..	98,000
Accumulated amortization, equipment[2]	32,000

[1] Remaining useful life 15 years; estimated residual value $50,000
[2] Remaining useful life six years; estimated residual value $15,000.

On September 28, 2012, a major renovation on the building was completed, costing $152,000 and increasing its estimated residual value to $120,000. The estimated useful life of the building was not affected by the renovation. At the beginning of 2012, it was determined that the remaining estimated life of the equipment should be 10 years and the residual value $5,000. Cascades Company calculates amortization using the straight-line method to the nearest month (round calculations to the nearest whole dollar).

Required
Prepare the entries to record amortization on the building and equipment for the year ended December 31, 2012.

Problem 12-12B
Revenue and capital expenditures; revising amortization rates
LO1, 2, 4

Golf World showed the following adjusted balances in selected capital asset accounts at January 1, 2011:

Equipment..	$450,000
Accumulated amortization, equipment[1]	140,000
Clubhouse	820,000
Accumulated amortization, clubhouse[2]	670,000

[1] Remaining useful life three years; estimated residual value $82,000
[2] Remaining useful life five years; estimated residual value $0

The following transactions occurred during 2011 and 2012 regarding the above assets:

2011		
June	10	Annual maintenance was performed on the equipment at a cost of $60,000 cash.
Nov.	1	The clubhouse was closed for the season and major renovations started; estimated total cost: $340,000.
	30	The renovations were completed on schedule but over-budget; total final cost $417,500. The remaining useful life and residual value were revised to 15 years and $0. The clubhouse was officially reopened on this date with a Winter Wonderland Gala, free and for members only, at a cost of $35,000 cash.
Dec.	31	Recorded straight-line amortization on the equipment and clubhouse.
2012		
Feb.	10	It was determined that the remaining useful life and residual value on the equipment for 2012 should be adjusted to five years and $40,000.
Oct.	15	The banquet hall in the clubhouse was repainted at a cost of $7,500; paid cash.
Dec.	31	Recorded straight-line amortization on the equipment and clubhouse.

Check figures:
Dec. 31/12 amortization expense:
Clubhouse, $36,000;
Equipment, $38,800

Required
Record the amortization expense at December 31, 2011, and December 31, 2012, for both the equipment and clubhouse.

Analysis component:
Assume that Golf World had revised the remaining useful life and residual value of the clubhouse to 30 years and $150,000 on December 31, 2011. Without doing calculations, explain the effect on the income statement and balance sheet. Is it important to estimate the useful life and residual value of capital assets correctly? Explain why.

Problem 12-13B
Revenue and capital expenditures; partial year's amortization; disposal
LO1, 2, 3, 5

On January 9, 2011, Gibbons purchased a used machine for $68,400. The next day, it was repaired at a cost of $8,100 and was mounted on a new platform that cost $6,300. Management estimated that the machine would be used for three years and would then have a $10,800 residual value. Amortization was to be charged on a straight-line basis to the nearest whole month. A full year's amortization was charged on December 31 of the first and second years of the machine's use, and on March 29, 2013, the machine was retired from service.

Check figures:
2. Dec. 31/11 Amort. Exp. $24,000
Mar. 29/13 Amort. Exp. $6,000
3a. Gain $6,450
3b. Loss $4,650
3c. Loss $6,750

Required
1. Prepare journal entries to record the purchase of the machine, the cost of repairing it, and the installation. Assume that cash was paid.
2. Prepare entries to record amortization on the machine on December 31, 2011, and on March 29, 2013. Assume amortization is calculated to the nearest whole month.
3. Prepare entries to record the retirement of the machine under each of the following unrelated assumptions:
   a. It was sold for $35,250.
   b. It was sold for $24,150.
   c. It was destroyed in a fire and the insurance company paid $22,050 in full settlement of the loss claim.

Tamboora Industries showed the following selected capital asset balances on January 31, 2011:

Van	$46,000
Accumulated amortization, van[1]	29,000
Machinery	92,000
Accumulated amortization, machinery[2]	14,600
Equipment	54,000
Accumulated amortization, equipment[3]	32,000

[1] Remaining estimated useful life is 40,000 kilometres with a residual value of $7,000; amortized using the units-of-production method.
[2] Total estimated useful life is 10 years with a residual value of $12,000; amortized using the double-declining-balance method to the nearest whole month.
[3] Remaining estimated useful life is three years with a residual value of $4,000; amortized using the straight-line method to the nearest whole month.

Required
Prepare the entries to record the following disposals:
1. The van was sold on March 2, 2011, for cash of $12,800. It had been driven 4,500 kilometres from January 31, 2011, to the date of sale.
2. The machinery was sold on August 27, 2011, for cash of $68,370.
3. The equipment was sold on June 29, 2011, for cash of $19,800.

Problem 12-14B
Partial period amortization; disposal of capital assets
LO2, 3, 5

Check figures:
1. Accum. Amort. $30,125;
2. Accum. Amort. $23,630;
3. Accum. Amort. $34,500

On January 1, 2011, Brodie purchased a used machine for $130,000. The next day, it was repaired at a cost of $3,390 and mounted on a new platform that cost $4,800. Management estimated that the machine would be used for seven years and would then have an $18,000 residual value. Amortization was to be charged on a straight-line basis to the nearest whole month. A full year's amortization was charged on December 31, 2011, through to December 31, 2015, and on April 1, 2016, the machine was retired from service.

Required
1. Prepare journal entries to record the purchase of the machine, the cost of repairing it, and the installation. Assume that cash was paid.
2. Prepare entries to record amortization on the machine on December 31, 2011, and on April 1, 2016 (round calculations to the nearest whole dollar).
3. Prepare entries to record the retirement of the machine under each of the following unrelated assumptions:
   a. It was sold for $30,000.
   b. It was sold for $50,000.
   c. It was destroyed in a fire and the insurance company paid $20,000 in full settlement of the loss claim.

Problem 12-15B
Disposal of capital assets
LO1, 2, 3, 5

Check figures:
2. Dec. 31/11 $17,170
Apr. 1/16 $4,293
3a. Loss $18,047
3b. Gain $1,953
3c. Loss $28,047

During 2011, Delton Hardware had the following transactions.

2011
Aug. 31   Delton traded in furniture with a cost of $21,000 and accumulated amortization of $12,900 recorded in the accounting records on this date. Delton paid $28,200 in cash for a computer system that was estimated to have a three-year life and a $9,600 trade-in value equal to the asset's fair value. The invoice for the exchange showed these items:

Price of the computer equipment	$37,200
Trade-in allowance granted on the furniture	(9,000)
Total paid in cash	$28,200

Sept. 4   Paid $3,690 for upgrades to the computer equipment, which increased its usefulness.
Dec. 31   Recorded straight-line amortization on the computer equipment to the nearest whole month. Round calculations to the nearest whole dollar.

Required
Prepare journal entries to record the transactions.

Problem 12-16B
Partial year's amortization; revising amortization; exchanging capital assets
LO2, 3, 4, 5

Check figures:
Aug. 31/11: Gain $900;
Dec. 31/11: Amort. Exp. $3,477

Problem 12-17B
Partial year's amortization; alternative methods; exchange/disposal of capital assets

LO2, 3, 5

Montreal Printing Co. completed the following transactions involving printing equipment:

Machine 366-90 was purchased for cash on May 1, 2011, at an installed cost of $48,600. Its useful life was estimated to be four years with a $5,400 trade-in value. Straight-line amortization was recorded for the machine at the end of 2011 and 2012.

On August 5, 2013, it was traded for machine 366-91, which had an installed cash price of $36,000. A trade-in allowance of $27,000 was received and the balance was paid in cash. The new machine's life was estimated at five years with a $6,300 trade-in value. Double-declining-balance amortization was recorded on each December 31 of its life. On February 1, 2016, it was sold for $9,000.

Machine 367-11 was purchased on February 1, 2016, at an installed cash price of $53,100. It was estimated that the new machine would produce 75,000 units during its useful life after which it would have a $5,400 trade-in value. Units-of-production amortization was recorded on the machine for 2016, a period in which it produced 7,500 units of product. Between January 1 and October 3, 2017, the machine produced 11,250 more units. On October 3, 2017, it was sold for $36,000.

Check figures:
1. Machine 366-90: $7,200;
Machine 366-91: $6,000;
Machine 367-11: $4,800

Required
Prepare journal entries to record:
1. The amortization expense recorded to the nearest whole month on the first December 31 of each machine's life (for units-of-production, round the rate per unit to two decimal places).
2. The purchase/exchange/disposal of each machine. Assume any trade-in values are equal to the asset's fair value.

Problem 12-18B
Natural resources

LO6

On May 8, 2011, Hubert Industries paid $1,080,000 for land estimated to contain nine million tonnes of recoverable ore. It installed machinery costing $187,500, which had an eight-year life and no residual value and was capable of exhausting the ore deposit in five years. The machinery was paid for on June 28, four days before mining operations began. The company removed 720,000 tonnes of ore during the first six months of operations.

Check figures:
3. $86,400
4. $15,000

Required
Prepare entries to record:
1. The purchase of the land
2. The installation of the machinery
3. The first six months' amortization on the mine under the assumption that the land will be valueless after the ore is mined, and
4. The first six months' amortization on the machinery, which will be abandoned after the ore is fully mined.

Problem 12-19B
Intangible assets

LO7

Check figure:
2. Total PPE = $612,500

On Febrary 3, 2011, Letsin Pharmacy Products purchased the patent for a new drug for cash of $184,000. Letsin expects the drug to be sold over the next 10 years.

Required
1. Prepare entries to record the:
   a. purchase of the patent, and
   b. amortization for the year ended December 31, 2011, calculated to the nearest whole month. Round to the nearest dollar.
2. On December 31, 2011, Letsin's adjusted trial balance showed the additional asset accounts shown below. Prepare the asset section of the balance sheet at December 31, 2011, including the patent purchased on February 3, 2011.

Accounts receivable	238,000
Accumulated amortization, equipment	216,000
Accumulated amortization, building	157,500
Allowance for doubtful accounts	7,000
Cash	86,000
Equipment	398,000
Building	496,000
Land	92,000
Merchandise inventory	113,000

Analytical and Review Problem

At the last meeting of the executive committee of Kearins, Ltd., the controller was severely criticized by both the president and vice-president of production about the recognition of periodic amortization. The president was unhappy with the fact that what he referred to as "a fictitious item" was deducted, resulting in depressed net income. In his words, "Amortization is a fiction when the assets being amortized are worth far more than we paid for them. What the controller is doing is unduly understating our net income. This in turn is detrimental to our shareholders because it results in the undervaluation of our shares on the market."

A & R Problem 12-1

The vice-president was equally adamant about the periodic amortization charges; however, she presented a different argument. She said, "Our maintenance people tell me that the level of maintenance is such that our plant and equipment will last virtually forever." She further stated that charging amortization on top of maintenance expenses is double-counting—it seems reasonable to charge either maintenance or amortization but not both.

The time taken by other pressing matters did not permit the controller to answer; instead, you were asked to prepare a report to the executive committee to deal with the issues raised by the president and vice-president.

Required

As the controller's assistant, prepare the required report.

Ethics Challenge

Marcia Diamond is a small business owner who handles all the books for her business. Her company just finished a year in which a large amount of borrowed funds were invested into a new building addition as well as numerous equipment and fixture additions. Marcia's banker requires that she submit semiannual financial statements for his file so he can monitor the financial health of her business. He has warned her that if profit margins erode, making the loan riskier from the bank's point of view, he might raise the interest rate on the borrowed funds. Marcia knows that her profit margin is likely to decline in this current year. As she posts year-end adjusting entries, she decides to apply the following amortization rule: All capital additions for the current year are considered put into service the first day of the following month.

EC 12-1

Required

1. Identify the decisions managers like Ms. Diamond must make in applying amortization methods.
2. Is Marcia's decision an ethical violation, or is it a legitimate decision that managers make in calculating amortization?
3. How will Marcia's amortization rule affect the profit margin of her business?

Focus on Financial Statements

FFS 12-1

GelCo's Capital Asset Subledger at January 1, 2011, appeared as follows:

		Cost Information					Amortization	
Description	Date of Purchase[1]	Amort. Method[2]	Original Cost[3]	Residual	Life	Accum. Amort. Balance Dec. 31, 2010	Amort. Expense for 2011
Land[4]	July 3/08		$140,000				
Building[4]	July 3/08	S/L	227,000	20,000	15 yr.		
Machinery[5]	Mar 20/08	Units	75,000	15,000	250,000 units		
Truck[6]	Mar 01/08	S/L	149,400	15,000	7 yr.		
Furniture[7,8]	Feb 18/08	DDB	12,000	1,500	5 yr.		
Patent	Nov 7/09		51,900	-0-	5 yr.		

Additional information:
[1] GelCo calculates amortization to the nearest whole month.
[2] S/L = Straight-Line; DDB = Double-Declining-Balance; Units = Units-of-Production
[3] There were no disposals or betterments prior to January 1, 2011.
[4] At the beginning of 2011, it was determined that the land and building would be used for five years less than originally estimated due to the need to expand.
[5] Actual units produced: 2008, 45,000; 2009, 55,000; 2010, 52,000; 2011, 65,000.
[6] A major overhaul costing $21,600 was performed on the truck on July 3, 2011, that would extend its useful life by four years (with no material change expected in the residual value). The overhaul of $21,600 has not been included in the cost of $149,400.
[7] Used office equipment and furniture were purchased on April 10, 2011, for a total of $57,000 at a bankruptcy sale. The appraised value of the office equipment was $48,000 and of the furniture $36,000. The old furniture was given to a charitable organization on April 12, 2011.
[8] The estimated useful lives and residual values of the April 10 purchases were four years and $5,000 for the office equipment, and five years and $2,000 for the furniture. These assets will be amortized using the DDB method.

Required
a. Complete the Capital Asset Subledger; round calculations to the nearest dollar.
b. Using the information from the Capital Asset Subledger completed in Part (a) and the following December 31, 2011, adjusted account balances, prepare a single-step income statement and statement of owner's equity for the year ended December 31, 2011, along with the December 31, 2011, classified balance sheet: Cash, $15,000; Accounts Receivable, $36,000; Prepaid Insurance, $7,800; Accounts Payable, $34,000; Unearned Revenue, $26,900; Notes Payable due in 2014, $142,000; Ted Gel, Capital, $232,190; Ted Gel, Withdrawals, $102,000; Fees Earned, $475,000; Salaries Expense, $147,000; Insurance Expense, $15,000; Loss on disposal of furniture, $2,592. Ted Gel, the owner, made no investments during 2011.

FFS 12-2

Refer to the financial statements and notes to the financial statements for each of Danier Leather and WestJet on pages I-I to I-16 and I-17 to I-39, respectively, in Appendix I at the end of the textbook.

Required
Answer the following questions.

Part 1
The June 25, 2005, balance sheet for Danier Leather reports $25,314 (thousand) of capital assets.
a. What does the $25,314 (thousand) represent (i.e., is it the cost of the capital assets)?
b. Which generally accepted accounting principle (GAAP) requires that information in addition to the $25,314 (thousand) must be reported and where must it be reported?
c. What amount did Danier report as amortization expense for the year ended June 25, 2005? Identify how you determined this amount.
d. What method(s) of amortization did Danier use to record 2005 amortization? Identify where this information is located in the financial statements.

Part 2

The December 31, 2005, balance sheet for WestJet reports $1,803,497 (thousand) of property and equipment.

a. What was the total cost of the property and equipment at December 31, 2005? What was the total accumulated amortization (depreciation)?

b. What was the total amortization expense recorded for the year ended December 31, 2005?

c. What method(s) of amortization did WestJet use to record 2005 amortization? Identify where this information is located in the financial statements.

Critical Thinking Mini Case

Two years ago, on March 1, 2009, General Waste Management Systems purchased five used trucks and debited the Trucks account for the total cost of $180,000. The estimated useful life and residual value per truck was determined to be five years and $5,000, respectively. $36,000 was paid for a two-year insurance policy covering the trucks effective March 1, 2009; this amount was also debited to the Trucks account since it related to the trucks. On February 1, 2010, new motors were installed in the trucks; parts cost $33,000 and labour was $7,000. New tires were also installed on this date at a total cost of $32,000, and each truck was given an oil change in addition to some minor brake work; the total cost was $2,500. All of these costs were debited to the Trucks account. Net income for the years ended December 31, 2010 and 2011, was $78,000 and $85,000. The manager of the business was paid a bonus equal to 15% of net income; the 2010 bonus was paid on February 1, 2011, and recorded on that date as a debit to Bonus Expense and credit to Cash; the 2011 amount was paid on February 1, 2012, and recorded on that date as a debit to Bonus Expense and credit to Cash.

Required

Using the elements of critical thinking described on the inside front cover, comment.

CHAPTER 13

Current Liabilities

Sometimes, "It's Not What You See; It's What You Don't See"!!!

Current liabilities include accounts payable, salaries and wages payable, interest payable, income taxes payable, GST and sales tax payable, as well as many others. According to John Douglas, a Chartered Accountant and Certified Fraud Examiner based in Toronto, Ontario, undisclosed current liabilities may significantly distort the true picture of financial statements used by decision makers such as analysts, banks, and investors, who evaluate the business based on these financial statements.

For example, when current liabilities are omitted, the working capital (current assets less current liabilities), quick ratio, and current ratio become inflated, giving the impression that the business has a favourable liquidity position when in fact the opposite might be true. Undisclosed current liabilities may also cause net income to be overstated, if the offset to the liability is an income statement item. The ultimate discovery of hidden or unrecorded liabilities was one of the contributing factors to the fall of Enron and other companies.

But why intentionally mislead users of financial statements by hiding liabilities? John Douglas's experience has been that sometimes when businesspeople face extreme pressures, they employ unethical accounting practices. They are required to prepare one set of financial statements to satisfy multiple audiences, each with goals that could be in conflict with the others'.

Because current liabilities have to be paid out of current assets, they have an immediate impact on a business. Therefore, it is important to manage these liabilities, and be sure that they are properly and completely recorded, and in the correct period. To do that, you have to understand how current liabilities arise and how to record them in accordance with GAAP.

—*John Douglas has carried out large and small fraud and other financial investigations, and has appeared in civil and criminal court as an expert witness. His Web site is www.johndouglas.ca.*

Student Success *Cycle*

Read the material

Do the exercises

Check your answers

Apply your critical thinking skills

CRITICAL THINKING CHALLENGE

How can current liabilities be hidden? Explain and provide examples.

learning objectives

LO1 Describe the characteristics of liabilities and explain the difference between current and long-term liabilities.

LO2 Identify and describe known current liabilities.

LO3 Prepare entries to account for short-term notes payable.

LO4 Account for estimated liabilities, including warranties and corporate income taxes.

LO5 Explain how to account for contingent liabilities.

*APPENDIX 13A

LO6 Explain and account for short-term notes payable issued at a discount.

chapter preview

Previous chapters introduced us to liabilities for accounts payable, notes payable, wages, and unearned revenues. In this chapter we define, classify, and measure these liabilities for the purpose of reporting useful information about them to decision makers. We also learn more about liabilities such as warranties, taxes, payroll liabilities, and contingent liabilities. Understanding liabilities is important for both preparers and users of financial information, according to John Douglas as described in the opening article.

Characteristics of Liabilities

This section discusses important characteristics of liabilities, how they are classified, and how they are reported.

LO1 | Describe the characteristics of liabilities and explain the difference between current and long-term liabilities.

Defining Liabilities

A **liability** is a future payment of assets or services that a company is currently obligated to make as a result of past transactions or events.[1] This definition includes three crucial elements as portrayed in Exhibit 13.1.

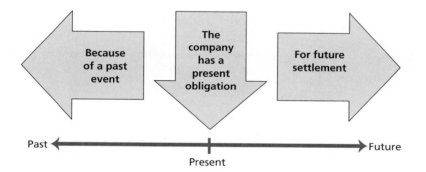

Exhibit 13.1

Characteristics of a Liability

Liabilities do not include *all* expected future settlements. For example, most companies expect to pay wages to their employees in upcoming months and years. But these future amounts are not liabilities because the revenue recognition principle says we record an event only when it occurs. Therefore, a future liability regarding an employee's work will be recorded only when the work has been performed (revenue recognition principle) and in the period in which it occurred (matching principle).

Classifying Liabilities as Current or Long-Term

Information about liabilities is more useful when the balance sheet P. 29 identifies them as either current or long-term. Decision makers need to know when obligations are due so they can plan for them and take appropriate action. Improper classification of liabilities can affect key ratios[2] used in financial statement analysis and decision making.

---

[1] *CICA Handbook*, section 1000, "Financial Statement Concepts," par. 32.

[2] For example, current liabilities are the denominator in the calculation of both the *current ratio* P. 216 and *acid-test ratio* P. 472. These ratios, commonly referred to as measures of *liquidity*, measure an organization's ability to pay current obligations with specific current assets. If current liabilities were understated because of a misclassification of liabilities, both ratios would overstate the company's liquidity.

Current Liabilities

Current liabilities, also called *short-term liabilities*, are obligations expected to be settled:

1. Within one year of the balance sheet date, or within the company's next operating cycle, whichever is longer,
2. Using current assets or by creating other current liabilities (e.g., replacing an account payable with a note payable).[3]

Examples of current liabilities are accounts payable, short-term notes payable, wages payable, warranty liabilities, lease liabilities, payroll and other taxes payable, unearned revenues, and the portion of long-term debt that is due within the next period.

Current liabilities and their classification on financial statements vary depending on the type of operations performed by the company and the desired detail. For instance, Gildan Activewear Inc. reported current liabilities on its October 2, 2005, balance sheet as shown in Exhibit 13.2. This means that Gildan Activewear expected to pay $112,888,000 of current liabilities using current assets during the year after the balance sheet date of October 2, 2005.

Exhibit 13.2

Liabilities of Gildan Activewear Inc. at October 2, 2005

www.gildan.com

Liabilities:		
Current Liabilities		
Bank indebtedness	$ 3,980,000	
Accounts payable and accrued liabilities	86,843,000	
Income taxes payable	2,206,000	
Current portion of long-term debt	19,859,000	
Total current liabilities		$112,888,000
Long-term debt		27,288,000

Long-Term Liabilities

A company's obligations *not* expected to be settled within the longer of one year of the balance sheet date or the next operating cycle are reported as **long-term liabilities**. Long-term liabilities such as long-term notes payable, lease liabilities, and bonds payable are expected to be settled out of current assets that do not yet exist. Sometimes long-term liabilities are reported on the balance sheet as a single item or they can be reported as individual amounts. Gildan Activewear reported long-term debt on its October 2, 2005, balance sheet as shown in Exhibit 13.2. This means Gildan expects to pay $27,288,000 after October 2, *2006*.

Long-term liabilities are discussed in greater detail in Chapter 17 but are introduced here because of their relationship to current liabilities.

Current Portion of Long-Term Debt

The **current portion of long-term debt** is the part of long-term debt that is due within the longer of one year of the balance sheet date or the next operating cycle and is reported under current liabilities. Exhibit 13.2 shows Gildan Activewear's *current portion of long-term debt* as part of current liabilities. This represents the principal

---

[3] *CICA Handbook*, section 1510, "Current Assets and Current Liabilities," par. .03.

amount of debt that will be paid by Gildan Activewear by October 2, 2006, which is *within one year from the balance sheet date*. The portion due after *October 2, 2006*, is reported on the balance sheet as long-term debt. Exhibit 13.3 illustrates the timing of current vs. long-term debt in comparison to the balance sheet date for Gildan Activewear.

Exhibit 13.3

Timing of Current vs. Long-Term Liabilities on Gildan Activewear Inc.'s October 2, 2005, Balance Sheet Date

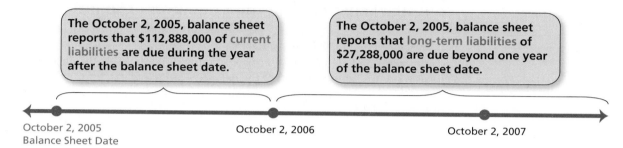

To illustrate further, let's assume a debt of $7,500 is issued on January 1, 2011. It is to be repaid in installments of $1,500 per year for five years each December 31. On December 31, 2011, the first principal payment of $1,500 was made (ignore interest), leaving a principal balance owing on December 31, 2011, of $6,000 (= $7,500 − $1,500). The December 31, 2011, balance sheet reports the $1,500 principal payment due in 2012 as the current portion of long-term debt under current liabilities as shown in Exhibit 13.4. The ***remaining*** $4,500 long-term portion of the principal (= $6,000 total liability − $1,500 current portion) will be reported under long-term liabilities on the December 31, 2011, balance sheet. The sum of the current and long-term portions equals the $6,000 total principal of the liability outstanding on December 31, 2011. No journal entry is necessary to split the current portion from the long-term portion. Instead, we properly classify the amounts for debt as either current or long-term when the balance sheet is prepared.

Exhibit 13.4

Determining Current vs. Long-Term Portions of Liabilities

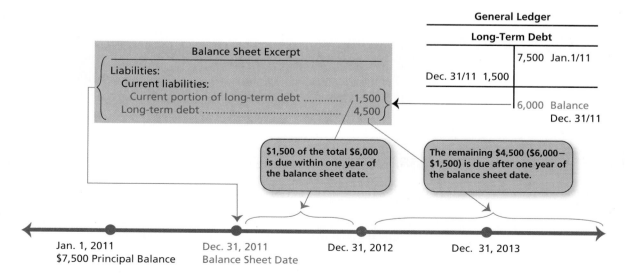

Dividing a liability between its current and long-term portions involves only the principal amount of the debt and not the anticipated future interest payments. Any interest that has accrued up to the date of the balance sheet is reported as *interest payable* under current liabilities.

Liabilities not having a fixed due date that are payable on the creditor's demand are known as **demand loans**. They are reported as current liabilities because the creditor may *demand* or require payment within a year from the balance sheet date or the company's next operating cycle; whichever is longer.

Balance Sheet Presentation of Current Liabilities

Exhibit 13.5 is based on the December 31, 2005, balance sheet of Loblaw Companies Limited. The actual balance sheet details the assets and shareholders' equity items and contains notes corresponding to items on the balance sheet. Our focus is on the liability section of the balance sheet. Note that current liabilities are listed according to their maturity or due dates similar to the current liabilities listed in Exhibit 13.2.[4]

Exhibit 13.5

Balance Sheet of Loblaw Companies Limited

Loblaw Companies Limited Balance Sheet December 31, 2005 ($millions)		
Assets..		$13,761
Liabilities:		
Current liabilities:		
Bank indebtedness..	$ 30	
Commercial paper..	436	
Accounts payable and accrued liabilities....................	2,535	
Income taxes..	-0-	
Current portion of long-term liabilities.....................	161	
Total current liabilities...		$ 3,162
Long-term debt..		4,194
Other liabilities...		519
Total liabilities...		$ 7,875
Shareholders' equity		5,886
Total liabilities and shareholders' equity		$13,761

CHECKPOINT   Read
              Apply   Do
              Check

1. What is a liability?
2. Is every expected future payment a liability?
3. If a liability is payable in 15 months, is it classified as current or long-term?

Do: QS 13-1, QS 13-2

Known (Determinable) Liabilities

LO2 | Identify and describe known current liabilities.

Accounting for liabilities involves addressing three important questions: Whom to pay? When to pay? How much to pay? Answers to these questions often are decided when a liability is incurred. For example, suppose a company has an account payable to a specific individual for $5,000, due on August 15, 2011.

---

[4] Listing current liabilities according to their maturity dates is not a GAAP requirement; there are alternatives for how current liabilities can be listed.

This liability is definite with respect to all three questions. The company *knows* whom to pay, when to pay, and how much to pay; these liabilities are called **known liabilities**. They are set by agreements, contracts, or laws, and are measurable and include accounts payable, payroll, sales taxes, unearned revenues, and notes payable. For other types of liabilities there may be *uncertainty* with respect to one or more of these three questions. This section discusses how we account for *known* liabilities. The next section will look at *uncertain* liabilities.

Trade Accounts Payable

Trade accounts payable, frequently shortened to *accounts payable*, are amounts owed to suppliers with whom we *trade* regarding products or services purchased on credit. Much of our discussion of merchandising activities in earlier chapters dealt with accounts payable. To review, assume Danier Leather purchases $12,000 of office supplies from Staples on November 14, 2011, on credit, terms n/30. Danier would record the transaction as follows:

DANIER

2011			
Nov. 14	Office Supplies	12,000	
	Accounts Payable—Staples....................		12,000
	To record the purchase of office supplies on credit: terms n/30.		

Because this account payable is due within 30 days (which is within the current period), it is reported as a current liability on the balance sheet.

Payroll Liabilities

A more detailed discussion of payroll liabilities than what follows is included in Chapter 11 of Volume 1. For your convenience, Chapter 11, including end-of-chapter materials, is available in PDF format on the online Student Success Centre.

Extend Your Knowledge

13-1

   Payroll represents employee compensation for work performed. **Payroll liabilities** are employee compensation amounts owing to employees. Employers are required by law to deduct (withhold) amounts regarding the employee's income taxes payable and Canada Pension Plan P. 559 (CPP) (or Quebec Pension Plan in Quebec) and Employment Insurance P. 560 (EI) contributions. Employers may withhold other amounts such as union dues and hospital insurance as authorized by the employee. All amounts withheld are remitted by the employer to the appropriate authorities. The difference between an employee's gross earnings and deductions taken equals an employee's net pay (or take-home pay).

   To illustrate the journal entry to record payroll liabilities, assume that on January 5, the end of its first weekly pay period in the year, Chandler Company's payroll records showed that its one office employee and two sales employees had each earned gross pay of $688, $880, and $648 respectively. The payroll records showed the following details:

	Deductions						Payment	Distribution	
Gross Pay	EI Premium[5]	Income Taxes[5]	Hosp. Ins.	CPP[5]	Union Dues	Total Deductions	Net Pay	Office Salaries	Sales Salaries
688.00	14.45	137.50	40.00	30.72	15.00	237.67	450.33	688.00	
880.00	18.48	203.35	40.00	40.23	15.00	317.06	562.94		880.00
648.00	13.61	124.80	40.00	28.74	15.00	222.15	425.85		648.00
2,216.00	46.54	465.65	120.00	99.69	45.00	776.88	1,439.12	688.00	1,528.00

[5] These values are based on assumed payroll deductions.

The journal entries to record the January 5 payroll liabilities are:

Jan.	5	Office Salaries Expense	688.00	
		Sales Salaries Expense	1,528.00	
		EI Payable		46.54
		Employees' Income Tax Payable		465.65
		Employees' Hospital Insurance Payable		120.00
		CPPPayable		99.69
		Employees' Union Dues Payable		45.00
		Salaries Payable		1,439.12
		To record January 5 payroll.		
	5	EI Expense	65.16	
		CPP Expense	99.69	
		EI Payable		65.16
		CPP Payable		99.69
		To record the employer's payroll taxes;		
		46.54 × 1.4 = 65.16 EI;		
		99.69 × 1 = 99.69 CPP.		

www.bombardier.com

Payroll liabilities are shown on the balance sheet under current liabilities. Bombardier detailed "Payroll related liabilities" of $395 million in Note 9 as part of its current liabilities at January 31, 2006.

Provincial Sales Tax (PST) and Federal Goods and Services Tax (GST) Payable

Canada has two levels of government—provincial and federal—that impose sales taxes on the same transactions. We will introduce and demonstrate *each independently* to avoid confusion.

Provincial Sales Tax (PST)

Provincial Sales Tax (PST) is a tax levied on sales to the *final* consumers of products. It is calculated as a percentage of the sale price of the item being sold.[6] PST percentages vary across the country, as detailed in Exhibit 13.6. All provinces (except Alberta) require retailers to collect PST from their customers and to forward this tax periodically to the appropriate provincial authority.

Exhibit 13.6

Provincial Sales Tax Rates

	PST Rate
Alberta	-0-
British Columbia	7%
Manitoba	7%
Northwest Territories	-0-
Nunavut	-0-
Ontario	8%
Prince Edward Island[6]	10%
Quebec[6]	7.5%
Saskatchewan	7%
Yukon Territory	-0-

Note: For New Brunswick, Nova Scotia, and Newfoundland and Labrador, a Harmonized Sales Tax (HST) of 14% is used (see Exhibit 13.7 for explanation of HST).

[6] In Quebec and PEI, PST = PST% × (Sales Price + GST).

To demonstrate, assume that Best Furniture, located in Maidstone, Saskatchewan, is a retailer of household furnishings. Best purchases merchandise inventory from several manufacturers including Holt Industries. Because Best Furniture is not the final consumer, it does not pay PST on purchases made from Holt Industries and its other suppliers. Customers purchasing from Best Furniture are the final consumer and will therefore pay the applicable PST. Best Furniture is required to collect and remit PST charged on sales to its customers. If Best Furniture's total cash sales on July 14, 2011, were $16,000 (cost of sales $12,000), the company would record the following entry (assuming a perpetual inventory system):

2011				
July	14	Cash...	17,120	
		Sales		16,000
		PST Payable..		1,120
		To record cash sales plus applicable PST;		
		16,000 × 7% = 1,120.		
	14	Cost of Goods Sold	12,000	
		Merchandise Inventory..........................		12,000
		To record cost of sales.		

When Best Furniture *remits* or forwards this tax to the provincial authority, the entry is (assume for simplicity that it is remitted on the same day):

2011				
July	14	PST Payable..	1,120	
		Cash		1,120
		To record remittance of sales tax		
		payable to provincial authority.		

Any balance in PST Payable at the end of the period is reported as a current liability on the balance sheet.

Federal Goods and Services Tax (GST)

The federal government levies a **Goods and Services Tax (GST)**, which is a tax on nearly all goods and services sold in Canada. To discuss GST, the related terminology must be understood and is summarized in Exhibit 13.7.

Exempt Supplies	GST-exempt services are educational, health care, and financial services.	**Exhibit 13.7** **Terminology Related to GST**
Harmonized Sales Tax (HST)	A combined GST and PST rate of 14% applied to taxable supplies. Currently, New Brunswick, Nova Scotia, and Newfoundland and Labrador apply HST.	
Input Tax Credit (ITC)	GST paid by the *registrant* on purchases of *taxable supplies*. Input tax credits are applied against (reduce) GST Payable. Input tax credits are also known as and recorded by the *registrant* as GST Receivable.	
Receiver General for Canada	Federal government authority to which GST Payable is remitted.	
Registrant	Registered[7] individual or entity selling *taxable supplies* that is responsible for collecting the GST on behalf of the government.	
Taxable Supplies	Taxable goods or services on which GST is calculated and includes everything except *zero-rated* and *exempt* supplies.	
Zero-Rated Supplies	Goods including groceries, prescription drugs, and medical devices, which have zero GST.	

---

[7] A business with sales of less than $30,000 per year does not have to register for GST purposes.

GST is calculated as 6% of taxable supplies. A registrant collects GST regarding a sale of taxable supplies. The same registrant also *pays* GST on purchases of taxable supplies but records an input tax credit (or GST Receivable) for the amount of GST paid. GST collected less input tax credits (GST paid) equals the balance to be remitted to (or refunded from) the Receiver General for Canada.[8]

We will now demonstrate the collection, payment, and final remittance of GST (*for simplicity, PST will be ignored for the moment*). On August 3, 2011, Best Furniture purchased $20,000 of merchandise inventory on credit from Holt Industries; terms n/30. Best Furniture records this transaction as:

2011				
Aug.	3	Merchandise Inventory....................................	20,000	
		GST Receivable..	1,200	
		Accounts Payable—Holt Industries		21,200
		To record purchase on credit plus applicable ITC; 20,000 × 6% = 1,200.		

The balance in GST Receivable after posting the August 3 transaction is (assuming a zero beginning balance):

GST Receivable (or ITC)			
Aug. 3	1,200		

On August 6, Best Furniture recorded total sales (all cash) of $45,000 (cost of sales $33,750) as:

2011				
Aug.	6	Cash..	47,700	
		Sales		45,000
		GST Payable..		2,700
		To record cash sales plus applicable GST; 45,000 × 6% = 2,700.		
	6	Cost of Goods Sold	33,750	
		Merchandise Inventory..........................		33,750
		To record cost of sales.		

The balance in GST Payable after posting the August 6 transaction is (assuming a zero beginning balance):

GST Payable			
	2,700	Aug. 6	

After posting the August 6 transaction, the GST accounts show a net balance *owing* to the Receiver General for Canada of $1,500 (GST Payable of $2,700 less GST Receivable or ITC of $1,200).[9]

---

[8] Businesses are required to remit quarterly, or for larger businesses, monthly. Certain businesses may elect to pay annually.

[9] Some businesses combine GST Receivable and GST Payable to achieve the same net result. For example, if Best Furniture had combined the GST accounts, as shown below, the same $1,500 net balance results.

GST Receivable/Payable			
Aug. 3	1,200	2,700	Aug. 6
		1,500	Balance

Assume Best Furniture remitted the balance to the Receiver General for Canada on August 7. The entry to record this transaction is:

2011			
Aug. 7	GST Payable...	2,700	
	Cash		1,500
	GST Receivable.......................................		1,200
	To record remittance of GST to Receiver General for Canada.		

The balances in GST Receivable and GST Payable would be zero after posting the August 7 entry.

If the balance in GST Receivable (ITC) exceeds the balance in GST Payable, Best Furniture would be entitled to receive a refund.

A net credit balance in the GST Payable account at the end of the period would be shown on the balance sheet as a current liability; a net debit balance would appear under current assets as GST Receivable.

Additional examples demonstrating PST/GST, by region in Canada, can be found online in Extend Your Knowledge 13-2 along with reinforcement exercises.

Extend Your Knowledge

13-2

Unearned Revenues

Unearned revenues[10] are amounts received in advance from customers for future products or services and are reported as current liabilities. Unearned revenues include advance ticket sales for sporting events, music concerts, or airline flights. For example WestJet, in Appendix I of the textbook, reported "Advance ticket sales" of $127,450,000 in its December 31, 2005, annual report. When WestJet sells $100,000 of advance tickets, its entry is:

Cash...	100,000	
Advance ticket sales		100,000
To record airline tickets sold in advance.		

If $40,000 in airline tickets purchased in advance are redeemed at a later date, the entry is:

Advance ticket sales..	40,000	
Passenger revenues		40,000
To record redemption of airline tickets sold in advance.		

Unearned revenues also arise with magazine publishers, construction projects, hotel reservations, and custom orders. Unearned revenue accounts are reported as current liabilities.

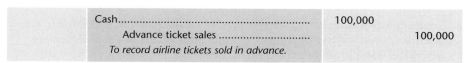

4. Masters Company collected $1,140 including taxes from a customer. Assuming that Masters pays a combined PST/GST rate of 14%, calculate (a) sales, and (b) harmonized sales taxes payable.

Do: QS 13-3, QS 13-4, QS 13-5, QS 13-6, QS 13-7

---

[10] Unearned revenues are also called **deferred revenues**, **collections in advance**, or *customer deposits*.

mid-chapter demonstration problem

Centrum Advertising Services, a Montreal business, has a December 31 year-end and prepares financial statements annually. Centrum gathered the following information to prepare the current liability section of its December 31, 2011, balance sheet.

a. Centrum borrowed $48,000 on January 2, 2011. Payments are made annually for five years each January 2.

Year	Annual Payment	Principal Portion of Payment	Interest Portion of Payment	Principal Balance at Year-End
2012	11,395	8,515	2,880	39,485
2013	11,395	9,026	2,369	30,459
2014	11,395	9,567	1,828	20,892
2015	11,395	10,142	1,253	10,750
2016	11,395	10,750	645	-0-

b. Property taxes of $8,650 were unpaid and unrecorded at December 31, 2011.

c. The payroll register showed the following total unpaid amounts as at December 31, 2011.

| Gross Pay | Deductions | | | | | Pay | Distribution | |
	EI Premiums[11]	Income Taxes[11]	United Way	CPP[11]	Total Deductions	Net Pay	Office Salaries	Sales Salaries
7,840.00	164.64*	3,196.25	320.00	384.75*	4,065.64	3,774.36	1,900.00	5,940.00

The employer's portions of EI and CPP are 1.4 times and 1 times the employee's portion respectively.

d. Centrum Advertising Services operates out of a small building in downtown Montreal. Total services provided to clients during the month of December were $186,000 excluding sales taxes. Assume GST and PST are paid on the fifteenth day of the month following sales.

e. The unadjusted trial balance P. 147 showed Unearned Service Revenue of $7,800. $5,200 of this amount had been earned by December 31.

Required

For each of the above, determine what will be included in the current liabilities section of Centrum's December 31, 2011, balance sheet. Hint: For (d), refer to Exhibit 13.6 to determine the appropriate PST rate.

Analysis component:

If the current portion of the long-term debt described in (a) above is not reported under current liabilities but reported as part of long-term liabilities, total liabilities would be correct. Therefore, is it acceptable to report the current portion of long-term liabilities as part of long-term debt? Why or why not?

solution to *Mid-Chapter Demonstration Problem* _____

a. Two amounts will appear in the current liabilities section as a result of this information:

Interest payable of $2,880; and
Current portion of long-term note $8,515.

[11] These values are based on assumed payroll deductions.

b. Property taxes payable of $8,650

c. Five amounts will be included in the "Payroll liabilities" amount appearing in the current liabilities section as a result of this information:

EI payable	$ 395.14*
Employees' income taxes payable	3,196.25
United Way payable	320.00
CPP payable	769.50**
Salaries payable	3,774.36
Total payroll liabilities	$8,455.25

*164.64 × 1.4 = 230.50 Employer's portion plus 164.64 Employees' portion.
**384.75 Employer's portion plus 384.75 Employees' portion.

d. GST = $186,000 × 6%   = $11,160.00
    PST = ($186,000 + $11,160) × 7.5%   =   14,787.00
    Total sales taxes payable $25,947.00

e. Unearned revenue = $7,800 − $5,200 = $ 2,600

Analysis component:

It is not acceptable to report the current portion of long-term liabilities as part of long-term debt even though total liabilities would be unaffected. Why? Because if current liabilities are understated then the liquidity position is overstated, which has the potential to create the impression that the business has the ability to cover its current obligations when it may not.

Short-Term Notes Payable

A **short-term note payable** is a written promise to pay a specified amount on a specified future date within one year or the company's operating cycle, whichever is longer, and is reported as a current liability on the balance sheet. Notes payable are interest-bearing to compensate for the time until payment is made. Less common are notes payable issued at a discount, which are discussed in Appendix 13A.

LO3 Prepare entries to account for short-term notes payable.

A company often issues a note payable to purchase merchandise inventory and other assets or to replace an account payable. Short-term notes payable also arise when money is borrowed from a bank.

Note Given to Extend Credit Period

A company can substitute an interest-bearing note payable to replace an overdue account payable that does not bear interest.

To illustrate, assume that on November 23, 2011, Weston Holdings asks to extend its past-due $6,000 account payable to TechNology Inc. After some negotiations, TechNology Inc. agrees to accept $1,000 cash and a 60-day, 12%, $5,000 note payable to replace the account payable. Weston Holdings records this transaction as:

2011			
Nov. 23	Accounts Payable—TechNology Inc.	6,000.00	
	Cash		1,000.00
	Notes Payable		5,000.00
	Gave $1,000 cash and a 60-day note to extend due date on account.		

Signing the note changes the form of the debt from an account payable to a note payable.

On December 31, 2011, Weston's year-end, accrued interest on the note (38 days from November 23 to December 31) is recorded as follows:

Dec.	31	Interest Expense.	62.47	
		Interest Payable....................................		62.47
		Accrued interest expense on note;		
		$5,000 × 12% × 38/365.		

To calculate interest, we used the formula in Exhibit 13.8.

Exhibit 13.8

Formula to Calculate Interest
($I = Prt$)

Interest	=	Principal of the Note	×	Annual Interest Rate	×	Time
$62.47	=	$5,000	×	12%	×	38/365

The balance sheet presentation on December 31, 2011, of the liabilities regarding the note payable is shown under current liabilities as in Exhibit 13.9. Interest is rounded to the nearest whole dollar for financial statement presentation purposes.

Exhibit 13.9

Balance Sheet Presentation of Short-Term Notes Payable and Interest Payable

Current liabilities:
    Notes payable, short-term $5,000
    Interest payable... 62

On the due date[12] of January 22, 2012, Weston pays the note and interest by giving TechNology a cheque for $5,098.63; $5,000 represents payment for the note payable and $98.63 is payment of the total interest for the 60-day note calculated at the rate of 12%.

The payment is recorded as:

Jan.	22	Notes Payable	5,000.00	
		Interest Payable...	62.47	
		Interest Expense	36.16	
		Cash		5,098.63
		Paid note with interest;		
		$5,000 × 12% × 22/365 = $36.16.		

---

[12] The due date or *maturity date* P. 519 of a note was discussed in Chapter 10. To review the calculation of the due date, assume the 60-day note above that is dated November 23. The due date or maturity date is January 22, calculated as:

Days in November...	30
Minus date of note	23
Days remaining in November	7
Add days in December..	31
	38
Days to equal 60 days or	
Maturity date, January 22.........................	22
Period of the note in days	60

Notice that $62.47 of the total interest being paid is for the interest liability that appeared on the December 31 balance sheet in Exhibit 13.9. $36.16 of the total interest is the interest expense for the accounting period beginning January 1, 2012. The matching principle P. 133 requires that the total interest expense be allocated over the term of the note as illustrated in Exhibit 13.10.

Exhibit 13.10

Matching of Interest Expense to the Proper Accounting Periods

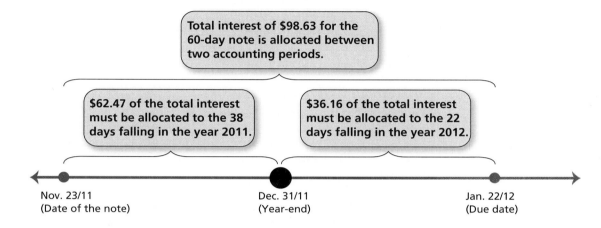

Total interest of $98.63 for the 60-day note is allocated between two accounting periods.

$62.47 of the total interest must be allocated to the 38 days falling in the year 2011.

$36.16 of the total interest must be allocated to the 22 days falling in the year 2012.

Nov. 23/11
(Date of the note)

Dec. 31/11
(Year-end)

Jan. 22/12
(Due date)

Note Given to Borrow from Bank

A bank requires a borrower to sign a promissory note P. 519 when making a loan. The borrowing company records its receipt of cash and the new liability with this entry:

Sept.	30	Cash..	2,000.00	
		Notes Payable		2,000.00
		Borrowed $2,000 cash with a 60-day,		
		12%, $2,000 note.		

When the note matures (or becomes due), the borrower repays the note plus interest. Journal entries regarding the accrual of interest expense at the end of the accounting period and repayment of the note on the due date are the same as described in the previous section for a note given to extend a credit period.

5. Why does a creditor want a past-due account replaced by a note?

6. A company borrows $10,000 by signing a note payable promising to repay the principal plus interest calculated at the rate of 8% in 180 days. What is the total interest expense?

Do: QS 13-8, QS 13-9

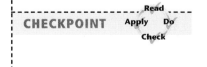

CHECKPOINT   Read   Apply   Do   Check

Estimated (or Uncertain) Liabilities

An **estimated liability** is a known obligation of an uncertain amount, but one that can be reasonably estimated. Common examples are warranties offered by a seller and income taxes. We discuss each of these in this section. Other examples of estimated liabilities include property taxes and certain contracts to provide future services.

LO4   Account for estimated liabilities, including warranties and corporate income taxes.

Warranty Liabilities

A warranty is an estimated liability of the seller. A **warranty** obligates a seller to pay for replacing or repairing the product (or service) when it fails to perform as expected within a specified period. Most cars, for instance, are sold with a warranty covering parts for a specified period of time.

To comply with the *matching principle*, the seller reports the expected expense of providing the warranty in the period when revenue from the sale of the product is reported. The seller reports this warranty obligation as a liability, even though there is uncertainty about existence, amount, payee P. 519, and date the obligation will be satisfied. The seller's warranty obligation does not require payments unless products fail and are returned for repairs. But future payments are probable and the amount of this liability can be estimated using, for instance, past experience with warranties.

Illustration of Warranty Liabilities

To illustrate, let's consider a dealer who sells a used car for $16,000 on December 1, 2011, with a one-year or 15,000-kilometre warranty covering parts and labour. This dealer's experience shows warranty expense averages 4% of a car's selling price or $640 (= $16,000 × 4%). The dealer records this estimated expense and liability with this entry:

2011			
Dec. 1	Warranty Expense..	640	
	Estimated Warranty Liability		640
	To record warranty expense and liability at 4% of selling price.		

This entry alternatively could have been made as part of end-of-period adjustments. Either way, it causes the estimated warranty expense to be reported on the 2011 income statement. Also, it results in a warranty liability on the balance sheet for December 31, 2011.

Suppose the customer returns the car for warranty repairs on January 9, 2012. The dealer performs this work by replacing parts costing $200 and using $180 for labour regarding installation of the parts. The entry to record partial settlement of the estimated warranty liability is:

2012			
Jan. 9	Estimated Warranty Liability	380	
	Auto Parts Inventory..............................		200
	Wages Payable		180
	To record costs of warranty repairs.		

This entry does not record any additional expense in the year 2012 but instead reduces the balance of the estimated warranty liability. Warranty expense was already recorded in 2011, the year the car was sold. The balance in the Estimated Warranty Liability account on January 9, 2012, after posting this entry is:

Estimated Warranty Liability			
Jan. 9/12	380	640	Dec. 1/11
		260	Balance

What happens if total warranty costs turn out to be more or less than the estimated 4% or $640? The answer is that management should monitor actual warranty costs to see whether the 4% rate is accurate. If experience reveals a large difference from estimates, the rate should be changed for future sales. This means that while differences are expected, they should be small.

The preceding example illustrated estimating warranty expense based on a percent of sales dollars. Warranty expense can also be based on a percent of *units* sold. For example, assume that Snowjammer Snowboards sold 7,600 snowboards during November 2011 for an average of $185 (cost: $120). Snowjammer provides a warranty that replaces any defective board with a new one. This company's experience shows that warranty expense averages 0.5% of the snowboards sold. The entry on November 30 to record the estimated warranty would be:

2011			
Nov. 30	Warranty Expense..	4,560	
	Estimated Warranty Liability		4,560
	To record warranty expense and liability		
	at 0.5% of units sold; 0.005 × 7,600		
	= 38 snowboards × $120 cost/board		
	= $4,560.		

Notice that the journal entries are the same for recording warranty expense based on a percent of sales dollars or on a percent of units sold. Which method is used depends on whether warranty expense is to be matched to sales dollars or units sold.

7. Estimated liabilities include an obligation to pay:

  a. An uncertain but reasonably estimated amount to a specific entity on a specific date.

  b. A known amount to a specific entity on an uncertain due date.

  c. A known amount to an uncertain entity on a known due date.

  d. All of the above.

8. A car is sold for $15,000 on June 1, 2010, with a one-year warranty covering parts and labour. Warranty expense is estimated at 1.5% of selling price. On March 1, 2011, the car is returned for warranty repairs for parts costing $75 and labour costing $60. The amount recorded as warranty expense at the time of the March 1 repairs is:

  a. $0   **d.** $135

  b. $60   **e.** $225

  c. $75

Do: QS 13-10, QS 13-11

Income Tax Liabilities for Corporations

Financial statements of both single proprietorships P. 4 and partnerships P. 5 do not include income taxes because these organizations do not directly pay income taxes. Instead, taxable income for these organizations is carried to the owners' personal tax returns and taxed at that level. But corporations P. 5 are subject to income taxes and must estimate their income tax liability when preparing financial statements. We explain this process in this section.

Income tax expense for a corporation creates a liability until payment is made to the government. Because this tax is created through earning taxable income, a liability is incurred when taxable income is earned. This tax must usually be paid monthly under federal regulations. The monthly installment is equal to one-twelfth of the corporation's estimated income tax liability for the year.

Illustration of Income Tax Liabilities

To illustrate, let's consider a corporation that prepares monthly financial statements. Based on its taxable income for 2010, this corporation estimates it will owe income taxes of $144,000 in 2011. In January 2011, the following adjusting entry records the estimated income tax:

2011			
Jan. 31	Income Tax Expense..	12,000	
	Income Tax Payable		12,000
	Accrued income tax based on 1/12 of		
	total estimated; $144,000 × 1/12.		

Assume that the tax installment is paid the next day and the entry to record its payment is:

Feb. 1	Income Tax Payable.......................................	12,000	
	Cash		12,000
	Paid income tax installment for January 2011.		

This process of accruing and then paying tax installments continues through the year. By the time annual financial statements are prepared at year-end, the corporation knows its total taxable income and the actual amount of income taxes it must pay. This information allows it to update the expense and liability accounts.

Suppose this corporation determines that its income tax liability for 2011 is a total of $156,700. The Income Tax Expense account reflects estimated taxes of $132,000 based on installments recorded at the rate of $12,000 per month for each of January to November. The entry to record the additional income tax for 2011 is as follows:

Dec. 31	Income Tax Expense..	24,700	
	Income Tax Payable		24,700
	To record additional tax expense and		
	liability; $156,700 − $132,000 = $24,700		
	balance owing.		

This liability of $24,700 is settled when the corporation makes its final payment, assumed to be on January 1, 2012.

CHECKPOINT   Read   Apply   Do   Check

9. Why does a corporation accrue an income tax liability for quarterly reports?
Do: QS 13-12, QS 13-13

Contingent Liabilities

LO5 | Explain how to account for contingent liabilities.

A **contingent liability** is a potential future liability caused by a past event. Any future payment of a contingent liability depends on uncertain future events. A typical example is a lawsuit pending in court. Here, a past transaction or event leads to a lawsuit whose result is uncertain because it is to be determined by the court.

Accounting for Contingent Liabilities

Accounting for contingent liabilities depends on the likelihood of a future event occurring along with our ability to estimate the amount owed in the future if it occurs. Typical examples include a lawsuit taken against a company or environmental liability concerns.

There are two main categories of contingent liabilities. Those that are:

1. Likely and *the amount can be reasonably estimated*, and
2. *Unlikely*.

The first category includes situations in which the contingency is likely (probable) and the amount can be reasonably estimated, in which case the amount is recorded on the balance sheet as a liability.[13] These amounts must be accrued because they meet the two criteria of being likely to occur **and** the amount can be reasonably estimated. The journal entry to record a likely contingent liability, which is estimated to be in the amount of $10,000, is:

Contingent Loss..	10,000	
Contingent Liability		10,000
To record a likely and estimable contingent loss.		

Recording this entry prevents income and net assets from being overstated, which is in accordance with the *conservatism principle* P. 351. If the potential future liability is likely but the amount is not measurable, then the contingent loss and liability should be disclosed in the notes to the financial statements because this information is relevant to users of financial statements. This is in accordance with the *full disclosure principle* P. 348.

According to the *CICA Handbook*, uncertainties such as warranties and doubtful accounts are not contingencies since they relate to normal business activities.[14]

The second category of contingent liabilities involves situations in which the future event is *unlikely* (remote or slight chance of occurrence). If the occurrence of a contingent loss is unlikely but would have a significant negative effect on the reporting company if the event were to occur, note disclosure is required. The reporting options for contingent liabilities are summarized in Exhibit 13.11.

In practice, accounting for contingencies is extremely difficult to apply. Canadian GAAP permit a business to apply judgement: Is a contingent liability likely? Can the amount be reasonably estimated? Management recognizes that recording and/or disclosing a contingent liability could affect decisions made by users of financial statements. For example, note disclosure regarding a pending lawsuit may cause share prices to decline. In applying judgement, the unethical manager may withhold information regarding uncertain future events.

For example, in Note 18 of its June 30, 2005, financial statements, Rentcash Inc. reported the following contingency regarding legal proceedings:

During fiscal 2004, the Company was served with three Statements of Claim on behalf of customers in Alberta, British Columbia, and Ontario alleging that the Company is in breach of the *Criminal Code* and *Fair Trading Act*. Subsequent to June 30, 2005, the claim in British Columbia was certified as a class proceeding. The Company believes that it conducts its business in accordance with applicable law and will defend each of the actions vigorously, however the likelihood of loss if any is not determinable. Accordingly, no provision has been made for these actions in the accounts.

Source: www.rentcash.com

---

[13] *CICA Handbook*, section 3290, "Contingencies," par. .06.

[14] In the United States, the FASB argues that contingencies include estimated liabilities such as warranties, vacation pay, premiums offered to customers, and income taxes. It claims that all estimated liabilities are contingencies because they represent potential liabilities.

Exhibit 13.11

Reporting of Contingencies[15]

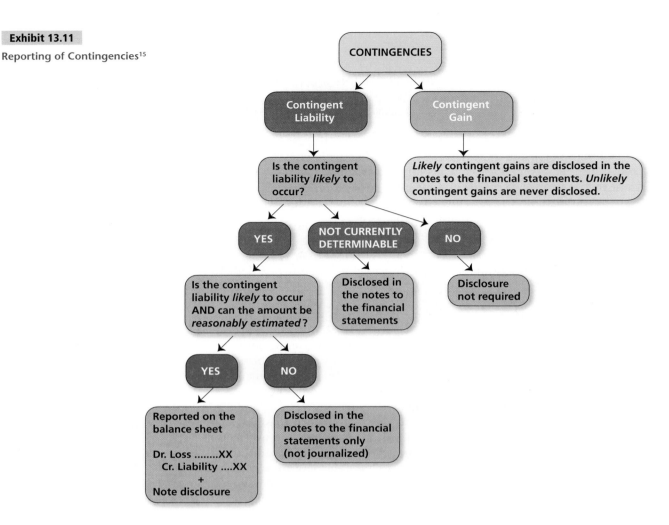

Gain Contingencies

Contingent gains should never be recorded until they are actually realized. Gain contingencies that are likely are disclosed in the notes to the financial statements but because of conservatism we should avoid any misleading implications about their realization.[16] For example, a plaintiff in a lawsuit should not disclose any expected gain until the courts settle the matter. Disclosure of *unlikely* contingent gains is prohibited.

CHECKPOINT   Read   Apply   Do   Check

10. A future payment is reported as a liability on the balance sheet if payment is contingent on a future event that:

    a. Is not likely but is reasonably possible and the payment cannot be reasonably estimated.

    b. Is likely and the payment can be reasonably estimated.

    c. Is not likely but the payment is known.

11. Under what circumstances is a future payment reported in the notes to the financial statements as a contingent liability?

Do: QS 13-14, QS 13-15

---

[15] *CICA Handbook*, section "Contingencies," par. 3290.12–15.
[16] *CICA Handbook*, par. 3290.18.

Eco Cops

What's it worth to be able to ski at Lake Louise? What's the cost when beaches are closed due to pollution? What's the life of a seal worth? These questions are part of measuring environmental liabilities of polluters. One method of measuring these liabilities is called contingent valuation, in which people are surveyed and asked to answer questions like these. Their answers are used by regulators to levy hefty fines, assess punitive damages, measure costs of clean-up, and assign penalties for damage to "environmental intangibles."

DID YOU KNOW?

Summary

LO1 **Describe the characteristics of liabilities and explain the difference between current and long-term liabilities.** Liabilities are highly probable future settlements of assets or services an entity is currently obligated to make as a result of past transactions or events. Current liabilities are due within one year of the balance sheet date or the next operating cycle, whichever is longer, and are settled using current assets. All other liabilities are long-term liabilities.

LO2 **Identify and describe known current liabilities.** Known current liabilities are set by agreements or laws and are measurable with little uncertainty. They include accounts payable, sales taxes payable, unearned revenues, notes payable, payroll liabilities, and the current portion of long-term debt.

LO3 **Prepare entries to account for short-term notes payable.** Short-term notes payable are current liabilities

and most bear interest. When a short-term note is interest-bearing, its face value equals the amount borrowed. This type of note also identifies a rate of interest to be paid at maturity.

LO4 **Account for estimated liabilities, including warranties and corporate income taxes.** Liabilities for warranties and corporate income taxes are recorded with estimated amounts and are recognized as expenses when incurred.

LO5 **Explain how to account for contingent liabilities.** If an uncertain future payment depends on a probable future event and the amount can be reasonably estimated, the payment is recorded as a liability. If the future payment is reported as a contingent liability, (a) the future event is reasonably possible but not probable, or (b) the event is probable but the amount of the payment cannot be reasonably estimated.

---

guidance answers to **CHECKPOINT**
Read Apply Do Check

1. Liabilities are probable future settlements of assets or services that an entity is currently obligated to make as a result of past transactions or events.

2. No, an expected future payment is not a liability unless an existing obligation was created by a past event or transaction.

3. In most cases, a liability due in 15 months is classified as long-term. But it is classified as a current liability if the company's operating cycle is 15 months or longer.

4. **a.** Sales = $1,140 ÷ 1.14 = $1,000

   b. HST = $1,140 − $1,000 = $140

5. A creditor might want to have a note payable instead of an account payable in order to (a) start charging interest and/or (b) have positive evidence of the debt and its terms.

6. The interest expense was $10,000 × 8% × 180/365 = $394.52.

7. *a*

8. *a*

9. A corporation accrues an income tax liability for its interim financial statements because income tax expense is incurred when income is earned, not just at the end of the year.

10. *b*

11. A future payment is reported as a contingent liability in the notes to the financial statements if (a) the uncertain future event is likely but the amount of payment cannot be reasonably estimated, or (b) the uncertain future event is not likely but has a reasonable possibility of occurring.

demonstration problem

The following series of transactions and other events took place at the Kern Company, located in Saskatchewan, during its calendar reporting year. Describe their effects on the financial statements by presenting the journal entries described in each situation, if any.

a. In September 2011, Kern sold $140,000 of merchandise that was covered by a 180-day warranty. Prior experience shows that the costs of fulfilling the warranty will equal 5% of the sales revenue. Calculate September's warranty expense and the increase in the warranty liability and show how it would be recorded with a September 30 adjusting entry. Also show the journal entry that would be made on October 8 to record an expenditure of $300 cash to provide warranty service on an item sold in September.

b. On October 12, 2011, Kern arranged with a supplier to replace an overdue $10,000 account payable by paying $2,500 cash and signing a note for the remainder. The note matured in 90 days and had a 12% interest rate. Show the entries that would be recorded on October 12, December 31, and the date the note matures.

c. In late December the company learns that it is facing a product liability suit filed by an unhappy customer. The company's lawyer is of the opinion that although the company will likely suffer a loss from the lawsuit, it is not possible to estimate the amount of the damages at the present time.

d. Kern Company recorded estimated income taxes at the end of each month, January through December inclusive, at the rate of 28% of income before tax. Total income before taxes for the year was estimated to be $896,000. At year-end, the actual income tax expense was determined to be $273,880. Record the year-end income tax expense adjustment entry for the company.

e. On November 1, Kern Company borrows $5,000 from the bank on a 90-day, 14% note. Record the issuance of the note on November 1, interest accrual on December 31, and repayment of the note with interest on the maturity date.

f. As of November 30, 2011, the account balances for GST Receivable, GST Payable, and PST Payable were $16,800, $9,660, and $8,280 respectively. During December, Kern Company purchased $196,000 of merchandise on credit and recorded credit sales of $295,000 (cost of sales $177,000). Kern Company remits GST and PST on the last day of each month regarding the previous month's transactions. Record the remittance or refund of sales taxes on December 31 as well as summary entries for the purchase and sale of merchandise during December. (Date the summary entries Dec. 31 for simplicity.)

Analysis component:

Part (a) requires that a warranty liability be recorded for September yet no warranty work regarding September sales has yet been performed and may not even result in the future. Would it be acceptable to defer recording warranty liabilities and related expenses until the warranty work actually results? Why or why not?

Planning the Solution

- For *(a)*, calculate the warranty expense for September and record it with an estimated liability. Record the October expenditure as a decrease in the liability.
- For *(b)*, eliminate the liability for the account payable and create the liability for the note payable. Calculate the interest expense for the 80 days that the note is outstanding in 2011 and record it as an additional liability. Determine the maturity date of the note. Record the payment of the note, being sure to include the interest for the 10 days in 2012.

- For (c), decide if the contingent liability for the company needs to be disclosed or accrued according to the two necessary criteria: how probable the loss and how reasonably the amount can be estimated.
- For (d), determine how much of the income tax expense is payable for the current year.
- For (e), record the note. Make the year-end adjustment for 60 days' accrued interest. Record the repayment of the note, being sure to include the interest for the 30 days in 2012.
- For (f), four entries are required. First, prepare separate entries to record the remittance or refund of GST and PST on December 31 based on the November 30, 2011, account balances. Next, prepare the entry to record the purchase of merchandise during December, including GST. Finally, prepare the entry to record the sale of merchandise during December, including GST and appropriate PST for Saskatchewan.
- Prepare an answer for the analysis component.

solution to *Demonstration Problem*

a. Warranty expense = 5% × $140,000 = $7,000

Sept.	30	Warranty Expense..	7,000.00	
		Estimated Warranty Liability		7,000.00
		To record warranty expense and liability at 5% of sales for the month.		
Oct.	8	Estimated Warranty Liability	300.00	
		Cash		300.00
		To record the cost of the warranty service.		

b. Interest expense for 2011 = 12% × $7,500 × 80/365 = $197.26
Interest expense for 2012 = 12% × $7,500 × 10/365 = $24.66

Oct.	12	Accounts Payable	10,000.00	
		Notes Payable		7,500.00
		Cash		2,500.00
		Paid $2,500 cash and gave a 90-day, 12% note to extend the due date on the account.		
Dec.	31	Interest Expense	197.26	
		Interest Payable.....................................		197.26
		To accrue interest on note payable; 7,500 × 0.12 × 80/365 = 197.26.		
Jan.	10	Notes Payable	7,500.00	
		Interest Payable..	197.26	
		Interest Expense	24.66	
		Cash		7,721.92
		Paid note with interest, including accrued interest payable.		

c. The pending lawsuit should be disclosed only in the notes to the financial statements. Although the loss is likely, no liability can be accrued since the loss cannot be reasonably estimated.

d.

Dec.	31	Income Tax Expense..	23,000.00	
		Income Taxes Payable		23,000.00
		To record income tax expense; $273,880 − ($896,000 × 28% = $250,880) = $23,000.		

e.

Nov.	1	Cash..	5,000.00	
		Notes Payable		5,000.00
		Borrowed cash with a 90-day 14% note.		
Dec.	31	Interest Expense	115.07	
		Interest Payable......................................		115.07
		To record accrued interest;		
		5,000 × 14% × 60/365 = 115.07.		
Jan.	30	Notes Payable	5,000.00	
		Interest Expense	57.53	
		Interest Payable...	115.07	
		Cash		5,172.60
		To record payment of note and accrued		
		interest; 5,000 × 14% × 30/365 = 57.53.		

f.

Dec.	31	GST Payable...	9,660	
		Cash..	7,140	
		GST Receivable......................................		16,800
		To record refund of GST from Receiver		
		General for Canada; $16,800 − $9,660		
		= $7,140.		
	31	PST Payable...	8,280	
		Cash		8,280
		To record remittance of sales tax payable		
		to provincial authority.		
	31	Merchandise Inventory..................................	196,000	
		GST Receivable...	11,760	
		Accounts Payable		207,760
		To record the purchase of merchandise on		
		credit; $196,000 × 6% = $11,760 GST.		
	31	Accounts Receivable	333,350	
		Sales		295,000
		PST Payable..		20,650
		GST Payable..		17,700
		To record the sale of merchandise on		
		credit; $295,000 × 6% GST = $17,700 GST;		
		$295,000 × 7% PST = $20,650 PST.		
	31	Cost of Goods Sold	177,000	
		Merchandise Inventory.........................		177,000
		To record the cost of sales.		

Analysis component:

Although warranty costs regarding September sales will not occur until a future date, the matching principle requires that expenses (and the related liability) be recorded in the period in which the corresponding sales were realized. Warranty work done in the future regarding September sales must be matched against September sales, otherwise income for September will be overstated.

APPENDIX 13A

Short-Term Notes Payable Issued at a Discount

A note often states that the signer of the note promises to pay principal (the amount borrowed) plus interest. In this case, the face value of the note equals principal. These are referred to as interest-bearing notes and were discussed in Chapter 13.

LO6 Explain and account for short-term notes payable issued at a discount.

A bank sometimes has a borrower sign a note with a face value that includes *both* principal and interest. In this case, the signer of the note receives *less than* the note's face value. The difference between the borrowed amount and the note's face value is interest. These are **short-term notes issued at a discount**. Since the borrowed amount is less than the note's face value, the difference is called a **discount on notes payable**.

To illustrate, let's assume a company needs $2,000 for a specific project and borrows this money from a bank at 12% annual interest by signing a discounted note. The loan is made on December 16, 2011, and is due in 60 days. The face value of the note will *include* interest. Therefore, the borrowing company signs a $2,039.45 note that includes a promise similar to: "I promise to pay $2,039.45 within 60 days after December 16." The note does not refer to the rate used to calculate the $39.45 of interest (= $2,000 × 12% × 60/365) included in the $2,039.45 face value. Because this note lacks a stated interest rate, it is sometimes called a **non–interest-bearing note**.

When recording this note, the company credits the $2,039.45 face value to Notes Payable and debits the $39.45 discount to a contra-liability account. This entry is:

2011			
Dec. 16	Cash...	2,000.00	
	Discount on Notes Payable............................	39.45	
	Notes Payable		2,039.45
	Borrowed $2,000 cash with a 60-day		
	discounted note.		

Discount on Notes Payable is a contra-liability account to the Notes Payable account. If a balance sheet is prepared on December 16, the $39.45 discount is subtracted from the $2,039.45 balance in the Notes Payable account to reflect the $2,000 net amount borrowed as follows:[17]

Note Payable..	$2,039.45	
Less: Discount on Note Payable...................................	39.45	$ 2,000

At year-end, the adjusting entry needed to record the accrual of 15 days of interest for 2011 is:

Dec. 31	Interest Expense	9.86	
	Discount on Notes Payable		9.86
	To record accrued interest on note; $2,000 ×		
	12% × 15/365 or $39.45 × 15/60.		

---

[17] We approximate the annual interest rate on a short-term loan as: ($ Interest paid ÷ $ Amount received) × (365 days ÷ Loan period in days).

Note that accrued interest is not credited to Interest Payable. Instead, this entry reduces the balance of the contra-liability account from $39.45 to $29.59 (= $39.45 − $9.86). This increases the net note liability to $2,009.86 (= $2,039.45 note less $29.59 discount).

When the note matures, we need an entry both to accrue interest expense for the last 45 days of the note and to record its payment:

2012				
Feb. 14	Interest Expense	29.59		
	Notes Payable	2,039.45		
	Discount on Notes Payable		29.59	
	Cash		2,039.45	
	Paid note with interest; $2,000 × 12% × 45/365 or $39.45 × 45/60.			

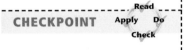

JUDGEMENT CALL

Answer—p. 676

Rock Band

You are a member of a rock band. Your band needs $15,000 to upgrade equipment. You receive loan approvals for $15,000 at two banks. One bank's proposed loan contract reads: "Band promises to pay $15,000 plus interest at 14% in six months." The competing bank's contract reads: "Band promises to pay $16,000 in six months." Which loan do you prefer?

CHECKPOINT   Read Apply   Do   Check

12. DuRight borrows $6,000 from a bank at 6% interest by signing a discounted note dated November 15, 2011, and due in 45 days. Record the November 15, 2011, entry by DuRight.

Do: *QS 13-16, *QS 13-17

Summary of Appendix 13A

LO6 **Explain and account for short-term notes payable issued at a discount.** Short-term notes payable are current liabilities. The face value of a short-term note payable issued at a discount includes both principal and interest. At the time of signing the note, the debtor receives less than the face value: the face value less the interest portion. When the note is repaid, the entire face value is repaid.

guidance answer to	JUDGEMENT CALL

Rock Band

Both banks have agreed to give the band $15,000, and both loans require repayment in six months. Provided terms in these contracts are similar, the only potential difference is in the amount of interest the band must pay. The second bank's contract makes this clear—since $15,000 is borrowed and the band must pay $16,000, the interest charged is $1,000. We must calculate interest on the first bank's contract—it is $1,050, calculated as $15,000 × 14% × 6/12. The band prefers the contract requiring less interest, which is the one reading: "Band promises to pay $16,000 in six months."

guidance answer to	CHECKPOINT Read Apply Do Check

12.

2011			
Nov. 15	Cash...	6,000.00	
	Discount on Notes Payable............................	44.38	
	Notes Payable		6,044.38
	$6,000 × 6% × 45/365 = $44.38		

Glossary

Collections in advance See *unearned revenues*. (p. 661)

Contingent gain A potential gain that depends on a future event arising out of a past transaction. Contingent gains are never recorded until actually realized. (p. 670)

Contingent liability A potential liability that depends on a future event arising out of a past transaction; it is not an existing liability. (p. 668)

Current liability Obligations due within a year of the balance sheet date or the company's next operating cycle, whichever is longer; paid using current assets or by creating other current liabilities. (p. 654)

Current portion of long-term debt The portion of long-term debt that is due within one year of the balance sheet date; reported under current liabilities on the balance sheet. (p. 654)

Deferred revenues See *unearned revenues*. (p. 661)

Demand loan A liability not having a fixed due date that is payable on the creditor's demand. (p. 656)

Discount on notes payable The difference between the face value of a non-interest-bearing note payable and the amount borrowed; represents interest that will be paid on the note over its life. (p. 675)

Estimated liability An obligation of an uncertain amount that can be reasonably estimated. (p. 665)

Exempt supplies GST-exempt services are educational, health care, and financial services. (p. 659)

Goods and Services Tax (GST) A value-added tax on nearly all goods and services sold in Canada. The tax is levied by the federal government. (p. 659)

Harmonized Sales Tax (HST) A combined GST and PST rate of 15% applied to taxable supplies. Currently, New Brunswick, Nova Scotia, and Newfoundland and Labrador apply HST. (p. 659)

Input Tax Credit (ITC) GST paid by the registrant on purchases of taxable supplies. Input tax credits are applied against (reduce) GST Payable. Also known as *GST Receivable*. (p. 659)

Known liability A company's obligations that have little uncertainty and are set by agreements, contracts, or laws; also called *definitely determinable liabilities*. (p. 657)

Liability A future payment of assets or services that a company is presently obligated to make as a result of past transactions or events. (p. 653)

Long-term liability Obligations of a company that do not require payment within the longer of one year or an operating cycle. (p. 654)

Non–interest-bearing note A note that does not have a stated rate of interest; the interest is included in the face value of the note. (p. 675)

Payroll Employee compensation for work performed. (p. 657)

Payroll liabilities Employee compensation amounts owing to employees and government and other agencies. (p. 657)

Provincial Sales Tax (PST) A consumption tax levied by provincial governments on sales to the final consumers of products; calculated as a percentage of the sale price of the item being sold. (p. 658)

Registrant Registered individual or entity selling taxable supplies that is responsible for collecting the GST on behalf of the government. A business with sales of less than $30,000 per year does not have to register for GST purposes. (p. 659)

Short-term note payable A current obligation in the form of a written promissory note. (p. 663)

Short-term notes issued at a discount See *non–interest-bearing note*. (p. 675)

Taxable supplies Taxable goods or services on which GST is calculated and includes everything except zero-rated and exempt supplies. (p. 659)

Trade accounts payable Amounts owed to suppliers regarding products or services purchased on credit. Commonly referred to as *accounts payable*. (p. 657)

Unearned revenues Amounts received in advance from customers for future products or services. (p. 661)

Warranty An agreement that obligates the seller or manufacturer to repair or replace a product when it breaks or otherwise fails to perform properly within a specified period. (p. 666)

Zero-rated supplies Goods including groceries, prescription drugs, and medical devices that have zero GST. (p. 659)

SSC

For more study tools, quizzes, and problem material, visit the **Student Success** *Centre* at
www.mcgrawhill.ca/studentsuccess/FAP

Questions

1. What is the difference between a current and a long-term liability?

2. What are the three important questions concerning the certainty of liabilities?

3. What amount does WestJet, in Appendix I, report as the current portion of long-term debt as at December 31, 2005? In what accounting period will this amount be paid?

4. Refer to Danier's balance sheet in   **DANIER**   Appendix I. Does Danier show any unpaid income tax? If so, what is the account name and the June 26, 2004, balance in the account?

5. What is an estimated liability?

6. Why are warranty liabilities usually recognized on the balance sheet as liabilities even when they are uncertain?

7. Suppose that a company has a facility located in an area where disastrous weather conditions often occur. Should it report a probable loss from a future disaster as a liability on its balance sheet? Why?

Quick Study

QS 13-1
Distinguishing between current and long-term liabilities
LO1

Which of the following items would normally be classified as a current liability for a company that has a 15-month operating cycle?
a. A note payable due in 18 months.
b. Salaries payable.
c. A payable that matures in two years.
d. A note payable due in 10 months.
e. The portion of a long-term note that is due to be paid in 12 months.

QS 13-2
Current portion of long-term debt
LO1

On January 1, 2011, Tetley Manufacturing borrowed $146,000 from the bank. Interest is calculated at the rate of 10% and the term of the note is four years. Four equal annual payments will be made in the amount of $46,059 each December 31. The payment schedule is shown below:

Year	Annual Payment	Principal Portion of Payment	Interest Portion of Payment	Principal Balance at Year-End
2011	46,059	31,459	14,600	114,541
2012	46,059	34,605	11,454	79,936
2013	46,059	38,065	7,994	41,871
2014	46,059	41,871	4,188	-0-

Show how Tetley Manufacturing will show the note on its year-end:
1. December 31, 2011, balance sheet.
2. December 31, 2012, balance sheet.

QS 13-3
Unearned revenue
LO2

MetroConcerts receives $2,000,000 in advance cash ticket sales for a four-date tour for Rita MacNeil. Record the advance ticket sales as a lump sum as of October 31, 2011. The concerts sold out and no additional ticket sales have been recorded. Record the revenue earned for the first concert date, November 16, 2011, assuming each concert date brings in the same amount of revenue.

QS 13-4
Accounting for sales tax payable
LO2

Palm Computing sells $5,000 of merchandise (with a cost of $4,450) for cash on September 30. The sales tax law requires Palm Computing to collect 14% harmonized sales tax on every dollar of merchandise sold. Record Palm's entries for the $5,000 sale and applicable sales tax (assume a perpetual inventory system).

QS 13-5
Sales tax payable
LO2

Saratoga Designers, located in Quebec, provided $3,400 of services on credit to a client on May 7, 2011. Record Saratoga's entry, including the appropriate GST and PST. Hint: Refer to Exhibit 13.6 for PST rates.

QS 13-6
Sales tax payable
LO2

On September 3, 2011, Metcalfe Retailers, operating out of Nunavut, sold $7,350 of goods for cash with a cost of $6,190. Record Metcalfe's entries, including all appropriate sales taxes.

Tecsey's has two employees and the payroll register showed the following information for the biweekly pay-period ended March 23, 2011:

QS 13-7
Payroll liabilities
LO²

Employee	Gross Pay	EI Premium	Income Taxes	CPP	Total Deductions	Net Pay	Salaries Expense
			Deductions			Pay	Distribution
Bently, A.	2,010.00	42.21	493.75	92.83	628.79	1,381.21	2,010.00
Craig, T.	2,115.00	44.42	532.65	98.03	675.10	1,439.90	2,115.00
Totals	4,125.00	86.63	1,026.40	190.86	1,303.89	2,821.11	4,125.00

Prepare the entry to record the payroll liability on March 23, 2011. Ignore employer's contributions payable on CPP and EI.

Jackson Textiles had an outstanding account in the amount of $14,800 owing to Nordon Manufacturing. On October 1, 2011, Nordon agreed to convert Jackson's account to an 8%, 45-day note having a face value of $14,800. Record Jackson's entries on October 1, 2011, and on the due date.

QS 13-8
Notes payable
LO³

On December 11, 2011, the Sydner Company borrowed $42,000 and signed a 60-day, 9% note payable. Calculate the accrued interest payable on December 31, 2011.

QS 13-9
Short-term note transactions
LO³

Vision Wear's product warranties state that defective glasses will be replaced free of charge for the life of the product. Vision Wear estimates that 2% of all items sold will require replacement. Each pair of glasses costs Vision Wear on average $40. During October 2011, Vision Wear sold 1,300 pairs of glasses at an average price of $120 per pair. Record the estimated warranty liability for October.

QS 13-10
Warranty liabilities
LO⁴

On December 20, 2011, The Net Department Store sold a computer for $3,500 with a one-year warranty that covers parts and labour. Warranty expense was estimated at 2% of sales. On March 2, 2012, the computer was taken in for repairs covered under the warranty that required $30 in parts and $10 of labour. Prepare the March 2 journal entry to record the warranty repairs.

QS 13-11
Warranty liabilities
LO⁴

Wang Corp. estimates income tax expense to be $285,600 for the year 2011. Record estimated income tax for January on January 31, 2011, and the payment on February 1, 2011.

QS 13-12
Recording an income tax liability
LO⁴

Delta Corp. recorded $36,000 in estimated income taxes on the last day of each month and made the payment on the 15th of the following month. On December 31, 2011, Delta's year-end, it was determined that total income tax expense for the year was $402,000. Record the income tax expense on December 31 (assuming no entry has yet been made in December to record tax) and the payment on January 15, 2012.

QS 13-13
Recording income tax liability
LO⁴

The following legal claims exist for the Doucet Company. Classify the required accounting treatment for each legal situation as (a) a liability should be recorded, or (b) the legal claim need only be described in the notes to the financial statements.
a. Doucet faces a likely loss on a pending lawsuit; however, the amount of the judgement cannot be reasonably estimated.
b. Doucet Company estimates that one lawsuit could result in a damage award of $1,200,000, and it is likely that the plaintiff will win the case.
c. Doucet Company estimates damages of another case at $3,000,000 with a likelihood of losing the case.

QS 13-14
Accounting for contingent liabilities
LO⁵

QS 13-15
Contingent liabilities
LO5

BioMed Pharmaceuticals was notified by its lawyers on November 18, 2011, that a lawsuit had been launched against the company. It was the opinion of the lawyers that BioMed would probably lose the case and that the plaintiff would settle for approximately $750,000. How should this be reported?

*QS 13-16
Discounting notes payable
LO6

Jerico Estates received $12,000 from the bank after signing a 60-day discounted note payable with a face value of $12,138 dated May 15, 2011. Record Jerico's entries on May 15 and on the due date.

*QS 13-17
Discounting notes payable
LO6

The Snyder Company signs a discounted note dated December 20, 2011, promising to pay $8,197 within 90 days. Record the signing of the note and the interest accrual on December 31, 2011. ($197 of interest is included in the note's face value of $8,197.)

Exercises

Exercise 13-1
Classifying liabilities
LO1

The following list of items might appear as liabilities on the balance sheet of a company that has a two-month operating cycle. Identify the proper classification of each item. In the space beside each item write a C if it is a current liability, an L if it is a long-term liability, or an N if it is not a liability.

_____ **a.** Wages payable.
_____ **b.** Notes payable in 60 days.
_____ **c.** Mortgage payable (payments due in the next 12 months).
_____ **d.** Notes receivable in 90 days.
_____ **e.** Note payable (matures in 5 years).
_____ **f.** Mortgage payable (payments due after the next 12 months).
_____ **g.** Notes payable due in 6 to 12 months.
_____ **h.** Income taxes payable.

Exercise 13-2
Financial statement presentation—
current liabilities
LO1

The Cambridge Cellular Company shows the following selected adjusted account balances as at December 31, 2011:

Accounts Payable...	$120,000
Salaries Payable	12,000
Accumulated Amortization, Equipment	36,000
Estimated Warranty Liability.............................	32,000
Mortgage Payable	300,000
Notes Payable, 6 months..................................	24,000

Check figure:
Total current liabilities = $236,000

Required
Prepare the current liability section of Cambridge's balance sheet. $48,000 in principal is due during 2012 regarding the mortgage payable. For simplicity, order the liabilities from largest to smallest.

Exercise 13-3
Current versus long-term
portions of debt
LO1

On January 2, 2011, the Bonnet Co. acquired land by issuing a 6%, three-year note for $120,000. The note will be paid in three annual payments of $44,893 each December 31. The payment schedule follows:

Year	Annual Payment	Principal Portion of Payment	Interest Portion of Payment	Principal Balance at Year-End
2011	44,893	37,693	7,200	82,307
2012	44,893	39,955	4,938	42,352
2013	44,893	42,352	2,541	-0-

An asterisk (*) identifies assignment material based on Appendix 13A.

Required
1. Prepare the entry to:
   a. Issue the note on January 2, 2011.
   b. Record the annual payment on December 31, 2011.
2. Show how the note will appear on the December 31, 2011, balance sheet.

The following alphabetized list of selected adjusted account balances is from the records of Assiniboine Company on December 31, 2011:

Accounts Payable	$ 40,000
Accumulated Amortization—Equipment	50,000
Estimated Warranty Liability	12,000
GST Payable	14,000
Mortgage Payable, $20,000 due Dec. 31, 2012	240,000
Notes Payable, due April 1, 2012	24,000
Notes Payable, due April 1, 2015	120,000
PST Payable	12,000
Warranty Expense	8,000

Exercise 13-4
Financial statement presentation—
current liabilities
LO1

Required
Prepare the current liability section of Assiniboine Company's 2011 balance sheet (for simplicity, list the accounts from largest to smallest).

Check figure:
Total current liabilities = $122,000

Analysis component:
Why is it important to categorize assets and liabilities?

James & Sons is a lucrative paving stone installation business that operates from about April to October each year. Clients arrange for their own paving stones and James & Sons is contracted to provide the installation. Because of the boom in the construction business, James & Sons has pre-booked customers for the next year and a half. Customers must pay 40% at the time of booking and the balance seven days prior to the start of the job. The December 31, 2011, balance sheet shows Unearned Revenues totalling $2,050,000. During 2012, $3,780,000 of cash was collected: $2,124,000 regarding work completed during the year, and the balance representing prepayments.

Exercise 13-5
Unearned revenues
LO2

Required
1. Prepare the entry to record the collection of cash in 2012.
2. Determine the balance in Unearned Revenue at December 31, 2012.

Billingsgate Fisheries had the following additional information at its November 30, 2011, year-end:
a. The Unearned Revenue account showed a balance of $48,000, which represented four months of services paid in advance by a client on October 15, 2011.
b. The payroll register showed the following unpaid amounts as at November 30:

Exercise 13-6
Various liabilities
LO2

EI* Premium	Income Taxes	CPP*	Total Deductions	Net Payable	Office Salaries	Sales Salaries
80.41	1,290.00	183.98	1,554.39	2,745.61	2,500.00	1,800.00

*The employer's portions of EI and CPP are 1.4 times and 1 times the employees' portion respectively.

c. The November utility bill in the amount of $1,380 was unpaid and unrecorded at November 30.

Required
Prepare the appropriate entries at year-end based on the above information.

Analysis component:
If the above entries are not recorded on November 30, 2011, what is the effect on the income statement and the balance sheet? Identify which GAAP would be violated.

Exercise 13-7
Sales taxes payable

LO²

Check figures:
a. HST Payable 25,200
b. PST Payable 12,600
c. PST Payable 19,080

Gelibrand Architectural Consultants provided $180,000 of consulting services to Carnegy Developments on April 14, 2011, on account.

Required
Journalize Gelibrand's April 14 transaction including applicable PST and GST or HST assuming it is located in:
a. Nova Scotia.
b. British Columbia.
c. Prince Edward Island.
Use the PST rates in Exhibit 13.6.

Exercise 13-8
Sales tax payable

LO²

On October 15, Lentron purchased $2,500 of merchandise on credit. The next day, it recorded sales of $1,700; cost of sales was $1,200. Record the October 15 and October 16 entries assuming each of the geographical areas noted in Exhibit 13.6. A chart similar to the following might be useful in organizing your answer.

Date	Description	Alberta		Etc.	

Exercise 13-9
Asset purchased with a note

LO², ³

The LaPierre Company purchased some machinery on March 10, 2011, that had a cost of $60,000 (ignore GST/PST). Show the journal entries that would record this purchase and payment under these three separate situations:
a. The company paid cash for the full purchase price.
b. The company purchased the machinery on credit with terms 1/30, n/60. Payment was made on April 9, 2011.
c. The company signed a 10%, one-year note for the full purchase price. The note was paid on March 10, 2012, the maturity date. Ignore year-end accruals.

Exercise 13-10
Notes payable

LO³

Check figure:
1. October 30

Peugot Boats borrowed $100,000 on September 15, 2011, for 45 days at 8% interest by signing a note.
1. On what date will this note mature?
2. How much interest expense is created by this note?
3. Prepare the journal entries for September 15, 2011, and the maturity date.

Exercise 13-11
Notes payable with year-end adjustments

LO³

Check figure:
1. March 1

Sobey Co. borrowed $30,000 on December 1, 2011, for 90 days at 10% interest by signing a note.
1. On what date will this note mature?
2. How much interest expense is created by this note in 2011?
3. How much interest expense is created by this note in 2012?
4. Prepare the journal entries on December 1, December 31 (Sobey Co.'s year-end), and the maturity date.

Exercise 13-12
Estimated warranties

LO⁴

Check figures:
c. $15,470
d. $9,750

Kendel Sunglasses extends a lifetime replacement warranty on all units sold. Using past experience, the company estimates that 0.5% of units sold will be returned and require replacement at an average cost of $130 per unit. On January 1, 2011, the balance in Kendel's Estimated Warranty Liability account was $15,600. During 2011, sales totalled $3,600,000 or 15,000 units. The actual number of units returned and replaced was 76.

Required
a. Prepare the entry to estimate warranty liabilities regarding the units sold for 2011. Assume the adjustment is made on December 31.
b. Record the replacement of the units returned in 2011 (use a date of December 31).
c. Calculate the balance in the Estimated Warranty Liability account at December 31, 2011.
d. What is the warranty expense that will appear on the income statement for the year ended December 31, 2011?

On December 6, 2011, Midinski Co. sold a computer for cash of $8,000 (cost $4,200) with a two-year parts and labour warranty. Based on prior experience, Midinski expects eventually to incur warranty costs equal to 5% of the selling price. The fiscal year P. 27 coincides with the calendar year P. 27. On January 20, 2012, the customer returned the computer for repairs that were completed the same day. The cost of the repairs consisted of $198 for the materials taken from the parts inventory and $40 of labour that was fully paid with cash. These were the only repairs required in 2012 for this computer.

Exercise 13-13
Warranty expense and liability
LO4

Required
1. How much warranty expense should the company report in 2011 for this computer?
2. How much is the warranty liability for this computer as of December 31, 2011?
3. How much warranty expense should the company report in 2012 for this computer?
4. How much is the warranty liability for this computer as of December 31, 2012?
5. Show the journal entries that would be made to record: (a) the sale (assume a perpetual inventory system); (b) the adjustment on December 31, 2011, to record the warranty expense; and (c) the repairs that occurred in January 2012. Ignore sales taxes.

Check figure:
4. Ending 2012 balance: $162

Dunn's Watch Repairs Ltd. prepares statements quarterly.

Exercise 13-14
Income taxes payable
LO4

Part A

Required
1. Based on 2010 results, Dunn's estimated tax liability for 2011 is $103,200. Dunn will accrue 1/12 of this amount at the end of each month (assume the installments are paid the next day). Prepare the entry on January 31, 2011, to accrue the tax liability and on February 1 to record the payment.
2. At year-end, December 31, the actual income tax for 2011 was determined to be $99,600. Prepare the adjusting entry on December 31 to record the accrual (assume 11 months have been accrued to date in 2011). Record the payment on January 1, 2012.

Part B

Required
3. Complete the following table assuming the company estimates its tax liability for the year 2011 to be $99,600.

Check figure:
5. $346,000

	Jan.–Mar.	Apr.–June	July–Sept.	Oct.–Dec.
Income before tax	$114,000	$68,000	$121,000	$164,500
Estimated income tax expense ...				
Net income				

4. Assuming that actual tax for the year 2011 was determined to be $121,500, prepare the appropriate adjusting entry at year-end to bring the balance in the Income Tax Expense account to the correct balance, assuming no accrual has yet been recorded for the fourth quarter.
5. Calculate the company's actual net income for the year 2011.

Whitby Company, located in Ontario, is preparing adjusting entries at December 31, 2011. An analysis reveals the following:
a. During December, Whitby sold 4,000 units of a product that carries a 60-day warranty. The sales for this product totalled $240,000. The company expects 8% of the units to need repair under warranty and it estimates that the average repair cost per unit will be $32.
b. A disgruntled employee is suing the company. Legal advisors believe that it is probable that the company will have to pay damages, the amount of which cannot be reasonably estimated.
c. The company needs to record previously unrecorded cash sales of $4,000,000 (cost of sales 65%) plus applicable PST and GST.
d. The company recognizes that $80,000 of $200,000 received in advance for products has now been earned.

Exercise 13-15
Various liabilities
LO2, 4, 5

Required
Prepare any required adjusting entries at December 31, 2011, for each of the above.

Check figure:
c. PST Payable $320,000

Exercise 13-16
Various liabilities
LO2, 4 ,5

Mackenzie Corp. is preparing the December 31, 2011, year-end financial statements. Following are selected unadjusted account balances:

Estimated warranty liability........	$ 6,460	120-day note payable, 6%	$ 75,000
Income tax expense	128,700	Unearned fees	345,000
Mortgage payable, 5%..............	680,000	Warranty expense.....................	7,392

Additional information:
a. $11,700 of income tax was accrued monthly from January through to November inclusive and paid on the 15th day of the following month. The actual amount of tax expense for the year is determined to be $147,350.
b. A customer is suing the company. Legal advisors believe that it is probable that the company will have to pay damages, the amount of which will approximate $500,000 given similar cases in the industry.
c. During December, Mackenzie had sales of $840,000. 5% of sales typically require warranty work equal to 20% of the sales amount.
d. Mortgage payments are made on the first day of each month.
e. $215,000 of the Unearned Fees remain unearned at December 31, 2011.
f. The 120-day note payable was dated November 15, 2011.

Required
a. Prepare any required adjusting entries at December 31, 2011, for each of the above.
b. Determine the adjusted amounts for total liabilities and net income assuming these were $940,000 and $620,000, respectively, prior to preparing the adjustments in (a) to (f) above.

Analysis component:
What is the effect on the income statement and balance sheet if the above entries are not recorded? Identify which GAAP, if any, would be violated if these entries are not recorded.

Exercise 13-17
Discounted notes payable
LO6

Check figure:
1. October 13

Gladiator Systems received $65,000 after signing a discounted note with a face value of $66,442 on July 15, 2011, for 90 days.

Required
1. On what date will this note mature?
2. How much interest expense is created by this note?
3. Prepare the journal entries for July 15, 2011, and the maturity date.

*Exercise 13-18
Discounted notes payable
LO6

Check figure:
1. January 19

Steinway Co. received $240,000 after signing a discounted note with a face value of $243,156 on November 20, 2011, for 60 days.

Required
1. On what date will this note mature?
2. How much interest expense is created by this note in 2011?
3. How much interest expense is created by this note in 2012?
4. Prepare the journal entries on November 20, December 31 (Steinway's year-end), and the maturity date.

Problems

Problem 13-1A
Current versus long-term portions of debt
LO1

On January 2, 2011, Forest Company acquired machinery by issuing an 8%, $200,000 note due in four years on December 31, 2014. Annual payments are $60,384 each December 31. The payment schedule is:

Year	Annual Payment	Principal Portion of Payment	Interest Portion of Payment	Principal Balance at Year-End
2011	$60,384	$44,384	$16,000	$155,616
2012	60,384	47,935	12,449	107,681
2013	60,384	51,770	8,614	55,911
2014	60,384	55,911	4,473	0

An asterisk (*) identifies assignment material based on Appendix 13A.

Required

Using the information provided, complete the following liabilities section of Forest Company's balance sheet at December 31:

	December 31			
	2011	**2012**	**2013**	**2014**
Current Liabilities:				
Current portion of long-term debt....				
Interest payable................................				
Long-term liabilities				
Long-term debt................................				

The Fifth Avenue Company entered into the following transactions involving short-term liabilities during 2011 and 2012:

	2011	
Mar.	14	Purchased merchandise on credit from Ferris Inc. for $25,000. The terms were 1/10, n/30 (assume a perpetual inventory system).
Apr.	14	Fifth Avenue paid $7,000 cash and replaced the $18,000 remaining balance of the account payable to Ferris Inc. with a 10%, 60-day note payable.
May	21	Borrowed $40,000 from Scotia Bank by signing a 12%, 90-day note.
	?	Paid the note to Ferris Inc. at maturity.
	?	Paid the note to the bank at maturity.
Dec.	15	Borrowed $70,000 and signed a 9%, 120-day note with National Bank.
Dec.	31	Recorded an adjusting entry for the accrual of interest on the note to National Bank.
	2012	
	?	Paid the note to National Bank at maturity.

Required

1. Determine the maturity dates of the three notes just described.
2. Present journal entries for each of the preceding dates.

Problem 13-2A
Transactions with short-term notes payable
LO3

On November 10, 2011, Muen Products began to buy and resell high-powered flashlights for $80 each. Muen uses the perpetual system to account for inventories. The flashlights are covered under a warranty that requires the company to replace any nonworking flashlight within 90 days. When a flashlight is returned, the company simply throws it away and mails a new one from inventory to the customer. The company's cost for a new flashlight is only $14. The manufacturer has advised the company to expect warranty costs to equal 18% of the units sold. These transactions occurred in 2011 and 2012 (ignore GST and PST):

Problem 13-3A
Estimated product warranty liabilities
LO4

	2011	
Nov.	15	Sold 200 flashlights for $16,000 cash.
	30	Recognized warranty expense for November with an adjusting entry.
Dec.	8	Replaced 15 flashlights that were returned under the warranty.
	15	Sold 550 flashlights.
	29	Replaced 40 flashlights that were returned under the warranty.
	31	Recognized warranty expense for December with an adjusting entry.
	2012	
Jan.	14	Sold 275 flashlights.
	20	Replaced 63 flashlights that were returned under the warranty.
	31	Recognized warranty expense for January with an adjusting entry.

Required

1. How much warranty expense should be reported for November and December 2011?
2. How much warranty expense should be reported for January 2012?
3. What is the balance of the estimated warranty liability as of December 31, 2011?
4. What is the balance of the estimated warranty liability as of January 31, 2012?
5. Prepare journal entries to record the transactions and adjustments.

Check figures:
2. $700
3. $1,120
4. $938

Problem 13-4A
Determining the effects of various
liabilities on financial statements
LO1, 4

Part 1

PEI Cameras manufactures and markets products throughout Canada. It was disclosed in notes to the company's financial statements that estimated warranty costs are accrued at the time products are sold. Assume that in 2011 warranty costs are estimated at $400,000 and that the related warranty work was actually paid for during 2012.

Required

Explain how financial statements are affected due to warranties in 2011 and 2012.

Part 2

Assume that Dobush Enterprises collected $6,000,000 during 2011 for magazines that will be delivered in future years. During 2012, Dobush delivered magazines based on these subscriptions amounting to $1,800,000.

Required

Explain how financial statements are affected in 2011 and 2012 by these subscriptions.

Problem 13-5A
Comprehensive
LO1, 2, 3, 4

Nissen Company's liabilities as reported on the June 30, 2011, balance sheet are shown below, along with its statement of owner's equity.

Accounts payable	$192,000
Notes payable, due 2013	500,000
Total liabilities	$692,000

NISSEN COMPANY Statement of Owner's Equity For Year Ended June 30, 2011	
Jen Nissen, capital, June 30, 2010	$598,000
Add: Net income	120,000
Total	$718,000
Less: Withdrawals	100,000
Jen Nissen, capital June 30, 2011	$618,000

Jen is selling the business. A potential buyer has hired an accountant to review the accounting records and the following was discovered:

a. Nissen Company began selling a new product line this past year that offered a warranty to customers. It is expected that $50,000 of warranty work will result next year based on first-year sales. No entry was prepared on June 30 to show this.

b. Annual property taxes of $19,680 are due July 31, 2011; the income statement shows only one month of property expense resulting from an entry correctly recorded on July 31, 2010.

c. Interest on the notes payable is paid quarterly. No entry has been recorded since the last quarterly payment of $8,700 on May 1, 2011.

d. $34,000 of new office furniture was purchased on account and received on June 28. This transaction has not been recorded .

e. Unearned revenue of $92,000 has been included on the income statement.

Check figure:
Total liabilities = $891,840

Required

Using the information provided, prepare a corrected statement of owner's equity and liabilities section of the balance sheet (ignore PST/GST).

Analysis component:

Which GAAP are violated when accrued liabilities are not recorded? Explain your answer.

Alternate Problems

On January 2, 2011, Wimberly Manufacturing acquired machinery by issuing a 10%, $250,000 note due in four years on January 2, 2015. Annual payments are $78,868 each January 2. The payment schedule is:

Problem 13-1B
Current versus long-term portions of debt
LO[1]

Year	Annual Payment	Principal Portion of Payment	Interest Portion of Payment	Principal Balance at Year-End
2012	78,868	53,868	25,000	196,132
2013	78,868	59,254	19,613	136,878
2014	78,868	65,180	13,688	71,698
2015	78,868	71,698	7,170	-0-

Required
Using the information provided, complete the following liabilities section of Wimberly Manufacturing's balance sheet:

	December 31			
	2011	2012	2013	2014
Current Liabilities:				
Current portion of long-term debt				
Interest payable................................				
Long-term liabilities				
Long-term debt................................				

Pap Company entered into the following transactions involving short-term liabilities during 2011 and 2012:

Problem 13-2B
Transactions with short-term notes payable
LO[3]

2011

Feb.	4	Purchased merchandise on credit from Shafai Products for $35,200. The terms were 2/10, n/60. Assume Pap uses a perpetual inventory system.
Mar.	2	Borrowed $120,000 from the First Provincial Bank by signing a note payable for 30 days at 14%.
Apr.	1	Paid the First Provincial Bank note.
	5	Gave Shafai Products $11,200 cash and a $24,000, 30-day, 12% note to secure an extension on Pap's past-due account.
May	5	Paid the note given to Shafai on April 5.
Nov.	16	Borrowed $108,000 at First Provincial Bank by signing a note payable for 60 days at 10%.
Dec.	1	Borrowed money at the Bank of Montreal by giving a $150,000, 90-day, 15% note payable.
	31	Recorded an adjusting entry for the accrual of interest on the note to the First Provincial Bank.
	31	Recorded an adjusting entry for the accrual of interest on the note to the Bank of Montreal.

2012

Jan.	15	Paid the November 16 note to First Provincial Bank.
Mar.	1	Paid the principal and interest on the December 1 note given to the Bank of Montreal.

Required
Prepare journal entries to record these transactions for Pap Company.

Problem 13-3B
Estimated product warranty liabilities

LO4

On November 9, 2011, Hubert Co. began to buy and resell toasters for $35 each. Hubert uses the perpetual method to account for inventories. The toasters are covered under a warranty that requires the company to replace any non-working toaster within 60 days. When a toaster is returned, the company simply throws it away and mails a new one from inventory to the customer. The company's cost for a new toaster is only $14. The manufacturer has advised the company to expect warranty costs to equal 20% of the total units sold. These transactions occurred in 2011 and 2012:

	2011	
Nov.	16	Sold 60 toasters for $2,100 cash.
	30	Recognized warranty expense for November with an adjusting entry.
Dec.	10	Replaced six toasters that were returned under the warranty.
	20	Sold 140 toasters.
	30	Replaced 17 toasters that were returned under the warranty.
	31	Recognized warranty expense for December with an adjusting entry.
	2012	
Jan.	6	Sold 50 toasters for $1,750 cash.
	20	Replaced 26 toasters that were returned under the warranty.
	31	Recognized warranty expense for January with an adjusting entry.

Check figures:
2. $140
3. $238
4. $14

Required
1. How much warranty expense should be reported for November and December 2011?
2. How much warranty expense should be reported for January 2012?
3. What is the balance of the estimated warranty liability as of December 31, 2011?
4. What is the balance of the estimated warranty liability as of January 31, 2012?
5. Prepare journal entries to record the transactions and adjustments.

Problem 13-4B
Contingencies and warranties

LO4, 5

Sam Aryee is the new manager of accounting and finance for a medium-sized manufacturing company. Now that the end of the year is approaching, his problem is determining whether and how to describe some of the company's contingencies and warranty estimates in the financial statements. The general manager, Sue Peebles, raised objections to one contingency and one warranty estimate in his preliminary proposal.

First, Peebles objected to the proposal to report nothing about a patent P. 617 infringement suit that the company has filed against a competitor. The manager's written comment on his proposal was, "We KNOW that we have them cold on this one! There is no way that we're not going to win a very large settlement!"

Second, she objected to his proposal to recognize an expense and a liability for warranty service on units of a new product that was just introduced in the company's fourth quarter. Her scribbled comment on this point was, "There is no way that we can estimate this warranty cost. Besides, we don't owe anybody anything until the products break down and are returned for service. Let's just report an expense if and when we do the repairs."

Required
Develop a written response for Aryee to the objections raised by the general manager.

Problem 13-5B
Comprehensive

LO1, 2, 3, 4

Picadilly Company's condensed income statement for the year ended November 30, 2011, is shown below.

PICADILLY COMPANY
Income Statement
For Year Ended November 30, 2011

Fees earned	$940,000
Operating expenses	830,000
Net income	$110,000

The liabilities reported on the November 30, 2011, balance sheet were:

Accounts payable	$ 36,000
Mortgage payable	300,000
Total liabilities...	$336,000

Louise Kinny, the owner, is looking for additional financing. A potential lender has reviewed Picadilly's accounting records and discovered the following:

a. Mortgage payments are made annually each December 1. The December 1, 2011, payment has not yet been made or recorded. A partial amortization schedule for the mortgage follows:

Year	Payment	Interest	Principal	Principal Balance, December 1
2010				300,000
2011	50,000	21,000	29,000	271,000
2012	50,000	18,970	31,030	239,970
2013	50,000	16,800	33,200	206,770

b. Fees earned included $170,000 received for work to be done in January and February 2012.
c. Accrued salaries at November 30, 2011, totalling $23,000 have not been recorded.
d. $14,000 of office supplies purchased on account were received November 28; this transaction was not recorded.
e. Annual property taxes of $15,000 are due each December 1; no property taxes have been included on the income statement.

Required
Using the information provided, prepare a corrected income statement and liabilities section of the balance sheet.

Analysis component:
If you were paid an annual bonus based on net income, what ethical dilemma would you face regarding the above items?

Ethics Challenge

Mike Thatcher is a sales manager for an automobile dealership in Alberta. Mike earns a bonus each year based on revenue generated by the number of vehicles sold in the year less related warranty expenses. The quality of automobiles sold each year seems to vary since the warranty experience related to vehicles sold is highly variable. The actual warranty expenses have varied over the past 10 years from a low of 3% of an automobile's selling price to a high of 10%. In the past, Mike has tended toward estimating warranty expenses on the high end just to be conservative. It is the end of the year and once again he must work with the dealership's accountant in arriving at the warranty expense accrual for the cars sold this year.

EC 13-1

Required
1. Does the warranty accrual decision present any kind of ethical dilemma for Mike Thatcher?
2. Since the warranty experience is not constant, what percent do you think Mike should choose for this year? Justify your response.

Focus on Financial Statements

FFS 13-1

On August 31, 2011, World Travel Consulting showed the adjusted account balances in alphabetical order:

Accounts payable	$ 3,100
Accounts receivable	29,000
Accumulated amortization, building	36,000
Accumulated amortization, equipment	13,000
Building	271,000
Cash	15,000
Equipment	38,000
GST receivable	840
Interest payable	1,400
Land	145,000
Long-term mortgage payable	116,000
Notes payable, due December 1, 2012	26,000
Notes payable, due March 1, 2012	17,000
Office supplies	1,800
Office supplies expense	14,000
Other operating expenses (including amortization)	101,000
Prepaid expenses	8,500
Salaries expense	126,000
Salaries payable	8,200
Sales	642,000

Required
1. Prepare the liability section of the balance sheet at August 31, 2011.
2. Charles World, the owner, is planning on expanding the business and has applied for a $2,000,000 bank loan. John Douglas, the Chartered Accountant and Certified Fraud Examiner featured in the chapter opening vignette on page 652, was contracted by the bank to review the financial statements of World Travel Consulting. John discovered that included in sales were the following:

Advance air ticket sales	114,000
Accommodation prepayments	96,000
Unearned bus tour revenue	36,000

He also noted the following excerpt from the amortization schedule of the long-term mortgage payable:

Year	Principal Balance at August 31
2010	$148,570
2011	116,000
2012	81,800
2013	45,900

Prepare a corrected balance sheet at August 31, 2011.

Analysis component:
Using your answers from Parts 1 and 2, discuss the implications of John's findings on the financial statements.

Required

Answer the following questions by referring to the June 25, 2005, and December 31, 2005, respective balance sheets for each of Danier Leather and WestJet on pages I-3 and I-20 in the textbook.

1. Danier reported $18,000,000 of *Accrued litigation provision and related expenses.* Explain what kind of liability this is.
2. WestJet shows *Advance ticket sales* of $127,450 (thousand) under current liabilities. Explain what this is.
3. WestJet shows *Current portion of long-term debt* of $114,115 (thousand) under current liabilities. Explain what this is and why it is classified as a current liability. Why is some of the debt listed as a current liability and the balance as long-term debt?

Critical Thinking Mini Case

Selected information taken from the December 31, 2011, financial statements for Mesa Company is shown below for the year just ended:

Current assets............................	$120,000	Long-term liabilities...................	$660,000
Property, plant and equipment...	840,000	Equity..	278,000
Intangibles	50,000	Revenues...................................	960,000
Current liabilities	72,000	Expenses	890,000

Mesa Company purchased $34,000 of merchandise inventory that was recorded as a debit to Merchandise Inventory and a credit to Accounts Payable on December 28; it was shipped FOB destination on December 28 and received on January 5. Because this liability was not due until 2012, it was listed as a long-term liability on the December 31, 2011, balance sheet. $50,000 of revenue earned but not recorded as of December 31, 2011, was recorded as a debit to Accounts Receivable and a credit to Revenue on December 31, 2011. $80,000 was collected on December 15 for services to be provided in February and March of 2012; this amount was recorded on December 15 as a debit to Cash and a credit to Revenue. $5,000 of interest accrued on a note payable during December and was recorded when it was paid on January 5, 2012, as a debit to Interest Expense and a credit to Interest Payable. $40,000 of payroll liabilities had accrued as of December 31, 2011, but had not been recorded. $430,000 of the long-term liabilities were due after December 31, 2012; the balance was current.

Required

Using the elements of critical thinking described on the inside front cover, comment.

Comprehensive Problem

Fast Exterminators
(Review of Chapters 1–13)

Fast Exterminators provides pest control services and sells pest extermination products manufactured by other companies. The following six-column table contains the company's unadjusted trial balance as of December 31, 2011.

	Unadjusted Trial Balance		Adjustments		Adjusted Trial Balance	
Fast Exterminators **Six-Column Table** **December 31, 2011**						
Cash..	$ 30,000					
Accounts receivable..	48,000					
Allowance for doubtful accounts		$ 6,128				
Merchandise inventory..................................	36,000					
Trucks...	44,000					
Accum. amortization, trucks..........................		-0-				
Equipment	150,000					
Accum. amort., equipment		43,000				
Accounts payable		12,000				
Interest payable...		-0-				
Estimated warranty liability...........................		2,400				
Unearned extermination services revenue		-0-				
Long-term notes payable...............................		120,000				
Ken Jones, capital		85,804				
Ken Jones, withdrawals..................................	42,000					
Extermination services revenue......................		140,000				
Interest earned		872				
Sales..		270,000				
Cost of goods sold	162,000					
Amort. expense, trucks..................................	-0-					
Amort. expense, equip.	-0-					
Wages expense..	90,000					
Interest expense	-0-					
Rent expense...	32,000					
Bad debts expense	-0-					
Miscellaneous expenses.................................	12,404					
Repairs expense...	22,000					
Utilities expense	11,800					
Warranty expense..	-0-					
Totals..	$680,204	$680,204				

The following information applies to the company and its situation at the end of the year:
a. The bank reconciliation P. 462 as of December 31, 2011, includes these facts:

Balance per bank...	$26,400
Balance per books	30,000
Outstanding cheques	5,200
Deposit in transit	7,000
Interest earned	88
Service charges (miscellaneous expense)	34

Included with the bank statement was a cancelled cheque that the company had failed to record. (This information allows you to determine the amount of the cheque, which was a payment of an account payable.)

b. An examination of customers' accounts shows that accounts totalling $5,000 should be written off as uncollectible. In addition, it has been determined that the ending balance of the Allowance for Doubtful Accounts account should be $8,600.

c. A truck was purchased and placed in service on July 1, 2011. Its cost is being amortized with the straight-line method using these facts and predictions:

Original cost...	$44,000
Expected residual value	12,000
Useful life (years)	4

d. Two items of equipment (a sprayer and an injector) were purchased and put into service early in January 2009. Their costs are being amortized with the straight-line method using these facts and predictions:

	Sprayer	Injector
Original cost..	$90,000	$60,000
Expected residual value	6,000	5,000
Useful life (years)	8	5

e. On October 1, 2011, the company was paid $5,280 in advance to provide monthly service on an apartment complex for one year. The company began providing the services in October. When the cash was received, the full amount was credited to the Extermination Services Revenue account.

f. The company offers a warranty for all of the products it sells. The expected cost of providing warranty service is 2% of sales. No warranty expense has been recorded for 2011. All costs of servicing products under the warranties in 2011 were properly debited to the liability account.

g. The $120,000 long-term note is a five-year, 8% note that was given to National Bank on December 31, 2009.

h. The ending inventory of merchandise was counted and determined to have a cost of $32,600. The difference is due to shrinkage; assume a perpetual inventory system.

Required

1. Use the preceding information to determine the amounts of the following items:
   a. The correct ending balance of Cash and the amount of the omitted cheque.
   b. The adjustment needed to obtain the correct ending balance of the Allowance for Doubtful Accounts.
   c. The annual amortization expense for the truck that was acquired during the year (calculated to the nearest month).
   d. The annual amortization expense for the two items of equipment that were used during the year.
   e. The correct ending balances of the Extermination Services Revenue and Unearned Extermination Services Revenue accounts.
   f. The correct ending balances of the accounts for Warranty Expense and Estimated Warranty Liability.
   g. The correct ending balance of the Interest Expense account. (Round amounts to the nearest whole dollar.)
   h. The cost of goods sold for the year.
2. Use the results of requirement 1 to complete the six-column table by first entering the appropriate adjustments for items *(a)* through *(h)* and then completing the adjusted trial balance columns. (Hint: Item *(b)* requires two entries.)
3. Present General Journal entries to record the adjustments entered on the six-column table.
4. Present a single-step income statement P. 273, a statement of owner's equity P. 29, and a classified balance sheet P. 206.

Check figures:
4. Net Income = $25,390
Total assets = $220,700

CHAPTER 14

Partnerships

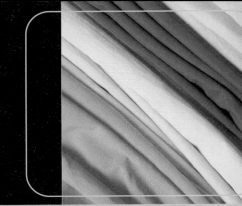

Go For It!

Toronto, ON—What do we say to an 18-year-old who wants some extra spending money? Maybe, "Check the *help wanted* at Zellers, McDonald's, or The Bay." But do we ever say, "What do *you* want to do?" Well, Jennifer Wong did what she wanted to do. Wong decided to block print cotton T-shirts and dresses in her parents' garage to be sold at craft shows and festivals. One would not normally expect much success from such a venture.

Wong's efforts paid off, however. In her first full year of business, at the ripe age of 19, her sales climbed to $110,000. In her second year, with a loan co-signed by her parents, she set up a small factory in a leased building in Scarborough. Jennifer formed a partnership with her friend, Malu Balizar, who invested $10,000 into the business. A partnership agreement was drawn up specifying how profits and losses would be divided between Jennifer and Malu and how the assets would be allocated if they decided to end the partnership. Wong has never looked back. Wong's clothing is funky, flowing, and artsy. Each product is individually hand block printed with evocative designs and symbols, and signed by the artist. Jennifer's clothing isn't cheap—a T-shirt can cost $60 and a dress, $200 to $300— but the style holds up from year to year. Wong says her clothing "is customer driven and says something meaningful about our times." All clothing is made with natural dyes and uses only organic cotton.

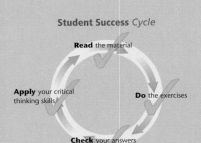

Student Success *Cycle*

Read the material

Do the exercises

Check your answers

Apply your critical thinking skills

CRITICAL THINKING CHALLENGE

Why would Jennifer form a partnership when her business appeared to be already doing well?

learning objectives

LO1 Identify characteristics of partnerships.

LO2 Prepare entries when forming a partnership.

LO3 Allocate and record income and loss among partners.

LO4 Account for the admission and withdrawal of a partner.

LO5 Prepare entries for partnership liquidation.

chapter preview

There are three common types of business organizations: corporations, partnerships, and proprietorships. In Chapter 1, we briefly discussed the following characteristics of these organizations:

	Sole Proprietorship	Partnership	Corporation
Business entity	yes	yes	yes
Legal entity	no	no	yes
Limited liability	no	no	yes
Unlimited life	no	no	yes
Business taxed	no	no	yes
One owner allowed	yes	no	yes

The opening article revealed Jennifer Wong's choice to form a partnership with her friend Malu, but there are disadvantages as well as advantages to this form of business organization. This chapter focuses on the partnership form of organization.

Partnership Form of Organization

A **partnership** is an unincorporated association of two or more persons to pursue a business for profit as co-owners. General partnerships are governed by provincial law and registration requirements. Many businesses are organized as partnerships. They are especially common in small retail and service businesses. Many professional practitioners such as physicians, lawyers, and accountants also organize their practices as partnerships.

Two forms of partnerships are recognized by Canadian law: *general partnerships* and *limited partnerships*.

Characteristics of General Partnerships

General partnerships offer certain advantages and disadvantages with their unique characteristics, as described in this section.

LO1 | Identify characteristics of partnerships.

Partnership Agreement

Forming a partnership requires that two or more legally competent persons agree to be partners. Their agreement becomes a **partnership contract**. While it should be in writing to protect partners in the event of disagreement or dissolution of the business, the contract is binding even if it is only expressed verbally.[1] Partnership agreements normally include the partners':

- names and contributions,
- rights and duties,
- sharing of income and losses,
- withdrawal provisions,
- dispute procedures,
- procedures for admission and withdrawal of new partners, and
- rights and duties of surviving partners in the event of a partner's death.

---

[1] Some courts have ruled that partnerships are created by the actions of partners even when there is no expressed agreement to form one.

Lawyers prepare partnership contracts but it is common for public accountants to review these contracts and advise partners on tax matters relating to their share of partnership income.

Limited Life

The life of a partnership is limited. Death,[2] bankruptcy, or any event taking away the ability of a partner to enter into or fulfill a contract ends a partnership. A partnership can also be terminated at will by any one of the partners. Conditions of termination may be specified in the partnership contract.

Taxation

A partnership is not subject to taxes on its income. It has the same tax status as a proprietorship. The income or loss of a partnership is allocated to the partners according to the partnership agreement, and is included for determining the taxable income of each partner's tax return.[3] Allocation of partnership income or loss is done each year whether or not cash is distributed to partners.

Co-Ownership of Property

Partnership assets are owned jointly by all partners. Any investment by a partner becomes the joint property of all partners. Partners have a claim on partnership assets based on the balances in their capital accounts.

Mutual Agency

The relationship between partners in a general partnership involves **mutual agency**. This means each partner is a fully authorized agent of the partnership. As its agent, a partner can commit or bind the partnership to any contract within the scope of the partnership's business. For instance, a partner in a merchandising business can sign contracts binding the partnership to buy merchandise, lease a store building, borrow money, or hire employees. These activities are all within the scope of business of a merchandising firm. However, a partner in a law firm, acting alone, cannot bind the other partners to a contract to buy snowboards for resale or rent an apartment for parties. These actions are outside the normal scope of a law firm's business.

Partners can agree to limit the power of any one or more of the partners to negotiate contracts for the partnership. This agreement is binding on the partners and on outsiders who know it exists, but it is not binding on outsiders who do not know it exists. Outsiders unaware of the agreement have the right to assume each partner has normal agency powers for the partnership. Because mutual agency exposes all partners to the risk of unwise actions by any one partner, people should evaluate each potential partner before agreeing to join a partnership.

Unlimited Liability

When a general partnership cannot pay its debts, the creditors can apply their claims to *personal* assets of partners, such as their homes. If a partner does not have enough assets to meet his or her share of the partnership debt, the creditors can apply their claims to the assets of the *other* partners. Because partners can be called on to pay the debts of a partnership, each partner is said to have **unlimited liability** for the partnership's debts. Mutual agency and unlimited liability are two main reasons why most partnerships have only a few members. Unlimited liability is considered a major disadvantage of the partnership form of organization. For a summary of advantages and disadvantages of partnerships see Exhibit 14.1.

---

[2] Partnership agreements may include special provisions regarding the death of a partner so that the partnership can continue after that event.

[3] The *Canada Income Tax Act* requires that proper records be maintained by partnerships and all other forms of business ownership that fall under its provisions.

Partnerships	
Advantages	**Potential Disadvantages**
• Ease of formation	• Unlimited liability for general partnerships creating personal obligations
• Low start-up costs	
• Access to more capital sources	• Hard to find suitable partners
• Broader base of management talent	• Possible development of conflict among partners
• Increased effectiveness from pooling talent	• Divided authority
• Less bureaucracy than corporations	• Partners can legally bind each other without prior approval
	• Lack of continuity

Exhibit 14.1

Advantages and Disadvantages of Partnerships

Limited Partnerships

Some individuals who want to invest in a partnership are unwilling to accept the risk of unlimited liability. Their needs may be met with a **limited partnership**. Limited partnerships are established under provincial statutes that require registration. A limited partnership has two classes of partners: general and limited. At least one partner must be a **general partner** who assumes management duties and unlimited liability for the debts of the partnership. The **limited partners** have no personal liability beyond the amounts they invest in the partnership. A limited partnership is managed by the general partner(s). Limited partners have no active role except as specified in the partnership agreement. A limited partnership agreement often specifies unique procedures for allocating incomes and losses between general and limited partners. The same basic accounting procedures are used for both limited and general partnerships.

Limited Liability Partnerships

Some provinces such as Ontario allow professionals such as lawyers and accountants to form a **limited liability partnership**. This is identified with the words "Limited Liability Partnership" or by "L.L.P." This type of partnership is designed to protect innocent partners from malpractice or negligence claims resulting from the acts of another partner. When a partner provides service resulting in a malpractice claim, that partner has personal liability for the claim. The remaining partners who are not responsible for the actions resulting from the claim are not personally liable. However, all partners are personally liable for other partnership debts. Accounting for a limited liability partnership is the same as for a general partnership.

1. Prepare a summary of the characteristics of a general partnership.
2. What is the difference between a *limited partnership* and a *limited liability partnership?*

Do: QS 14-1, QS 14-2

CHECKPOINT

Basic Partnership Accounting

Accounting for a partnership is the same as accounting for a proprietorship except for transactions directly affecting partners' equity. Because ownership rights in a partnership are divided among partners, partnership accounting:

- Uses a capital account for each partner.
- Uses a withdrawals account for each partner.
- Allocates net income or loss to partners according to the partnership agreement.

This section describes partnership accounting for organizing a partnership, distributing income and losses, and preparing financial statements P. 26.

Organizing a Partnership

LO2 | Prepare entries when forming a partnership.

When partners invest in a partnership, their capital accounts are credited for the invested amounts. Partners can invest both assets and liabilities. Each partner's investment is recorded at an agreed upon value, normally the fair market value P. 137 of the assets and liabilities at their date of transfer to the partnership.

To illustrate, on January 11, 2011, Olivia Tsang and David Breck organize as a partnership called The Landing Zone. Their business offers year-around facilities for skateboarding and snowboarding. Tsang's initial net investment in The Landing Zone is $30,000, made up of $7,000 in cash, equipment with a fair value of $33,000, and a $10,000 note payable reflecting a bank loan for the business due in six months. Breck's initial investment is cash of $10,000. These amounts are the values agreed upon by both partners. The entries to record these investments are:

	2011			
Jan.	11	Cash..	7,000	
		Equipment	33,000	
		Notes payable.......................................		10,000
		Olivia Tsang, Capital		30,000
		To record investment of Tsang.		
	11	Cash..	10,000	
		David Breck, Capital.............................		10,000
		To record investment of Breck.		

The balance sheet for the partnership would appear as follows immediately after the initial investment on January 11, 2011:

The Landing Zone
Balance Sheet
January 11, 2011

Assets		**Liabilities**		
Current assets:		Notes payable		$10,000
Cash	$17,000	**Partners' Equity**		
Capital assets:		Olivia Tsang, capital...........................	$30,000	
Equipment.....................................	33,000	David Breck, capital	10,000	
Total assets..	$50,000	Total partners' equity		40,000
		Total liabilities and partners' equity		$50,000

3. Partners A and B invested cash of $50,000 and equipment worth $75,000, respectively. Partner C transferred land worth $180,000 along with the related $100,000 note payable to the partnership. Calculate the total partnership equity for Partners A, B, and C.

Do: QS 14-3

After a partnership is formed, accounting for its transactions is similar to a proprietorship. The differences include:

1. Partners' withdrawals of assets are debited to their *individual* withdrawals accounts (as opposed to *one* withdrawals account for a sole proprietorship P. 4).
2. In closing the accounts at the end of a period, *each* partner's capital account is credited or debited for his or her share of net income or loss (as opposed to *one* capital account for a sole proprietorship).
3. The withdrawals account of *each* partner is closed to that partner's capital account (as opposed to *one* withdrawals account and *one* capital account for a sole proprietorship).

In the following sections, we will demonstrate that the basic accounting procedures related to the recording of withdrawals and closing of the accounts at the end of a period are similar for a partnership as for a proprietorship.

Dividing Income or Loss

Partners are not employees of the partnership. They are its owners. Partnership agreements generally include a provision for rewarding partners for their service and capital contributions to the partnership. If partners devote their time and services to their partnership, they are understood to do so for profit, not for salary. This means that when partners calculate the net income of a partnership, the amounts that they withdraw from the partnership assets are **not** expenses on the income statement.[4] They are recorded by debiting the partner's withdrawals account. Assume, for example, that on December 15, 2011, Olivia Tsang withdrew $20,000 and David Breck withdrew $18,000. The journal entry to record the withdrawals is:

LO3 | Allocate and record income and loss among partners.

	2011			
Dec.	15	Olivia Tsang, Withdrawals..............................	20,000	
		David Breck, Withdrawals.............................	18,000	
		Cash		38,000
		To record the withdrawal of cash by each partner.		

When net income or loss of a partnership is allocated among partners, the partners can agree to be assigned *salary allowances* as part of their allocation. *These salary allowances simply represent allocations of income; they are not actual distributions of cash.* Partners also can agree that division of partnership earnings includes a return based on the amount invested. These are called *interest allowances*. Their partnership agreement can provide for interest allowances based on their capital

---

[4] Withdrawals are frequently called *salary allowances* but they should not be confused with salary expense. Salaries taken out of the partnership are simply withdrawals.

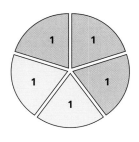

or

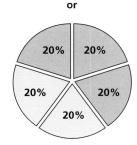

balances. For instance, since Tsang contributes three times the investment of Breck, it is only fair that this fact be considered when earnings are allocated between them. Like salary allowances, these interest allowances are *not* expenses on the income statement and they are *not* actual distributions of cash.

Partners can agree to any method of dividing income or loss. In the absence of an agreement, the law says that income or loss of a partnership is shared equally by the partners. If partners agree on how they share income but say nothing about losses, then losses are shared in the same way as income. Several methods of sharing partnership income or loss are used. Three frequently used methods divide income or loss using: (1) a stated fractional basis, (2) the ratio of capital investments, or (3) salary and interest allowances and any remainder in a fixed ratio.

1. Allocated on a Stated Fractional Basis

One way to divide partnership income or loss is to give each partner a fraction of the total. Partners must agree on the fractional share each receives. A fractional basis can be expressed as a ratio, a fraction, or a percentage. As an example, assume a 3:2 ratio as illustrated in Exhibit 14.2. This means that 3/5 or 60% (3 ÷ 5 = 0.60 × 100% = 60%) is allocated to one partner and 2/5 or 40% (2 ÷ 5 = 0.40 × 100% = 40%) is allocated to the other partner.

Assume the partnership agreement of Olivia Tsang and David Breck is based on a ratio of 3:2. This means Tsang receives three-fifths or 60%, and Breck two-fifths or 40%, of partnership income and loss. If their partnership's net income for the year ended December 31, 2011, is $70,000, it is allocated to the partners and the Income Summary account is closed with the following entry:

2011				
Dec.	31	Income Summary...	70,000	
		Olivia Tsang, Capital		42,000
		David Breck, Capital.............................		28,000
		To allocate income and close the Income Summary account.		

2. Allocated on the Ratio of Capital Investments

Partners can also allocate income or loss on the ratio of the relative capital investments of each partner. Assume Tsang and Breck agreed to share earnings on the ratio of their beginning capital investments. Since Tsang invested $30,000 and Breck invested $10,000, this means Tsang receives three-fourths [$30,000/($30,000 + $10,000)] or 75% of any income or loss and Breck receives one-fourth [$10,000/($30,000 + $10,000)] or 25%.

3. Allocated Using Salaries, Interest Allowance, and a Fixed Ratio

Service contributions (the amount of work each partner does) and capital contributions of partners often are not equal. Salary allowances can make up for differences in service contributions and interest allowances can make up for unequal capital contributions. When both service and capital contributions are unequal, the allocation of income and loss can include *both* salary and interest allowances.

In the new partnership formed by Olivia Tsang and David Breck, assume both partners agree that Tsang's services are worth an annual salary of $40,000. Since Breck is less experienced in the business, his services are valued at $25,000 annually. To compensate Tsang and Breck fairly given these differences in service and capital contributions, they agree to share income or loss as per Exhibit 14.3.

1. Annual salary allowances of $40,000 to Tsang and $25,000 to Breck.

2. Interest allowances equal to 10% of each partner's beginning-of-year capital balance.

3. Any remaining balance of income or loss to be shared 3:1.

Exhibit 14.3

Partnership Agreement Between Tsang and Breck

The provisions for salaries and interest in this partnership agreement are called *allowances*. Allowances are *not* reported as salaries and interest expense on the income statement. They are a means of dividing the income or loss of a partnership so each partner's capital account can be allocated its share.

Illustration When Income Exceeds Allowance

Recall that Tsang's original investment was $30,000 and Breck's $10,000. If The Landing Zone has first-year income of $70,000 and Tsang and Breck apply the partnership agreement as per Exhibit 14.3, they would allocate income or loss as shown in Exhibit 14.4 with the accompanying entry following.

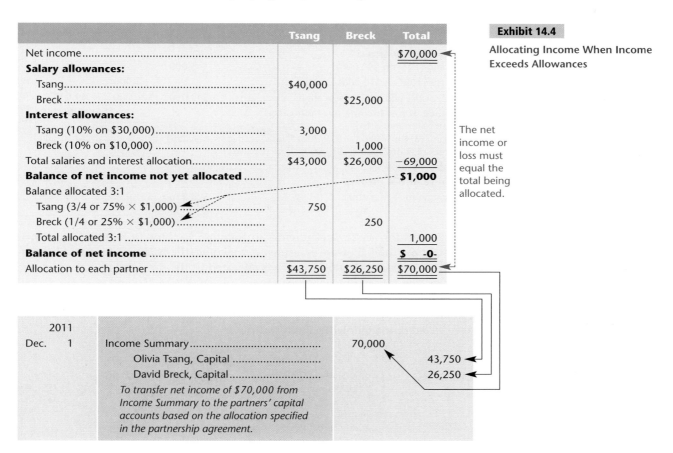

Exhibit 14.4

Allocating Income When Income Exceeds Allowances

Tsang is *allocated* $43,750 and Breck $26,250 of the $70,000 total; they do not *receive* these amounts. Remember that the purpose of the calculation in Exhibit 14.4 is to determine the amount of income or loss to be allocated to each partner's capital account at the end of the accounting period. Therefore, the entry to allocate the $70,000 net income between the partners and to close the Income Summary account on December 31, 2011, is as shown in Exhibit 14.4.

The balance in each of Tsang's and Breck's capital accounts at December 31, 2011, after posting all closing entries P. 197 is reflected in Exhibit 14.5.

Exhibit 14.5

Partners' Post-Closing Capital Balances at December 31, 2011

Olivia Tsang, Capital		
		30,000 Jan. 11/11 Partner investment
Dec. 31/11 Withdrawal[5]	20,000	43,750 Dec. 31/11 Allocation of income
		53,750 Post-Closing Balance Dec. 31/11

David Breck, Capital		
		10,000 Jan. 11/11 Partner investment
Dec. 31/11 Withdrawal[5]	18,000	26,250 Dec. 31/11 Allocation of income
		18,250 Post-Closing Balance Dec. 31/11

Illustration When Allowances Exceed Income

The method of sharing agreed to by Tsang and Breck must be followed even if net income is less than the total of the allowances. If The Landing Zone's first-year net income is $50,000 instead of $70,000, it is allocated to the partners as shown in Exhibit 14.6. The net income or loss must equal the total being allocated.

Exhibit 14.6

Allocating Income When Allowances Exceed Income

	Tsang	Breck	Total
Net income..			**$50,000**
Salary allowances:			
Tsang...	$40,000		
Breck		$25,000	
Interest allowances:			
Tsang (10% on $30,000)....................	3,000		
Breck (10% on $10,000)		1,000	
Total salaries and interest allocation........	$43,000	$26,000	−69,000
Balance of net income over allocated			**$(19,000)**
Balance allocated 3:1			
Tsang (3/4 or 75% × −$19,000)	(14,250)		
Breck (1/4 or 25% × −$19,000).........................		(4,750)	
Total allocated 3:1			19,000
Balance of net income			$ -0-
Allocation to each partner..	$28,750	$21,250	$ 50,000

The net income or loss must equal the total being allocated.

Calculations for salaries and interest are identical to those in Exhibit 14.4. When we apply the total allowances against net income, the balance of income is negative. This negative $19,000 balance is allocated in the same manner as a positive balance. The 3:1 sharing agreement means negative $14,250 and negative $4,750 are allocated to the partners to determine the final allocation. In this case, Tsang's capital account is credited with $28,750 and Breck's capital account with $21,250 as reflected in the following closing entry:

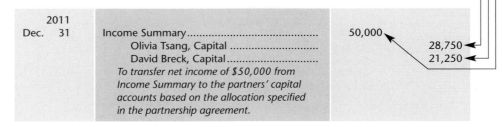

2011			
Dec. 31	Income Summary..	50,000	
	Olivia Tsang, Capital		28,750
	David Breck, Capital..............................		21,250
	To transfer net income of $50,000 from Income Summary to the partners' capital accounts based on the allocation specified in the partnership agreement.		

[5] Recall that the closing entry for withdrawals would have been:

2011			
Dec. 31	Olivia Tsang, Capital..	20,000	
	David Breck, Capital	18,000	
	Olivia Tsang, Withdrawals		20,000
	David Breck, Withdrawals.......................		18,000
	To record withdrawals to each partner's capital account.		

Illustration When There is a Net Loss

If The Landing Zone had experienced a loss, then it would have been shared by Tsang and Breck in the same manner as the $50,000 income. The only difference is that they would have begun with a negative amount because of the loss. Specifically, the partners would still have been allocated their salary and interest allowances, further adding to the negative balance of the loss. This *total* negative balance *after* salary and interest allowances would have been allocated 3:1 (75% and 25%) between the partners. These allocations would have been applied against the positive numbers from any allowances to determine each partner's share of the loss. Exhibit 14.7 illustrates how a $6,000 net loss would be divided between Tsang and Breck.

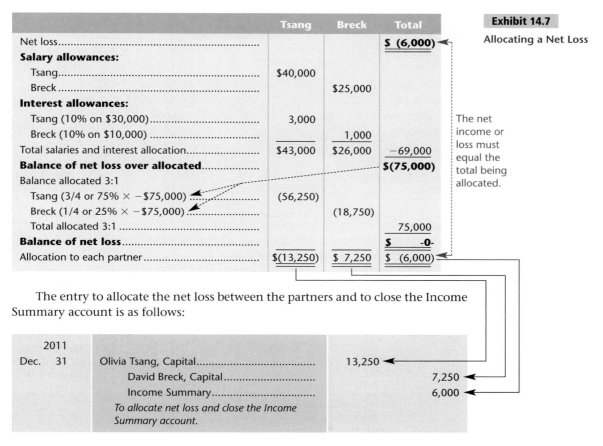

	Tsang	Breck	Total
Net loss..			$ (6,000)
Salary allowances:			
Tsang...	$40,000		
Breck		$25,000	
Interest allowances:			
Tsang (10% on $30,000)...................................	3,000		
Breck (10% on $10,000)		1,000	
Total salaries and interest allocation.......................	$43,000	$26,000	−69,000
Balance of net loss over allocated.................			$(75,000)
Balance allocated 3:1			
Tsang (3/4 or 75% × −$75,000)	(56,250)		
Breck (1/4 or 25% × −$75,000)		(18,750)	
Total allocated 3:1			75,000
Balance of net loss...			$ -0-
Allocation to each partner	$(13,250)	$ 7,250	$ (6,000)

Exhibit 14.7

Allocating a Net Loss

The net income or loss must equal the total being allocated.

The entry to allocate the net loss between the partners and to close the Income Summary account is as follows:

2011			
Dec. 31	Olivia Tsang, Capital..	13,250	
	David Breck, Capital...............................		7,250
	Income Summary....................................		6,000
	To allocate net loss and close the Income Summary account.		

When a net loss is allocated to the partners' capital accounts, you would expect each partner's capital account to decrease (a debit). However, notice that this entry causes Breck's capital account to increase (a credit) even though the partnership incurred a $6,000 loss. This occurs because Breck's 25% share of the $75,000 negative remaining balance is less than his $26,000 salaries and interest allocation. If the net loss had been, for example, $60,000, both Tsang's and Breck's capital accounts would have decreased as a result of the closing entry.

CHECKPOINT Read Apply Do Check

4. Ben and Jerry form a partnership by contributing $70,000 and $35,000, respectively. They agree to an interest allowance equal to 10% of each partner's capital balance at the beginning of the year with the remaining income shared equally. Allocate first-year income of $40,000 to each partner.

5. What fraction does each receive if three partners share on a 1:2:2 basis?

6. What percentage does each receive if three partners share on a 1:2:2 basis?

Do: QS 14-4, QS 14-5, QS 14-6

Partnership Financial Statements

Partnership financial statements are very similar to those of a proprietorship. The **Statement of Partners' Equity** is one exception. It shows each partner's capital balance at the beginning of the period, any additional investments made by each partner, each partner's allocation of the income or loss, withdrawals made by each partner, and the ending capital balance for each partner. To illustrate, Exhibit 14.8 shows the statement of partners' equity for The Landing Zone prepared according to the sharing agreement of Exhibit 14.3. Recall that The Landing Zone's first-year income was $70,000. Also, Tsang withdrew $20,000 and Breck $18,000 at the end of the first year as reflected in the T-accounts of Exhibit 14.5.

Exhibit 14.8

Statement of Partners' Equity

The Landing Zone
Statement of Partners' Equity
For Year Ended December 31, 2011

	Tsang	Breck	Total
Capital, January 1	$ -0-	$ -0-	$ -0-
Add: Investments by partners	30,000	10,000	40,000
Net income	43,750	26,250	70,000
Total	$ 73,750	$ 36,250	$110,000
Less: Partners' withdrawals	(20,000)	(18,000)	(38,000)
Capital, December 31	$53,750	$18,250	$ 72,000

The owners' equity section of the balance sheet of a partnership usually shows the separate capital account balance of each partner. In the case of The Landing Zone, both Olivia Tsang, Capital and David Breck, Capital are listed in the partners' equity section along with their balances of $53,750 and $18,250, respectively. This information appears on the December 31, 2011, balance sheet as shown in Exhibit 14.9.

> The ending capital balances on the statement of partners' equity are listed on the balance sheet.

Exhibit 14.9

Balance Sheet for The Landing Zone at December 31, 2011

The Landing Zone
Balance Sheet
December 31, 2011

Assets			Liabilities		
Current assets:			Long-term notes payable		$ 8,000
Cash		$50,000	**Partners' Equity**		
Capital assets:			Olivia Tsang, capital	$53,750	
Equipment	$33,000		David Breck, capital	18,250	
Less: Accumulated amortization	3,000	30,000	Total partners' equity		72,000
Total assets		$80,000	Total liabilities and partners' equity		$80,000

mid-chapter demonstration problem

Claudia Parker and Tom Poon began a partnership several years ago called The Gift Consultants. Adjusted trial balance information for the year ended September 30, 2011, appears below.

Account	Balance*	Account	Balance*
Accounts payable	$ 18,000	Expenses	$94,000
Accounts receivable	47,000	Notes payable, due March 2014	25,000
Accumulated amortization, office furniture	6,000	Office furniture	33,000
Accumulated amortization, vehicles	21,000	Prepaid rent	12,000
Allowance for doubtful accounts	3,000	Tom Poon, capital	72,000**
Cash	34,000	Tom Poon, withdrawals	75,000
Claudia Parker, capital	47,000	Unearned fees	7,000
Claudia Parker, withdrawals	50,000	Vehicles	68,000
Consulting revenue	214,000		

*Assume all account balances are normal.
**Tom Poon invested $10,000 during the year.

1. Prepare calculations that show how the income should be allocated to the partners assuming the partnership agreement states that incomes/losses are to be shared by allowing an $85,000 per year salary allowance to Parker, a $15,000 per year salary allowance to Poon, 10% interest on beginning of the year capital balances, and the remainder equally.

2. Prepare the journal entry to close the Income Summary account to the partners' capital accounts.

3. Prepare a statement of partners' equity and a classified balance sheet.

Analysis component:

Why are each of the partners' withdrawals different than the salary allowance identified in the partnership agreement?

Planning the Solution

- Set up a column for each partner as well as a column to keep track of allocated income.
- Allocate income to each partner according to the terms of the partnership agreement.
- Prepare the entry to close the Income Summary to the partners' capital accounts.
- Prepare the statement of partners' equity for the year ended September 30, 2011, and a classified balance sheet for September 30, 2011.
- Answer the analysis question.

solution to *Mid-Chapter Demonstration Problem* _____

1.

	Parker	Poon	Total
Net income..			**$120,000**
Salary allowances:			
Parker...	$ 85,000		
Poon		$ 15,000	
Interest allowances:			
Parker (10% on $47,000)	4,700		
Poon (10% on [$72,000 − $10,000])		6,200	
Total salaries and interest allocation	$ 89,700	$ 21,200	−110,900
Balance of net income over allocated			**$ 9,100**
Balance allocated equally:			
Parker (50% × $9,100)	4,550		
Poon (50% × $9,100)...		4,550	
Total allocated equally			9,100
Balance of net income			**$ -0-**
Allocation to each partner..........................	**$94,250**	**$25,750**	**$120,000**

must be equal

To closing
entry

2.

2011			
Dec. 31	Income Summary...	120,000	
	Claudia Parker, Capital		**94,250**
	Tom Poon, Capital		**25,750**
	To transfer net income of $120,000 from		
	Income Summary to the partners' capital		
	accounts.		

To statement of
partners' equity

3.

From income allocation in Part 1 and resulting closing entry in Part 2

THE GIFT CONSULTANTS
Statement of Partners' Equity
For Year Ended September 30, 2011

	Parker	Poon	Total
Capital, October 1, 2010	$ 47,000	$ 62,000	$ 109,000
Plus:			
Investments by owners	-0-	10,000	10,000
Net income	94,250	25,750	120,000
Total	$ 141,250	$ 97,750	$ 239,000
Less: Partners' withdrawals	50,000	75,000	125,000
Capital, September 30, 2011	$ 91,250	$ 22,750	$114,000

THE GIFT CONSULTANTS
Balance Sheet
September 30, 2011

Assets

Current assets:			
Cash		$ 34,000	
Accounts receivable	$47,000		
Less: Allowance for doubtful accounts	3,000	44,000	
Prepaid rent		12,000	
Total current assets			$ 90,000
Property, plant and equipment:			
Vehicles	$68,000		
Less: Accumulated amortization	21,000	$ 47,000	
Office furniture	$33,000		
Less: Accumulated amortization	6,000	27,000	
Total property, plant and equipment			74,000
Total assets			$ 164,000

Liabilities

Current liabilities:			
Accounts payable	$18,000		
Unearned fees	7,000	$ 25,000	
Total current liabilities			
Long-term liabilities:			
Notes payable, due March 2014		25,000	
Total liabilities			$ 50,000
Partners' Equity			
Claudia Parker, capital		$91,250	
Tom Poon, capital		22,750	
Total partners' capital			114,000
Total liabilities and partners' equity			$ 164,000

Analysis component:

The withdrawals represent the assets actually withdrawn by the partners from the partnership. The salary allowance in the partnership agreement is *assumed* and used only as one of the variables for calculating how much of the net income is to be allocated to each partner's capital account.

Admission and Withdrawal of Partner

LO4 | Account for the admission and withdrawal of a partner.

A partnership is based on a contract between individuals. When a partner is added or a partner withdraws, the old partnership ends. Still, the business can continue to operate as a new partnership among the remaining partners. This section looks at how we account for the addition and withdrawal of a partner.

Admission of a Partner

There are two ways in which a new partner is admitted to a partnership. First, a new partner can purchase an interest from one or more current partners. Second, a new partner can invest cash or other assets in the partnership.

Purchase of a Partnership Interest

The purchase of a partnership interest is a *personal transaction between one or more current partners and the new partner* that involves a reallocation of current partners' capital. To become a partner, the purchaser must be accepted by the current partners.

To illustrate, assume that at the end of The Landing Zone's third year, David Breck has a capital balance of $20,000 and he sells *one-half* of his partnership interest to Cris Davis for $18,000 on January 4, 2014. Breck is selling a $10,000 recorded interest (= $20,000 × 1/2) in the partnership. The partnership records this as:

2014			
Jan. 4	David Breck, Capital	10,000	
	Cris Davis, Capital		10,000
	To record admission of Davis by purchase.		

The effect of this transaction on partners' equity is as follows:

	Olivia Tsang, Capital	David Breck, Capital	Cris Davis, Capital	Total Partners' Equity
Balance *before* January 4 transaction...	$52,000	$20,000	$ -0-	$72,000
January 4 tranaction............................	-0-	(10,000)	+10,000	-0-
Balance *after* January 4 transaction	$52,000	$10,000	$10,000	$72,000

Two aspects of this transaction are important. First, the $18,000 Davis paid to Breck is *not* recorded by the partnership. The partnership's assets, liabilities, and total equity are not affected by this transaction. Second, Tsang and Breck must agree if Davis is to become a partner. If they agree to accept Davis, a new partnership is formed and a new contract with a new income-and-loss-sharing agreement is prepared. If Tsang or Breck refuses to accept Davis as a partner, then Davis gets Breck's sold share of partnership income and loss. If the partnership is liquidated, Davis gets Breck's sold share of partnership assets. However, Davis gets no voice in managing the company until being admitted as a partner.

Investing Assets in a Partnership

Admitting a partner by an investment of assets is a *transaction between the new partner and the partnership*. The invested assets become partnership property. To illustrate, if Tsang (with a $52,000 interest) and Breck (with a $20,000 interest) agree to accept Davis as a partner in The Landing Zone with her investment of $28,000, the entry to record Davis' investment is:

2014			
Jan. 4	Cash..	28,000	
	Cris Davis, Capital..................................		28,000
	To record admission of Davis by investment.		

After this entry is posted, both assets (cash) and owners' equity (Cris Davis, Capital) increase by $28,000 as shown in the following schedule:

	Net Assets	Olivia Tsang, Capital	David Breck, Capital	Cris Davis, Capital	Total Partners' Equity
Balance *before* January 4 transaction...	$ 72,000	$52,000	$20,000	$ -0-	$ 72,000
January 4 tranaction.............................	+28,000	-0-	-0-	+28,000	+28,000
Balance *after* January 4 transaction	$100,000	$52,000	$20,000	$28,000	$100,000

Davis now has 28% equity in the net assets of the business, calculated as $28,000 divided by the entire partnership equity of $100,000 (= $52,000 + $20,000 + $28,000). However, she does not necessarily have a right to 28% of income. Dividing income and loss is a separate matter on which partners must agree.

Bonus to Old Partners

When the current market value of a partnership is greater than the recorded amounts of equity, the partners usually require a new partner to pay a bonus (premium) for the privilege of joining. This situation exists when the market value of net assets exceeds their book value. To illustrate, let's say Tsang and Breck agree to accept Davis as a partner with a 25% interest in The Landing Zone, but they require Davis to invest $48,000. Recall that the partnership's accounting records show Tsang's equity in the business to be $52,000 and Breck's equity to be $20,000. Davis' equity is determined as follows:

Equities of existing partners ($52,000 + $20,000)...	$ 72,000
Investment of new partner..	48,000
Total partnership equity	$120,000
Equity of Davis (25% × $120,000)	$ 30,000

Although Davis invests $48,000, her equity in the recorded net assets of the partnership is only $30,000. The difference of $18,000 is called a bonus (or premium) and is allocated to the existing partners according to their net income/loss share ratio. Assume this to be 50:50. The entry to record this is:

2014			
Jan. 4	Cash..	48,000	
	Cris Davis, Capital..................................		30,000
	Olivia Tsang, Capital		9,000
	David Breck, Capital..............................		9,000
	To record admission of Davis and bonus to old partners; $18,000 × 1/2 = $9,000.		

The effects of this transaction on the accounts are summarized as follows:

	Net Assets	Olivia Tsang, Capital	David Breck, Capital	Cris Davis, Capital	Total Partners' Equity
Balance *before* January 4 transaction...	$ 72,000	$52,000	$20,000	$ -0-	$ 72,000
January 4 tranaction............................	+48,000	+9,000	+9,000	+30,000	+48,000
Balance *after* January 4 transaction	$120,000	$61,000	$29,000	$30,000	$120,000

Bonus to New Partner

Existing partners can give a bonus (premium) to a new partner so that the new partner gets a larger equity than the amount invested. This usually occurs when additional cash is needed or the new partner has exceptional talents. To illustrate, let's say Tsang and Breck agree to accept Davis as a partner with a 25% interest in the partnership's equity, but they require Davis to invest only $18,000. Davis' equity is determined as:

Equities of existing partners ($52,000 + $20,000)	$72,000
Investment of new partner	18,000
Total partnership equity	$90,000
Equity of Davis (25% × $90,000)..	$22,500

Davis receives a bonus of $4,500 (= $22,500 − $18,000). The entry to record Davis' investment is:

2014			
Jan. 4	Cash..	18,000	
	Olivia Tsang, Capital...	2,250	
	David Breck, Capital	2,250	
	Cris Davis, Capital		22,500
	To record Davis' admission and bonus;		
	$4,500 × 1/2 = $2,250.		

The effect of this transaction on the accounts follows:

	Net Assets	Olivia Tsang, Capital	David Breck, Capital	Cris Davis, Capital	Total Partners' Equity
Balance *before* January 4 transaction...	$72,000	$52,000	$20,000	$ -0-	$72,000
January 4 tranaction............................	+18,000	−2,250	−2,250	+22,500	+18,000
Balance *after* January 4 transaction	$90,000	$49,750	$17,750	$22,500	$90,000

Davis' bonus of $4,500 is contributed by the old partners in their income-and-loss-sharing ratio. Davis' 25% equity doesn't necessarily entitle her to 25% of any income or loss. This is a separate matter for agreement by the partners.

7. When a 'bonus' is given to a new partner being admitted, what is the effect on the existing partners' capital accounts?

Do: QS 14-7, QS 14-8, QS 14-9, QS 14-10

Withdrawal of a Partner

There are generally two ways in which a partner withdraws from a partnership. First, the withdrawing partner can sell his or her interest to another person who pays for it in cash or other assets. For this, we debit the withdrawing partner's capital account and credit the new partner's capital account (as already described in our discussion on the purchase of partnership interests). The second case is when cash or other assets of the partnership are given to the withdrawing partner in settlement of his or her equity interest. This section explains the accounting for the second case.

To illustrate, let's assume that on October 31, 2014, Breck withdraws from the partnership of The Landing Zone. The three partners share income and loss equally. The accounts show the following capital balances immediately prior to Breck's withdrawal:

	Olivia Tsang, Capital	David Breck, Capital	Cris Davis, Capital	Total Partners' Equity
Capital balances immediately **prior** to Breck's withdrawal...............	$84,000	$38,000	$38,000	$160,000

Accounting for the withdrawal depends on whether a bonus is paid or not. We describe three possibilities, summarized as follows:

1. No Bonus

If Breck withdraws and receives cash of $38,000

Oct.	31	David Breck, Capital	38,000	
		Cash		38,000

2. Bonus to Remaining Partners

If Breck withdraws and receives cash of $34,000

Oct.	31	David Breck, Capital	38,000	
		Cash		34,000
		Olivia Tsang, Capital		2,000
		Cris Davis, Capital		2,000

3. Bonus to Withdrawing Partner

If Breck withdraws and receives cash of $40,000

Oct.	31	David Breck, Capital	38,000	
		Olivia Tsang, Capital.................................	1,000	
		Cris Davis, Capital	1,000	
		Cash		40,000

A withdrawing partner is sometimes willing to take less than the recorded value of his or her equity just to get out of the partnership or because the recorded values of some assets are overstated. When this occurs, the withdrawing partner in effect gives a bonus to remaining partners equal to the equity left behind as shown in the second situation above.

The third case shows a bonus to the withdrawing partner. This bonus might arise for two reasons:

- if the recorded equity of the partnership is understated, or
- if the remaining partners want to remove a partner, which may require giving assets of greater value than the withdrawing partner's recorded equity.

Death of a Partner

A partner's death dissolves a partnership if the partnership agreement does not provide otherwise. A deceased partner's estate is entitled to receive his or her equity based on provisions that are stated in the partnership contract. These provisions include methods for: (a) closing of the books to determine income or loss since the end of the previous period up to the date of death, and (b) determining current values for assets and liabilities. The remaining partners and the deceased partner's estate then must agree to a settlement of the deceased partner's equity. This can involve selling the equity to remaining partners or to an outsider, or it can involve withdrawing assets. The journal entries regarding the death of a partner are the same as those for the withdrawal of a partner.

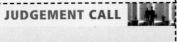

JUDGEMENT CALL

Answer—p. 716

Lawyer

You are a lawyer hired by the two remaining partners of a three-member partnership. The third partner recently died. The three partners shared income and loss in the ratio of their capital balances, which were equal. The partnership agreement says a deceased partner's estate is entitled to the "partner's percent share of partnership assets." The estate argues it is entitled to one-third of the current value of the partnership's total assets. The remaining partners say the distribution should use the asset's book values, which are only 75% of current value. They also point to partnership liabilities, which equal 40% of the assets' book value, and 30% of current value. How would you resolve this situation?

CHECKPOINT   Read   Apply   Do   Check

8. Partners X and Y have respective capital balances of $40,000 and $20,000. If Partner X withdraws and receives cash from the partnership of $30,000, what is the journal entry?

Do: QS 14-11, QS 14-12, QS 14-13

Liquidation of a Partnership

LO5 | Prepare entries for partnership liquidation.

Partnership liquidation is the process of closing down a business; it involves selling partnership assets, paying business debts, and distributing any remaining cash to owners. When a partnership is liquidated, its business is ended. Four steps are involved:

1. Non-cash assets are sold for cash and a gain or loss on liquidation is recorded.
2. Gain or loss on liquidation is allocated to partners using their income-and-loss ratio.
3. Liabilities are paid.
4. Remaining cash is distributed to partners based on their capital balances.

Partnership liquidation often follows one of two different cases described next.

No Capital Deficiency

No capital deficiency means that all partners have credit balances in their capital accounts before final distribution of cash. To illustrate, let's assume Tsang, Breck, and Davis operate their partnership in The Landing Zone for several years, sharing income and losses equally. The partners decide to liquidate on January 15, 2016. On that date, the books are closed, and income from operations is transferred to the partners' capital accounts. A summary of account balances immediately *prior* to liquidation are:

		Assets			= Liabilities +	Partners' Equity		
	Cash	Sporting Facilities	Accum. Amort. Sporting Facilities	Land	Accounts Payable	Olivia Tsang, Capital	David Breck, Capital	Cris Davis, Capital
Account balances immediately *prior* to liquidation	$168,000	$33,000	$18,000	$25,000	$20,000	$70,000	$66,000	$52,000

Following the four-step liquidation process, we first record the sale of the non-cash assets that occurred on January 15 for cash of $46,000. The entry is:

2016				
Jan.	15	Cash...	46,000	
		Accumulated Amortization, Sporting Facilities	18,000	
		Sporting Facilities...................................		33,000
		Land		25,000
		Gain From Liquidation		6,000
		Sold non-cash assets at a gain.		

Second, we record the allocation of the resulting gain from liquidation against the partners' capital accounts:

Jan.	15	Gain From Liquidation....................................	6,000	
		Olivia Tsang, Capital		2,000
		David Breck, Capital...............................		2,000
		Cris Davis, Capital		2,000
		To allocate liquidation gain to partners.		

The balances in the accounts after Steps 1 and 2 are recorded and summarized in Exhibit 14.10.

Step 3 in the liquidation process requires that liabilities be paid. Because creditors have claim to partnership assets before the partners do, they are paid first. The entry to record payment to the creditors is:

Jan.	15	Accounts Payable	20,000	
		Cash		20,000
		To pay claims of creditors.		

Exhibit 14.10 shows the account balances after Step 3, payment of creditors.

Exhibit 14.10

Liquidation of a Partnership—No Capital Deficiency

	Assets				= Liabilities +	Partners' Equity		
	Cash	Sporting Facilities	Accum. Amort., Sporting Facilities	Land	Accounts Payable	Olivia Tsang, Capital	David Breck, Capital	Cris Davis, Capital
Account balances immediately **prior** to liquidation.............................	$168,000	$33,000	$18,000	$25,000	$20,000	$70,000	$66,000	$52,000
1. & 2. Sale of non-cash assets for a gain of $6,000..............	+46,000	−33,000	−18,000	−25,000		+2,000	+2,000	+2,000
Balance.....................................	$214,000	$ -0-	$ -0-	$ -0-	$20,000	$72,000	$68,000	$54,000
3. Payment of Accounts Payable.................................	−20,000				−20,000			
Balance.....................................	$194,000	$ -0-	$ -0-	$ -0-	$ -0-	$72,000	$68,000	$54,000
4. Distribution of cash to partners.....................................	−194,000					−72,000	−68,000	−54,000
Final balance...........................	$ -0-	$ -0-	$ -0-	$ -0-	$ -0-	$ -0-	$ -0-	$ -0-

Step 4 in the liquidation process is to **divide the remaining cash of $194,000 among the partners according to their capital account balances** as follows:

Jan.	15	Olivia Tsang, Capital..	72,000 ◄	
		David Breck, Capital	68,000 ◄	
		Cris Davis, Capital	54,000 ◄	
		Cash		194,000
		To distribute remaining cash to partners.		

The account balances after distribution of cash to the partners are summarized in Exhibit 14.10.

Capital Deficiency

Capital deficiency means that at least one partner has a debit balance in his or her capital account before the final distribution of cash. This can arise from liquidation losses, excessive withdrawals before liquidation, or recurring losses in prior periods.

Assume that the partners of The Landing Zone decide to liquidate. Davis' capital account shows a deficiency of $3,000 immediately prior to the final distribution of cash. Davis' capital deficiency means that she owes the partnership $3,000. The final distribution of cash depends on whether the deficient partner can pay the deficiency or not.

Partner Pays Deficiency

Davis should pay $3,000 into the partnership to cover the deficiency. If Davis is willing and able to pay, the partners' capital balances after the payment are:

	Cash	Olivia Tsang, Capital	David Breck, Capital	Cris Davis, Capital
Account balances immediately **prior** to distribution of cash to partners	$24,000	$19,000	$8,000	$(3,000)
Davis pays deficiency	+3,000			+3,000
Balance...	$27,000	$19,000	$8,000	$ -0-

The entry to record the final cash distributions to partners is:

Jan.	15	Olivia Tsang, Capital.....................................	19,000	
		David Breck, Capital	8,000	
		Cash		27,000
		To distribute remaining cash to partners.		

Partner Cannot Pay Deficiency

Because of unlimited liability in a partnership, a partner's unpaid deficiency is absorbed by the remaining partners with credit balances. If Davis is unable to pay the $3,000 deficiency, it is shared by Tsang and Breck based on their income-and-loss-sharing ratio. Since they share equally, this is recorded as:

Jan.	15	Olivia Tsang, Capital.....................................	1,500	
		David Breck, Capital	1,500	
		Cris Davis, Capital		3,000
		To transfer Davis' deficiency to Tsang		
		and Breck.		

After Davis' deficiency is absorbed by Tsang and Breck, the capital account balances of the partners are:

	Cash	Olivia Tsang, Capital	David Breck, Capital	Cris Davis, Capital
Account balances immediately **prior** to distribution of cash to partners	$24,000	$19,000	$8,000	$(3,000)
Transfer Davis' deficiency to Tsang and Breck		−1,500	−1,500	+3,000
Balance...	$24,000	$17,500	$6,500	$ -0-

The entry to record the final cash distributions to the partners is:

Jan.	15	Olivia Tsang, Capital.....................................	17,500	
		David Breck, Capital	6,500	
		Cash		24,000
		To distribute remaining cash to partners.		

The inability of Davis to cover her deficiency does not relieve her of the liability. If she becomes able to pay at some future date, Tsang and Breck can each collect $1,500 from her. If Davis does not comply, then Tsang and Breck may have to resort to legal action.

The sharing of an insolvent partner's deficit by the remaining partners in their original income-and-loss-sharing ratio is generally regarded as equitable.

CHECKPOINT

9. Assume that assets, liabilities, and equity prior to liquidation were $50,000; $10,000; and $40,000. Calculate total assets, liablities, and equity after the payment of the liabilities.

Do: QS 14-14, QS 14-15

Summary

LO1 | **Identify characteristics of partnerships.** A partnership is a voluntary association between the partners that is based on a contract. The life of a partnership is limited by agreement or by the death or incapacity of a partner. Normally, each partner can act as an agent of the other partners and commit the partnership to any contract within the apparent scope of its business. All partners in a general partnership are personally liable for all the debts of the partnership. Limited partnerships include one or more general partners plus one or more (limited) partners whose liabilities are limited to the amounts of their investments in the partnership. The risk of becoming a partner results in part from the fact that partnership characteristics include mutual agency and unlimited liability.

LO2 | **Prepare entries when forming a partnership.** The initial investment of partnership assets is recorded by debiting the assets contributed at the fair market value and crediting the partners' capital accounts.

LO3 | **Allocate and record income and loss among partners.** A partnership's net incomes or losses are allocated to the partners according to the terms of the partnership agreement. The agreement may specify that each partner will receive a given fraction, or that the allocation of incomes and losses will reflect salary allowances and/or interest allowances. When salary and/or interest allowances

are granted, the residual net income or loss usually is allocated equally or on a stated fractional basis.

LO4 | **Account for the admission and withdrawal of a partner.** When a new partner buys a partnership interest directly from one or more of the existing partners, the amount of cash paid from one partner to another does not affect the total recorded equity of the partnership. The recorded equity of the selling partner(s) is simply transferred to the capital account of the new partner. Alternatively, a new partner may purchase an equity interest in the partnership by investing additional assets in the partnership. When this occurs, part of the new partner's investment may be credited as a bonus to the capital accounts of the existing partners. Also, to gain the participation of the new partner, the existing partners may give the new partner a bonus whereby portions of the existing partners' capital balances are transferred to the new partner's capital account.

LO5 | **Prepare entries for partnership liquidation.** When a partnership is liquidated, losses and gains from selling the partnership assets are allocated to the partners according to the partnership income-and-loss-sharing ratio. If a partner's capital account has a deficit balance that the partner cannot pay, the other partners must share the deficit in their relative income-and-loss-sharing ratio.

guidance answer to   **JUDGEMENT CALL**

Lawyer

The partnership agreement apparently fails to mention liabilities or use the term "net assets." Still, to give the estate one-third of total assets is not fair to the remaining partners. This is because if the partner had lived and the partners had decided to liquidate, the liabilities would have had to be paid first. Also, a settlement based on the

recorded equity of the deceased partner would fail to recognize excess of current value over book value. These value increases would be realized if the partnership were liquidated. A fair settlement would be a payment to the estate for the balance of the deceased partner's equity based on the *current value of net assets*.

guidance answers to | **CHECKPOINT** | Read · Apply · Do · Check

1. A summary of the characteristics of a general partnership is as follows:

Partnership	A contract exists between the partners agreement and in its absence, incomes and losses are shared equally.
Limited life	The life of a partnership is limited subject to terms in the partnership contract.
Taxation	A partnership is not subject to tax.
Co-ownership of property	Partnership assets are owned jointly by the partners.
Mutual agency	Each partner is an authorized agent of the partnership.
Unlimited liability	Partners can be called on to pay the debts of the partnership.

2. A limited partnership has one general partner who assumes management duties and unlimited liability for the debts of the partnership; the limited partners have no personal liability beyond the amounts they invest in the partnership. In a limited liability partnership, liability is limited to the partner(s) responsible for any malpractice or negligence claims; innocent partners are not liable. However, all partners in a limited liability partnership are personally liable for other partnership debts.

3. $50,000 + $75,000 + ($180,000 − $100,000) = $205,000

4.

	Ben	Jerry	Total	
Net income.....................			$ 40,000	
Interest allowance...........	$ 7,000	$ 3,500	−10,500	must be equal
Remaining balance			**$29,500**	
Balance allocated equally	14,750	14,750	29,500	
Remaining balance..........			$ -0-	
Shares of partners	**$21,750**	**$18,250**	**$40,000**	

5. 1/5, 2/5, 2/5

6. 20%, 40%, 40%

7. A 'bonus' to a new partner being admitted causes the existing partners' capital accounts to decrease.

8.

Partner X....................................	40,000	
Partner Y............................		10,000
Cash		30,000

9. Assets = $50,000 − $10,000 = $40,000;
Liabilities = $10,000 − $10,000 = $0;
Equity = $40,000.

demonstration problem

Read · Apply · Do · Check

Part 1

On a work sheet similar to that shown below, include eight columns to show the effects of the following on the partners' capital accounts over a four-year period.

Date	Transaction	Ries, Capital	Bax, Capital	Royce, Capital	Murdock, Capital	Elway, Capital	Total Partners' Equity

Apr. 13/11	Ries, Bax, and Royce create RB&R Co. Ries and Bax each invest $10,000 while Royce invests $24,000. They agree that each will get a 10% interest allowance on each partner's beginning-of-year capital balance. In addition, Ries and Bax are to receive $5,000 salary allowances. The remainder of the income is to be divided evenly.
Dec. 31/11	The partnership's income for the year is $39,900, and withdrawals at year-end are: Ries, $5,000; Bax, $12,500; and Royce, $11,000.
Jan. 1/12	Ries sells her interest to Murdock for $20,000, who is accepted by Bax and Royce as a partner in the new BR&M Co. The profits are to be shared equally after Bax and Royce each receive $25,000 salaries.
Dec. 31/12	The partnership's income for the year is $35,000, and their withdrawals are: Bax, $2,500; and Royce, $2,000.
Jan. 1/13	Elway is admitted as a partner after investing $60,000 cash in the new Elway & Associates partnership. Elway is given a 60% interest in capital after the other partners transfer $9,180 to his account from each of theirs. A 20% interest allowance (on the beginning-of-year capital balances) will be used in sharing profits, but there will be no salaries. Elway will get 40% of the remainder, and the other three partners will each get 20%. (Note: The interest allowance is to be calculated on each partner's capital balance immediately after the admission of Elway.)
Dec. 31/13	Elway & Associates earns $127,600 for the year, and year-end withdrawals are: Bax, $25,000; Royce, $27,000; Murdock, $15,000; and Elway, $40,000.
Jan. 1/14	Elway buys out Bax and Royce for the balances of their capital accounts, paying them $92,000 cash from personal funds. Murdock and Elway will share future profits on a 1:9 ratio.
Feb. 29/14	The partnership has earned $10,000 of income since the beginning of the year. Murdock retires and receives partnership cash equal to her capital balance. Elway takes possession of the partnership assets in his own name, and the business is dissolved.

Part 2

Journalize the transactions affecting the partnership for the year ended December 31, 2012.

Analysis component:

Why would the partnership agreement allocate different salary allowances to each of Bax, Royce, and Murdock ($25,000, $25,000, and $0, respectively)?

Planning the Solution

- Evaluate each transaction's effects on the capital accounts of the partners.
- Each time a new partner is admitted or a partner withdraws, allocate any bonus based on the income-or-loss-sharing agreement.
- Each time a new partner is admitted or a partner withdraws, allocate subsequent net incomes or losses in accordance with the new partnership agreement.
- Prepare the journal entries to record the transactions for the year 2012.
- Answer the analysis question.

solution to *Demonstration Problem*

Part 1

Date	Event	Ries, Capital	Bax, Capital	Royce, Capital	Murdock, Capital	Elway, Capital	Total Partners' Equity
Apr. 13/11	Investment	$10,000	$10,000	$24,000			$ 44,000
Dec. 31/11	$39,900 income allocation:						39,900
	– 10% interest	1,000	1,000	2,400			
	– salary allowance	5,000	5,000	-0-			
	– $25,500 remainder equally	8,500	8,500	8,500			
	Withdrawals:	(5,000)	(12,500)	(11,000)			(28,500)
	Balance:	$19,500	$12,000	$23,900			$ 55,400
Jan. 1/12	Ries sells to Murdock	(19,500)			$19,500		-0-
Dec. 31/12	$35,000 income allocation:						35,000
	– salary allowance		25,000	25,000	-0-		
	– ($15,000) remainder equally		(5,000)	(5,000)	(5,000)		
	Withdrawals:		(2,500)	(2,000)	-0-		(4,500)
	Balance:		$29,500	$41,900	$14,500		$ 85,900
Jan. 1/13	Elway admitted as partner		(9,180)	(9,180)	(9,180)	$ 87,540	60,000
Dec. 31/13	$127,600 income allocation:						127,600
	– 20% interest allowance		4,064	6,544	1,064	17,508	
	– remainder 40% Elway;						
	20% others		19,684	19,684	19,684	39,368	
	Withdrawals:		(25,000)	(27,000)	(15,000)	(40,000)	(107,000)
	Balance:		$19,068	$31,948	$11,068	$104,416	$166,500
Jan. 1/14	Elway buys out Bax and Royce		(19,068)	(31,948)		51,016	-0-
	Balance:		$ -0-	$ -0-	$11,068	$155,432	$166,500
Feb. 29/14	$10,000 income allocation:				1,000	9,000	10,000
	Adjusted balance:				$12,068	$164,432	$176,500
	Murdock retires:				(12,068)	-0-	(12,068)
	Adjusted balance:				$ -0-	$164,432	$164,432
	Partnership dissolved					(164,432)	(164,432)
	Final balance					$ -0-	$ -0-

Part 2

2012				
Jan. 1	Ries, Capital	19,500	
	Murdock, Capital		19,500
	To record entrance of Murdock in place of Ries.		
Dec. 31	Bax, Capital..	2,500	
	Royce, Capital	2,000	
	Bax, Withdrawals		2,500
	Royce, Withdrawals..............................		2,000
	To close partners' withdrawal accounts		
	to their capital.		
Dec. 31	Income Summary..	35,000	
	Murdock, Capital	5,000	
	Bax, Capital...		20,000
	Royce, Capital		20,000
	To close Income Summary to partners' capital.		

Analysis component:

The partnership agreement allocates different salary allowances to each of the partners likely because each partner's direct involvement in the operation of the partnership varies.

Glossary

General partner A partner who assumes unlimited liability for the debts of the partnership; also, the general partner in a limited partnership is responsible for its management. (p. 697)

General partnership A partnership in which all partners have mutual agency and unlimited liability for partnership debts. (p. 695)

Limited liability partnership A partnership in which each partner is not personally liable for malpractice or negligence claims unless the partner was responsible for providing the service that resulted in the claim. (p. 697)

Limited partners Partners who have no personal liability for debts of the partnership beyond the amounts they have invested in the partnership. (p. 697)

Limited partnership A partnership that has two classes of partners: limited partners and general partners. (p. 697)

Mutual agency The legal relationship among the partners whereby each partner is an agent of the partnership and is able to bind the partnership to contracts within the apparent scope of the partnership's business. (p. 696)

Partnership An unincorporated association of two or more persons to pursue a business for profit as co-owners. (p. 695)

Partnership contract The agreement between partners that sets forth the terms under which the affairs of the partnership will be conducted. (p. 695)

Partnership liquidation The dissolution of a business partnership by: (1) selling non-cash assets for cash, (2) allocating the gain or loss according to partners' income-and-loss ratio, (3) paying liabilities, and (4) distributing remaining cash to partners based on capital balances. (p. 712)

Statement of partners' equity A financial statement that shows the total capital balances at the beginning of the period, any additional investment by the partners, the net income or loss of the period, the partners' withdrawals during the period, and the ending capital balances. (p. 704)

Unlimited liability of partners The legal relationship among general partners that makes each of them responsible for paying all the debts of the partnership if the other partners are unable to pay their shares. (p. 696)

For more study tools, quizzes, and problem material,
visit the **Student Success** *Centre* at
www.mcgrawhill.ca/studentsuccess/FAP

Questions

1. Amey and Lacey are partners. Lacey dies, and her son claims the right to take his mother's place in the partnership. Does he have this right? Why?
2. If a partnership contract does not state the period of time over which the partnership is to exist, when does the partnership end?
3. As applied to a partnership, what does the term *mutual agency* mean?
4. Can partners limit the right of a partner to commit their partnership to contracts? Would the agreement be binding: (a) on the partners, and (b) on outsiders?
5. What does the term *unlimited liability* mean when it is applied to members of a partnership?
6. How does a general partnership differ from a limited partnership?
7. George, Burton, and Dillman have been partners for three years. The partnership is being dissolved. George is leaving the firm, but Burton and Dillman plan to carry on the business. In the final settlement, George places a $75,000 salary claim against the partnership. He contends that he has a claim for a salary of $25,000 for each year because he devoted all of his time for three years to the affairs of the partnership. Is his claim valid? Why?
8. The partnership agreement of Jenny Nelmida and Fei Abella provides for a two-thirds/one-third sharing of income but says nothing about losses. The first year of partnership operations resulted in a loss and Nelmida argues that the loss should be shared equally because the partnership agreement said nothing about sharing losses. What do you think?
9. If the partners in Blume Partnership want the financial statements to show the procedures used to allocate the partnership income among the partners, on what financial statement should the allocation appear?
10. After all partnership assets are converted to cash and all liabilities have been paid, the remaining cash should equal the sum of the balances of the partners' capital accounts. Why?
11. Kay, Kat, and Kim are partners. In a liquidation, Kay's share of partnership losses exceeds her capital account balance. She is unable to meet the deficit from her personal assets, and the excess losses are shared by her partners. Does this relieve Kay of liability?
12. A partner withdraws from a partnership and receives assets of greater value than the book value of his equity. Should the remaining partners share the resulting reduction in their equities in the ratio of their relative capital balances or in their income-and-loss-sharing ratio?

Quick Study

Bowen and Campbell are partners in operating a store. Without consulting Bowen, Campbell enters into a contract for the purchase of merchandise for the store. Bowen contends that he did not authorize the order and refuses to take delivery. The vendor sues the partners for the contract price of the merchandise. Will the partnership have to pay? Why? Does your answer differ if Bowen and Campbell are partners in a public accounting firm?

QS 14-1
Partnership liability
LO1

Pourier organized a limited partnership and is the only general partner. Hillier invested $20,000 in the partnership and was admitted as a limited partner with the understanding that he would receive 10% of the profits. After two unprofitable years, the partnership ceased doing business. At that point, partnership liabilities were $85,000 larger than partnership assets. How much money can the creditors of the partnership obtain from the personal assets of Hillier in satisfaction of the unpaid partnership debts?

QS 14-2
Liability in limited partnerships
LO1

Len Peters and Beau Silver form a partnership to operate a catering business. Peters invests $20,000 cash and Silver invests $30,000 cash on March 1, 2011. Prepare the journal entry to record the formation of the partnership.

QS 14-3
Journal entry when forming a partnership
LO2

Bill Ace and Dennis Bud are partners in AMPAC Company. Net income for the year ended March 31, 2011, is $120,000.
a. How much net income should be allocated to each partner assuming there is no partnership agreement?
b. Prepare the entry to allocate the net income.
c. Prepare the entry to allocate the $120,000 assuming it is a net loss.

QS 14-4
Partnership income allocation
LO3

Lisa Montgomery and Joel Calmar had a partnership and shared incomes and losses based on an agreement that gave Lisa a salary allowance of $45,000 and Joel $10,000 with any unallocated income (loss) shared equally. Prepare the entry to close the Income Summary account at December 31, 2011, assuming a credit balance of $48,000.

QS 14-5
Allocation of net income
LO3

Jenn Smith and Mike Yang had a partnership and shared incomes and losses based on an agreement that gave Jenn a salary allowance of $115,000 and Mike $90,000 with any unallocated income (loss) shared 3:2. Prepare the entry to close the Income Summary account at December 31, 2011, assuming a debit balance of $80,000.

QS 14-6
Allocation of net loss
LO3

Ramos and Briley are equal partners, each with $30,000 in his partnership capital account. Fontaine is admitted to the partnership on October 1, 2011, after paying $30,000 to the partnership for a one-third interest. Prepare the entry to show Fontaine's admission to the partnership.

QS 14-7
Admission of a partner
LO4

On March 12, 2011, Fontaine agrees to pay Ramos and Briley $12,000 each for a one-third interest in the existing Ramos–Briley partnership. At the time Fontaine is admitted, each partner has a $30,000 capital balance. Prepare the journal entry to record Fontaine's purchase of the partners' interest. *Note: Fontaine is paying Ramos and Briley, he is not paying the partnership.*

QS 14-8
Admission of a partner
LO4

On June 17, 2011, Bishop agrees to invest $30,000 into a partnership for a 40% interest in total partnership equity. At the time Bishop is admitted, the existing partners, Pollard and Mission, each have a $30,000 capital balance. Prepare the entry on June 17 to record Bishop's admission to the partnership. Any bonus is to be shared equally by Pollard and Mission.

QS 14-9
Admission of a partner—bonus to new partner
LO4

QS 14-10
Admission of a partner—bonus
to old partners
LO⁴

On April 21, 2011, Wilson agrees to invest $30,000 into a partnership for a 20% interest in total partnership equity. At the time Wilson is admitted, the existing partners, Beacon and Metcalf, each have a $30,000 capital balance. Prepare the entry on April 21 to record Wilson's admission to the partnership. Any bonus is to be shared equally by Beacon and Metcalf.

QS 14-11
Partner withdrawal
LO⁴

Lector, Wylo, and Stuart are partners with capital balances of $25,000, $40,000, and $35,000 respectively. They share income and losses equally. Stuart is retiring and has agreed to accept $35,000 cash for his share of the partnership. Record Stuart's withdrawal on November 23, 2011.

QS 14-12
Partner withdrawal—bonus
to remaining partners
LO⁴

Oliver, Peter, and Wendell are partners in NewTech Company. Their capital balances are $30,000, $22,000, and $15,000 respectively on November 23, 2011. They share income and losses in the ratio of 3:2:1. Peter retires on November 23, 2011, and has agreed to accept $15,000 for his share of the partnership. Record Peter's retirement and calculate the resulting balances in the capital accounts.

QS 14-13
Partner withdrawal—bonus
to leaving partner
LO⁴

Linda, Sue, and Darlene are partners in Designs Unlimited. Their capital balances are $150,000, $140,000, and $250,000 respectively on March 15, 2011. They share income and losses in the ratio of 2:2:2. Darlene retires on March 15, 2011, and has agreed to accept $300,000 for her share of the partnership. Record Darlene's retirement and calculate the resulting balances in the capital accounts.

QS 14-14
Partnership liquidation—gain
on sale of equipment
LO⁵

Sam, Andrews, and Mary were partners in Gana Company. The partners shared profits and losses 3:2:3, respectively. On April 1, 2011, the partnership showed the following account balances just prior to liquidation:

	Cash	Equipment	Accum. Amort. Equipment	Sam, Capital	Andrews, Capital	Mary, Capital
Account balances immediately ***prior*** to liquidation..........................	$32,000	$151,000	$36,000	$65,000	$48,000	$34,000

Equipment was sold for $175,000. Prepare the journal entry to record the final distribution of cash.

QS 14-15
Partnership liquidation—loss on
sale of equipment
LO⁵

Assume the same information as in QS 14-14 except that the *Equipment* was sold for $85,000 on April 1, 2011. Prepare the journal entry to record the final distribution of cash.

Exercises

Exercise 14-1
Forms of organization
LO¹

For each scenario below, recommend a form of business organization: sole proprietorship, partnership, or corporation. Along with each recommendation explain how business profits would be taxed if the form of organization recommended were adopted by the owners. Also list several advantages that the owners would enjoy from the form of business organization that you recommend.
1. Keith, Scott, and Brian are new university graduates in computer science. They are thinking of starting a Web-page creation company. They all have quite a few university debts and currently do not own any of the computer equipment that they will need to get the company started.
2. Dr. Marble and Dr. Sampson are new graduates from medical residency programs. They are both family practice physicians and would like to open a clinic in an underserved rural area. Although neither has any funds to bring to the new venture, a banker has expressed interest in making a loan to provide start-up funds for the practice.

3. Matthew has been out of school for about five years and has become quite knowledgeable about the commercial real estate market. Matthew would like to organize a company that buys and sells real estate. Matthew feels that he has the expertise to manage the company but needs funds to invest in the commercial property.

On February 1, 2011, Tessa Williams and Audrey To formed a partnership in the province of Ontario. Williams contributed $105,000 cash and To contributed land valued at $120,000 and a small building valued at $135,000. Also, the partnership assumed responsibility for To's $45,000 long-term note payable associated with the land and building. The partners agreed to share profits as follows: Williams is to receive an annual salary allowance of $52,500, both are to receive an annual interest allowance of 20% of their original capital investments, and any remaining profit or loss is to be shared equally. On November 20, 2011, Williams withdrew cash of $60,000 and To withdrew $45,000. After the adjusting entries and the closing entries to the revenue and expense accounts, the Income Summary account had a credit balance of $102,000.

Exercise 14-2
Journalizing partnership entries
LO2, 3

Required
1. Present General Journal entries to record the initial capital investments of the partners, their cash withdrawals, and the December 31 closing of the Income Summary and withdrawals accounts.
2. Determine the balances of the partners' capital accounts as of the end of 2011.

Check figures:
1. Share of income:
   Williams: $66,750;
   To: $35,250

Newton and Scampi began a partnership by investing $52,000 and $78,000, respectively. During its first year, the partnership recorded net income of $180,000.

Exercise 14-3
Income allocation in a partnership
LO3

Required
Prepare calculations showing how the income should be allocated to the partners under each of the following plans for sharing net incomes and losses:
a. The partners failed to agree on a method of sharing income.
b. The partners agreed to share incomes and losses in proportion to their initial investments.
c. The partners agreed to share income by allowing an $85,000 per year salary allowance to Newton, a $65,000 per year salary allowance to Scampi, 10% interest on their initial investments, and the balance equally.

Check figures:
c. To Newton: $98,700;
   To Scampi: $81,300

Lowe and Bentley began a partnership by investing $80,000 and $140,000, respectively. They agreed to share net incomes and losses by allowing yearly salary allowances of $85,000 to Lowe and $65,000 to Bentley, 15% interest allowances on their investments, and the balance 3:2.

Exercise 14-4
Income allocation in a partnership
LO3

Check figures:
1. To Lowe: $74,380;
   To Bentley: $70,920
2. To Lowe: $(36,920);
   To Bentley: $(3,280)

Required
1. Determine each partner's share if the first-year net income was $145,300.
2. Independently of (1), determine each partner's share if the first-year net loss was $40,200.

Josh Stevens and Kit Sharp formed a partnership by investing $40,000 and $200,000 respectively. They agreed to share income based on an allocation to Josh of an annual salary allowance of $130,000, interest allowance to both Josh and Kit equal to 15% of their beginning-of-year capital balance, and any balance based on a 1:3 ratio respectively. At the end of their first year, December 31, 2011, the Income Summary had a credit balance of $30,000. Josh withdrew $7,000 during the year and Kit $24,000.

Exercise 14-5
Income allocation
LO3

Required
1. Prepare the entry to close the Income Summary on December 31, 2011.
2. Calculate the balance in each partner's capital account at the end of their first year.

Check figures:
1. Share of income:
   To Stevens: $102,000;
   To Sharp: $(72,000)

Debra and Glen are partners who agree that Debra will receive a $100,000 salary allowance after which remaining incomes or losses will be shared equally. If Glen's capital account is credited $8,000 as his share of the net income (loss) in a given period, how much net income (loss) did the partnership earn?

Exercise 14-6
Income allocation
LO3

Exercise 14-7
Income allocation, statement of partners' equity, balance sheet
LO³

Shawna Jensen and Mike Yang were students when they formed a partnership several years ago for a part-time business called Downloads Etc. Adjusted trial balance information for the year ended December 31, 2011, appears below.

Account	Balance*	Account	Balance*
Accounts payable	$ 350	Office equipment	$ 8,600
Accumulated amortization	3,500	Office supplies	1,370
Cash	12,200	Revenues	96,000
Expenses	32,400	Shawna Jensen, capital**	3,800
Mike Yang, capital**	4,600	Shawna Jensen, withdrawals	31,000
Mike Yang, withdrawals	26,000	Utilities payable	120
Note payable, due May 2013***	3,200		

*Assume all account balances are normal.
**The partners made no investments during the year.
***$2,000 of the note payable is due in May 2012.

Check figures:
1. Share of income:
   To Jensen, $38,160;
   To Yang, $25,440
3. Total assets = $18,670

Required
1. Prepare calculations that show how the income should be allocated to the partners assuming the partnership agreement states that incomes/losses are to be shared by allowing a $30,000 per year salary allowance to Jensen, a $20,000 per year salary allowance to Yang, and the remainder on a 3:2 ratio.
2. Prepare the journal entry to close the Income Summary account to the partners' capital accounts.
3. Prepare a statement of partners' equity and a classified balance sheet.

Analysis component:
Why might the partners' capital accounts be so small relative to the amount of the withdrawals made?

Exercise 14-8
Admission of a new partner
LO⁴

The Hagan–Baden Partnership has total partners' equity of $380,000, which is made up of Hagan, Capital, $300,000, and Baden, Capital, $80,000. The partners share net incomes and losses in a ratio of 75% to Hagan and 25% to Baden. On July 1, Megan is admitted to the partnership and given a 20% interest in equity.

Check figures:
b. Cr Baden, Capital: 4,000
c. Dr Baden, Capital: 8,000

Required
Prepare the journal entry to record the admission of Megan under each of the following unrelated assumptions, in which Megan invests cash of:
a. $95,000
b. $115,000
c. $55,000

Exercise 14-9
Admission of a new partner
LO⁴

Gunnar & Dietar Consulting showed the following partners' equity at August 31, 2011:

Gunnar Schwiede, Capital	$100,000
Dietar Loris, Capital	390,000

Gunnar and Dietar share net incomes and losses in a 2:3 ratio respectively. On September 1, 2011, Wil Court is admitted to the partnership with a cash investment of $210,000.

Required
Prepare the journal entry to record the admission of Wil under each of the following unrelated assumptions, where he is given:
a. a 30% interest in equity
b. a 20% interest in equity
c. a 50% interest in equity

The partners in the Magesty Partnership have agreed that partner Prince may sell his $70,000 equity in the partnership to Queen, for which Queen will pay Prince $55,000. Present the partnership's journal entry to record the sale on April 30.

Exercise 14-10
Sale of a partnership interest
LO4

Barth, Holt, and Tran have been partners sharing net incomes and losses in a 6:2:2 ratio. On November 30, the date Tran retires from the partnership, the equities of the partners are: Barth, $100,000; Holt, $65,000; and Tran, $25,000. Present General Journal entries to record Tran's retirement under each of the following unrelated assumptions:
a. Tran is paid $25,000 in partnership cash for his equity.
b. Tran is paid $30,000 in partnership cash for his equity.
c. Tran is paid $22,500 in partnership cash for his equity.

Exercise 14-11
Retirement of a partner
LO4

Check figures:
b. Dr Holt, Capital: 1,250
c. Cr Holt, Capital: 625

Barb Rusnak, Len Peters, and Doug Morris are partners in RPM Dance Studios. They share net incomes and losses in a 40:40:20 ratio. Doug retires from the partnership on October 14, 2011, and receives $40,000 cash plus a car with a book value of $20,000 (original cost was $42,000).

Exercise 14-12
Retirement of a partner
LO4

Required
For each of the following unrelated situations, present the journal entry to record Doug's retirement assuming the equities of the partnership on October 14 are:
a. Rusnak, $150,000; Peters, $200,000; Morris, $60,000
b. Rusnak, $50,000; Peters, $60,000; Morris, $80,000
c. Rusnak, $65,000; Peters, $80,000; Morris; $30,000

Les Wallace, Mavis Dunn, and Sig Jensen were partners and showed the following account balances as of December 31, 2011:

Exercise 14-13
Liquidation of a partnership
LO5

	Cash	Equipment	Accum. Amort. Equipment	Accounts Payable	Notes Payable	Les Wallace, Capital	Mavis Dunn, Capital	Sig Jensen, Capital
Account balances December 31, 2011...	$26,000	$304,000	$178,000	$14,000	$24,000	$62,000	$28,000	$24,000

Due to several unprofitable periods, the partners decided to liquidate the partnership. The equipment was sold for $112,000 on January 1, 2012. The partners share any income (loss) in the ratio of 2:1:1 for Wallace, Dunn, and Jensen respectively.

Required
Prepare the liquidation entries (sale of equipment, allocation of gain/loss, payment of creditors, final distribution of cash).

Martha Wheaton, Bess Jones, and Sam Dun were partners and showed the following account balances as of December 31, 2011:

Exercise 14-14
Liquidation of a partnership
LO5

	Cash	Building	Accum. Amort. Building	Land	Accounts Payable	Martha Wheaton, Capital	Bess Jones, Capital	Sam Dun, Capital
Account balances December 31, 2011 ..	$92,000	$412,000	$240,000	$104,000	$64,000	$158,000	$(26,000)	$172,000

Due to difficulties, the partners decided to liquidate the partnership. The land and building were sold for $340,000 on January 1, 2012. The partners share any income (loss) in the ratio of 2:1:1 for Wheaton, Jones, and Dun respectively.

Required
Prepare the entry to distribute the remaining cash to the partners assuming any deficiencies are paid by the partners.

Check figure:
Dr Martha Wheaton, Capital: 190,000

Exercise 14-15
Liquidation of a partnership
LO5

Check figure:
Dr Martha Wheaton, Capital: 183,333

Assume the same information as in Exercise 14-14 except that capital deficiencies at liquidation are absorbed by the remaining partners according to their income (loss) ratio.

Required
Prepare the entry to distribute the remaining cash to the partners. Round calculations to the nearest whole dollar.

Exercise 14-16
Liquidation of a partnership
LO5

Check figure:
3b. Dr Boom, Capital: 5,100

The Whiz–Bam–Boom partnership began with investments by the partners as follows: Whiz, $115,600; Bam, $88,600; and Boom, $95,800. The first year of operations did not go well, and the partners finally decided to liquidate the partnership, sharing all losses equally. On December 31, after all assets were converted to cash and all creditors were paid, only $30,000 in partnership cash remained.

Required
1. Calculate the capital account balances of the partners after the liquidation of assets and payment of creditors.
2. Assume that any partner with a deficit pays cash to the partnership to cover the deficit. Present the General Journal entries on December 31 to record the cash receipt from the deficient partner(s) and the final disbursement of cash to the partners.
3. Now make the contrary assumption that any partner with a deficit is not able to reimburse the partnership. Present journal entries: (a) to transfer the deficit of any deficient partners to the other partners, and (b) to record the final disbursement of cash to the partners.

Problems

Problem 14-1A
Methods of allocating partnership income
LO3

Check figure:
c. Cr Curtis Wall, Capital: $119,880

Curtis Wall, Jen Dock, and Lori Kent invested $132,800, $116,200, and $83,000, respectively, in a partnership. During its first year, the firm recorded net income of $351,000.

Required
Prepare entries to close the firm's Income Summary account as of December 31 and to allocate the net income to the partners under each of the following assumptions:
a. The partners did not produce any special agreement on the method of sharing incomes.
b. The partners agreed to share net incomes and losses in the ratio of their beginning investments.
c. The partners agreed to share income by: providing annual salary allowances of $104,000 to Wall, $116,000 to Dock, and $90,000 to Kent; allowing 10% interest on the partners' beginning investments; and sharing the remainder equally.

Problem 14-2A
Allocating partnership incomes and losses; sequential years
LO3

Check figures:
d. Year 1: To Bowtell: $(63,650);
   To Locke: $23,650
d. Year 2: To Bowtell: $16,350;
   To Locke: $103,650
d. Year 3: To Bowtell: $51,350;
   To Locke: $138,650

Avice Bowtell and Reece Locke are in the process of forming a partnership to which Bowtell will devote one-third time and Locke will devote full time. They have discussed the following alternative plans for sharing net incomes and losses.
a. In the ratio of their initial investments, which they have agreed will be $66,000 for Bowtell and $99,000 for Locke.
b. In proportion to the time devoted to the business.
c. A salary allowance of $7,000 per month to Locke and the balance in accordance with their initial investment ratio.
d. A $7,000 per month salary allowance to Locke, 10% interest on their initial investments, and the balance equally.
The partners expect the business to generate income as follows: Year 1, $40,000 net loss; Year 2, $120,000 net income; and Year 3, $190,000 net income.

Required
Prepare four schedules with the following column headings:

Year	Calculations	Share to Bowtell	Share to Locke	Total

Complete a schedule for each of the four plans being considered by showing how the partnership net income or loss for each year would be allocated to the partners. Round your answers to the nearest whole dollar.

Ben Conway, Ida Chan, and Clair Seghal formed CCS Consulting by making capital contributions of $490,000, $560,000, and $350,000, respectively. They anticipate annual net income of $780,000 and are considering the following alternative plans of sharing net incomes and losses:
a. Equally;
b. In the ratio of their initial investments; or
c. Salary allowances of $190,000 to Conway, $92,000 to Chan, and $120,000 to Seghal and interest allowances of 12% on initial investments, with any remaining balance shared equally.

Required
1. Prepare a schedule with the following column headings:

Income/Loss Sharing Plan	Calculations	Share to Conway	Share to Chan	Share to Seghal

Use the schedule to show how a net income of $780,000 would be distributed under each of the alternative plans being considered.
2. Prepare a statement of partners' equity showing the allocation of income to the partners, assuming they agree to use alternative (c) and the net income actually earned for the year ended December 31, 2011, is $780,000. During the year, Conway, Chan, and Seghal withdraw $80,000, $60,000, and $40,000, respectively.
3. Prepare the December 31, 2011, journal entry to close Income Summary assuming they agree to use alternative (c) and the net income is $780,000. Also, close the withdrawals accounts.

Problem 14-3A
Partnership income allocation, statement of partners' equity, and closing entries
LO2, 3

Check figures:
1c. To Conway: $318,800;
    To Chan: $229,200;
    To Seghal: $232,000

Zeller, Acker, and Benton are partners with capital balances as follows: Zeller, $168,000; Acker, $138,000; and Benton, $294,000. The partners share incomes and losses in a 3:2:5 ratio. Dent is admitted to the partnership on May 1, 2011, with a 25% equity. Prepare General Journal entries to record the entry of Dent into the partnership under each of the following unrelated assumptions:
a. Dent invests $200,000.
b. Dent invests $145,000.
c. Dent invests $262,000.

Problem 14-4A
Admission of a partner
LO4

Check figures:
b. Dr Zeller, Capital $12,375
c. Cr Zeller, Capital $13,950

On June 1, 2011, Jill Bow and Aisha Amri formed a partnership, contributing $140,000 cash and $180,000 of equipment, respectively. Also, the partnership assumed responsibility for a $20,000 note payable associated with the equipment. The partners agreed to share profits as follows: Bow is to receive an annual salary allowance of $75,000, both are to receive an annual interest allowance of 8% of their original capital investments, and any remaining profit or loss is to be shared 40/60 (to Bow and Amri, respectively). On November 20, 2011, Amri withdrew cash of $50,000. At year-end, May 31, 2012, the Income Summary account had a credit balance of $190,000. On June 1, 2012, Peter Wilems invested $60,000 and was admitted to the partnership for a 20% interest in equity.

Required
Prepare journal entries for the following dates:
a. June 1, 2011
b. November 20, 2011
c. May 31, 2012
d. June 1, 2012

Problem 14-5A
Partnership entries, income allocation, admission of a partner
LO2, 3, 4

Check figures:
c. Cr Bow: $122,600
   Cr Amri: $67,400
d. Dr Amri: $16,800

Gale, McLean, and Lux are partners with capital balances as follows: Gale, $168,000; McLean, $138,000; and Lux, $294,000. The partners share incomes and losses in a 3:2:5 ratio. McLean decides to withdraw from the partnership. Prepare General Journal entries to record the May 1, 2011, withdrawal of McLean from the partnership under each of the following unrelated assumptions:
a. McLean sells his interest to Freedman for $336,000 after Gale and Lux approve the entry of Freedman as a partner (where McLean receives the cash personally from Freedman).
b. McLean gives his interest to a son-in-law, Park. Gale and Lux accept Park as a partner.
c. McLean is paid $138,000 in partnership cash for his equity.
d. McLean is paid $264,000 in partnership cash for his equity.
e. McLean is paid $54,500 in partnership cash plus computer equipment that is recorded on the partnership books at $230,000 less accumulated amortization of $166,000.

Problem 14-6A
Withdrawal of a partner
LO4

Check figures:
d. Dr Gale, Capital $47,250
e. Cr Gale, Capital $7,312.50

Problem 14-7A
Liquidation of a partnership
LO5

Vonne, Kent, and Johnson plan to liquidate their partnership. They have always shared losses and gains in a 1:4:5 ratio, and on the day of the liquidation their balance sheet appeared as follows:

VKJ Partnership
Balance Sheet
June 30, 2011

Assets			Liabilities		
Cash..		$ 55,000	Accounts payable		$104,300
Truck..	$471,000		**Partners' Equity**		
Less: Accumulated Amortization ...	110,000	361,000	Jim Vonne...	$ 61,000	
Total assets		$416,000	Milton Kent, capital.........................	160,700	
			Ty Johnson, capital...........................	90,000	
			Total partners' equity....................		311,700
			Total liabilities and partners' equity......		$416,000

Required

Part 1
Under the assumption that the truck is sold and the cash is distributed to the proper parties on June 30, 2011, complete the schedule provided below.

	Cash	Truck (net)	Accounts Payable	Jim Vonne, Capital	Milton Kent, Capital	Ty Johnson, Capital
Account balances June 30, 2011.....						

Check figures:
a. Cash to Vonne: $63,950
b. Cash to Vonne: $54,900
c. Cash to Vonne: $41,900
d. Cash to Vonne: $36,800

Show the sale, the gain or loss allocation, and the distribution of the cash in each of the following unrelated cases:
a. The truck is sold for $390,500.
b. The truck is sold for $300,000.
c. The truck is sold for $170,000, and any partners with resulting deficits can and do pay in the amount of their deficits.
d. The truck is sold for $150,000, and the partners have no assets other than those invested in the business.

Part 2
Prepare the entry to record the final distribution of cash assuming case (a) above.

Problem 14-8A
Liquidation of a partnership
LO5

Trish Craig and Ted Smith have a partnership and share income and losses in a 3:1 ratio. They decide to liquidate their partnership on December 31, 2011, when the balance sheet shows the following:

Craig and Smith Consulting
Balance Sheet
December 31, 2011

Assets			Liabilities		
Cash..		$ 76,000	Accounts payable..........................		$ 42,000
Property, plant, and equipment........	$428,000		**Partners' Equity**		
Less: Accumulated amortization....	166,000	262,000	Trish Craig, capital...........................	$204,000	
Total assets.......................................		$338,000	Ted Smith, capital............................	92,000	
			Total partners' equity....................		296,000
			Total liabilities and partners' equity...		$338,000

Required
Prepare the entries on December 31, 2011, to record the liquidation under each of the following independent assumptions:
a. Property, plant, and equipment are sold for $600,000.
b. Property, plant, and equipment are sold for $120,000.

Check figures:
Re: final distribution of cash
a. Dr Craig, Capital $457,500
b. Dr Craig, Capital $97,500

Alternate Problems

Paula Jones, Roy Rodgers, and Anne Jackson invested $92,400, $74,800, and $52,800, respectively, in a partnership. During its first year, the firm earned $135,000.

Required
Prepare entries to close the firm's Income Summary account as of December 31 and to allocate the net income to the partners under each of the following assumptions.
a. The partners did not specify any special method of sharing incomes.
b. The partners agreed to share net incomes and losses in the ratio of their beginning investments.
c. The partners agreed to share income by: providing annual salary allowances of $75,000 to Jones, $40,500 to Rodgers, and $45,500 to Jackson; allowing 10% interest on the partners' beginning investments; and sharing the remainder equally.

Problem 14-1B
Methods of allocating partnership income
LO3

Check figure:
c. Cr Roy Rodgers, Capital: $31,980

Harriet Monroe and Ozzie Young are in the process of forming a partnership to which Monroe will devote one-third time and Young will devote full time. They have discussed the following alternative plans for sharing net incomes and losses.
a. In the ratio of their initial investments, which they have agreed will be $49,800 for Monroe and $74,700 for Young.
b. In proportion to the time devoted to the business.
c. A salary allowance of $5,250 per month to Young and the balance in accordance with their initial investment ratio.
d. A $5,250 per month salary allowance to Young, 10% interest on their initial investments, and the balance equally.
The partners expect the business to generate income as follows: Year 1, $30,500 net income; Year 2, $82,500 net loss; and Year 3, $215,000 net income.

Problem 14-2B
Allocating partnership incomes and losses; sequential years
LO3

Required
Prepare four schedules with the following column headings:

Check figures:
d. Year 1: To Monroe: $(17,495);
    To Young: $47,995
d. Year 2: To Monroe: $(73,995);
    To Young: $(8,505)
d. Year 3: To Monroe: $74,755;
    To Young: $140,245

Year	Calculations	Share to Monroe	Share to Young	Total

Complete a schedule for each of the four plans being considered by showing how the partnership income or loss for each year would be allocated to the partners. Round your answers to the nearest whole dollar.

Problem 14-3B
Partnership income allocation, statement of partners' equity, and closing entries
LO2, 3

Check figures:
1c. To Vacon: $65,371;
    To Masters: $51,667;
    To Ramos: $77,962

Milton Vacon, Milford Masters, and Marita Ramos formed the VMR Partnership by making capital contributions of $116,640, $129,600, and $142,560, respectively on January 7, 2011. They anticipate annual net incomes of $195,000 and are considering the following alternative plans of sharing net incomes and losses:
a. Equally;
b. In the ratio of their initial investments (do not round the ratio calculations); or
c. Salary allowances of $35,000 to Vacon, $20,000 to Masters, and $45,000 to Ramos; interest allowances of 10% on initial investments, with any remaining balance shared equally.

Required
1. Prepare a schedule with the following column headings:

Income/Loss Sharing Plan	Calculations	Share to Vacon	Share to Masters	Share to Ramos	Total

Use the schedule to show how a net income of $195,000 would be distributed under each of the alternative plans being considered. Round your answers to the nearest whole dollar.
2. Prepare a statement of partners' equity showing the allocation of income to the partners, assuming they agree to use alternative (c) and the net income actually earned for the year ended December 31, 2011, is $195,000. During 2011, Vacon, Masters, and Ramos withdrew $15,000, $20,000, and $23,000, respectively.
3. Prepare the December 31, 2011, journal entry to close Income Summary, assuming they agree to use alternative (c) and the net income is $195,000. Also, close the withdrawals accounts.

Problem 14-4B
Admission of a Partner
LO4

Check figures:
b. Dr Burke, Capital $4,500.00
c. Cr Burke, Capital $9,300.00

Burke, Comeau, and LeJeune are partners with capital balances as follows: Burke, $153,000; Comeau, $51,000; and LeJeune, $102,000. The partners share incomes and losses in a 1:2:1 ratio. Sung is admitted to the partnership on November 30 with a 20% equity. Prepare General Journal entries to record the entry of Sung under each of the following unrelated assumptions:
a. Sung invests $76,500.
b. Sung invests $54,000.
c. Sung invests $123,000.

Problem 14-5B
Partnership entries, income allocation, admission of a partner
LO2, 3, 4

Check figures:
a. Cr Goth: $80,000
b. Cr To: $32,000
c. Cr Goth: $15,000

On November 1, 2011, James Goth, Hum To, and Gina Selcido formed a partnership by contributing $80,000 in cash, $130,000 of equipment, and a truck worth $60,000, respectively. The partners agreed to share profits and losses as follows: To and Selcido were to receive an annual salary allowance of $70,000 each and any remaining profit or loss was to be shared 5:2:3. On October 31, 2012, the partnership's first year-end, the Income Summary account had a debit balance of $50,000. On November 1, 2012, Goth withdrew from the partnership and received $10,000 from the partnership.

Required
Prepare journal entries for the following dates:
a. November 1, 2011
b. October 31, 2012
c. November 1, 2012

Problem 14-6B
Withdrawal of a partner
LO4

Check figures:
d. Dr Burke, Capital $9,000
e. Cr Burke, Capital $11,000

Burke, Comeau, and LeJeune are partners with capital balances as follows: Burke, $153,000; Comeau, $51,000; and LeJeune, $102,000. The partners share incomes and losses in a 1:2:1 ratio. LeJeune decides to withdraw from the partnership. Prepare General Journal entries to record the November 30 withdrawal of LeJeune from the partnership under each of the following unrelated assumptions:
a. LeJeune sells her interest to Devereau for $42,800 after Burke and Comeau approve the entry of Devereau as a partner.
b. LeJeune gives her interest to a daughter-in-law, Shulak. Burke and Comeau accept Shulak as a partner.
c. LeJeune is paid $102,000 in partnership cash for her equity.
d. LeJeune is paid $129,000 in partnership cash for her equity.
e. LeJeune is paid $36,000 in partnership cash plus manufacturing equipment recorded on the partnership books at $78,000 less accumulated amortization of $45,000.

Poppy, Sweetbean, and Olive, who have always shared incomes and losses in a 3:1:1 ratio, plan to liquidate their partnership. Just prior to the liquidation their balance sheet appeared as follows:

Problem 14-7B
Liquidation of a partnership
LO5

Poppy, Sweetbean, and Olive
Balance Sheet
October 15, 2011

Assets		Liabilities		
Cash	$ 13,500	Accounts payable		$ 56,700
Equipment (net)*	237,600	**Partners' Equity**		
Total assets	$251,100	Ernie Poppy, capital..........................	$91,200	
		Lynn Sweetbean, capital...................	60,000	
		Ned Olive, capital	43,200	
		Total partners' equity.....................		194,400
		Total liabilities and partners' equity		$251,100

*Accumulated amortization = $58,000

Required

Part 1

Under the assumption that the equipment is sold and the cash is distributed to the proper parties on October 15, 2011, complete the schedule provided below.

	Cash	Equipment (net)	Accounts Payable	Ernie Poppy, Capital	Lynn Sweetbean, Capital	Ned Olive, Capital
Account balances October 15, 2011						

Show the sale, the gain or loss allocation, and the distribution of the cash in each of the following unrelated cases:
a. The equipment is sold for $270,000.
b. The equipment is sold for $170,100.
c. The equipment is sold for $72,600, and any partners with resulting deficits can and do pay in the amount of their deficits.
d. The equipment is sold for $55,200, and the partners have no assets other than those invested in the business.

Check figures:
a. Cash to Olive $49,680
b. Cash to Olive $29,700
c. Cash to Olive $10,200
d. Cash to Olive $0

Part 2

Prepare the entry to record the final distribution of cash assuming case (a) above.

Leslie Bjorn, Jason Douglas, and Tom Pierce have a partnership and share income and losses in a 3:1:1 ratio. They decide to liquidate their partnership on March 31, 2011. The balance sheet appeared as follows on the date of liquidation:

Problem 14-8B
Liquidation of a partnership
LO5

BDP Architects
Balance Sheet
March 31, 2011

Assets			Liabilities		
Cash..		$ 79,000	Accounts payable..........................		$ 46,000
Property, plant, and equipment........	$389,000		**Partners' Equity**		
Less: Accumulated amortization....	214,000	175,000	Leslie Bjorn, capital..........................	$ 92,000	
Total assets......................................		$254,000	Jason Douglas, capital	106,000	
			Tom Pierce, capital	10,000	
			Total partners' equity...................		208,000
			Total liabilities and partners' equity...		$254,000

Check figures:
Re: final distribution of cash
a. Dr Bjorn, Capital 257,000
b. Dr Bjorn, Capital 53,000

Required
Prepare the entries on March 31, 2011, to record the liquidation under each of the following independent assumptions:
a. Property, plant, and equipment is sold for $450,000.
b. Property, plant, and equipment is sold for $110,000.
Assume that any deficiencies are paid by the partners.

Analytical and Review Problems

A & R Problem 14-1
Liquidation of a partnership

Prince, Count, and Earl are partners who share incomes and losses in a 1:3:4 ratio. After lengthy disagreements among the partners and several unprofitable periods, the partners decided to liquidate the partnership. Before the liquidation, the partnership balance sheet showed: total assets, $238,000; total liabilities, $200,000; Prince, Capital, $8,000; Count, Capital, $10,000; and Earl, Capital, $20,000. The cash proceeds from selling the assets were sufficient to repay all but $45,000 to the creditors. Calculate the loss from selling the assets, allocate the loss to the partners, and determine how much of the remaining liability should be paid by each partner.

A & R Problem 14-2
Liquidation of a limited partnership

Assume that the Prince, Count, and Earl partnership of A & R Problem 14-1 is a limited partnership. Prince and Count are general partners and Earl is a limited partner. How much of the remaining $45,000 liability should be paid by each partner?

A & R Problem 14-3
Income allocation

Keith Scott and David McPeek agreed to share the annual net incomes or losses of their partnership as follows: If the partnership earned a net income, the first $60,000 would be allocated 40% to Scott and 60% to McPeek to reflect the time devoted to the business by each partner. Income in excess of $60,000 would be shared equally. Also, the partners have agreed to share any losses equally.

Required
1. Prepare a schedule showing how net income of $72,000 for 2011 should be allocated to the partners.
2. Sometime later in 2012, the partners discovered that $80,000 of accounts payable had existed on December 31, 2011, but had not been recorded. These accounts payable relate to expenses incurred by the business. They are now trying to determine the best way to correct their accounting records, particularly their capital accounts. McPeek suggested that they make a special entry crediting $80,000 to the liability account, and debiting their capital accounts for $40,000 each. Scott, on the other hand, suggested that an entry should be made to record the accounts payable and retroactively correct the capital accounts to reflect the balance that they would have had if the expenses had been recognized in 2011. If they had been recognized, the partnership would have reported a loss of $8,000 instead of the $72,000 net income.
   a. Present the journal entry suggested by McPeek for recording the accounts payable and allocating the loss to the partners.
   b. Give the journal entry to record the accounts payable and correct the capital accounts according to Scott's suggestion. Show how you calculated the amounts presented in the entry.
3. Which suggestion do you think complies with their partnership agreement? Why?

Ethics Challenge

EC 14-1

Paul, Frank, and Basil formed a partnership 10 years ago and Paul is about to retire. Paul is not financially minded but he knows that he is entitled to one-third of partnership assets upon his retirement. Total assets have a book value of $900,000 and Paul feels that he is entitled to his share. Frank and Basil are aware that the market value of the firm's net assets approximates $1,500,000. Frank and Basil plan to form a new partnership.

Required
What are the financial and ethical implications of distributing $300,000 to Paul upon his retirement?

Focus on Financial Statements

Les Waruck, Kim Chau, and Leena Manta formed a partnership, WCL Sales, on January 11, 2011, by investing $68,250, $109,200, and $95,550 respectively. The partnership agreement states that incomes and losses are to be shared on the basis of a salary allowance of $40,000 for Waruck, $80,000 for Chau, and $40,000 for Manta, with any remainder shared on the ratio of beginning-of-period capital balance. Following is the December 31, 2011, adjusted trial balance, in alphabetical order:

FFS 14-1

Account	Balance*	Account	Balance*
Accounts payable	14,000	Leena Manta, capital	95,550
Accounts receivable	46,000	Leena Manta, withdrawals	10,000
Accumulated amortization, fixtures	3,000	Les Waruck, capital	68,250
Accumulated amortization, furniture	6,000	Les Waruck, withdrawals	30,000
Accumulated amortization, patent	6,000	Merchandise inventory	22,000
Allowance for doubtful accounts	1,200	Notes payable, due 2014**	34,000
Amortization expense, fixtures	3,000	Patent	20,000
Amortization expense, furniture	6,000	Prepaid rent	36,000
Amortization expense, patent	2,000	Rent expense	84,000
Bad debt expense	2,800	Sales	102,000
Cash	14,000	Sales discounts	3,400
Fixtures	31,000	Unearned sales	3,000
Furniture	69,000	Wages expense	49,000
Kim Chau, capital	109,200		
Kim Chau, withdrawals	14,000		

*Assume all accounts have a normal balance.
**$7,000 is due during 2012.

Required
Prepare the December 31, 2011, classified balance sheet, showing all appropriate supporting calculations.

Analysis component
Assuming that the assets of businesses similar to WCL Sales are financed 60% by debt and 40% by equity, does WCL Sales compare favourably or unfavourably to the industry average? What is the relationship between type of financing and risk?

Refer to the financial statements for Danier Leather and WestJet in Appendix I at the end of the textbook.

FFS 14-2

Required
Answer the following questions.
1. Is Danier Leather a partnership? Explain why or why not.
2. Is WestJet a sole proprietorship, partnership, or corporation? Explain.

Critical Thinking Mini Case

Josh and Ben Mooth are brothers. They each have $75,000 to invest in a business together: Northern Canadian Extreme Adventures. They estimate that an additional $200,000 is required to get the business operating but have yet to determine how to get this additional financing.

Required
Using the elements of critical thinking described on the inside front cover, comment.

CHAPTER 15

Organization and Operation of Corporations

Staying Private

The word *corporation* conjures up images of Canadian giants like the Toronto-Dominion Bank, Alcan Inc., Bombardier Inc., or Air Canada. These are examples of *public* corporations, which means ownership is achieved through the purchase of *publicly traded* shares (shares that are bought and sold on a stock exchange). The shareholders, or owners, can be from anywhere across Canada or around the globe. There are, however, corporations that do not trade their shares publicly, like McCain Foods Limited and Birks . . . these are *private* corporations. Friesens, specializing in book manufacturing and retailing, is also a private corporation. It is located in Altona, Manitoba. Some of the books it prints include the *Company's Coming* cookbook series and, with over 20 million copies printed to date, the incredibly successful book *Love You Forever* from Canadian children's author Robert Munsch.

Friesens' 15 million shares are available only to its 500 employees. David Friesen, the CEO, believes that it is people who make the company a success and with sales approaching $100 million annually, it's tough to argue against that philosophy. Through the hard work and dedication of the employees (alias owners, alias shareholders!), Friesens' share values have increased an average of 10% per year over the past decade. And that's good news for the shareholders (the employees!), who receive total annual dividends equal to 8% of the share value.

www.friesens.com

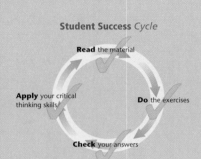

Student Success *Cycle*

Read the material

Apply your critical thinking skills

Do the exercises

Check your answers

CRITICAL THINKING CHALLENGE

What would cause Friesens' share values to increase an average of 10% per year over the past decade? What are dividends and why do shareholders receive them?

---

learning objectives

LO¹ Identify characteristics of corporations and their organization.

LO² Describe and contrast the specialized components of corporate financial statements.

LO³ Record the issuance of common and preferred shares and describe their presentation in shareholders' equity on the balance sheet.

LO⁴ Describe and account for cash dividends.

LO⁵ Distribute dividends between common and preferred shares.

LO⁶ Record closing entries for a corporation.

*APPENDIX 15A

*LO⁷ Calculate book value and explain its use in analysis.

chapter preview

There are three common types of business organizations: corporations, partnerships, and proprietorships. This chapter explains corporations. Corporations are fewest in number but, with dollar sales at least 10 times the combined sales of unincorporated companies, they are very important players in our global economy. Understanding the advantages and disadvantages of the forms of business organization was important for D.W. Friesen, the founder of Friesens described in the opening article. This chapter begins by providing general information to help us make the decision as to which form of organization best satisfies our needs. We then analyze financial statements for corporations in contrast to those for the unincorporated form of organization. The basic journal entries specific to corporations are illustrated, including those related to issuing shares, dividends, and closing the accounts.

Corporate Form of Organization

A corporation is an entity that is created by law and is separate from its owners. It has most of the rights and privileges granted to individuals. Owners of corporations are called **shareholders**. Each unit of ownership in a corporation is called a **share**. **Share capital**, also referred to as **capital stock**, is a general term referring to all types (or classes) of a corporation's shares. *Common shares* and *preferred shares*, explained in a later section, are names given to two classes of shares issued (sold) by corporations to shareholders. Corporations can be separated into *privately held* and *publicly held* corporations. A **privately held** corporation, also called **closely held**, does not offer its shares for public sale and usually has few shareholders. A **publicly held** corporation offers its shares for *public sale* and can have thousands of shareholders. **Public sale** refers to trading in an organized stock market such as the Montreal or Toronto stock exchanges.

LO¹ Identify characteristics of corporations and their organization.

Characteristics of Corporations

Corporations are important because of advantages created by the unique characteristics of the corporate structure of ownership. We describe these characteristics in this section.

Separate Legal Entity

A corporation is a separate legal entity that conducts its affairs with the same rights, duties, and responsibilities as a person. A corporation takes actions through its agents, who are its officers and managers.

Limited Liability of Shareholders

Because a corporation is a separate legal entity, it is responsible for its own acts and its own debt. Because shareholders are not liable for either, the corporate form of organization is also known as a *limited company*. Shareholders invest in the business by contributing cash or other assets in return for ownership rights in the corporation. If the business fails, the amount contributed by shareholders is the maximum loss to the shareholders. If there are insufficient assets to pay business creditor claims, creditors have no claim on the shareholders' personal assets, an important advantage of the corporate form.

www.td.com

Ownership Rights Are Transferable

Ownership of a corporation is evidenced by shares that are usually easily bought or sold. The transfer of shares from one shareholder to another usually has no effect on the corporation or its operations.[1] Many corporations have thousands or even millions of their shares bought and sold daily in major stock exchanges throughout the world. For example, it is not uncommon for over 2,000,000 Toronto-Dominion Bank shares to trade in one day.

Continuous Life

A corporation's life can continue indefinitely because it is not tied to the physical lives of its owners. This means a corporation can exist as long as it continues to be successful.

Shareholders Are Not Corporate Agents

A corporation acts through its agents, who are the officers or managers of the corporation. Shareholders who are not officers or managers of the corporation do not have the power to bind the corporation to contracts. This is also referred to as *lack of mutual agency* P. 696.

Ease of Capital Accumulation

www.alcan.com

Buying shares in a corporation often is attractive to investors because of the advantages of the corporate form of organization, as summarized in Exhibit 15.1. These advantages make it possible for some corporations to accumulate large amounts of capital from the total investments of many shareholders. Alcan Inc. for example, a Canadian company involved in ventures such as bauxite mining, alumina refining, and power generation, had by 2005 accumulated about $6,181 million from common shareholders who own 371,921,000 shares.[2]

Exhibit 15.1

Summary of Advantages and Disadvantages of the Corporate Form of Organization

Advantages	Disadvantages
Limited liability of shareholders	Government regulation
Ownership rights are easily transferable	Corporate taxation
Continuous life	Separation of management and ownership
Lack of mutual agency	
Ease of capital accumulation	

Governmental Regulation

Corporations must meet requirements of provincial or federal incorporation laws. Single proprietorships P. 4 and partnerships P. 5 escape some of these regulations. Private corporations, however, are exempt from most of the security and corporate legislation reporting requirements. According to the *Canada Business Corporations Act* (CBCA), any publicly traded company with gross revenues of $10 million or assets exceeding $5 million must make public its financial statements, which have been prepared according to Canadian Generally Accepted Accounting Principles P. 31. All public corporations that are registered with one of the provincial securities bodies, depending on which province, must file annual audited financial statements within 140–170 days of their fiscal year-end P. 27.

Many Canadian companies are listed on U.S. stock exchanges as well and are also required to file their annual reports with U.S. regulators. Some of these companies—such as Nortel, Corel, and Alcan—actually issue their annual reports in U.S. dollars.

---

[1] A transfer of ownership can create significant effects if it brings about a change in who controls the company's activities.

[2] *Annual Report*, Alcan Inc., 2005.

Corporate Taxation

Corporations are subject to the same property, payroll, and consumption taxes (PST P. 658 and GST P. 659) as proprietorships and partnerships. Corporations are subject to an *additional* tax not levied on either of these two forms, however, that is, income tax expense (normally referred to as just *tax expense*).

The tax situation of a corporation is *usually* a disadvantage. But in some cases it can be an advantage to shareholders because corporate and individual tax rates are *progressive*. A **progressive tax** means higher levels of income are taxed at higher rates and lower levels of income are taxed at lower rates. This suggests that taxes can be saved or at least delayed if a large amount of income is divided among two or more tax-paying entities. A person who has a large personal income and pays a high rate of tax can benefit if some of the income is earned by a corporation the person owns, so long as the corporation avoids paying dividends[3] or pays tax at a lower rate than the individual's rate.

Corporate income tax is an expense that appears on the income statement. However, income tax expense is *not* an operating expense because income tax expense is determined by government rather than by how the business operates. It is therefore reported as a separate expense as shown in the excerpt below taken from the income statement of a key Canadian retailer for its year ended January 31, 2006.

(thousands of dollars)	
Earnings (loss) before income taxes	$(202,057)
Income taxes	27,189
Net earnings	$(174,868)

Choosing the proper form of entity for a business is crucial. Many factors should be considered including taxes, liability, tax and fiscal year-end, ownership structure, estate planning, business risks, and earnings and property distributions. The chart below gives a summary of several important characteristics of business organizations:

	Proprietorship	**Partnership**	**Corporation**
Business entity	yes	yes	yes
Legal entity	no	no	yes
Limited liability	no	no	yes
Business taxed	no	no	yes
One owner allowed	yes	no	yes

Organizing a Corporation

This section describes incorporation and treatment of organization costs.

Incorporation

A corporation may be created under either provincial law or federal laws. Those incorporated federally must comply with the *Canada Business Corporations Act* (CBCA). Most of the provincial laws are modelled after the federal statute. Requirements vary across provinces and from the CBCA, but essentially a legal document known as a charter, articles of incorporation, letters patent, or memorandum of association is completed and signed by the prospective shareholders. A

---

[3] If a shareholder receives dividends, the shareholder must include the dividend amount as income and pay income tax, except in certain situations that are better discussed in a tax course.

corporation's charter *authorizes* the number and types (or classes[4]) of shares to be issued. **Authorized shares** are the total number of shares that a corporation is permitted to sell. When all of the legal requirements are satisfied, investors purchase the corporation's shares, meet as shareholders, and elect a board of directors. Directors are responsible for guiding a corporation's affairs.

Organization Costs

The costs of organizing a corporation are **organization costs**. They include legal fees, promoters' fees, and amounts paid to obtain a charter. Assuming a corporation paid $15,000 in organization costs on April 15, 2011, the entry would be:

2011			
April 15	Organization Costs...	15,000	
	Cash		15,000
	To record payment of costs regarding the		
	organization of the corporation.		

www.rentcash.ca

For example, Rentcash Inc., a provider of short-term cash advances to consumers, reported organization costs of $114,963 as an intangible asset at June 30, 2005.

Collectively, organization costs are an intangible asset that benefits the corporation, and the costs are amortized over their estimated useful life. Because organization costs usually are small in amount, the materiality principle P. 337 supports an arbitrary short amortization period P. 136.[5] Sometimes a corporation gives shares to promoters in exchange for their services in selling shares of the corporation. The entry to record this transaction would credit the appropriate share capital account instead of the Cash account.

Management of a Corporation

Ultimate control of a corporation rests with its shareholders through election of the *board of directors*. Individual shareholders' rights to affect management are limited to a vote in shareholders' meetings, where each shareholder has one vote for each common share owned. This relation is shown in Exhibit 15.2.

Exhibit 15.2

Corporation Authority Structure

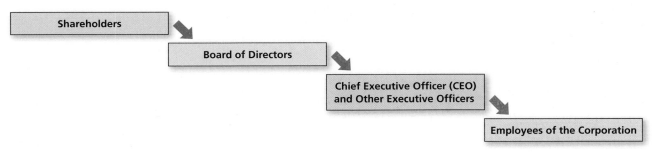

A corporation's board of directors is responsible for and has final authority for managing the corporation's activities but usually limits its actions to establishing broad policy and hiring the external auditors and corporate executive officers. It can act only as a collective body and an individual director has no power to transact corporate business.

---

[4] There is no limit on the number of classes of shares that can be set out in the articles of incorporation. Shares may be alphabetized by class such as *Class A* and *Class B* or may be assigned names such as *common shares* and *preferred shares*. ClubLink, for instance, is authorized to issue an unlimited number of each of preferred and common shares. Bombardier reported in its January 31, 2003, annual report that it is authorized to issue 12 million each of Series 2 and Series 3 preferred shares, 9.4 million Series 4 preferred shares, and 1,792 million each of Class A and Class B common shares.

[5] Organization costs can be expensed if they are very small in amount relative to other assets on the balance sheet. This treatment would be in accordance with the materiality principle.

A group of shareholders owning or controlling votes of more than 50% of a corporation's shares can elect the board and control the corporation. However, in many corporations few shareholders actually get involved in the voting process, which means a much smaller percentage is often able to dominate the election of board members. Shareholders may delegate their voting rights to an agent by signing a document called a **proxy**.

Rights of Shareholders

According to the *Canada Business Corporations Act*, shareholders have three basic rights: the right to vote, the right to receive dividends that have been declared, and the right to receive property of the corporation after its closure. When there is more than one class of shares, each of these three basic rights is assigned to at least one class but not necessarily to all. When a corporation has only one class of shares, those shares are identified as **common shares**. Shareholders are also entitled to receive timely reports on the corporation's financial position and results of operations. These reports take the form of financial statements and are the topic of the next section.

> **1.** Since organization costs are an intangible asset, what method of amortization should be used?
>
> **Do: QS 15-1, QS 15-2**

CHECKPOINT   Read · Apply · Do · Check

Corporate Financial Statements

The financial statements for the corporate form of organization are similar to those of unincorporated businesses. The differences all relate to *who owns* each form of business organization. We focus on these differences by comparing the assumed statements for ABC Corporation to those of a single proprietorship, Dell's Servicing.

LO² | Describe and contrast the specialized components of corporate financial statements.

Income Statement

The income statements in Exhibit 15.3 are identical except for income tax expense. Corporations are required by law to pay tax because they are a separate legal entity. Application of corporate tax rules can be complex. Therefore, to show how tax

Exhibit 15.3

Comparison of Income Statements

ABC Corporation Income Statement For Year Ended December 31, 2011		
Revenues		$116
Operating expenses..................................		40
Income from operations		$ 76
Other revenues and expenses:[6]		
Gain on sale of capital assets	$ 7	
Interest revenue	3	
Loss on sale of capital assets	(12)	
Interest expense	(14)	(16)
Income before tax		$ 60
Income tax expense....................................		12
Net income		$ 48

Dell's Servicing Income Statement For Year Ended December 31, 2011		
Revenues..		$116
Operating expenses		40
Income from operations...........................		$ 76
Other revenues and expenses:[6]		
Gain on sale of capital assets..........................	$ 7	
Interest revenue..	3	
Loss on sale of capital assets	(12)	
Interest expense	(14)	(16)
Net income...		$ 60

The income statements are identical except for the $12 of income tax expense.

[6] Some companies will divide this section on their income statement between *Other Revenues and Gains* and *Other Expenses and Losses*. The *CICA Handbook* permits flexibility in this regard.

expense appears on the income statement for a corporation, we have simplified the calculation and assumed a 20% flat tax rate. The 20% tax rate is applied to *income before tax* (20% × $60 = $12). The resulting tax expense of $12 is subtracted from *income before tax* to arrive at *net income*. Therefore, the term *net income* for a corporation means income after tax. Because the single proprietorship and partnership forms of business organization are not taxed (the owners are taxed), the net income for these two business organizations excludes income tax expense.

Statement of Retained Earnings

A single proprietorship prepares a Statement of Owner's Equity P. 29 to show how equity changed during the accounting period. The equity of the owners, regardless of the form of business organization, changes because of:

- net incomes or losses,
- distributions of income (known as withdrawals for a single proprietorship), and
- owner investments.

A single proprietorship includes all three of these activities in one account, the owner's capital account.

The equity of a corporation also changes because of net incomes or losses, distributions of income (called *dividends*), and owner investments. However, net incomes or losses and dividends are recorded in the *Retained Earnings* account while shareholder (or owner) investments are recorded in a share capital account, either common shares or preferred shares. **Retained Earnings** represents the income to date that has been kept (retained) by the corporation for the purpose of reinvestment. The **Statement of Retained Earnings** shows how retained earnings have changed during an accounting period as shown in Exhibit 15.4.

Exhibit 15.4

Comparison of Statement of Retained Earnings and Statement of Owner's Equity

ABC Corporation Statement of Retained Earnings For Year Ended December 31, 2011	
Retained earnings, January 1	$-0-
Add: Net income	48
Total...	$48
Less: Dividends	40
Retained earnings, December 31	$ 8

Dell's Servicing Statement of Owner's Equity For Year Ended December 31, 2011		
Ivor Dell, capital, January 1		$ -0-
Add: Owner investment	$500	
Net income...	60	
Total		$560
Less: Withdrawals		40
Ivor Dell, capital, December 31		$520

> Notice that both statements include net income (losses) and distributions of income (called *dividends* for a corporation and *withdrawals* for a single proprietorship). Owner investments are included as part of Ivor Dell, Capital, for the single proprietorship but, for the corporation, investments by shareholders are *not* part of Retained Earnings.

Balance Sheet

The balance sheets for the corporation and the single proprietorship are identical except for the equity section. The equity section for the single proprietorship is called *owner's equity* because the equity belongs to the owner. The equity section is called **Shareholders' Equity** for a corporation because the equity belongs to a group of owners known as shareholders. Assume the owner of the single proprietorship invested $500 into the business. This $500 investment is included as part of Ivor Dell, Capital, as shown in Exhibit 15.4. The shareholders of ABC Corporation also invested $500. Their investment is recorded in a share capital account, which is shown on the balance sheet as part of Shareholders' Equity in Exhibit 15.5.

Exhibit 15.5

Comparison of Balance Sheets

ABC Corporation Balance Sheet December 31, 2011		
Assets		
Cash..		$148
Other assets		600
Total assets		$748
Liabilities................................		$240
Shareholders' Equity		
Share capital	$500	
Retained earnings.....................	8	
Total shareholders' equity		508
Total liabilities and shareholders' equity		$748

Dell's Servicing Balance Sheet December 31, 2011	
Assets	
Cash	$160
Other assets	600
Total assets...............................	$760
Liabilities	$240
Owner's Equity	
Ivor Dell, Capital......................	520
Total liabilities and owner's equity	$760

> Shareholders' Equity and Owner's Equity include the same transactions in total: net incomes (losses), distributions of income, and owner investments.

In summary, the transactions that affect shareholders' equity for the corporate form of organization are the same as for an unincorporated business. The difference is into which accounts the transactions are recorded. A corporation records net incomes (losses) and dividends in Retained Earnings and shareholder investments are recorded in a share capital account. How we record shareholder investments is the topic of the next section. Dividends are discussed later in the chapter.

CHECKPOINT

2. Refer to Exhibit 15.5. Explain why there is a difference of $12 between *Total liabilities and shareholders' equity* on the corporate balance sheet and *Total liabilities and owner's equity* on the single proprietorship balance sheet.

3. Explain the difference between the income statement for a corporation and that for an unincorporated business.

4. How is the Statement of Retained Earnings similar to the Statement of Owner's Equity?

5. Explain the differences between Shareholders' Equity and Owner's Equity on the balance sheets for a corporation and a single proprietorship.

Do: QS 15-3, QS 15-4, QS 15-5, QS 15-6, QS 15-7

Issuing Shares

When investors buy a corporation's shares, they sometimes receive a *share certificate* as proof they purchased shares. Issuance of certificates is becoming less common. Instead, most shareholders maintain accounts with the corporation or their stockbrokers and never receive certificates. If a corporation's shares are traded on a major stock exchange, the corporation must have a *registrar* who keeps shareholder records and prepares official lists of shareholders for shareholders' meetings and dividend payments.

The selling or issuing of shares by a corporation is referred to as **equity financing** because assets are increased (financed) through shareholder (equity) investment. For instance, assume ABC Corporation issued shares to shareholders in exchange for $100,000 cash. The balance sheet prepared for ABC Corporation immediately after this transaction shows the $100,000 cash having been provided through shareholders' equity.

ABC Corporation Balance Sheet December 31, 2011	
Assets	
Cash..	$100,000
Total assets...	$100,000
Liabilities...	$ -0-
Shareholders' Equity	
Share capital..	100,000
Total liabilities and shareholders' equity	$100,000

The next section introduces us to the terminology and basic accounting for the issuance of common and preferred shares.

Accounting for Shares

LO3 | Record the issuance of common and preferred shares and describe their presentation in shareholders' equity on the balance sheet.

Corporations can sell shares either *directly* or *indirectly* to shareholders at the *market value per share*. To **sell shares directly**, a corporation advertises its share issuance directly to potential buyers, which is most common with privately held corporations. To **sell shares indirectly**, a corporation pays a brokerage house (investment banker) to issue its shares. Some brokerage houses **underwrite** an indirect issuance of shares, meaning they buy the shares from the corporation and take all gains or losses from the shares' resale to shareholders.

Market value per share is the price at which a share is bought or sold. Market value is influenced by a variety of factors, including expected future earnings, dividends, growth, and other company and economic events. Market values of frequently traded shares are reported online and in daily newspapers such as *The Globe & Mail*. For example, WestJet Airlines' trading history over a three-year period ending March 2006 is illustrated in a chart format below. The first chart shows the changes in share price over three years. During that time, the market price per share has fluctuated between a low of $10.80 per share to about $21.00 per share. The second chart shows how many shares were trading (called volume) over that same time period.

Source: www.tsx.com, March 2006.

Market values of shares not actively traded are more difficult to determine. Several techniques are used to estimate the value of these and other shares but most use accounting information as an important input. *We must remember that the buying and selling of shares **between** investors does not impact that corporation's shareholders' equity accounts.*

Common Shares

Recall that if a corporation has only one class of shares, they are known as common shares. Common shares represent *residual equity*, or what is left over after creditors and other shareholders (if any) are paid when a corporation is liquidated (or closed). Common shares have certain rights, which are summarized in Exhibit 15.10 on page 746.

Issuing Common Shares for Cash

The *Canada Business Corporations Act* (CBCA) requires that all shares be of **no par value** or nominal value. **Par value** is an arbitrary value a corporation places on each share of its share capital. Par value shares are rare in Canada and will be addressed in an online Student Success Centre supplement.

Shares are most commonly issued in exchange for cash. For example, assume that on June 4, 2011, Dillon Snowboards Ltd. was granted a charter to issue an unlimited number of both common and preferred shares. The entry to record Dillon Snowboards' immediate issuance of 30,000 common shares for $300,000 on June 5, 2011, is:

Extend Your Knowledge

15-1

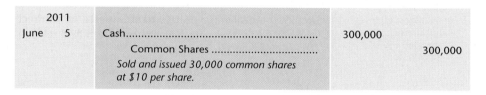

2011			
June 5	Cash..	300,000	
	Common Shares		300,000
	Sold and issued 30,000 common shares at $10 per share.		

Many important terms and phrases are used in the shareholders' equity section of a balance sheet. Exhibit 15.6 details each of these using the shareholders' equity section of Dillon Snowboards Ltd. at June 30, 2011, assuming net income for June of $65,000 and no dividend payments.

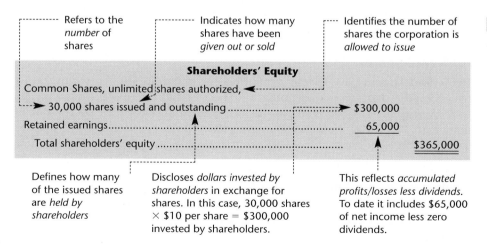

Exhibit 15.6

Shareholders' Equity of Dillon Snowboards Ltd. at June 30, 2011

Shares outstanding are explained in detail in Appendix 15A. For simplicity, we will assume that **outstanding shares** (or shares held by shareholders) will be equal to the shares issued (or sold) unless otherwise noted.

Issuing Common Shares for Non-Cash Assets

A corporation can receive assets other than cash in exchange for its shares.[7] The corporation records the assets acquired at the assets' fair market values as of the date of the transaction.[8]

To illustrate, here is the entry to record Dillon Snowboards' receipt of land on July 2, 2011, valued at $105,000 in return for immediate issuance of 4,000 common shares:

2011				
July	2	Land...	105,000	
		Common Shares		105,000
		Exchanged 4,000 common shares for land.		

Exhibit 15.7 shows the shareholders' equity of Dillon Snowboards at July 31, 2011, assuming net income earned during July of $82,000.

Exhibit 15.7

Shareholders' Equity of Dillon Snowboards Ltd. at July 31, 2011

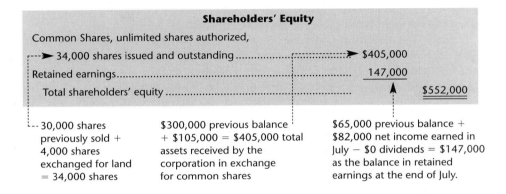

Shareholders' Equity
Common Shares, unlimited shares authorized,
34,000 shares issued and outstanding.................................. $405,000
Retained earnings.. 147,000
Total shareholders' equity $552,000

30,000 shares previously sold + 4,000 shares exchanged for land = 34,000 shares

$300,000 previous balance + $105,000 = $405,000 total assets received by the corporation in exchange for common shares

$65,000 previous balance + $82,000 net income earned in July − $0 dividends = $147,000 as the balance in retained earnings at the end of July.

CHECKPOINT Read · Apply · Do · Check

6. Refer to Exhibit 15.7. What was the average issue price per common share at July 31, 2011?

7. A company issues 7,000 common shares and a $40,000 note payable in exchange for equipment valued at $105,000. The entry to record this transaction includes a credit to: (a) Retained Earnings for $65,000; (b) Common Shares for $65,000; or (c) Common Shares for $105,000.

Do: QS 15-8, QS 15-9

Preferred Shares

Preferred shares have special rights that give them priority (or senior status) over common shares in one or more areas. Special rights typically include a preference for receiving dividends and for the distribution of assets if the corporation is liquidated. Because of these special rights, preferred shares are always listed before common shares in the shareholders' equity section. Most preferred shares do not have the right to vote.

Issuing Preferred Shares for Cash

A separate account is used to record preferred shares. To illustrate, if on August 3, 2011, Dillon Snowboards issued 5,000 preferred shares with a dividend preference of $3 per share for a total of $125,000 cash, the entry is:

---

[7] It can also assume liabilities on assets received such as a mortgage on property.

[8] Fair market value is determined by the current value of the item given up. If the current value for the item being given up cannot be determined, then the fair value of the item received is used. In the example above, the fair market value of the shares being given up cannot be determined so the $105,000 value of the land is used.

2011			
Aug.	3	Cash..	125,000	
		Preferred Shares		125,000
		Issued 5,000 preferred shares for total		
		cash of $125,000.		

Issuing preferred shares for non-cash assets is treated like similar entries for common shares.

The preferred shares account is included as part of contributed capital. The equity section of the balance sheet at August 31, 2011, for Dillon Snowboards—assuming net income earned during August of $156,000—would appear as shown in Exhibit 15.8.

When more than one class of shares has been issued, the shareholders' equity section is classified by grouping the share capital accounts under the heading *contributed capital*. **Contributed capital** is the total amount of cash and other assets received by the corporation from its shareholders in exchange for common and/or preferred shares.

The notation "$3" is the dividend preference, which means preferred shareholders are entitled to dividends at the rate of $3 per year per preferred share when declared.

Exhibit 15.8

Shareholders' Equity with Common and Preferred Shares

Shareholders' Equity

Contributed capital:		
Preferred shares, $3, unlimited shares authorized,		
5,000 shares issued and outstanding...	$125,000	
Common shares, unlimited shares authorized,		
34,000 shares issued and outstanding.....................................	405,000	
Total contributed capital..		$530,000
Retained earnings..		303,000
Total shareholders' equity...		$833,000

Net income of $65,000 for June + $82,000 net income for July + $156,000 net income for August − $0 dividends = $303,000 as the balance in retained earnings at August 31, 2011.

Exhibit 15.9

Shareholders' Equity on August 31, 2011, Balance Sheet

Dillon Snowboards Ltd.
Balance Sheet
August 31, 2011

Assets

Current assets:		
Cash		
Total current assets		
Capital assets:		
Land		
Total capital assets		
Total assets	$	
Liabilities		
Current liabilities:		
Accounts payable............................		
Total current liabilities.....................		
Long-term liabilities:		
Total liabilities		
Shareholders' Equity		
Contributed capital:		
Preferred shares	$125,000	
Common shares	405,000	
Total contributed capital..................		$530,000
Retained earnings..............................		303,000
Total shareholders' equity....................		$833,000
Total liabilities and shareholders' equity		$

An *abbreviated* example of how Dillon Snowboards' shareholders' equity might appear within the balance sheet at August 31, 2011, is illustrated here in Exhibit 15.9.

On December 1, Z-Tech's date of payment, the following entry is recorded:

Dec. 1	Common Dividends Payable........	5,000		or	Dec. 1	Common Dividends Payable........	5,000	
	Cash......................................		5,000			Cash......................................		5,000
	Paid cash dividend to common shareholders.					*Paid cash dividend to common shareholders.*		

At the end of the reporting period, the balance of Z-Tech's Cash Dividends account is closed to Retained Earnings as follows:

Dec. 31	Retained Earnings	5,000		or	Dec. 31	No entry	
	Cash Dividends......................		5,000			*Because Retained Earnings was debited directly on the date of declaration, no closing entry is required when using this alternative approach.*	
	To close Cash Dividends account.						

CANADIAN
WESTERN
BANK

www.cwbankgroup.com

Because dividends cause retained earnings to decrease, they are subtracted on the statement of retained earnings as shown previously for ABC Corporation in Exhibit 15.4. For example, Canadian Western Bank's retained earnings were decreased by $11,573,000 for the year ended October 31, 2005, because of a cash dividend declared and paid to common shareholders.

The entries regarding cash dividends on preferred shares would be recorded in the same way as shown for common shares.

Deficits and Cash Dividends

A corporation with a debit (abnormal) balance in Retained Earnings is said to have a **deficit**. A deficit arises when a company has cumulative losses greater than total profits earned in prior years. A deficit is deducted on a corporation's balance sheet as shown in Exhibit 15.12.

Exhibit 15.12

Rent-A-Wreck Capital Inc.
—Deficit Illustrated

www.rentawreck.ca

Rent-A-Wreck Capital Inc. **Shareholders' Equity** **September 30, 2005**	
Share capital..	$ 702,173
Deficit..	(831,566)

A corporation with a deficit is not allowed to pay a cash dividend to its shareholders in most jurisdictions. This legal restriction is designed to protect creditors of the corporation by preventing distribution of assets to shareholders at a time when the company is in financial difficulty.

Special Features of Preferred Shares

Preferred shares can have a number of special features such as being cumulative or non-cumulative, participating, callable, and convertible. These characteristics are unique to preferred shares and are discussed in this section.

Dividend Preference

In exchange for voting rights, preferred shares usually carry a **dividend preference**, which means a dividend cannot be paid to common shareholders unless preferred shareholders are paid first. The dividend preference is usually expressed as a dollar amount per share as illustrated in Exhibit 15.13.

Stake Technology Ltd.
Shareholders' Equity
April 30, 2011

Contributed capital:		
Preferred shares, $2.20, 25,000 shares authorized;		
7,000 shares issued and outstanding	$ 84,000	
Common shares, unlimited shares authorized;		
80,000 shares issued and outstanding	760,000	
Total contributed capital..		$844,000
Retained earnings..		49,000
Total shareholders' equity..		$893,000

Exhibit 15.13

Presentation of Dividend Preference

The preferred shareholders are entitled to receive $2.20 per share annually when dividends are declared.

A preference for dividends does not guarantee dividends. If the directors do not declare a dividend, neither the preferred nor the common shareholders receive one. However, if dividends are not declared on preferred shares, the undeclared dividends from prior periods plus current dividends may be paid if the preferred shares have a *cumulative* feature. The features known as cumulative and non-cumulative dividends are the topic of the next section.

Cumulative or Non-Cumulative Dividend

Many preferred shares carry a *cumulative* dividend right. **Cumulative preferred shares** have a right to be paid both current and all prior periods' undeclared dividends before any dividend is paid to common shareholders. When preferred shares are cumulative and the directors either do not declare a dividend to preferred shareholders or declare a dividend that does not satisfy the cumulative dividend, then the unpaid dividend amount is called a **dividend in arrears**. Accumulation of dividends in arrears on cumulative preferred shares does not guarantee they will be paid. Some preferred shares are *non-cumulative*. **Non-cumulative preferred shares** have no right to prior periods' unpaid dividends if they were not declared.

LO5 Distribute dividends between common and preferred shares.

To illustrate and show the difference between cumulative and non-cumulative preferred shares, refer to the assumed information regarding the shares of Stake Technology Ltd. in Exhibit 15.13.

During the year ended April 30, 2011, the first year of the corporation's operations, the directors declared and paid total cash dividends of $31,400. During the years ended April 30, 2012 and 2013, total dividends declared and paid were $0 and $110,800 respectively. Allocations of total dividends are shown in Exhibit 15.14 under two assumptions:

a. the preferred shares are non-cumulative, and
b. the preferred shares are cumulative.

Exhibit 15.14

Allocation of Dividends Between
Preferred and Common Shares

a. If non-cumulative preferred:

	Preferred	Common	Total
Year ended 2011:			
7,000 shares × $2.20/share	$15,400		
Remainder to common		$16,000	$ 31,400
Year ended 2012:..	-0-	-0-	$ -0-
Year ended 2013:			
7,000 shares × $2.20/share	$15,400		
Remainder to common		$95,400	$110,800

b. If cumulative preferred:

	Preferred	Common	Total
Year ended 2011:			
7,000 shares × $2.20/share	$15,400		
Remainder to common		$16,000	$ 31,400
Year ended 2012:..	-0-	-0-	$ -0-
Year ended 2013:			
Dividends in arrears = $15,400			
+ Current year dividends of $15,400	$30,800		
Remainder to common		$80,000	$110,800

With non-cumulative preferred shares, the preferred shareholders in Exhibit 15.14 never receive the $15,400 not declared for the year ended 2012. Undeclared dividends are *lost* if preferred shares are non-cumulative.

When preferred shares are cumulative, undeclared dividends are not lost because they go into arrears. In Exhibit 15.14, the $15,400 not declared in 2012 is paid during the year ended 2013 before the common shareholders receive a dividend.

Financial Statement Disclosure of Dividends

A liability for a dividend does not exist until the directors declare a dividend. This means that if a preferred dividend date passes and the corporation's board fails to declare the dividend on its cumulative preferred shares, the dividend in arrears is not a liability. When preparing financial statements, the *full disclosure principle* P. 348 requires the corporation to report the amount of preferred dividends in arrears as of the balance sheet date. This information is usually in a note.

CHECKPOINT   Read Apply Do Check

10. The Cash Dividends account is normally: (a) reported on the balance sheet as a liability; (b) closed to Income Summary; or (c) closed to Retained Earnings.

11. What three dates are involved in the process of paying a cash dividend?

12. When does a dividend become a legal obligation of the company?

13. A corporation has issued 9,000 shares of $5 cumulative preferred shares for a total of $450,000 and 27,000 common shares for a total of $270,000. No dividends have been declared for 2009 and 2010. During 2011, the corporation declares a $288,000 dividend. The amount paid to common shareholders is: (a) $198,000; (b) $153,000; or (c) $108,000.

Do: QS 15-11, QS 15-12, QS 15-13

In addition to being cumulative or non-cumulative, preferred shares can have other features. This is the topic of the next section.

Other Features of Preferred Shares

Participating or Non-Participating Dividends on Preferred Shares

Non-participating preferred shares have dividends limited to a maximum amount each year. This maximum is often stated as a specific dollar amount per share. Once preferred shareholders receive this amount, the common shareholders receive any and all additional dividends.

Participating preferred shares have a feature in which preferred shareholders share with common shareholders in any dividends paid in excess of the dollar amount specified for the preferred shares. This participating feature does not apply until common shareholders receive dividends in a ratio equal to the preferred shares' dividend. While many corporations are authorized to issue participating preferred shares, they are rarely issued.

Convertible Preferred Shares

Preferred shares are more attractive to investors if they carry a right to exchange preferred shares for a fixed number of common shares. **Convertible preferred shares** give holders the option of exchanging their preferred shares into common shares at a specified rate. This feature offers holders of convertible preferred shares a higher potential return. When a company prospers and its common shares increase in value, convertible preferred shareholders can share in this success by converting their preferred shares into more valuable common shares. Also, these holders benefit from increases in the value of common shares without converting their preferred shares because the preferred shares' market value is affected by changes in the value of common shares.

To illustrate the entries to record the conversion of preferred shares to common, assume that the preferred shares in Exhibit 15.15 were convertible at the rate of two common shares for each preferred share.

Stake Technology Ltd. **Shareholders' Equity** **April 30, 2011**	**Exhibit 15.15** Presentation of Dividend Preference

Contributed capital:		
Preferred shares, $2.20, 25,000 shares authorized;		
7,000 shares issued and outstanding	$ 84,000	
Common shares, unlimited shares authorized;		
80,000 shares issued and outstanding	760,000	
Total contributed capital		$844,000
Retained earnings		49,000
Total shareholders' equity		$893,000

The average issue price of the preferred shares is used as the basis of the calculation to record the conversion of 1,000 preferred shares into common shares on May 1, 2011:

2011				
May	1	Preferred Shares	12,000	
		Common Shares		12,000
		To record the conversion of preferred shares into common; $84,000/7,000 shares = $12/share average issue price; $12/share × 1,000 shares = $12,000.		

This entry transfers $12,000 from the Preferred Shares account to the Common Shares account. Total shareholders' equity does not change.

Callable Preferred Shares

Callable preferred shares, also known as **redeemable preferred shares**, give the issuing corporation the right to purchase (retire) these shares from their holders at specified future prices and dates. Many issues of preferred shares are callable. The amount paid to call and retire a preferred share is its **call price**, or *redemption value*. This amount is set at the time the shares are issued. The call price normally includes the issue price of the shares plus a premium giving holders additional return on their investment. When the issuing corporation calls and retires preferred shares, it must pay the call price *and* any dividends in arrears.

For instance, in Note 15 of its December 31, 2005, annual report, TransCanada Pipelines Limited reports that on or after October 15, 2013, for the Series U shares, and on or after March 5, 2014, for the Series Y shares, the company may redeem the shares at $50 per share.

TransCanada

In business to deliver ™

www.transcanada.com

Closing Entries for Corporations

LO6 | Record closing entries for a corporation.

Extend Your Knowledge

SSC

15-2

Recall that the closing process involves closing all temporary accounts. This includes closing revenues and expenses to the Income Summary account. For the corporate form of organization, the balance in the Income Summary account is closed to Retained Earnings. To demonstrate, assume Weber Inc. had the adjusted trial balance at December 31, 2011, as shown below. After closing all of the revenue and expense accounts, the Income Summary account would appear as shown to the right.

Acct. No.	Account	Debit	Credit
101	Cash	$ 40,000	
106	Prepaid rent	57,000	
153	Trucks	137,000	
154	Accumulated amortization, trucks		$ 16,000
201	Accounts payable		20,000
307	Common shares		75,000
315	Preferred shares		40,000
318	Retained earnings		30,000
319	Cash dividends	10,000	
401	Fees earned		238,000
640	Rent expense	120,000	
611	Amortization expense, trucks	35,000	
695	Income taxes expense	20,000	
	Totals	$419,000	$419,000

Income Summary

Dec 31/11	175,000	238,000	Dec. 31/11
			Bal.
		63,000	Dec. 31/11

The entry to close the Income Summary account is:[9]

2011			
Dec. 31	Income Summary..	63,000	
	Retained Earnings..................................		63,000
	To close net income to Retained Earnings.		

After posting the closing entries, the Income Summary will show a balance of $0, as illustrated in the T-account below.

Income Summary

Dec 31/11	175,000	238,000	Dec. 31/11
			Bal.
Dec. 31/11	63,000	63,000	Dec. 31/11
			Bal.
		0	Dec. 31/11

The final step in the closing process would be to close dividends as follows (unless Retained Earnings had been debited directly as described on page 749):

2011			
Dec. 31	Retained Earnings..	10,000	
	Cash Dividends		10,000
	To close the Cash Dividends account to Retained Earnings.		

Retained Earnings

			Bal.
Dec. 31/11	10,000	30,000	Dec. 31/11
		63,000	Dec. 31/11
			Bal.
		83,000	Dec. 31/11

The post-closing balance in Retained Earnings after posting these entries is reflected in the T-account to the left.

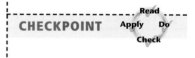

14. Assume Retained Earnings had a January 1, 2011, balance of $5,000. During January, dividends of $3,000 were declared but not paid and a net income of $7,000 was realized. What is the January 31, 2011, post-closing balance in Retained Earnings?

Do: QS 15-14, QS 15-15, QS 15-16

CHECKPOINT

---

[9] If, instead, Weber Inc. had realized a net loss during the accounting period of $14,000, the balance in the Income Summary account would have been a debit after closing all revenues and expenses. The entry to close the Income Summary account in this instance would be:

2011			
Dec. 31	Retained Earnings..	14,000	
	Income Summary...................................		14,000
	To close net loss to Retained Earnings.		

Summary

LO¹ **Identify characteristics of corporations and their organization.** Corporations are separate legal entities and their shareholders are not liable for corporate debts. Shares issued by corporations are easily transferred between shareholders, and the life of a corporation does not end with the incapacity or death of a shareholder. A corporation acts through its agents, who are its officers and managers, not its shareholders. Corporations are regulated by the government and are subject to income taxes.

LO² **Describe and contrast the specialized components of corporate financial statements.** The income statement for a corporation is similar to that of an unincorporated organization except for the inclusion of income tax expense. A corporation, like a proprietorship, records net incomes (losses), distributions of net income (in the form of dividends) to its owners (shareholders), and owner (shareholder) investments. Accumulated net incomes less losses and dividends are recorded in Retained Earnings and summarized on the statement of retained earnings. Shareholder investments are recorded in share capital accounts, either common shares or preferred shares, in shareholders' equity on the balance sheet. An unincorporated business records these three activities in the owner's capital account.

LO³ **Record the issuance of common and preferred shares and describe their presentation in shareholders' equity on the balance sheet.** When only one class of shares is issued, they are called common shares. Shares, both common and preferred, can be issued for cash or other assets. The number of shares authorized, issued, and outstanding, along with the dollar value contributed by the

shareholders, is shown under the heading Contributed Capital in the shareholders' equity section on the balance sheet. Preferred shares have a priority (or senior status) relative to common shares in one or more areas. The usual areas include preference as to (a) dividends and (b) assets in case of liquidation. They do not have voting rights.

LO⁴ **Describe and account for cash dividends.** The board of directors makes all decisions regarding dividends. The date of declaration is the date the liability to pay dividends is created. All shareholders holding shares as of the date of record are eligible to receive the declared dividend. The dividend payment date is when dividends are actually paid.

LO⁵ **Distribute dividends between common and preferred shares.** Preferred shareholders usually hold the right to receive dividend distributions before common shareholders. This right is known as dividend preference. When preferred shares are cumulative and in arrears, the amount in arrears must be distributed to preferred shareholders before any dividends are distributed to common shareholders. Preferred shares can also be convertible or callable. Convertibility permits the holder to convert preferred shares to common shares. Callability permits the issuer to buy preferred shares under specified conditions.

LO⁶ **Record closing entries for a corporation.** Revenues and expenses are closed to the Income Summary account as for an unincorporated organization. The balance in Income Summary is closed to Retained Earnings. Dividends are closed to Retained Earnings, as well.

---

guidance answer to | **JUDGEMENT CALL**

Concert Organizer

Because you wish to maintain control of the company, you want to issue shares in a way that does not interfere with your ability to run the company the way you desire. You have two basic options: (1) different classes of common shares, or (2) common and preferred shares. Your

objective in this case is to issue a class of shares to yourself that has all or a majority of the voting power. The other class of shares you issue would carry limited or no voting rights. In this way you maintain complete control and are able to raise your necessary funds.

---

guidance answers to | **CHECKPOINT** | Read Apply Do Check

1. Straight-line amortization is normally used to amortize intangible assets.

2. All transactions are identical for both organizations except for the $12, which represents the income tax expense imposed on the corporation but not on the unincorporated form of organization.

3. The income statement of a corporation includes Income Tax Expense but the income statement for an unincorporated business does not. This is because a corporation must pay taxes on its income, whereas an unincorporated business does not since it is not a separate legal entity.

4. Both statements include net incomes (losses) less distributions of earnings (called *withdrawals* for an unincorporated organization and *dividends* for the corporation).

5. Shareholders' equity shows investments by the owners (shareholders) separately from net incomes (losses) and dividends. Shareholder investments are recorded in share capital accounts, either common shares or preferred shares, and net incomes (losses) less dividends are summarized in the Retained Earnings account. Owner's equity shows all three activities in one account, the owner's capital account.

6. The average issue price per common share at July 31, 2011, was $405,000/34,000 = $11.91 (rounded).

7. *b*

8. Special rights include a preference for receiving dividends and for the distribution of assets if the corporation's assets are liquidated.

9. *a*

10. *c*

11. The three dates are the date of declaration, date of record, and date of payment.

12. A dividend becomes a legal obligation of the company when it is declared by the board of directors on the date of declaration.

13. *b*

Total dividend...	$288,000
To preferred shareholders	135,000*
Remainder to common shareholders	$153,000

\$9,000 × \$5 × 3 = \$135,000

14. $5,000 − $3,000 + $7,000 = $9,000.

demonstration problem

Read
Apply   Do
Check

Barton Corporation was created on January 1, 2011. Barton is authorized by its articles of incorporation to issue 100,000 shares of $10 cumulative preferred shares and an unlimited number of common shares. The following transactions relating to shareholders' equity occurred during the first two years of the company's operations.

2011		
Jan.	2	Issued 200,000 common shares at $12 per share.
	2	Issued 100,000 common shares in exchange for a building valued at $820,000 and merchandise inventory valued at $380,000.
	3	Paid a cash reimbursement to the company's founders for $100,000 of organization costs; these costs are to be amortized over 10 years.
	3	Issued 12,000 preferred shares for cash at $110 per share.
Dec.	31	The Income Summary account for 2011 had a $125,000 credit balance before being closed to Retained Earnings; no dividends were declared on either common or preferred shares.
2012		
June	4	Issued 100,000 common shares for cash at $15 per share.
Dec.	10	Declared total cash dividends of $540,000 payable on January 10, 2013.
	31	The Income Summary account for 2012 had a $1 million credit balance before being closed to Retained Earnings.

Required

1. Prepare the journal entries to record these transactions.
2. Prepare statements of retained earnings for the years ended December 31, 2011 and 2012.
3. Prepare the balance sheet presentation of the organization costs, liabilities, and shareholders' equity as at December 31, 2011 and 2012. Include appropriate notes to the financial statements (regarding any dividends in arrears).

Analysis component:

What effect does the declaration and subsequent payment of cash dividends have on the income statement and balance sheet?

Planning the Solution

- Record journal entries for the transactions in 2011 and 2012.
- Close the accounts related to retained earnings at the end of each year.
- Prepare the statements of retained earnings for the years 2011 and 2012.
- Determine the balances for the 2011 and 2012 contributed capital accounts for the balance sheet including information about the number of shares issued.
- Prepare the shareholders' equity section of the 2011 and 2012 balance sheet including a note regarding any dividends in arrears.
- Prepare an answer for the analysis component.

solution to **Demonstration Problem**

1.

2011				
Jan.	2	Cash...	2,400,000	
		Common Shares		2,400,000
		Issued 200,000 common shares;		
		200,000 × $12.		
	2	Building	820,000	
		Merchandise Inventory..................................	380,000	
		Common Shares		1,200,000
		Issued 100,000 common shares.		
	3	Organization Costs..	100,000	
		Cash		100,000
		Reimbursed the founders for organization		
		costs.		
	3	Cash...	1,320,000	
		Preferred Shares		1,320,000
		Issued 12,000 preferred shares;		
		12,000 × $110.		
Dec.	31	Income Summary...	125,000	
		Retained Earnings..................................		125,000
		Close the Income Summary account and		
		update Retained Earnings.		
2012				
June	4	Cash...	1,500,000	
		Common Shares		1,500,000
		Issued 100,000 common shares;		
		100,000 × $15.		
Dec.	10	Cash Dividends (or Retained Earnings)	540,000	
		Preferred Dividend Payable		240,000
		Common Dividend Payable...................		300,000
		Declared current dividends and dividends		
		in arrears to common and preferred		
		shareholders, payable on January 10, 2013;		
		Preferred = $10/share × 12,000 shares ×		
		2 years; Common = $ 540,000 − $ 240,000.		

31	Income Summary..	1,000,000	
	Retained Earnings..................................		1,000,000
	To close the Income Summary account and update Retained Earnings.		
31	Retained Earnings...	540,000	
	Cash Dividends		540,000
	To close to Retained Earnings the Cash Dividends.		

2.

Barton Corporation
Statement of Retained Earnings
For Years Ended December 31,

	2012	2011
Retained earnings, January 1......................................	$ 125,000	$ -0-
Add: Net income	1,000,000	125,000
Total	$1,125,000	$125,000
Less: Dividends	540,000	-0-
Retained earnings, December 31	$ 585,000	$125,000

3. Balance sheet presentations:

Barton Corporation
Balance Sheet
As of December 31,

	2012	2011
Assets		
Organization costs	$ 80,000	$ 90,000
Liabilities		
Preferred dividend payable	$ 240,000	$-0-
Common dividend payable	300,000	-0-
Shareholders' Equity		
Contributed capital:		
Preferred shares, $10 cumulative, 100,000 shares authorized; 12,000 shares issued and outstanding	$1,320,000	$1,320,000
Common shares, unlimited shares authorized; 400,000 shares issued and outstanding in 2012; 300,000 shares issued and outstanding in 2011	5,100,000	3,600,000
Total contributed capital.......................................	$6,420,000	$4,920,000
Retained earnings (see Note 1)	585,000	125,000
Total shareholders' equity......................................	$7,005,000	$5,045,000

Note 1: As of December 31, 2011, there were $120,000 of dividends in arrears on the preferred shares.

Analysis component:

The declaration and subsequent payment of cash dividends will not affect the income statement in any way. On the balance sheet, assets will decrease because cash is paid to the shareholders and equity will decrease—specifically, Retained Earnings.

APPENDIX 15A

Book Value Per Share

LO⁷ | Calculate book value and explain its use in analysis.

This section explains how we calculate book value and use it for analysis. We first focus on book value per share for corporations with only common shares outstanding, and then look at book value per share when both common and preferred shares are outstanding.

Book Value Per Share When Only Common Shares Are Outstanding

Book value per common share is the recorded amount of shareholders' equity applicable to common shares divided by the number of common shares outstanding. This ratio is defined in Exhibit 15A.1.

Exhibit 15A.1

Book Value Per Common Share Formula

$$\text{Book value per common share} = \frac{\text{Shareholders' equity applicable to common shares}}{\text{Number of common shares outstanding}}$$

For instance, we can calculate the book value per common share for Dillon Snowboards at June 30, 2011, using data in Exhibit 15.6. Dillon has 30,000 outstanding common shares and the shareholders' equity applicable to common shares is $365,000. Common shares are entitled to total shareholders' equity when there are no preferred shares outstanding. Dillon's book value per common share is $12.17, calculated as $365,000 divided by 30,000 shares.

Book Value Per Share When Both Common and Preferred Shares Are Outstanding

To calculate book value when both common and preferred shares are outstanding, we must first allocate total shareholders' equity between these two kinds of shares. The **book value per preferred share** is calculated first, and its calculation is shown in Exhibit 15A.2.

Exhibit 15A.2

Book Value Per Preferred Share Formula

$$\text{Book value per preferred share} = \frac{\text{Shareholders' equity applicable to preferred shares*}}{\text{Number of preferred shares outstanding}}$$

Stated another way, the numerator could be described as: Call price of preferred shares plus dividends in arrears or, if there is no call price then: Paid-in capital from preferred shares plus dividends in arrears.

The shareholders' equity applicable to preferred shares equals the preferred shares' call price (or average paid-in amount if the preferred shares are not callable) plus any cumulative dividends in arrears. The remaining shareholders' equity is the portion applicable to common shares.

Calculation of Book Value—Call Price

To illustrate, let us look at the December 31, 2011, shareholders' equity section of Music Live! as shown in Exhibit 15A.3. The preferred shares of Music Live! are callable at $108 per share, and since no dividends were declared during 2010 and 2011, there are two years of cumulative preferred dividends in arrears.

Music Live!	
Shareholders' Equity	
December 31, 2011	
Contributed capital:	
Preferred shares, $7 cumulative, $108 call price, 2,000 shares authorized, 1,000 shares issued and outstanding...	$105,000
Common shares, 12,000 shares authorized, 10,000 shares issued and outstanding...	260,000
Total contributed capital	$365,000
Retained earnings	82,000
Total shareholders' equity	$447,000

Exhibit 15A.3

Shareholders' Equity with Preferred and Common Shares

The book values of Music Live! preferred and common shares are calculated in Exhibit 15A.4. Note the need to allocate equity to preferred shares before we calculate the book value of common shares.

Total shareholders' equity		$447,000
Less equity applicable to preferred shares:		
Call price (1,000 × $108)...	$108,000	
Cumulative dividends in arrears (1,000 × $7 × 2)...............	14,000	(122,000)
Equity applicable to common shares.............................		$325,000
Book value per preferred share ($122,000/1,000)..........................		$122.00
Book value per common share ($325,000/10,000)........................		$32.50

Exhibit 15A.4

Calculating Book Value Per Share, Call Price

Calculation of Book Value—No Call Price

Let's use the same information for Music Live! except we'll assume that the preferred shares have no call price. The new book values are calculated in Exhibit 15A.5.

Total shareholders' equity		$447,000
Less equity applicable to preferred shares:		
Paid-in amount..	$105,000	
Cumulative dividends in arrears (1,000 × $7 × 2)...............	14,000	(119,000)
Equity applicable to common shares.............................		$328,000
Book value per preferred share ($119,000/1,000)..........................		$119.00
Book value per common share ($328,000/10,000)........................		$32.80

Exhibit 15A.5

Calculating Book Value Per Share, No Call Price

Book value per share is often used in analysis of a company. It is the starting point in many share valuation methods. Other uses include merger negotiations, price setting for public utilities, and loan contracts. The main limitation in using book values is likely differences between book values and market values for both assets and liabilities. Professionals often adjust their analyses and the accounting numbers to reflect these differences.

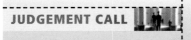

Answer—p. 762

Investor

You are considering investing in Ride Ltd., a leading manufacturer of snowboards. Ride's current book value per common share is about $4, yet its common shares are priced at about $7 per share on the stock exchange. From this information, can you say whether Ride's net assets are priced higher or lower than their recorded values?

CHECKPOINT   Read Apply Do Check

15. A corporation's outstanding shares include $90,000 of cumulative preferred shares consisting of 1,000 shares and 12,000 common shares. Preferred shares have a call price of $90 and dividends of $18,000 are in arrears. Total shareholders' equity is $630,000. What is the book value per common share?

16. The price at which a share is bought or sold is the (a) call price, (b) redemption value, or (c) market value.

Do: *QS 15-17

Summary of Appendix 15A --

LO7 | **Calculate book value and explain its use in analysis.** Book value per common share is shareholders' equity applicable to common shares divided by the number of outstanding common shares. Book value per preferred share is shareholders' equity applicable to preferred shares divided by the number of outstanding preferred shares.

---

guidance answer to   **JUDGEMENT CALL**

Investor

Book value reflects recorded values. Ride's book value is about $4 per common share. The share price reflects the market's expectation of current and future values. Ride's market value is about $7 per common share. Comparing these figures suggests that market perception of Ride's value is much higher than its recorded values ($7 vs. $4 per share, respectively).

---

guidance answers to   **CHECKPOINT**   Read Apply Do Check

15.

Total shareholders' equity		$630,000
Less equity applicable to preferred shares:		
Call price (1,000 × $90)	$90,000	
Dividends in arrears	18,000	108,000
Equity applicable to common shares		$522,000
Book value of common shares ($522,000/12,000)		$43.50

16. *c*

Glossary

Authorized shares   The total number of shares that a corporation's charter authorizes it to sell. Federally incorporated companies are authorized to issue an unlimited number. (p. 738)

Book value per common share   The recorded amount of shareholders' equity applicable to common shares divided by the number of common shares outstanding. (p. 760)

Book value per preferred share   The amount of shareholders' equity applicable to preferred shares (equals the preferred share's call price or issue price if the preferred share is not callable, plus any cumulative dividends in arrears) divided by the number of preferred shares outstanding. (p. 760)

Callable preferred shares   Preferred shares that the issuing corporation, at its option, may retire by paying a specified amount (the call price) to the preferred shareholders plus any dividends in arrears. (p. 754)

Call price   The amount that must be paid to call and retire a preferred share. (p. 754)

Capital stock   See *share capital*. (p. 735)

Closely held shares   See *privately held shares*. (p. 735)

Common shares   Shares of a corporation when there is only one class of shares. (p. 739)

Contributed capital   The total amount of cash and other assets received by the corporation from its shareholders in exchange for common and/or preferred shares. (p. 745)

Convertible preferred shares   Preferred shares that give holders the option of exchanging their preferred shares for common shares at a specified rate. (p. 753)

Cumulative preferred shares   Preferred shares on which undeclared dividends accumulate until they are paid; common shareholders cannot receive a dividend until all cumulative dividends have been paid. (p. 751)

Date of declaration   The date the directors vote to pay a dividend. (p. 749)

Date of payment   The date when shareholders receive the dividend payment. (p. 749)

Date of record   The future date specified by the directors for identifying those shareholders listed in the corporation's records to receive dividends. (p. 749)

Deficit   Arises when a corporation has a debit (abnormal) balance for retained earnings. (p. 750)

Dividend in arrears   An unpaid dividend on cumulative preferred shares; it must be paid before any current dividends on the preferred shares and before any dividends on the common shares are paid. (p. 751)

Dividend preference   The rate per share at which dividends are paid when declared. (p. 751)

Equity financing   Obtaining capital, or money, by issuing shares. (p. 741)

Financial leverage   Achieving an increased return on common shares by paying dividends on preferred shares or interest on debt at a rate that is less than the rate of return earned with the assets that were invested in the corporation by the preferred shareholders or creditors. (p. 747)

Market value per share   The price at which stock is bought or sold. (p. 742)

Non-cumulative preferred shares   Preferred shares on which the right to receive dividends is lost for any year that the dividends are not declared. (p. 751)

Non-participating preferred shares   Preferred shares on which dividends are limited to a maximum amount each year. (p. 753)

No par value   A class of shares that has not been assigned a par value by the corporate charter. (p. 743)

Organization costs   The costs of bringing a corporation into existence, including legal fees, promoters' fees, and amounts paid to the incorporating legal jurisdiction. (p. 738)

Outstanding shares   The number of shares held by shareholders. (p. 743)

Participating preferred shares   Preferred shares with a feature that allows preferred shareholders to share with common shareholders in any dividends paid in excess of the percent stated on the preferred shares. (p. 753)

Par value   An arbitrary value a corporation places on each of the corporation's shares. (p. 743)

Preemptive right   The right to purchase additional common shares issued by the corporation in the future. (p. 746)

Preferred shares   Shares that give their owners a priority status over common shareholders in one or more ways, such as the payment of dividends or the distribution of assets on liquidation. (p. 744)

Privately held shares   When a corporation offers its shares to only a few shareholders; shares are not for public sale; also called *closely held shares*. (p. 735)

Progressive tax   Higher levels of income are taxed at higher rates and lower levels of income are taxed at lower rates. (p. 737)

Proxy   A legal document that gives an agent of a shareholder the power to exercise the voting rights of that shareholder's shares. (p. 739)

Publicly held shares   When a corporation offers its shares for public sale, which can result in thousands of shareholders. (p. 735)

Public sale   Refers to trading in an organized stock market. (p. 735)

Redeemable preferred shares   See *callable preferred shares*. (p. 754)

Retained earnings   The cumulative net income less losses and dividends retained by a corporation. (p. 740)

Sell shares directly   When a corporation advertises its shares' issuance directly to potential buyers. This is most common with privately held corporations. (p. 742)

Sell shares indirectly   When a corporation pays a brokerage house (investment banker) to issue its shares. (p. 742)

Share   One unit of ownership in a corporation. (p. 735)

Share capital   Refers to all types (or classes) of a corporation's shares; also called *capital stock*. (p. 735)

Shareholder(s)   The owners of a corporation. (p. 735)

Shareholders' equity   The equity of a corporation; also called *corporate capital*. (p. 740)

Statement of retained earnings   A financial statement unique to the corporate form of organization that reconciles retained earnings for the period by taking retained earnings at the beginning of the period, plus net income for the period (or less net loss), less dividends declared for the period, to arrive at retained earnings at the end of the period. (p. 740)

Underwrite   When a brokerage house buys the shares from the corporation and takes all gains or losses from its resale to shareholders. (p. 742)

For more study tools, quizzes, and problem material, visit the **Student Success** *Centre* at
www.mcgrawhill.ca/studentsuccess/FAP

Questions

1. Who is responsible for directing the affairs of a corporation?

2. What are organization costs? List examples of these costs.

3. How are organization costs classified on the balance sheet?

4. List the general rights of common shareholders.

5. What is the preemptive right of common shareholders?

6. What is the meaning of the *call price* of a share?

7. Why would an investor find convertible preferred shares attractive?

8. Examine the balance sheet for WestJet Airlines in Appendix I at the end of the book and determine the average issue price for the $429,613,000 in share capital at December 31, 2005.

9. Refer to the financial statements for Danier Leather in Appendix I at the end of the book. What were the total cash dividends declared and paid during the year ended June 25, 2005?

WEST JET

DANIER

Quick Study

QS 15-1
Characteristics of corporations
LO¹

Of the following statements, which are true for the corporation form of business?
a. Capital often is more easily accumulated than with other forms of organization.
b. It has a limited life.
c. Owners have unlimited liability for corporate debts.
d. It is a separate legal entity.
e. Ownership rights cannot be easily transferred.

QS 15-2
Organization of corporations
LO¹

Bentley Inc. incorporated on January 2, 2011. Total costs regarding organization were $56,000. The organizers accepted cash of $50,000 and common shares for the balance. Record Bentley's entries on January 2 and on December 31, the year-end, assuming the organization costs were to be amortized over five years using the straight-line method.

QS 15-3
Corporate financial statements
LO²

Ludwig Ltd. showed the following amounts for its year just ended October 31, 2011. Prepare a multi-step income statement assuming a tax rate of 25%.

Cost of goods sold	$420,000	Operating expenses	$162,000
Gain on sale of capital assets	4,000	Sales	982,000
Interest expense......................	6,200		

QS 15-4
Components of shareholders' equity
LO²

From the following list of selected accounts for X-cell Inc., identify the shareholders' equity accounts. Use "CC" for contributed capital, "RE" for retained earnings, and "X" if not a shareholders' equity account.

_____ Cash		_____ Preferred shares	
_____ Common shares		_____ Retained earnings	
_____ Common dividend payable		_____ Preferred dividend payable	
_____ Deficit		_____ Preferred shares, $5 non-cumulative	

Vision Consulting began operations on January 1, 2011. Complete the following schedule with journal entries detailing the transactions during 2011 for Vision Consulting under two forms of organization: as a single proprietorship (owned by Ian Smith), and as a corporation.

QS 15-5
Corporate financial statements
LO²

Transaction	FORM OF BUSINESS ORGANIZATION	
	Single Proprietorship	**Corporation**
Jan. 1, 2011: The owner(s) invested $10,000 into the new business		
During 2011: Revenues of $50,000 were earned; all cash		
During 2011: Expenses of $30,000 were incurred; all cash		
Dec. 15, 2011: $15,000 cash was distributed to the owner(s)		
Dec. 31, 2011, Year-End: All temporary accounts were closed -Close Revenue account		
-Close Expense account		
-Close Income Summary account to appropriate equity account(s)		
-Close Withdrawal/Cash Dividends Declared account		
Equity section on the balance sheet at December 31, 2011 after the first year of operations.	**Vision Consulting** **Partial Balance Sheet** **December 31, 2011**	**Vision Consulting Inc.** **Partial Balance Sheet** **December 31, 2011**

Benson Inc. had a credit balance in Retained Earnings on December 31, 2011, of $48,000. During 2012, Benson recorded net income of $146,000 and declared and paid dividends of $47,000. During 2013, the company recorded a net loss of $15,000. No dividends were declared or paid in 2013. Calculate the balance in Retained Earnings at December 31, 2013.

QS 15-6
Retained earnings
LO²

The Retained Earnings account for Callaho Inc. is shown below:

QS 15-7
Analyzing retained earnings
LO²

Retained Earnings		
50,000	120,000	(Balance Jan. 1/11)
	X	
	300,000	(Balance Dec. 31/11)

1. Calculate X.
2. What does X represent?
3. What caused the debit of $50,000?

QS 15-8
Issuance of common shares
LO3

On February 1, Excel Corporation issued 37,500 common shares for $252,440 cash. On February 12, an additional 47,000 common shares were issued for cash of $7.25 per share. Present the entries to record these transactions and calculate the average issue price per common share.

QS 15-9
Interpreting journal entries for share issuances
LO3

Each of these entries was recently recorded by a different corporation. Provide an explanation for the transaction described by each entry.

a.	Apr.	1	Cash..	60,000	
			Common Shares		60,000
b.	Apr.	3	Organization Costs...........................	90,000	
			Common Shares		90,000
c.	Apr.	5	Merchandise Inventory.....................	90,000	
			Machinery.......................................	130,000	
			Notes Payable		144,000
			Common Shares		76,000

QS 15-10
Issuance of preferred shares in exchange for land
LO3

On October 3, 2011, Allarco Inc. issued 4,000 of its preferred shares for cash of $15 each. On November 19 the company issued 3,400 preferred shares in exchange for land with a fair market value of $52,480.
a. Prepare the entries for October 3 and November 19.
b. Calculate the average issue price per preferred share.

QS 15-11
Accounting for cash dividends
LO4

Prepare journal entries to record the following transactions for Desmond Corporation:

Apr.	15	Declared a $48,000 cash dividend payable to common shareholders.
June	30	Paid the dividend declared on April 15.
Dec.	31	Closed the Cash Dividends account.

QS 15-12
Dividend allocation between classes of shareholders
LO5

The shareholders' equity section of the Holden Ltd. balance sheet includes 75,000 shares of $0.40 cumulative preferred shares that had been issued for $375,000 and 200,000 common shares issued for a total of $720,000. Holden did not declare any dividends during the prior year and now declares and pays a $108,000 cash dividend.
a. Determine the amount distributed to each class of shareholders.
b. Repeat the calculations assuming the preferred shares were non-cumulative.

QS 15-13
Components of shareholders' equity
LO3, 4, 5

Reese Corporation
Shareholders' Equity
December 31, 2011

Contributed capital:	
Preferred shares, $0.50 cumulative; 20,000 shares authorized, issued, and outstanding..	$ 200,000
Common shares, unlimited shares authorized; 150,000 shares issued and outstanding..	750,000
Total contributed capital...	$ 950,000
Retained earnings	890,000
Total shareholders' equity	$1,840,000

Explain each of the following terms included in the shareholders' equity section above:
a. $0.50 cumulative   **d.** 150,000 shares issued and outstanding
b. total contributed capital   **e.** retained earnings
c. 20,000 shares authorized   **f.** unlimited shares authorized

Peter Puck Inc. showed the following adjusted information on May 31, 2011, its year-end:

Assets		Liabilities		Common Shares	
120,000			40,500		13,000

Preferred Shares		Retained Earnings		Cash Dividends	
	7,000		29,000	3,500	

Revenues		Expenses		Income Summary	
	92,000	58,000			

a. Prepare the appropriate closing entries.
b. Prepare a statement of retained earnings for the year ended May 31, 2011.

QS 15-14
Statement of retained earnings, closing entries for a corporation—net income
LO2, 6

Morris Inc. showed the following adjusted information on November 30, 2011, its year-end:

Assets		Liabilities		Common Shares	
95,000			18,000		48,000

Preferred Shares		Retained Earnings		Cash Dividends	
	10,000		42,000	14,000	

Revenues		Expenses		Income Summary	
	87,000	96,000			

a. Prepare the appropriate closing entries.
b. Prepare a statement of retained earnings for the year ended November 30, 2011.

QS 15-15
Statement of retained earnings, closing entries for a corporation—net loss
LO2, 6

Velor Ltd. showed the following adjusted information on August 31, 2011, its year-end:

Assets		Liabilities		Common Shares	
75,000			23,000		48,000

Preferred Shares		Retained Earnings		Cash Dividends	
	10,000		12,000	-0-	

Revenues		Expenses		Income Summary	
	76,000	94,000			

a. Prepare the appropriate closing entries.
b. Prepare a statement of retained earnings for the year ended August 31, 2011.

QS 15-16
Statement of retained earnings, closing entries for a corporation—net loss and deficit
LO2, 6

*QS 15-17
Book value per common share
LO7

Courtland Corporation **Shareholders' Equity** **December 31, 2011**		
Contributed capital:		
Preferred shares, $5 cumulative, 10,000 shares authorized, issued and outstanding......		$100,000
Common shares, 100,000 shares authorized; 75,000 shares issued and outstanding		375,000
Total contributed capital......		$475,000
Retained earnings		445,000
Total shareholders' equity		$920,000

Using the information provided, calculate book value per common share assuming:
a. there are no dividends in arrears.
b. there are three years of dividends in arrears.
c. the preferred shares have a $30 call price and there are no dividends in arrears.

Exercises

Exercise 15-1
Comparative entries for
partnership and corporation
LO2

Tom Seabrink and Joan Miller began a new business on February 14 when each of them invested $125,000 in the company. On December 20, it was decided that $48,000 of the company's cash would be distributed equally between the owners. Two cheques for $24,000 were prepared and given to the owners on December 23. On December 31, the company reported a $96,000 net income.

Prepare two sets of journal entries to record the investments by the owners, the distribution of cash to the owners, the closing of the Income Summary account, and the withdrawals or dividends under these alternative assumptions:
a. the business is a partnership, and
b. the business is a corporation that issued 1,000 common shares.

Exercise 15-2
Issuing shares
LO3

Prepare journal entries for each of the following selected transactions that occurred during Z-Bar Inc.'s first year of operations:

	2011	
Jan.	15	Issued 2,000 common shares to the corporation's promoters in exchange for their efforts in creating it. Their efforts are estimated to be worth $22,500.
Feb.	21	15,000 common shares were issued for cash of $10 per share.
Mar.	9	6,000 preferred shares were issued for cash totalling $79,000.
Aug.	15	55,000 common shares were issued in exchange for land, building, and equipment with appraised values of $225,000, $300,000, and $80,000 respectively.

Exercise 15-3
Share transactions, shareholders'
equity
LO2, 3

ABC Inc. was authorized to issue 50,000 $2.00 preferred shares and 300,000 common shares. During 2011, its first year of operations, the following selected transactions occurred:

Jan.	1	5,000 of the preferred shares were issued at $10.00 per share; cash.
Feb.	5	15,000 of the common shares were issued for a total of $105,000; cash.
Mar.	20	3,000 of the common shares were given to the organizers of the corporation regarding their efforts. The shares were valued at a total of $24,000.
May	15	12,000 preferred shares and 20,000 common shares were issued at $11.00 and $8.00 respectively; cash.
Dec.	31	The Income Summary account was closed; it showed a debit balance of $235,000. December 31 is ABC Inc.'s year-end.

An asterisk (*) identifies assignment material based on Appendix 15A.

Required

a. Journalize the above transactions.

b. Prepare the shareholders' equity section of the ABC Inc. balance sheet at December 31, 2011.

c. The preferred shares are described as "*$2.00 preferred shares.*" Explain what the $2.00 means.

Check figure:
b. Total shareholders' equity = $236,000

On March 1, the board of directors declared a cash dividend of $0.50 per common share to shareholders of record on March 10, payable March 31. There were 50,000 shares issued and outstanding on March 1 and no additional shares had been issued during the month. Record the entries for March 1, 10, and 31.

Exercise 15-4
Cash dividend
LO4

Hanson Inc. began operations on June 5, 2011. Journalize the following shareholders' equity transactions that occurred during the first month of operations:

Exercise 15-5
Issuing shares
LO3, 4

	2011	
June	5	Gave 4,000 common shares to the organizers of the corporation in exchange for accounting and legal services valued at $65,000.
	15	Received $17 cash per share for the issuance of 75,000 common shares.
	16	Issued 10,000 preferred shares for cash of $30 per share.
	17	8,000 common shares were issued to a creditor who was owed $100,000.
	18	The board of directors declared a cash dividend of $15,000 on the preferred shares and $5,000 on the common shares to shareholders of record on June 20, payable July 1.
	30	150,000 common shares were issued in exchange for machinery with a fair market value of $2,000,000. The shares were actively trading on this date at $13.20 per share.
July	1	The dividends declared on June 18 were paid.

Lindsay Ltd. was authorized to issue an unlimited number of common shares. During January 2011, its first month of operations, the following selected transactions occurred:

Exercise 15-6
Issuing shares; shareholders' equity
LO2, 3, 4

Jan.	1	1,000 shares were issued to the organizers of the corporation. The total value of the shares was determined to be $8,000.
	5	15,000 shares were sold to various shareholders for $9.00 each.
	15	The board of directors declared a cash dividend of $0.50 per common share to shareholders of record on January 19, payable January 31.
	20	4,000 shares were issued in exchange for land valued at $32,000. The shares were actively trading on this date at $10.75 per share.
	31	Closed the Income Summary account, which showed a credit balance of $110,000.
	31	Paid the dividends declared on January 19.

Required

a. Journalize the above transactions.

b. Prepare the shareholders' equity section of the balance sheet of Lindsay Ltd. at January 31, 2011.

c. What was the average issue price per common share?

Check figure:
b. Total shareholders' equity = $288,000

Exercise 15-7
Retained earnings, dividend distribution
LO2, 5

The December 31, 2011, shareholders' equity section of the balance sheet of Maritime Inc. appears below.

Maritime Inc.
Shareholders' Equity
December 31, 2011

Contributed capital:	
Preferred shares, $4.50 cumulative, 40,000 shares authorized and issued	$2,000,000
Preferred shares, $12 non-cumulative, 8,000 shares authorized and issued	800,000
Common shares, 400,000 shares authorized and issued	2,000,000
Total contributed capital	$4,800,000
Retained earnings	890,000
Total shareholders' equity	$5,690,000

Check figure:
1. Total dividends = $736,000

Required

All the shares were issued on January 1, 2009 (when the corporation began operations). No dividends had been declared during the first two years of operations (2009 and 2010). During 2011, the cash dividends declared and paid totalled $736,000.

1. Calculate the amount of cash dividends paid during 2011 to each of the three classes of shares.
2. Assuming net income earned during 2011 was $1,500,000, determine the December 31, 2010, balance in retained earnings.
3. Prepare a statement of retained earnings for the year ended December 31, 2011.

Exercise 15-8
Share transactions, distribution of dividends, shareholders' equity
LO2, 3, 5

Blue Iguana Inc. showed the following shareholders' equity as at December 31, 2011:

Blue Iguana Inc.
Shareholders' Equity
December 31, 2011

Contributed capital:	
Preferred shares, $3.00 non-cumulative; 100,000 shares authorized 75,000 shares issued and outstanding	A
Common shares; unlimited shares authorized; E shares issued and outstanding	B
Total contributed capital	$6,250,000
Retained earnings	C
Total shareholders' equity	D

Other information:
a. The preferred shares had sold for an average price of $30.00.
b. The common shares had sold for an average price of $16.00.
c. Retained Earnings at December 31, 2010, was $160,000. During 2011, net income earned was $1,440,000. The board of directors declared a total cash dividend of $450,000.

Required
Calculate A, B, C, D, and E.

Selected T-accounts for Watson Corporation at December 31, 2011, are duplicated below.

Preferred Shares, $5 cumulative 10,000 shares authorized 8,000 shares issued		
	160,000	Dec. 31/10 Bal.
	160,000	Dec. 31/11 Bal.

Common Shares, 50,000 shares authorized 45,000 shares issued		
	450,000	Dec. 31/10 Bal.
	450,000	Dec. 31/11 Bal.

Retained Earnings		
	105,000	Dec. 31/10 Bal.
	????	Dec. 31/11 Bal.

Note: • Dividends were not paid during 2009 or 2010. Dividends of $4 per common share were declared and paid for the year ended December 31, 2011.
       • 2009 was the first year of operations.
       • All shares were issued in the first year of operations.

Required
Using the information provided, answer the following questions.
1. What is the total amount of dividends that the preferred shareholders are entitled to receive per year?
2. Are there any dividends in arrears at December 31, 2010? If yes, calculate the dividends in arrears.
3. Calculate total dividends paid during 2011 to the:
   a. Preferred shareholders.
   b. Common shareholders.
4. During 2011, the company earned a net income of $340,000. Calculate the balance in the Retained Earnings account at the end of 2011.
5. Calculate Total Contributed Capital at the end of 2011.
6. Calculate Total Shareholders' Equity at December 31, 2011.
7. How many more preferred shares are available for issue at December 31, 2011?
8. What was the average issue price per share of the preferred shares at December 31, 2011?

The outstanding share capital of Prestige Sales Corporation includes 47,000 shares of $8 cumulative preferred and 82,000 common shares, all issued during the first year of operations. During its first four years of operation, the corporation declared and paid the following amounts in dividends:

Year	Total Dividends Declared
2011	$ -0-
2012	400,000
2013	840,000
2014	400,000

Determine the total dividends paid in each year to each class of shareholders. Also determine the total dividends paid to each class over the four years.

Determine the total dividends paid in each year to each class of shareholders of Exercise 15-10 under the assumption that the preferred shares are non-cumulative. Also determine the total dividends paid to each class over the four years.

Exercise 15-12
Identifying characteristics of preferred shares
LO5

Match each of the numbered descriptions with the characteristic of preferred shares that it best describes. Indicate your answer by writing the letter for the correct characteristic in the blank space next to each description.

A. Callable or redeemable   D. Non-cumulative
B. Convertible   E. Non-participating
C. Cumulative   F. Participating

_____ 1. The holders of the shares can exchange them for common shares.
_____ 2. The issuing corporation can retire the shares by paying a prearranged price.
_____ 3. The holders of the shares are entitled to receive dividends in excess of the stated rate under some conditions.
_____ 4. The holders of the shares are not entitled to receive dividends in excess of the stated rate.
_____ 5. The holders of the shares lose any dividends that are not declared.
_____ 6. The holders of the shares are entitled to receive current and all past dividends before common shareholders receive any dividends.

Exercise 15-13
Dividend allocation
LO5

Almarat Trading Corporation has the following outstanding shares:

15,000 shares, $4.50 cumulative preferred
35,000 shares, common

During 2011, Almarat declared and paid $150,000 in dividends. Dividends were in arrears for the previous year (2010) only. No new shares have been issued since the first year of operations.

Required
1. What was the total amount paid to the preferred shareholders as dividends in 2011?
2. What was the total amount paid to the common shareholders as dividends in 2011?

Exercise 15-14
Closing entries for a corporation
LO6

Gildan Corp. showed the following alphabetized list of adjusted account balances at December 31, 2011:

Accounts Payable	18,400	Income Tax Expense	29,000
Accounts Receivable	28,000	Land	84,000
Accum. Amort., Equip.	7,600	Notes Payable, due in 2014	24,000
Accum. Amort., Warehouse	15,200	Operating Expenses	78,000
Cash	6,000	Preferred Shares	28,000
Cash Dividends	14,000	Retained Earnings	19,800
Common Shares	80,000	Revenue	194,000
Equipment	56,000	Warehouse	92,000

Check figure:
Retained earnings,
Dec. 31/11 = $92,800

Required
Assuming normal balances, prepare the closing entries at December 31, 2011, Gildan's year-end. Also, calculate the post-closing balance in Retained Earnings at December 31, 2011.

Exercise 15-15
Analysis of shareholders' equity
LO1, 2, 3, 4, 5, 6

Check figure:
Total assets = $243,200

Using the information in Exercise 15-14, prepare a classified balance sheet at December 31, 2011, and then answer each of the following questions (assume that the preferred shares are non-cumulative):
1. What percentage of the total assets is owned by the shareholders?
2. What percentage of Gildan Corp. is equity financed?
3. What percentage of Gildan Corp. is financed by debt?
4. The common shareholders own what percentage of the total assets?
5. What percentage of the assets is financed by the preferred shareholders?
6. What are the advantages to the common shareholders of issuing preferred shares over additional common shares?

The shareholders' equity section of the balance sheet for TGIF Inc. showed the following on December 31, 2010:

Exercise 15-16
Share transactions, distribution of dividends, shareholders' equity, closing
LO1, 2, 3, 4, 5, 6

TGIF Inc.
Shareholders' Equity
December 31, 2010

Contributed capital:

Preferred shares, $0.25 cumulative; 80,000 shares authorized; 60,000 shares issued and outstanding	$150,000
Common shares; 250,000 shares authorized; 120,000 shares issued and outstanding	120,000
Total contributed capital	$270,000
Retained earnings	92,500
Total shareholders' equity	$362,500

During the year 2011, TGIF Inc. had the following transactions affecting shareholders' equity accounts:

Jan.	3	Sold 20,000 common shares for a total of $21,500 cash
Mar.	1	Sold 5,000 preferred shares at $3.00 each; cash.
June	15	Exchanged 7,000 common shares for equipment with a fair market value of $10,000. The last common share trade was dated March 15 at $3.05.
Dec.	31	Closed the Income Summary account, which showed a credit balance of $175,000.

The board of directors had not declared dividends for the past two years (2010 and 2011).

Required
1. Journalize the above transactions.
2. Prepare the shareholders' equity section as at December 31, 2011.
3. How many preferred shares are available for issue at December 31, 2011?
4. How many common shares are available for issue at December 31, 2011?

Check figure:
2. Total shareholders' equity = $584,000

ABC Inc. began a very lucrative consulting operation on October 1, 2011. It is authorized to issue 100,000 shares of $0.50 cumulative preferred shares and 500,000 common shares.

Exercise 15-17
Share transactions, dividend distribution, balance sheet, closing
LO2, 3, 4, 5, 6

Part A

Required
Prepare journal entries for each of the transactions listed.

Oct.	1	Issued for cash, 1,000 shares of the preferred shares at $4.00 each.
	10	Issued for cash, 50,000 shares of the common stock at $3.00 per share.
	12	The accountant responsible for organizing the corporation accepted 2,500 preferred shares in exchange for her services valued at $11,250.
	15	ABC Inc. purchased land for $155,000, paying cash of $55,000 and borrowing the balance from the bank (to be repaid in two years).
	20	15,000 preferred shares were issued today for total cash proceeds of $70,500.
	24	In addition to the declaration of the annual dividend on the preferred shares, dividends of $22,400 were declared on the common shares today, payable November 15, 2011.
	31	Revenues of $750,000 were earned during the month; all cash. Expenses, all cash, totalling $250,000 were incurred in October. Close the Income Summary and dividend accounts.

Part B

Required
Based on the transactions in Part A, prepare the balance sheet as at October 31, 2011.

Check figure:
B. Total assets = $835,750; Total shareholders' equity = $704,100

*Exercise 15-18
Book value per share
LO⁷

Check figures:
a. Book value of common shares = $32.13
b. Book value of common shares = $31.00

Oma Corp. Shareholders' Equity December 31, 2011		
Contributed capital:		
Preferred shares, $3.00 cumulative, $60 call price, 5,000 shares issued and outstanding		$ 250,000
Common shares, 40,000 shares issued and outstanding		800,000
Total contributed capital		$1,050,000
Retained earnings		535,000
Total shareholders' equity		$1,585,000

Using the information above, calculate the book value per share of the preferred and common shares under these two situations:
a. No preferred dividends are in arrears.
b. Three years of preferred dividends are in arrears.

Problems

Problem 15-1A
Corporate balance sheet preparation
LO²

Required
Using the information from the alphabetized post-closing trial balance below, prepare a classified balance sheet for Southgate Inc. as at March 31, 2011. *Be sure to use proper form, including all appropriate subtotals.*

Account Description	Account Balance*
Accounts payable	$ 17,000
Accounts receivable	56,000
Accumulated amortization, equipment	124,000
Accumulated amortization, franchise	42,000
Accumulated amortization, vehicles	52,000
Advertising payable	2,500
Allowance for doubtful accounts	3,000
Cash	24,000
Common shares, 100,000 shares authorized; 25,000 shares were issued at an average price of $8; market price per share on March 31, 2011, was $9	?
Equipment	390,000
Franchise	96,000
Income tax payable	46,000
Notes payable**	120,000
Prepaid rent	46,000
Retained earnings	?
Unearned revenues	23,000
Vehicles	68,000

*Assume that all accounts have normal balances.
**$50,000 of the notes payable will be paid by March 31, 2012.

Check figure:
Total assets = $459,000

Analysis component:
1. What percent of assets are financed by debt?
2. What percent of assets are financed by equity?
3. Assuming that 37% of Southgate's assets were financed by debt at March 31, 2010, has the balance sheet been strengthened over the current year? *Note: When a balance sheet is said to have been* strengthened, *it means, in general, that total liabilities (or risk associated with debt financing) have decreased and shareholders' equity has increased.*

An asterisk (*) identifies assignment material based on Appendix 15A.

The equity sections from the 2011 and 2012 balance sheets of Chum Corporation appeared as follows:

Problem 15-2A
Retained earnings, dividends
LO2, 4

Chum Corporation
Shareholders' Equity
December 31, 2011

Contributed capital:

Common shares, unlimited shares authorized,
  96,000 shares issued and outstanding $1,376,000

Retained earnings 1,117,216

Total shareholders' equity $2,493,216

Chum Corporation
Shareholders' Equity
December 31, 2012

Contributed capital:

Common shares, unlimited shares authorized,
  115,200 shares issued and outstanding $1,667,840

Retained earnings 919,200

Total shareholders' equity $2,587,040

On March 16, June 15, September 5, and again on November 22, 2012, the board of directors declared $0.40 per share cash dividends on the outstanding common shares. On October 14, 2012, 19,200 additional common shares were issued.

Required
Under the assumption that there were no transactions affecting retained earnings other than the ones given, determine the 2012 net income (net loss) of Chum Corporation. Show your calculations.

Problem 15-3A
Convertible preferred shares
LO4, 5

Wild Corp.
Shareholders' Equity
March 31, 2011

Contributed capital:

Preferred shares, $16 cumulative, 2,500 shares
  authorized, issued and outstanding .... $ 500,000

Common shares, unlimited shares authorized,
  40,000 shares issued and outstanding 800,000

Total contributed capital $1,300,000

Retained earnings 385,000

Total shareholders' equity $1,685,000

Required
Refer to the shareholders' equity section above. Assume that the preferred are convertible into common at a rate of eight common shares for each share of preferred. If 1,000 shares of the preferred are converted into common on April 1, 2011, prepare the entry and describe how this affects the shareholders' equity section of the balance sheet (immediately after the conversion).

Analysis component:
If you are a common shareholder in this company, and the company plans to pay total cash dividends of $600,000, does it make any difference to you whether or not the conversion takes place before the dividend declaration? Why?

Problem 15-4A
Analyzing shareholders' equity,
dividend allocation
LO2, 5

Use the information provided below to answer the following questions.

Northstar Corp.
Partial Balance Sheet
October 31, 2011

Shareholders' Equity

Contributed capital:

Preferred shares, $2.50 non-cumulative; unlimited shares authorized,

 A shares issued and outstanding .... $ 450,000

Common shares, unlimited shares authorized,

325,000 shares issued and outstanding .... B

Total contributed capital... C

Deficit... D

Total shareholders' equity $2,890,000

Other information:
- All of the shares were issued during the first year of operations (year ended October 31, 2010).
- The common shares were issued for an average price of $8 per share.
- The preferred shares were issued for an average price of $15 per share.
- Retained Earnings at October 31, 2010, was $320,000. No dividends had been paid for the year ended October 31, 2011.

Required
1. Calculate A.
2. Calculate B.
3. Calculate C.
4. Calculate D.
5. Calculate Net Income (Net Loss) for the year ended October 31, 2011.
6. Assume cash dividends of $100,000 were paid during the year ended October 31, 2010. Calculate the total dividends actually paid during the year ended October 31, 2010 to the:
   a. preferred shareholders.
   b. common shareholders.
7. Referring to your answers in Part 6 above, calculate the dividends *per share* actually received by the:
   a. preferred shareholders.
   b. common shareholders.
8. Are there any dividends in arrears as at October 31, 2011? If yes, calculate the amount of the arrears.
9. Explain the difference between "Retained Earnings" and "Deficit."
10. Explain the difference between "dividends in arrears" and "dividends payable."

Problem 15-5A
Dividend allocation
LO5

Island Corp. has the following shares, taken from the shareholders' equity section of its balance sheet dated December 31, 2011.

Preferred shares, $5.60 non-cumulative,

45,000 shares authorized and issued*.. 3,600,000

Common shares,

80,000 shares authorized and issued*.. 1,600,000

*All shares were issued during 2009.

During its first three years of operations, Island Corp. declared and paid total dividends as shown in the last column of the following schedule.

Required

Part A

Complete the following schedule by filling in the shaded areas.

1. Calculate the total dividends paid in each year to the preferred and to the common shareholders.

Year	Preferred Dividend	Common Dividend	Total Dividend
2009			200,000
2010			500,000
2011			700,000
Total for three years			1,400,000

2. Calculate the dividends paid *per share* to both the preferred and the common shares in 2011.

Part B

Repeat the requirements in Part A assuming the preferred shares are cumulative.

Analysis component:

Which shares would have a greater market value: cumulative or non-cumulative? Explain.

The balance sheet for the Clarke Corporation reported the following components of shareholders' equity on December 31, 2011:

Common shares, unlimited shares authorized, 20,000 shares issued and outstanding......	$460,000
Retained earnings......	270,000
Total shareholders' equity......	$730,000

Problem 15-6A
Share transactions, dividends, statement of retained earnings, shareholders' equity
LO2, 3, 4, 5, 6

In 2012, Clarke Corporation had the following transactions affecting shareholders and the shareholder equity accounts:

Jan.	5	The directors declared a $4.00 per share cash dividend payable on Feb. 28 to the Feb. 5 shareholders of record.
Feb.	28	Paid the dividend declared on January 5.
July	6	Sold 750 common shares at $48 per share.
Aug.	22	Sold 1,250 common shares at $34 per share.
Sept.	5	The directors declared a $4.00 per share cash dividend payable on Oct. 28 to the Oct. 5 shareholders of record.
Oct.	28	Paid the dividend declared on September 5.
Dec.	31	Closed the $434,000 credit balance in the Income Summary account.
	31	Closed the Cash Dividends account.

Required

1. Prepare journal entries to record the transactions and closings for 2012.
2. Prepare a statement of retained earnings for the year ended December 31, 2012.
3. Prepare the shareholders' equity section of the corporation's balance sheet as of December 31, 2012.

Check figures:
2. Retained earnings, December 31/12 = $536,000
3. Total shareholders' equity = $1,074,500

Analysis component:

Explain the relationship between assets and retained earnings; use your answer in Part 3 above as part of the explanation.

Problem 15-7A
Share transactions, statement of retained earnings, shareholders' equity, dividend distribution, closing
LO2, 3, 4, 5, 6

Wrightson Corp. was legally incorporated on January 2, 2011. Its articles of incorporation granted it the right to issue an unlimited number of common shares and 100,000 shares of $12 non-cumulative preferred shares. The following transactions are among those that occurred during the first three years of operations:

2011

Jan.	12	Issued 40,000 common shares at $4 each.
	20	Issued 6,000 common shares to promoters who provided legal services that helped to establish the company. These services had a fair value of $30,000.
	31	Issued 80,000 common shares in exchange for land, building, and equipment, which have fair market values of $300,000, $400,000, and $40,000 respectively.
Mar.	4	Purchased equipment at a cost of $6,800 cash. This was thought to be a special bargain price. It was felt that at least $9,000 would normally have had to be paid to acquire this equipment.
Dec.	31	During 2011, Wrightson Corp. incurred a net loss of $80,000. The Income Summary account was closed.

2012

Jan.	4	Issued 5,000 preferred shares at $60 per share.
Dec.	31	The Income Summary account was closed. Net income for 2012 was $180,000.

2013

Dec.	4	The company declared a cash dividend of $0.10 per share on the common shares payable on December 18 and also declared the required dividend on the preferred shares.
	18	Paid the dividends declared on December 4.
	31	Net income for the year ended December 31, 2013, was $160,000. The Income Summary and Cash Dividends accounts were closed.

Check figures:
2. Retained earnings,
Dec. 31/13 = $187,400
3. Total shareholders'
equity = $1,417,400

Required
1. Journalize the transactions for the years 2011, 2012, and 2013.
2. Prepare the statement of retained earnings for the year ended December 31, 2013.
3. Prepare the shareholders' equity section as of December 31, 2013.

Analysis component:
Determine the net assets of Wrightson Corp. for 2011, 2012, and 2013. Is the trend favourable or unfavourable? Explain.

Problem 15-8A
Share transactions, dividends, statement of retained earnings, shareholders' equity
LO2, 3, 4, 5, 6

The balance sheet for the Techno Corporation, provincially incorporated in 2009, reported the following components of shareholders' equity on December 31, 2010.

Techno Corporation
Shareholders' Equity
December 31, 2010

Contributed capital:	
Preferred shares, $1.50 cumulative, unlimited shares authorized; 20,000 shares issued and outstanding	$ 280,000
Common shares, unlimited shares authorized; 75,000 shares issued and outstanding.	525,000
Total contributed capital	$ 805,000
Retained earnings	270,000
Total shareholders' equity	$1,075,000

In 2011 and 2012, Techno Corporation had the following transactions affecting shareholders and the shareholder equity accounts:

2011		
Jan.	1	Sold 30,000 common shares at $7.60 per share.
	5	The directors declared a total cash dividend of $165,000 payable on Feb. 28 to the Feb. 5 shareholders of record. Dividends had not been declared for the years 2009 and 2010. All of the preferred shares had been issued during 2009.
Feb.	28	Paid the dividends declared on January 5.
July	1	Sold preferred shares for a total of $112,000. The average issue price was $16 per share.
Dec.	31	Closed the dividend accounts along with the $412,000 credit balance in the Income Summary account.
2012		
Sept.	5	The directors declared the required cash dividend on the preferred shares and a $1.00 per common share cash dividend payable on Oct. 28 to the Oct. 5 shareholders of record.
Oct.	28	Paid the dividends declared on September 5.
Dec.	31	Closed the Cash Dividends account along with the $388,000 credit balance in the Income Summary account.

Required

1. Prepare journal entries to record the transactions and closings for 2011 and 2012.
2. Prepare a statement of retained earnings for the year ended December 31, 2012.
3. Prepare the shareholders' equity section of the company's balance sheet as of December 31, 2012.

Check figures:
2. Retained earnings, Dec. 31/12 = $759,500
3. Shareholders' equity, Dec. 31/12 = $1,904,500

Ryniak Corporation's common shares are currently selling on a stock exchange at $85 per share, and a recent balance sheet shows the following information:

*Problem 15-9A
Book value per share
LO7

Ryniak Corporation
Shareholders' Equity
April 30, 2011

Contributed capital:	
Preferred shares, $2.50 cumulative, 1,000 shares authorized, issued and outstanding	$ 50,000
Common shares, 4,000 shares authorized, issued, and outstanding	80,000
Total contributed capital	$130,000
Retained earnings...	150,000
Total shareholders' equity	$280,000

Required

Preparation component:

1. What is the market value of the corporation's common shares?
2. How much capital was contributed by the residual owners of the company?
3. If no dividends are in arrears, what are the book values per share of the preferred shares and the common shares?
4. If two years' preferred dividends are in arrears, what are the book values per share of the preferred shares and the common shares?
5. If two years' preferred dividends are in arrears and the preferred shares are callable at $55 per share, what are the book values per share of the preferred shares and the common shares?
6. If two years' preferred dividends are in arrears and the board of directors declares dividends of $10,000, what total amount will be paid to preferred and common shareholders? What is the amount of dividends per share for the common shares?

Analysis component:
What are some factors that may contribute to the difference between the book value of common shares and their market value?

Check figures:
3. Book value per common share = $57.50
4. Book value per common share = $56.25
5. Book value per common share = $55.00

An asterisk (*) identifies assignment material based on Appendix 15A.

*Problem 15-10A
Calculating book value
LO7

On December 31, 2011, Monnex Inc. showed the following:

Monnex Inc. Shareholders' Equity December 31, 2011		
Contributed capital:		
Preferred shares, $4, unlimited shares authorized, 10,000 shares issued and outstanding*		$ 220,000
Common shares, unlimited shares authorized, 25,000 shares issued and outstanding*		325,000
Total contributed capital		$ 545,000
Retained earnings		680,000
Total shareholders' equity		$1,225,000

*All of the shares had been issued early in 2010.

Check figures:
Book value per common
a. $37.00
c. $40.20
e. $33.80

Required

Part 1:
Calculate book value per common share and preferred share at December 31, 2011, assuming no dividends were declared for the years ended December 31, 2010 or 2011, and that the preferred shares are:
a. Cumulative,
b. Non-cumulative.

Part 2 (independent of Part 1):
Calculate book value per common share and preferred share at December 31, 2011, assuming total dividends of $65,000 were declared and paid in each of the years ended December 31, 2010 and 2011, and that the preferred shares are:
c. Cumulative,
d. Non-cumulative.

Part 3 (independent of Parts 1 and 2):
e. Calculate book value per common share and preferred share at December 31, 2011, assuming:
- Preferred shares are cumulative, and callable at $30 per share, and
- Dividends were not declared for the years ended December 31, 2010 and 2011.

Alternate Problems

Problem 15-1B
Corporate balance sheet
preparation
LO2

Using the information from the alphabetized post-closing trial balance below, prepare a classified balance sheet for JenStar Inc. as at October 31, 2011. Be sure to use proper form, including all appropriate subtotals.

Check figures:
Total assets = $4,561,000;
Total shareholders'
equity = $3,695,000

Account Description	Account Balance*
Accounts Payable	$ 158,000
Accounts Receivable	225,000
Accumulated Amortization—Building	833,000
Accumulated Amortization—Machinery	763,000
Building	2,875,000
Cash	355,000
Common shares (unlimited shares authorized; 50,000 shares issued at an average price of $32 per share; market price per share on October 31, 2011, $57)	?
Land	1,000,000
Long-Term Notes Payable (due in 2015)	550,000
Machinery	1,600,000
Office Supplies	85,000
Preferred Shares ($1.50 non-cumulative, unlimited shares authorized; 30,000 shares issued at an average price of $40 per share; market price per share on October 31, 2011, $60)	?
Prepaid Insurance	17,000
Retained Earnings	?
Unearned Fees	28,000
Wages Payable	130,000

*Assume all accounts have normal balances.

The equity sections from the 2011 and 2012 balance sheets of Henns Corporation appeared as follows:

Problem 15-2B
Retained earnings, dividends
LO2, 4

Henns Corporation
Shareholders' Equity
December 31, 2011

Contributed capital:	
Common shares, unlimited shares authorized, 350,000 shares issued	$ 8,750,000
Retained earnings	1,960,720
Total shareholders' equity	$10,710,720

Henns Corporation
Shareholders' Equity
December 31, 2012

Contributed capital:	
Common shares, unlimited shares authorized, 385,000 shares issued	$ 9,660,000
Retained earnings	2,200,500
Total shareholders' equity	$11,860,500

On February 11, May 24, August 13, and again on December 12, 2012, the board of directors declared $0.25 per share cash dividends on the outstanding shares. 15,000 common shares were issued on August 1, 2012, and another 20,000 were issued on November 2, 2012.

Required
Under the assumption that there were no transactions affecting retained earnings other than the ones given, determine the 2012 net income of Henns Corporation. Show your calculations.

Problem 15-3B
Convertible preferred shares
LO4, 5

Sembaluk Corp.
Shareholders' Equity
November 30, 2011

Contributed capital:		
Preferred shares, $11 cumulative, 2,000 shares authorized and issued		$ 200,000
Common shares, unlimited shares authorized; 60,000 shares issued		600,000
Total contributed capital		$ 800,000
Retained earnings		420,000
Total shareholders' equity		$1,220,000

Required
Refer to the shareholders' equity section above. Assume that the preferred shares are convertible into common at a rate of eight common shares for each share of preferred. If 1,000 shares of the preferred are converted into common shares on December 1, 2011, prepare the entry and describe how this affects the shareholders' equity section of the balance sheet (immediately after the conversion).

Analysis component:
If you are a common shareholder in this company, and it plans to pay total cash dividends of $487,000, does it make a difference to you whether or not the conversion takes place before the dividend declaration? Why?

Problem 15-4B
Analyzing shareholders' equity,
dividend allocation
LO2, 5

JenCo Inc.
Partial Balance Sheet
October 31, 2011

Shareholders' Equity

Contributed capital:

Preferred shares, $8 cumulative, unlimited shares authorized,
45,000 shares issued and outstanding.. | A |

Preferred shares, $5 non-cumulative, unlimited shares authorized,
| B | shares issued and outstanding:... 3,800,000

Common shares, unlimited shares authorized,
265,000 shares issued and outstanding.. | C |

Total contributed capital... | D |

Retained earnings... | E |

Total shareholders' equity .... | F |

Required
1. Calculate *A* assuming an average issue price of $20 per share.
2. Calculate *B* assuming an average issue price of $100 per share.
3. Calculate *C* assuming the average issue price was $5 per share.
4. Calculate *D*.
5. Calculate *E* assuming that JenCo Inc. showed net incomes (losses) for the years ended October 31, 2008, 2009, 2010, and 2011, of $2,500,000, $1,750,000, $1,300,000, and ($2,200,000) respectively. Dividends totalling $1,200,000 were declared and paid during the first year ended October 31, 2008. No other dividends have been declared to date.
6. Calculate *F*.
7. Calculate any dividends in arrears as at October 31, 2011 (all of the shares were issued early in 2008).

Problem 15-5B
Dividend allocation
LO5

XYZ Corporation has issued and outstanding a total of 40,000 shares of $12 preferred shares and 120,000 of common shares. The company began operations and issued both classes of shares on January 1, 2010.

Required
1. Calculate the total dividends to be paid to each group of shareholders in each year by completing the following chart. Assume that the preferred shares are cumulative.

Year	Dividends Declared and Paid	Preferred Dividends	Common Dividends
2010	600,000		
2011	100,000		
2012	250,000		
2013	1,500,000		

2. Calculate the total dividends to be paid to each group of shareholders in each year by completing the following chart. Assume that the preferred shares are non-cumulative.

Year	Dividends Declared and Paid	Preferred Dividends	Common Dividends
2010	600,000		
2011	100,000		
2012	250,000		
2013	1,500,000		

The balance sheet for Caldwell Corp. reported the following components of shareholders' equity on December 31, 2011:

Common shares, unlimited shares authorized, 100,000 shares issued and outstanding	$ 800,000
Retained earnings	1,080,000
Total shareholders' equity	$1,880,000

Problem 15-6B
Share transactions, statement of retained earnings, shareholders' equity, dividend distribution, closing
LO2, 3, 4, 5, 6

The company completed these transactions during 2012:

Mar.	2	The directors declared a $1.50 per share cash dividend payable on March 31 to the March 15 shareholders of record.
	31	Paid the dividend declared on March 2.
Nov.	11	Issued 12,000 common shares at $13 per share.
	25	Issued 8,000 common shares at $9.50 per share.
Dec.	1	The directors declared a $2.50 per share cash dividend payable on January 2, 2013, to the December 10 shareholders of record.
	31	Closed the $536,000 credit balance in the Income Summary account to Retained Earnings.
	31	Closed the Cash Dividends account.

Required
1. Prepare General Journal entries to record the transactions and closings for 2012.
2. Prepare a statement of retained earnings for the year ended December 31, 2012.
3. Prepare the shareholders' equity section of the company's balance sheet as of December 31, 2012.

Analysis component:
How much of Caldwell's assets are financed by the common shareholders at December 31, 2012? Explain what other sources of financing are available.

Check figures:
2. Retained earnings, December 31 = $1,166,000
3. Total shareholders' equity = $2,198,000

Solar Energy Company Inc. is authorized to issue an unlimited number of common shares and 100,000 shares of $10 non-cumulative preferred. The company completed the following transactions:

Problem 15-7B
Share transactions, statement of retained earnings, shareholders' equity, dividend distribution, closing
LO2, 3, 4, 5, 6

2011			
Feb.	5	Issued 70,000 common shares at $10 for cash.	
	28	Gave the corporation's promoters 3,750 common shares for their services in organizing the corporation. The directors valued the services at $40,000.	
Mar.	3	Issued 44,000 common shares in exchange for the following assets with the indicated reliable market values: land, $80,000; buildings, $210,000; and machinery, $155,000.	
Dec.	31	Closed the Income Summary account. A $27,000 loss was incurred.	
2012			
Jan.	28	Issued for cash 4,000 preferred shares at $100 per share.	
Dec.	31	Closed the Income Summary account. A $98,000 net income was earned.	
2013			
Jan.	1	The board of directors declared a $10 per share cash dividend to preferred shares and $0.20 per share cash dividend to outstanding common shares, payable on February 5 to the January 24 shareholders of record.	
Feb.	5	Paid the previously declared dividends.	
Dec.	31	Closed the Cash Dividends and Income Summary accounts. A $159,000 net income was earned.	

Required
1. Prepare General Journal entries to record the transactions.
2. Prepare a statement of retained earnings for the year ended December 31, 2013.
3. Prepare the shareholders' equity section of the balance sheet as of the close of business on December 31, 2013.

Analysis component:
Calculate the net assets of Solar Energy for 2011, 2012, and 2013. Is the trend favourable or unfavourable? Explain.

Check figures:
2. Retained earnings, December 31 = $166,450
3. Total shareholders' equity = $1,751,450

Problem 15-8B
Share transactions, dividends, statement of retained earnings, shareholders' equity
LO2, 3, 4, 5, 6

Francois Corp. began operations in 2010. Its balance sheet reported the following components of shareholders' equity on December 31, 2010:

Francois Corp.
Shareholders' Equity
December 31, 2010

Contributed capital:

Preferred shares, $0.75 non-cumulative, unlimited shares authorized; 100,000 shares issued and outstanding....................................	$1,300,000
Common shares, unlimited shares authorized; 650,000 shares issued and outstanding...	2,925,000
Total contributed capital	$4,225,000
Retained earnings..	1,135,000
Total shareholders' equity..	$5,360,000

The corporation completed these transactions during 2011 and 2012:

2011

Jan.	1	Sold 130,000 common shares at $4.75 per share.
	5	The directors declared the first cash dividend totalling $270,000 payable on Feb. 28 to the Feb. 5 shareholders of record.
Feb.	28	Paid the dividends declared on January 5.
July	1	Issued preferred shares for a total of $675,000. The average issue price was $13.50 per share.
Dec.	31	Closed the dividend accounts along with the Income Summary account, which reflected net income earned during 2011 of $320,000.

2012

Sept.	5	The directors declared a $0.75 cash dividend per preferred share and a $0.25 per common share cash dividend payable on Oct. 28 to the Oct. 5 shareholders of record.
Oct.	28	Paid the dividends declared on September 5.
Dec.	31	Closed the dividend accounts along with the $480,000 debit balance in the Income Summary account.

Check figures:
2. Retained earnings, Dec. 31/12 = $397,500
3. Shareholders' equity, Dec. 31/12 = $5,915,000

Required

1. Prepare journal entries to record the transactions and closings for 2011 and 2012.
2. Prepare the statement of retained earnings for the year ended December 31, 2012.
3. Prepare the shareholders' equity section of the company's balance sheet as of December 31, 2012.

*Problem 15-9B
Book value per share
LO7

The balance sheet of Global Filter Company Ltd. at November 30, 2011, includes the following information:

Global Filter Company Ltd.
Shareholders' Equity
November 30, 2011

Contributed capital:

Preferred shares, $11 cumulative, 2,000 shares authorized and issued	$200,000
Common shares, 60,000 shares authorized and issued...................................	600,000
Total contributed capital	$800,000
Retained earnings..	120,000
Total shareholders' equity..	$920,000

An asterisk (*) identifies assignment material based on Appendix 15A.

Required

Assume that the preferred shares have a call price of $106. Calculate the book value per share of the preferred and common under each of the following assumptions:

a. No dividends are in arrears on the preferred shares.
b. One year's dividends are in arrears on the preferred shares.
c. Three years' dividends are in arrears on the preferred shares.

Check figures:
a. Book value per common
share = $11.80
b. Book value per common
share = $11.43
c. Book value per common
share = $10.70

On December 31, 2011, Abbotsfield Corp. showed the following:

*Problem 15-10B
Calculating book value
LO7

> **Abbotsfield Corp.**
> **Shareholders' Equity**
> **December 31, 2011**
>
> Contributed capital:
>
> Preferred shares, $0.75, unlimited shares authorized,
>   50,000 shares issued and outstanding* $400,000
>
> Common shares, unlimited shares authorized,
>   125,000 shares issued and outstanding* 525,000
>
> Total contributed capital .... $ 925,000
> Retained earnings.. 875,000
> Total shareholders' equity.. $1,800,000

*All of the shares had been issued early in 2010.

Required

Part 1:

Calculate book value per common share and preferred share at December 31, 2011, assuming no dividends were declared for the years ended December 31, 2010 or 2011, and that the preferred shares are:

a. Cumulative,   **b.** Non-cumulative.

Check figures:
Book value per common share
a. $10.60
c. $11.00
e. $9.60

Part 2 (independent of Part 1):

Assume no dividends were declared for the year ended December 31, 2010, and total dividends of $50,000 were declared and paid for the year ended December 31, 2011. Calculate book value per common share and preferred share at December 31, 2011, if preferred shares are:

c. Cumulative,   **d.** Non-cumulative.

Part 3 (independent of Parts 1 and 2):

e. Calculate book value per common share and preferred share at December 31, 2011, assuming:
  − Preferred shares are cumulative and callable at $12 per share, and
  − there were no dividends in arrears.

Analytical and Review Problems

Fargo Inc. showed the following income statement information for its first three years of operation:

A & R 15-1

	For the Years Ended December 31		
	2012	2011	2010
Net Sales	$5,000,000	$4,000,000	$3,000,000
Cost of Goods Sold.................................	3,000,000	2,400,000	1,650,000
Operating Expenses................................	1,400,000	1,300,000	900,000
Other Revenues (Expenses).....................	(200,000)	(220,000)	50,000
Income Tax Expense...............................	80,000	16,000	100,000

An asterisk (*) identifies assignment material based on Appendix 15A.

Partial information regarding Fargo's shareholders' equity for the past three years follows:

	Dec. 31 2012	Dec. 31 2011	Dec. 31 2010
Contributed capital:			
Preferred shares, $2 non-cumulative; 100,000 shares authorized; 20,000* shares issued and outstanding	$400,000	$400,000	$400,000
Common shares, 500,000 shares authorized; 100,000* shares issued and outstanding	550,000	550,000	550,000
Total contributed capital................................	?	?	?
Retained earnings**	?	?	?
Total shareholders' equity	?	?	?

*Issued on January 1, 2010
**Cash dividends of $100,000 were declared and paid for the year ended Dec. 31, 2010. Dividends
  were not declared for the years ended Dec. 31, 2011, or Dec. 31, 2012.

Required
1. Calculate Gross Profit, Operating Income, Income Before Tax, and Net Income for the years ended December 31, 2010, 2011, and 2012.
2. Calculate Contributed Capital as at December 31, 2010, 2011, and 2012.
3. Calculate Retained Earnings as at December 31, 2010, 2011, and 2012.
4. Calculate Total Shareholders' Equity as at December 31, 2010, 2011, and 2012.

Analysis component:
Assume total liabilities in 2012, 2011, and 2010 were $1,123,200, $936,000, and $900,000, respectively. Identify whether the balance sheet has been strengthened from 2010 to 2012. Explain what this means.

Ethics Challenge

EC 15-1

Jack and Bill are partners in a computer software company. They developed a word processing program that is remarkably similar to a Corel product. Jack telephones Bill at home one evening and says, "We should convert our partnership into a corporation before we launch this new word processing software. Let's withdraw most of our assets from the business before forming a corporate entity. If we are sued by Corel, our liability will be limited to our business assets." Bill feels a little uneasy and replies, "Let's meet at 9 A.M. sharp to discuss this matter."

Focus on Financial Statements

FFS 15-1

Barry Bowtie incorporated his business under the name BowTie Fishing Expeditions Corp. on March 1, 2011. It was authorized to issue 30,000 $2 cumulative preferred shares and an unlimited number of common shares. During March, the following shareholders' equity transactions occurred:
a. 50,000 common shares were issued for cash of $3 per share.
b. 10,000 preferred shares were issued for $5,000 cash plus equipment with a fair market value of $37,000.
c. The corporation reported net income for the month of $190,000.
d. Total cash dividends of $45,000 were declared payable on April 15 to shareholders of record on March 31.

Required

Using the information provided in (a) through (d) plus the following March 31, 2011, selected account balances[1], prepare the statement of retained earnings for the month ended March 31, 2011, along with the March 31, 2011, balance sheet:

Accounts Payable	$17,000	Building	$148,600
Accounts Receivable	36,000	Cash	15,000
Accumulated Amortization,		Customer Deposits	28,000
Building	12,000	Equipment	140,000
Accumulated Amortization,		Estimated Warranty	
Equipment	2,000	Liabilities	3,400
Accumulated Amortization,		Furniture	75,000
Furniture	5,000	Land	105,000
Accumulated Amortization,		Notes Payable[2]	90,000
Patent	2,000	Patent	14,000
Allowance for Doubtful		Prepaid Rent	9,000
Accounts	1,200		

1. This list of accounts is incomplete; you will have to add several accounts based on the information provided in (a) through (d).
2. The note payable is due in principal installments of $30,000 beginning March 1, 2012.

Analysis component:

Use your financial statements prepared above to answer each of the following questions:
1. What percentage of the total assets is equity financed?
2. What percentage of the total assets are financed by debt?
3. Assume that 30% of BowTie Fishing (the previous proprietorship) was financed by debt at March 31, 2010. Has the risk associated with debt financing increased or decreased from 2010 to 2011? Explain.
4. The common shareholders own what percentage of the total assets?
5. What percentage of the assets is financed by the preferred shareholders?

Refer to the financial statements and notes to the financial statements for Danier Leather on pages I-1 to I-16 in Appendix I at the end of the textbook.

FFS 15-2

Required
1. How many shares were issued as of June 25, 2005, regarding the paid-in amount of $22,493 (thousand)?
2. **a.** What were the total dividends declared during 2005?
   b. Were all of the dividends declared in 2005 paid in 2005? Explain.
   c. What are dividends?
3. Danier reported a net loss of $185 (thousand) for the year ended June 25, 2005. What effect does a net loss have on equity? Explain.

Critical Thinking Mini Case

Jones Inc. needs $100,000 to finance the purchase of new equipment. The finance manager is considering two options:
1. Borrowing the funds over a five-year term and paying interest at the rate of 6% per year, or
2. Issuing 6,000 shares of $1 cumulative preferred shares.
The equipment is estimated to have a life of five years and no residual value. Income before interest expense and tax is expected to be $80,000. The tax rate is assumed to be 25%.

Required
Using the elements of critical thinking described on the inside front cover, respond.

CHAPTER 16

Corporate Reporting: Income, Earnings Per Share, and Retained Earnings

Strategic Buybacks

Cognos, with its head office in Ottawa, is a world leader in the creation of business software applications. The company has over 3,400 employees and serves more than 23,000 customers in over 135 countries. On October 6, 2005, Cognos announced that it would spend up to U.S.$100 million to repurchase and cancel up to 4 million common shares from October 10, 2005, to October 9, 2006. The company repurchased 1,154,000 shares for a total price of $42,735,000 during its fiscal year ended February 28, 2005. By buying back its shares, Cognos reduced its equity base so that profits were spread over fewer shares. That increased its return on equity and earnings per share, which are two key ratios used to determine a company's financial health and investment rating. In addition, share buybacks can lead to increases in share price since there are fewer shares on the market.

www.cognos.com

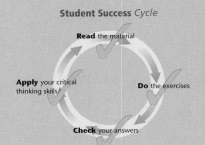

Student Success *Cycle*

Read the material

Do the exercises

Check your answers

Apply your critical
thinking skills

CRITICAL THINKING CHALLENGE

What factors, other than the repurchase of shares, cause basic earnings per share to increase or decrease?

---

learning objectives

LO¹ Describe and account for share dividends and share splits.

LO² Describe and account for retirement of shares.

LO³ Calculate earnings per share and describe its use.

LO⁴ Explain the form and content of a comprehensive corporate income statement.

LO⁵ Explain the items reported in retained earnings.

*APPENDIX 16A

*LO⁶ Record the purchase and reissue of treasury shares.

chapter preview

This chapter begins by describing share transactions that affect the calculation of an important ratio, earnings per share, that is included as part of the corporate income statement. Earnings per share is described in more detail in the third section of the chapter. Corporations constantly evaluate their performance and make decisions to keep pace with changes in their global marketplace. This ongoing process often results in activities that include income-related transactions that go beyond a company's continuing, normal operations. The income statement needs to provide useful information to help users understand both current and past transactions, and to predict future performance. The fourth section of this chapter focuses on the reporting of additional income information. The final section describes special issues regarding the statement of retained earnings. Understanding these topics helps us read, interpret, and use financial statements for decision making, and helps shareholders when they evaluate the performance of companies like Cognos as described in the opening article.

Additional Share Transactions

In order to discuss completely the earnings per share calculation explained later in this chapter, we need to understand share transactions that occur in addition to the issuance of those discussed in Chapter 15. These additional share transactions affect the calculation of earnings per share and include share dividends, share splits, and the retirement of shares. We describe share dividends and share splits in the next section. The retirement of shares is then discussed.

Share Dividends

In Chapter 15, we described cash dividends. However, a corporation's directors can also declare a **share dividend**, also called a *stock dividend*, in which a company distributes additional shares to its shareholders without receiving any payment in return. Share dividends and cash dividends are different: A share dividend does not reduce a corporation's assets and shareholders' equity, while a cash dividend reduces both. A share dividend simply transfers a portion of equity from retained earnings to contributed capital. This is sometimes described as *capitalizing* retained earnings because it increases a company's contributed capital.

> **LO1** Describe and account for share dividends and share splits.

For example, on July 26, 2005, Petro-Canada announced a 100% share dividend, distributable on September 14, 2005, to shareholders of record on September 3, 2005. The effect of this share dividend would double the number of common shares outstanding.

www.petro-canada.ca

Reasons for Share Dividends

If share dividends do not affect assets or total shareholders' equity, then why declare and distribute them? Reasons include the following:

1. Directors are said to use share dividends to keep the market price of the shares affordable. For example, if a profitable corporation grows but does not pay cash dividends, the price of its common shares continues to increase. The price of such shares may become so high that it discourages some investors from buying them. When a corporation declares a share dividend, it increases the number of outstanding shares and lowers the market price of its shares.

2. Issuing share dividends conserves cash for business expansion that might lead to positive returns on shareholder investment.

3. A share dividend provides evidence of management's confidence that the company is doing well.

Entries for Share Dividends

To illustrate share dividends, we use the shareholders' equity section of the balance sheet for X-Quest Ltd., shown in Exhibit 16.1, just *before* the company's declaration of a share dividend.

Exhibit 16.1

Shareholders' Equity Before the Share Dividend

X-Quest Ltd.
Shareholders' Equity
December 31, 2011

Contributed capital:	
Common shares, unlimited shares authorized, 10,000 shares issued and outstanding	$108,000
Retained earnings	35,000
Total shareholders' equity	$143,000

Let's assume the directors of X-Quest Ltd. declare a 10% share dividend on December 31, 2011. This share dividend of 1,000 shares, calculated as 10% of its 10,000 outstanding shares P. 743, is to be distributed on January 20 to the shareholders of record on January 15. The *Canada Business Corporations Act* requires that the value to be assigned to a share dividend be equal to the market value P. 137 of the shares on the date of declaration. Since the market price of X-Quest's shares on December 31 is $15 per share, the dividend declaration is recorded as:

Dec. 31	Share Dividends	15,000		*or*	Dec. 31	Retained Earnings	15,000	
	Common Share Dividends Distributable		15,000			Common Share Dividends Distributable		15,000
	To record declaration of a share dividend of 1,000 common shares.					*To record declaration of a share dividend of 1,000 common shares.*		

The debit is recorded in the temporary (contra equity) account called Share Dividends. This account serves the same purpose as the Cash Dividends account. As shown above, an alternative entry is to debit Retained Earnings directly to eliminate the need to close the Share Dividends account at the end of the accounting period. The $15,000 credit is an increase to a contributed capital account called Common Share Dividends Distributable. This account balance exists only until the shares are actually issued.

A share dividend is *never a liability* because shareholders will be given shares in the future; shareholders receiving a share dividend are *not* owed any assets. Share dividends affect equity accounts only. The shareholders' equity section of X-Quest's December 31, 2011, balance sheet immediately *after* the declaration of the share dividend appears in Exhibit 16.2.

Exhibit 16.2

Shareholders' Equity After
Declaring a Share Dividend

X-Quest Ltd.
Shareholders' Equity
December 31, 2011

Contributed capital:	
Common shares, unlimited shares authorized,	
10,000 shares issued and outstanding	$108,000
Common share dividends distributable, 1,000 shares	15,000
Total contributed capital..	$123,000
Retained earnings	20,000
Total shareholders' equity	$143,000

As part of the year-end closing process, X-Quest Ltd. closes the Share Dividends account to Retained Earnings with the following entry:

Dec. 31	Retained Earnings...	15,000	
	Share Dividends		15,000
	To close the Share Dividends account.		

Note that if Retained Earnings had been debited on the date of declaration instead of Share Dividends, the above closing entry would not be required. No entry is made on the date of record for a share dividend. On January 20, the date of distribution,[1] X-Quest distributes the new shares to shareholders and records this with the entry:

Jan. 20	Common Share Dividends Distributable.........	15,000	
	Common Shares		15,000
	To record distribution of a 1,000-share *common share dividend.*		

The combined effect of these two share dividend entries is to transfer (or capitalize) $15,000 of retained earnings to contributed capital. Share dividends have no effect on *total* shareholders' equity as shown in Exhibit 16.3. Nor do they affect the percent of the company owned by individual shareholders.

Exhibit 16.3

Shareholders' Equity Before
and After Distribution of
Share Dividend

X-Quest Ltd.
Shareholders' Equity

	Dec. 31, 2011, Before Declaration of Share Dividend	Jan. 20, 2012, After Declaration of Share Dividend
Contributed capital:		
Common shares, unlimited shares authorized,		
Dec. 31, 2011: 10,000 shares issued and outstanding......................................	$108,000	
Jan. 20, 2012: 11,000 shares issued and outstanding......................................		$123,000
Retained earnings...	35,000	20,000
Total shareholders' equity...............................	$143,000	$143,000

[1] For a share dividend, additional shares are issued (no cash is paid). Therefore, January 20 is referred to as the date of distribution and not the date of payment.

Share Splits

A **share split** is the distribution of additional shares to shareholders according to their percent ownership. When a share split occurs, the corporation calls in its out-standing shares and issues more than one new share in exchange for each old share.[2] Splits can be done in any ratio including two-for-one (expressed as 2:1), three-for-one (expressed as 3:1), or higher. There are no journal entries for a share split but note disclosure is required and should state the number of shares distributed. For example:

> Note 6: As a result of a two-for-one share split declared by the board of directors, the company issued an additional 200,000 common shares on July 1, 2011.

To illustrate the effect of a share split on shareholders' equity, assume the information in Exhibit 16.4 for CLT Inc. at December 31, 2011, immediately prior to the declaration of a share split. CLT Inc.'s board of directors declared a 3:1 share split on December 31, 2011, to be issued on January 4, 2012. Notice that the share split simply replaces the 20,000 shares issued on December 31, 2011, with 60,000 shares on January 4, 2012. A share split does not affect individual shareholders' percent ownership. The Contributed Capital and Retained Earnings accounts are unchanged by a split. The only effect of a share split on the accounts is a change in the number of common shares. However, the market will respond by reducing the market value of the shares in proportion to the share split. For example, if CLT Inc.'s shares were trading on December 31, 2011, for $21 per share, the market value would be reduced to about $7 ($21 ÷ 3) per share after the share split.

Exhibit 16.4

Shareholders' Equity for CLT Inc. Before and After Share Split

	CLT Inc. Shareholders' Equity	
	Dec. 31, 2011 **Before Share Split**	**Jan. 4, 2012** **After Share Split**
Contributed capital:		
Common shares, unlimited shares authorized,		
Dec. 31, 2011: 20,000 shares issued and outstanding.....................................	$240,000	
Jan. 4, 2012: 60,000 shares issued and outstanding.....................................		$240,000
Retained earnings..	90,000	90,000
Total shareholders' equity..............................	$330,000	$330,000

A **reverse share split** is the opposite of a share split. It increases both the market value per share and the issued value per share. It does this by specifying the ratio to be less than one-to-one, such as one-for-two. This means shareholders end up with fewer shares after a reverse share split.

---

[2] To reduce administrative cost, most splits are done by issuing new certificates to shareholders for the additional shares they are entitled to receive. The shareholders keep the old certificates.

CHECKPOINT   Read Apply Do Check

1. Which of the following statements is correct?

   a. A share split increases the market value per share.

   b. Share dividends and share splits have the same effect on the total assets and retained earnings of the issuing corporation.

   c. A share dividend does not transfer corporate assets to the shareholders but does require that retained earnings be capitalized.

2. What distinguishes a share dividend from a share split?

3. What amount of retained earnings is capitalized for a share dividend?

Do: QS 16-1, QS 16-2

Repurchase of Shares

Under the *Canada Business Corporations Act*, a corporation may repurchase shares of its own outstanding share capital. Shares can be repurchased and then retired; this is referred to as a retirement or **cancelling of shares**.

LO2 | Describe and account for retirement of shares.

DANIER

For example, Note 7(c) of Danier's 2005 financial statements included in Appendix I at the end of the text states that Danier repurchased and cancelled 402,400 shares.

Retiring shares reduces the number of issued shares. Purchases and retirements of shares are allowed under the *Canada Business Corporations Act* only if they do not jeopardize the interests of creditors and shareholders and are therefore limited by the balance of retained earnings. Corporations buy back their own shares for several reasons: they can repurchase shares to avoid a hostile takeover by an investor, or they can buy shares to maintain a strong or stable market. By buying shares, management shows its confidence in the price of its shares.

Retiring Shares

To demonstrate the accounting for the **retirement of shares**, assume that Delta Inc. originally issued its common shares at an average price per share of $12.[3] If, on May 1, the corporation purchased and retired 1,000 of these shares at the same price for which they were issued, the entry would be:

May	1	Common Shares..	12,000	
		Cash		12,000
		Purchased and retired 1,000 common shares equal to the average issue price; $12 × 1,000 shares.		

---

[3] Shares are often issued at different amounts per share. Therefore when retiring shares, the average issue price per share is used to determine the amount to be debited to the share capital account. Average issue price per share is equal to Total share capital ÷ Total number of shares issued.

Earnings Per Share When There Is No Change in Common Shares Outstanding

Consider Lescon Inc., with shares issued as shown in Exhibit 16.6.

Exhibit 16.6

Shareholders' Equity of Lescon Inc. at December 31, 2011

Lescon Inc. Shareholders' Equity December 31, 2011	
Contributed capital:	
Common shares, unlimited shares authorized, 500,000 shares issued and outstanding	$6,500,000
Retained earnings	480,000
Total shareholders' equity	$6,980,000

Exhibit 16.7 illustrates the earnings per share presentation for Lescon Inc. for the year ended December 31, 2011, calculated as $750,000/500,000 shares = $1.50.

Exhibit 16.7

Income Statement with Earnings Per Share Information

Lescon Inc. Income Statement For Year Ended December 31, 2011	
Sales	$8,500,000
Cost of goods sold	4,600,000
Net income	$ 750,000
Earnings per common share	$1.50

DANIER

Danier Leather reported basic earnings per share of ($0.03) for the year ended June 25, 2005, as shown in its annual report found in Appendix I at the end of this textbook. WestJet reported basic earnings per share of $0.19 for the year ended December 31, 2005.

When common shares outstanding are constant throughout the year, the calculation of earnings per share is straightforward because the denominator of the ratio, weighted-average common shares outstanding, is equal to the reported number of shares outstanding. The next section demonstrates the calculation of earnings per share when the number of shares outstanding *changes* during the year.

Earnings Per Share When There Are Changes in Common Shares Outstanding

The number of shares outstanding can change because of:

- The issuance of additional shares,
- Share dividends,
- Share splits, and/or
- The retirement of shares.

We consider the effect of each on the denominator of the earnings per share calculation.

When Shares Are Sold or Purchased in the Period

When a company sells or repurchases shares during the year, the denominator of the basic earnings per share formula must equal the *weighted-average number of outstanding shares*. The idea behind this calculation is to measure the average amount of earnings to the average number of shares outstanding during the year. Why do we need a weighted-average calculation? To illustrate, assume you have $100 to invest in a 12% savings account at the bank. What is the earning power of your investment? The earning power is dependent on how long the money is in the savings account. If you deposit the money on January 1, 2011, the interest revenue earned by December 31, 2011, is $12 ($100 × 12%). If the money is invested on December 1, 2011, $1 ($100 × 12% × 1/12) of earnings would be realized by December 31, 2011. The earning power of an investment is greater the longer the funds are invested. Shares represent investments made by shareholders in the corporation. The longer those investments are in the company, the greater their potential impact on earnings.

Assume Lescon Inc. reported net income of $880,000 for the year ended December 31, 2012. During 2012, Lescon issued 50,000 preferred and 40,000 additional common shares and retired 30,000 common shares, as shown in Exhibit 16.8. Dividends were declared on the preferred shares only.

Exhibit 16.8

Shareholders' Equity of Lescon Inc. at December 31, 2012

Lescon Inc.
Shareholders' Equity
December 31, 2012

Contributed capital:	
Preferred shares, $5 cumulative, unlimited shares authorized, 50,000 shares issued and outstanding	$1,000,000
Common shares, unlimited shares authorized, 510,000 shares issued and outstanding*	7,200,000
Total contributed capital	$8,200,000
Retained earnings	1,110,000
Total shareholders' equity	$9,310,000

*500,000 shares were issued and outstanding on January 1, 2012; 40,000 common shares were issued on April 1, 2012; 30,000 common shares were repurchased and retired on November 1, 2012.

To calculate the weighted-average number of shares outstanding, we need to determine the number of months that each group of common shares was outstanding during the year. Exhibit 16.9 shows us how to calculate Lescon's weighted-average number of shares outstanding for the year 2012.

Exhibit 16.9

Calculating Weighted-Average Number of Shares Outstanding

Time Period	Outstanding Shares	Fraction of Year Outstanding	Weighted Average
January–March	500,000	× 3/12	= 125,000
April–October	540,000	× 7/12	= 315,000
November–December	510,000	× 2/12	= 85,000
Weighted-average outstanding shares			525,000

We can then calculate Lescon's basic earnings per share for the year ended December 31, 2012, as:

$$\text{Basic earnings per share} = \frac{\$880,000 \text{ net income} - \$250,000 \text{ preferred dividends declared*}}{525,000}$$

$$= \$1.20$$

*Note: Because the preferred shares are cumulative, the annual dividends of $250,000 would be subtracted even if the dividends had not been declared.

Lescon reports the $1.20 basic earnings per share number on the face of its December 31, 2012, income statement, similar to that shown in Exhibit 16.7.

Share Dividends or Splits in the Period

The number of outstanding shares is also affected by a share split or share dividend. Earnings for the year are spread over a larger number of shares as a result of a share dividend or share split. This affects our calculation of the weighted-average number of shares outstanding. We handle a share split or share dividend by restating the number of shares outstanding during the year to reflect the share split or dividend *as if it had occurred at the beginning of the year.*

To illustrate, let's assume Lescon declared a two-for-one share split effective December 1, 2012. The calculations in Exhibit 16.9 would change as shown in Exhibit 16.10. Notice that the only change in calculating weighted-average shares outstanding is the additional multiplication. This shows the split as if it had occurred at the beginning of the year. The December outstanding shares already reflect the split and do not require any adjustment.

Exhibit 16.10

Calculating Weighted-Average Number of Shares Outstanding With Share Split

Time Period	Outstanding Shares	Effect of Split	Fraction of Year	Weighted Average
January–March	500,000	× 2	× 3/12	= 250,000
April–October	540,000	× 2	× 7/12	= 630,000
November	510,000	× 2	× 1/12	= 85,000
December	1,020,000	× 1	× 1/12	= 85,000
Weighted-average outstanding shares				1,050,000

Lescon's basic earnings per share for the year 2012 under the assumption of the two-for-one share split is:

$$\text{Basic earnings per share} = \frac{\$880,000 \text{ net income} - \$250,000 \text{ preferred dividends declared}}{1,050,000}$$

$$= \underline{\$0.60}$$

Exhibit 16.11 shows the calculation of weighted-average shares outstanding if the two-for-one share split had been a 10% share dividend. The December outstanding shares already reflect the share dividend and do not require any adjustment.

Exhibit 16.11

Calculating Weighted-Average Number of Shares With Share Dividend

Time Period	Outstanding Shares	Effect of Share Dividend	Fraction of Year	Weighted Average
January–March	500,000	× 1.10	× 3/12	= 137,500
April–October	540,000	× 1.10	× 7/12	= 346,500
November	510,000	× 1.10	× 1/12	= 46,750
December	561,000	× 1	× 1/12	= 46,750
Weighted-average outstanding shares				577,500

Earnings per share under the assumption of the 10% share dividend would be:

$$\text{Basic earnings per share} = \frac{\$880,000 \text{ net income} - \$250,000 \text{ preferred dividends declared}}{577,500}$$

$$= \underline{\$1.09^*}$$

*rounded to two decimal places

CHECKPOINT

5. During 2011, FDI reports net income of $250,000 and pays $70,000 in current year preferred dividends. On January 1, 2011, the company had 25,000 outstanding common shares and retired 5,000 shares on July 1, 2011. The 2011 basic earnings per share is: (a) $8; (b) $9; or (c) $10.

6. In addition to the facts in Checkpoint 5, assume a 3:1 share split occurred on August 1, 2011. The 2011 weighted-average number of common shares outstanding is: (a) 60,000; (b) 117,500; or (c) 67,500.

7. How are share splits and share dividends treated in calculating the weighted-average number of outstanding common shares?

Do: QS 16-5, QS 16-6, QS 16-7, QS 16-8, QS 16-9, QS 16-10

Earnings Per Share and Extraordinary Items

Extraordinary items are a special type of gain or loss that is reported separately on the income statement with corresponding earnings per share data as shown in Exhibit 16.12.

The *CICA Handbook* identifies an **extraordinary gain or loss** as an item that has all of the following three characteristics:

- It is not expected to occur frequently over several years,
- It does not typify the normal business activities of the entity, and
- It does not depend primarily on decisions or determinations by management or owners.[4]

Few items qualify as extraordinary because they must meet both criteria of *unusual* and *infrequent*. An **unusual gain or loss** is abnormal or otherwise unrelated to the ordinary activities and environment of the business. An **infrequent gain or loss** is one that is not expected to occur again. The list of items usually considered extraordinary include:

- Expropriation (taking away) of property by a foreign government.
- Condemning of property by a domestic government body.
- Prohibition against using an asset by a newly enacted law.
- Losses or gains from an unusual and infrequent calamity ("act of God").

Gains or losses that result from the risks of normal business activities are not extraordinary and are reported in continuing operations *but* below the normal revenues and expenses. The following are examples of items *not* considered extraordinary:

- Write-downs of inventories.
- Write-offs of receivables.
- Gains or losses from exchanging foreign currencies.
- Effects of labour strikes.
- Accrual adjustments on long-term contracts.
- Sale of equipment.

[4] *CICA Handbook*, section 3480.

Exhibit 16.12 shows how extraordinary items are reported in the income statement along with the corresponding earnings per share presentation for Gallivan Inc.

Exhibit 16.12

Income Statement Presentation of Earnings Per Share and Extraordinary Items

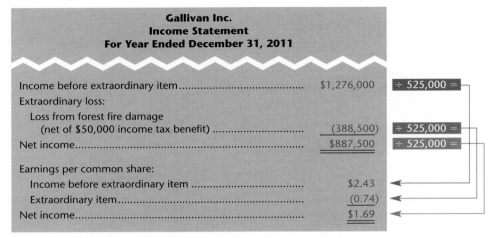

Gallivan Inc.
Income Statement
For Year Ended December 31, 2011

Income before extraordinary item	$1,276,000 ÷ 525,000 =
Extraordinary loss:	
Loss from forest fire damage (net of $50,000 income tax benefit)	(388,500) ÷ 525,000 =
Net income	$887,500 ÷ 525,000 =
Earnings per common share:	
Income before extraordinary item	$2.43
Extraordinary item	(0.74)
Net income	$1.69

Assume there are no preferred shares and the weighted-average number of common shares outstanding is 525,000 shares.

CHECKPOINT   Read Apply Do Check

8. Which of the following is an extraordinary item? (a) A settlement paid to a customer injured while using a company's product; (b) A loss from damages to a plant caused by a meteorite; or (c) A loss from selling old equipment.

Do: QS 16-11

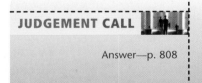

JUDGEMENT CALL

Answer—p. 808

Farmer

You are a farmer with an orchard in Kentville, Nova Scotia. This winter, a bad frost wiped out about half your trees. You are currently preparing an income statement for a bank loan. Can you claim the loss of apple trees as extraordinary and separate from continuing operations?

The next section discusses some additional income reporting issues and how they affect the income statement.

Reporting Income Information

LO4 Explain the form and content of a comprehensive corporate income statement.

The basic corporate income statement of Exhibit 16.13 shows the revenues, expenses, and income generated by the company's **continuing operations**. Prior chapters have explained the nature of the items and measures included in income from these continuing operations.

Exhibit 16.13

Corporate Income Statement
Showing Continuing Operations

Amanda Corporation
Income Statement
For Year Ended December 31, 2011

Sales		$100
Cost of goods sold		40
Gross profit		$ 60
Operating expenses		18
Income from operations		$ 42
Other revenues and expenses:[5]		
Gain on sale of capital assets	$4	
Interest revenue	3	
Loss on sale of capital assets	(7)	
Interest expense	(2)	(2)
Income before tax		$ 40
Income tax expense		10
Net income		$ 30

Continuing operations

When a company's activities include income-related transactions that are not part of a company's continuing, normal operations, the income statement needs to be expanded to include different sections to provide more useful information to users. The most important of these additional sections include: *discontinued operations*, *extraordinary items*, and *earnings per share*. Discontinued operations and extraordinary items will be discussed in this section. Earnings per share was described in detail in the previous section. Exhibit 16.14 shows the additional income statement items as reported for CanComp for its year ended December 31, 2011.

Exhibit 16.14

Comprehensive Income
Statement for a Corporation

CanComp Corporation
Income Statement
For Year Ended December 31, 2011

Net sales		$8,440,000
Cost of goods sold		5,950,000
Gross profit		$2,490,000
Operating expenses		570,000
Operating income		$1,920,000
Other revenues and expenses:		
Loss on relocating a plant		(45,000)
Income from continuing operations before income tax		$1,875,000
Income tax expense		397,000
Income from continuing operations		$1,478,000

① Continuing operations

Discontinued operations:		
Income from operating Division A		
(net of $180,000 income taxes)	$420,000	
Loss on disposal of Division A		
(net of $66,000 tax benefit)	(154,000)	266,000
Income before extraordinary items		$1,744,000

② Discontinued operations

Extraordinary items:		
Gain on sale of land taken by government		
(net of $61,200 income taxes)		142,000
Net income		$1,886,000

③ Extraordinary items

Earnings per common share	
(200,000 outstanding shares):	
Income from continuing operations	$7.39
Income from discontinued operations	1.33
Income before extraordinary item	$8.72
Extraordinary item	0.71
Net income (basic earnings per share)	$9.43

④ Earnings per share

---

5 Some companies will divide this section on the income statement between *Other Revenues and Gains* and *Other Expenses and Losses*. The *CICA Handbook* permits flexibility in this regard.

www.clublink.com

www.lionsgatefilms.com

Many companies have several different lines of business or operating *segments* that deal with different groups of customers. A **segment of a business** is a part of a company's operations that serves a particular line of business or class of customers and is of interest to users of financial statements. For instance, ClubLink reports two operating segments in Note 16 of its 2005 financial statements: golf club operations and golf resort operations. Lions Gate Entertainment reports its operations in three business segments: Motion Pictures, Television, and Studio Facilities.

Discontinued Operations

When an operating segment of the business is discontinued, a **discontinued operation** results and two items must be reported in a separate section of the income statement:[6]

1. The gain or loss from selling or closing down a segment, and

2. The income from operating the discontinued segment prior to its disposal.

The income tax effects of each are also reported net of tax separate from continuing operations as shown in Section 2 of Exhibit 16.14. When an amount is shown **net of tax**, it means that it has been adjusted for the income tax effect. The income tax effect can be an additional expense or a benefit (reduction of total tax expense). For example, in the case of the $420,000 reported in Section 2 as the *Income from Operating Division A*, it is *net of $180,000 income tax expense*. This means that the gross income (or before-tax amount) was $600,000 ($420,000 net amount + $180,000 income tax expense). For the *Loss on Disposal of Division A*, the $154,000 is reported net of a *$66,000 tax benefit*. Because a loss reduces net income, it also reduces income tax expense—therefore a tax *benefit* results.

The purpose of reporting discontinued operations separately is to clearly isolate the results of discontinued operations from continuing operations. Additional information regarding the transaction must be disclosed in the notes to the financial statements.[7] For instance, on its income statement for the year ended June 25, 2005, and in Note 2, Danier Leather reported as discontinued operations the sale of three shopping mall stores—two on Long Island, New York, and one in Paramus, New Jersey.

DANIER

Extraordinary Items

Section 3 of the income statement in Exhibit 16.14 reports extraordinary items. Reporting extraordinary items in a separate category helps users predict future performance, without the effects of extraordinary items. Extraordinary items, like gains or losses resulting from discontinued segments, are reported net of income tax expense or benefit. For example, QLT Inc. reported an extraordinary gain of $12,517,000 on its income statement for the year ended December 31, 2004, which caused a 7% decrease in the net loss shown for the period.[8]

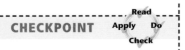
CHECKPOINT

9. Identify the four major sections of the income statement that are potentially reported.

Do: QS 16-12

---

[6] *CICA Handbook*, section 1700.

[7] *CICA Handbook*, section 3475, "Discontinued Operations."

[8] This information was reported in the CICA's 2005 *Financial Reporting in Canada*.

Statement of Retained Earnings

Recall that the statement of retained earnings shows the details of how the Retained Earnings account changes over the accounting period. Retained earnings are part of the shareholders' claim on the company's net assets. A common error is to think that retained earnings represent cash. Retained earnings are not cash. Retained earnings do not imply that there is a certain amount of cash available to pay shareholders, nor any other asset. They simply describe how much of the assets are owned by the shareholders as a result of earnings that have been *retained* for the purpose of reinvestment.

LO5   Explain the items reported in retained earnings.

The statement of retained earnings is often combined with the income statement, as shown in Exhibit 16.15.

Petro Inc. Statement of Income and Retained Earnings For Year Ended December 31, 2011	
Sales	$9,000,000
Cost of goods sold	6,500,000
Net income	$1,250,000
Retained earnings, January 1	1,200,000
Less: Cash dividends	(350,000)
Retained earnings, December 31	$2,100,000
Earnings per common share	$5.25

Exhibit 16.15

Statement of Retained Earnings Presented in Combination with the Income Statement

For additional examples of how the statement of retained earnings is combined with the income statement, refer to the WestJet and Danier Leather statements provided in Appendix I at the end of this textbook.

DANIER

The next section describes important items affecting retained earnings. It also explains how we include these as part of the statement of retained earnings.

Restricted Retained Earnings

To protect creditors' interests in assets of a corporation, incorporating acts sometimes place *restrictions* on retained earnings. **Restrictions** are limits that identify how much of the retained earnings balance is not available for dividends or the repurchase of shares. Restrictions are usually disclosed in the notes to the financial statements. There are three kinds of restrictions:

1. *Statutory restrictions* are imposed by a regulatory body. For example, dividends are limited to the balance of retained earnings.

2. *Contractual restrictions* occur when certain contracts, such as loan agreements, restrict retained earnings such that the payment of dividends is limited to a certain amount or percent of retained earnings.

3. *Voluntary restrictions* are placed on retained earnings by a corporation's directors to limit dividends because of a special need for cash, such as for the purchase of new facilities.

Accounting Changes

Another issue that can affect retained earnings is that of accounting changes. There are three types of accounting changes but only two have the potential to affect retained earnings. Exhibit 16.16 summarizes accounting changes and their appropriate treatment:

Exhibit 16.16

Guidelines for the Treatment of Accounting Changes[9]

Accounting Change	Accounting Treatment
1. Change in Accounting Policy	–Retroactive restatement of financial statements,
	–Disclosure requiring description of change and effect on financial statements,
2. Correction of Error(s) in Prior Financial Statements	–New policy or corrected amount is reported in current year's operating results, and
	–Charged or credited (net of tax) to opening balance of Retained Earnings.
3. Change in Estimate	Accounted for in period of change and future.

1. Change in Accounting Policy

A *change in accounting policy* occurs if, for example, a company changes from FIFO to the weighted-average method for calculating the cost of sales and merchandise inventory. A change in accounting policy is represented by a change from an existing accounting policy to an alternative one. *Consistency* P. 31 requires a company to continue applying the same accounting policies once they are chosen to ensure financial statements are comparable from one accounting period to the next. A company can change from one acceptable accounting policy to another as long as the change improves the usefulness of information in its financial statements. The accounting treatment for a change in accounting policy is noted in Exhibit 16.16.

2. Correction of Error(s) in Prior Financial Statements

Sometimes errors occur. For instance, assume Lashburn Ltd. makes an error in a 2011 journal entry for the purchase of land by incorrectly debiting an expense account for $240,000. This error was discovered in 2012 and requires correction as per the guidelines outlined in Exhibit 16.16. The entry to record the correction is:

2012			
Dec. 31	Land..	240,000	
	Income Tax Payable*		
	($240,000 × 25%)		60,000
	Retained Earnings.................................		180,000
	To adjust for error in 2011 journal entry that expensed the purchase of land.		

*Assuming a flat tax rate of 25% for simplicity.

To correct the error, the 2011 financial statements are restated, appropriate note disclosure is included explaining the error, and retained earnings are restated as per Exhibit 16.17. There is no effect on the current year's operating results in this particular instance.

---

[9] *CICA Handbook*, section 1506.

Lashburn Ltd.
Statement of Retained Earnings
For Year Ended December 31, 2012

Retained earnings, December 31, 2011, as previously stated............................	$4,745,000
Add: Correction of error:	
Cost of land incorrectly expensed	
(net of $60,000 income tax expense)	180,000
Retained earnings, December 31, 2011, as restated	$4,925,000
Add: Net income..	1,162,500
Less: Cash dividends	240,000
Retained earnings, December 31, 2012..	$5,847,500

Exhibit 16.17

Presentation of Accounting Changes on the Statement of Retained Earnings

3. Change in Estimate

Many items reported in financial statements are based on estimates. Future events are certain to reveal that some of these estimates were inaccurate even when based on the best data available at the time. Because these inaccuracies are not the result of mistakes, they are considered to be **changes in accounting estimates** and *not* accounting errors. For example, if the estimated useful life of a capital asset changed because of new information, this would be identified as a change in estimate.

10. A company that has used FIFO for the past 15 years decides to switch to LIFO. Which of the following statements describes the effect of this event on past years' net income?

    a. The cumulative effect is reported as an adjustment to ending retained earnings for the prior period.

    b. The cumulative effect is ignored as it is a change in an accounting estimate.

    c. The cumulative effect is reported only on the current year's income statement.

Do: QS 16-13, QS 16-14

CHECKPOINT   Read · Apply · Do · Check

Summary

LO¹ | **Describe and account for share dividends and share splits.** Both a share dividend and a share split divide a company's outstanding shares into smaller pieces. The total value of the company is unchanged, but the price of each new share is smaller. Share dividends and share splits do not transfer any of the corporation's assets to shareholders and do not affect assets, total shareholders' equity, or the equity attributed to each shareholder. Share dividends are recorded by capitalizing retained earnings equal to the market value of the distributed shares. Share splits are not recorded with journal entries but do require note disclosure.

LO² | **Describe and account for retirement of shares.** When a corporation purchases its own previously issued outstanding shares for the purpose of retirement, the share capital account is debited based on the original issue price. If the amount paid by the corporation is less than the original issue price, the excess is credited to the Contributed Capital from Retirement of Shares account. If the amount paid is greater than the original issue price, Contributed Capital from Retirement of Shares is debited to the extent a credit balance exists in that account and any remaining amount is debited to Retained Earnings.

LO³ | **Calculate earnings per share and describe its use.** Corporations calculate basic earnings per share by dividing net income less any preferred dividends by the weighted-average number of outstanding common shares.

LO4 | **Explain the form and content of a comprehensive corporate income statement.** Corporate income statements are similar to those for proprietorships and partnerships except for the inclusion of income taxes. The income statement consists of four potential sections: (1) continuing operations, (2) discontinued segments, (3) extraordinary items, and (4) earnings per share.

LO5 | **Explain the items reported in retained earnings.** Retained earnings are sometimes restricted to limit

dividends and reacquisition of shares or to protect creditors. Corporations may voluntarily restrict retained earnings as a means of informing shareholders why dividends are not larger. Accounting changes that affect retained earnings of prior years include (1) change in accounting policy/procedure, and (2) correction of an error. A change in accounting estimate, also a type of accounting change, does not affect retained earnings of prior years.

---

guidance answer to : **JUDGEMENT CALL**

Farmer

The frost loss is probably not extraordinary. Nova Scotia experiences enough frost damage that it would be difficult to argue that this event is both unusual and infrequent. Nevertheless, you would want to highlight the frost loss, and hope the bank would view this uncommon event separately from your continuing operations.

---

guidance answers to : **CHECKPOINT**   Read Apply Do Check

1. *c*

2. A share dividend increases the number of shares issued and outstanding and requires a journal entry to transfer (or capitalize) a portion of retained earnings to contributed capital. A share split does not involve a journal entry and simply increases the number of shares issued and outstanding.

3. Retained earnings equal to the market value of the distributable shares should be capitalized.

4. The number of shares outstanding is reduced by the number of shares retired and cancelled.

5. *a*

Calculations: ($250,000 − $70,000)/22,500* = $8.00

*

Time Period	Outstanding Shares	Fraction of Year Outstanding	Weighted Average
January–June	25,000	× 6/12	= 12,500
July–December	20,000	× 6/12	= 10,000
Weighted-average outstanding shares			22,500

6. *c*

Calculations:

Time Period	Outstanding Shares	Effect of Split	Fraction of Year	Weighted Average
January–June	25,000	× 3	× 6/12	= 37,500
July	20,000	× 3	× 1/12	= 5,000
August–December	60,000	× 1	× 5/12	= 25,000
Weighted-average outstanding shares				67,500

7. The number of shares previously outstanding is retroactively restated to reflect the share split or share dividend as if it had occurred at the beginning of the year.

8. *b*

9. The four major sections are Income from Continuing Operations, Discontinued Segments, Extraordinary Items, and Earnings Per Share.

10. *a*

demonstration problem

Read
Apply   Do
Check

X-On Ltd. began 2011 with the following balances in its shareholders' equity accounts:

Common shares, unlimited shares authorized,	
500,000 shares issued and outstanding	$3,000,000
Retained earnings	2,500,000

The following share-related transactions occurred during the year:

Date	Transaction
March 1	Issued at $20 per share 100,000 $2.50 non-cumulative preferred shares with an unlimited number authorized.
May 1	Issued 50,000 common shares at $15 per share.
Sept. 1	Repurchased and retired 150,000 common shares at $16 per share.
Nov. 30	Declared and distributed a 3:1 share split on the common shares.

Required

a. Calculate the weighted-average number of shares outstanding using the information above.

b. Using the information provided, prepare an income statement for 2011 similar to Exhibit 16.14:

Cumulative effect of a change in amortization method	
(net of $26,000 tax benefit)..	$ (136,500)
Operating expenses (related to continuing operations)	(2,072,500)
Extraordinary gain on expropriated land	
(net of $71,000 tax expense)...	275,500
Gain on disposal of discontinued operations' assets	
(net of $8,600 tax expense)...	37,500
Gain on sale of investment in shares...	400,000
Loss from operating discontinued operations	
(net of $40,000 tax benefit)...	(182,500)
Income taxes on income from continuing operations....................................	(660,000)
Revenues..	5,375,000
Loss from sale of plant assets*..	(650,000)

The assets were items of equipment replaced with new technology.

Analysis component:

Why are extraordinary items shown separately on the income statement?

Planning the Solution

- Based on the shares outstanding at the beginning of the year and the transactions during the year, calculate the weighted-average number of outstanding shares for the year.

- Calculate earnings per share.

- Assign each of the listed items to an appropriate income statement category.

- Prepare an income statement similar to Exhibit 16.14, including separate sections for continued operations, discontinued operations, extraordinary items, and earnings per share.

- Answer the analysis component.

solution to **Demonstration Problem**

a. Calculate the weighted-average number of outstanding shares:

Time Period	Outstanding Shares	Effect of Split	Fraction of Year	Weighted Average
January–April	500,000	× 3	× 4/12	= 500,000
May–August	550,000	× 3	× 4/12	= 550,000
September–November	400,000	× 3	× 3/12	= 300,000
December	1,200,000	× 1	× 1/12	= 100,000
Weighted-average outstanding shares				1,450,000

b. Prepare an income statement for 2011:

X-On Ltd.
Income Statement
For Year Ended December 31, 2011

Revenues		$5,375,000
Operating expenses		2,072,500
Income from operations		$3,302,500
Other revenues and expenses:		
Gain on sale of investment in shares	$ 400,000	
Loss from sale of plant assets	(650,000)	(250,000)
Income from continuing operations before tax		$3,052,500
Income tax expense		660,000
Income from continuing operations		$2,392,500
Discontinued operations:		
Loss from operating discontinued operations		
(net of $40,000 tax benefit)	$(182,500)	
Gain on disposal of discontinued operations' assets		
(net of $8,600 tax)	37,500	(145,000)
Income before extraordinary items		$2,247,500
Extraordinary items:		
Extraordinary gain on expropriated land		
(net of $71,000 tax)		275,500
Net income		$2,523,000
Earnings per share		
(1,450,000 average shares outstanding):		
Income from continuing operations		$1.65[1]
Loss from discontinued segment		(0.10)[2]
Income before extraordinary gain		$1.55
Extraordinary gain		0.19[3]
Net income		$1.74

[1] $2,392,500/1,450,000 = $ 1.65
[2] $(145,000)/1,450,000 = $(0.10)
[3] $275,500/1,450,000 = $ 0.19

Analysis component:

Extraordinary items are shown separately on the income statement to ensure users can interpret performance based on ongoing activities. Including extraordinary gains and losses as part of continuing operations could distort analyses.

A P P E N D I X 1 6 A

Treasury Shares

In some provincial jurisdictions, a corporation may buy back shares without having to retire them. These reacquired shares are called **treasury shares**.[10] Treasury shares *have been issued* but *are not outstanding* since they are not held by shareholders; instead they are held by the corporation. Because voting rights and dividend entitlements apply to outstanding shares only, treasury shares are not entitled to receive dividends or vote.

LO6 Record the purchase and reissue of treasury shares.

Purchasing Treasury Shares

The *Treasury Shares* account is a contra shareholders' equity account. Therefore, purchasing treasury shares for cash reduces the corporation's assets and shareholders' equity by equal amounts.[11] We illustrate these effects on the balance sheet of Cyber Corporation. Exhibit 16A.1 shows Cyber's account balances before any treasury shares are purchased.

Cyber Corporation
Balance Sheet
May 1, 2011

Assets

Cash	$ 30,000
Other assets	95,000
Total assets	$125,000
Liabilities	$ -0-
Shareholders' equity	
Common shares, unlimited shares authorized; 10,000 issued and outstanding	$100,000
Retained earnings	25,000
Total liabilities and shareholders' equity	$125,000

Exhibit 16A.1

Balance Sheet Before
Purchasing Treasury Shares

On May 2, 2011, Cyber purchased 1,000 of its own common shares at $11.50 per share. The entry to record this purchase is:

May	2	Treasury Shares, Common	11,500	
		Cash		11,500
		Purchased 1,000 treasury shares at $11.50 per share.		

Exhibit 16A.2 shows the effects of this transaction on Cyber's balance sheet.

---

[10] Treasury shares are not common in Canada.
[11] We describe the *cost method* of accounting for treasury shares. It is the method most widely used. The *par value method* is another method explained in advanced courses.

Exhibit 16A.2

Balance Sheet After Purchasing Treasury Shares

Cyber Corporation
Balance Sheet
May 2, 2011

Assets

Cash..	$ 18,500
Other assets...	95,000
Total assets...	$113,500

Liabilities.. $ -0-

Shareholders' equity

Contributed capital:

Common shares, unlimited shares authorized; 10,000 shares issued; 9,000 shares outstanding......................	$100,000
Retained earnings, of which $11,500 is restricted by treasury shares purchased	25,000
Total..	$125,000
Less: 1,000 treasury shares..	11,500
Total shareholders' equity	$113,500
Total liabilities and shareholders' equity	$113,500

The number of shares *issued* is the same before *and* after the purchase of treasury shares

The number of shares outstanding is decreased by the purchase of treasury shares.

The treasury share purchase reduces Cyber's cash and total equity by $11,500. This purchase does not reduce the balance of either the Common Shares account or the Retained Earnings account. Note that there are only 9,000 shares outstanding (10,000 issued less 1,000 in treasury).[12] Recall from Chapter 15 that *issued* shares have been *sold*. The retained earnings description tells us it is partly restricted.

Reissuing Treasury Shares

Treasury shares can be reissued. They can be sold at cost, above cost, or below cost.

If, on May 20, Cyber reissues 100 of the treasury shares at $11.50 per share, their cost on May 1, the entry is:

May	20	Cash..	1,150	
		Treasury Shares, Common......................		1,150
		Reissued 100 treasury shares at cost.		

If, on June 3, 400 treasury shares are reissued at $12 per share, which is above their cost on May 1, the entry is:

June	3	Cash..	4,800	
		Treasury Shares, Common......................		4,600
		Contributed Capital, Treasury Shares.....		200
		Reissued 400 treasury shares above cost; *400 × $11.50 = $4,600; 400 × $12* *= $4,800.*		

The Contributed Capital, Treasury Shares account is reported as a separate item in the contributed capital section of shareholders' equity. No gain is ever reported from the sale of treasury shares.

---

[12] Recall from Chapter 15 that *issued* shares have been *sold*. Treasury shares have been issued but are not *held* by shareholders; treasury shares are held by the issuing corporation. Only shares held by shareholders are said to be *outstanding*.

If, on July 10, 300 treasury shares are reissued at $11 per share, which is below their cost on May 1, the entry is:

July	10	Cash..	3,300	
		Contributed Capital, Treasury Shares..............	150	
		Treasury Shares, Common.....................		3,450
		Reissued 300 treasury shares below cost;		
		300 × $11.50 = $3,450; 300 × $11		
		= $3,300.		

The debit to the Contributed Capital, Treasury Shares account cannot exceed the credit balance present in the account (in this case, the July 10 debit of $150 does not exceed the June 3 credit balance of $200; a credit of $50 remains). In a case where the credit balance in the contributed capital account is eliminated, the remaining difference between the cost and the selling price is debited to Retained Earnings.

For example, if, on July 15, 100 treasury shares are reissued at $10 per share, the entry is:

July	15	Cash..	1,000	
		Contributed Capital, Treasury Shares..............	50	
		Retained Earnings...	100	
		Treasury Shares, Common.....................		1,150
		Reissued 100 treasury shares below cost.		

CHECKPOINT   Read · Apply · Do · Check

11. Purchase of treasury shares: (a) has no effect on total assets; (b) reduces total assets and total shareholders' equity by equal amounts; or (c) is recorded with a debit to Retained Earnings.

12. Southern Inc. purchases shares of Northern Corp. Should these shares be classified as treasury shares by either company?

13. How do treasury shares affect the number of shares authorized, issued, and outstanding?

Do: *QS 16-15, *QS 16-16

Summary of Appendix 16A

LO6   **Record the purchase and reissue of treasury shares.** When a corporation purchases its own previously issued outstanding shares, the cost of these shares is debited to Treasury Shares. The balance of Treasury Shares is subtracted from total shareholders' equity in the balance sheet. If treasury shares are later reissued, the amount of any proceeds in excess of cost is credited to Contributed Capital, Treasury Shares. If the proceeds are less than cost, the difference is debited to Contributed Capital, Treasury Shares to the extent a credit balance exists in that account. Any remaining amount is debited to Retained Earnings.

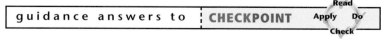

guidance answers to   CHECKPOINT   Read · Apply · Do · Check

11. *b*

12. No. The shares are an investment for Southern Inc. and issued and outstanding shares for Northern Corp.

13. Treasury shares do not affect the number of either authorized or issued shares. They reduce the amount of outstanding shares only.

Glossary

Basic earnings per share Calculated with the formula: (Net income − Preferred dividends) ÷ Weighted-average common shares. (p. 797)

Cancelling of shares See *retirement of shares*. (p. 793)

Changes in accounting estimates Corrections to previous estimates or predictions about future events and outcomes, such as salvage values and the useful lives of operating assets; the changes are accounted for in the current and future periods. (p. 807)

Continuing operations That section of an income statement that shows the revenues, expenses, and income generated by the company's day-to-day operating activities. (p. 802)

Discontinued operations When a company with operations in different segments sells a segment, the sold segment is known as a discontinued operation. (p. 804)

Earnings per share The amount of income earned by each share of a company's outstanding common shares; commonly abbreviated as *EPS*. (p. 797)

EPS See *earnings per share*. (p. 797)

Extraordinary gain or loss A gain or loss that is reported separately from continuing operations because it is not expected to occur frequently over several years, does not typify the normal business activities of the entity, and does not depend primarily on decisions or determinations by management or owners. (p. 801)

Extraordinary item See *extraordinary gain or loss*. (p. 801)

Infrequent gain or loss A gain or loss that is not expected to occur again, given the operating environment of the business and does not qualify as an extraordinary gain or loss. (p. 801)

Net of tax An amount reported net of tax means the income tax expense (benefit) has already been subtracted. (p. 804)

Restrictions Legal or contractual limitations that cause a portion of the retained earnings balance not to be available for dividends or the repurchase of shares. No journal entry is required but note disclosure is necessary. (p. 805)

Retirement of shares Occurs when a corporation repurchases and cancels its own shares. (p. 793)

Reverse share split An act by a corporation to call in its shares and replace each share with less than one new share; reverse splits are opposite of share splits as they increase both the market value per share and the issued value per share. (p. 792)

Segment of a business A component of a company's operations that serves a particular line of business or class of customers and that has assets, activities, and financial results of operations that can be distinguished from other parts of the business. (p. 804)

Share dividend A corporation's distribution of its own shares to its shareholders without receiving any payment in return. Also called a *stock dividend*. (p. 789)

Share split An act by a corporation to call in its shares and replace each share with more than one new share; a share split will decrease the market value per share and also the book value per share. (p. 792)

Treasury shares Shares that were reacquired and are still held by the issuing corporation. (p. 811)

Unusual gain or loss A gain or loss that is abnormal or otherwise unrelated to the ordinary activities and environment of the business but does not qualify as an extraordinary gain or loss. (p. 801)

For more study tools, quizzes, and problem material,
visit the **Student Success** *Centre* at
www.mcgrawhill.ca/studentsuccess/FAP

Questions

1. What is the difference between a share dividend and a share split?
2. What effects does declaring a share dividend have on the corporation's assets, liabilities, and total shareholders' equity? What effects does the distribution of the shares have?
3. Refer to the financial statements **DANIER** for Danier Leather in Appendix I at the end of the book. What is the balance of retained earnings as of June 25, 2005? What amount of dividends was declared during the year ended June 25, 2005?
4. How are earnings per share results calculated for a corporation with a simple capital structure?

5. Refer to the financial statements **DANIER** for Danier Leather in Appendix I. Did basic EPS increase or decrease from 2004 to 2005?
6. Where on the income statement would a company report an unusual gain that is not expected to occur more often than once every two years?
7. After taking five years' straight-line amortization expense for an asset that was expected to have an eight-year useful life, a company decided that the asset would last another six years. Is this decision a change in accounting policy? How would the financial statements describe this change?
*8. How does the purchase of treasury shares affect the purchaser's assets and total shareholders' equity?
*9. Why do legal jurisdictions place limits on purchases of treasury shares?

An asterisk (*) identifies assignment material based on Appendix 16A.

Quick Study

Information taken from Jamestown Corp.'s balance sheet as of April 1, 2011, follows:

Common shares, 375,000 shares authorized,	
150,000 shares issued and outstanding	$1,102,500
Retained earnings..	633,000

On April 1, Jamestown declares and distributes a 10% share dividend. The market value of the shares on this date is $25. Prepare the shareholders' equity section for Jamestown immediately following the share dividend (assume all dividends are debited directly to Retained Earnings).

QS 16-1
Accounting for a share dividend
LO¹

Vector Ltd. showed the following shareholders' equity account balances on December 31, 2011:

Common shares, 100,000 shares authorized;	
28,000 shares issued and outstanding..	$476,000
Retained earnings..	85,000

On January 2, 2012, Vector declared and distributed a 3:1 share split. Prepare a comparative shareholders' equity section immediately before and after the share split similar to Exhibit 16.4.

QS 16-2
Share split
LO¹

On September 2, Garrett Corporation purchased and retired 2,000 of its own shares for $18,000. The shares had been issued at an average price of $5. Prepare the September 2 entry for the purchase and retirement of the shares (assuming this is the first retirement ever recorded by Garrett).

QS 16-3
Repurchase and retirement of shares
LO²

Amex Inc. had 180,000 common shares issued and outstanding as at December 31, 2011. The shares had been issued for $9.80 each. On September 12, 2012, Amex repurchased and retired 40,000 of these shares at $9.10 each, the first retirement ever recorded by Amex. Amex also repurchased and retired 20,000 shares at $11.40 on December 17, 2012. Record the entries on September 12 and December 17.

QS 16-4
Repurchase and retirement of shares
LO²

Nelson Corp. earned a net income of $450,000. The number of common shares outstanding all year long was 200,000 and preferred shareholders received a dividend totalling $10,000. Calculate the basic earnings per share for Nelson Corp.

QS 16-5
Basic earnings per share
LO³

Bellevue Ltd. reported net income of $860,000 for its year ended December 31, 2011. Calculate earnings per share given the following additional information at December 31, 2011:

Preferred shares, $2 cumulative, 50,000 shares authorized;	
26,000 shares issued and outstanding...	$286,000
Common shares, 300,000 shares authorized,	
160,000 shares issued and outstanding*	544,000
Retained earnings**...	180,000

*There was no change in the outstanding shares during the year.
**Dividends totalling $100,000 were declared during 2011. There were no dividends in arrears.

QS 16-6
Basic earnings per share
LO³

On January 1, Harmon Corp. had 100,000 common shares outstanding. On February 1, Harmon Corp. issued 40,000 additional common shares. On June 1, another 80,000 common shares were issued. Calculate Harmon Corp.'s weighted-average shares outstanding. Round calculations to the nearest whole share.

QS 16-7
Weighted average shares outstanding
LO³

QS 16-8
Weighted-average common shares
outstanding—share dividend
LO3

On January 1, Harrell Corp. had 75,000 common shares issued and outstanding. On April 1, it issued 24,000 additional shares and on June 1, declared and distributed a 20% share dividend. Calculate Harrell's weighted-average outstanding shares for the year.

QS 16-9
Weighted-average common shares
outstanding—share split
LO3

On January 1, Star Corp. had 50,000 common shares issued and outstanding. On April 1, it issued 4,000 additional shares and on June 5, declared and distributed a two-for-one share split. Calculate Star's weighted-average outstanding shares for the year.

QS 16-10
Weighted-average common shares
outstanding—repurchase
LO3

On January 1, 2011, Wonsto Mining Corp. had 580,000 common shares issued and outstanding. On April 30, it issued an additional 220,000 shares and on October 1 it repurchased and cancelled 100,000 shares. Calculate Wonsto's weighted-average shares outstanding for the year ended December 31, 2011. Round calculations to the nearest whole share.

QS 16-11
Extraordinary items
LO3

Using the information provided, identify which of the following would be reported as extraordinary items:
a. Inventory costing $185,000 was determined to be obsolete.
b. Tenants were given notice that they had to vacate the building because it had been condemned by the municipality.
c. A bottling company was required by recently enacted environmental legislation to purchase new equipment that prevented the pull-tabs on cans of beverages from being removed easily.
d. A tornado, never before experienced in this region, destroyed a lumber mill.
e. $890,000 of receivables were written off.

QS 16-12
Income statement categories
LO4

Using the numbers to represent each section of a comprehensive income statement, identify where each of items (a) through (l) should be reported:
1. Continuing operations   3. Extraordinary items
2. Discontinued operations   4. Earnings per share

a. Gain on sale of Division E   _____   g. Earnings per share   _____
b. Operating expenses   _____   h. Cost of goods sold   _____
c. Extraordinary loss   _____   i. Loss from operating Division E   _____
d. Loss on sale of equipment   _____   j. Income tax expense   _____
e. Interest revenue   _____   k. Gain on sale of warehouse   _____
f. Amortization expense   _____   l. Interest expense   _____

QS 16-13
Accounting for estimate changes
and error adjustments
LO5

Answer the questions about each of the following items related to a company's activities for the year:
a. After using an expected useful life of seven years and no residual value to amortize its office equipment over the preceding three years, the company decided early this year that the equipment would last only two more years. How should the effects of this decision be reported in the current financial statements?
b. An account receivable in the amount of $180,000 was written off two years ago. It was recovered this year. The president believes this should be reported as an error. How should the proceeds be reported in the current year's financial statements?

QS 16-14
Accounting changes
LO5

Barton Inc. changed the method of calculating amortization on its equipment from straight-line to double-declining-balance during 2011. The cumulative effect of the change is an additional expense of $46,000 related to prior years. The tax benefit is $13,000. Record the entry on December 31, 2011.

On May 3, Nicholson Corp. purchased 3,000 of its own shares for $27,000 to be held as treasury shares. On November 4, Nicholson reissued 750 treasury shares for $7,080. Prepare the November 4 journal entry Nicholson should make to record the sale of the treasury shares.

*QS 16-15
Purchase and sale of treasury shares
LO6

Arcon Ltd. had 45,000 common shares issued and outstanding that had been issued for $7.50 each. On September 25, 2011, Arcon repurchased 15,000 shares at $7.80 per share to be held as treasury shares. 10,000 of these shares were reissued to employees of the company on November 14 at $3.00 per share. Record the entries on September 25 and November 14 (assuming this is the first repurchase ever recorded by Arcon).

*QS 16-16
Treasury shares
LO6

Exercises

Delware Inc.'s shareholders' equity section at December 31, 2010, showed the following information:

Common shares, unlimited shares authorized,	
150,000 shares issued and outstanding	$1,850,000
Retained earnings..	475,000

Exercise 16-1
Share dividends
LO1

On January 15, 2011, Delware's board of directors declared a 5% share dividend to the shareholders of record on January 20 to be distributed on January 30. The market prices of the shares on January 15, 20, and 30 were $15.00, $13.50, and $14.25, respectively.

Required
1. Prepare the required entries for January 15, 20, and 30.
2. Prepare the shareholders' equity section at January 31, 2011, assuming net income earned during January 2011 was $650,000.

Check figure:
2. Retained earnings = $1,012,500

Analysis component:
What effect did the share dividend have on the market price of Delware's shares and why?

Stingray Inc.'s shareholders' equity section at October 31, 2011, showed the following information:

Common shares, unlimited shares authorized,	
500,000 shares issued and outstanding..	$600,000
Retained earnings...	75,000

Exercise 16-2
Share splits
LO1

On November 15, 2011, Stingray's board of directors declared a 3:1 share split to the shareholders of record on November 20 to be distributed on November 29. The market prices of the shares on November 15, 20, and 29 were $1.50, $0.48, and $0.52, respectively.

Required
1. Prepare the required entries for November 15, 20, and 29.
2. Prepare the shareholders' equity section at November 30, 2011, assuming net income earned during November 2011 was $125,000.

Check figure:
2. Retained earnings = $200,000

Analysis component:
What effect did the share split have on the market price of Stingray's shares and why?

An asterisk (*) identifies assignment material based on Appendix 16A.

Exercise 16-3
Share dividend, share split,
shareholders' equity
LO1

Fargo Inc. showed the following shareholders' equity information at December 31, 2010.

Common shares, unlimited shares authorized; 4,000,000 shares issued and outstanding	$1,255,600
Retained earnings...	1,640,000

On April 1, 2011, 200,000 common shares were issued at $0.75 per share. On June 1, the board of directors declared a 15% share dividend to shareholders of record on June 15; the distribution date was July 1. The market prices of the shares on June 1, June 15, and July 1 were $2.60, $2.20, and $2.45, respectively. On December 11, the board of directors declared a 2:1 share split to shareholders of record on December 15; the distribution date was December 20. Net income earned during the year was $1,750,000.

Check figure:
Shareholders' equity
Dec. 31/11 = $4,795,600

Required
Prepare the company's shareholders' equity section at December 31, 2011.

Analysis component:
What are the benefits to Fargo Inc. of declaring a share dividend as opposed to a cash dividend?

Exercise 16-4
Retirement of shares
LO2

Information taken from Tickets-4-Sale Inc.'s January 31, 2011, balance sheet follows:

Common shares, 600,000 shares authorized, 30,000 shares issued and outstanding..	$270,000
Retained earnings	52,900

On February 1, 2011, the company repurchased and retired 400 common shares (the first retirement the company has recorded).

Check figure:
c. Dr Common Shares $3,600

Required
Prepare General Journal entries to record the repurchase and retirement under each of the following independent assumptions.
The shares were repurchased for:
a. $6 per share   **b.** $9 per share   **c.** $12 per share

Exercise 16-5
Share split, retirement of shares
LO1, 2

The Precision Company of Canada Inc. had the following balances in its shareholders' equity accounts at December 31, 2010:

Common shares, unlimited shares authorized; 200,000 shares issued and outstanding	$3,000,000
Retained earnings...	500,000

During 2011, the following shareholders' equity transactions occurred:

Apr.	15	Repurchased and retired 15,000 common shares at $13 per share.
May	1	Repurchased and retired 25,000 common shares at $17 per share.
Nov.	1	The board of directors declared a 2:1 share split effective on this date.

Check figure:
2. Retained earnings,
Dec. 31/11 = $310,000

Required
1. Prepare journal entries to account for the transactions during 2011.
2. Prepare the company's shareholders' equity section at December 31, 2011, assuming a net loss for the year of $170,000.

Analysis component:
What does a share repurchase and retirement accomplish for Precision Company?

Exercise 16-6
Share dividends, share splits,
retirements, shareholders' equity
LO1, 2

ScubaPro Inc. showed the following shareholders' equity account balances at December 31, 2010:

Common shares, unlimited authorized shares, 680,000 shares issued and outstanding	$6,800,000
Retained earnings...	3,600,000

During 2011, the following selected transactions occurred:

Apr.	1	Repurchased and retired 280,000 common shares at $10.50 per share; this is the first retirement recorded by ScubaPro.
June	1	Declared a 2:1 share split to shareholders of record on June 12, distributable June 30.
Dec.	1	Declared a 10% share dividend to shareholders of record on December 10, distributable December 20. The market prices of the shares on December 1, December 10, and December 20 were $5.50, $4.80, and $5.20 respectively.
	20	Distributed the share dividend declared December 1.
	31	Closed the credit balance of $1,620,000 in the Income Summary account.

Required

a. Journalize the transactions above.

b. Prepare the shareholders' equity section at December 31, 2011.

Check figure:
Shareholders' equity,
Dec. 31/11 = $9,080,000

Northside Corporation's 2011 income statement, excluding the earnings per share portion of the statement, was as follows:

Exercise 16-7
Reporting earnings per share
LO3, 4

Revenues		$475,000
Expenses:		
Amortization	$ 51,900	
Income taxes...	65,100	
Other expenses	205,000	322,000
Income from continuing operations.............................		$153,000
Loss from operating discontinued business segment		
(net of $23,500 tax benefit)	$ 56,000	
Loss on sale of business segment (net of $9,400 tax benefit)	22,000	(78,000)
Income before extraordinary items		$ 75,000
Extraordinary gain (net of $18,400 taxes)......................		43,200
Net income		$118,200

The weighted-average number of common shares outstanding during the year was 100,000. Present the earnings per share portion of the 2011 income statement.

Check figure:
EPS = $1.18

Peony Inc. reported $262,300 net income in 2011 and declared preferred dividends of $43,000. The following changes in common shares outstanding occurred during the year:

Exercise 16-8
Weighted-average shares outstanding and earnings per share
LO3

Jan.	1	60,000 common shares were outstanding.
June	30	Sold 20,000 common shares.
Sept.	1	Declared and issued a 20% common share dividend.
Nov.	2	Sold 12,000 common shares.

Calculate the weighted-average number of common shares outstanding during the year and earnings per share.

Check figure:
Weighted-average outstanding
shares = 86,000

Kingsley Production Corp. reported $741,500 net income in 2011 and declared preferred dividends of $66,500. The following changes in common shares outstanding occurred during the year.

Exercise 16-9
Weighted-average shares outstanding and earnings per share
LO3

Jan.	1	60,000 common shares were outstanding.
Mar.	1	Declared and issued a 30% common share dividend.
Aug.	1	Sold 20,000 common shares.
Nov.	1	Sold 40,000 common shares.

Calculate the weighted-average number of common shares outstanding during the year and earnings per share. Round calculations to two decimal places.

Check figure:
Weighted-average outstanding
shares = 93,000

Analysis component:
What is the effect of a share dividend on earnings per share?

Exercise 16-10
Weighted-average shares outstanding and earnings per share
LO1, 3

Excalibre Inc. reported $1,343,775 of net income for 2011. On November 2, 2011, it declared and paid the annual preferred dividends of $195,000. On January 1, 2011, Excalibre had 80,000 and 270,000 outstanding preferred and common shares, respectively. The following transactions changed the number of shares outstanding during the year:

Feb.	1	Declared and issued a 10% common share dividend.
Apr.	30	Sold 180,000 common shares for cash.
May	1	Sold 50,000 preferred shares for cash.
Oct.	31	Sold 99,000 common shares for cash.

Check figure:
b. Weighted-average outstanding shares = 433,500

a. What is the amount of net income available for distribution to the common shareholders?
b. What is the weighted-average number of common shares for the year?
c. What is the basic earnings per share for the year?

Analysis component:
Did the sale of preferred shares on May 1, 2011, affect the basic earnings per common share?

Exercise 16-11
Weighted-average shares outstanding and earnings per share
LO3

A company reported $480,000 of net income for 2011. It also declared $65,000 of dividends on preferred shares for the same year. At the beginning of 2011, the company had 50,000 outstanding common shares. These three events changed the number of outstanding shares during the year:

June	1	Sold 30,000 common shares for cash.
Aug.	31	Purchased and retired 13,000 common shares.
Oct.	1	Completed a three-for-one share split.

Check figure:
c. EPS = $2.19

a. What is the amount of net income available for distribution to the common shareholders?
b. What is the weighted-average number of common shares for the year?
c. What is the basic earnings per share for the year?

Analysis component:
What is the effect of a share split on earnings per share?

Exercise 16-12
Income statement categories
LO4

Check figure:
Income before extraordinary items = $62,430

The following list of items was extracted from the December 31, 2011, trial balance of Wesson Corp. Using the information contained in this listing, prepare Wesson's multiple-step income statement for 2011. You need not complete the earnings per share calculations.

	Debit	Credit
Salaries expense	$ 33,350	
Income tax expense (continuing operations)	34,190	
Loss from operating Division C (net of $5,100 tax benefit)	12,000	
Sales		$350,120
Total effect on prior years' income of change from declining-balance to straight-line amortization (net of $4,800 tax)		16,200
Extraordinary gain on provincial condemnation of land owned by Wesson Corp. (net of $12,400 tax)		34,000
Amortization expense	31,050	
Gain on sale of Division C (net of $9,850 tax)		33,000
Cost of goods sold	210,100	

In preparing the annual financial statements for Elite Electronics Inc., the correct manner of reporting the following items was not clear to the company's employees. Explain where each of the following items should appear in the financial statements.

a. After amortizing office equipment for three years based on an expected useful life of eight years, the company decided this year that the office equipment should last seven more years. As a result, the amortization for the current year is $8,000 instead of $10,000.

b. This year, the accounting department of the company discovered that last year, an installment payment on the five-year note payable had been charged entirely to interest expense. The after-tax effect of the charge to interest expense was $15,400.

c. The company keeps its repair trucks for several years before disposing of the old trucks and buying new trucks. On June 1 of this year, for the first time in 10 years, it sold old trucks for a gain of $19,900. New trucks were purchased in August of the same year.

Exercise 16-13
Classifying income items not related to continuing operations
LO4

During 2011, Magna Data Inc. sold its interest in a chain of wholesale outlets. This sale took the company out of the wholesaling business completely. The company still operates its retail outlets. Following is a lettered list of sections of an income statement:

a. Income from continuing operations
b. Income from operating a discontinued operation
c. Gain or loss from disposing of a discontinued operation
d. Extraordinary gain or loss

Indicate where each of the eight income-related items for the company would appear on the 2011 income statement by writing the letter of the appropriate section in the blank beside each item.

Exercise 16-14
Income statement categories
LO4

		Debit	Credit
____	1. Amortization expense	$131,250	
____	2. Gain on sale of wholesale operation (net of $112,500 income taxes)		$ 337,500
____	3. Loss from operating wholesale operation (net of $92,500 tax benefit)	277,500	
____	4. Salaries expense	270,000	
____	5. Sales		1,350,000
____	6. Gain on expropriation of company property (net of $55,000 income taxes)		165,000
____	7. Cost of goods sold	690,000	
____	8. Income taxes expense	103,500	

Use the data for Magna Data Inc. in Exercise 16-14 to present a multiple-step income statement for 2011. You need not complete the earnings per share calculations.

Exercise 16-15
Income statement presentation
LO4

Check figure:
Income from continuing operations (after tax) = $155,250

Bell Corporation showed the following shareholders' equity account balances at December 31, 2010:

Exercise 16-16
Statement of retained earnings
LO5

Common shares, unlimited shares authorized, 70,000 shares issued and outstanding..	$680,000
Retained earnings	94,000

Bell Corporation issued long-term debt during 2011 that requires a retained earnings restriction of $60,000. Share dividends declared but not distributed during 2011 totalled 7,000 shares capitalized for a total of $70,000.

a. Prepare a statement of retained earnings for the year ended December 31, 2011, assuming net income earned during the year was $104,000.
b. Prepare the shareholders' equity section at December 31, 2011.
c. What is the maximum amount of dividends that Bell Corporation can declare during 2012?

Check figure:
b. Total shareholders' equity = $878,000

Exercise 16-17
Accounting for a change in
accounting policy
LO⁵

Canadian Home Company Ltd. put an asset in service on January 1, 2009. Its cost was $225,000, its predicted service life was six years, and its expected residual value was $22,500. The company decided to use double-declining-balance amortization. After consulting with the company's auditors, management decided to change to straight-line amortization in 2011, without changing either the predicted service life or residual value.

Required
Explain how and where this change should be accounted for.

Exercise 16-18
Accounting changes
LO⁵

Selected information regarding the accounts of Sedge Corp. follows:

Common dividends declared and paid during 2011	$100,000
Cumulative effect of change in accounting estimate	
(net of $6,000 tax)...	(28,000)
Net income for the year ended December 31, 2011	285,000
Preferred dividends declared and paid during 2011	60,000
Retained earnings, December 31, 2010 (as originally reported)	490,000

Prepare a statement of retained earnings for the year ended December 31, 2011.

*Exercise 16-19
Treasury shares
LO⁶

On October 10, 2011, the shareholders' equity account balances for Affiliated Systems, Inc., showed the following:

Common shares, unlimited shares authorized,	
36,000 shares issued, and outstanding..	$468,000
Retained earnings	432,000

On October 11, 2011, the corporation repurchased for treasury 4,500 common shares at $30 per share.

Check figures:
a. Total shareholders'
equity = $765,000
b.(iii) Dr. Retained Earnings $6,000

Required
a. Prepare the shareholders' equity section on October 11, 2011, after the repurchase.
b. Journalize the following transactions for Affiliated Systems, Inc.:
  (i) The purchase of the treasury shares on October 11.
  (ii) The sale of 1,500 treasury shares on November 1 for cash at $38 per share.
  (iii) The sale of all the remaining treasury shares on November 25 for cash at $24 per share.

*Exercise 16-20
Treasury shares
LO⁶

Sudbury Inc. began 2011 with the following balances in its shareholders' equity accounts:

Common shares, 500,000 shares authorized;	
200,000 shares issued and outstanding	$1,500,000
Retained earnings..	2,500,000

All of the outstanding shares were issued for $7.50.

Required
Prepare journal entries to account for the following transactions during 2011:

June	30	Purchased 30,000 treasury shares at $10 per share.
Aug.	31	Sold 10,000 treasury shares at $10 per share.
Nov.	30	Sold 15,000 treasury shares at $11 per share.

An asterisk (*) identifies assignment material based on Appendix 16A.

Problems

Except for the earnings per share statistics, the 2012, 2011, and 2010 income statements of Formula-1 Corp. were originally presented as follows:

	2012	2011	2010
Sales	$998,900	$687,040	$466,855
Costs and expenses..	323,570	234,500	157,420
Income from continuing operations	?	?	?
Loss on discontinued operations	(107,325)	—	—
Income (loss) before extraordinary items................	?	?	?
Extraordinary gains (losses)	—	80,410	(156,191)
Net income (loss)...	?	?	?

Information on Common Shares*	
Shares outstanding on December 31, 2009..	14,400
Purchase and retirement of shares on March 1, 2010	− 1,440
Sale of shares on June 1, 2010..	+ 6,240
Share dividend of 5% on August 1, 2010	+ ?
Shares outstanding on December 31, 2010..	?
Sale of shares on February 1, 2011	+ 2,880
Purchase and retirement of shares on July 1, 2011...	− 720
Shares outstanding on December 31, 2011..	?
Sale of shares on March 1, 2012...	+ 8,280
Purchase and retirement of shares on September 1, 2012	− 1,800
Share split of 3:1 on October 1, 2012	+ ?
Shares outstanding on December 31, 2012..	?

No preferred shares have been issued.

Required
1. Calculate the 14 missing amounts.
2. Calculate the weighted-average number of common shares outstanding during
   a. 2010   **b.** 2011 and   **c.** 2012.
3. Prepare the earnings per share income statement presentations for
   a. 2010;   **b.** 2011; and   **c.** 2012.

Analysis component:
Income from continuing operations increased from 2011 to 2012 yet there was a decrease in the earnings per share calculated for this amount for the same years. Explain.

Problem 16-1A
Earnings per share calculations and presentation
LO1, 2, 3, 4

Note: Problem 16-1B covers LO1, 3 with no retirement of shares.

Check figures:
Weighted-average outstanding shares:
2. a. 17,682
   b. 22,440
   c. 85,860

Problem 16-2A
Earnings per share
LO1, 3

Churchill Corp.'s financial statements for the current year ended December 31, 2011, have been completed and submitted to you for review. The shareholders' equity account balances a year ago, at December 31, 2010, are as follows:

Preferred shares, $2.80 non-cumulative, 10,000 shares authorized, issued and outstanding	$498,700
Common shares, unlimited shares authorized, 120,000 shares issued and outstanding..	946,900
Retained earnings	450,530

The only share transactions during 2011 were the declaration and distribution of a 24,000 common share dividend on July 1 and the issuance of 12,000 common shares for cash on October 31. Churchill's 2011 net income was $413,400. A cash dividend on the preferred shares was declared on December 1, but was not paid as of December 31. Earnings per share for 2011 were calculated as follows:

$$\frac{\text{Net income}}{\text{Common shares outstanding on Dec. 31, 2011}} = \frac{\$413,400}{156,000} = \$2.65$$

Required
1. Explain what is wrong with the earnings per share calculation, indicating what corrections should be made to both the numerator and the denominator. Round calculations to two decimal places.
2. Explain how your answer to requirement 1 would be different if there had not been a cash dividend declaration to preferred shares and if the share dividend had taken place on January 2, 2011.

Problem 16-3A
Dividends, retirement, statement of retained earnings, shareholders' equity
LO1, 2, 5

Note: Problem 16-3B covers LO1, 5 with no retirement of shares.

The accounts for the Kent Corporation reported the following shareholders' equity account balances on December 31, 2010:

Preferred shares, $3 cumulative, unlimited shares authorized...............................	$ -0-
Common shares, unlimited shares authorized, 20,000 shares issued and outstanding...	460,000
Retained Earnings	270,000

In 2011, Kent Corporation had the following transactions affecting shareholders and the shareholders' equity accounts:

Jan.	1	Purchased and retired 2,000 common shares at $30 per share.
	14	The directors declared a 10% share dividend distributable on February 5 to the January 30 shareholders of record. The shares were trading at $38 per share.
	30	Date of record regarding the 10% share dividend.
Feb.	5	Date of distribution regarding the 10% share dividend.
July	6	Sold 5,000 preferred shares at $50 per share.
Sept.	5	The directors declared a total cash dividend of $40,000 payable on October 5 to the September 20 shareholders of record.
Oct.	5	The cash dividend declared on September 5 was paid.
Dec.	31	Closed the $388,000 credit balance in the Income Summary account to Retained Earnings.
	31	Closed the dividend accounts.

Check figures:
2. Dec. 31/11 Retained Earnings = $535,600
3. Total shareholders' equity = $1,268,000

Required
1. Prepare journal entries to record the transactions and closings for 2011.
2. Prepare a statement of retained earnings for the year ended December 31, 2011.
3. Prepare the shareholders' equity section of the company's balance sheet as of December 31, 2011.

The following table shows the balances from various accounts in the adjusted trial balance for Depew Corp. as of December 31, 2011:

	Debit	Credit
a. Interest earned..		$ 24,000
b. Amortization expense, equipment..	$ 72,000	
c. Loss on sale of office equipment..	49,500	
d. Accounts payable...		84,000
e. Other operating expenses..	195,000	
f. Accumulated amortization, equipment		147,000
g. Gain from settling a lawsuit..		84,000
h. Cumulative effect of change in accounting principle (pre-tax)...		126,000
i. Accumulated amortization, buildings		327,000
j. Loss from operating a discontinued operation (pre-tax)	39,000	
k. Gain on expropriation of land and building by government (pre-tax)..		57,000
l. Sales		1,941,000
m. Amortization expense, buildings	108,000	
n. Correction of overstatement of prior year's sales (pre-tax)...	30,000	
o. Gain on sale of discontinued operation's assets (pre-tax)...		66,000
p. Loss from settling a lawsuit	48,000	
q. Income taxes expense..	?	
r. Cost of goods sold	975,000	

Required

1. Assuming that the company's income tax rate is 30%, what are the tax effects and after-tax measures of the items labelled as pre-tax?
2. Prepare a multi-step income statement for the year ended December 31, 2011.

Problem 16-4A
Presenting items in an income statement
LO4

Check figure:
Income from continuing operations before tax = $601,500

The income statement for Pelzer Inc.'s year ended December 31, 2011, was prepared by an inexperienced bookkeeper. As the new accountant, your immediate priority is to correct the statement. All amounts included in the statement are before tax (assume a rate of 30%). Pelzer Inc. had 100,000 common shares issued and outstanding throughout the year, as well as 20,000 shares of $1.00 cumulative preferred shares issued and outstanding. Retained earnings at December 31, 2010, were $274,000.

Problem 16-5A
Combined statement of income and retained earnings
LO4, 5

Pelzer Inc.
Income Statement
December 31, 2011

Revenues:		
Sales	$960,000	
Gain on sale of equipment...	12,000	
Interest revenue...	5,600	
Extraordinary gain	118,000	
Operating income on discontinued operation.............	24,200	$1,119,800
Expenses:		
Cost of goods sold..	$290,000	
Selling and administrative expenses	150,000	
Sales discounts..	9,800	
Loss on sale of discontinued operation.......................	30,000	
Dividends	100,000	579,800
Net income..		$ 540,000
Earnings per share..		$5.40

Required

Prepare a corrected income statement and statement of retained earnings including earnings per share information. Round earnings per share calculations to the nearest whole cent.

Check figures:
Income before discontinued operation = $369,460;
Earnings per common share = $4.28

Problem 16-6A
Dividends, statement of retained earnings, shareholders' equity
LO1, 5

Hayes Inc. had the following shareholders' equity account balances at December 31, 2010:

Preferred shares, $1.75, non-cumulative,	
Authorized: 20,000 shares	
Issued and outstanding: 5,000 shares..	$ 25,000
Common shares,	
Authorized: Unlimited	
Issued and outstanding: 85,000 shares..	205,496
Retained earnings	29,000

On February 1, 2011, 5,000 preferred shares were issued at $5.50 each. The board of directors declared and paid the annual cash dividend on the preferred shares on June 30, 2011, and a 12% common share dividend was declared and distributed on the same day when the market price per common share was $3.00. On October 1, 2011, 20,000 common shares were issued at $3.10 each. Net income earned during 2011 was $292,000.

Check figures:
1. Retained earnings,
Dec. 31/11 = $272,900
2. Total contributed capital,
Dec. 31/11 = $350,596

Required
Using the information provided, prepare the:
1. Statement of retained earnings for the year ended December 31, 2011.
2. Shareholders' equity section of the balance sheet at December 31, 2011.

Problem 16-7A
Retirement of shares, retained earnings analysis
LO1, 2, 5

Note: Problem 16-7B covers LO1, 5 with no retirement of shares.

The equity sections from the 2011 and 2012 balance sheets of Seghal Corporation appeared as follows:

Seghal Corporation Shareholders' Equity December 31		
	2012	**2011**
Contributed capital:		
Common shares, 50,000 shares authorized; 22,200 and		
20,000 shares issued and outstanding, respectively...............	$347,800	$280,000
Retained earnings	400,000	320,000

The following transactions occurred during 2012:

Jan.	5	A $1.00 per share cash dividend was declared, and the date of record was five days later.
Mar.	20	1,500 common shares were repurchased and retired at $14 per share.
Apr.	5	A $1.00 per share cash dividend was declared, and the date of record was five days later.
July	5	A $1.00 per share cash dividend was declared, and the date of record was five days later.
	31	A 20% share dividend was declared when the market value was $24 per share.
Aug.	14	The share dividend was issued.
Oct.	5	A $1.00 per share cash dividend was declared, and the date of record was five days later.

Check figure:
1. Outstanding shares
Oct. 5 = 22,200

Required
1. How many shares were outstanding on each of the cash dividend dates?
2. How much net income did the company earn during 2012?

*Problem 16-8A
Cash dividends, treasury share transactions
LO5, 6

Li Corporation, which was provincially incorporated, reported the following shareholders' equity account balances on December 31, 2010:

Common shares, unlimited shares authorized,	
20,000 shares issued and outstanding..	$460,000
Retained Earnings	270,000

An asterisk (*) identifies assignment material based on Appendix 16A.

In 2011, Li Corporation had the following transactions affecting shareholders and the shareholders' equity accounts:

Jan.	1	Purchased 2,000 treasury shares at $40 per share.
	5	The directors declared a $4.00 per share cash dividend payable on Feb. 28 to the Feb. 5 shareholders of record.
Feb.	28	Paid the dividend declared on January 5.
July	6	Sold 750 of the treasury shares at $48 per share.
Aug.	22	Sold 1,250 of the treasury shares at $34 per share.
Dec.	31	Closed the $388,000 credit balance in the Income Summary account to Retained Earnings.
	31	Closed the Cash Dividends account.

Required

1. Prepare journal entries to record the transactions and closings for 2011.
2. Prepare a statement of retained earnings for the year ended December 31, 2011.
3. Prepare the shareholders' equity section of the company's balance sheet as of December 31, 2011.

Check figures:
2. Retained earnings, December 31 = $584,500
3. Total shareholders' equity = $1,044,500

Alternate Problems

The original income statements for Titus, Inc., presented the following information when they were first published in 2010, 2011, and 2012:

Problem 16-1B
Earnings per share calculations and presentation
LO1, 3, 4

	2012	2011	2010
Sales	$400,000	$300,000	$250,000
Expenses	270,000	215,000	160,000
Income from continuing operations	?	?	?
Loss on discontinued segment	—	—	(26,145)
Income before extraordinary items..........................	?	?	?
Extraordinary gain (loss)...	(37,125)	14,100	—
Net income..	?	?	?

The company also experienced some changes in the number of outstanding common shares over the three years through the following activities:*

Outstanding shares on December 31, 2009	10,000
2010	
Issued shares on July 1..	+ 1,000
Issued shares on September 30	+ 3,500
20% share dividend on December 1	?
Outstanding shares on December 31, 2010	?
2011	
Issued shares on March 31	+ 4,000
Outstanding shares on December 31, 2011	?
2012	
Issued shares on July 1..	+ 3,200
2:1 split on November 1	?
Outstanding shares on December 31, 2012	?

No preferred shares have been issued.

Required

1. Calculate the 14 missing amounts.
2. Calculate the weighted-average number of common shares outstanding during:
   a. 2010   **b.** 2011   **c.** 2012
3. Present the earnings per share income statement presentations for:
   a. 2010;   **b.** 2011; and   **c.** 2012.

Check figure:
Weighted-average outstanding shares:
2. a. 13,650
   b. 20,400
   c. 46,000

Problem 16-2B
Earnings per share
LO1, 3

Computex Corporation has tentatively prepared its financial statements for the year ended December 31, 2011, and has submitted them to you for review. The shareholders' equity account balances at December 31, 2011, are as follows:

Preferred shares, $2.50 cumulative, 30,000 shares authorized, 18,000 shares issued and outstanding...	$520,100
Common shares, unlimited shares authorized; 132,000 shares issued and outstanding..	777,840
Retained earnings...	996,200

Computex Corporation's 2011 net income was $600,000 and no cash dividends were declared. The only share transaction that occurred during the year was the issuance of 24,000 common shares on March 31, 2011. Earnings per share for 2011 was calculated as follows:

$$\frac{\text{Net income}}{\text{Common plus preferred shares outstanding on Dec. 31}} = \frac{\$600,000}{132,000 + 18,000} = \$4.00$$

Required
1. Explain what is wrong with the earnings per share calculation, indicating what corrections should be made to both the numerator and the denominator.
2. Explain how your answer to requirement 1 could be different if the preferred shares were not cumulative and if the issuance of 24,000 shares had been a share dividend.

Problem 16-3B
Dividends, share dividend, share split, statement of retained earnings, shareholders' equity
LO1, 5

The shareholders' equity accounts for Caldwell Corp. showed the following balances on December 31, 2010:

Preferred shares, $2.50 non-cumulative, unlimited shares authorized	$ -0-
Common shares, unlimited shares authorized, 100,000 shares issued and outstanding	800,000
Retained earnings..	1,080,000

The company completed these transactions during 2011:

Jan.	10	Issued 20,000 common shares at $12 cash per share.
	15	The directors declared a 10% share dividend to the January 30 shareholders of record, distributable on February 15. The market price of the shares on January 15 was $12.25.
Feb.	15	Distributed the share dividend.
Mar.	2	The directors declared a $1.50 per share cash dividend payable on March 31 to the March 15 shareholders of record.
	31	Paid the dividend declared on March 2.
Apr.	10	The directors announced a 3:1 share split to the April 20 shareholders of record. The shares were trading just prior to the announcement at $12.50 per share.
Nov.	11	Issued 12,000 preferred shares at $25 per share.
Dec.	1	The board of directors declared total dividends of $228,000 payable December 15, 2011.
	15	Paid the dividends declared on December 1.
	31	Closed the $1,450,000 credit balance in the Income Summary account.
	31	Closed the Cash Dividends account.

Check figures:
2. Dec. 31/11 Retained earnings = $1,957,000
3. Total shareholders' equity = $3,444,000

Required
1. Prepare General Journal entries to record the transactions and closings for 2011.
2. Prepare a statement of retained earnings for 2011.
3. Prepare the shareholders' equity section of the company's balance sheet as of December 31, 2011.

The following table shows the balances from various accounts in the adjusted trial balance for Barbour Corp. as of December 31, 2011:

Problem 16-4B
Presenting items in an income statement
LO4

	Debit	Credit
a. Accumulated amortization, buildings		$ 200,000
b. Interest earned		10,000
c. Cumulative effect of change in accounting policy (pre-tax)		46,000
d. Sales..		1,320,000
e. Income taxes expense	$?	
f. Loss on condemnation of property (pre-tax)..........................	32,000	
g. Accumulated amortization, equipment.................................		110,000
h. Other operating expenses	164,000	
i. Amortization expense, equipment.......................................	50,000	
j. Loss from settling a lawsuit..	18,000	
k. Gain from settling a lawsuit..		34,000
l. Loss on sale of office equipment.......................................	12,000	
m. Loss from operating a discontinued operation (pre-tax).............	60,000	
n. Amortization expense, buildings..	78,000	
o. Correction of overstatement of prior year's expense (pre-tax)....		24,000
p. Cost of goods sold...	520,000	
q. Loss on sale of discontinued operation's assets (pre-tax)	90,000	
r. Accounts payable		66,000

Required
1. Assuming that the company's income tax rate is 25%, what are the tax effects and after-tax measures of the items labelled as pre-tax?
2. Prepare a multi-step income statement for the year ended December 31, 2011.

Check figure:
Income from continuing operations before tax = $522,000

After returning from vacation, the accountant of Bosworth Inc. was dismayed to discover that the income statement for the year ended December 31, 2011, was prepared incorrectly. All amounts included in the statement are before tax (assume a rate of 40%). Bosworth Inc. had 200,000 common shares issued and outstanding throughout the year as well as 70,000 $2.00 cumulative preferred shares. Dividends had not been paid for the past two years (2009 and 2010). Retained earnings at December 31, 2010, were $342,000.

Problem 16-5B
Combined statement of income and retained earnings
LO3, 4, 5

Bosworth Inc.
Income Statement
December 31, 2011

Revenues:		
Sales..	$1,800,000	
Gain on sale of discontinued operation (pre-tax)	240,000	
Accumulated amortization, equipment.....................................	45,000	
Operating income on discontinued operation (pre-tax).............	636,000	$2,721,000
Expenses:		
Cost of goods sold..	$ 480,000	
Selling and administrative expenses.......................................	180,000	
Sales returns and allowances	14,000	
Extraordinary loss (pre-tax)...	80,000	
Dividends...	95,000	849,000
Net income		$1,872,000
Earnings per share		$9.36

Required
Prepare a corrected income statement, using a multi-step format, and statement of retained earnings including earnings per share information. Round all earnings per share calculations to the nearest whole cent.

Check figures:
Income before discontinued operation = $675,600;
Earnings per share = $5.07

Problem 16-6B
Dividends, statement of retained earnings, shareholders' equity
LO1, 5

BusCom Corp. had the following shareholders' equity account balances at December 31, 2010:

Preferred shares, $0.50, cumulative,	
Authorized: 100,000 shares	
Issued and outstanding: 45,000 shares..	$360,000
Common shares,	
Authorized: Unlimited	
Issued and outstanding: 300,000 shares...	898,200
Retained earnings	218,000

On November 1, 2011, the board of directors declared and paid the current year's cash dividend on the preferred shares plus the two years of dividends in arrears. On the same day, a 10% common share dividend was declared and distributed; the market price per common share was $3.50. On December 1, 2011, 100,000 common shares were issued at $3.60. Net income earned during 2011 was $200,000.

Check figures:
1. Retained earnings,
Dec. 31/11 = $245,500
2. Total contributed capital,
Dec. 31/11 = $1,723,200

Required
Using the information provided, prepare the:
1. Statement of retained earnings for the year ended December 31, 2011.
2. Shareholders' equity section of the balance sheet at December 31, 2011.

Problem 16-7B
Retained earnings analysis
LO1, 5

The equity sections from the 2010 and 2011 balance sheets of Thornhill Corporation appeared as follows:

Thornhill Corporation
Shareholders' Equity
December 31

	2011	2010
Contributed capital:		
Common shares, unlimited shares authorized, 18,900 and		
8,500 shares issued and outstanding, respectively.................	$224,100	$200,000
Retained earnings	400,000	135,000
Total shareholders' equity	$624,100	$335,000

The following events occurred during 2011:

Feb.	15	A $0.40 per share cash dividend was declared, and the date of record was five days later.
Mar.	2	500 common shares were issued at $23 per share.
May	15	A $0.40 per share cash dividend was declared, and the date of record was five days later.
Aug.	15	A 2:1 share split was declared and distributed to shareholders of record five days later.
Oct.	4	A 5% share dividend was declared when the market value was $14 per share.
	20	The dividend shares were issued.
Nov.	15	A $0.40 per share cash dividend was declared, and the date of record was five days later.

Check figure:
1. Outstanding shares
May 15 = 9,000

Required
1. How many shares were outstanding on each of the cash dividend dates?
2. How much net income did the company earn during 2011?

Lavigne Corp. reported the following shareholders' equity account balances on December 31, 2010:

Common shares, unlimited shares authorized;	
100,000 shares issued and outstanding	$ 800,000
Retained earnings...	1,080,000

*Problem 16-8B
Dividends, treasury shares transactions
LO5, 6

The company completed these transactions during 2011:

Jan.	10	Purchased 20,000 treasury shares at $12 cash per share.
Mar.	2	The directors declared a $1.50 per share cash dividend payable on March 31 to the March 15 shareholders of record.
	31	Paid the dividend declared on March 2.
Nov.	11	Sold 12,000 of the treasury shares at $13 per share.
	25	Sold 8,000 of the treasury shares at $9.50 per share.
Dec.	1	The directors declared a $2.50 per share cash dividend payable on January 2, 2012, to the December 10 shareholders of record.
	31	Closed the $536,000 credit balance in the Income Summary account to Retained Earnings.
	31	Closed the Cash Dividends account.

Required
1. Prepare General Journal entries to record the transactions and closings for 2011.
2. Prepare a statement of retained earnings for 2011.
3. Prepare the shareholders' equity section of the company's balance sheet as of December 31, 2011.

Check figures:
2. Retained earnings = $1,238,000
3. Total shareholders' equity = $2,038,000

Analytical and Review Problem

The following adjusted trial balance information (with accounts in alphabetical order) for Willis Tour Co. Inc. as at December 31, 2011, was made available after its second year of operations:

A & R 16-1

Account	Debit	Credit
Accounts Payable..		$ 2,500
Accumulated Amortization, Office Equipment		8,000
Cash...	$ 17,500	
Common Shares, 20,000 authorized;		
10,000 issued and outstanding...		12,500
Dividends Payable		4,500
Gain on Expropriation of Land and Building (net of $5,000 tax).....		20,000
Income Tax Expense	7,000	
Income Tax Payable..		2,000
Loss on Sale of Office Equipment..	13,500	
Notes Payable (due in 18 months)..		8,500
Office Equipment	56,000	
Operating Expenses...	195,500	
Preferred Shares, $0.25 non-cumulative; 5,000 shares		
authorized; 2,000 shares issued and outstanding		10,000
Prepaid Rent..	22,500	
Retained Earnings		14,500
Ticket Sales...		229,500
Totals...	$312,000	$312,000

Required
Willis follows the practice of debiting retained earnings directly for the annual dividend declaration. Prepare an income statement (in multi-step format), a statement of retained earnings, and a classified balance sheet for Willis Tour Co. Inc. using the information provided. Include the appropriate presentation for earnings per share.

Check figure:
Net income = $33,500

An asterisk (*) identifies assignment material based on Appendix 16A.

Ethics Challenge

EC 16-1

JenStar's management team has decided that its income statement would be more useful if amortization were calculated using the double-declining-balance method instead of the straight-line method. This change in accounting policy adds $156,000 to net income in the current year. As the auditor of the company, you are reviewing the decision to make the change in accounting policy. You review the equipment in question and realize that it is a piece of high-tech equipment and the risk of obsolescence in the near future is relatively high. You are also aware that all members of top management receive year-end bonuses based on net income.

Required
As an auditor in this situation, would you support the change in policy or ask management to continue using the straight-line method? Justify your response.

Focus on Financial Statements

FFS 16-1

LR Enterprises Inc. had the following shareholders' equity account balances at December 31, 2010:

Preferred shares, $1.75, non-cumulative,	
Authorized: 100,000 shares	
Issued and outstanding: 45,000 shares	$ 675,000
Common shares,	
Authorized: Unlimited	
Issued and outstanding: 800,000 shares	1,320,000
Retained earnings...	645,000

Sales during 2011 totalled $1,560,000 and operating expenses were $998,000. Assume that income tax is accrued at year-end at the rate of 30% of annual operating income. On March 1, 2011, 200,000 of the common shares were repurchased at $1.70 each and then cancelled. The board of directors declared and paid the annual cash dividend on the preferred shares on December 1 and an 8% common share dividend was declared and distributed on the same day when the market price per common share was $1.80.

Required

Preparation component:
Use the information provided to prepare:
1. An income statement for the year ended December 31, 2011, including appropriate earnings per share information.
2. A statement of retained earnings for the year ended December 31, 2011.
3. A classified balance sheet at December 31, 2011, assuming the following adjusted account balances: Cash, $168,000; Accounts Receivable, $102,000; Allowance for Doubtful Accounts, $3,500; Prepaid Insurance, $36,000; Land, $1,000,000; Building, $500,000; Accumulated Amortization, Building, $241,000; Machinery, $1,909,600; Accumulated Amortization, Machinery, $653,850; Furniture, $78,000; Accumulated Amortization, Furniture, $44,000; Accounts Payable, $41,000; Notes Payable (due March 2013), $27,000.

Analysis component:
4. What percent of the assets is financed by debt?
5. What percent of the assets is financed by equity?

Refer to the financial statements and notes to the financial statements for Danier Leather in   **FFS 16-2**
Appendix I at the end of the textbook.

Required
Answer the following questions.
1. **a.** Did retained earnings increase or decrease from June 26, 2004, to June 25, 2005?
   b. The 2005 retained earnings were decreased by a share repurchase of $2,883 (thousand). Explain what this means.
2. Prepare the entry that might have been recorded regarding the share repurchase.
3. Danier's 2005 income statement shows the basic weighted-average number of common shares outstanding to be 6,726,658. Explain the actual composition of this amount.

Critical Thinking Mini Case

CanaCo showed the following shareholders' equity at December 31, 2011:

Contributed capital	
Preferred shares, $2 non-cumulative	
Authorized: 50,000	
Issued and outstanding: 0	$ -0-
Common shares	
Authorized: Unlimited	
Issued and outstanding: 50,000	6,800,000
Total contributed capital	$ 6,800,000
Retained earnings	3,800,000
Total shareholders' equity...	$10,600,000

The shareholders of CanaCo expressed concerns to the board of directors at the recent annual meeting that the market price of their shares has not changed significantly over the past 18 months, yet the company is very profitable. Net income for each of the past three years has been $1,800,000, $2,300,000, and $3,500,000, respectively. Cash dividends were paid in each of these years equal to 50% of net income.

Required
Using the elements of critical thinking described on the inside front cover, comment.

CHAPTER 17

Bonds and Long-Term Notes Payable

Then and Now . . .

On its December 31, 2002, balance sheet, Air Canada had total assets of $7.4 billion. That's a lot of assets and sounds very impressive . . . until you look further: liabilities totalled $9.7 billion and shareholders' equity was $(2.3) billion!

As a result of mounting debt and an inability to pay creditors, Air Canada obtained creditor protection on April 1, 2003. The December 31, 2003, balance sheet showed assets of $6.9 billion, liabilities of $11 billion, and shareholders' equity of $(4.1) billion. Note 1 of these financial statements stated that ". . . there is substantial doubt about the Corporation's ability to continue as a going concern." The situation was spiralling downward despite efforts to keep Air Canada afloat.

Then, on June 29, 2004, an agreement was reached and ACE Aviation Holdings Inc. was incorporated and became the parent of Air Canada and its subsidiaries. Under a new plan, the December 31, 2004, balance sheet showed a reversal: total assets of $9.4 billion, liabilities of $9.2 billion, and equity of $0.2 billion. Under ACE, Air Canada's debt was creatively restructured, making a recovery seem possible.

As of September 30, 2005, the balance sheet has been further strengthened so that liabilities are 89% of total assets (an improvement over 98% at December 31, 2004). Liabilities, when managed well, can help grow a company, but as we see with Air Canada, they can also almost destroy it.

http://www.aircanada.com/en/about/investor/reports.html

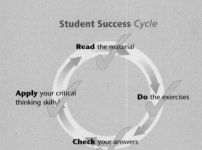

Student Success *Cycle*

Read the material

Do the exercises

Check your answers

Apply your critical thinking skills

CRITICAL THINKING CHALLENGE

What does "Air Canada obtained creditor protection" mean? Describe why "the Corporation's ability to continue as a going concern" was in question. Explain the statement: "Liabilities, when managed well, can help grow a company . . . ." What was the likely cause of the increase in negative equity from December 31, 2002 to 2003?

learning objectives

LO1 Compare bond versus share financing.

LO2 Explain the types of bonds and their issuing procedures.

LO3 Prepare entries to record bonds issued at par.

LO4 Determine the price of a bond.

LO5 Prepare entries to record bonds issued at a discount.

LO6 Prepare entries to record bonds issued at a premium.

LO7 Record the retirement of bonds.

LO8 Explain and record notes.

*APPENDIX 17B

*LO9 Prepare entries to record lease liabilities.

chapter preview

In Chapters 15 and 16, we learned that companies can get funds through equity financing: by issuing shares and by increasing retained earnings through profitable operations. This chapter discusses another major source of funds—debt financing: issuing bonds. Companies and governments issue bonds to finance their activities. In return for money, bonds promise to repay the amount borrowed plus interest. This chapter explains the basics of bonds and the accounting for their issuance and retirement. We explain how present value concepts affect bonds' accounting and reporting. The chapter also describes long-term notes and installment notes. Understanding how liabilities can be used to the advantage of a company if well managed, as shown in the opening article, is an important goal of this chapter.

Basics of Bonds

A **bond** is a written promise to pay an amount identified as the *par value* of the bond along with interest at a stated annual rate. A bond is a liability to the borrowing or issuing corporation. The **par value** of the bond, also called the *face amount* or *face value*, is paid at a specified future date known as the *maturity date of the bond*. The total amount of interest P. 519 paid each year is determined by multiplying the par value of the bond by the bond's stated rate of interest. The **stated interest rate**—sometimes called the **contract rate**, **nominal rate**, or **coupon rate**—is quoted as an annual rate. Interest can be paid annually, semi-annually, or for some other fraction of the year. For example, let's suppose a company issues a $1,000 bond with a contract interest rate of 8% to be paid semi-annually. For this bond, the annual interest of $80 (= 8% × $1,000) is paid in two semi-annual payments of $40 each. The document that specifies the issuer's name, the bond's par value, the contract interest rate, and the maturity date is called a **bond certificate**.

This section explains both advantages and disadvantages of bond financing.

Advantages of Bonds

There are three main advantages of bond financing over share financing.

LO1 Compare bond versus share financing.

1. *Bonds do not affect shareholder control.* Shares reflect an ownership right in the corporation, and affect equity. A *bondholder* lends the company money, which increases liabilities on the issuing corporation's balance sheet.

2. *Interest on bonds is tax deductible.* Bond interest is tax deductible, but dividends to shareholders are not. To illustrate the importance of this, let's assume a company that pays tax at the rate of 40% issued $1,000,000 of bonds that pay interest at 10%. Interest expense will be $100,000 (= $1,000,000 × 10%). Because interest expense is tax deductible, the company's income tax expense will be reduced by the amount of the interest expense times the tax rate or $40,000 (= $100,000 × 40%). Because the corporation saves $40,000 in taxes, the true cost (or after-tax cost) of borrowing is $60,000 (= $100,000 interest expense less $40,000 tax saving). If the same amount of money were raised by issuing shares instead of bonds, $100,000 paid out as dividends would not be tax deductible and the net costs of raising the $1,000,000 would be the full amount of the dividends.

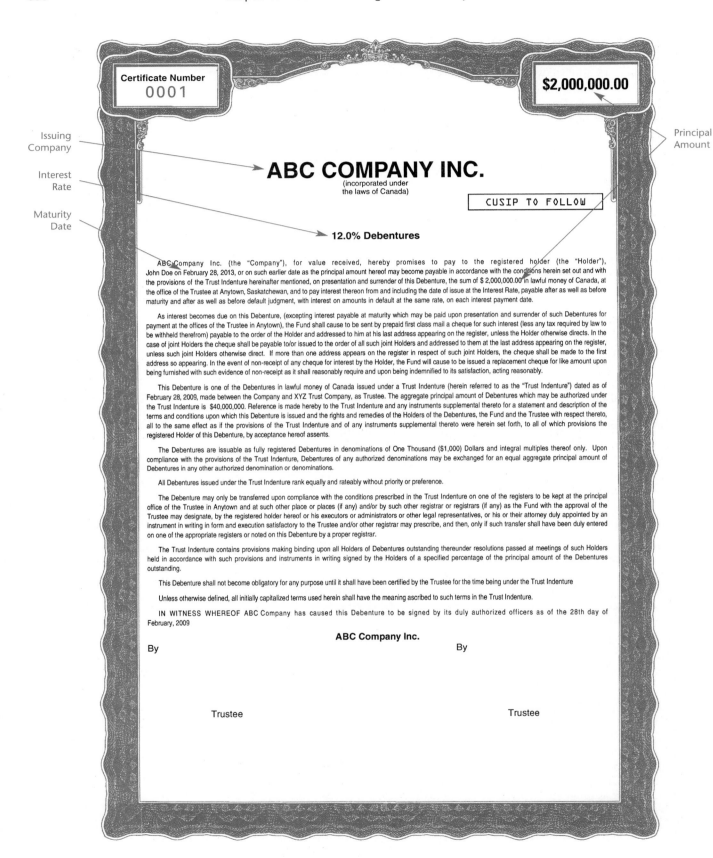

Certificate Number
0001

$2,000,000.00

Issuing Company

Interest Rate

Maturity Date

Principal Amount

ABC COMPANY INC.

(incorporated under
the laws of Canada)

CUSIP TO FOLLOW

12.0% Debentures

ABC Company Inc. (the "Company"), for value received, hereby promises to pay to the registered holder (the "Holder"), John Doe on February 28, 2013, or on such earlier date as the principal amount hereof may become payable in accordance with the conditions herein set out and with the provisions of the Trust Indenture hereinafter mentioned, on presentation and surrender of this Debenture, the sum of $ 2,000,000.00 in lawful money of Canada, at the office of the Trustee at Anytown, Saskatchewan, and to pay interest thereon from and including the date of issue at the Interest Rate, payable after as well as before maturity and after as well as before default judgment, with interest on amounts in default at the same rate, on each interest payment date.

As interest becomes due on this Debenture, (excepting interest payable at maturity which may be paid upon presentation and surrender of such Debentures for payment at the offices of the Trustee in Anytown), the Fund shall cause to be sent by prepaid first class mail a cheque for such interest (less any tax required by law to be withheld therefrom) payable to the order of the Holder and addressed to him at his last address appearing on the register, unless the Holder otherwise directs. In the case of joint Holders the cheque shall be payable to/or issued to the order of all such joint Holders and addressed to them at the last address appearing on the register, unless such joint Holders otherwise direct. If more than one address appears on the register in respect of such joint Holders, the cheque shall be made to the first address so appearing. In the event of non-receipt of any cheque for interest by the Holder, the Fund will cause to be issued a replacement cheque for like amount upon being furnished with such evidence of non-receipt as it shall reasonably require and upon being indemnified to its satisfaction, acting reasonably.

This Debenture is one of the Debentures in lawful money of Canada issued under a Trust Indenture (herein referred to as the "Trust Indenture") dated as of February 28, 2009, made between the Company and XYZ Trust Company, as Trustee. The aggregate principal amount of Debentures which may be authorized under the Trust Indenture is $40,000,000. Reference is made hereby to the Trust Indenture and any instruments supplemental thereto for a statement and description of the terms and conditions upon which this Debenture is issued and the rights and remedies of the Holders of the Debentures, the Fund and the Trustee with respect thereto, all to the same effect as if the provisions of the Trust Indenture and of any instruments supplemental thereto were herein set forth, to all of which provisions the registered Holder of this Debenture, by acceptance hereof assents.

The Debentures are issuable as fully registered Debentures in denominations of One Thousand ($1,000) Dollars and integral multiples thereof only. Upon compliance with the provisions of the Trust Indenture, Debentures of any authorized denominations may be exchanged for an equal aggregate principal amount of Debentures in any other authorized denomination or denominations.

All Debentures issued under the Trust Indenture rank equally and rateably without priority or preference.

The Debenture may only be transferred upon compliance with the conditions prescribed in the Trust Indenture on one of the registers to be kept at the principal office of the Trustee in Anytown and at such other place or places (if any) and/or by such other registrar or registrars (if any) as the Fund with the approval of the Trustee may designate, by the registered holder hereof or his executors or administrators or other legal representatives, or his or their attorney duly appointed by an instrument in writing in form and execution satisfactory to the Trustee and/or other registrar may prescribe, and then, only if such transfer shall have been duly entered on one of the appropriate registers or noted on this Debenture by a proper registrar.

The Trust Indenture contains provisions making binding upon all Holders of Debentures outstanding thereunder resolutions passed at meetings of such Holders held in accordance with such provisions and instruments in writing signed by the Holders of a specified percentage of the principal amount of the Debentures outstanding.

This Debenture shall not become obligatory for any purpose until it shall have been certified by the Trustee for the time being under the Trust Indenture

Unless otherwise defined, all initially capitalized terms used herein shall have the meaning ascribed to such terms in the Trust Indenture.

IN WITNESS WHEREOF ABC Company has caused this Debenture to be signed by its duly authorized officers as of the 28th day of February, 2009

ABC Company Inc.

By

By

Trustee

Trustee

3. *Bonds can increase return on equity.* **Return on equity** is net income available to common shareholders divided by common shareholders' equity.[1] When a company earns a higher return with the borrowed funds than it is paying in interest, it increases its return on equity. This process is called **financial leverage**.

To illustrate the effect on return on equity, let's look at Magnum Skates Corp. Magnum's income before tax is $100,000 per year and it has no interest expense. It has $1 million in equity, and is planning a $500,000 expansion to meet increasing demand for its product. Magnum predicts the $500,000 expansion will provide $125,000 in additional income before paying any interest and tax. Magnum is considering three plans:

- Plan A is not to expand.
- Plan B is to expand, and raise $500,000 from issuing shares.
- Plan C is to sell $500,000 worth of bonds paying 10% annual interest, or $50,000.

Exhibit 17.1 shows us how these three plans affect Magnum's net income, equity, and return on equity (Net income ÷ Equity).

	Plan A: Do Not Expand	Plan B: Increase Equity	Plan C: Issue Bonds
Income before interest expense and tax...............	$ 100,000	$ 225,000	$ 225,000
Interest expense...	—	—	(50,000)
Income before tax..	$ 100,000	$ 225,000	$ 175,000
Equity	$1,000,000	$1,500,000	$1,000,000
Return on equity (Net income ÷ Equity)	**10.0%**	**15.0%**	**17.5%**

Exhibit 17.1

Financing With Bonds or Shares

Analysis of these plans shows that the corporation will earn a higher return on equity if it expands. The preferred plan of expansion is to issue bonds. Why? Even though the projected income before tax under Plan C of $175,000 is smaller than the $225,000 under Plan B, the return on equity is larger because of less shareholder investment. This is an important example of financial leverage and proves a general rule: Return on equity increases when the expected rate of return from the new assets is greater than the rate of interest on the bonds. Issuing bonds also allows the current owners to remain in control.

Disadvantages of Bonds

There are two main disadvantages of bond financing over share financing.

1. *Bonds* **require** *payment of* **both** *annual interest and par value at maturity.* Bond payments can be a burden when a company's income is low. Shares, on the other hand, do not require payment of dividends because they are declared at the discretion of the board of directors.

2. *Bonds can decrease return on equity.* When a company earns a lower return with the borrowed funds than it is paying in interest, it decreases its return on equity. This is a risk of bond financing and is more likely to arise when a company has periods of low income.

[1] Ratios are discussed in more detail in Chapter 20.

A company must weigh the risks of these disadvantages against the advantages of bond financing when deciding how to finance operations.

Types of Bonds

Bonds appear on the balance sheets of companies such as Air Canada, Bell Canada Enterprises, Bombardier, Canadian Tire, and Magna International. We describe the more common kinds of bonds in this section.

Secured and Unsecured Bonds

LO2 | Explain the types of bonds and their issuing procedures.

Secured bonds have specific assets of the issuing company pledged (or *mortgaged*) as *collateral* (a guarantee). This arrangement gives bondholders added protection if the issuing company fails to pay interest or par value. In the event of non-payment, secured bondholders can demand that the secured assets be sold and the proceeds be used to pay the bond obligation.

Unsecured bonds, also called **debentures**, are supported by the issuer's general credit standing. Because debentures are unsecured, a company generally must be financially strong to issue debentures successfully at a favourable rate of interest.

Term and Serial Bonds

Term bonds make up a bond issue that becomes due at a single specified date. **Serial bonds** comprise a bond issue whose component parts mature at several different dates (in series). For instance, $1 million of serial bonds might mature at the rate of $100,000 each year from Year 6 until all the bonds are fully repaid in Year 15.

Registered Bonds and Bearer Bonds

Bonds issued in the names and addresses of their owners are **registered bonds**. The issuing company makes bond payments by sending cheques to these registered owners.

Bonds payable to whomever holds them (the *bearer*) are called **bearer bonds**, or *unregistered bonds*. Since there may be no record of sales or exchanges, the holder of a bearer bond is presumed to be its rightful owner. As a result, lost or stolen bearer bonds are difficult to replace. Bearer bonds are now uncommon.

Many bearer bonds are also **coupon bonds**. This term reflects interest coupons that are attached to these bonds. Each coupon matures on a specific interest payment date. The owner detaches each coupon when it matures and presents it to a bank or broker for collection.

Convertible and Callable Bonds

Bondholders can exchange **convertible bonds** for a fixed number of the issuing company's common shares. Convertible bonds offer bondholders the potential to participate in future increases in the shares' market value. If the shares do not appreciate and the bonds are not converted, bondholders continue to receive periodic interest and will receive the par value when the bond matures. In most cases, the bondholders decide whether and when to convert the bonds to shares. **Callable** or **redeemable bonds** have an option under which they can be retired at a stated dollar amount prior to maturity. In the case of callable bonds, the issuer has the option of retiring them; in the case of redeemable bonds, it is the purchaser who has the option of retiring them.

A summary of types of bonds and their features is presented in Exhibit 17.2.

Types of Bonds	Explanation
1. Secured or Unsecured	
a. Secured	a. Assets are pledged as a guarantee of payment by the issuing company.
b. Unsecured (called debentures)	b. Backed not by specific assets but only by the earning capacity and credit reputation of the issuer.
2. Term and Serial	
a. Term	a. Principal of all bonds is due in a lump sum at a specified single date.
b. Serial	b. Principal is due in installments at several different dates.
3. Registered and Bearer	
a. Registered	a. Bonds issued registered in the names of the buyers. Ownership records are kept up to date.
b. Bearer	b. Bonds payable to whomever possesses them. No records are kept for change of ownership. Many are coupon bonds, meaning that interest is paid to the holder of attached coupons.
4. Convertible, Callable, Redeemable	
a. Convertible	a. Bonds that allow the buyer to exchange the bond for common shares at a fixed ratio.
b. Callable	b. Bonds that may be called for early retirement at the option of the issuing corporation.
c. Redeemable	c. Bonds that may be retired early at the option of the purchaser.

Exhibit 17.2

Summary of Bond Features

Bond Issuing Procedures

Issuing company bonds usually requires approval by both the board of directors and shareholders and is governed by provincial and federal laws that require registration with a securities commission. Registration with the securities commission requires that it be informed of the number of bonds authorized, their par value, and the contract interest rate. Bonds are typically issued in par value units of $1,000 or $5,000.

The legal document (contract) identifying the rights and obligations of both the bondholders and the issuer is called the **bond indenture**. The issuing company normally sells the bonds to an investment firm such as BMO Nesbitt Burns, called an *underwriter*, which resells them to the public or directly to investors. The bondholders' interests are represented and protected by a *trustee* who monitors the issue to ensure it complies with the obligations in the bond indenture. Most trustees are large banks or trust companies.

www.bmonesbittburns.com

Bond Trading

The offering of bonds to the public is called *floating an issue*. Because bonds are exchanged in the market, they have a market value (price). For convenience, bond market values are expressed as a percent of their par (face) value. For example, a company's bonds might be trading at 103½, which means they can be bought or sold for 103.5% of their par value. Bonds that trade above par value are said to trade at a **premium**. Bonds trading below par value trade at a **discount**. For instance, if a company's bonds are trading at 95, they can be bought or sold at 95% of their par value.

The **market rate of interest**, or **effective interest rate**, is the amount of interest borrowers are willing to pay and lenders are willing to earn for a particular bond given its risk level. When the contract rate and market rate are equal, the bonds sell at their par value, or 100%. When the contract rate does not equal the market rate, the bonds sell at either above or below their par values (greater or less than 100%) as detailed in Exhibit 17.3.

Exhibit 17.3

Relation Between Bond Issue Price, Contract Rate, and Market Rate

Contract rate is:		Bond sells:	
Above market rate	➡	At a premium	(> 100% of face value)
Equal to market rate	➡	At par value	(= 100% of face value)
Below market rate	➡	At a discount	(< 100% of face value)

For example, assuming a 6% contract rate (or *bond interest* rate, also commonly known as the *coupon rate*), a $1,000 face value bond would sell as follows given various market interest rates:

Contract rate is 6%:		Bond sells:	
If the market rate is 4%	➡	At a premium	(e.g., 101%* or $1,010)
If the market rate is 6%	➡	At par value	(e.g., 100% or $1,000)
If the market rate is 7%	➡	At a discount	(e.g., 98%* or $980)

*Assumed

CHECKPOINT

1. Unsecured bonds supported only by the issuer's general credit standing are called: (a) Serial bonds; (b) Debentures; (c) Registered bonds; (d) Convertible bonds; (e) Bearer bonds.
2. How do you calculate the amount of interest a bond issuer pays each year?
3. When the contract interest rate is above the market interest rate, do bonds sell at a premium or a discount? Do purchasers pay more or less than the par value of the bonds?

Do: QS 17-1, QS 17-2, QS 17-3

Issuing Bonds at Par

LO3 Prepare entries to record bonds issued at par.

This section explains accounting for bond issuances at par. We first show the accounting for bonds issued on the stated date and then show how to account for bonds that are issued between interest dates. Later in the chapter we will explain accounting for bonds issued below par and above par.

To illustrate an issuance of bonds at par value, let's suppose Barnes Corp. receives authorization to issue $800,000 of 9%, 20-year bonds. The bonds are dated January 1, 2011, and are due in 20 years on January 1, 2031. They pay interest semi-annually each June 30 and December 31. If all bonds are sold at their par value, Barnes Corp. makes this entry to record the sale:

	2011			
Jan.	1	Cash...	800,000	
		Bonds Payable.....................................		800,000
		Sold bonds at par.		

This entry reflects increases in the company's cash and long-term liabilities.

Six months later, the first semi-annual interest payment is made, and Barnes records the payment as:

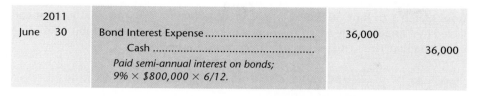

2011			
June 30	Bond Interest Expense....................................	36,000	
	Cash..		36,000
	Paid semi-annual interest on bonds;		
	9% × $800,000 × 6/12.		

Barnes pays and records the semi-annual interest every six months until the bonds mature.

When the bonds mature 20 years later, Barnes Corp. records its payment of the maturity value with this entry:

2031			
Jan. 1	Bonds Payable..	800,000	
	Cash..		800,000
	Paid bonds at maturity.		

Issuing Bonds Between Interest Dates

Many bonds are sold on an interest payment date. But when a company sells its bonds on a date other than an interest payment date, the purchasers pay the issuer the purchase price plus any interest accrued since the prior interest payment date. This accrued interest is then repaid to the bondholders by the issuing corporation on the next interest date.

To illustrate, let's suppose that Canadian Tire has $100,000 of 9% bonds available for sale on January 1. Interest is payable semi-annually on each June 30 and December 31. If the bonds are sold at par on March 1, two months after the original issue date of January 1, the issuer collects two months' interest from the buyer at the time of the sale. This amount is $1,500 (= $100,000 × 9% × 2/12) as shown in Exhibit 17.4.

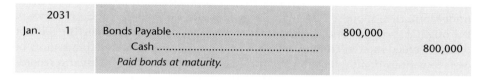

Stated issue date January 1	Date of sale March 1		First interest date June 30
	$1,500 accrued	**$3,000 earned**	
	Bondholder pays $1,500 to issuer		Issuer pays $4,500 to bondholder

Exhibit 17.4

Accruing Interest Between Interest Dates

Canadian Tire's entry to record the sale of its bonds on March 1 is:

Mar. 1	Cash...	101,500	
	Interest Payable[2]...................................		1,500
	Bonds Payable......................................		100,000
	Sold $100,000 of bonds at par with two		
	months' accrued interest.		

Liabilities for interest payable and the bonds are recorded in separate accounts.

---

[2] When selling bonds between interest dates, *Interest Expense* could be credited instead of *Interest Payable*.

When the June 30 semi-annual interest date arrives, Canadian Tire pays a full six months' interest of $4,500 (= $100,000 × 9% × 6/12) to the bondholder. This payment includes the four months' interest of $3,000 earned by the bondholder from March 1 to June 30 plus the repayment of two months' accrued interest collected by Canadian Tire when the bonds were sold, as shown in Exhibit 17.4.

Canadian Tire's entry to record this first interest payment is:

June	30	Interest Payable...	1,500	
		Bond Interest Expense......................................	3,000	
		Cash		4,500
		Paid semi-annual interest on the bonds.		

The practice of collecting and then repaying accrued interest with the first interest payment is done to simplify the bond issuer's administrative efforts. To understand this, suppose Canadian Tire sold bonds on 20 different dates between the original issue date and the first interest payment date. If Canadian Tire did not collect accrued interest from buyers, it would need to pay 20 different amounts of cash to various bondholders on the first interest payment date. The extra record-keeping this would involve is avoided by having each buyer pay accrued interest at the time of purchase. Issuers then pay interest of equal amounts to all purchasers, regardless of when the bonds were purchased.

CHECKPOINT

4. Assume a $200,000, 7%, five-year bond is dated and issued on November 1, 2011. Interest is paid quarterly beginning February 1, 2012. What is the total amount of interest paid on February 1, 2012?

Do: QS 17-4, QS 17-5

Bond Pricing

LO4 Determine the price of a bond.

Extend Your Knowledge

17-1

Prices for bonds that are traded on an organized exchange are published in newspapers and available through online services. This information includes the bond price (called *quote*), its contract rate, and its market rate (called *yield*). Only a fraction of bonds outstanding are actually traded on an organized exchange, however; many others are rarely traded. To calculate the price of a bond, we need to apply present value concepts. This can be done using special bond pricing tables or through calculating the present value of a bond's cash flows. The *market* interest rate is used to find the present value of a bond. The *contract* interest rate is used to calculate the cash interest payments produced by the bond. This section explains how we use *present value concepts* to price a *discount bond* and a *premium bond*.

Present Value of a Discount Bond

The issue price of a bond is found by calculating the present value of the bond's future cash payments. To illustrate, Fila Corp. announces an offer to issue bonds with a $100,000 par value, an 8% annual contract rate with interest payable *semi-annually*, and a three-year life. The market rate for Fila's bonds is 10%, meaning the bonds will sell at a discount since the contract rate (8%) is less than the market rate (10%).[3] When calculating the present value of the Fila bond, we work with semi-annual compounding periods because the time between interest payments is six months. This means the annual market rate of 10% is equal to a semi-annual rate of 5% and the three-year life of the bonds is equal to six semi-annual periods.

---

[3] The difference between the contract rate and the market rate of interest on a new bond issue is usually a fraction of a percent. However, here we use a difference of 2% to emphasize the effects.

The two steps involved in calculating the issue price are to find the present values of the:

1. $100,000 maturity payment and
2. Six interest payments of $4,000 each (= $100,000 × 8% × 6/12).

These present values can be determined by using present value functions found on business calculators,[4] by keying in present value formulas on basic calculators that have a power key, by using the present value function in an Excel worksheet,[5] or by using present value tables. Appendix 17A lists two present value tables for those who choose not to use calculators to find the present value factors. Table 17A.1 is used to calculate the present value of the single $100,000 maturity payment, and Table 17A.2 is used to calculate the present value of the $4,000 series of equal interest payments that form an *annuity*. An **annuity** is a series of equal payments occurring at equal time intervals.

The bond price is calculated as the present value of the principal plus the present value of the cash interest payments. The present value is found by multiplying the cash flow amounts by the corresponding table values as shown in Exhibit 17.5.

Cash Flow	Table	Table Value	Amount	Present Value
$100,000 par value	17A.1	0.7462	$100,000	$ 74,620
$4,000 interest payments...................	17A.2	5.0757	4,000	20,303*
Issue price of bond				**$94,923**[6]

*Rounded to the nearest whole dollar.

Exhibit 17.5

Calculating Fila's Bond Price

This analysis shows that if 5% is the semi-annual market rate for Fila bonds, the maximum price that buyers will pay (and the minimum price the issuer will accept) is $94,923. At this price the cash flow for the Fila bonds will provide investors a 5% semi-annual rate of return (or 10% annual return) on the $94,923 they have lent Fila.

Present Value of a Premium Bond

Assume that Hydro Quebec issues bonds with a $50,000 par value, a 14% annual contract rate with interest payable *annually*, and a four-year life. The market rate for Hydro Quebec bonds is 12% on the issue date, meaning the bonds will sell at a premium because the contract rate (14%) is greater than the market rate (12%). This means buyers of these bonds will bid up the market price until the yield equals the market rate. We estimate the issue price of Hydro Quebec bonds by using the market rate to calculate the present value of its future cash flows. Recall that the Fila bond paid interest semi-annually, every six months. In contrast, interest is paid annually on the Hydro Quebec bonds. Therefore, when calculating the present value of the Hydro Quebec bond, we work with *annual* compounding periods because 12 months or one year is the time between interest payments.

Extend Your Knowledge

17-2
17-3

---

[4] Many inexpensive calculators provide present value functions for easy calculation of bond prices. Extend Your Knowledge 17-2 provides a present value tutorial using a Sharp EL 733A calculator.
[5] Extend Your Knowledge 17-3 provides a tutorial with supporting exercises to reinforce the use of the present value function in Excel.
[6] Because of rounding, the present value tables will often result in a slightly different bond price than using the present value function on a calculator. In this case, a calculator would indicate a bond price of $94,924.

The two-step process for calculating the issue price of a bond sold at a premium is the same as shown previously for a discount and is summarized in Exhibit 17.6.

Exhibit 17.6

Calculating Hydro Quebec
Bond Price

Cash Flow	Table	Table Value	Amount	Present Value
$50,000 par value	17A.1	0.6355	$50,000	$ 31,775
$7,000 interest payments..................	17A.2	3.0373	7,000	21,261*
Issue price of bond				**$53,036**[7]

*Rounded to the nearest whole dollar.

This analysis shows that if 12% is the annual market rate for Hydro Quebec bonds, the maximum price that buyers will pay (also the minimum price the issuer will accept) is $53,036.

CHECKPOINT   Read   Apply   Do   Check

5. Using the tables in Appendix 17A on page 869, calculate the present value of a 9%, $400,000 bond with a three-year term issued when the market rate of interest was 8%. Interest is paid quarterly.

Do: QS 17-6, QS 17-7

Issuing Bonds at a Discount

LO5   Prepare entries to record bonds issued at a discount.

A **discount on bonds payable** occurs when a company issues bonds with a contract rate less than the market rate. This means the issue price is less than the bonds' par value (or < 100%).

To illustrate, let's assume that the Fila bonds discussed earlier are issued on December 31, 2011, at the discounted price of $94,923 (94.923% of par value). Fila records the bond issue as follows:

	2011			
	Dec. 31	Cash..	94,923	
		Discount on Bonds Payable	5,077	
		Bonds Payable..		100,000
		Sold bonds at a discount on the original issue date.		

These bonds obligate the issuer to pay out two different future cash flows:

1. $100,000 face amount at the end of the bonds' three-year life, and
2. $4,000 interest (8% × $100,000 × 6/12) at the end of each six-month interest period of the bonds' three-year life.

The pattern of cash flows for Fila's bonds is shown in Exhibit 17.7.

Exhibit 17.7

Cash Flows of Fila's Bonds

---

[7] Using the present value function on a calculator would result in a bond price of $53,037.

These bonds are reported in the *long-term liability* section of the issuer's December 31, 2011, balance sheet, as shown in Exhibit 17.8.

			Exhibit 17.8
Long-term liabilities:			Balance Sheet Presentation of
Bonds payable, 8%, due December 31, 2014	$100,000		Bond Discount
Less: Discount on bonds payable	**5,077**	$94,923	

The discount is deducted from the par value of the bonds to produce the **carrying** *(or book)* **value** of the bonds payable. Discount on Bonds Payable is a *contra liability account*. The book value of the bonds at the date of issue is always equal to the cash price of the bonds. You will learn in the next section that the carrying value of bonds issued at a discount or premium changes over the life of the bond issue.

Amortizing a Bond Discount

The issuer (Fila) received $94,923 for its bonds and will pay bondholders the $100,000 face amount after three years plus interest payments totalling $24,000 (= $4,000 × 6 interest payments). Because the $5,077 discount is eventually paid to bondholders at maturity, it is part of the cost of using the $94,923 for three years. The upper portion of Exhibit 17.9 shows that the total interest cost of $29,077 is the difference between the total amount repaid to bondholders ($124,000) and the amount borrowed from bondholders ($94,923). Alternatively, we can calculate total bond interest expense as the sum of the interest payments and the bond discount. This alternative calculation is shown in the lower portion of Exhibit 17.9.

		Exhibit 17.9
Amount repaid:		Total Bond Interest Expense for
Six interest payments of $4,000	$ 24,000	Bonds Issued at a Discount
Par value at maturity...	100,000	
Total repaid to bondholders..	$124,000	
Less: Amount borrowed from bondholders	94,923	
Total bond interest expense	$ 29,077	
Alternative Calculation		
Six payments of $4,000	$ 24,000	
Add: Discount..	5,077	
Total bond interest expense	$ 29,077	

Accounting for Fila's bonds must include two procedures:

1. Allocating the total bond interest expense of $29,077 across the six six-month periods in the bonds' life, and

2. Updating the carrying value of the bonds at each balance sheet date.

To allocate the total bond interest expense over the life of the bonds, known as amortizing the bond discount, either the straight-line or effective interest method can be used. Both methods reduce the discount on the bonds over the life of the bonds.

Straight-Line Method

The **straight-line method** of allocating interest allocates an equal portion of the total bond interest expense to each of the six-month interest periods.

To apply the straight-line method to Fila's bonds, we divide the total expense of $29,077 by 6 (the number of semi-annual periods in the bonds' three-year life). This gives us a total bond interest expense of **$4,846 per period**.[8] Alternatively, we can find this number by dividing the $5,077 original discount by 6. The resulting $846 is the amount of discount to be amortized in each interest period. When the $846 of amortized discount is added to the $4,000 cash interest payment, the total bond interest expense for each six-month period is $4,846.

The issuer records bond interest expense and updates the balance of the bond liability for each semi-annual cash payment with this entry:

2012			
June 30	Bond Interest Expense.....................................	4,846	
	Discount on Bonds Payable..................		846
	Cash		4,000
	To record six months' interest and discount amortization.		

Fila incurs a $4,846 bond interest expense each period but pays only $4,000. The $846 unpaid interest each period is part of the amount to be repaid when the bond becomes due ($5,077 discount + $94,923 issue price = $100,000 total face amount to be paid at maturity).

The $846 credit to the Discount on Bonds Payable account *increases* the bonds' carrying value as shown in Exhibit 17.10. This increase occurs because we *decrease* the balance of the Discount on Bonds Payable (contra) account, which is subtracted from the Bonds Payable account. Exhibit 17.10 shows this pattern of decreases in the Discount on Bonds Payable account (the unamortized discount), along with increases in the bonds' carrying value.

Exhibit 17.10

Bond Discount and Carrying Value Under Straight-Line

Period Ending	(A) Cash Interest Paid $100,000 × 4%	(B) Period Interest Expense $29,077/6	(C) Discount Amort. $5,077/6	(D) Unamortized Discount	(E) Carrying Value 100,000 − (D)
Dec. 31/11				$5,077	$ 94,923
Jun. 30/12	$ 4,000	$ 4,846	$ 846	4,231[1]	95,769
Dec. 31/12	4,000	4,846	846	3,385[2]	96,615
Jun. 30/13	4,000	4,846	846	2,539	97,461
Dec. 31/13	4,000	4,846	846	1,693	98,307
Jun. 30/14	4,000	4,846	846	847	99,153
Dec. 31/14	4,000	4,847[3]	847[3]	-0-	100,000
Totals	$24,000	$29,077	$5,077		

[1] 5,077 − 846 = 4,231
[2] 4,231 − 846 = 3,385
[3] Adjusted for rounding.

[8] For simplicity, all calculations are rounded to the nearest whole dollar. **Do the same when solving the exercises and problems at the end of the chapter.**

We can summarize the following points in applying straight-line amortization to the discount on Fila's bonds over its life of six semi-annual periods:

1. The $94,923 cash received from selling the bonds equals the $100,000 par value of the bonds less the initial $5,077 discount from selling the bonds for less than par.

2. Semi-annual bond interest expense of $4,846 equals total bond interest expense of $29,077 divided by six semi-annual periods (alternatively calculated as the periodic cash interest paid of $4,000 plus the periodic discount amortization of $846).

3. Semi-annual credit of $846 to the Discount on Bonds Payable account equals the total discount of $5,077 divided by six semi-annual periods.

4. Semi-annual $4,000 interest payment equals the bonds' $100,000 par value multiplied by the 4% semi-annual contract rate.

5. Carrying (or book) value of bonds continues to grow each period by the $846 discount amortization until it equals the par value of the bonds when they mature as shown in Exhibit 17.10.

Effective Interest Method

The straight-line method yields changes in the bonds' carrying value (see Exhibit 17.10) while the amount for bond interest expense does not change (always equal to $4,846 for Fila bonds). This gives the impression of a changing interest rate when users divide a constant bond interest expense over a changing carrying value. As a result, the straight-line method should only be used when its results do not differ materially from those obtained by using the effective interest method.

The **effective interest method** allocates bond interest expense over the life of the bonds in a way that yields a constant rate of interest. *This constant rate of interest is the market rate at the issue date.* The effect of selling bonds at a premium or discount is that the issuer incurs the prevailing market rate of interest at issuance and not the contract rate. Bond interest expense for a period is found by multiplying the balance of the liability at the end of the last period by the bonds' original market rate. An amortization table can be constructed to help us keep track of interest allocation and the balances of bond-related accounts.

Exhibit 17.11 shows an amortization table for the Fila bonds. The key difference between the effective interest and straight-line methods lies in the calculation of bond interest expense. Instead of assigning an equal amount of interest to each interest period, the effective interest method assigns an increasing amount of interest over the Fila bonds' life because the balance of the liability increases over these three years. But both methods allocate the same $29,077 of total expense across the three years.

Exhibit 17.11

Effective Interest Amortization of Bond Discount

Period Ending	Cash Interest Paid $100,000 × 4% (A)	Period Interest Expense E × 5% (B)	Discount Amort. B − A (C)	Unamortized Discount (D)	Carrying Value 100,000 − (D) (E)
Dec. 31/11				$5,077	$ 94,923
Jun. 30/12	$ 4,000	$ 4,746[1]	$ 746	4,331	95,669
Dec. 31/12	4,000	4,783[2]	783	3,548	96,452
Jun. 30/13	4,000	4,823	823	2,725	97,275
Dec. 31/13	4,000	4,864	864	1,861	98,139
Jun. 30/14	4,000	4,907	907	954	99,046
Dec. 31/14	4,000	4,954[3]	954	-0-	100,000
	$24,000	$29,077	$5,077		

[1] 94,923 × 0.05 = 4,746
[2] 95,669 × 0.05 = 4,783
[3] Adjusted for rounding.

Column (A) is the bonds' par value ($100,000) multiplied by the semi-annual contract rate (4%).

Column (B) is the bonds' prior period carrying value multiplied by the semi-annual market rate (5%).

Column (C) is the difference between bond interest expense and interest paid, or [(B) − (A)].

Column (D) is the prior period's unamortized discount less the current period's discount amortization.

Column (E) is the bonds' par value less unamortized discount, or [$100,000 − (D)].

The amortization table shows how the balance of the discount (column D) is amortized by the effective interest method until it reaches zero. The bonds' carrying value changes each period until it equals par value at maturity. Total bond interest expense is $29,077, comprising $24,000 of semi-annual cash interest payments and $5,077 of the original discount below par value.

Except for differences in amounts, journal entries recording the expense and updating the liability balance are the same under the effective interest method and the straight-line method. For instance, the entry to record the interest payment at the end of the first interest period is:

2012			
June 30	Bond Interest Expense	4,746	
	Discount on Bonds Payable		746
	Cash		4,000
	To record six months' interest and discount amortization.		

We use the numbers in Exhibit 17.11 to make similar entries throughout the three-year life of the bonds. We can also use information in this exhibit to prepare comparative balance sheet information. For example, we prepare the bonds payable section of long-term liabilities for 2013 and 2012 as shown in Exhibit 17.12. Note that the carrying value of the bonds payable increases as the discount on bonds payable gets smaller.

	Dec. 31 2013	Dec. 31 2012
Long-term liabilities:		
Bonds payable, 8%, due December 31, 2014	$100,000	$100,000
Less: Discount on bonds payable..	1,861	3,548
Carrying value...	$ 98,139	$ 96,452

Exhibit 17.12

Balance Sheet Presentation of Bond Discount

Use this information to answer Checkpoint Questions 6, 7, and 8: Five-year, 6% bonds with a $100,000 par value are issued at a price of $91,893. Interest is paid semi-annually, and the market rate is 8% on the issue date.

6. Are these bonds issued at a discount or a premium? Explain why.

7. What is the issuer's journal entry to record the sale?

8. What is the amount of bond interest expense recorded at the first semi-annual cash payment using the (a) straight-line method and (b) effective interest method?

Do: QS 17-8, QS 17-9, QS 17-10

Issuing Bonds at a Premium

When bonds carry a contract rate greater than the market rate, the bonds sell at a price greater than par value (or > 100%). The difference between par and market value is the **premium on bonds**. Buyers bid up the price of bonds above the bonds' par value until it reaches a level yielding the market rate.

LO6 Prepare entries to record bonds issued at a premium.

To illustrate, let's assume that the Hydro Quebec bonds discussed earlier are issued on December 31, 2011, at 106.072 (106.072% of par value), which amounts to $53,036. Hydro Quebec records the bond issue with this entry:

2011			
Dec. 31	Cash...	53,036	
	Premium on Bonds Payable..................		3,036
	Bonds Payable......................................		50,000
	Sold bonds at a premium on the original issue date.		

Hydro Quebec's bonds obligate it to pay out two different future cash flows:

1. $50,000 face amount at the end of the bonds' four-year life.

2. $7,000 (= 14% × $50,000) at the end of each annual interest period of the bonds' four-year life.

The pattern of cash flows for Hydro Quebec bonds is shown in Exhibit 17.13.

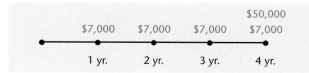

Exhibit 17.13

Cash Flows of Hydro Quebec Bonds

These bonds are reported in the long-term liability section of the issuer's December 31, 2011, balance sheet, as shown in Exhibit 17.14.

Exhibit 17.14

Balance Sheet Presentation of Bond Premium

Long-term liabilities:		
Bonds payable, 14%, due December 31, 2015................................	$50,000	
Add: Premium on bonds payable...	**3,036**	**$53,036**

The premium is added to the par value of the bonds to produce the carrying (book) value of the bonds payable. Premium on Bonds Payable is an adjunct (also called accretion) liability account.

Amortizing a Bond Premium

The issuer (Hydro Quebec) receives $53,036 for its bonds and will pay bondholders the $50,000 face amount after four years have passed plus interest payments totalling $28,000. Because the $3,036 premium is not repaid to bondholders at maturity, it reduces the expense of using the $53,036 for four years.

The upper portion of Exhibit 17.15 shows that total bond interest expense of $24,964 is the difference between the total amount repaid to bondholders ($78,000) and the amount borrowed from bondholders ($53,036). Alternatively, we can calculate total bond interest expense as the sum of the interest payments less the bond premium. The premium is subtracted because it will not be paid to the bondholders when the bonds mature. This alternative calculation is shown in the lower portion of Exhibit 17.15. Total bond interest expense is allocated over the four annual periods with either the straight-line or the effective interest method.

Exhibit 17.15

Total Bond Interest Expense for Bonds Issued at a Premium

Amount repaid:	
Four interest payments of $7,000	$28,000
Par value at maturity..	50,000
Total repaid to bondholders..	$78,000
Less: Amount borrowed from bondholders	53,036
Total bond interest expense	$24,964
Alternative Calculation	
Four payments of $7,000	$28,000
Less: Premium	3,036
Total interest expense..	$24,964

Straight-Line Method

We explained how the straight-line method allocates an equal portion of total bond interest expense to each of the bonds' interest periods. To apply the straight-line method to Hydro Quebec's bonds, we divide the four years' total bond interest expense of $24,964 by 4 (the number of annual periods in the bonds' life). This gives us a total bond interest expense of $6,241 per period.

The issuer records bond interest expense and updates the balance of the bond liability for each annual cash payment with this entry:

2012			
Dec. 31	Bond Interest Expense.....................................	6,241	
	Premium on Bonds Payable............................	759	
	Cash		7,000
	To record annual interest and premium amortization; 3,036/4 = 759.		

This is the entry made at the end of each of the four annual interest periods. The $759 debit to the Premium on Bonds Payable account decreases the bonds' carrying value. Exhibit 17.16 shows an amortization table using the straight-line method for the Hydro Quebec bonds.

Exhibit 17.16

Bond Premium and Carrying Value Under Straight-Line

Period Ending	(A) Cash Interest Paid $50,000 × 14%	(B) Period Interest Expense 24,964/4	(C) Premium Amort. 3,036/4	(D) Unamortized Premium	(E) Carrying Value $50,000 + (D)
Dec. 31/11				$3,036	$53,036
Dec. 31/12	$ 7,000	$ 6,241	$ 759	2,277[1]	52,277
Dec. 31/13	7,000	6,241	759	1,518[2]	51,518
Dec. 31/14	7,000	6,241	759	759	50,759
Dec. 31/15	7,000	6,241	759	-0-	50,000
Totals	$28,000	$24,964	$3,036		

[1] $3,036 - 759 = 2,277$
[2] $2,277 - 759 = 1,518$

Effective Interest Method

Exhibit 17.17 shows an amortization table using the effective interest method for the Hydro Quebec bonds.

Exhibit 17.17

Effective Interest Amortization of Bond Premium

Period Ending	(A) Cash Interest Paid $50,000 × 14%	(B) Period Interest Expense (E) × 12%	(C) Premium Amort. (A) − (B)	(D) Unamortized Premium	(E) Carrying Value $50,000 + (D)
Dec. 31/11				$3,036	$53,036
Dec. 31/12	$ 7,000	$ 6,364[1]	$ 636	2,400	52,400
Dec. 31/13	7,000	6,288[2]	712	1,688	51,688
Dec. 31/14	7,000	6,203	797	891	50,891
Dec. 31/15	7,000	6,109[3]	891	-0-	50,000
Totals	$28,000	$24,964	$3,036		

[1] $53,036 × 0.12 = 6,364$
[2] $52,400 × 0.12 = 6,288$
[3] Adjusted for rounding.

Column (A) is the bonds' par value ($50,000) multiplied by the annual contract rate (14%).

Column (B) is the bonds' prior period carrying value multiplied by the annual market rate (12%).

Column (C) is the difference between interest paid and bond interest expense, or [(A) − (B)].

Column (D) is the prior period's unamortized premium less the current period's premium amortization.

Column (E) is the bonds' par value plus unamortized premium, or [$50,000 + (D)].

The amount of cash paid (Column A) is larger than bond interest expense (Column B) because the cash payment is based on the higher 14% contract rate.

The effect of premium amortization on the bond interest expense and the bond liability is seen in the journal entry on December 31, 2012, when the issuer makes the first interest payment:

2012			
Dec. 31	Bond Interest Expense......................................	6,364	
	Premium on Bonds Payable............................	636	
	Cash		7,000
	To record annual interest and premium amortization.		

Similar entries are recorded at each payment date until the bonds mature at the end of 2015. The effective interest method yields decreasing amounts of bond interest expense and increasing amounts of premium amortization over the bonds' life.

CHECKPOINT

9. When the period interest expense is constant over the term of a bond, is the straight-line or effective interest method being used to calculate amortization?

Do: QS 17-11, QS 17-12, QS 17-13

Summary of Bond Discount and Premium Behaviour

The Fila and Quebec Hydro bond examples have shown that bond discounts and premiums behave in opposite ways over the term of a bond and therefore affect the bond's carrying value differently. The graphs presented in Exhibit 17.18 summarize these behaviour patterns.

Accruing Bond Interest Expense

If a bond's interest period does not coincide with the issuing company's accounting period, an adjusting entry is necessary to recognize bond interest expense accruing since the most recent interest payment.

To illustrate, let's assume that the Hydro Quebec bonds described in Exhibit 17.17 were issued on December 31, 2011. If Hydro Quebec's year-end is April 30, four months of bond interest and premium amortization accrue (from December 31, 2011, to April 30, 2012). An adjusting entry is needed to capture:

1. Four months of interest equal to $2,121 (= $6,364 from Column B of Exhibit 17.17 × 4/12), and
2. Four months of premium amortization equal to $212 (= $636 from Column C of Exhibit 17.17 × 4/12).

The resulting interest payable is $2,333, the sum of the $2,121 interest expense and $212 premium amortization (also calculated as $7,000 from Column A of Exhibit 17.17 × 4/12). We record these effects with this adjusting entry:

2012			
Apr. 30	Bond Interest Expense......................................	2,121	
	Premium on Bonds Payable............................	212	
	Interest Payable......................................		2,333
	To record four months' accrued interest and premium amortization.		

Similar entries are made on each April 30 year-end throughout the three-year life of the bonds.

Exhibit 17.18

Graphic Comparison of Bond Discount and Premium Behaviour

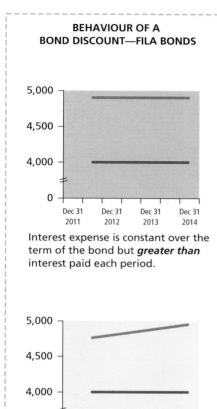

BEHAVIOUR OF A BOND DISCOUNT—FILA BONDS

Interest expense is constant over the term of the bond but **greater than** interest paid each period.

Interest expense is **increasing** over the term of the bond **and greater than** interest paid each period.

As the discount is amortized each period, the **carrying value of the bond increases** as it approaches par value.

BEHAVIOUR OF A BOND PREMIUM—HYDRO QUEBEC BONDS

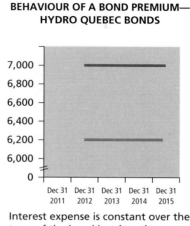

Interest expense is constant over the term of the bond but **less than** interest paid each period.

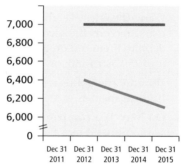

Interest expense is **decreasing** over the term of the bond **and less than** interest paid each period.

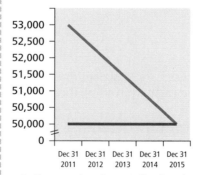

As the premium is amortized each period, the **carrying value of the bond decreases** as it approaches par value.

Straight-Line Amortization

— Cash interest paid
— Period interest expense

vs. Effective Interest Amortization

Carrying vs. Par Value

— Carrying value
— Par value

When the $7,000 cash payment occurs on the December 31, 2012, interest date, the journal entry recognizes the bond interest expense and amortization for May through December, a total of eight months. It must also eliminate the interest payable liability created by the April 30 adjusting entry. In this case we make the following entry to record payment on December 31, 2012:

2012			
Dec. 31	Interest Payable...	2,333	
	Bond Interest Expense ($6,364 × 8/12)	4,243	
	Premium on Bonds Payable ($636 × 8/12)	424	
	Cash		7,000
	To record eight months' interest and amortization and eliminate the accrued interest liability.		

Use this information to solve Checkpoint Questions 10, 11, and 12: On December 31, 2011, a company issued 16%, 10-year bonds with a par value of $100,000. Interest is paid on June 30 and December 31. The bonds are sold at an issue price of $110,592 to yield a 14% annual market rate.

10. Are these bonds issued at a discount or a premium? Explain why.

11. Using the effective interest method of allocating bond interest expense, the issuer records the second interest payment (on December 31, 2012) with a debit to Premium on Bonds Payable in the amount of: (a) $7,470; (b) $7,741; (c) $259; (d) $530; or (e) $277.

12. How are the bonds reported in the long-term liability section of the issuer's balance sheet as of December 31, 2012?

13. On May 1, a company sells 9% bonds with a $500,000 par value that pay semi-annual interest on each January 1 and July 1. The bonds are sold at par value plus interest accrued since January 1. The bond issuer's entry to record the first semi-annual interest payment on July 1 includes: (a) a debit to Interest Payable for $15,000; (b) a debit to Bond interest expense for $22,500; or (c) a credit to Interest Payable for $7,500.

Do: QS 17-14, QS 17-15, QS 17-16, QS 17-17

Bond Retirements

LO7 | Record the retirement of bonds.

This section describes the retirement of bonds: (1) at maturity, (2) before maturity, and (3) by converting them to shares.

Bond Retirement at Maturity

The carrying value of bonds at maturity will always equal their par value. Both Exhibits 17.11 (a discount) and 17.17 (a premium) show that the carrying value of these bonds at the end of their life equals the bonds' par value.

The entry to record the retirement of the Hydro Quebec bonds in Exhibit 17.17 at maturity, assuming interest is already paid and recorded, is:

2015			
Dec. 31	Bonds Payable...	50,000	
	Cash		50,000
	To record retirement of bonds at maturity.		

Bond Retirement Before Maturity

Companies sometimes wish to retire some or all of their bonds prior to maturity. For instance, if interest rates decline significantly, a company may wish to replace old high-interest paying bonds with new low-interest bonds. Two common ways of retiring bonds before maturity are to:

1. Exercise a call option, or

2. Purchase them on the open market.

In the first instance, a company can reserve the right to retire bonds early by issuing callable bonds. This means the bond indenture gives the issuing company an option to call the bonds before they mature by paying the par value plus a *call premium* to the bondholders. In the second case, the issuer retires bonds by repurchasing them on the open market at their current price. When there is a difference between the bonds' carrying value and the amount paid in a bond retirement transaction, the issuer records a gain or loss equal to the difference. Any unrecorded discount or premium up to the date of the call must be recorded to bring the carrying value of the bond up to date.

To illustrate bond retirement before maturity, let's assume a company has issued callable bonds with a par value of $100,000. The call option requires the issuer to pay a call premium of $3,000 to bondholders in addition to the par value. Immediately after the June 30, 2011, interest payment, the bonds have a carrying value of $104,500. On July 1, 2011, the issuer calls these bonds and pays $103,000 to bondholders. The issuer recognizes a $1,500 gain from the difference between the bonds' carrying value of $104,500 and the retirement price of $103,000. The entry to record this bond retirement is:

July	1	Bonds Payable..	100,000	
		Premium on Bonds Payable............................	4,500	
		Gain on Retirement of Bonds		1,500
		Cash		103,000
		To record retirement of bonds before maturity.		

A company generally must call all of its bonds when it exercises a call option. But a company can retire as many or as few bonds as it desires through open market transactions. If it retires less than the entire set of bonds, it recognizes a gain or loss for the difference between the carrying value of those bonds retired and the amount paid to acquire them.

Bond Retirement by Conversion to Shares

Convertible bonds are those that give bondholders the right to convert their bonds to a specified number of common shares. When conversion occurs, the carrying value of bonds is transferred from long-term liability accounts to contributed capital accounts and no gain or loss is recorded.

To illustrate, on January 1 the $100,000 par value bonds of Converse Corp., with a carrying value of $100,000, are converted to 15,000 common shares. The entry to record this conversion is:

Jan.	1	Bonds Payable..	100,000	
		Common Shares		100,000
		To record retirement of bonds by conversion into common shares.		

Notice that the market prices of the bonds and shares have no bearing on this entry. Any related bond discount or premium must also be removed. For example if there had been a $4,000 balance in Discount on Bonds Payable, it must be credited as shown in the following entry:

Jan.	1	Bonds Payable...	100,000	
		Discount on Bonds Payable...................		4,000
		Common Shares		96,000
		To record retirement of bonds by conversion into common shares.		

14. Six years ago, a company issued $500,000 of 6%, eight-year bonds at a price of 95. The current carrying value is $493,750. The company retired 50% of the bonds by buying them on the open market at a price of 102½. What is the amount of gain or loss on retirement of these bonds?

Do: QS 17-18, QS 17-19

mid-chapter demonstration problem

On February 1, 2011, Enviro-Engineering Inc. has available for issue a $416,000, 5%, two-year bond. Interest is to be paid quarterly beginning May 1, 2011.

Required

Part 1

Calculate the issue price of the bonds assuming a market interest rate of:

a. 5%   **b.** 4%   **c.** 8%

Part 2

Assuming the bonds were issued on April 1, 2011, at a market interest rate of 5%, prepare the entries for the following dates:

a. April 1, 2011 (date of issue)   **b.** May 1, 2011 (interest payment date)

Part 3

Assuming the bonds were issued on Feb. 1, 2011, at a market interest rate of 4%:

a. Prepare an amortization schedule using the straight-line method.

b. Record the entries for the following dates:

  i.   February 1, 2011 (date of issue)

  ii. May 1, 2011 (interest payment date)

  iii. May 31, 2011 (Enviro's year-end)

Part 4

Assuming the bonds were issued on February 1, 2011, at a market interest rate of 8%:

a. Prepare an amortization schedule using the effective interest method.

b. Record the entries for the following dates:

   i.   February 1, 2011 (date of issue)

   ii. May 1, 2011 (interest payment date)

   iii. May 31, 2011 (Enviro's year-end)

Part 5

Assume the bonds issued in Part 4 were retired on August 1, 2012, for cash of $410,500. Record the retirement (assume the August 1 interest payment had been journalized).

Analysis component:

When bonds sell at a premium, the total interest expense related to the bond is reduced. Explain.

Preparing the Solution:

- Calculate the issue price of the bonds using the PV tables in Appendix 17A or a calculator.
- Record the journal entries for bonds issued at par (market interest rate of 5%).
- Using the straight-line method, prepare an amortization schedule for bonds issued at a premium (market rate of 4%).
- Using the straight-line amortization schedule, record the journal entries for bonds issued at a premium.
- Using the effective interest method, prepare an amortization schedule for bonds issued at a discount (market interest rate of 8%).
- Using the effective interest amortization schedule, record the journal entries for bonds issued at a discount.
- Record the retirement of the bonds.
- Answer the analysis component.

s o l u t i o n t o *Mid-Chapter Demonstration Problem* _____

Part 1

a. $416,000

b.

PV of face amount (Table 17A.1)...................	$416,000	×	0.9235	=	$384,176
PV of interest annuity (Table 17A.2)	$ 5,200[1]	×	7.6517	=	39,789
					$423,965[2]

[1]$416,000 × 5% × 3/12 = $5,200
[2]Using the present value function on a calculator would result in a bond price of $423,958.

c.

PV of face amount (Table 17A.1)...................	$416,000	×	0.8535	=	$355,056
PV of interest annuity (Table 17A.2)	$ 5,200[1]	×	7.3255	=	38,093
					$393,149[2]

[1]$416,000 × 5% × 3/12 = $5,200
[2]Using the present value function on a calculator would result in a bond price of $393,144.

Part 2—Issued at a market interest rate of 5% (par).

a.

2011			
April 1	Cash..	419,467	
	Interest Payable		
	($416,000 × 5% × 2/12).....................		3,467
	Bonds Payable..		416,000

b.

May 1	Interest Payable...	3,467	
	Bond Interest Expense		
	($416,000 × 5% × 1/12)....................	1,733	
	Cash		5,200

Part 3—Issued at a market interest rate of 4% (premium).

a.

Period Ending	(A) Cash Interest Paid $416,000 × 5% × 3/12	(B) Period Interest Expense $33,635/8	(C) Premium Amort. $7,965/8	(D) Unamortized Premium	(E) Carrying Value $416,000 + (D)
Feb. 01/11				7,965	423,965
May 01/11	5,200	4,204	996	6,969	422,969
Aug. 01/11	5,200	4,204	996	5,973	421,973
Nov. 01/11	5,200	4,204	996	4,977	420,977
Feb. 01/12	5,200	4,204	996	3,981	419,981
May 01/12	5,200	4,204	996	2,985	418,985
Aug. 01/12	5,200	4,204	996	1,989	417,989
Nov. 01/12	5,200	4,204	996	993	416,993
Feb. 01/13	5,200	4,207*	993	0	416,000
Totals	41,600	33,635	7,965		

Adjusted for rounding.

b.

	2011			
i.	Feb. 1	Cash..	423,965	
		Premium on Bonds Payable...................		7,965
		Bonds Payable..		416,000
ii.	May 1	Bond Interest Expense	4,204	
		Premium on Bonds Payable...........................	996	
		Cash		5,200
iii.	May 31	Bond Interest Expense ($4,204 × 1/3)	1,401	
		Premium on Bonds Payable ($996 × 1/3)	332	
		Interest Payable ($5,200 × 1/3).............		1,733

Part 4—Issued at a market interest rate of 8% (discount).

a.

Period Ending	(A) Cash Interest Paid $416,000 × 5% × 3/12	(B) Period Interest Expense (E) × 8% × 3/12	(C) Discount Amort. (B) − (A)	(D) Unamortized Discount	(E) Carrying Value $416,000 − (D)
Feb. 01/11				22,851	393,149
May 01/11	5,200	7,863	2,663	20,188	395,812
Aug. 01/11	5,200	7,916	2,716	17,472	398,528
Nov. 01/11	5,200	7,971	2,771	14,701	401,299
Feb. 01/12	5,200	8,026	2,826	11,875	404,125
May 01/12	5,200	8,082	2,882	8,993	407,007
Aug. 01/12	5,200	8,140	2,940	6,053	409,947
Nov. 01/12	5,200	8,199	2,999	3,054	412,946
Feb. 01/13	5,200	8,254*	3,054	0	416,000
Totals	41,600	64,451	22,851		

*Adjusted for rounding.

b.

	2011			
i.	Feb. 1	Cash..	393,149	
		Discount on Bonds Payable	22,851	
		Bonds Payable..		416,000
ii.	May 1	Bond Interest Expense....................................	7,863	
		Discount on Bonds Payable		2,663
		Cash		5,200
iii.	May 31	Bond Interest Expense ($7,916 × 1/3)	2,639	
		Discount on Bonds Payable		
		($2,716 × 1/3)		906*
		Interest Payable ($5,200 × 1/3)		1,733

*Adjusted for rounding.

Part 5

	2012			
	Aug. 1	Bonds Payable...	416,000	
		Loss on Retirement of Bonds	553	
		Discount on Bonds Payable		6,053
		Cash		410,500
		To record retirement of bonds prior to maturity.		

Analysis component:

Cash greater than the face value of the bond is received by the issuing corporation when it sells bonds at a premium. However, when the bond matures, only the face value of the bond is repaid to the bondholders. The excess cash received reduces the interest expense associated with the bond. This is accomplished by amortizing the bond premium against bond interest expense over the term of the bond.

Long-Term Notes Payable

Like bonds, companies issue notes payable to finance operations. But, unlike signing a bond, signing a note payable is typically a transaction with a single lender such as a bank, insurance company, or pension fund. A note is initially measured and recorded at its selling price. Over the life of a note, the amount of interest expense allocated to each period is calculated by multiplying the interest rate of the note by the beginning-of-period balance of the note.

Interest-Bearing Notes

LO8 | Explain and record notes.

Let's assume Taco Bell buys on January 2, 2011, equipment with a fair market value of $45,000 by issuing an 8%, three-year note with a face value of $45,000 to the equipment seller. The company records the purchase with this entry:

	2011				
Jan.	2	Equipment		45,000	
		Notes Payable			45,000
		Issued a $45,000, three-year, 8% note payable for equipment.			

The company (note issuer) reports annual interest expense equal to the original interest rate times each year's beginning balance of the note over the life of the note. Exhibit 17.19 shows this interest expense calculation and allocation.

Exhibit 17.19

Interest-Bearing Note—Interest Paid at Maturity

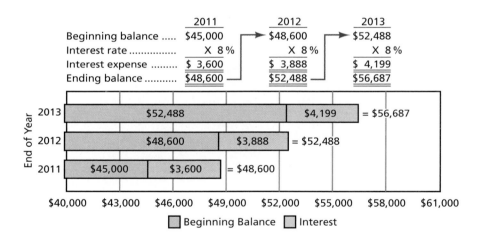

Interest is calculated by multiplying each year's beginning balance by the original 8% interest rate. Interest is then added to the beginning balance to calculate the ending balance. A period's ending balance becomes next period's beginning balance. Because the balance grows by compounding, the amount of interest allocated to each year increases over the life of the note. The final ending balance of $56,687 equals the original $45,000 borrowed plus total interest of $11,687.[9] A note like this one that delays interest payments is more common for lower-risk companies who wish to delay cash payments until some later period. It is often backed with assets as collateral.

[9] Using the present value/future value functions on a calculator will yield the same results.

CHECKPOINT

15. On January 1, 2011, a company signs a $6,000 three-year note payable bearing 6% annual interest. The original principal and all interest is paid on December 31, 2013. Interest is compounded annually. How much interest is allocated to year 2012? (a) $0; (b) $360; (c) $381.60; (d) $741.60.

Do: QS 17-20

Installment Notes

An **installment note** is an obligation requiring a series of periodic payments to the lender. Installment notes are common for franchises and other businesses where costs are large and the owner desires to spread these costs over several periods. For example, in Note 4 of its financial statements found in Appendix I at the back of this textbook, WestJet reports the installment details regarding loans totalling $1,158,834,000 at December 31, 2005.

To illustrate, let's assume CanBowl, a bowling alley operator, borrows $60,000 from a bank to purchase AMF and Brunswick bowling equipment. CanBowl signs an 8% installment note with the bank requiring three annual payments and records the note's issuance as:

2010			
Dec. 31	Cash..	60,000	
	Notes Payable		60,000
	Borrowed $60,000 by signing an 8% installment note.		

Payments on an installment note normally include the interest expense accruing to the date of the payment plus a portion of the amount borrowed (the *principal*). Generally, we can identify two types of payment patterns:

1. Accrued interest plus equal principal payments, and

2. Equal payments.

The remainder of this section describes these two patterns and how we account for them.

Accrued Interest Plus Equal Principal Payments

This payment pattern creates cash flows that decrease in size over the life of the note. This decrease occurs because each payment reduces the note's principal balance, yielding less interest expense for the next period.

To illustrate, let's assume the $60,000, 8% note signed by CanBowl requires it to make three payments at the end of each year equal to *accrued interest plus $20,000 of principal*. Exhibit 17.20 describes these payments, interest, and changes in the balance of this note.

This table shows that total interest expense is $9,600 and total principal is $60,000. This means total cash payments are $69,600. Notice the decreasing total payment pattern, decreasing accrued interest, and constant principal payments of $20,000.

Exhibit 17.20

Installment Note—Accrued Interest Plus Equal Principal Payments

	(A)	(B)	(C)	(D)	(E)
		Debit	*Debit*	*Credit*	
	Beginning	**Interest**	**Notes**		**Ending**
	Balance	**Expense**	**Payable**	**Cash**	**Balance**
Period Ending	**Prior (E)**	**8% × (A)**	**$60,000/3**	**(B) + (C)**	**(A) − (C)**
Dec. 31/11	$60,000	$4,800	$20,000	$24,800	$40,000
Dec. 31/12	40,000	3,200	20,000	23,200	20,000
Dec. 31/13	20,000	1,600	20,000	21,600	-0-
		$9,600	$60,000	$69,600	

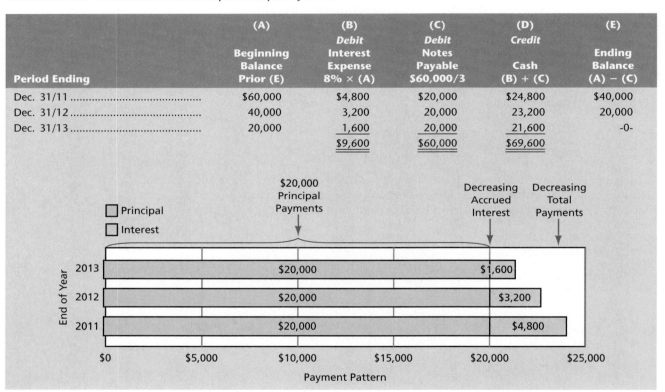

CanBowl (borrower) records the effects of the first payment with this entry:

2011			
Dec. 31	Interest Expense	4,800	
	Notes Payable	20,000	
	Cash		24,800
	To record first installment payment.		

After all three payments are recorded, the balance of the Notes Payable account is zero.

Equal Total Payments

Installment notes that require the borrower to make a series of equal payments consist of changing amounts of interest and principal.

To illustrate, let's assume the previous $60,000 note requires CanBowl to make three equal total payments at the end of each year. Table 17A.2 is used to calculate the series of three payments equal to the present value of the $60,000 note at 8% interest. We go to Row 3 of the table and go across to the 8% column, where the table value is 2.5771. We solve for the payment by dividing $60,000 by 2.5771. The resulting $23,282 payment includes both interest and principal. Exhibit 17.21 shows that while all three payments are equal, the accrued interest decreases each year because the principal balance of the note is declining. As the amount of interest decreases each year, the amount applied to the principal increases.

Exhibit 17.21

Installment Note—Equal Total Payments

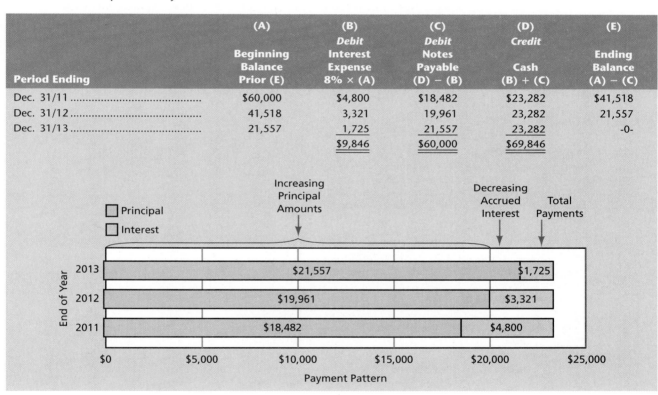

Period Ending	(A) Beginning Balance Prior (E)	(B) *Debit* Interest Expense 8% × (A)	(C) *Debit* Notes Payable (D) − (B)	(D) *Credit* Cash (B) + (C)	(E) Ending Balance (A) − (C)
Dec. 31/11	$60,000	$4,800	$18,482	$23,282	$41,518
Dec. 31/12	41,518	3,321	19,961	23,282	21,557
Dec. 31/13	21,557	1,725	21,557	23,282	-0-
		$9,846	$60,000	$69,846	

The amounts in Exhibit 17.21 are used to show how we record the journal entry for the first payment toward this note:

2011			
Dec. 31	Interest Expense	4,800	
	Notes Payable	18,482	
	Cash		23,282
	To record first installment payment.		

The borrower records similar entries for each of the remaining payments. After three years, the Notes Payable account balance is zero.

It is interesting to compare the two payment patterns graphed in Exhibits 17.20 and 17.21. The series of equal total payments leads to a greater amount of interest expense over the life of the note. This is because the first three payments in Exhibit 17.21 are smaller and do not reduce the principal as quickly as the first three payments in Exhibit 17.20.

Mortgage Notes

A **mortgage** is a legal agreement that helps protect a lender if a borrower fails to make the required payments on bonds or notes. A mortgage gives the lender the right to be paid out of the cash proceeds from the sale of a borrower's specific assets identified in the mortgage. A separate legal document, called a *mortgage contract*, describes the terms of a mortgage.

Mortgage notes include a mortgage contract pledging title to specific assets as security for the note. This contract usually requires the borrower to pay all property taxes on the mortgaged assets, to maintain them properly, and to carry adequate insurance against fire and other types of losses. These requirements are designed to keep the property from losing value and avoid diminishing the lender's security. Mortgage notes are especially popular in the purchase of homes and in the acquisition of plant assets by companies.

For example, Note 10 to Boardwalk REIT's December 31, 2005, financial statements states:

10. Mortgages Payable		
AS AT	December 31, 2005	December 31, 2004
(a) Revenue producing properties	(thousands)	
Mortgages payable bearing interest at a weighted average of 5.39% (December 31, 2004—5.49%) per annum, payable in monthly principal and interest installments totalling $9.7 million (December 31, 2004—$9.4 million), mature from 2005 to 2020 and are secured by specific charges against specific properties.		
	$1,423,237	$1,412,358

Accounting for mortgage notes and bonds is essentially the same as accounting for unsecured notes and bonds. The primary difference is that the mortgage agreement needs to be disclosed to users of financial statements.

CHECKPOINT   Read · Apply · Do · Check

16. Which of the following is true for an installment note requiring a series of equal payments?

   a. Payments consist of an increasing amount of interest and a decreasing amount of principal.

   b. Payments consist of changing amounts of principal, but the interest portion remains constant.

   c. Payments consist of a decreasing amount of interest and an increasing amount of principal.

17. How is the interest portion of an installment note payment calculated?

18. When a borrower records a periodic interest payment on an installment note, how are the balance sheet and income statement affected?

Do: QS 17-21

Lease Liabilities

Leasing is one alternative to purchasing an asset and, in certain situations, is reported like a known liability P. 657. A company can lease an asset by agreeing to make a series of rental payments to the property owner, called the *lessor*. Because a lease gives the asset's user (called the *lessee*) exclusive control over the asset's usefulness, the lessee can use it to earn revenues. A lease creates a liability if it has essentially the same characteristics as a purchase of an asset on credit. Appendix 17B illustrates basic accounting for leases.

Summary --

LO1 **Compare bond versus share financing.** Bond financing is used to fund business activities. Advantages of bond financing versus common shares include (a) no effect on shareholders' control, (b) tax savings, and (c) increased earnings due to financial leverage. Disadvantages include (a) required interest and principal payments, and (b) decreased earnings when operations turn less profitable.

LO2 **Explain the types of bonds and their issuing procedures.** An issuer's bonds usually are sold to many investors. Certain bonds are secured by the issuer's assets, while other bonds, called *debentures,* are unsecured. Serial bonds mature at different points in time while term bonds mature together. Registered bonds have each bondholder's name and address recorded by the issuing company, while bearer bonds are payable to whomever holds the bonds. Convertible bonds are exchangeable by bondholders for shares of the issuing company's shares. Callable bonds can be retired by the issuer at a set price. Bonds are often issued by an underwriter, and a bond certificate is evidence of the issuer's obligation.

LO3 **Prepare entries to record bonds issued at par.** When bonds are issued at par, Cash is debited and Bonds Payable is credited for the bonds' par value. At the bonds' interest payment dates, Bond Interest Expense is debited and Cash credited for an amount equal to the bonds' par value multiplied by the bonds' contract rate. The cash paid to bondholders on semi-annual interest payment dates is calculated as one-half of the result of multiplying the par value of the bonds by their contract rate.

LO4 **Determine the price of a bond.** The price of a bond is determined by summing the present values of two amounts: (1) the present value of the interest payments (an annuity), and (2) the present value of the face value of the bond that is received at the bond's maturity date. Both amounts are discounted to present value using the market rate of interest.

LO5 **Prepare entries to record bonds issued at a discount.** Bonds are issued at a discount when the contract rate is less than the market rate. This is the same as saying the issue (selling) price is less than par. When this occurs, the issuer records a credit to Bonds Payable (at par) and debits both to Discount on Bonds Payable and to Cash. The amount of bond interest expense assigned to each period is calculated using either the straight-line or effective interest method. Straight-line can only be used if the results are not materially different from the effective interest method. Bond interest expense using the effective interest method equals the bonds' beginning-of-period carrying value multiplied by the original market rate at time of issuance.

LO6 **Prepare entries to record bonds issued at a premium.** Bonds are issued at a premium when the contract rate is higher than the market rate. This means that the issue (selling) price is greater than par. When this occurs, the issuer records a debit to Cash and credits both to Premium on Bonds Payable and to Bonds Payable (at par). The amount of bond interest expense assigned to each period is calculated using either the straight-line or effective interest method. The balance of the Premium on Bonds Payable is allocated to reduce bond interest expense over the life of the bonds.

LO7 **Record the retirement of bonds.** Bonds are retired at maturity with a debit to Bonds Payable and a credit to Cash for the par value of the bonds. Bonds can be retired early by the issuer by exercising a call option or by purchases on the open market. The issuer recognizes a gain or loss for the difference between the amount paid out and the bonds' carrying value. Alternatively, bondholders can retire bonds early by exercising a conversion feature on convertible bonds.

LO8 **Explain and record notes.** Notes can require repayment of principal and interest (a) at the end of a period of time, or (b) gradually over a period of time in either equal or unequal amounts. Notes repaid over a period of time are called installment notes and usually follow one of two payment patterns: (a) decreasing payments of interest plus equal amounts of principal, or (b) equal total payments. Interest is allocated to each period in a note's life by multiplying its carrying value by its interest rate.

The entry to record the lease payment at the end of 2011 is:

Dec.	31	Lease Liability	2,205	
		Interest Expense	795	
		Cash		3,000
		To record annual payment of the lease.		

The balance sheet presentation of the leased asset at the end of 2011 is as follows:

Assets:		
Equipment	$9,936	
Less: Accumulated amortization	2,484	$7,452
Liabilities:		
Current liabilities:		
Lease liability—current portion...		$2,382
Long-term liabilities:		
Lease liability...		$5,349

Summary of Appendix 17B

LO⁹ **Prepare entries to record lease liabilities.** Lease liabilities are one type of long-term liability often used as an alternative to purchase assets. Capital leases are recorded as assets and liabilities. Other leases, called *operating leases*, are recorded as rent expense when the asset is leased.

Glossary

Annuity A series of equal payments occurring at equal time intervals. (p. 843)

Bearer bonds Bonds that are made payable to whoever holds them (called the *bearer*); also called *unregistered bonds*. (p. 838)

Bond A written promise to pay an amount identified as the par value of the bond along with interest at a stated annual amount; usually issued in denominations of $1,000. (p. 835)

Bond certificate A document containing information about the bond, such as the issuer's name, the bond's par value, the contract interest rate, and the maturity date. (p. 835)

Bond indenture The contract between the bond issuer and the bondholders; it identifies the rights and obligations of the parties. (p. 839)

Callable bonds Bonds that give the issuer an option of retiring them at a stated dollar amount prior to maturity. (p. 838)

Capital lease A lease that gives the lessee the risks and benefits normally associated with ownership. (p. 870)

Carrying value The net amount at which bonds are reflected on the balance sheet; equals the par value of the bonds less any unamortized discount or plus any unamortized premium; also called the *book value* of the bonds. (p. 845)

Contract rate The interest rate specified in the bond indenture; it is multiplied by the par value of the bonds to determine the amount of interest to be paid each year; also called the *coupon rate*, the *stated rate*, or the *nominal rate*. (p. 835)

Convertible bonds Bonds that can be exchanged by the bondholders for a fixed number of shares of the issuing company's common shares. (p. 838)

Coupon bonds Bonds that have interest coupons attached to their certificates; the bondholders detach the coupons when they mature and present them to a bank or broker for collection. (p. 838)

Coupon rate See *contract rate*. (p. 835)

Debentures See *unsecured bonds*. (p. 838)

Discount/Discount on bonds payable The difference between the par value of a bond and its lower issue price; arises when the contract rate is lower than the market rate. (pp. 839, 844)

Effective interest method Allocates interest expense over the life of the bonds in a way that yields a constant rate of interest; interest expense for a period is found by multiplying the balance of the liability at the beginning of the period by the bonds' original market rate. (p. 847)

Effective interest rate See *market rate of interest*. (p. 839)

Financial leverage When a company earns a higher return with borrowed funds than it is paying in interest, the result is an increase in return on equity. (p. 837)

Installment note An obligation requiring a series of periodic payments to the lender (p. 861)

Market rate of interest The interest rate that borrowers are willing to pay and that lenders are willing to earn for a particular bond given its risk level. Also called the *effective interest rate*. (p. 839)

Mortgage A legal agreement that protects a lender by giving the lender the right to be paid out of the cash proceeds from the sale of the borrower's specific assets identified in the mortgage. (p. 864)

Nominal rate See *contract rate*. (p. 835)

Operating lease A short-term lease that does not require the lessee to record the right to use the property as an asset or to record any liability for future lease payments. (p. 870)

Par value of a bond The amount that the bond issuer agrees to pay at maturity and the amount on which interest payments are based; also called the *face amount* or *face value*. (p. 835)

Premium/Premium on bonds The difference between the par value of a bond and its higher issue price; arises when the contract rate is higher than the market rate. (pp. 839, 849)

Redeemable bonds Bonds that give the purchaser an option of retiring them at a stated dollar amount prior to maturity. (p. 838)

Registered bonds Bonds owned by investors whose names and addresses are recorded by the issuing company; the interest payments are made with cheques to the registered owners. (p. 838)

Return on equity A ratio calculated as net income available to common shareholders divided by common shareholders' equity; measures how much income is being generated for the common shareholders by their investment. (p. 837)

Secured bonds Bonds that have specific assets of the issuing company pledged as collateral. (p. 838)

Serial bonds Bonds that mature at different dates with the result that the entire debt is repaid gradually over a number of years. (p. 838)

Stated interest rate See *contract rate*. (p. 835)

Straight-line method (interest allocation) A method of amortization that allocates an equal amount of interest to each accounting period in the life of bonds. (p. 846)

Term bonds Bonds that are scheduled for payment (mature) at a single specified date. (p. 838)

Unsecured bonds Bonds that are backed by the issuer's general credit standing; unsecured bonds are almost always more risky than secured bonds; also called *debentures*. (p. 838)

For more study tools, quizzes, and problem material,
visit the **Student Success** *Centre* at
www.mcgrawhill.ca/studentsuccess/FAP

Questions

1. What is the difference between notes payable and bonds payable?
2. What is the primary difference between a share and a bond?
3. What is the main advantage of issuing bonds instead of obtaining funds from the company's owners?
4. What is a bond indenture? What provisions are usually included in an indenture?
5. What are the duties of a trustee for bondholders?
6. What obligation do issuing corporations have to bondholders?
7. Refer to the annual report for WestJet presented in Appendix I. Is there any indication that the company has issued bonds?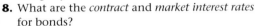
8. What are the *contract* and *market interest rates* for bonds?
9. What factors affect the market interest rates for bonds?
10. If you know the par value of bonds, the contract rate, and the market interest rate, how can you estimate the market value of the bonds?
11. Does the straight-line or effective interest method produce an allocation of interest that creates a constant rate of interest over a bond's life? Explain your answer.
12. What is the cash price of a $2,000 bond that is sold at 98¼? What is the cash price of a $6,000 bond that is sold at 101½?
13. Why does a company that issues bonds between interest dates collect accrued interest from the bonds' purchasers?
14. Describe two alternative payment patterns for installment notes.
15. Refer to the annual report for WestJet presented in Appendix I. How many long-term loans are outstanding? What is the total dollar amount? Are these loans secured?
*16. How would a lease create an asset and a liability for the lessee?

When solving the exercises and problems
1. *Round all dollar amounts to the nearest whole dollar, and*
2. *Assume that none of the companies uses reversing entries.*

Quick Study

QS 17-1
Calculating bond interest
LO¹

A $15,000 bond with a contract interest rate of 6% was issued on March 1, 2011. Calculate the cash paid on the first interest payment date if interest is paid:
a. annually
b. semi-annually
c. quarterly
d. monthly

QS 17-2
Bond financing
LO¹

Curtis Ltd. issued $100,000 of 8% bonds at face value on October 1, 2011. Interest is paid each March 31 and September 30. If Curtis's tax rate is 40%, what is the annual after-tax borrowing cost (a) in percentage terms and (b) in dollars?

QS 17-3
Bond terms and identifications
LO²

Match the following terms and phrases by entering the letter of the phrase that best describes each term in the blank next to the term.

_____ Serial bonds   _____ Secured bonds
_____ Convertible bonds   _____ Debentures
_____ Registered bonds   _____ Bond indenture
_____ Bearer bonds

a. Issuer records the bondholders' names and addresses.
b. Unsecured; backed only by the issuer's general credit standing.
c. Varying maturity dates.
d. Identifies the rights and responsibilities of the issuer and bondholders.
e. Can be exchanged for shares of the issuer's common shares.
f. Unregistered; interest is paid to whomever possesses them.
g. Specific assets of the issuer are mortgaged as collateral.

An asterisk (*) identifies assignment material based on Appendix 17B.

On March 1, 2011, JenStar Inc. issued at par an $80,000, 6%, three-year bond. Interest is to be paid quarterly beginning May 31, 2011. JenStar's year-end is July 31. A partial payment schedule is shown below:

Period Ending	Cash Interest Paid*	Carrying Value
Mar. 1/11		$80,000
May 31/11	$ 1,200	80,000
Aug. 31/11	1,200	80,000
Aug. 31/13	1,200	80,000
Nov. 30/13	1,200	80,000
Feb. 28/14	1,200	80,000
Total	$14,400	

*$80,000 $\times$ 6% $\times$ 3/12

a. Record the issuance of the bond on March 1, 2011.
b. Record the payment of interest on May 31, 2011.
c. Record the accrual of bond interest on July 31, 2011, JenStar's year-end, and the subsequent payment of interest on August 31, 2011.

Presley Corp. issued $200,000 of 6% bonds on November 1, 2011, at par value. The bonds were dated October 1, 2011, and pay interest each April 1 and October 1. Record the issue of the bonds on November 1, 2011.

On August 1, 2011, Blancard Inc. issued $520,000 of 10%, seven-year bonds. Interest is to be paid semi-annually. Calculate the issue price of the bonds if the market interest rate was:
a. 12%
b. 10%
c. 14%

On February 1, 2011, Seemac Corp. issued $750,000 of 11%, eight-year bonds. Interest is to be paid quarterly. Calculate the issue price of the bonds if the market interest rate was:
a. 6%
b. 11%
c. 13%

Wilhelm Inc. issued $400,000 of 10%, five-year bonds on January 1, 2011, at 97. The bonds were dated January 1, 2011, and pay interest each June 30 and December 31. Wilhelm Inc. uses the straight-line method to amortize bond discounts and premiums. Record the issuance of the bonds and the first payment of interest.

Bellevue Corp. issued $600,000 of 6%, four-year bonds for $579,224 on July 1, 2011, the day the bonds were dated. The market interest rate on this date was 7%. Interest is paid quarterly beginning October 1, 2011. Bellevue uses the effective interest method to amortize bond discounts and premiums. Record the issuance of the bonds and the first payment of interest.

Alberta Industries Ltd. issued 10%, 10-year bonds with a par value of $200,000 and semi-annual interest payments. On the issue date, the annual market rate of interest for the bonds was 12%, and the selling price was $177,059. The straight-line method is used to allocate the interest.
a. What is the total amount of bond interest expense that will be recognized over the life of the bonds?
b. What is the total bond interest expense recorded on the first interest payment date?

QS 17-4
Issuance of bond at par, recording interest payment and accrual
LO³

QS 17-5
Issue of bonds at par between interest dates
LO³

QS 17-6
Calculating the price of a bond using PV tables (or business calculator PV function)
LO⁴

QS 17-7
Calculating the price of a bond using business calculator PV function
LO⁴

QS 17-8
Issuance of bonds at a discount, payment of interest—straight-line amortization
LO⁵

QS 17-9
Issuance of bonds at a discount, payment of interest—effective interest amortization
LO⁵

QS 17-10
Bond transactions—discount
LO⁵

QS 17-11
Issuance of bonds at a premium, payment of interest—straight-line amortization
LO6

Jordan Inc. issued $300,000 of 8%, 10-year bonds on January 1, 2011, at 101. The bonds were dated January 1, 2011, and pay interest quarterly beginning April 1, 2011. Jordan uses the straight-line method to amortize bond discounts and premiums. Record the issuance of the bonds and the first payment of interest.

QS 17-12
Issuance of bonds at a premium, payment of interest—effective interest amortization
LO6

Maier Corporation issued $700,000 of 6%, six-year bonds for $735,902 on July 1, 2011, the day the bonds were dated. The market interest rate was 5%. Interest is paid semi-annually beginning December 31, 2011. Maier uses the effective interest method to amortize bond discounts and premiums. Record the issuance of the bonds and the first payment of interest.

QS 17-13
Bond transactions—premium
LO6

Dawson Limited issued 12%, 10-year bonds with a par value of $60,000 and semi-annual interest payments. On the issue date, the annual market rate of interest for the bonds was 10%, and they sold for $67,478. The effective interest method is used to allocate the interest.
a. What is the total amount of bond interest expense that will be recognized over the life of the bonds?
b. What is the amount of bond interest expense recorded on the first interest payment date?

QS 17-14
Issuance of bond at discount, recording interest payment and accrual—straight-line amortization
LO5

Holiday Corporation issued a $95,000, 7%, four-year bond on September 1, 2011, for cash of $92,300. Interest is to be paid semi-annually beginning March 1, 2012. Assume a year-end of April 30. The amortization schedule, using the straight-line method, is shown below:

Period Ending	(A) Cash Interest Paid $95,000 × 7% × 6/12	(B) Period Interest Expense $29,300/8	(C) Discount Amort. $2,700/8	(D) Unamortized Discount	(E) Carrying Value $95,000 − (D)
Sept. 1/11				2,700	92,300
Mar. 1/12	3,325	3,663	338	2,362	92,638
Sept. 1/12	3,325	3,663	338	2,024	92,976
Mar. 1/13	3,325	3,663	338	1,686	93,314
Sept. 1/15	3,325	3,659*	334*	-0-	95,000
Totals	26,600	29,300	2,700		

*Adjusted for rounding.

a. Record the issuance of the bond on September 1, 2011.
b. Record the payment of bond interest on March 1, 2012.
c. Record the accrual of bond interest and discount amortization on April 30, 2012, the year-end, and the subsequent payment of interest on September 1, 2012.

Bozena Inc. issued a $200,000, 8%, three-year bond on November 1, 2011, for cash of $194,792. Interest is to be paid quarterly. The annual market rate of interest is 9%. Assume a year-end of December 31. The amortization schedule, using the effective interest method, is shown below:

QS 17-15
Issuance of bond at discount, recording interest payment and accrual—effective interest amortization
LO5

Period Ending	(A) Cash Interest Paid $200,000 × 8% × 3/12	(B) Period Interest Expense (E) × 9% × 3/12	(C) Discount Amort. (B) − (A)	(D) Unamortized Discount	(E) Carrying Value $200,000 − (D)
Nov. 1/11				5,208	194,792
Feb. 1/12	4,000	4,383	383	4,825	195,175
Aug. 1/14	4,000	4,478	478	492	199,508
Nov. 1/14	4,000	4,492*	492	-0-	200,000
Totals	**48,000**	**53,208**	**5,208**		

*Adjusted for rounding.

a. Record the issuance of the bond on November 1, 2011.
b. Record the accrual of bond interest at year-end, December 31, 2011, and the subsequent payment on February 1, 2012.

On May 1, 2011, Darroch Corporation issued a $386,000, 15%, four-year bond for cash of $394,600. Interest is to be paid semi-annually. Assume a year-end of August 31. The amortization schedule, using the straight-line method, is shown below:

QS 17-16
Issuance of bond at premium, accrual and payment of interest—straight-line amortization
LO6

Period Ending	(A) Cash Interest Paid $386,000 × 15% × 6/12	(B) Period Interest Expense $223,000/8	(C) Premium Amort. $8,600/8	(D) Unamortized Premium	(E) Carrying Value $386,000 + (D)
May 1/11				8,600	394,600
Nov. 1/11	28,950	27,875	1,075	7,525	393,525
May 1/12	28,950	27,875	1,075	6,450	392,450
May 1/15	28,950	27,875	1,075	-0-	386,000
Totals	**231,600**	**223,000**	**8,600**		

a. Record the issuance of the bond on May 1, 2011.
b. Record the accrual of bond interest and premium amortization on August 31, 2011, the year-end, and the subsequent payment of interest on November 1, 2011.

QS 17-17
Issuance of bond at premium, accrual and payment of interest—effective interest amortization
LO6

Henderson Inc. issued a $652,000, 14% 10-year bond on October 1, 2011, for cash of $697,701. Interest is to be paid quarterly. The annual market rate of interest is 12.75%. Assume a year-end of February 28. A partial amortization schedule, using the effective interest method, is shown below.

Period Ending	(A) Cash Interest Paid $652,000 × 14% × 3/12	(B) Period Interest Expense (E) × 12.75% × 3/12	(C) Premium Amort. (A) − (B)	(D) Unamortized Premium	(E) Carrying Value $652,000 + (D)
Oct. 1/11				45,701	697,701
Jan. 1/12	22,820	22,239	581	45,120	697,120
Apr. 1/12	22,820	22,221	599	44,521	696,521
July 1/12	22,820	22,202	618	43,903	695,903
Oct. 1/21	22,820	20,845	1,975	-0-	652,000
Totals	912,800	867,099	45,701		

a. Record the issuance of the bond on October 1, 2011.
b. Record the accrual of bond interest and premium amortization on February 28, 2012, the year-end, and the subsequent payment of interest on April 1, 2012.

QS 17-18
Retiring bonds before maturity
LO7

On July 1, 2011, Loudre Ltd. exercises a $4,000 call option on its outstanding bonds, which have a carrying value of $206,000 and par value of $200,000. Loudre exercises the call option immediately after the semi-annual interest is paid on June 30, 2011. Record the journal entry to show the retirement of the bonds.

QS 17-19
Bond retirement by share conversion
LO7

On January 1, 2011, the $1,000,000 par value bonds of Sinclair Corporation with a carrying value of $950,000 are converted to 500,000 common shares. Journalize the conversion of the bonds.

QS 17-20
Calculating the amount due on an interest-bearing note
LO8

On January 1, 2011, the Pareto Company borrowed $80,000 in exchange for an interest-bearing note. The note plus interest compounded at an annual rate of 8% is due on December 31, 2013. Calculate the amount that Pareto will pay on the due date.

QS 17-21
Installment note with equal payments
LO8

Calvin Corp. borrowed $80,000 from a bank and signed an installment note that calls for five annual payments of equal size, with the first payment due one year after the note was signed. Use Table 17A.2 or a calculator to calculate the size of the annual payment for each of the following annual interest rates:
a. 5%
b. 7%
c. 10%

Exercises

Exercise 17-1
Bonds issued at par
LO3

On January 1, 2011, Sharma Ltd. issued $600,000 of 20-year bonds that pay 8% interest semi-annually on June 30 and December 31. The bonds were sold to investors at their par value.
a. How much interest will Sharma pay to the holders of these bonds every six months?
b. Show the journal entries that Sharma would make to record: (1) the issuance of the bonds on January 1, 2011; (2) the first interest payment on June 30, 2011; and (3) the second interest payment on December 31, 2011.

On March 1, 2011, Marham Ltd. issued bonds dated January 1, 2011. The bonds have a $600,000 par value, mature in 20 years, and pay 8% interest semi-annually on June 30 and December 31. The bonds were sold to investors at their par value plus the two months' interest that had accrued since the original issue date.

a. How much accrued interest was paid to Marham by the purchasers of these bonds on March 1, 2011?

b. Show the journal entries that Marham would make to record: (1) the issuance of the bonds on March 1, 2011; (2) the first interest payment on June 30, 2011; and (3) the second interest payment on December 31, 2011.

Exercise 17-2
Bond issued at par between interest dates
LO3

South Corporation had a $1,350,000, 5% bond available for issue on September 1, 2011. Interest is to be paid quarterly beginning November 30. All of the bonds were issued at par on October 1. Prepare the appropriate entries for:

a. October 1, 2011
b. November 30, 2011
c. December 31, 2011 (South Corporation's year-end)
d. February 28, 2012

Exercise 17-3
Bonds issued at par between interest dates
LO3

Delta Corporation had an $856,000, 7% bond available for issue on April 1. Interest is to be paid on the last day of each month. On April 14 and 25, bonds with a face value of $650,000 and $206,000, respectively, were issued at par. Record the entries for April 14, 25, and 30.

Exercise 17-4
Bonds issued at par between interest dates
LO3

On October 1, 2011, Allar Inc. has available for issue $618,000 bonds due in four years. Interest at the rate of 4% is to be paid quarterly. Calculate the issue price if the market interest rate is:

a. 5%
b. 4%
c. 3%

Exercise 17-5
Calculating the issue price using business calculator PV function
LO4

Check figure:
c. $641,213

Morelee Inc. has available for issue a $2,500,000 bond due in eight years. Interest at the rate of 6% is to be paid semi-annually. Calculate the issue price if the market interest rate is:

a. 5.5%
b. 6%
c. 6.75%

Exercise 17-6
Calculating the issue price using business calculator PV function
LO4

Check figure:
a. $2,580,029

The Kitchener Corp. issued bonds on March 1, 2011, with a par value of $150,000. The bonds mature in 15 years and pay 8% annual interest in two semi-annual payments. On the issue date, the annual market rate of interest for the bonds turned out to be 10%.

a. What is the size of the semi-annual interest payment for these bonds?
b. How many semi-annual interest payments will be made on these bonds over their life?
c. Use the information about the interest rates to decide whether the bonds were issued at par, at a discount, or at a premium.
d. Estimate the market value of the bonds as of the date they were issued.
e. Present the journal entry that would be made to record the bonds' issuance.

Exercise 17-7
Calculating the present value of a bond and recording the issuance
LO4, 5

Check figure:
e. Discount = $23,055

Connelly Ltd. issued bonds with a par value of $100,000 on January 1, 2011. The annual contract rate on the bonds is 8%, and the interest is paid semi-annually on June 30 and December 31. The bonds mature after three years. The annual market interest rate at the date of issuance was 12%, and the bonds were sold for $90,165.

a. What is the amount of the original discount on these bonds?
b. How much total bond interest expense will be recognized over the life of these bonds?
c. Present an amortization table for these bonds; use the straight-line method of allocating the interest and amortizing the discount.

Exercise 17-8
Straight-line allocation of interest for bonds sold at a discount
LO5

Check figure:
b. Total interest expense = $33,835

Exercise 17-9
Effective interest method
allocation of interest for bonds
sold at a discount

LO5

Check figure:
b. Total interest expense = $8,723

Burlington Corporation issued bonds with a par value of $30,000 on January 1, 2011. The annual contract rate on the bonds is 8%, and the interest is paid semi-annually. The bonds mature after three years. The annual market interest rate at the date of issuance was 10%, and the bonds were sold for $28,477.

a. What is the amount of the original discount on these bonds?
b. How much total bond interest expense will be recognized over the life of these bonds?
c. Present an amortization table for these bonds; use the effective interest method of allocating the interest and amortizing the discount.

Exercise 17-10
Straight-line amortization table
and accrued interest

LO5

Check figure:
a. Total interest expense = $185,265

Towbell Corp. issued bonds with a par value of $500,000 and a five-year life on May 1, 2011. The contract interest rate is 7%. The bonds pay interest on October 31 and April 30. They were issued at a price of $489,734. Towbell Corp.'s year-end is December 31.

a. Prepare an amortization table for these bonds that covers their entire life. Use the straight-line method of allocating interest.
b. Show the journal entries that the issuer would make to record the entries on: October 31, 2011; December 31, 2011; and April 30, 2012.

Exercise 17-11
Amortization of bond discount—
straight-line method

LO5

Check figure:
a. $588,857

On November 1, 2011, Inca Ltd. issued a $600,000, 5%, two-year bond. Interest is to be paid semi-annually each May 1 and November 1.

Required
a. Calculate the issue price of the bond assuming a market interest rate of 6% on the date of the bond issue.
b. Using the straight-line method, prepare an amortization schedule similar to Exhibit 17.10.

Exercise 17-12
Amortization of bond discount—
straight-line method

LO5

Check figures:
a. $696,742
b. Total interest expense = $398,408

On October 1, 2011, Binbishr Inc. issued a $735,000, 7%, seven-year bond. Interest is to be paid annually each October 1.

Required
a. Calculate the issue price of the bond assuming a market interest rate of 8% on the date of the bond issue.
b. Using the straight-line method, prepare an amortization schedule similar to Exhibit 17.10.

Exercise 17-13
Recording bonds issued at a
discount—straight-line
amortization

LO5

Check figure:
a. Discount = $38,258

Refer to the amortization schedule prepared in Exercise 17-12. Binbishr Inc. has a November 30 year-end.

Required

Part 1
Record the following entries:
a. issuance of the bonds on October 1, 2011,
b. adjusting entry to accrue bond interest and discount amortization on November 30, 2011,
c. payment of interest on October 1, 2012.

Part 2
Show how the bond will appear on the balance sheet under long-term liabilities at November 30, 2015.

Exercise 17-14
Amortization of bond discount—
effective interest method

LO5

Check figures:
a. $3,859,570 (using PV tables) or
$3,859,606 (using a calculator)
b. Total interest expense = $940,430

On March 1, 2011, Lenderyou Inc. issued a $4,000,000, 5%, four-year bond. Interest is to be paid semi-annually beginning August 31, 2011.

Required
a. Calculate the issue price of the bond assuming a market interest rate of 6% on the date of the bond issue.
b. Using the effective interest method, prepare an amortization schedule similar to Exhibit 17.11.

Refer to the amortization schedule prepared in Exercise 17-14. Assume a year-end of June 30.

Required

Part 1

Record the following entries:
a. issuance of the bonds on October 1, 2011,
b. accrual of interest on June 30, 2011, the year-end,
c. payment of interest on August 31, 2011.

Part 2

Show how the bonds will appear on the balance sheet under long-term liabilities at June 30, 2014.

Exercise 17-15
Recording bonds issued at a discount—effective interest amortization
LO5

Check figure:
a. Discount = $140,430

On January 1, 2011, Wallace Ltd. issued $600,000 of 20-year bonds that pay 8% interest semi-annually on June 30 and December 31. Assume the bonds were sold at: (1) 98; and (2) 102. Journalize the issuance of the bonds at 98 and 102.

Exercise 17-16
Journal entries for bond issuances
LO5, 6

Check figure:
b. Premium = $12,000

Allen Ice Ltd. issued bonds on September 1, 2011, with a par value of $25,000. The bonds mature in 15 years and pay 8% annual interest in two semi-annual payments. On the issue date, the annual market rate of interest for the bonds turned out to be 6%.
a. What is the semi-annual interest payment for these bonds?
b. How many semi-annual interest payments will be made on these bonds over their life?
c. Use the information about the interest rates to decide whether the bonds were issued at par, at a discount, or at a premium.
d. Estimate the market value of the bonds as of the date they were issued.
e. Present the journal entry that would be made to record the bonds' issuance.

Exercise 17-17
Computing the present value of a bond and recording the issuance
LO4, 6

Check figure:
e. Cash = $29,900

MegaMax Ltd. issued bonds with a par value of $250,000 on January 1, 2011. The annual contract rate on the bonds was 12%, and the interest is paid semi-annually. The bonds mature after three years. The annual market interest rate at the date of issuance was 10%, and the bonds were sold for $262,689.
a. What is the amount of the original premium on these bonds?
b. How much total bond interest expense will be recognized over the life of these bonds?
c. Present an amortization table for these bonds (similar to Exhibit 17.17); use the effective interest method of allocating the interest and amortizing the premium.

Exercise 17-18
Effective interest method allocation of interest for bonds sold at a premium
LO6

Check figure:
b. Total interest expense = $77,311

On November 1, Lendrome Inc. issued a $300,000, 5%, two-year bond. Interest is to be paid quarterly each February 1, May 1, August 1, and November 1.

Required
a. Calculate the issue price of the bond assuming a market interest rate of 4% on the date of the bond issue.
b. Using the straight-line method, prepare an amortization schedule similar to Exhibit 17.16.

Exercise 17-19
Amortization of bond premium—straight-line method
LO4, 6

Check figure:
a. $305,744 (using PV tables) or $305,739 (using a calculator)

On October 1, 2011, Sharden Inc. issued a $735,000, 7%, seven-year bond. Interest is to be paid annually each October 1.

Required
a. Calculate the issue price of the bond assuming a market interest rate of 6% on the date of the bond issue.
b. Using the straight-line method, prepare an amortization schedule similar to Exhibit 17.16.

Exercise 17-20
Amortization of bond premium—straight-line method
LO6

Check figures:
a. $776,063 (using PV tables) or $776,031 (using a calculator)
b. Total interest expense = $319,087

Exercise 17-21
Recording bonds issued at
a premium—straight-line
amortization
LO6

Check figures:
1c. Premium = $4,888
2. Premium = $16,621

Refer to the amortization schedule prepared in Exercise 17-20. Assume a November 30 year-end.

Required

Part 1
Record the following entries:
a. issuance of the bonds on October 1, 2011,
b. adjusting entry to accrue bond interest and premium amortization on November 30, 2011,
c. payment of interest on October 1, 2012.

Part 2
Show how the bond will appear on the balance sheet under long-term liabilities at November 30, 2015.

Exercise 17-22
Amortization of bond premium—
effective interest method
LO4, 6

Check figures:
a. $557,874 (using PV tables) or
$557,864 (using a calculator)
b. Total interest expense = $187,140

On October 1, 2011, Terra Inc. issued a $500,000, 7%, seven-year bond. Interest is to be paid annually each October 1.

Required
a. Calculate the issue price of the bond assuming a market interest rate of 5%.
b. Prepare an amortization schedule similar to Exhibit 17.17 using the effective interest method.

Exercise 17-23
Recording bonds issued at a
premium—effective interest
amortization
LO6

Check figure:
a. Cash = $557,874

Refer to the amortization schedule prepared in Exercise 17-22. Assume a November 30 year-end.

Required

Part 1
Record the following entries:
a. issuance of the bonds on October 1, 2011.
b. adjusting entry to accrue bond interest and premium amortization on November 30, 2011.
c. payment of interest on October 1, 2012.

Part 2
Show how the bond will appear on the balance sheet under long-term liabilities at November 30, 2016.

Exercise 17-24
Retiring bonds for cash
LO7

Check figure:
a. Dr Premium = $4,312

Porsha Inc. issued a $400,000, 7%, 10-year bond on October 1, 2011. Interest is paid annually each October 1.

Required
Using the partial amortization schedule provided below, record the entry to retire the bonds on October 1, 2018, for cash of:
a. $407,000
b. $404,312
c. $400,000

Period Ending	Cash Interest Paid	Period Interest Expense	Premium Amort.	Unamortized Premium	Carrying Value
Oct. 1/11				$14,378	$414,378
Oct. 1/12	$28,000	$29,438	$1,438	12,940	412,940
Oct. 1/13	28,000	29,438	1,438	11,502	411,502
Oct. 1/17	28,000	29,438	1,438	5,750	405,750
Oct. 1/18	28,000	29,438	1,438	4,312	404,312
Oct. 1/19	28,000	29,438	1,438	2,874	402,874

Jazz Inc. issued a $900,000, 5%, five-year bond on October 1, 2011. Interest is paid annually each October 1. Jazz's year-end is December 31.

Required
Using the amortization schedule provided below, record the entry to retire the bonds on October 1, 2014, for cash of:
a. $881,000
b. $883,500
c. $886,900

Exercise 17-25
Retiring bonds for cash
LO7

Check figure:
c. Loss = $3,400

Period Ending	Cash Interest Paid	Period Interest Expense	Discount Amort.	Unamortized Discount	Carrying Value
Oct. 1/11				$37,911	$862,089
Oct. 1/12	$ 45,000	$ 51,725	$ 6,725	31,186	868,814
Oct. 1/13	45,000	52,129	7,129	24,057	875,943
Oct. 1/14	45,000	52,557	7,557	16,500	883,500
Oct. 1/15	45,000	53,010	8,010	8,490	891,510
Oct. 1/16	45,000	53,491	8,490	0	900,000
	$225,000	$262,911	$37,911		

On January 1, 2011, Dutch Ltd., issued $700,000 of 10%, 15-year bonds at a price of 95 1/2. Interest is to be paid semi-annually. Three years later, on January 1, 2014, the corporation retired 30% of these bonds by buying them on the open market at 105 3/4. All interest had been properly accounted for and paid through December 31, 2013, the day before the purchase. The straight-line method was used to allocate the interest and amortize the original discount.
a. How much money did the company receive when it first issued the entire group of bonds?
b. How large was the original discount on the entire group of bonds?
c. How much amortization did the company record on the entire group of bonds between January 1, 2011, and December 31, 2013?
d. What was the carrying value of the entire group of bonds as of the close of business on December 31, 2013? What was the carrying value of the retired bonds on this date?
e. How much money did the company pay on January 1, 2014, to purchase the bonds that it retired?
f. What is the amount of the gain or loss from retiring the bonds?
g. Provide the General Journal entry that the company would make to record the retirement of the bonds.

Exercise 17-26
Retiring bonds payable
LO7

Check figure:
g. Loss = $19,635

Denston Inc. showed the following on its December 31, 2011, balance sheet:

Bonds payable, convertible..	$5,000,000	
Less: Unamortized discount..	18,000	$4,982,000

Exercise 17-27
Conversion of bonds payable
LO7

Required
1. Assuming the bonds are convertible into 500,000 common shares, journalize the conversion on January 1, 2012, when the market value per common share was $10.25.
2. How will the conversion of bonds into common shares affect the elements of the balance sheet (assets, liabilities, equity)?

Exercise 17-28
Conversion of bonds payable
LO7

Van Bruen Inc.'s December 31, 2011, adjusted trial balance shows the following:

Account Description	Balance*
Bonds payable, convertible...	$1,500,000
Premium on bonds payable...	20,000

*Assume normal balances.

Required
1. What is the carrying value of the bonds on December 31, 2011?
2. The bonds were converted into 150,000 common shares on January 1, 2012. Journalize the entry assuming the market value per common share on this date was $9.10.

Exercise 17-29
Installment note with payments of accrued interest and equal amounts of principal
LO8

Check figure:
b. Total interest expense = $2,000

On December 31, 2011, Morgan Inc. borrowed $16,000 by signing a four-year, 5% installment note. The note requires annual payments of accrued interest and equal amounts of principal on December 31 of each year from 2012 through 2015.
a. How much principal will be included in each of the four payments?
b. Prepare an amortization table for this installment note like the one presented in Exhibit 17.20.

Exercise 17-30
Journal entries for an installment note with payments of accrued interest and equal amounts of principal
LO8

Use the data in Exercise 17-29 to prepare journal entries that Morgan Inc. would make to record the loan on December 31, 2011, and the four payments starting on December 31, 2012, through the final payment on December 31, 2015.

Exercise 17-31
Installment note with equal payments
LO8

Check figure:
b. Total interest expense = $2,560

On December 31, 2011, Logan Corp. borrowed $20,000 by signing a four-year, 5% installment note. The note requires four equal payments of accrued interest and principal on December 31 of each year from 2012 through 2015.
a. Calculate the size of each of the four equal payments.
b. Prepare an amortization table for this installment note like the one presented in Exhibit 17.20.

Exercise 17-32
Journal entries for an installment note with equal payments
LO8

Use the data in Exercise 17-31 to prepare journal entries that Logan Corp. would make to record the loan on December 31, 2011, and the four payments starting on December 31, 2012, through the final payment on December 31, 2015.

*Exercise 17-33
Liabilities from leasing
LO9

Check figures:
a. 22,745
c. 2,843

On December 31, 2011, a day when the available interest rate was 10%, Kowloon Printing Company leased equipment with an eight-year life. The contract called for a $6,000 annual lease payment at the end of each of the next five years, with the equipment becoming the property of the lessee at the end of that period. Prepare entries to record: (a) the leasing of the equipment, (b) amortization expense for 2012 assuming straight-line and a zero residual value, (c) the December 31, 2012, lease payment, including the recognition of interest expense on the lease liability on December 31, 2012, and (d) prepare an amortization schedule.

An asterisk (*) identifies assignment material based on Appendix 17B.

Problems

Applet Inc. issued bonds on January 1, 2011, that pay interest semi-annually on June 30 and December 31. The par value of the bonds is $80,000, the annual contract rate is 8%, and the bonds mature in 10 years.

Required
For each of these three situations, (a) determine the issue price of the bonds and (b) show the journal entry that would record the issuance, assuming the market interest rate at the date of issuance was

1. 6%
2. 8%
3. 10%

Problem 17-1A
Calculating bond prices and recording issuance with journal entries
LO3, 5, 6

Check figures:
1a. $91,904
2a. $80,000
3a. $70,031

The Costello Corporation issued $250,000 of bonds that pay 6% interest. The date of issuance was January 1, 2011, and the interest is paid each June 30 and December 31. The bonds mature after 10 years and were issued at the price of $232,235.

Required
1. Prepare a General Journal entry to record the issuance of the bonds.
2. Calculate the cash payment, discount amortization amount using straight-line amortization, and bond interest expense to be recognized every six months.
3. Determine the total bond interest expense that will be recognized over the life of these bonds.
4. Show the beginning and ending balances of the Discount on Bonds Payable account for the first four semi-annual periods.
5. Prepare the first two years of an amortization table based on the straight-line method of allocating the interest.
6. Present the journal entries that Costello would make to record the first two interest payments. Assume a December 31 year-end.

Problem 17-2A
Straight-line method of allocating bond interest and amortizing a bond discount
LO5

Check figure:
3. Total interest expense = $167,765

Gordon Corp. issued $100,000 of bonds that pay 4% semi-annual interest each June 30 and December 31. The date of issuance was January 1, 2011. The bonds mature after four years. The market interest rate was 6%.

Required

Preparation component:
1. Calculate the issue price of the bond.
2. Prepare a General Journal entry to record the issuance of the bonds.
3. Determine the total bond interest expense that will be recognized over the life of these bonds.
4. Prepare the first two years of an amortization table based on the effective interest method.
5. Show the beginning and ending balances of the discount on bonds payable account for the first four amortization periods.
6. Present the journal entries Gordon would make to record the first two interest payments.

Analysis component:
Now assume that the market interest rate on January 1, 2011, was 3% instead of 6%. Without presenting any specific numbers, describe how this change would affect the amounts presented on Gordon's financial statements.

Problem 17-3A
Effective interest method of allocating bond interest and amortizing a bond discount
LO4, 5

Check figure:
1. $92,979 (using PV tables) or $92,980 (using a calculator)

On February 1, 2011, Wafi Inc. issued a $490,000, 10%, four-year bond. Interest is to be paid quarterly beginning May 1, 2011.

Required
a. Calculate the issue price of the bond assuming a market interest rate of 11%.
b. Using the straight-line method, prepare an amortization schedule similar to Exhibit 17.10.

Problem 17-4A
Amortization of bond discount—straight-line method (using business calculator PV function)
LO4, 5

Check figures:
a. $474,314
b. Total interest expense = $211,686

Problem 17-5A
Recording bonds issued at a discount—straight-line amortization

LO5

Check figures:
1a. Cash = $474,314
1b. Cash = $12,250

Refer to the amortization schedule prepared in Problem 17-4A. Assume Wafi Inc. has a June 30 year-end.

Required

Part 1
Record the following entries:
a. issuance of the bonds on February 1, 2011,
b. payment of interest on May 1, 2011,
c. adjusting entry to accrue bond interest and discount amortization on June 30, 2011,
d. payment of interest on August 1, 2011.

Part 2
Show how the bonds will appear on the balance sheet under liabilities at June 30, 2014.

Problem 17-6A
Amortization of bond discount—effective interest method (using business calculator PV function)

LO4, 5

Check figures:
a. $351,286
b. Total interest expense = $151,550

On June 1, 2011, Seghal Inc. issued a $360,000 12%, three-year bond. Interest is to be paid semi-annually beginning December 1, 2011.

Required
a. Calculate the issue price of the bond assuming a market interest rate of 13%.
b. Using the effective interest method, prepare an amortization schedule similar to Exhibit 17.11.

Problem 17-7A
Recording bonds issued at a discount—effective interest method

LO5

Check figures:
1a. Cash = $351,286
1b. Cash = $21,600

Refer to the amortization schedule prepared in Problem 17-6A. Assume Seghal Inc. has a January 31 year-end.

Required

Part 1
Record the following entries:
a. issuance of the bonds on June 1, 2011,
b. payment of interest on December 1, 2011,
c. adjusting entry to accrue bond interest and discount amortization on January 31, 2012,
d. payment of interest on June 1, 2012.

Part 2
Show how the bonds will appear on the balance sheet under long-term liabilities at January 31, 2013.

Problem 17-8A
Bond premium amortization and finding the present value of remaining cash flows—effective interest method

LO6

Check figure:
2. Total interest expense = $64,756

Cloze Ltd. issued 8.5% bonds with a par value of $160,000 and a five-year life on January 1, 2011, for $163,244. The bonds pay interest on June 30 and December 31. The market interest rate was 8% on the original issue date.

Required
1. Calculate the total bond interest expense over the life of the bonds.
2. Prepare an amortization table using the effective interest method similar to Exhibit 17.17.
3. Show the journal entries that Cloze Ltd. would make to record the first two interest payments assuming a December 31 year-end.
4. Use the original market interest rate to calculate the present value of the remaining cash flows for these bonds as of December 31, 2013. Compare your answer with the amount shown on the amortization table as the balance for that date and explain your findings.

Problem 17-9A
Bonds issued at a premium and discount—effective interest (using business calculator PV function)

LO4, 5, 6

On March 1, 2011, Fefferman Inc. issued a $400,000, 8%, three-year bond. Interest is payable semi-annually beginning September 1, 2011.

Required

Part 1
a. Calculate the bond issue price assuming a market interest rate of 7% on the date of issue.
b. Using the effective interest method, prepare an amortization schedule.
c. Record the entry for the issuance of the bond on March 1, the adjusting entry to accrue bond interest and related amortization on April 30, 2011, Fefferman's year-end, and the payment of interest on September 1, 2011.

Part 2

a. Calculate the bond issue price assuming a market interest rate of 8.5% on the date of issue.

b. Using the effective interest method, prepare an amortization schedule.

c. Record the entries for the issuance of the bond on March 1, the adjusting entry to accrue bond interest and related amortization on April 30, 2011, Fefferman's year-end, and the payment of interest on September 1, 2011.

Check figures:
1a. = $410,657
2a. = $394,800

Shop-a-lot Inc. has a July 31 year-end. It showed the following partial amortization schedules regarding two bond issues:

Problem 17-10A
Recording bonds
LO5, 6, 7

Bond Issue A

Period Ending	(A) Cash Interest Paid $680,000 × 9% × 6/12	(B) Period Interest Expense (E) × 8% × 6/12	(C) Amort. (A) − (B)	(D) Unamortized Balance	(E) Carrying Value $680,000 ÷ (D)
June 1/11				$43,042	$723,042
Dec. 1/11	$ 30,600	$ 28,922	$ 1,678	41,364	721,364
Dec. 1/17	30,600	27,913	2,687	15,137	695,137
June 1/18	30,600	27,805	2,795	12,342	692,342
Dec. 1/18	30,600	27,694	2,906	9,436	689,436
June 1/19	30,600	27,577	3,023	6,413	686,413
Dec. 1/19	30,600	27,457	3,143	3,270	683,270
June 1/20	30,600	27,330	3,270	0	680,000
Totals	$550,800	$507,758	$43,042		

Bond Issue B

Required

Period Ending	(A) Cash Interest Paid $540,000 × 8% × 3/12	(B) Period Interest Expense $467,361 ÷ 40	(C) Amort. $35,361 ÷ 40	(D) Unamortized Balance	(E) Carrying Value $540,000 − (D)
Apr. 1/09				$35,361	$504,639
July 1/09	$ 10,800	$ 11,684	$ 884	34,477	539,116
Apr. 1/17	10,800	11,684	884	7,073	539,116
July 1/17	10,800	11,684	884	6,189	539,116
Oct. 1/17	10,800	11,684	884	5,305	539,116
Jan. 1/18	10,800	11,684	884	4,421	539,116
Apr. 1/18	10,800	11,684	884	3,537	539,116
July 1/18	10,800	11,684	884	2,653	539,116
Oct. 1/18	10,800	11,684	884	1,769	539,116
Jan. 1/19	10,800	11,684	884	885	539,116
Apr. 1/19	10,800	11,685*	885*	0	539,115
Totals	$432,000	$467,361	$35,361		

*Adjusted for rounding

Answer the following for each bond issue:

a. Were the bonds issued at a premium and/or discount?

b. Journalize the issuance of bond issue A and B on June 1, 2011, and April 1, 2009, respectively.

c. What is the contract interest rate for each bond issue?

d. The premium and/or discount is amortized using what method (straight-line and/or effective interest) for each bond issue?

e. Interest of how much is paid how often for each bond issue?

f. What is the term of each bond issue?

g. Show how each of the bonds would appear on the balance sheet under long-term liabilities at July 31, 2017.

h. Calculate the total bond interest expense that would appear on the income statement for the year ended July 31, 2018.

i. Independent of (a) through (h), assume both bond issues were retired on December 1, 2018, at 97. Record the entries.

Problem 17-11A
Installment notes
LO8

Check figure:
2. Total interest expense = $31,696

On November 30, 2011, Calibaut Ltd. borrowed $100,000 from a bank by signing a four-year installment note bearing interest at 12%. The terms of the note require equal payments each year on November 30, starting November 30, 2012.

Required
1. Calculate the size of each installment payment.
2. Complete an installment note amortization schedule for this note similar to Exhibit 17.21.
3. Present the journal entries that Calibaut would make to record accrued interest as of December 31, 2011 (the end of the annual reporting period), and the first payment on the note.
4. Now assume that the note does not require equal payments but does require four payments that include accrued interest and an equal amount of principal in each payment. Complete an installment note amortization schedule for this note similar to Exhibit 17.20. Present the journal entries that Calibaut would make to record accrued interest as of December 31, 2011, (the end of the annual reporting period) and the first payment on the note.

*Problem 17-12A
Lease liabilities
LO9

Check figure:
2. Total interest expense = $28,880

Laporte Engineering Company leased a machine on January 1, 2011, under a contract calling for four annual payments of $30,000 on December 31, 2011 through 2014. The machine becomes the property of the lessee after the fourth payment. The machine was predicted to have a service life of six years and no residual value, and the interest rate available to Laporte Engineering was 12% on the day the lease was signed. The machine was delivered on January 10, 2011, and was immediately placed in service. On January 4, 2016, it was overhauled at a total cost of $5,000. The overhaul did not increase the machine's efficiency but it did add two additional years to the expected service life. On June 30, 2018, the machine was traded in on a similar new machine having an $84,000 cash price. A $6,000 trade-in allowance was received, and the balance was paid in cash.

Required
1. Determine the initial net liability created by the lease and the cost of the leased asset.
2. Prepare a table showing the calculation of the amount of interest expense allocated to each year the lease is in effect and the carrying amount of the liability at the end of each of those years.
3. Prepare the entry to record the leasing of the machine.
4. Prepare entries that would be made on December 31, 2012, to record the annual amortization on a straight-line basis, and the recording of the lease payment. Also show how the machine and the lease liability should appear on the December 31, 2012, balance sheet.
5. Prepare the entries to record the machine's overhaul in 2016 and amortization at the end of that year.
6. Prepare the entries to record the exchange of the machines on June 30, 2018.

Alternate Problems

Stevens Limited issued a group of bonds on January 1, 2011, that pay interest semi-annually on June 30 and December 31. The par value of the bonds is $50,000, the annual contract rate is 10%, and the bonds mature in 10 years.

Required
For each of these three situations, (a) determine the issue price of the bonds, and (b) show the journal entry that would record the issuance, assuming the market interest rate at the date of issuance was:
1. 8%
2. 10%
3. 12%

Problem 17-1B
Calculating bond prices and recording issuance with journal entries
LO3, 5, 6

Check figures:
1a. $56,796
2a. $50,000
3a. $44,265

Sontag Corp. issued $3.7 million of bonds that pay 12.9% annual interest with two semi-annual payments. The date of issuance was January 1, 2011, and the interest is paid on June 30 and December 31. The bonds mature after 10 years and were issued at the price of $3,890,952. The market interest rate was 12%.

Required
1. Show how the bond price was calculated and prepare a General Journal entry to record the issuance of the bonds.
2. Calculate the cash payment, premium amortization amount using straight-line amortization, and bond interest expense to be recognized every six months.
3. Determine the total bond interest expense that will be recognized over the life of these bonds.
4. Prepare the first two lines of an amortization table based on the straight-line method.
5. Present the journal entries that Sontag Corp. would make to record the first two interest payments.
6. Show the beginning and ending balances of the Premium on Bonds Payable account for the first four semi-annual periods.

Problem 17-2B
Straight-line method of allocating interest and amortizing a bond premium
LO4, 6

Check figure:
1. Cash = $3,890,952 (using a PV table) or $3,890,974 (using a calculator)

Cape Breton Corp. issued $800,000 of bonds that pay 9.7% annual interest with two semi-annual payments. The date of issuance was January 1, 2011, and the interest is paid on June 30 and December 31. The bonds mature after 10 years and were issued at the price of $785,045. The market interest rate was 10% and the company uses the effective interest method of amortization.

Required
1. Show how the bond price was determined and prepare a General Journal entry to record the issuance of the bonds.
2. Determine the total bond interest expense that will be recognized over the life of these bonds.
3. Prepare the first two lines of an amortization table based on the effective interest method.
4. Present the journal entries that Cape Breton Corp. would make to record the first two interest payments.

Problem 17-3B
Effective interest method of allocating interest and amortizing a bond discount (using business calculator PV function)
LO4, 5

Check figure:
1. Cash = $785,045

On May 1, 2011, Rooniak Corporation issued a $625,000, 12%, three-year bond. Interest is payable quarterly beginning August 1, 2011.

Required
a. Calculate the bond issue price assuming a market interest rate of 11% on the date of issue.
b. Using the straight-line method, prepare an amortization schedule similar to Exhibit 17.16.

Problem 17-4B
Amortization of bond premium—straight-line method (using business calculator PV function)
LO4, 6

Check figures:
a. $640,788
b. Total interest expense = $209,212

Problem 17-5B
Recording bonds issued at a premium—straight-line method
LO6

Check figures:
1a. Cash = $640,788
1b. Cash = $18,750

Refer to the amortization schedule prepared in Problem 17-4B. Rooniak Corporation's year-end is August 31.

Required

Part 1
Record the following entries:
a. issuance of the bonds on May 1, 2011,
b. payment of interest on August 1, 2011,
c. adjusting entry to accrue bond interest and premium amortization on August 31, 2011,
d. payment of interest on November 1, 2011.

Part 2
Show how the bond will appear on the balance sheet at August 31, 2013.

Problem 17-6B
Amortization of bond premium—effective interest method (using business calculator PV function)
LO4, 6

Check figures:
a. $365,828
b. Total interest expense = $194,172

On September 1, 2011, Messner Corp. issued a $350,000, 15%, four-year bond. Interest is payable semi-annually beginning March 1, 2012.

Required
a. Calculate the bond issue price assuming a market interest rate of 13.5% on the date of issue.
b. Using the effective interest method, prepare an amortization schedule similar to Exhibit 17.17.

Problem 17-7B
Recording bonds issued at a premium—effective interest amortization
LO6

Check figures:
1a. Cash = $365,828
1c. Cash = $26,250

Refer to the amortization schedule prepared in Problem 17-6B. Assume a January 31 year-end.

Required

Part 1
Record the following entries:
a. issuance of the bonds on September 1, 2011,
b. adjusting entry to accrue bond interest and premium amortization on January 31, 2012,
c. payment of interest on March 1, 2012.

Part 2
Show how the bond will appear on the balance sheet under long-term liabilities at January 31, 2014.

Problem 17-8B
Bond discount amortization and finding the present value of remaining cash flows—effective interest method (using business calculator PV function)
LO4, 5

Check figure:
2. Total interest expense = $140,660

Dipchand Ltd. issued bonds with a par value of $320,000 and a five-year life on January 1, 2011. The bonds pay interest on June 30 and December 31. The contract interest rate is 8%. The market interest rate was 9% on the original issue date.

Required
1. Calculate the issue price and the total bond interest expense over the life of the bonds.
2. Prepare an amortization table using the effective interest method similar to Exhibit 17.11.
3. Show the journal entries that Dipchand would make to record the first two interest payments. Assume a December 31 year-end.
4. Use the original market interest rate to calculate the present value of the remaining cash flows for these bonds as of December 31, 2013. Compare your answer with the amount shown on the amortization table as the balance for that date, and explain your findings.

Problem 17-9B
Bonds issued at a premium and discount—effective interest (using business calculator PV function)
LO4, 5, 6

On February 1, 2011, Giant Corp. issued an $800,000, 5%, two-year bond. Interest is payable quarterly each May 1, August 1, November 1, and February 1.

Required

Part 1
a. Calculate the bond issue price assuming a market interest rate of 6% on the date of issue.
b. Using the effective interest method, prepare an amortization schedule.
c. Record the entry for the issuance of the bond on February 1, the adjusting entry to accrue bond interest and related amortization on March 31, 2011, Giant Corp.'s year-end, and the payment of interest on May 1, 2011.

Part 2
d. Calculate the bond issue price assuming a market interest rate of 4.5% on the date of issue.
e. Using the effective interest method, prepare an amortization schedule.
f. Record the entries for the issuance of the bond on February 1, the adjusting entry to accrue bond interest and related amortization on March 31, 2011, Giant Corp.'s year-end, and the payment of interest on May 1, 2011.

Maritime Inc. has a December 31 year-end. It showed the following partial amortization schedules regarding its two bond issues:

Problem 17-10B
Recording bonds
LO5, 6, 7

Bond Issue 1

Period Ending	(A) Cash Interest Paid $650,000 × 7% × 3/12	(B) Period Interest Expense (E) × 8% × 3/12	(C) Amortization (B) − (A)	(D) Unamortized Balance	(E) Carrying Value $650,000 − (D)
Sept. 1/12				26,571	623,429
Dec. 1/12	11,375	12,469	1,094	25,477	624,523
Dec. 1/16	11,375	12,876	1,501	4,685	645,315
Mar. 1/17	11,375	12,906	1,531	3,154	646,846
June 1/17	11,375	12,937	1,562	1,592	648,408
Sept. 1/17	11,375	12,967*	1,592	-0-	650,000
Totals	**227,500**	**254,071**	**26,571**		

*Adjusted for rounding.

Bond Issue 2

Period Ending	(A) Cash Interest Paid $780,000 × 11% × 6/12	(B) Period Interest Expense $644,133/16	(C) Amortization $42,267/16	(D) Unamortized Balance	(E) Carrying Value $780,000 + (D)
May 1/10				42,267	822,267
May 1/16	42,900	40,258	2,642	10,563	790,563
Nov. 1/16	42,900	40,258	2,642	7,921	787,921
May 1/17	42,900	40,258	2,642	5,279	785,279
Nov. 1/17	42,900	40,258	2,642	2,637	782,637
May 1/18	42,900	40,263*	2,637	-0-	780,000
Totals	**686,400**	**644,133**	**42,267**		

*Adjusted for rounding.

Required
Answer the following for each bond issue:
a. Were the bonds issued at a premium and/or discount?
b. Journalize the issuance of bond issue 1 and 2 on September 1, 2012, and May 1, 2010, respectively.
c. What is the contract interest rate for each bond issue?
d. The premium and/or discount is amortized using what method (straight-line and/or effective interest) for each bond issue?
e. Interest of how much is paid how often for each bond issue?
f. What is the term of each bond issue?
g. Show how each of the bonds would appear on the balance sheet at December 31, 2016.
h. Calculate the total bond interest expense that would appear on the income statement for the year ended December 31, 2017.
i. Independent of (a) through (h), assume both bond issues were retired on December 1, 2016, at 101. Record the entries.

Problem 17-11B
Installment notes
LO8

Check figure:
2. Total interest expense = $74,744

On May 31, 2011, Venice Ltd. borrowed $220,000 from a bank by signing a four-year installment note bearing interest at 14%. The terms of the note require equal semi-annual payments each year beginning on November 30, 2011.

Required
1. Calculate the size of each installment payment.
2. Complete an installment note amortization schedule for this note similar to Exhibit 17.21.
3. Present the journal entries that Venice Ltd. would make to record the first payment on the note, the accrued interest as of December 31, 2011 (the end of the annual reporting period), and the second payment on the note.
4. Now assume that the note does not require equal payments but does require eight payments that include accrued interest and an equal amount of principal in each payment. Complete an installment note amortization schedule for this note similar to Exhibit 17.20. Present the journal entries that Venice Ltd. would make to record the first payment on the note and the accrued interest as of December 31, 2011 (the end of the annual reporting period).

*Problem 17-12B
Lease liabilities
LO9

Check figure:
2. Total interest expense = $196,831

Stoney Point Services Company leased a machine on January 1, 2011, under a contract calling for six annual payments of $130,000 on December 31, 2011 through 2016. The machine becomes the property of the lessee after the sixth payment. The machine was predicted to have a service life of seven years and no residual value, and the interest rate available to Stoney Point Services Company for equipment loans was 9% on the day the lease was signed. The machine was delivered on January 8, 2011, and was immediately placed in service. On January 2, 2014, it was overhauled at a total cost of $29,200. The overhaul did not increase the machine's efficiency but it did add an additional three years to the expected service life. On September 30, 2017, the machine was traded in on a similar new machine having a $330,000 cash price. A $65,000 trade-in allowance was received, and the balance was paid in cash.

Required
1. Determine the initial net liability created by the lease and the cost of the leased asset.
2. Prepare a table showing the calculation of the amount of interest expense allocated to each year the lease is in effect and the carrying amount of the liability at the end of each of those years.
3. Prepare the entry to record the leasing of the machine.
4. Prepare entries that would be made on December 31, 2012, to record the annual amortization on a straight-line basis, and the recording of the lease payment. Also show how the machine and the lease liability should appear on the December 31, 2012, balance sheet.
5. Prepare the entries to record the machine's overhaul in 2014 and amortization at the end of that year.
6. Prepare the entries to record the exchange of the machines on September 30, 2017.

Ethics Challenge

EC 17-1

A few years ago, the politicians needed a new headquarters building for their municipal government. The price tag for the building approached $24 million. The politicians felt that the voters were unlikely to approve a bond issue to raise money for the headquarters since approving the bond issue would cause taxes to increase. The politicians opted for a different approach. They had a bank issue $24 million worth of securities to pay for the construction of the building. The municipality then agreed to make a yearly lease payment (comprising repayment of principal and interest) to repay the obligation. Unlike conventional municipal bonds, the lease payments are not binding obligations on the municipal government and, therefore, no voter approval is required.

Required
1. Do you think the actions of the politicians and the investment bankers were ethical in this situation?
2. How does the security issued to pay for the building compare in riskiness to a regular municipal bond issued by a municipal government?

Focus on Financial Statements _____

ZedCon Inc. intends to raise $10,000,000 for the purpose of expanding operations internation-   **FFS 17-1**
ally. Two options are available:

- Plan 1: Issue $10,000,000 of 5% bonds payable due in 2021, or
- Plan 2: Issue 100,000 common shares at $100 per share.

The expansion is expected to generate additional annual income before interest and tax of
$800,000. ZedCon's tax rate is 35%. The assumed adjusted trial balance at December 31, 2012,
one year after the expansion under each of Plan 1 and Plan 2, is shown below:

Account	Balance* Plan 1	Balance* Plan 2
Accounts payable	$ 33,000	$ 33,000
Accounts receivable	48,000	48,000
Accumulated amortization, buildings	78,000	78,000
Accumulated amortization, equipment	202,000	202,000
Accumulated amortization, international assets	100,000	100,000
Additional income as a result of expansion	800,000	800,000
Allowance for doubtful accounts	5,200	5,200
Amortization expense	127,000	127,000
Bad debt expense	3,200	3,200
Bonds payable	10,000,000	-0-
Buildings...	150,000	150,000
Cash	312,000	812,000
Cash dividends..	92,000	92,000
Cash over/short...	100	100
Common shares (1,000 shares issued and outstanding)**	100,000	—
Common shares (101,000 shares issued and outstanding)**....	—	10,100,000
Cost of goods sold	48,000	48,000
Delivery expense..	700	700
Dividends payable..	31,000	31,000
Equipment	273,000	273,000
Fees earned...	1,050,000	1,050,000
Income tax expense	?	?
Income tax payable..	?	?
Interest expense..	506,100	6,100
Interest receivable	300	300
Interest revenue	800	800
International property, plant and equipment assets	10,000,000	10,000,000
Land	32,000	32,000
Merchandise inventory..	32,000	32,000
Mortgage payable ($14,000 due in 2013)..............................	60,000	60,000
Notes receivable, due October 2016	14,000	14,000
Patent	7,000	7,000
Petty cash	800	800
Retained earnings..	25,600	25,600
Salaries expense	916,000	916,000
Sales	59,000	59,000
Sales discounts..	1,400	1,400
Unearned fees...	19,000	19,000

*Assume normal account balances.
**Assume all shares were outstanding for the entire year.

Required

Preparation component:

1. Prepare a single-step income statement for 2012 (showing salaries expense, amortization expense, cost of goods sold, interest expense, and other expenses) and a classified balance sheet at December 31, 2012, assuming:
   a. Plan 1, and then
   b. Plan 2.

Analysis component:
Which financing plan should ZedCon Inc. choose assuming its goal is to:
a. maximize earnings per share, or
b. maximize net income.
Explain your answers showing any relevant calculations (rounded to the nearest whole cent).

FFS 17-2

Required
Answer the following questions by referring to the 2005 financial statements for each of Danier and WestJet in Appendix I in the back of the textbook.
1. How much of Danier's total assets are financed by debt? by equity?
2. How much long-term debt does WestJet report on its balance sheet?
3. How much of WestJet's total assets are financed by debt? by equity?
4. Which of the two companies has the *stronger* balance sheet?* Is it reasonable to compare these two balance sheets? Why or why not?

*When a balance sheet is said to have been **strengthened**, it means, in general, that total liabilities (or risk associated with debt financing) have decreased and shareholders' equity has increased.

Critical Thinking Mini Case

5-Star Adventures Inc. financed its $1,000,000 expansion by issuing on January 1, 2011, a 5%, 10-year, bond dated the same day with annual interest payments to be made each December 31. The market interest rate at the time of issue was 7%. You are one of the major shareholders and are a member of the board of directors. At the December 31, 2012, board meeting, a draft set of financial statements was presented for the board's review and you immediately ask: "The $1,000,000 bond payable is reported on the December 31, 2012, draft balance sheet as $869,695 and the income statement reports bond interest expense of $50,000? In Note 7 to the financial statements it indicates that total interest expense to be recognized over the 10-year term on this bond is $500,000."

Required
Using the elements of critical thinking described on the inside front cover, respond.

CHAPTER 18

Accounting for Debt and Share Investments

Investing: The Next Generation

Teck Cominco Limited has its head office in Vancouver, British Columbia, and is one of the largest steel producers in the world. With assets exceeding $8 billion, and cash representing 31% of that amount at September 30, 2005, Teck was looking to use excess cash in November 2005 to buy Inco, a Canadian nickel producer based in Toronto, which was looking to buy Falconbridge, another nickel producer that operates out of Calgary, Alberta. Inco's cash balance on December 31, 2004, represented 10% of its almost $11 billion in assets. Soaring commodity prices have generated large cash balances for mining companies. Dofasco Inc., a Canadian steel producer operating out of Hamilton, Ontario, was the victim of a hostile bid for its shares—in November 2005 by ThyssenKrupp AG, Germany's largest steel producer—for the amount of $4.8 billion, which was 40% higher than a hostile bid made by Arcelor earlier in the same month. The Canadian mining industry was likely to open 2006 as a very different group of players!

www.teckcominco.com

www.dofasco.com

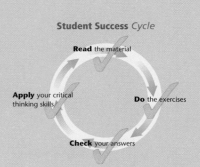

Student Success *Cycle*

Read the material

Apply your critical thinking skills

Do the exercises

Check your answers

CRITICAL THINKING CHALLENGE

Is the proposed purchase by Teck Cominco Limited of Inco a strategic or passive investment? If ThyssenKrupp were successful in acquiring Dofasco, how would the investor likely classify its investment of the investee in this case?

---

learning objectives

LO1 Describe and explain the purpose of debt and share investments.

LO2 Identify and describe the investment classifications.

LO3 Account for and report trading investments.

LO4 Account for and report held-to-maturity investments.

LO5 Describe the accounting for available-for-sale investments.

LO6 Account for significant influence investments.

LO7 Describe the accounting for controlled and joint venture investments.

*APPENDIX 18A

*LO8 Explain and record foreign exchange transactions.

chapter preview

This chapter focuses on the recording and reporting of investments in debt and shares. Many companies have investments in the form of debt and shares issued by other companies. Our understanding of the topics in this chapter is important to our ability to read and interpret financial statements. This knowledge is the type used by Teck Cominco as described in the opening article for investment decisions in shares and bonds.

Purpose of Debt and Share Investments

LO1 | Describe and explain the purpose of debt and share investments.

Corporations frequently purchase debt and shares of other corporations. These are called **intercorporate investments**. A **debt investment** (or **debt security**) such as a bond represents an amount owed and arises when one company lends money to another. A **share investment** (or **equity security**) represents one company's purchase of the shares in another company. The company that purchases as an investment the debt or shares of another is called the **investor**, and the company whose debt (i.e., bonds) or shares (common or preferred) are being purchased is called the **investee**. For instance, if you own shares in WestJet, then you are the investor and WestJet is the investee.

Investments are made in other corporations for various reasons. Examples include:

Passive Investments

- To earn greater interest or dividend income on available excess cash than can be earned by leaving the cash in a typical bank account.
- To earn a gain over the original purchase price on the eventual sale of purchased shares.
- To earn interest on long-term debt.

Strategic Investments

- To participate in new markets or new technologies.
- To build a favourable business relationship, generally with a major customer or supplier.
- To achieve non-controlling interest with the investee by acquiring enough shares to be influential to the investee's operating, financing, and investing decisions.
- To acquire a controlling interest in the investee.

An investor has made a **passive investment** when they cannot significantly influence or control the operations of the investee company. A **strategic investment** has occurred when the investee is controlled by, significantly influenced by, or in a joint venture with the investor. In order to account for investments, we must understand how equity and debt investments are classified. This is the topic of the next section.

Classification of Investments

LO2 | Identify and describe the investment classifications.

Passive investments are of three types: *trading*, *held-to-maturity*, and *available-for-sale*. **Trading investments** are the shares or debt of another corporation purchased by the investor for the short term. This group of securities is subject to **active trading**, which means there is frequent buying and selling. Profits may be realized from trading investments primarily because of short-term changes in price[1] and secondarily through receipt of dividend or interest revenue. **Held-to-maturity investments** are debt securities, such as bonds, where interest and principal payments are specified along with the maturity date. The investor's intent is to hold these investments until maturity. An investment in shares cannot be a held-to-maturity investment. **Available-for-sale investments**, according to the *CICA Handbook*, are investments in the shares or debt of another corporation but are not trading investments or held-to-maturity investments.

Strategic investments include the following three categories: *significant influence*, *control*, and *joint venture*. *Significant influence investments* occur when the investor can affect the strategic operating, investing, and/or financing policies of the investee. The general rule for determining significant influence is that it exists if 20% to 50% of the investee's shares are held by the investor.[2] This is a general rule because an owner with 40% ownership could have no influence if all of the other shares were held by one owner. A *control investment* exists when the investor owns sufficient shares to determine the investee's strategic operating, investing, and financing policies without the cooperation of others.[3] Again, the *general* rule is that control exists when more than 50% of the shares are owned by a single investor. A **joint venture** investment is where two or more venturers jointly control the resulting economic activity. For example, the Syncrude Project is a joint venture producing crude oil within the Athabasca Oil Sands Region. Its venturers include those shown in Exhibit 18.1 with corresponding co-ownership interests. During 2004, Syncrude generated revenues of $4.57 billion.

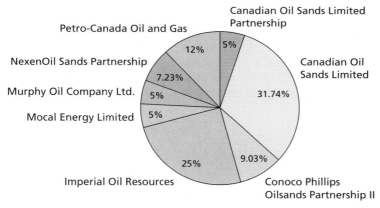

Exhibit 18.1

Joint Venturers in Syncrude Project

Source: www.syncrude.ca (accessed November 26, 2005)

The accounting for each of these investments is described in the next sections.

---

1. What is the main difference between passive and strategic investments?
2. How are trading investments different from held-to-maturity investments?
3. Explain why the *20% to 50% rule* to determine significant influence does not always hold true.

Do: QS 18-1, QS 18-2

CHECKPOINT   Read   Apply   Do   Check

---

[1] *CICA Handbook*, section 3855, par.20
[2] *CICA Handbook*, section 3051, par.05
[3] *CICA Handbook*, section 1590.

Accounting for Trading Investments

LO3 | Account for and report trading investments.

This section explains the basics of accounting for trading investments in both equity and debt securities. Recall that the main distinguishing feature of this group of investments is that the investor's intent is to generate profit *primarily* through short-term changes in fair values; the receipt of dividend and/or interest revenue is secondary. The investor records trading investments using the *fair value method*. The **fair value method** when applied to trading investments records the purchase at cost excluding any brokerage fees and commissions. Brokerage fees and commissions, also known as transaction costs, should be expensed when incurred for trading investments.[4] Both realized and unrealized gains and losses are recognized in income.

Purchase of Equity Investments

Equity investments classified as trading investments are recorded using the fair value method as described above. For example, on June 2, 2011, TechCom purchased 300 Cameco Corporation common shares at $50 per share plus a $50 commission. TechCom intends to hold these shares for six to twelve months for the purpose of realizing a gain in share price fluctuation. The entry to record this purchase is:

2011			
June 2	Trading Investment—Cameco[5]	15,000	
	Brokerage Fees Expense..................................	50	
	Cash		15,050
	Purchased shares to be held as trading investment; $50 × 300 shares = $15,000.		

Note that the commission is recorded in a separate account for trading investments.[6] Assume that on December 12, TechCom received a $0.40 cash dividend per share on its Cameco share investment. This dividend is credited to a revenue account as follows:

Dec. 31	Cash...	120	
	Dividend Revenue		120
	$0.40 × 300 shares.		

Purchase of Debt Investments

Debt investments classified as trading investments are recorded using the fair value method as described previously. TechCom Company, for instance, paid $29,500 plus a brokerage fee of $75 to buy Power Corp. 7% bonds payable with a $30,000 par value on September 1, 2011. The bonds pay interest semi-annually on August 31 and February 28, and will mature on February 28, 2015. TechCom intends to trade these bonds within the next six to nine months, therefore they are trading investments as opposed to held-to-maturity investments. The entry to record this purchase is:

2011			
Sept. 1	Trading Investment—Power Corp..................	29,500	
	Brokerage Fees Expense..................................	75	
	Cash		29,575
	Purchased bonds to be held as trading investment.		

---

[4] *CICA Handbook*, section 3855, par.56 effective October 2006.
[5] In reality, there would be a General Ledger control account for Trading Investments supported by a subledger.
[6] *CICA Handbook*, section 3855, par.56 effective October 2006.

Again, notice that the commission is recorded in a separate account because this is a trading investment.[7] On December 31, 2011, at the end of its accounting period, TechCom accrues interest receivable on the Power Corp. bond in the following entry:

Dec. 31	Interest Receivable..	700	
	Interest Revenue		700
	$30,000 × 7% × 4/12.		

Balance Sheet Presentation of Trading Investments

An additional adjustment is required at the end of the accounting period regarding trading investments. After recording the purchase, an entity should measure investments that are classified as held for trading at their fair values.[8] Any gain or loss on a trading investment should be recognized in net income for the period in which it arises.[9] To demonstrate, assume that TechCom's investment in the Cameco shares and the Power Corp. bond had fair values, also known as market values, on December 31, 2011, of $53 and 97, respectively. The unadjusted balances and market values at December 31, 2011, of TechCom's trading investments can be summarized as follows:

	Unadjusted Balance	Fair Value	Difference
Cameco shares	$15,000	$15,900*	$ 900
Power Corp. bond	29,500	29,100**	(400)
Net unrealized gain (loss)	$44,500	$45,000	$ 500

*$53 × 300 shares = $15,900
**$30,000 face value × 97% = $29,100

The entry to record the valuation adjustment is:

Dec. 31	Trading Investment—Cameco	900	
	Trading Investment—Power Corp.		400
	Unrealized Holding Gain		500
	To record the net unrealized holding gain resulting from adjustment of trading investments to fair value.		

Because the Cameco shares increased in value, the increase is added or debited to the *Trading Investment—Cameco* account. The Power Corp. bond decreased in value, so the decrease is subtracted from or credited to the *Trading Investment—Power Corp.* account. The result is that the trading investment accounts will reflect December 31, 2011, fair values on the balance sheet. The net difference of the valuation adjustments is a gain of $500 that is recorded on the income statement as an **unrealized gain**. It is unrealized because no transaction has occurred. When the investments are sold, a **realized gain** or loss will be recorded on the income statement.

On the December 31, 2011, balance sheet, TechCom would report the combined adjusted balances of the trading investment accounts as shown below.

Current assets:	
Trading investments, at market value..	$45,000

[7] Ibid.
[8] *CICA Handbook*, section 3855, par.66.
[9] *CICA Handbook*, section 3855, par.76(a).

Investors can obtain the market prices of share and debt investments from a number of sources. Exhibit 18.2 shows an example of share transactions that was obtained online from a newspaper.

Exhibit 18.2

Market Prices of Share Transactions

(Trades of 100,000 or more shares worth at least $1 million)					
Stock	**Symbol**	**Buyer**	**Seller**	**Volume (000s)**	**Price**
CIBC	CM	TD Securit	TD Securit	100	42.20
Cott Corp	BCB	NesBurns	NesBurns	111	26.20
Iamgold	IMG	NesBurns	NesBurns	396	7.34
Norske Skog	NS	NesBurns	NesBurns	316	4.89
Nortel Netwk	NT	CSFB	CSFB	500	3.67
Royal Bank	RY	CIBC World	CIBC World	121	56.55
Suncor Enr	SU	CIBC World	CIBC World	126	25.82
TD Bank	TD	CIBC World	CIBC World	118	34.11
Wstrn Oil	WTO	NesBurns	NesBurns	123	23.75

SOURCE: www.globeandmail.com

Real-time prices in a variety of formats are available from other online sources such as the graphs in Exhibit 18.3.

Exhibit 18.3

Online Share Price Information

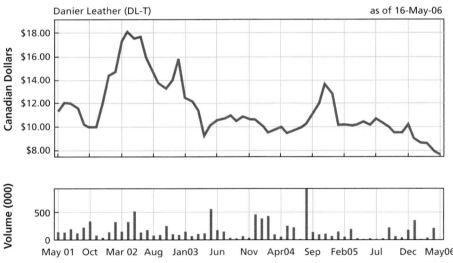

SOURCE: www.tsx.com, accessed May 16, 2006.

Sale of Trading Investments

To demonstrate the entries for the sale of trading investments, assume that on January 14, 2012, TechCom sold 200 of its Cameco shares at $52 per share and paid a commission of $90. The entry to record this is:

	2012			
Jan.	14	Cash..	10,310	
		Brokerage Fees Expense.....................................	90	
		Loss on sale of trading investments	200	
		Trading Investment—Cameco		10,600
		$52 × 200 shares = $10,400 − $90 =		
		$10,310; $15,900 × 200/300 = $10,600.		

Recall that the balance in *Trading Investment—Cameco* was adjusted to $15,900 on December 31, 2011 (originally recorded at $15,000 plus valuation adjustment of $900 = $15,900). Since TechCom sold 200 of the total 300 shares, the related amounts must be removed from the accounting records. To do this, we credit *Trading Investment—Cameco* for the proportion of the $15,900 balance sold.[10]

4. Explain how transaction costs such as brokerage fees and commissions are accounted for regarding trading investments.

5. How are unrealized gains and losses upon valuation of trading investments at year-end accounted for? Why are these gains and losses referred to as *unrealized*?

Do: QS 18-3, QS 18-4, QS 18-5, QS 18-6, QS 18-7

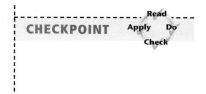

Accounting for Held-to-Maturity Investments

Recall that purchases of debt securities intended to be held until maturity are classified as held-to-maturity investments; the basic accounting for these is discussed in this section.

LO4 Account for and report held-to-maturity investments.

Purchases of Held-to-Maturity Investments

Purchases of held-to-maturity investments are recorded using the *cost method*. The cost method records investments at cost and interest revenue is recorded as time passes, including any premium or discount amortization. The *CICA Handbook* states that transaction costs are recognized either in net income (as was illustrated for trading investments in a previous section) or added to the cost of the investment being purchased.[11] For consistency, transaction costs will be added to the cost of all held-to-maturity investments referred to in this chapter.

To demonstrate the accounting for held-to-maturity investments, assume that on January 1, 2011, Music City paid $28,477 to buy an 8%, three-year, Intella Inc. $30,000 par value bond when the market interest rate was 10%. Interest is paid semi-annually each June 30 and December 31. The entry to record the purchase is:

2011			
Jan. 1	Held-to-Maturity Investment—Intella Inc........	28,477	
	Cash		28,477
	Purchased a bond at a discount to be held as a held-to-maturity investment.		

After initial recognition, an entity should measure held-to-maturity investments at amortized cost using the effective interest method.[12] Therefore, on June 30, 2011, the first interest receipt date, Music City would record:

June 30	Cash..	1,200	
	Held-to-Maturity Investment—Intella Inc........	224	
	Interest Revenue		1,424
	Recorded receipt of interest and amortization of bond discount using the effective interest method; 30,000 × 8% × 6/12 = 1,200; 28,477 × 10% × 6/12 = 1,424.		

[10] An alternative calculation would be to take the $15,900 total balance and divide by 300 total shares to get an average per share of $53.00 × 200 shares sold = $10,600.
[11] *CICA Handbook*, section 3855, par.57.
[12] *CICA Handbook*, section 3855, par.66(a).

The calculation of the $224 discount amortization is based on the amortization schedule using the effective interest method shown in Exhibit 18.4.[13]

Exhibit 18.4

Amortization Schedule Using Effective Interest Method—Intella Inc. Bond[14]

Period Ending	Cash Interest Received	Period Interest Revenue	Discount Amort.	Unamortized Discount	Carrying Value
Jan. 1/11				$1,523	$28,477
June 30/11	$1,200	$1,424	$ 224	1,299	28,701
Dec. 31/11	1,200	1,435	235	1,064	28,936
June 30/12	1,200	1,447	247	817	29,183
Dec. 31/12	1,200	1,459	259	558	29,442
June 30/13	1,200	1,472	272	286	29,714
Dec. 31/13	1,200	1,486	286	0	30,000
Totals	$7,200	$8,723	$1,523		

Notice that because the bond was purchased at a discount, the discount amortization on each interest receipt date is added or debited to the investment account. This will cause the balance in the investment account to approach face value until maturity.

At maturity, the entries recorded by Music City would be:

2013			
Dec. 31	Cash..	1,200	
	Held-to-Maturity Investment—Intella Inc.........	286	
	Interest Revenue		1,486
	Recorded receipt of interest and amortization of bond discount using the effective interest method; 30,000 × 8% × 6/12 = 1,200; 29,714 × 10% × 6/12 = 1,486.		

AND

Dec. 31	Cash..	30,000	
	Held-to-Maturity Investment—Intella Inc.		30,000
	Record collection of cash resulting from maturity of investment in bond.		

Balance Sheet Presentation of Held-to-Maturity Investments

Held-to-maturity investments are not subject to valuation adjustments except for special situations that are beyond the scope of this textbook.[15] They are normally reported on the balance sheet at their amortized cost. For instance, Music City would have reported its investment in the Intella Inc. bond on its December 31, 2011, balance sheet as:

Long-term investments:	
Held-to-maturity investments, at amortized cost...	$28,936

---

[13] To review the concepts and calculations involved regarding bond premiums and discounts, refer to Chapter 17 of the textbook.

[14] *CICA Handbook*, section 3855, par.66(a).

[15] *CICA Handbook*, section 3855, par.77.

Sale of Held-to-Maturity Investments

Recall that the distinguishing feature of held-to-maturity investments is that *they are held to maturity*. Therefore, they would not normally be sold prior to maturity so gains and losses are a non-issue for these investments. If held-to-maturity investments are sold prior to maturity, special rules come into effect that are intermediate accounting issues and as such are beyond the scope of this textbook.

---

6. Explain how transaction costs such as brokerage fees and commissions are accounted for regarding held-to-maturity investments.

7. How are held-to-maturity investments reported on the balance sheet? Explain.

Do: QS 18-8, QS 18-9, QS 18-10

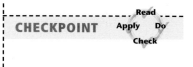

CHECKPOINT   Read   Apply   Do   Check

Accounting for Available-for-Sale Investments

As discussed earlier, available-for-sale investments consist of debt and equity investments that are not trading investments or held-to-maturity investments.[16] These investments are accounted for using the *fair value method*. The fair value method is applied to available-for-sale investments in a different manner than what was done for trading investments. The purchase of available-for-sale investments is recorded at cost as was done for trading investments. Transaction costs are dealt with differently. The *CICA Handbook* states that transaction costs are either recognized in net income (as was illustrated for trading investments in a previous section) or added to the cost of the asset being purchased.[17] The second difference is that any unrealized gains or losses resulting from valuation at year-end are recognized as *other comprehensive income* and subsequently closed to a shareholders' equity account called *Accumulated Other Comprehensive Income*. Recall that any unrealized gains or losses for trading investments were recognized directly in net income. The accounting and reporting of available-for-sale concepts is beyond the scope of this textbook, however, for those who are interested, this information is available online in Extend Your Knowledge 18-1 along with reinforcement exercises.

LO5 Describe the accounting for available-for-sale investments.

Extend Your Knowledge

18-1

---

8. Where are unrealized holding gains (losses) on available-for-sale investments reported on the financial statements?

CHECKPOINT   Read   Apply   Do   Check

---

[16] *CICA Handbook,* Section 3855, par.19(i)
[17] *CICA Handbook,* Section 3855, par.57

mid-chapter demonstration problem

The following transactions relate to Brown Company's investment activities during
2011 and 2012. Brown did not own any debt or share investments prior to 2011.

	2011		
Jan.	1	Purchased a 5%, three-year, $60,000 Bioware bond paying $61,680; the market interest rate is 4%. Interest is paid semi-annually each June 30 and December 31. The bond will be held to maturity.
June	30	Received semi-annual interest on Bioware bond.
Oct.	2	Purchased as a trading investment 2,000 shares of MT&T common shares for $60,000 cash plus a brokerage fee of $75.
	17	Purchased as a trading investment 1,000 shares of Four Seasons Hotels common shares for $40,000 cash plus brokerage fees of $30.
Nov.	30	Received $3,000 cash dividend from MT&T.
Dec.	15	Received $1,400 cash dividend from Four Seasons.
	17	Sold the MT&T shares at $33 per share; brokerage fees were $50.
	31	Received semi-annual interest on Bioware bond.
	31	Market values for the investments are: Four Seasons Hotels, $45,000; and Bioware, $61,200.
	2012		
Mar.	1	Purchased as a trading investment 7,000 shares of Zoey Inc. common shares at $11 per share plus a brokerage fee of $80.
June	30	Received semi-annual interest on Bioware bond.
Aug.	17	Sold the Four Seasons shares for $52,000 cash less a $50 brokerage fee.
Dec.	31	Received semi-annual interest on Bioware bond.
	31	Market values for the investments are: Zoey Inc., $69,000; and Bioware, $61,340.

Required

Show the appropriate journal entries that describe these transactions.

Analysis component:

On December 31, 2011, the fair value of the Bioware bonds is different from the
amortized cost on the same date, yet this investment would be reported on the
balance sheet at amortized cost. Explain why.

Planning the Solution

- Prepare an amortization schedule using the effective interest method for the
  Bioware bond.

- Account for the investments in MT&T, Four Seasons Hotels, Zoey, and Loblaw
  as trading investments using the fair value method with revaluation gains
  (losses) recognized in income.

- Account for the investment in the Bioware bond using the cost method; held-
  to-maturity investments are not subject to valuation gains (losses) because they
  are normally reported at their amortized cost.

- Answer the analysis component question.

solution to *Mid-Chapter Demonstration Problem*

Amortization schedule for Bioware bond:

Period Ending	Cash Interest Received	Period Interest Revenue	Premium Amort.	Unamortized Premium	Carrying Value
Jan. 1/11				$1,680	$61,680
June 30/11	$1,500	$1,234	$ 266	1,414	61,414
Dec. 31/11	1,500	1,228	272	1,142	61,142
June 30/12	1,500	1,223	277	865	60,865
Dec. 31/12	1,500	1,217	283	582	60,582
June 30/13	1,500	1,212	288	294	60,294
Dec. 31/13	1,500	1,206	294	0	60,000
Totals	$9,000	$7,320	$1,680		

Journal entries:

2011				
Jan. 1	Trading Investment—Bioware Bond	61,680		
	Cash		61,680	
	Purchased bonds as a held-to-maturity investment.			
June 30	Cash..	1,500		
	Held-to-Maturity Investment— Bioware Bond...		266	
	Interest Revenue		1,234	
	60,000 × 5% × 6/12 = 1,500; 61,680 × 4% × 6/12 = 1,234.			
Oct. 2	Trading Investment—MT&T Shares	60,000		
	Brokerage Fees Expense..................................	75		
	Cash		60,075	
	Purchased shares as a trading investment.			
17	Trading Investment—Four Seasons Shares	40,000		
	Brokerage Fees Expense..................................	30		
	Cash		40,030	
	Purchased shares as a trading investment.			
Nov. 30	Cash..	3,000		
	Dividend Revenue		3,000	
	Received dividends on MT&T shares.			
Dec. 15	Cash..	1,400		
	Dividend Revenue		1,400	
	Received dividends on Four Seasons shares.			
17	Cash..	65,950		
	Brokerage Fees Expense..................................	50		
	Trading Investment—MT&T Shares.......		60,000	
	Gain on Sale of Trading Investment.......		6,000	
	33 × 2,000 = 66,000 − 50 = 65,950.			

	31	Cash..	1,500	
		Held-to-Maturity Investment—		
		Bioware Bond...		272
		Interest Revenue		1,228
		60,000 × 5% × 6/12 = 1,500; 61,414 × *4% × 6/12 = 1,228.*		
	31	Trading Investment—Four Seasons Shares	5,000	
		Unrealized Holding Gain		5,000
		45,000 − 40,000 = 5,000.		
2012				
Mar.	1	Trading Investment—Zoey Shares	77,000	
		Brokerage Fees Expense...................................	80	
		Cash		77,080
		11 × 7,000 = 77,000.		
June	30	Cash..	1,500	
		Held-to-Maturity Investment—		
		Bioware Bond...		277
		Interest Revenue		1,223
		60,000 × 5% × 6/12 = 1,500; 61,142 × *4% × 6/12 = 1,223.*		
Aug.	17	Cash..	51,950	
		Brokerage Fee Expense	50	
		Trading Investment—Four Seasons Shares..		45,000
		Gain on Sale of Investment		7,000
		To record sale of trading investment.		
Dec.	31	Cash..	1,500	
		Held-to-Maturity Investment—		
		Bioware Bond...		283
		Interest Revenue		1,217
		60,000 × 5% × 6/12 = 1,500; 60,685 × *4% × 6/12 = 1,217.*		
	31	Unrealized Holding Loss	8,000	
		Trading Investment—Zoey Shares		8,000
		77,000 − 69,000 = 8,000.		

Analysis component:

The Bioware bonds will be reported on the December 31, 2011, balance sheet at the amortized cost of $61,142 instead of the fair value on the same date of $61,200 because they are a held-to-maturity investment; Bioware will actually collect the face value of the bond upon maturity, so the fair value until that time is irrelevant.

Accounting for Significant Influence Investments

Investors that hold 20% to 50% of an investee's shares are said to have **significant influence**. The **equity method** of accounting and reporting is used for long-term share investments with significant influence.[18] Under the equity method, shares are recorded at cost when they are purchased. To illustrate, Micron Company purchased 3,000 shares (30%) of JVT common shares for a total cost of $70,650 on January 1, 2011. The entry to record this purchase on Micron's books is:

LO6 Account for significant influence investments.

	2011			
Jan.	1	Investment in JVT Common Shares................	70,650	
		Cash		70,650
		Purchased 3,000 shares.		

Under the equity method, the investor records its share of the investee's earnings and dividends. This means that when JVT closes its books and reports net income of $20,000 for 2011, Micron records its 30% share of those earnings in its investment account as:

Dec.	31	Investment in JVT Common Shares................	6,000	
		Earnings from Investment in JVT...........		6,000
		To record 30% equity in investee's		
		earnings of $20,000.		

The debit reflects the increase in Micron's equity in JVT caused by JVT's $20,000 increase in equity through net income. Micron must debit the investment account for its proportionate share in that equity (JVT's net income). The credit shows the source of the increase in the investment account.

If the investee incurs a net loss instead of a net income, the investor records its share of the loss and reduces (credits) its investment account.

The receipt of cash dividends is not recorded as revenue when using the equity method because the investor has already recorded its share of the earnings reported by the investee. When the investee pays dividends its retained earnings are reduced by the amount of the dividend. The investee's equity is reduced and therefore the investment of the investor must also be reduced. Dividends received from an investee change the form of the investor's asset from a shares investment to cash. This means dividends reduce the balance of the investment account, but increase cash. To illustrate, JVT declared and paid $10,000 in cash dividends on its common shares. Micron's entry to record its 30% share of these dividends received on January 9, 2012, is:

	2012			
Jan.	9	Cash..	3,000	
		Investment in JVT Common Shares		3,000
		To record receipt of 30% of $10,000		
		dividend paid by JVT.		

The book value of an investment in equity securities when using the equity method is equal to the cost of the investment plus the investor's equity in the undistributed earnings of the investee. Once we record the above transactions for Micron, its investment account appears as in Exhibit 18.5.

---

[18] Note that in situations where there is a large number of small share holdings, significant influence is possible for an investor that owns less than 20% of the investee. Also, an investor may not be able to exert significant influence with a shareholding of greater than 20% if another shareholder owns a 51% block of shares in the investee.

Exhibit 18.5

Investment in JVT Common Shares Ledger Account

Date	Explanation	Debit	Credit	Balance
2011				
Jan. 1	Investment	70,650		70,650
Dec. 31	Share of earnings.....................................	6,000		76,650
2012				
Jan. 9	Share of dividends...................................		3,000	73,650

If a balance sheet were prepared on this date, Micron would report its investment in JVT on the balance sheet after total current assets but before capital assets. Any investment revenue would be reported on the income statement as shown in the bottom section of Exhibit 18.6.

Exhibit 18.6

Statement Presentation of Long-Term Investment and Investment Revenue

Partial Balance Sheet	
Assets	
Total current assets......................................	$ ×××,×××
Long-term investments.............................	73,650
Capital assets...	×××,×××
Total assets..	$×,×××,×××

Partial Income Statement	
Income from operations................................	$ ×××,×××
Other revenues and expenses:	
Earnings from equity investment	6,000

Recording the Sale of An Equity Investment

When an investment in equity securities is sold, the gain or loss is calculated by comparing proceeds from the sale with the book value of the investment on the date of sale. Care should be taken to ensure that the investment account is brought up to date in terms of earnings and dividends before recording the sale. If Micron sells its JVT shares for $80,000 on January 10, 2012, the entry to record the sale is:

Jan. 10	Cash...	80,000	
	Investment in JVT Common Shares		73,650
	Gain on Sale of Investments		6,350
	Sold 3,000 shares for $80,000.		

Comparison of Entries for Fair Value and Equity Methods

Exhibit 18.7 uses a side-by-side comparison to emphasize the differences between the fair value and equity methods of accounting for share investments. It is assumed that:

1. Maclean Company purchases a 20% interest in the shares of Lee Corp. for $30,000. If Maclean does not have significant influence over Lee Corp., the investment should be accounted for using the fair value method. If Maclean can significantly influence Lee Corp., then the investment should be accounted for using the equity method.

2. Lee earns a $40,000 net income during the first year of operations, and

3. Lee pays a dividend of $8,000.

Exhibit 18.7

Illustration of Fair Value and Equity Methods

	Fair Value Method		**Equity Method**	
1.	Investment in Lee Corp. Shares	30,000	Investment in Lee Corp. Shares	30,000
	Cash	30,000	Cash	30,000

To record purchase of 20% interest for $30,000.

2.	No entry		Investment in Lee Corp. Shares	8,000
			Earnings from Investment in Lee Corp......	8,000

To record 20% share of investee's $40,000 net income.

3.	Cash	1,600	Cash..	1,600
	Dividend Revenue..................	1,600	Investment in Lee Corp. shares.................	1,600

To record 20% share of $8,000 dividends received from Lee Corp.

---

9. What method is used to account for significant influence investments and how is it different from the fair value method?

10. ABC Inc. owns 50,000 of the 140,000 shares issued and outstanding of Alliance Corp. Does this represent significant influence? Explain why or why not.

Do: QS 18-11, QS 18-12

CHECKPOINT Read Apply Do Check

Accounting for Controlled and Joint Venture Investments

An investor with a long-term share investment that represents more than 50% of the investee's voting shares has *control* over the investee. **Control** is more than influence. The controlling investor can dominate all other shareholders in electing the corporation's board of directors and has control over the investee corporation's management. The controlling corporation (investor) is known as the **parent company** and the company whose shares are held by the parent is referred to as a **subsidiary** (investee).

A company owning all the outstanding shares of a subsidiary can take over the subsidiary's assets, cancel the subsidiary's shares, and merge the subsidiary into the parent company, creating potential financial, legal, and tax advantages.

When a business operates as a parent company with subsidiaries, separate accounting records are maintained by each entity. From a legal viewpoint, the parent and each subsidiary are still separate entities with all the rights, duties, and responsibilities of individual companies. However, investors in the parent company are indirect investors in the subsidiaries. To evaluate their investments, parent company investors must consider the financial status and operations of the subsidiaries as well as the parent. This information is provided in *consolidated financial statements*.

Consolidated financial statements show the financial position, results of operations, and cash flows of all companies under the parent's control, including all subsidiaries. These statements are prepared as if the company were organized as one entity. The parent uses the equity method in its accounts, but the investment account is *not* reported on the parent's consolidated financial statements. Instead, the individual assets and liabilities of the parent and its subsidiaries are combined on one balance sheet. Their revenues and expenses also are combined on one income statement and their cash flows are combined on one cash flow statement. The detailed procedures for preparing consolidated financial statements are included in advanced courses. Some of the basic procedures are provided in Extend Your Knowledge 18-2 on the online Student Success Centre.

LO7 Describe the accounting for controlled and joint venture investments.

Extend Your Knowledge

18-2

Recall that a joint venture investment is one where two or more venturers jointly control the resulting economic activity. Each venturer, or investor, would use *proportionate consolidation* to account for its investment in the joint venture. **Proportionate consolidation** combines the financial statements of an investor company and a joint venture enterprise based on the investor's proportionate share of the financial statements of the joint venture. The accounting for joint ventures is an advanced accounting issue and is beyond the scope of this textbook.

CHECKPOINT

11. ABC Inc. purchased 80,000 of the 80,000 common shares issued and outstanding of Ellai Inc. This would be classified as what type of investment by ABC Inc.?

   a. Significant influence

   b. Consolidation

   c. Held-to-maturity

   d. Control

   e. None of the above

Accounting Summary for Investments in Securities

Exhibit 18.8 summarizes the accounting for investments in securities. Recall that many investments can be classified as either short-term or long-term depending on management's intent and ability to convert them into cash in the future.

Exhibit 18.8

Summary of Accounting for Debt and Share Investments

	Investment Type	Accounting Method	Accounting Method Described
Passive Investments	Trading	Fair Value	Initially recorded at cost; transaction costs recognized as expense; adjusted to fair value each reporting date; realized and unrealized gains/losses recognized in income
	Held-to-Maturity	Cost	Recorded at cost; transaction costs recognized as expense OR capitalized; interest revenue is recorded as time passes including amortization of premium or discount using effective interest method
	Available-for-Sale	Fair Value	Initially recorded at cost; transaction costs recognized as expense OR capitalized; adjusted to fair value each reporting date; realized gains/losses recognized in income; unrealized gains/losses recognized in OCI
Strategic Investments	Significant Influence	Equity	Initially recorded at cost; investor's share of investee's earnings added to investment account (subtracted when loss); investor's receipt of dividends from investee reduces the investment account
	Control	Consolidation	Financial statements of subsidiary combined with parent
	Joint Venture	Proportionate Consolidation	Investor's proportionate share of joint venture financial statements combined with those of the investor

Summary

LO1 **Describe and explain the purpose of debt and share investments.** Debt investments (or debt securities) reflect a creditor relationship and include investments in notes, bonds, and certificates of deposit. Debt investments are issued by governments, companies, and individuals. Share investments (or equity securities) reflect an ownership relationship and include shares issued by corporations. Investments can be passive or strategic in nature.

LO2 **Identify and describe the investment classifications.** Passive investments include trading investments, held-to-maturity investments, and available-for-sale investments. Trading investments are shares or debt purchased primarily to realize gains from short-term changes in price. Held-to-maturity debt investments are held to maturity for the purpose of earning interest. Available-for-sale equity or debt investments are those that are not classified as trading or held-to-maturity. Strategic investments include significant influence, control, and joint ventures. Significant influence generally exists when the investor owns 20% to 50% of the investee's shares. Control exists when more than 50% of the investee's shares are owned by the investor, in general. Joint ventures are contractual investments as opposed to an investment in shares or debt securities.

LO3 **Account for and report trading investments.** Trading investments are initially recorded at cost. Transaction costs are recognized as an expense when incurred. Trading investments are adjusted to fair value each reporting date and any unrealized gains/losses are recognized in income. Realized gains/losses at the time of sale are recorded in income as well.

LO4 **Account for and report held-to-maturity investments.** Held-to-maturity investments are recorded at cost with transaction costs recognized as an expense when incurred or capitalized. Interest revenue is recorded as time

passes and included the amortization of premium or discount using the effective interest method.

LO5 **Describe the accounting for available-for-sale investments.** Available-for-sale investments are initially recorded at cost with transaction costs recognized as an expense when incurred or capitalized. These investments are adjusted to fair value each reporting date with any unrealized gains/losses recognized in other comprehensive income. Realized gains/losses at the time of sale are recognized in income.

LO6 **Account for significant influence investments.** The equity method is used when an investor has a significant influence over an investee. This usually exists when an investor owns 20% or more of the investee's voting shares, but not exceeding 50%. Under the equity method, the investor records its share of the investee's earnings with a debit to the investment account and a credit to a revenue account. Dividends received reduce the investment account balance and the investor debits its share of annual earnings (credits its share of losses) to the investment account.

LO7 **Describe the accounting for controlled and joint venture investments.** If an investor owns more than 50% of another company's voting shares and controls the investee, the investor's financial reports are prepared on a consolidated basis. These reports are prepared as if the company were organized as one entity. The individual financial statements of the parent and its subsidiaries are combined into one balance sheet, one income statement, and one cash flow statement. A joint venture investment results from a contractual arrangement where two or more venturers jointly control an economic activity. Each venturer, or investor, will use proportionate consolidation to combine the financial statements of the investee on a proportionate basis into the investor's statements.

---

guidance answers to **CHECKPOINT**

1. Investors in passive investments cannot significantly influence or control the operations of the investee company, while investors in strategic investments can.

2. Trading investments are held for the short term only and can be investments in debt or shares, while held-to-maturity investments can be debt investments only and are held until maturity.

3. The *20% to 50% rule* to determine significant influence does not always hold true because an investor

could hold 10% of the shares and be able to exert significant influence if all other investors have very small percentage holdings and, conversely, a 30% holding may not have significant influence if another investor has 60%.

4. Transaction costs such as brokerage fees and commissions are debited to an expense account regarding the purchase and sale of trading investments.

5. At year-end, unrealized gains (losses) upon valuation of trading investments are credited (debited) to an Unrealized Gain (Loss) account that appears on the income statement and debited (credited) to the trading investment account, which adjusts it to its fair value on the balance sheet.

6. Brokerage fees and commissions regarding held-to-maturity investment transactions can be debited to an expense account or added to the cost of the investment. For consistency, the textbook adds all such costs to held-to-maturity investments.

7. Held-to-maturity investments are reported on the balance sheet at their amortized cost.

8. Unrealized gains or losses resulting from valuation at year-end on available-for-sale investments are recognized as *other comprehensive income* and subsequently closed to a shareholder equity account called *Accumulated Other Comprehensive Income*.

9. The equity method is used to account for significant influence investments. As is the case for the fair value method, shares are recorded at cost when they are purchased under the equity method but the investor records its share of the investee's earnings and dividends.

10. ABC's ownership in Alliance Corp. represents a 35.7% interest, which qualifies as significant influence.

11. *d*

demonstration problem

Conestoga Inc. had excess cash and made the decision to begin investing in debt and shares. The following investment transactions occurred during 2011. Prepare the journal entries.

	2011		
Jan.	1	Purchased 5,000 Lindel Inc. common shares for $320,000 cash. These shares represent 35% of Lindel's outstanding shares.
Oct.	2	Purchased 12,000 LG common shares paying cash of $3.50 per share plus a $300 brokerage fee. Conestoga Inc. plans to hold the shares for less than a year.
	15	Purchased 50,000 Wall Corp. shares for $25,000 cash, which included a $75 brokerage fee. Conestoga will sell the shares after Wall Corp. declares and pays dividends in January 2012.
Nov.	30	Received a cash dividend of $3.50 per share from Lindel Inc.
Dec.	15	Received $0.40 cash dividend per share from LG.
	31	Lindel Inc. reported a net income of $820,000 for the year ended December 31, 2011.
	31	Market values per share for the investments are: Lindel Inc., $65; LG, $3.45; and Wall Corp. $0.50.
	2012	
Jan.	5	Wall Corp. declared dividends of $0.10 per share to the January 18 shareholders of record payable on January 25.
	25	Conestoga Inc. received the Wall Corp. dividend.
Feb.	10	Sold the Wall Corp. shares for $24,750 cash after subtracting a $50 brokerage fee.
Mar.	1	Sold 8,000 of the LG common shares at $3.75 per share less a brokerage fee of $200.
May	2	Purchased 16,000 of the 40,000 issued and outstanding Delta Corp. common shares for $38 cash per share.
Aug.	1	Purchased a $150,000, 7%, five-year BCE Inc. bond paying cash of $146,966. Interest is paid annually each July 31. The market interest rate is 7.5%. Conestoga Inc. plans to hold the bond until July 31, 2013.

Analysis component:

The sale of the Wall Corp shares on February 10, 2012, resulted in a loss. Does this indicate that this was a poor investment decision? Explain using calculations as appropriate.

Planning the Solution

- Account for the equity investment in Lindel Inc. and Delta Corp. using the equity method; equity investments are not generally subject to revaluation adjustments at year-end.

- Account for the trading investments in LG, Wall Corp., and BCE Inc. using the fair value method, making sure to apply revaluation adjustments at year-end as appropriate.

- Answer the analysis component question.

solution to *Demonstration Problem*

Journal entries:

	2011			
Jan.	1	Investment in Lindel Inc. Shares	320,000	
		Cash		320,000
		To record purchase of 35% interest for $320,000.		
Oct.	2	Trading Investment—LG Shares......................	42,000	
		Brokerage Fees Expense..................................	300	
		Cash		42,300
		12,000 × 3.50 = 42,000 + 300 = 42,300.		
	15	Trading Investment—Wall Corp. Shares..........	24,925	
		Brokerage Fees Expense..................................	75	
		Cash		25,000
		Purchased shares as a trading investment.		
Nov.	30	Cash...	17,500	
		Investment in Lindel Inc. Shares		17,500
		5,000 × 3.50 = 17,500.		
Dec.	15	Cash...	4,800	
		Dividend Revenue		4,800
		12,000 × 0.40 = 4,800.		
	31	Investment in Lindel Inc. Shares	287,000	
		Earnings from Investment in Lindel Inc....		287,000
		To record 35% share of investee's $820,000 net income; 820,000 × 35% = 287,000.		
	31	Unrealized Holding Loss	525	
		Trading Investment—Wall Corp. Shares..........	75	
		Trading Investment—LG Shares.............		600
		To apply valuation adjustment at year-end as per the following calculations:		

	Unadjusted Balance	Fair Value	Difference
LG Shares..	$42,000	$41,400*	$(600)
Wall Corp..	24,925	25,000**	75
Net unrealized gain (loss)....................	$66,925	$66,400	$(525)

*12,000 × 3.45 = 41,400
**50,000 × 0.50 = 25,000

2012				
Jan.	5	No entry		
	25	Cash...		5,000	
		Dividend Revenue			5,000
		50,000 × 0.10 = 5,000.			
Feb.	10	Cash...		24,750	
		Brokerage Fees Expense.................................		50	
		Loss on Sale of Investment		200	
		Trading Investment—Wall Corp. Shares...			25,000
		To record the sale of a trading investment.			
Mar.	1	Cash...		29,800	
		Brokerage Fees Expense.................................		200	
		Trading Investment—LG Shares.............			27,600
		Gain on Sale of Investment			2,400
		8,000 × 3.75 = 30,000 − 200 = 29,800;			
		41,400/12,000 = 3.50 × 8,000 = 27,600.			
May	2	Investment in Delta Corp.		608,000	
		Cash			608,000
		To record purchase of 40% interest for			
		$608,000; 16,000/40,000 = 0.40 × 100			
		= 40%; 16,000 × 38 = 608,000.			
Aug.	1	Trading Investment—BCE Inc. Bond		146,966	
		Cash			146,966
		Purchased bond as a trading investment.			

Analysis component:

The sale of the Wall Corp. shares on February 10, 2012, did result in a loss, however, this was not a poor investment decision because the investment generated a cash inflow of $4,750 over the investment period (calculated as $25,000 cash paid initially plus $5,000 dividends received plus $24,750 cash proceeds from sale).

Foreign Exchange Transactions

Many companies, from small entrepreneurs to large corporations, conduct business internationally. The operations of some large corporations take place in so many different countries that they are called **multinational businesses**. Many of us, for example, think of Alcan, Bombardier, and Nortel as primarily Canadian companies. Yet these companies earn over three-quarters of their sales from outside Canada. Others corporations such as Magna, McCain Foods; CAE Elecronics, and Molson are also major players in the world of international business.

Accounting for sales or purchases listed in a foreign currency is an accounting challenge that arises when companies have international operations. For ease in discussion of this challenge, we use companies with a base of operations in Canada and with a need to prepare financial statements in Canadian dollars. This means the *reporting currency* of these companies is the Canadian dollar.

*LO8 | Explain and record foreign exchange transactions.

Exchange Rates Between Currencies

Markets for the purchase and sale of foreign currencies exist all over the world. In these markets, Canadian dollars can be exchanged for U.S. dollars, British pounds, Japanese yen, or any other legal currencies. The price of one currency stated in terms of another currency is called a **foreign exchange rate**.

Exhibit 18A.1 lists foreign exchange rates for selected currencies at May 16, 2006. In recent years the Canadian currency has risen relative to the other currencies in the list but has fallen relative to the U.S. currency. We say that a currency is strong if it is rising in relation to the currency of other countries. We see in Exhibit 18A.1 that the exchange rate for British pounds into Canadian dollars was $2.09117 on that date. This rate means that one British pound could be purchased for Cdn$2.09117. Foreign exchange rates fluctuate due to changing economic and political conditions. These include the supply of and demand for currencies and expectations about future events.

Country (unit)	Price in Canadian dollars
Britain (pound)	$2.09117
U.S. (dollar)	1.1112
India (rupee)	0.0246659
Sweden (krona)	0.15158
Mexico (peso)	0.100525
Japan (yen)	0.0100954
Taiwan (dollar)	0.0349984
Europe (euro)	1.42422

Rates for May 16, 2006, http://www.x-rates.com/d/CAD/table.html

Exhibit 18A.1

Foreign Exchange Rates for Selected Currencies

Sales or Purchases Listed in a Foreign Currency

When a Canadian company makes a credit sale to an international customer, accounting for the sale and the account receivable requires special treatment when the terms of the sale require payment in a foreign currency.

Consider the case of the Canadian-based manufacturer, Quebec Company, which makes credit sales to London Outfitters, a British retail company. A sale occurred on December 12, 2011, for a price of £10,000, payment due on February 10, 2012. Quebec Company keeps its accounting records in Canadian dollars. To record the sale, Quebec Company must translate the sale price from pounds to dollars. This is done using the exchange rate on the date of the sale. Assuming the exchange rate on December 12, 2011, is $2.36, Quebec records this sale as:

Dec.	12	Accounts Receivable—London Outfitters	23,600	
		Sales (£10,000 × $2.36)		23,600
		To record a sale at £10,000, when the exchange rate equals $2.36.		

Quebec Company prepares its annual financial statements on December 31, 2011. On that date, the current exchange rate increases to $2.38. This means the current dollar value of Quebec Company's receivable is $23,800 (= 10,000 × $2.38). This amount is $200 greater than the amount recorded on December 12. Generally accepted accounting principles require a receivable to be reported in the balance sheet at its current dollar value. Quebec Company must make the following entry to record the increase in the dollar value of this receivable:

Dec.	31	Accounts Receivable—London Outfitters	200	
		Foreign Exchange Gain or Loss..............		200
		To record the increased value of the British pound on the receivable.		

Quebec Company receives London Outfitters' payment of £10,000 on February 10, 2012. Quebec Company immediately exchanges the pounds for Canadian dollars. On this date, the exchange rate for pounds is $2.35. This means Quebec Company receives only $23,500 (= 10,000 × $2.35). It records the cash receipt and the loss associated with the decline in the exchange rate as follows:

Feb.	10	Cash...	23,500	
		Foreign Exchange Gain or Loss.......................	300	
		Accounts Receivable— London Outfitters.................................		23,800
		Received foreign currency payment of an account and converted it into dollars.		

Gains and losses from foreign exchange transactions are accumulated in the Foreign Exchange Gain or Loss account and reported on the income statement as other revenues and expenses.

Accounting for credit purchases from an international supplier is treated in the same way as a credit sale to an international customer.

12. If a Canadian company makes a credit sale of merchandise to a French customer and the sales terms require payment in euros:

a. The Canadian company incurs an exchange gain if the foreign exchange rate between euros and dollars increases from $1.50123 at the date of sale to $1.52156 at the date the account is settled.

b. The French company may eventually need to record an exchange gain or loss.

c. The Canadian company may be required to record an exchange gain or loss on the date of the sale.

Do: *QS 18-13, *QS 18-14

Summary of Appendix 18A

*LO8 **Explain and record foreign exchange transactions.** A foreign exchange rate is the price of one currency stated in terms of another. A company with transactions in a foreign currency when the exchange rate changes between the time of the transactions and their settlement will experience an exchange gain or loss. When a company makes a credit sale to a foreign customer and sales terms call for payment in a foreign currency, the company must translate the foreign currency into dollars to record the receivable. If the exchange rate changes before payment is received, foreign exchange gains or losses are recognized in the year they occur.

guidance answers to **CHECKPOINT**

12. *a*

Glossary

Active trading When there is frequent buying and selling of shares or debt. (p. 896)

Available-for-sale investments Are investments in shares or debt but are not trading investments or held-to-maturity investments. (p. 897)

Consolidated financial statements Financial statements that show the results of all operations under the parent's control, including those of any subsidiaries; assets and liabilities of all affiliated companies are combined on a single balance sheet, revenues and expenses are combined on a single income statement, and cash flows are combined on a single cash flow statement as if the business were in fact a single company. (p. 909)

Control When an investor can dominate all other shareholders in electing the corporation's board of directors and has control over the investee corporation's management. (p. 909)

Debt investment Represents an amount owed and arises when one company lends money to another, such as in the case of a bond. Also called *debt security*. (p. 896)

Debt security See *debt investment*. (p. 896)

Equity method An accounting method used for long-term investments when the investor has significant influence over the investee; the investment account is initially debited for cost and then is increased to reflect the investor's share of the investee's earnings and decreased to reflect the investor's receipt of dividends paid by the investee. (p. 907)

Equity security See *share investment*. (p. 896)

Fair value method An accounting method for recording trading investments and available-for-sale investments. The application of the fair value method varies for each of these types of investments. (p. 898)

Foreign exchange rate The price of one currency stated in terms of another currency. (p. 915)

Held-to-maturity investments Are debt securities intended to be held by the investor until maturity; interest and principal payments are specified along with the maturity date. (p. 897)

Intercorporate investments Debt and shares of one corporation purchased by another corporation. (p. 896)

Investee The company whose debt or shares are being purchased. (p. 896)

Investor The company that purchases as an investment the debt or shares of another. (p. 896)

Joint venture An investment where two or more venturers jointly control the resulting economic activity. (p. 897)

Multinational business A company that operates in a large number of different countries. (p. 915)

Parent company A corporation that owns a controlling interest in another corporation (more than 50% of the voting shares is required). (p. 909)

Passive investment An investment where the investor cannot significantly influence or control the operations of the investee company. (p. 896)

Proportionate consolidation A method of accounting for joint ventures that combines the financial statements of an investor company and a joint venture based on the investor's proportionate share of the financial statement of the joint venture. (p. 910)

Realized gain (loss) A gain (or loss) recorded when debt or share investments are sold for more than (or less than) the value on the books. (p. 899)

Share investment Represents one company's purchase of the shares in another company. Also called *equity security*. (p. 896)

Significant influence The ability of the investor to influence the investee even though the investor owns less than 50% of the investee's voting shares. (p. 907)

Strategic investment An investment where the investee is controlled by, significantly influenced by, or is in joint venture with the investor. (p. 896)

Subsidiary A corporation that is controlled by another corporation (the parent) because the parent owns more than 50% of the subsidiary's voting shares. (p. 909)

Trading investments Are shares or debt of another corporation purchased for the short term so are *traded actively*. Profits can be realized through short-term changes in price and through receipt of dividend or interest revenue. (p. 896)

Unrealized gain (loss) A gain (or loss) recorded at the end of the accounting period based on a valuation adjustment; it is recorded although no transaction has occurred. (p. 899)

For more study tools, quizzes, and problem material,
visit the **Student Success** *Centre* at
www.mcgrawhill.ca/studentsuccess/FAP

Questions

1. Identify the classes for debt and share investments.
2. What is the difference between an equity investment and a debt investment?
3. How is interest recognized on long-term debt investments?
4. When trading investments are accounted for using the fair value method, when should revenue be recognized?
5. When share investments are accounted for using the cost method, when should revenue be recognized?
6. In accounting for common share investments, when should the equity method be used?
7. When share investments are accounted for using the equity method, when should revenue be recognized? What accounts are debited and credited?
8. Using the equity method, dividends received are not recorded as revenue. Explain why this is true.

9. Under what circumstances would a company prepare consolidated financial statements?
*10. What is a basic problem of accounting for international operations?
*11. If a Canadian company makes a credit sale to a foreign customer and the customer is required to make payment in Canadian dollars, can the Canadian company have an exchange gain or loss as a result of the sale?
*12. A Canadian company makes a credit sale to a foreign customer, and the customer is required to make payment in a foreign currency. The foreign exchange rate was $1.40 on the date of the sale and is $1.30 on the date the customer pays the receivable. Will the Canadian company record an exchange gain or an exchange loss?

Quick Study

ABC Inc. engaged in the following selected transactions during the year. Identify whether each of 1 through 8 represents an equity investment (E), investment in a debt security (D), or neither (N) from ABC Inc.'s perspective. If you answer 'N', explain.

QS 18-1
Share vs. debt investments
LO1

1. _____ Purchased 5,000 shares of Douglas Inc. shares to be held for about 30 days.
2. _____ Purchased at par a $100,000, 5% five-year bond; interest is payable quarterly and the bond will be held until maturity.
3. _____ Purchased 50,000 of the 80,000 authorized shares of Dolby Inc.
4. _____ Purchased equipment costing $140,000 by issuing shares.
5. _____ Purchased land costing $289,000 by borrowing $200,000 from the bank and issuing shares for the balance.
6. _____ Signed a contract with two other organizations regarding a project to develop and market a new computer program; each investor has a 1/3 share in the project costs and revenues.
7. _____ Purchased 80,000 Inco shares to be held for several years; Inco has over 5 million shares issued and outstanding;
8. _____ Purchased 3,000 Perdu shares, representing a 25% ownership interest.

Refer to QS 18-1. Identify how each investment would be classified from ABC Inc.'s perspective: trading (T), held-to-maturity (H), available-for-sale (A), significant influence (S), control (C), joint venture (J), or not applicable (NA).

QS 18-2
Classification of investments
LO2

On February 1, 2011, Shinko Inc. purchased 4% Telus bonds with a face value of $5,000 at 98 as a trading investment. Interest is paid quarterly beginning May 1, 2011. The bonds mature February 1, 2021. Shinko paid a brokerage fee of $50. Record the entries on February 1 and May 1.

QS 18-3
Debt investments—trading
LO3

On May 2, Sysco Industries Inc. acquired 1,200 common shares of Computer Web Corp. at $40.50 per share and paid a brokerage fee of 0.5%. Sysco's intent is to sell the shares within eight to ten months. On August 7, Sysco received dividends of $0.50 per share regarding the Computer Web investment. Record the entries on May 2 and August 7.

QS 18-4
Equity investments—trading
LO3

An asterisk (*) identifies assignment material based on Appendix 18A.

QS 18-5
Fair value valuation—trading
LO3

Delware Inc. prepared the summary shown below regarding its trading investments on December 31, 2011, its year-end. Prepare the appropriate entry on December 31, 2011, to record the valuation adjustment.

Trading Investments	Unadjusted Balance at Dec. 31/11	Market Values At Dec. 31/11
Zelco shares.................................	$102,000	$ 98,000
IMC bonds	540,000	547,000
Petra shares	96,000	48,000

QS 18-6
Fair value valuation—trading
LO3

Min Industries had selected unadjusted balances as shown below at year-end. A search on the Internet showed market values on December 31, 2011, of: CashCo, $18; Delta bonds, 89; Wells, $0.70. Prepare the appropriate entry on December 31, 2011, to record the valuation adjustment.

Trading Investments	Unadjusted Balance at Dec. 31/11
CashCo shares (21,250 shares)	$340,000
Delta bonds (200,000 face value bond)	175,000
Wells shares (45,000 shares)	34,000

QS 18-7
Balance sheet presentation—trading investments
LO3

Refer to the information in QS 18-6. Show how the trading investments will be presented on the December 31, 2011, balance sheet.

QS 18-8
Held-to-maturity investments—premium
LO4

On January 1, 2011, Gildan Activewear purchased a 12%, $40,000 Telus bond with a three-year term for $42,030. There were no brokerage fees. Interest is to be paid semi-annually each June 30 and December 31. Gildan is planning to hold the bond until maturity. Record the entries on January 1, 2011, June 30, 2011, and December 31, 2013, using the amortization schedule provided below.

Period Ending	Cash Interest Received	Period Interest Revenue	Premium Amort.	Unamortized Premium	Carrying Value
Jan. 1/11				$2,030	$42,030
June 30/11	$ 2,400	$ 2,102	$ 298	1,732	41,732
Dec. 31/11	2,400	2,087	313	1,419	41,419
June 30/12	2,400	2,071	329	1,090	41,090
Dec. 31/12	2,400	2,055	345	745	40,745
June 30/13	2,400	2,037	363	382	40,382
Dec. 31/13	2,400	2,018	382	0	40,000
Totals	$14,400	$12,370	$2,030		

QS 18-9
Held-to-maturity investments—discount
LO4

On January 1, 2011, Nickelada Inc. purchased a 4%, $50,000 Imax bond for $46,490. There were no brokerage fees. Interest is to be paid semi-annually each June 30 and December 31. Nickelada Inc. is planning to hold the bond until maturity. Record the entries on January 1, 2011, and June 30, 2011, based on the partial amortization schedule shown below.

Period Ending	Cash Interest Received	Period Interest Revenue	Discount Amort.	Unamortized Discount	Carrying Value
Jan. 1/11				$3,510	$46,490
June 30/11	$1,000	$1,395	$395	3,115	46,885
Dec. 31/11	1,000	1,407	407	2,708	47,292

Refer to the information in QS 18-9. Show how the investment will be presented on the December 31, 2011, balance sheet.

QS 18-10
Balance sheet presentation—
held-to-maturity investments
LO4

On January 2, 2011, Nassau Corp. paid $500,000 cash to acquire 10,000 of Suffolk Corporation's 40,000 outstanding common shares. Assume that Nassau has significant influence over Suffolk as a result. On October 12, 2011, Suffolk Corp. paid a $100,000 dividend and on December 31, 2011, it reported net income of $400,000 for 2011. Prepare Nassau's entries on January 2, October 12, and December 31.

QS 18-11
Significant influence—equity method
LO6

On January 2, 2011, Balla Corp. paid cash of $1,200,000 to acquire 704,000 of Dofasco Inc.'s 3,200,000 outstanding common shares. Assume that Balla has significant influence over Dofasco as a result. On March 15, 2011, Dofasco paid dividends of $0.20 per common share and on December 31, 2011, it reported a net loss of $1,675,000 for 2011. Prepare Balla's entries on January 2, March 15, and December 31.

QS 18-12
Significant influence—equity method
LO6

On November 21, 2011, a Canadian company, NCN, made a sale with credit terms requiring payment in 30 days to a Swedish corporation, Ehler Corp. The amount of the sale was 50,000 Swedish krona. Assuming the exchange rate in Exhibit 18A.1 on the date of sale and $0.160121 on December 21, prepare the entries to record the sale and the cash receipt on December 21. *For simplicity, round all final calculations to the nearest dollar.*

*QS 18-13
Foreign currency transactions
LO8

A Canadian corporation sells a British corporation a product with the transaction listed in British pounds. On August 31, 2011, the date of the sale, the transaction of $20,912 was billed at £10,000, reflecting an exchange rate as shown in Exhibit 18A.1. Show the entry to record the sale and also the receipt of the payment on September 28 when the exchange rate has risen to $2.20234. *For simplicity, round all final calculations to the nearest dollar.*

*QS 18-14
Foreign currency transactions
LO8

Exercises

Prepare entries to record the following trading investment transactions of Aryee Corporation:

Exercise 18-1
Trading investments
LO3

	2011	
Mar.	1	Paid $60,980 to purchase a $60,000 two-year, 7% bond payable of Cordy Corporation dated March 1. Interest is paid quarterly beginning June 1.
Apr.	16	Bought 2,000 common shares of Windsor Motors at $25.50 plus a $150 brokerage fee.
May	2	Paid $38,968 to purchase a five-year, 4.5%, $40,000 bond payable of Bates Corporation. Interest is paid annually each April 30.
June	1	Received a cheque from Cordy Corporation regarding quarterly interest.
Aug.	1	Windsor Motors' board of directors declared a dividend of $0.75 per share to shareholders of record on August 10, payable August 15.
	15	Received the Windsor Motors dividend.
Sept.	1	Received a cheque from Cordy Corporation regarding quarterly interest.
	17	Purchased 25,000 Delta Inc. common shares at $3.20 plus a brokerage fee of $200.
Oct.	20	Sold the Windsor Motors shares at $31.00 less a brokerage fee of $110.
Dec.	1	Received a cheque from Cordy Corporation regarding quarterly interest.
	1	Sold the Cordy Corporation bond at 101.
	31	Accrued interest on the Bates bond. Market values of the debt and equity securities on this date were: Bates, 99.5; Delta, $3.50.
	2012	
Apr.	30	Received a cheque from Bates Corporation regarding annual interest.

Analysis component:
If the adjusting entry on December 31, 2011, was not recorded, what would the effect be on the income statement and balance sheet? Based on your understanding of GAAP, would it be better or worse to omit an unrealized holding loss than an unrealized holding gain? Explain.

Check figure:
Dec. 31/11 Unrealized holding gain = $8,332

An asterisk (*) identifies assignment material based on Appendix 18A.

Exercise 18-2
Trading investments
LO³

Prepare entries to record the following trading investment transactions of Wiki Inc.:

	2011	
Feb.	1	Paid $120,200 to purchase a $124,000 four-year, 3% bond payable of Wella Inc. dated Feb. 1. Interest is paid semi-annually beginning August 1.
Mar.	29	Bought 100,000 common shares of Regina Inc. for a total of $85,600, which included a $600 brokerage fee.
May	7	Regina Inc.'s board of directors declared a total dividend of $525,000 regarding the total 3,500,000 shares issued and outstanding. The date of record is May 30, payable June 15.
June	1	Paid $139,000 to purchase a five-year, 6%, $136,000 bond payable of Yates Corporation. Interest is paid annually each May 30.
	15	Received a cheque regarding the dividends declared on May 7.
Aug.	1	Received a cheque from Wella Inc. regarding semi-annual interest.
	1	Sold the Wella Inc. bond at 98 less a brokerage fee of $110.
	17	Purchased 75,000 Tech Inc. common shares at $6.00 plus a brokerage fee of $1,500.
Dec.	1	Sold 75,000 of the Regina Inc. shares at $0.95 less a brokerage fee of $200.
	31	Accrued interest on the Yates bond. Market values of the debt and equity securities on this date were: Regina, $0.95; Yates, 101.5; Tech Inc., $5.50.
	2012	
May	30	Received a cheque from Yates Corporation regarding annual interest.

Check figure:
Dec. 31/11 Unrealized holding
loss = $35,960

Analysis component:
How would the financial statements have been affected differently if the dividends received on June 15 were from a significant influence investment as opposed to a trading investment?

Exercise 18-3
Revaluation adjustments at year-end
LO³

Roe Inc.'s trading investments as of December 31, 2011, are as follows:

	Cost	Fair Value
Nortel common shares..	$17,600	$19,450
Northern Electric common shares..	42,750	42,050
Imperial Oil common shares...	25,200	24,250
Inco Limited common shares...	34,800	31,950

Roe Inc. had no trading investments prior to 2011.

Check figure:
Dec. 31/11 Unrealized holding
loss = $2,650

Required
1. Prepare the valuation adjustment at December 31, 2011, based on the information provided.
2. Illustrate how the trading investments will be reported on the December 31, 2011, balance sheet.

Exercise 18-4
Revaluation adjustments at year-end
LO³

The cost and fair value of trading investments of IP Corporation on December 31, 2011, and December 31, 2012, are as follows:

	Cost	Fair Value
On December 31, 2011	$23,500	$22,000
On December 31, 2012	26,500	27,350

Check figures:
2. Dec. 31/11 = $22,000
Dec. 31/12 = $27,350

Required
1. Prepare the valuation adjustment at December 31, 2011, and December 31, 2012, based on the information provided.
2. Illustrate how the trading investments will be reported on the December 31, 2011, and December 31, 2012, balance sheets.

Prepare entries to record the following held-to-maturity investment transactions of Corona Inc.:

2011

Jan.	1	Purchased for $78,141 an 8%, $75,000 bond that matures in 10 years from Hanna Corporation when the market interest rate was 7.4%. Interest is paid semi-annually beginning June 30, 2011.
June	30	Received interest on the Hanna bond.
July	1	Paid $118,047 for a Tillemanns Inc. bond with a par value of $120,000. The bond pays interest quarterly beginning September 30, 2011 at the annual rate of 7.8%; the market interest rate on the date of purchase was 8.2%.
Sept.	30	Received interest on the Tillemanns bond.
Dec.	31	Received interest on the Hanna and Tillemanns bonds.
	31	The fair values of the bonds on this date were: Hanna bond, $78,200; Tillemanns bond, $117,980.

Exercise 18-5
Held-to-maturity investments
LO4

Required

1. For each of the bond investments, prepare an amortization schedule showing only 2011 and 2012.
2. Prepare the entries to record the transactions described above.
3. Show how the investments would be reported on Corona's December 31, 2011, balance sheet.

Analysis component:
Will the total revenue that the Hanna Corporation investment will generate for the investee over the time the investment will be held be different than if it were a trading investment? Explain.

Check figure:
3. Dec. 31/11 = $196,128

Gerges Inc. engaged in the following trading and held-to-maturity investment transactions during 2011:

2011

Jan.	1	Purchased for $406,894 a 6%, $400,000 Jarvis Corp. bond that matures in five years when the market interest rate was 5.6%. Interest is paid semi-annually beginning June 30, 2011. Gerges Inc. plans to hold this investment until maturity.
Mar.	1	Bought 6,000 shares of Medley Corp., paying $32.50 per share plus a brokerage fee of $975.
May	7	Received dividends of $0.90 per share on the Medley Corp. shares.
June	1	Paid $316,000 plus a $1,264 brokerage fee for 21,000 shares of Xtrapa common shares.
	30	Received interest on the Jarvis bond.
Aug.	1	Sold the Medley Corp. shares for $32.75 per share less a brokerage fee of $982.
Dec.	31	Received interest on the Jarvis bond.
	31	The fair values of Gerges Inc.'s investments on this date were: Jarvis bond; 101.5%; Xtrapa shares, $14.80.
2012		
Jan.	14	Sold the Xtrapa shares for $14.60 less a brokerage fee of $1,226.

Exercise 18-6
Held-to-maturity and trading investments
LO3, 4

Required

1. Prepare an amortization schedule for the Jarvis bond showing only 2011 and 2012.
2. Prepare the entries to record the transactions described above.
3. Show how the investments would be reported on Gerges' December 31, 2011, balance sheet.

Check figure:
2. Jan. 14/12 Loss on sale of investment = $4,200

Exercise 18-7
Reporting held-to-maturity investments
LO⁴

Trinista Developments purchased a five-year, 4.5%, $500,000 Magna Inc. bond on January 1, 2011, when the market interest rate was 5.2%; interest is paid annually each December 31. Trinista intends to hold this investment until December 31, 2015. The following additional information is available regarding the bond:

Period Ending	Cash Interest Received	Period Interest Revenue	Discount Amort.	Unamortized Discount	Carrying Value
Jan. 1/11				$15,070	$484,930
Dec. 31/11	$ 22,500	$ 25,216	$ 2,716	12,354	487,646
Dec. 31/12	22,500	25,358	2,858	9,496	490,504
Dec. 31/13	22,500	25,506	3,006	6,490	493,510
Dec. 31/14	22,500	25,663	3,163	3,327	496,673
Dec. 31/15	22,500	25,827	3,327	0	500,000
Totals	$112,500	$127,570	$15,070		

Check figure:
3. $493,510

Required
1. Based on the information provided, Trinista will have recorded the Magna Inc. bond as what type of investment?
2. Prepare Trinista's entries to record the purchase on January 1, 2011, and the collection of interest on December 31, 2011. Assume that there were no brokerage fees.
3. Illustrate how this investment will be reported on the December 31, 2013, balance sheet.

Exercise 18-8
Share investment transactions; equity method
LO⁶

The following events are for Toronto Inc.:

	2011	
Jan.	14	Purchased 18,000 shares of Queen's Inc. common shares for $156,900 plus a broker's fee of $1,000. Queen's has 90,000 common shares outstanding and has acknowledged the fact that its policies will be significantly influenced by Toronto.
Oct.	1	Queen's declared and paid a cash dividend of $2.60 per share.
Dec.	31	Queen's announced that net income for the year amounted to $650,000.
	2012	
April	1	Queen's declared and paid a cash dividend of $2.70 per share.
Dec.	31	Queen's announced that net income for the year amounted to $733,100.
	31	Toronto sold 6,000 shares of Queen's for $104,320.

Check figure:
Dec. 31: Loss = $8,720

Required
Prepare General Journal entries to record each transaction.

*Exercise 18-9
Receivables listed in a foreign currency
*LO⁸

Check figures:
Quarter ended June 30/11:
Gain = $432;
Quarter ended Dec. 31/11:
Loss = $421;
Net gain for all quarters = $592

On June 2, 2011, Comco Inc. (a Canadian corporation) made a credit sale to Phang (a Taiwanese corporation). The terms of the sale required Phang to pay 980,000 Taiwanese dollars on January 3, 2012. Comco prepares quarterly financial statements on March 31, June 30, September 30, and December 31. The foreign exchange rates for Taiwanese dollars during the time the receivable was outstanding were:

June 2, 2011....................................	$0.040114
June 30, 2011.................................	0.040555
September 30, 2011........................	0.040675
December 31, 2011	0.040246
January 3, 2012..............................	0.040718

Calculate the foreign exchange gain or loss that Comco should report on each of its quarterly income statements during the last three quarters of 2011 and the first quarter of 2012. Also calculate the amount that should be reported on Comco's balance sheets at the end of the last three quarters of 2011. *For simplicity, round final calculations to the nearest dollar.*

An asterisk (*) identifies assignment material based on Appendix 18A.

Donham Corporation of Montvale, New Brunswick, sells its products to customers in Canada and in the U.S. On December 3, 2011, Donham sold merchandise on credit to Swensons, Ltd., of Maine, at a price of U.S.$6,500. The exchange rate on that day was U.S.$1 for Cdn$1.3852. On December 31, 2011, when Donham prepared its financial statements, the exchange rate was U.S.$1 for Cdn$1.2964. Swensons paid its bill in full on January 3, 2012, at which time the exchange rate was U.S.$1 for Cdn$1.3041. Donham immediately exchanged the U.S.$6,500 for Canadian dollars. Prepare journal entries on December 3, December 31, and January 3, to account for the sale and account receivable on Donham's books. *For simplicity, round final calculations to the nearest dollar. Ignore cost of goods sold.*

*Exercise 18-10
Foreign currency transactions
*LO8

Check figure:
Jan. 3/12: Gain = $50

Sudbury Metals, a Canadian-based company, purchases ore from a Malaysian-based company; the terms are n/45. The following selected purchases of ore (raw materials inventory) occurred during 2011:

*Exercise 18-11
Payables listed in a foreign currency
*LO8

Date of Purchase	Dollar Amount of Purchase (Malaysian Ringgit)	Exchange Rate on Date of Purchase (in Canadian $)	Exchange Rate on Date of Payment (in Canadian $)
January 15	14,800,000	0.3087	0.3088
June 17	46,900,000	0.3093	0.3088

Required
Record the purchases and subsequent payments.

Check figure:
1. Aug. 1/11 Foreign exchange gain = $23,450

Boudreau Corp. is a Canadian corporation that has customers in several foreign countries. Following are some of Boudreau's 2011 and 2012 transactions (ignore cost of sales):

*Exercise 18-12
Foreign currency transactions
*LO8

	2011	
June	6	Sold merchandise to Lejeune Inc. of France for 125,000 euros to be received in 60 days. The exchange rate for euros was $1.50938.
June	14	Purchased inventory from the United States costing U.S. $260,000 payable in six months. The exchange rate on this date for American dollars into Canadian dollars was $1.0065.
Aug.	1	Received Lejeune Inc.'s payment for its purchase of June 6 and exchanged the euros for dollars. The current foreign exchange rate for euros into dollars was $1.51067.
Oct.	25	Sold merchandise on credit to British Imports, Ltd., a company located in London, England. The price of £3,000 was to be paid 90 days from the date of sale. On Nov. 18, the exchange rate for pounds into dollars was $1.7730.
Dec.	14	Paid the amount owing regarding the June 14 purchase. The exchange rate on this date for American dollars into Canadian dollars was $0.9216.
Dec.	31	Prepared the adjusting entry to recognize the exchange gain or loss on the annual financial statements. Rate for exchanging British pounds into dollars was $1.7125.
	2012	
Jan.	23	Received full payment from British Imports for the sale of October 25 and immediately exchanged the pounds for dollars. The exchange rate for pounds was $1.7628.

Required
Prepare General Journal entries to account for these transactions of Boudreau Corp. (For simplicity, ignore cost of sales.)

Analysis component:
What actions might Boudreau consider to reduce its risk of foreign exchange gains or losses?

Check figures:
Aug. 1/11: Gain = $161.25
Aug. 1/12: Gain = $150.90

An asterisk (*) identifies assignment material based on Appendix 18A.

Problems

Problem 18-1A
Trading and held-to-maturity
investments
LO2, 3, 4

Landers Inc. had the following transactions involving trading and held-to-maturity investments during 2011:

	2011	
Apr.	1	Paid $100,000 to buy a 90-day term deposit, $100,000 principal amount, 5%, dated April 1.
	12	Purchased 3,000 common shares of Dofasco Ltd. at $22.25 plus a $1,948 brokerage fee.
June	9	Purchased 1,800 common shares of Power Corp. at $49.50 plus a $1,235 brokerage fee.
	20	Purchased 700 common shares of Westburne Ltd. at $15.75 plus a $466 brokerage fee.
July	1	Purchased for $67,412 a 7%, $65,000 Littleton Inc. bond that matures in eight years when the market interest rate was 6.4%. Interest is paid semi-annually beginning December 31, 2011. Landers Inc. plans to hold this investment until maturity.
	3	Received a cheque for the principal and accrued interest on the term deposit that matured on June 30.
	15	Received a $0.95 per share cash dividend on the Dofasco common shares.
	28	Sold 1,500 of the Dofasco common shares at $26.00 less a $912 brokerage fee.
Sept.	1	Received a $2.10 per share cash dividend on the Power Corp. common shares.
Dec.	15	Received a $1.35 per share cash dividend on the remaining Dofasco common shares owned.
	31	Received the interest on the Littleton bond.
	31	The fair values of Landers Inc.'s investments on this date were: Dofasco shares, $24.60; Power Corp. shares, $42.35; Westburne shares, $16.05; Littleton bond, 1.02%.
	2012	
Feb.	16	Sold the remaining Dofasco shares at $26.25 less a brokerage fee of $200.

Check figure:
2. Feb. 16/12 Gain on sale of
investment = $2,475

Required
1. Prepare an amortization schedule for the Littleton bond showing only 2011 and 2012.
2. Prepare journal entries to record the preceding transactions.
3. Show how Landers Inc.'s investments will appear on its December 31, 2011, balance sheet.

Analysis component:
How is the unrealized loss recorded on the Dofasco shares on December 31, 2011, different than the loss on sale of investment recorded on February 16, 2012?

Problem 18-2A
Trading and held-to-maturity
investments
LO2, 3, 4

Sellers Corporation had relatively large idle cash balances and invested them as follows in securities to be held as both trading and held-to-maturity investments:

	2011	
Feb.	7	Purchased 2,200 common shares of Royal Bank at $26.50 plus a $500 commission.
	19	Purchased 1,200 common shares of Imperial Oil at $51.75 plus a $600 commission.
Apr.	1	Paid $88,758 for a 6.8%, four-year, $90,000 Minco Inc. bond that pays interest quarterly beginning June 30. The market rate of interest on this date was 7.2%. Sellers Corporation plans to hold this investment until maturity.
May	26	Purchased 2,000 common shares of BCE at $13.38 plus a $250 brokerage fee.
June	1	Received a $0.25 per share cash dividend on the Royal Bank common shares.
	17	Sold 1,200 Royal Bank common shares at $27.00 less a $300 brokerage fee.
	30	Received interest on the Minco Inc. bond.
Aug.	5	Received a $0.50 per share cash dividend on the Imperial Oil common shares.
Sept.	1	Received a $0.275 per share cash dividend on the remaining Royal Bank common shares.
	30	Received interest on the Minco Inc. bond.
Dec.	31	Received interest on the Minco Inc. bond.

On December 31, 2011, the market prices of the investments held by Sellers Corporation were: Royal Bank, $27.50; Imperial Oil, $50.13; BCE, $13.50; and Minco, 99%.

Required
1. Prepare an amortization schedule for the Minco Inc. bond showing only 2011.
2. Prepare journal entries to record the investment activity including the appropriate valuation adjustment on December 31.
3. Show how the investments will be reported on the December 31, 2011, balance sheet.

Analysis component:
If the valuation adjustment is not recorded by Sellers Corporation, what is the impact on its financial statements?

Check figure:
Dec. 31/11 Unrealized holding loss = $704

On January 1, 2011, Liu Corporation paid $241,960 to acquire bonds of Peverdo with a par value of $240,000. The annual contract rate on the bonds is 6% and interest is paid semi-annually on June 30 and December 31. The bonds mature after three years. The market rate of interest was 5.7%. Liu Corporation intends to hold the bonds until maturity.

Problem 18-3A
Held-to-maturity investments
LO4

Required
1. Prepare an amortization schedule for the investment showing only 2011.
2. Prepare Liu's entries to record: (a) the purchase of the bonds, (b) the receipt of the first two interest payments.
3. Show how the investment will appear on the December 31, 2011, balance sheet.

Check figure:
3. $241,343

Johnson Inc.'s trading investment portfolio at December 31, 2010, consisted of the following:

Problem 18-4A
Trading and significant influence investments
LO3, 6

Debt and Equity Investments*	Cost	Fair Value
10,000 Xavier Corporation common shares	$163,500	$145,000
1,250 Young Inc. common shares	65,000	62,000
120,000 Zed Corp. common shares	40,000	35,600

*The valuation adjustments were recorded on December 31, 2010.

Johnson had no other debt and equity investments at December 31, 2010, other than those shown above. During 2011, Johnson engaged in the following transactions:

	2011	
Jan.	17	Sold 750 common shares of Young Inc. for $36,000 less a brokerage fee of $180. Johnson Inc. planned to hold these shares for less than one year.
Mar.	3	Purchased 5,000 common shares of Allen Corp. for $300,000. The shares represent a 30% ownership in Allen Corp.
June	7	Received dividends from Allen Corp. at the rate of $2.50 per share.
Aug.	14	Sold the remaining Young Inc. shares at $31.50 less a brokerage fee of $50.
Nov.	28	Purchased a 5% ownership in Davis Corp. by acquiring 10,000 common shares at a total of $89,000 plus a brokerage fee of $445. Johnson Inc. will sell these shares in six to nine months.
Dec.	30	Sold 10,000 shares of Xavier Corporation for $160,000 less a brokerage fee of $800.
	31	Allen Corp. announced a net profit of $280,000 for the year.

Required
Journalize the above transactions.

Analysis component:
Assume the Allen Corp. shares were sold on January 16, 2012, for $364,000. Calculate the gain or loss and explain whether it is unrealized.

Check figure:
Dec. 30/11 Gain on sale of investment = $15,000

Problem 18-5A
Accounting for share investments
LO6

Hamilton Ltd. was organized on January 2, 2011. The following investment transactions and events subsequently occurred:

	2011	
Jan.	6	Hamilton paid $575,500 for 50,000 shares (20%) of Ginto Inc. outstanding common shares.
Apr.	30	Ginto declared and paid a cash dividend of $1.10 per share.
Dec.	31	Ginto announced that its net income for 2011 was $480,000. Market value of the shares was $11.80 per share.
	2012	
Oct.	15	Ginto declared and paid a cash dividend of $0.70 per share.
Dec.	31	Ginto announced that its net income for 2012 was $630,000. Market value of the shares was $12.18 per share.
	2013	
Jan.	5	Hamilton sold all of its investment in Ginto for $682,000 cash.

Assume that Hamilton has a significant influence over Ginto with its 20% share.

Check figure:
2. Carrying value per share, $14.15

Required
1. Give the entries to record the preceding transactions in Hamilton's books.
2. Calculate the carrying value per share of Hamilton's investment as reflected in the investment account on January 4, 2013.
3. Calculate the change in Hamilton's equity from January 6, 2011, through January 5, 2013, resulting from its investment in Ginto.

*Problem 18-6A
Foreign currency transactions
*LO8

Lupold Inc. is a Canadian corporation that has customers in several foreign countries. The corporation had the following transactions in 2011 and 2012:

	2011	
May	22	Sold merchandise to Weishaar Imports of Holland for 15,000 euros on credit. The exchange rate for euros was $1.50041.
Aug.	25	Received Weishaar Imports' payment for its purchase of May 22, and exchanged the euros for dollars. The current exchange rate for euros was $1.53211.
Sep.	9	Sold merchandise to Campos Inc. of Mexico for $24,780 cash. The exchange rate for pesos was $0.114002 on this date.
Nov.	29	Sold merchandise on credit to ONI Corp. located in Japan. The price of 1.1 million yen was to be paid 60 days from the date of sale. The exchange rate for yen was $0.009195 on November 29.
Dec.	23	Sold merchandise for 158,000 ringgit to Martinique Corp. of Malaysia, payment in full to be received in 30 days. On this day, the foreign exchange rate for ringgit was $0.375521.
	31	Prepared adjusting entries to recognize exchange gains or losses on the annual financial statements. Rates for exchanging foreign currencies on this day included the following:

Peso (Mexico)	$0.125226
Yen (Japan)............................	0.011867
Ringgit (Malaysia)..................	0.364473
Euro (EU)...............................	1.52156

	2012	
Jan.	24	Received full payment from Martinique for the sale of December 23 and immediately exchanged the ringgit for dollars. The exchange rate for ringgit was $0.342125.
	30	Received ONI's full payment for the sale of November 29 and immediately exchanged the yen for dollars. The exchange rate for yen was $0.012004.

An asterisk (*) identifies assignment material based on Appendix 18A.

Required

1. Prepare General Journal entries to account for these transactions on Lupold's books. *Round calculations to the nearest whole cent.*
2. Calculate the foreign exchange gain or loss to be reported on Lupold's 2011 income statement.

Analysis component:
What actions might Lupold consider to reduce its risk of foreign exchange gains or losses?

Alternate Problems

Musli Inc. had the following transactions involving trading and held-to-maturity investments during 2011:

Problem 18-1B
Trading and held-to-maturity investments
LO2, 3, 4

	2011	
Feb.	1	Paid $70,000 to buy a 60-day term deposit, $70,000 principal amount, 6.23%, dated Feb. 1.
	21	Purchased 6,000 common shares of Hilton Ltd. at $11.25 plus a $540 brokerage fee.
Apr.	2	Received a cheque for the principal and accrued interest on the term deposit that matured today.
	15	Purchased 8,200 common shares of Elder Corp. at $9.75 plus a $475 brokerage fee.
	20	Purchased 14,000 common shares of Venture Ltd. at $3.40 plus a $220 brokerage fee.
July	1	Purchased for $67,069 a 6.8%, $68,000 Barker Inc. bond that matures in four years when the market interest rate was 7.2%. Interest is paid semi-annually beginning December 31, 2011. Musli Inc. plans to hold this investment until maturity.
	15	Received a $0.30 per share cash dividend on the Hilton common shares.
	28	Sold 4,000 of the Hilton common shares at $11.15 less a $300 brokerage fee.
Dec.	1	Received a $0.30 per share cash dividend on the remaining Hilton common shares owned.
	31	Received the interest on the Barker bond.
	31	The fair values of Musli Inc.'s investments on this date were: Hilton shares, $12.60; Elder shares, $10.30; Venture shares, $3.20; Barker bond, 98.65%.
	2012	
Feb.	16	Sold the remaining Hilton shares at $12.65 less a brokerage fee of $200.

Required

1. Prepare an amortization schedule for the Barker bond showing only 2011 and 2012.
2. Prepare journal entries to record the preceding transactions.
3. Show how Musli Inc.'s investments will appear on its December 31, 2011, balance sheet.

Analysis component:
Musli Inc. purchased the Barker Inc. bond for less than its face value. Explain why.

Problem 18-2B
Trading and held-to-maturity investments
LO2, 3, 4

Thornhill Corporation has excess cash resulting from extremely successful operations. It has decided to invest this cash in debt and equity securities as follows to be held as both trading and held-to-maturity investments:

		2011	
Jan.	18	Purchased 16,000 common shares of Logitech at $1.40 plus a $672 commission.
Feb.	27	Purchased 500 common shares of Gildan Activewear at $103 plus an $870 commission.
Apr.	26	Purchased 1,000 common shares of Winston at $18.00 plus a $550 brokerage fee.
	30	Received a $0.10 per share cash dividend on the Logitech common shares.
June	4	Sold 10,000 Logitech common shares at $1.15 less a $380 brokerage fee.
July	1	Paid $142,933 for a 7.2%, five-year, $140,000 Sharp Inc. bond that pays interest semi-annually beginning December 31. The market rate of interest on this date was 6.7%. Thornhill Corporation plans to hold this investment until maturity.
	17	Received a $7.25 per share cash dividend on the Gildan Activewear shares.
Sept.	1	Received a $0.10 per share cash dividend on the remaining Logitech shares.
Dec.	31	Received interest on the Sharp Inc. bond.
		2012	
Feb.	6	Sold the remaining Logitech shares at $0.85 less a $100 commission.
June	30	Received interest on the Sharp Inc. bond.

On December 31, 2011, the market prices of the investments held by Thornhill Corporation were: Logitech, $0.90; Gildan Activewear, $101; Winston, $14.00; and Sharp, 102.25%.

Check figure:
Dec. 31/11 Unrealized holding loss = $8,000

Required
1. Prepare an amortization schedule for 2011 and 2012 regarding the Sharp Inc. bond.
2. Prepare journal entries to record the investment activity, including the appropriate valuation adjustment on December 31, 2011.
3. Show how the investments will be reported on the December 31, 2011, balance sheet.

Analysis component:
If the December 31, 2011, valuation adjustment on the Logitech shares were not recorded by Thornhill Corporation, would the February 6, 2012, journal entry be affected? Explain.

Problem 18-3B
Held-to-maturity investments
LO4

On April 1, 2011, JoeLite Corporation paid $851,560 to acquire bonds of Luxem Inc. with a par value of $860,000. The annual contract rate on the bonds is 6.5% and interest is paid quarterly beginning June 30, 2011. The bonds mature in six years. The market rate of interest at the time of purchase was 6.7%. JoeLite Corporation plans to hold the bonds until they mature.

Check figure:
3. $852,440

Required
1. Prepare an amortization schedule for the investment showing only 2011.
2. Prepare JoeLite's entries to record: (a) the purchase of the bonds, and (b) the receipt of the first three interest payments.
3. Show how the investment will appear on the December 31, 2011, balance sheet.

Problem 18-4B
Trading and significant influence investments
LO3, 6

Irving Inc.'s trading investment portfolio at December 31, 2010, consisted of the following:

Debt and Equity Investments*	Cost	Fair Value
50,000 Cumber Corporation common shares	$138,000	$145,000
18,000 Olds Inc. common shares	124,200	118,900
45,000 Wyeth Corp. common shares	265,500	261,000

*The valuation adjustments were recorded on December 31, 2010.

Irving Inc. had no other debt and equity investments at December 31, 2010, other than those shown above. During 2011, Irving engaged in the following transactions:

	2011	
Feb.	2	Sold 45,000 of the Cumber Corporation shares for $2.48 per share less a brokerage fee of $940.
June	27	Purchased 280,000 common shares of Kestler Corp. for $540,000. The shares represent a 38% ownership in Kestler Corp.
	30	Received dividends of $0.45 per share from Kestler Corp.
July	3	Sold the remaining Cumber Corporation shares for $14,680 less a brokerage fee of $250.
Aug.	7	Purchased a 15% ownership in Amber Corp. by acquiring 45,000 common shares at $14.50 per share plus a brokerage fee of $3,300. Irving Inc. plans to sell these shares in six to nine months.
Dec.	30	Sold 25,000 shares of Wyeth Corp. for $5.40 per share less a brokerage fee of $725.
	31	Kestler Corp. announced a net loss of $40,000 for the year.

Required
1. Calculate the total unrealized holding gain (loss) that was recorded on December 31, 2010.
2. Journalize the 2011 transactions as detailed above.

Check figure:
Dec. 30/11 Loss on sale of investment = $10,000

River Corporation was organized on January 2, 2011. River Corporation issued 50,000 common shares for $250,000 on that date. The following investment transactions and events subsequently occurred:

Problem 18-5B
Accounting for share investments
LO6

	2011	
Jan.	12	River Corporation acquired 12,000 shares of Turner Ltd. at a cost of $250,000. This investment represented 24% of Turner's outstanding shares.
Mar.	31	Turner Ltd. declared and paid a cash dividend of $1.00 per share.
Dec.	31	Turner Ltd. announced that its net income for 2011 was $125,000.
	2012	
Aug.	15	Turner Ltd. declared and paid a cash dividend of $0.80 per share.
Dec.	31	Turner Ltd. announced that its net loss for 2012 was $95,000.
	2013	
Jan.	6	River Corporation sold all of its investment in Turner Ltd. for $230,000 cash.

Assume that River Corporation has a significant influence over Turner Ltd. with its 24% share.

Required
1. Give the entries to record the preceding transactions in River Corporation's books.
2. Calculate the carrying value per share of River Corporation's investment as reflected in the investment account on January 1, 2013.
3. Calculate the change in River Corporation's equity from January 12, 2011, through January 6, 2013, resulting from its investment in Turner Ltd.

Check figure:
2. Carrying value per share, $19.63

*Problem 18-6B
Foreign currency transactions
*LO8

Global Enterprises Ltd. is a Canadian corporation that has customers in several foreign countries. It showed the following transactions for 2011 and 2012:

2011

July	13	Sold merchandise for 950,000 yen to Shisedu Inc. of Japan, with payment in full to be received in 60 days. On this day, the foreign exchange rate for yen was $0.012514.
Aug.	21	Sold merchandise to Klaus Retailers of France for $9,500 cash. The foreign exchange rate for euros was $1.54189.
Sept.	11	Received Shisedu Inc.'s payment for its purchase of July 13, and exchanged the yen for dollars. The current exchange rate for yen was $0.010681.
Oct.	6	Sold merchandise on credit to Trafalgar Distributors, a company located in London, England. The price of £5,000 is to be paid 90 days from the date of sale. On October 6, the foreign exchange rate for pounds was $2.21694.
Nov.	18	Sold merchandise for 30,000 Australian dollars to Belgique Suppliers of Australia, payment in full to be received in 60 days. The exchange rate for Australian dollars was $0.887613.
Dec.	31	Prepared adjusting entries to recognize exchange gains or losses on the annual financial statements. Rates of exchanging foreign currencies on this day are:

Pounds (Britain).....................	$2.18455
Euro (EU)..............................	1.52156
Yen (Japan)...........................	0.011867
Dollar (Australia)...................	0.898866

2012

Jan.	4	Received full payment from Trafalgar Distributors for the October 6 sale and immediately exchanged the pounds for dollars. The exchange rate for pounds was $2.22183.
	17	Received full payment in Australian dollars from Belgique Suppliers for the sale of November 18 and immediately exchanged the Australian dollars for Canadian dollars. The exchange rate for Australian dollars was $0.88985.

Check figure:
2. Total foreign exchange loss, $1,565.71

Required
1. Prepare General Journal entries to account for these transactions on the books of Global Enterprises. *Round calculations to the nearest whole cent.*
2. Calculate the foreign exchange gain or loss to be reported on Global Enterprises' 2011 income statement.

Analysis component:
What actions might Global Enterprises consider to reduce its risk of foreign exchange gains or losses?

Analytical and Review Problems

A & R 18-1

On January 1, 2011, Hinke Ltd. purchased 30% of Deveau Ltd.'s outstanding common shares. The balance in Hinke Ltd.'s Investment in Deveau Ltd. account was $500,000 as of December 31, 2012. The following information is available for years 2011 and 2012 for Deveau Ltd.:

	Net Income	Dividends Paid
2011...	$300,000	$100,000
2012...	$400,000	$100,000

Required
Calculate the purchase price paid by Hinke Ltd. for Deveau Ltd. shares on January 1, 2011.

An asterisk (*) identifies assignment material based on Appendix 18A.

On January 2, Pedro Inc. purchased a 40% interest (7,500 shares) in Zapata Inc.'s common shares for $236,250. The following entries were recorded in 2011 and 2012.

A & R 18-2

2011				
June	8	Cash...	10,500	
		Dividend Revenue		10,500
		To record dividends received.		
Dec.	31	Investment in Zapata Inc.	26,250	
		Investment Revenue		26,250
		To record increase in market value of		
		Zapata shares.		
2012				
June	8	Cash...	10,500	
		Dividend Revenue		10,500
		To record dividends received.		
Dec.	31	Investment in Zapata Inc.	45,750	
		Investment Revenue		45,750
		To record increase in market value of		
		Zapata shares.		

Zapata Inc.'s results for 2011 and 2012 were as follows:

	2011	2012
Net Income...	$70,500	$52,500
Cash Dividends Paid...	26,250	26,250

Required
a. Identify any errors you feel that Pedro Inc. may have made with respect to the entries shown in the problem.
b. Prepare any correcting entries as of December 31, 2012, assuming the books have not yet been closed.

Ethics Challenge

Jack Phelps is the controller for Jayhawk Corporation. Jayhawk has numerous held-to-maturity investments. About 18 months ago, the company had significant amounts of idle cash that were invested in 16%, 10-year Delta Inc. bonds. Management's intent was to hold the bonds until maturity. Jack is preparing the year-end financial statements. In accounting for investments, he knows he must review the fair values of the investments. Since the bonds were purchased, Delta Inc.'s success has declined significantly and it may go into receivership. Jack earns a bonus each year that is calculated as a percent of the net income of the corporation.

EC 18-1

Required
1. Will Jack's bonus be affected in any way by a revaluation of the debt securities?
2. What criteria should Jack consider when reviewing the fair value of investments?
3. Are there any likely checks in the corporation to review how Jack has treated the securities for year-end?

Focus on Financial Statements

FFS 18-1

Delta Corporation showed the following adjusted trial balance at its year-end, December 31, 2011:

DELTA CORPORATION Adjusted Trial Balance December 31, 2011 (000s)	
Account	**Balance[1]**
Accounts payable	96
Accounts receivable	71
Accumulated amortization—equipment	76
Allowance for doubtful accounts	8
Cash	70
Cash dividends	40
Common shares	100
Cost of goods sold	395
Earnings from investment in Tildon Inc.[2]	40
Equipment	101
Fees earned	160
Held-to-maturity—Investment—Delta Inc. bonds, due 2021	56
Income tax expense	52
Income taxes payable	7
Interest expense	5
Investment income	134
Investment in Tildon Inc. shares[2]	238
Merchandise inventory	28
Notes payable, due March 2016	74
Operating expenses	218
Preferred shares	44
Prepaid rent	6
Retained earnings	82
Sales	460
Trading—Investment—Cornerstone Inc. shares	15
Unearned fees	12
Unrealized holding gains[3]	2

[1] *Assume all balances are normal.*
[2] *Delta owns 36% of the outstanding shares of Tildon Inc.*
[3] *Relates to trading investments.*

Required
Using the information provided, prepare a single-step income statement, a statement of retained earnings, and a classified balance sheet, in thousands.

Analysis component:
Explain the impact on the financial statements if the held-to-maturity investments were listed instead as trading investments.

Alcan Inc., a major global corporation in the aluminum business, reported the following in **FFS 18-2**
Note 19 of its December 31, 2005, financial statements:

Investments comprise the following elements:	(millions of $US)		
	2005	2004	2003
Companies accounted for under the equity method	1,470	1,690	724
Investments accounted for under the cost method	41	57	84

Required
1. What type of investments are those 'accounted for under the equity method'? Explain.
2. What type of investments are those 'accounted for under the cost method'? Explain.

Critical Thinking Mini Case

You are the chairman of the board of CT Inc., a Canadian-based multinational corporation, which
has excess cash totalling $75 million. The company is interested in investing some or all of this in
Delmar Corp., one of CT's key suppliers. The following statements are available for your review.

Delmar Corp. Comparative Balance Sheet Information November 30 (millions of $)		
	2011	2010
Cash	$ 15	$ 5
Accounts receivable (net)	46	10
Inventory	80	75
Prepaid rent	30	15
Capital assets (net)	300	350
Accounts payable	40	22
Accrued liabilities	35	50
Income tax payable	7	2
Common shares[1]	150	150
Retained earnings[2]	239	231

Delmar Corp. Income Statement Year ended November 30, 2011 (millions of $)		
Sales		$500
Cost of goods sold		190
Gross profit		$310
Operating expenses:		
Amortization expense[3]	$ 50	
Other expenses	170	
Total operating expenses		220
Income from operations		$ 90
Income tax expense		10
Net income		$ 80

[1] There were 25 million common shares issued and outstanding; no new shares were issued during 2010 or 2011. Market price on November 30, 2011: $8.50 per share

[2] Dividends totalling $72 million were declared and paid during 2011.

[3] Delmar Inc. uses straight-line amortization; no capital assets have been purchased or sold since 2003.

Required
Using the elements of critical thinking described on the inside front cover, comment.

Reporting and Analyzing Cash Flows

Flying High

Calgary-based WestJet Airlines Ltd. is Canada's leading low-fare airline. It realized a 32% increase in revenues from the year ended December 31, 2004, to December 31, 2005, with a corresponding $41 million increase in net income. In order to satisfy this growth in its business, WestJet used $661 million of cash for aircraft additions plus another $46 million for other capital asset additions during 2005. The main sources of this cash were the issuance of debt and common shares: specifically, $256 million of long-term debt plus $21 million in common shares. So what is WestJet's secret? Prudent cash management.

WestJet's director of treasury Derek Payne says, "As the airline industry by nature is highly cyclical and capital intensive, it is imperative that airlines keep sufficient cash reserves on hand to fund day-to-day operations. Through the use of a mixture of debt, equity, and lease financing, WestJet has utilized appropriate levels of leverage to finance the growth of the airline, without sacrificing the overall strength of its balance sheet. Continuous monitoring of cash flow along with current and projected key financial ratios ensures the company plans financing options prudently. In addition, the strength of WestJet's balance sheet allows for a range of low-cost financing options and allows the company to secure future financing with ease."

In other words, Derek Payne and his colleagues at WestJet ensure cash flow strategies for the uncertainties of tomorrow are planned for today to keep WestJet flying high!

www.westjet.ca

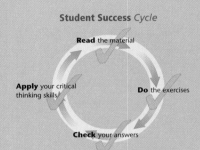

Student Success *Cycle*

Read the material

Apply your critical thinking skills

Do the exercises

Check your answers

CRITICAL THINKING CHALLENGE

How does debt financing affect cash flow? How does equity financing affect cash flow? What effect does debt versus equity financing have on the strength of the balance sheet?

---

learning objectives

LO1 | Explain the purpose and importance of cash flow information.

LO2 | Distinguish among operating, investing, and financing activities.

LO3 | Identify and disclose non-cash investing and financing activities.

LO4 | Describe and prepare the cash flow statement.

LO5 | Calculate cash flows from operating activities using the indirect method.

LO6 | Determine cash flows from both investing and financing activities.

*APPENDIX 19A

*LO7 | Calculate cash flows from operating activities using the direct method.

chapter preview

Profitability is a primary goal of most managers, but it is not the only goal. A company cannot achieve or maintain profits without careful management of cash. Managers and other users of information pay close attention to a company's cash position and the transactions affecting cash. Information about these transactions is reported in the cash flow statement. This chapter explains how we prepare, analyze, and interpret a cash flow statement using the indirect method that is entrenched in practice, although the direct method is recommended by the *CICA Handbook*. It also discusses the importance of cash flow information for predicting future performance and making managerial decisions. Developing cash flow strategies based upon an understanding of the cash flow statement is especially important, as described by Derek Payne, WestJet's director of treasury, in the opening article.

Basics of Cash Flow Reporting

This section describes the basics of cash flow reporting including its purpose, measurement, classification, format, and preparation.

Purpose of the Cash Flow Statement

The purpose of the **cash flow statement** (CFS) is to report detailed information about the major cash receipts (inflows) and cash payments (outflows) during a period. This includes separately identifying the cash flows related to operating, investing, and financing activities.

LO1 | Explain the purpose and importance of cash flow information.

The cash flow statement helps financial statement users evaluate the liquidity and solvency of an enterprise and assess the enterprise's ability to generate cash from internal sources, to repay its liabilities, and to reinvest and make distributions to owners.

We can examine balance sheets at the beginning and end of a year to determine by how much cash has changed, but the cash flow statement gives the details about individual cash flows that helps users answer questions such as:

- How does a company obtain its cash?
- Where does a company spend its cash?
- What is the change in the cash balance?

The cash flow statement addresses these important questions by summarizing, classifying, and reporting a company's periodic cash inflows and outflows; it is an analytical tool used to assess, evaluate, and analyze performance for decision making.

Importance of Cash Flows

Information about cash flows, and its inflows and outflows, can influence decision makers in important ways. For instance, we look more favourably at a company that is financing its expenditures with cash from operations than one that does it by selling its capital assets P. 136. Information about cash flows helps users decide whether a company has enough cash to:

- pay its existing debts as they mature,
- meet unexpected obligations,
- pursue unexpected opportunities
- plan day-to-day operating activities, and
- make long-term investment decisions.

There are many striking examples of how careful analysis and management of cash flows has led to improved financial stability. ACE Aviation Holdings Inc., the successor company to Air Canada, took the business from a bankruptcy protection situation to a much improved net income of $258 million and corresponding $675 million cash inflow from operating activities for the year ended December 31, 2005.

Measuring Cash Flows

The cash flow statement details the difference between the beginning and ending balances of cash and *cash equivalents*. While we continue to use the terms *cash flows* and *cash flow statement*, we must remember that both terms refer to cash and cash equivalents.

A **cash equivalent**[1] is an investment that must be:

1. readily convertible to a known amount of cash, and
2. sufficiently close to its maturity date P. 519 so its market value is not significantly affected by interest rate changes.

In most cases cash and cash equivalents include cash and temporary investments[2] of three months or less from the date of acquisition. Share investments are not included as cash equivalents because their values are subject to risk of changes in market prices. Cash subject to restrictions that prevent its use for current purposes, such as compensating balances, is also excluded from cash equivalents. Classifying short-term, highly liquid investments as cash equivalents is based on the idea that companies make these investments to earn a return on idle cash balances, yet they can be converted into cash quickly.

Classifying Cash Flows

LO² | Distinguish among operating, investing, and financing activities.

All individual cash receipts and payments (except cash paid/received for the purchase/sale of cash equivalents) are classified and reported on the statement as operating, investing, or financing activities. A net cash inflow (source) occurs when the receipts in a category exceed the payments. A net cash outflow (use) occurs when the payments in a category exceed receipts.

Operating Activities

Operating activities are the principal revenue generating activities of the enterprise.[3] They include the cash effects of transactions that determine net income. But not all items in income, such as unusual gains and losses, are operating activities. We discuss these exceptions later in the chapter.

Examples of **operating activities** are the production and purchase of merchandise, the sale of goods and services to customers, and administrative expenses of the business. Changes in current assets and current liabilities are normally the result of operating activities. Exhibit 19.1 lists the more common cash inflows and outflows from operating activities.

---

[1] *CICA Handbook* section 1540, "Cash Flow Statements (CFS)," was issued in June 1998 to replace the previously required "Statement of Changes in Financial Position (SCFP)." The revised section is based on International Accounting Standard 7—Cash Flow Statements. The *CICA Handbook* defines cash equivalents as, "short-term, highly liquid investments that are readily convertible to known amounts of cash and which are subject to an insignificant risk of changes in value."

[2] In recent years, cash equivalents have been determined net of short-term borrowings. Short-term borrowings will no longer be deducted.

[3] *CICA Handbook*, section 1540, par. 06.

Cash Inflows	Cash Outflows
From customers' cash sales	To employees for salaries and wages
From collection on credit sales	To suppliers for goods and services
From cash dividends received	To governments for taxes and fines
From borrowers for interest	To lenders for interest
From suppliers for refunds	To customers for refunds
From lawsuit settlements	To charities

Exhibit 19.1

Cash Flows from Operating Activities

Investing Activities

Investing activities include:

a. purchase and sale of capital assets,

b. purchase and sale of investments, other than cash equivalents, and

c. lending and collecting on loans (receivables).

Changes in long-term assets are normally caused by investing activities. Exhibit 19.2 lists examples of cash flows from investing activities. Proceeds from collecting the principal P. 519 amounts of loans deserve special attention. If the loan results from sales to customers, its cash receipts are classified as operating activities whether short-term or long-term. But if the loan results from a loan to another party, then its cash receipts from collecting the principal of the note are classified as an investing activity. Collection of interest on a loan, however, is not reported as an investing activity but rather as an operating activity.

Cash Inflows	Cash Outflows
From selling long-term productive assets	To purchase long-term productive assets
From selling equity investments	To purchase equity investments
From selling debt investments	To purchase debt investments
From collecting principal on loans	To make loans
From selling (discounting) of loans	

Exhibit 19.2

Cash Flows from Investing Activities*

Investing activities exclude transactions in trading securities.

Financing Activities

Financing activities are those that affect a company's owners and creditors. They include (a) obtaining cash from issuing debt and repaying the amounts borrowed, and (b) obtaining cash from or distributing cash to owners. Transactions with creditors that affect net income are classified as operating activities. For example, interest expense on a company's debt is classified as an operating rather than a financing activity because interest is deducted as an expense in calculating net income. Also, cash payments to settle credit purchases of merchandise, whether on account or by note, are operating activities because they are more related to a company's ongoing operations. Changes in long-term debt and equity and short-term debt not involving operating activities are normally a result of financing activities. Exhibit 19.3 lists examples of cash flows from financing activities.

Cash Inflows	Cash Outflows
From issuing its own shares	To pay cash dividends to shareholders
From issuing bonds and notes	To repurchase shares
From issuing short- and long-term liabilities	To repay cash loans
	To pay withdrawals by owners

Exhibit 19.3

Cash Flows from Financing Activities

Non-Cash Investing and Financing Activities

LO3 | Identify and disclose non-cash investing and financing activities.

Companies sometimes enter into direct exchange transactions in which non-current balance sheet items are exchanged but cash is not affected. Yet because of their importance and the full disclosure principle P. 348, these important non-cash investing and financing activities are disclosed in a note to the cash flow statement. One example of such a transaction is the purchase of long-term assets by giving a long-term note payable. Exhibit 19.4 lists some transactions that are disclosed as non-cash investing and financing activities.[4]

Exhibit 19.4

Examples of Non-Cash Investing and Financing Activities

- Retirement of debt by issuing shares.
- Conversion of preferred shares P. 744 to common shares.
- Purchase of long-term asset by issuing note payable.
- Exchange of non-cash assets for other non-cash assets.
- Purchase of non-cash assets by issuing shares or debt.
- Declaration and issuance of share dividend.

To illustrate, let's assume Burton Company purchases machinery for $12,000 by paying cash of $5,000 and trading in old machinery with a market value of $7,000. The cash flow statement reports only the $5,000 cash outflow for the purchase of machinery. This means the $12,000 investing transaction is only partially described in the body of the cash flow statement. Yet this information is potentially important to users in that it changes the makeup of assets.

Companies disclose non-cash investing and financing activities not reported in the body of the cash flow statement in either (1) a note, or (2) a separate schedule attached to the statement. In the case of Burton Company, it could either describe the transaction in a note or include a small schedule at the bottom of its statement that lists the $12,000 asset investment along with financing of $5,000 and a $7,000 trade-in of old machinery.

JUDGEMENT CALL

Answer—p. 956

Community Activist

You are a community activist trying to raise public awareness of pollution emitted by a local manufacturer. The manufacturer complains about the high costs of pollution controls and points to its recent $4 million annual loss as evidence. But you also know its net cash flows were a positive $8 million this past year. How are these results possible?

Format of the Cash Flow Statement

LO4 | Describe and prepare the cash flow statement.

Accounting standards require companies to include a cash flow statement in a complete set of financial statements. Refer to the cash flow statement that forms part of WestJet's complete set of financial statements in Appendix I at the end of the textbook.

Exhibit 19.5 shows us the usual format that reports cash inflows and cash outflows from three activities: operating, investing, and financing. The statement explains how transactions affect the beginning-of-period cash (and cash equivalents) balance to produce its end-of-period balance.

---

[4] *CICA Handbook*, section 1540, par. 47.

Company Name
Cash Flow Statement
Period Covered

Cash flows from operating activities:

[List of individual inflows and outflows]

Net cash inflow (outflow) from operating activities .... $ ###

Cash flows from investing activities:

[List of individual inflows and outflows]

Net cash inflow (outflow) from investing activities ....   ###

Cash flows from financing activities:

[List of individual inflows and outflows]

Net cash inflow (outflow) from financing activities ....   ###

Net increase (decrease) in cash (and cash equivalents) .... $ ###

Cash (and cash equivalents) balance at beginning of period ....   ###

Cash (and cash equivalents) balance at end of period .... $ ###

Note disclosure of *non-cash investing and financing transactions*, for example, "Note 4. Purchased new equipment by issuing bonds"

Exhibit 19.5

Format of the Cash Flow Statement

CHECKPOINT   Read Apply Do Check

1. Does a cash flow statement disclose payments of cash to purchase cash equivalents? Does it disclose receipts of cash from selling cash equivalents?

2. Identify the categories of cash flows reported separately on the cash flow statement.

3. Identify the category for each of the following cash flow activities: (a) purchase of equipment for cash; (b) payment of wages; (c) issuance of common shares for cash; (d) receipt of cash dividends from share investment; (e) collection of cash from customers; (f) issuance of bonds for cash.

Do: QS 19-1, QS 19-2, QS 19-3, QS 19-4

Preparing the Cash Flow Statement

The information we need to prepare a cash flow statement comes from:

- comparative balance sheets at the beginning and end of the period,
- an income statement for the period, and
- a careful analysis of additional information.

Preparation of a cash flow statement involves five steps:

1. Calculate the net increase or decrease in cash and cash equivalents;

2. Calculate and report net cash inflows (outflows) from operating activities using either the
   a. indirect method or
   b. direct method.

3. Calculate and report net cash inflows (outflows) from investing activities.

4. Calculate and report net cash inflows (outflows) from financing activities.

5. Calculate net cash flow by combining net cash inflows (outflows) from operating, investing, and financing activities and then prove it by adding it to the beginning cash balance to show it equals the ending cash balance.

Non-cash investing and financing activities are disclosed in a note to the statement or in a separate schedule to the statement, as shown at the bottom of Exhibit 19.5.

The remaining sections of this chapter explain these important steps in preparing the cash flow statement using the 2011 income statement of Genesis Corp. along with its December 31, 2010 and 2011, balance sheets shown in Exhibit 19.6. Our objective with the cash flow statement is to explain the increase or decrease in cash during 2011.

Exhibit 19.6

Financial Statements

In addition to providing its income statement and comparative balance sheet, Genesis Corp. also discloses additional information about year 2011 transactions:

a. All accounts payable balances result from merchandise purchases.

b. Capital assets costing $70,000 are purchased by paying $10,000 cash and issuing $60,000 of bonds payable.

c. Capital assets with an original cost of $30,000 and accumulated amortization of $12,000 are sold for $12,000 cash. This yields a $6,000 loss.

d. Proceeds from issuing 3,000 common shares are $15,000.

e. Paid $18,000 to retire bonds with a book value of $34,000. This yields a $16,000 gain from bond retirement.

f. Cash dividends of $14,000 are declared and paid.

GENESIS CORP.
Income Statement
For Year Ended December 31, 2011

Sales		$590,000
Cost of goods sold	$300,000	
Wages and other operating expenses	216,000	
Interest expense	7,000	
Income taxes expense	15,000	
Amortization expense	24,000	(562,000)
Loss on sale of capital assets		(6,000)
Gain on retirement of bonds		16,000
Net income		$ 38,000

GENESIS CORP.
Balance Sheet
December 31, 2011 and 2010

	2011	2010
Assets		
Current assets:		
Cash	$ 17,000	$ 12,000
Accounts receivable	60,000	40,000
Merchandise inventory	84,000	70,000
Prepaid expenses	6,000	4,000
Total current assets	$167,000	$126,000
Long-term assets:		
Capital assets	$250,000	$210,000
Less: Accumulated amortization	(60,000)	(48,000)
Total assets	$357,000	$288,000
Liabilities		
Current liabilities:		
Accounts payable	$ 35,000	$ 40,000
Interest payable	3,000	4,000
Income taxes payable	22,000	12,000
Total current liabilities	$ 60,000	$ 56,000
Long-term liabilities:		
Bonds payable	90,000	64,000
Total liabilities	$150,000	$120,000
Shareholders' Equity		
Contributed capital:		
Common shares	$ 95,000	$ 80,000
Retained earnings	112,000	88,000
Total shareholders' equity	207,000	168,000
Total liabilities and shareholders' equity	$357,000	$288,000

1. Calculate the Net Increase or Decrease in Cash

The increase or decrease in cash equals the current period's cash balance minus the prior period's cash balance. This is the *bottom line* figure for the cash flow statement and is a helpful check on the accuracy of our work. To illustrate, the summarized cash account of Genesis Corp. in Exhibit 19.7 shows a net increase in cash of $5,000 for the year ended December 31, 2011 ($17,000 balance, Dec. 31, 2011, less the $12,000 balance, Dec. 31, 2010).

Summarized Cash Account			
Balance, Dec. 31/10	12,000		
Receipts from customers	570,000	319,000	.................Payments for merchandise
Proceeds from asset sales	12,000		Payments for wages and
Proceeds from share issuance	15,000	218,000	..............................operating expenses
		8,000	................................Interest payments
		5,000	....Tax payments
		10,000	...........................Payments for assets
		18,000	...............Payments to retire bonds
		14,000	...........................Dividend payments
Balance, Dec. 31/11	17,000		

Exhibit 19.7

Summarized Cash Account

2. Calculate and Report Net Cash Inflows (Outflows) from Operating Activities

On the income statement, net income is calculated using accrual basis accounting P. 133. Accrual basis accounting recognizes revenues when earned and expenses when incurred. But revenues and expenses do not necessarily coincide with the receipt and payment of cash. Both the *indirect* and *direct* methods convert accrual net income to the same amount of cash provided by operating activities. The CICA recommends and encourages the use of the direct method because it provides greater detail regarding operating cash flows.

The **indirect method** calculates the net cash inflows (outflows) from operating activities by adjusting accrual net income to a cash basis. The indirect method reports the necessary adjustments to reconcile net income to net cash inflows (outflows) from operating activities.

The **direct method** separately lists each major item of operating cash receipts (such as cash received from customers) and each major item of operating cash payments (such as cash paid for merchandise). The cash payments are subtracted from cash receipts to determine the net cash inflows (outflows) from operating activities. The operating activities section is a restatement of net income from an accrual basis (as reported on the income statement) to a cash basis.

Although the direct method is *recommended* by the CICA, the indirect method is used by most companies because the direct method is not *required*. We therefore illustrate the indirect method in this chapter by preparing the operating activities section of the cash flow statement for Genesis. The direct method will be demonstrated in Appendix 19A.

Extend Your Knowledge

SSC

19-1

Indirect Method of Reporting Operating Cash Flows

We draw on the financial statements of Genesis Corp. in Exhibit 19.6 to illustrate application of the indirect method. The indirect method of reporting begins with net income of $38,000 for Genesis and then adjusts it to get net cash inflows (outflows)

LO⁵ | Calculate cash flows from operating activities using the indirect method.

from operating activities. Exhibit 19.8 highlights the results of the indirect method of reporting operating cash flows for Genesis. The net cash inflows from operating activities are $20,000. This amount is the same as that for the direct method of reporting operating cash flows detailed in Appendix 19A (see Exhibit 19A.1). *The two methods always yield the same net cash inflows (outflows) from operating activities.* Only the calculations and presentation are different.

Exhibit 19.8

Cash Flow Statement—Indirect Method of Reporting Operating Cash Flows

Genesis Corp. Cash Flow Statement For Year Ended December 31, 2011		
Cash flows from operating activities:		
Net income..		$38,000
Adjustments to reconcile net income to net cash provided by operating activities:		
Increase in accounts receivable.................................		(20,000)
Increase in merchandise inventory............................		(14,000)
Increase in prepaid expenses		(2,000)
Decrease in accounts payable....................................		(5,000)
Decrease in interest payable		(1,000)
Increase in income taxes payable..............................		10,000
Amortization expense..		24,000
Loss on sale of capital assets		6,000
Gain on retirement of bonds		(16,000)
Net cash inflow from operating activities		$20,000
Cash flows from investing activities:		
Cash received from sale of capital assets	$12,000	
Cash paid for purchase of capital assets....................	(10,000)	
Net cash inflow from investing activities		2,000
Cash flows from financing activities:		
Cash received from issuing shares	$15,000	
Cash paid to retire bonds...	(18,000)	
Cash paid for dividends	(14,000)	
Net cash outflow from financing activities.................		(17,000)
Net increase in cash		$ 5,000
Cash balance at beginning of 2011		12,000
Cash balance at end of 2011		$17,000

The indirect method adjusts net income for three types of adjustments:

1. Adjustments for changes in non-cash current assets and current liabilities relating to operating activities.

2. Adjustments to income statement items involving operating activities that do not affect cash inflows or outflows during the period.

3. Adjustments to eliminate gains and losses resulting from investing and financing activities (those not part of operating activities).

This section describes each of these three types of adjustments in applying the indirect method.

Adjustments for Changes in Non-Cash Current Assets

Changes in non-cash current assets are normally the result of operating activities. Under the indirect method for reporting operating cash flows:

Decreases in non-cash current assets are added to net income.

Increases in non-cash current assets are subtracted from net income.

To demonstrate, we now look at the individual non-cash current assets of Genesis as shown in Exhibit 19.6.

Accounts Receivable   Accounts Receivable of Genesis *increased* $20,000 in the period, from a beginning balance of $40,000 to an ending balance of $60,000. This increase implies Genesis collected less cash than its reported sales amount for this period. It also means some of these sales were in the form of accounts receivable, leaving Accounts Receivable with an increase. This lesser amount of cash collections compared with sales is reflected in the Accounts Receivable account as shown here:

Accounts Receivable			
Balance, Dec. 31/10	40,000		
Sales, 2011	590,000	570,000	= Collections
Balance, Dec. 31/11	60,000		

This $20,000 increase in Accounts Receivable is subtracted from net income as part of our adjustments to get net cash inflows from operating activities. Subtracting it adjusts sales to the cash receipts amount.

Merchandise Inventory   Merchandise Inventory *increased* $14,000 in the period, from a beginning balance of $70,000 to an ending balance of $84,000. This increase implies Genesis had a greater amount of cash purchases than goods sold this period. This greater amount of cash purchases ended up in the form of inventory, resulting in an inventory increase. This greater amount of cash purchases compared to the amount subtracted from income as cost of goods sold is reflected in the Merchandise Inventory account increase:

Merchandise Inventory			
Balance, Dec. 31/10	70,000		
Purchases =	314,000	300,000	Cost of goods sold
Balance, Dec. 31/11	84,000		

The $14,000 increase in inventory is subtracted from net income as part of our adjustments to get net cash inflows from operating activities.

Prepaid Expenses   Prepaid Expenses *increased* $2,000 in the period, from a beginning balance of $4,000 to an ending balance of $6,000. This increase implies Genesis' cash payments exceeded its operating expenses incurred this period. These larger cash payments ended up increasing the amount of prepaid expenses. This is reflected in the Prepaid Expenses account:

Prepaid Expenses			
Balance, Dec. 31/10	4,000		
Payments =	218,000		
		216,000	Wages and other operating expenses
Balance, Dec. 31/11	6,000		

This $2,000 increase in prepaid expenses is subtracted from net income as part of our adjustments to get net cash inflows from operating activities. Subtracting it adjusts operating expenses to the cash payments amount.

Adjustments for Changes in Current Liabilities

Changes in current liabilities P. 209 are normally the result of operating activities. Under the indirect method for reporting operating cash flows:

> **Increases in current liabilities are added to net income.**

> **Decreases in current liabilities are subtracted from net income.**

To demonstrate, we now analyze the individual current liabilities of Genesis as shown in Exhibit 19.6.

Accounts Payable   Accounts Payable of Genesis *decreased* $5,000 in the period, from a beginning balance of $40,000 to an ending balance of $35,000. This decrease implies its cash payments exceeded its merchandise purchases by $5,000 for the period. This larger amount for cash payments compared to purchases is reflected in the Accounts Payable account:

Accounts Payable			
		40,000	Balance, Dec. 31/10
Payments =	319,000	314,000	Purchases
		35,000	Balance, Dec. 31/11

The $5,000 decrease in Accounts Payable is subtracted from net income as part of our adjustments to get net cash inflows from operating activities.

Interest Payable   Interest Payable *decreased* $1,000 in the period, from a beginning balance of $4,000 to an ending balance of $3,000. This decrease indicates cash payments for interest exceeded interest expense for the period by $1,000. This larger cash payment compared to the reported interest expense is reflected in the Interest Payable account:

Interest Payable			
		4,000	Balance, Dec. 31/10
Interest paid =	8,000	7,000	Interest expense
		3,000	Balance, Dec. 31/11

The $1,000 decrease in Interest Payable is subtracted from net income as part of our adjustments to get net cash inflows from operating activities.

Income Taxes Payable   Income Taxes Payable *increased* $10,000 in the period, from a beginning balance of $12,000 to an ending balance of $22,000. This increase implies the amount owed for income taxes exceeded the cash payments for the period by $10,000. This smaller cash payment compared to income taxes owed is reflected in the Income Taxes Payable account:

Income Taxes Payable			
		12,000	Balance, Dec. 31/10
Income taxes paid =	5,000	15,000	Income taxes expense
		22,000	Balance, Dec. 31/11

The $10,000 increase in income taxes payable is added to net income as part of our adjustments to get net cash inflows from operating activities.

Adjustments for Operating Items Not Providing or Using Cash

The income statement usually includes certain expenses that do not reflect cash outflows in the period. Examples are amortization of capital assets, amortization of bond discount, and bad debts expense. The indirect method for reporting operating cash flows requires that:

Expenses with no cash outflows are added back to net income.

To see this logic, recall that items such as amortization and bad debts are recorded with debits to expense accounts and credits to non-cash accounts. There is no cash effect in these entries. Yet because items such as amortization expense are proper deductions in calculating accrual income, we need to add them back to net income when calculating net cash flows from operations. Adding them back cancels their deductions.

Similarly, when net income includes revenues that do not reflect cash inflows in the period, the indirect method for reporting operating cash flows requires that:

Revenues with no cash inflows are subtracted from net income.

For example, a sale on credit is recorded as a debit to accounts receivable and a credit to sales. This transaction increases net income yet there is no cash inflow. Therefore, we need to subtract transactions with no cash inflows from accrual net income to determine the actual cash generated from (or used in) operating activities.

We now look at the individual operating items of Genesis that fit this category and do not provide or use cash.

Amortization   Amortization expense P. 136 is the only operating item for Genesis that does not affect cash flows in the period. Our discussion indicates that we must add $24,000 amortization expense back to net income as part of our adjustments to get net cash inflows from operating activities.

Adjustments for Non-Operating Items

The income statement sometimes includes losses that are not part of operating activities. Examples are a loss from sale of a capital asset and a loss from retirement of a bond payable. Under the indirect method for reporting operating cash flows:

Non-operating losses are added back to net income.

To see the logic, consider items such as a capital asset sale and bond retirement. We record these transactions by recognizing the cash, removing capital asset or bond accounts, and recognizing the loss or gain. The cash received or paid is not part of operating activities but is recorded under either investing or financing activities. There is no operating cash flow effect. But because the non-operating loss is a deduction in calculating accrual income, we need to add it back to net income when calculating the net cash flow effect from operations. Adding it back cancels the deduction.

Similarly, when net income includes gains that are not part of operating activities, under the indirect method for reporting operating cash flows:

Non-operating gains are subtracted from net income.

These net income adjustments are part of calculations to get net cash provided by operating activities. We now look at the individual non-operating items of Genesis.

Loss on Sale of Capital Assets   Genesis reports a $6,000 loss on sale of capital assets in its income statement. This loss is a proper deduction in calculating net income, but it is *not part of operating activities*. Instead, a sale of capital assets is part of investing activities. This means the $6,000 non-operating loss is added back to net income as part of our adjustments to get net cash inflows from operating activities. Adding it back cancels the recorded loss. Earlier in the chapter we explained how the cash inflow from the capital asset sale was reported in investing activities.

Gain on Retirement of Bonds   There is a $16,000 gain on retirement of bonds reported in the income statement of Genesis. This gain is properly included in net income, but it is *not part of operating activities*. This means the $16,000 non-operating gain is subtracted from net income as part of our adjustments to get net cash inflows from operating activities. Subtracting it cancels the recorded gain. Earlier in the chapter we describe how the cash outflow to retire the bond was reported in financing activities.

While the calculations in determining net cash inflows (outflows) from operating activities are different for the indirect and direct methods, the results are identical. Both methods yield the same $20,000 figure for net cash inflows (outflows) from operating activities; see Exhibits 19.8 (indirect method) and 19A.1 (direct method). An approach used to prepare a cash flow statement is a detailed T-account analysis. A spreadsheet can also be used to organize information needed to prepare a cash flow statement. Both of these alternatives are described online in the Student Success Centre.

Extend Your Knowledge

SSC

19-2 & 19-3

DID YOU KNOW?

Cash or Income

The difference between net income and operating cash flows can be large. For example, Alcan reported a net income of $129 million for the year ended December 31, 2005, but operating cash flows were $1,655 million. Alcan is a Canadian company that reports in U.S. dollars.

CHECKPOINT   Read   Apply   Do   Check

4. Is the direct or indirect method of reporting operating cash flows more informative? Explain. Which method is more common in practice?

5. Determine the net cash inflows (outflows) from operating activities using the following data:

Net income	$74,900
Decrease in accounts receivable	4,600
Increase in inventory	11,700
Decrease in accounts payable	1,000
Loss on sale of equipment	3,400
Payment of dividends	21,500

6. Why are expenses such as amortization added to net income when cash flow from operating activities is calculated by the indirect method?

7. A company reports net income of $15,000 that includes a $3,000 gain on the sale of capital assets. Why is this gain subtracted from net income in calculating cash flow from operating activities using the indirect method?

Do: QS 19-5, QS 19-6, QS 19-7, QS 19-8

mid-chapter demonstration problem

Read
Apply   Do
Check

Mitchell Corporation Comparative Balance Sheet Information		
Assets	Dec. 31, 2011	Dec. 31, 2010
Cash	$ 15,000	$ 20,000
Accounts receivable	23,000	25,000
Merchandise inventory.......................	37,000	34,000
Prepaid expenses	6,000	8,000
Long-term investments	39,000	40,000
Capital assets	191,000	170,000
Accumulated amortization	(31,000)	(25,000)
Total assets.......................................	$280,000	$272,000
Liabilities and Shareholders' Equity		
Accounts payable...............................	$ 38,000	$ 30,000
Accrued liabilities	68,000	65,000
Bonds payable	100,000	90,000
Common shares..................................	40,000	37,000
Retained earnings	34,000	50,000
Total liabilities and shareholders' equity	$280,000	$272,000

Mitchell Corporation Income Statement For Year Ended December 31, 2011	
Sales...	$250,000
Cost of goods sold...	165,000
Gross profit	$ 85,000
Operating expenses..	40,000
Operating income before taxes	$ 45,000
Gain on sale of investment	8,000
Income before taxes	$ 53,000
Income taxes..	14,800
Net income	$ 38,200

Additional information:

a. Amortization expense of $6,000 is included in operating expenses.

b. There were no gains or losses other than the $8,000 gain on sale of investment reported on the income statement.

Required

Prepare the operating activities section of the cash flow statement for the year ended December 31, 2011, using the indirect method.

Analysis component:

What is the significance of *net income* versus *net cash inflow from operations*?

solution to *Mid-Chapter Demonstration Problem* _____

Net income...	$38,200
Adjustments:	
Amortization	$6,000
Gain on sale of investment	(8,000)
Decrease in accounts receivable[1]	2,000
Increase in merchandise inventory[2] ...	(3,000)
Decrease in prepaid expenses[3]	2,000
Increase in accounts payable[4]	8,000
Increase in accrued liabilities[5]	3,000
Net cash inflow from operations	$48,200

[1] 23,000 − 25,000 = 2,000 decrease
[2] 37,000 − 34,000 = 3,000 increase
[3] 6,000 − 8,000 = 2,000 decrease
[4] 38,000 − 30,000 = 8,000 increase
[5] 68,000 − 65,000 = 3,000 increase

Analysis component:

The *net income* comes from the income statement, which is prepared using accrual accounting; transactions are recorded when they occur regardless of whether cash is received or paid. For example, a credit sale increases net income but does not affect cash. The *net cash inflow from operations* represents the actual cash generated from operating activities; it is the accrual basis net income adjusted to a cash basis net income.

3. Cash Flows from Investing Activities

LO6 | Determine cash flows from both investing and financing activities.

The third major step in preparing the cash flow statement is to calculate and report net cash flows from investing activities. We normally do this by identifying changes in all non-current asset accounts. Changes in these accounts are then analyzed using available information to determine their effect, if any, on cash. Results of this analysis are reported in the investing activities section of the statement. *Reporting of investing activities is identical under the direct method and indirect method.*

Investing activities include transactions such as those listed in Exhibit 19.2. Information to calculate cash flows from investing activities is usually taken from beginning and ending balance sheets and from the income statement. Information provided earlier in the chapter about the transactions of Genesis reveals it both purchased and sold capital assets during the period. Both transactions are investing activities.

Capital Asset Transactions

We use a three-step process in determining net cash inflows (outflows) from investing activities: (1) identify changes in investing-related accounts; (2) explain these changes using reconstruction analysis; (3) report cash flow effects.

For capital assets, we need to deal with both the capital asset account and its related accumulated amortization account. Comparative balance sheet information for these accounts is in Exhibit 19.6. The first step reveals a $40,000 increase in capital assets from $210,000 to $250,000, and a $12,000 increase in accumulated amortization from $48,000 to $60,000. We need to explain these changes.

The second step begins by reviewing ledger accounts and any additional information at our disposal. A capital asset account is affected by both purchases and sales of capital assets. An accumulated amortization account is increased by amortization and reduced by removing accumulated amortization on asset disposals. Items (b) and (c) from the additional information reported with Exhibit 19.6 on page 942 for Genesis are relevant for these accounts. To explain changes in these accounts and to help us understand the cash flow effects, we prepare *reconstructed entries*. A reconstructed entry is our reproduction of an entry from a transaction; *it is not the actual entry made by the preparer*. Item (b) reports that Genesis purchased capital assets costing $70,000 by issuing $60,000 in bonds payable to the seller and paying $10,000 in cash. The reconstructed entry for our analysis of item (b) is:

Capital Assets..	70,000	
Bonds Payable..		60,000
Cash		**10,000**

This entry reveals a $10,000 cash outflow for assets purchased. It also reveals a non-cash investing and financing transaction involving $60,000 bonds given up for $60,000 of capital assets.

Item (c) on page 942 reports that Genesis sold capital assets costing $30,000 (with $12,000 of accumulated amortization) for cash received of $12,000, resulting in a loss of $6,000. The reconstructed entry for item (c) is:

Cash...	**12,000**	
Accumulated Amortization...	12,000	
Loss on Sale of Capital Assets	6,000	
Capital Assets		30,000

This entry reveals a $12,000 cash inflow for assets sold. The $6,000 loss is calculated by comparing the asset book value to the cash received, and does not reflect any cash inflow or outflow.

We can also reconstruct the entry for amortization expense using information from the income statement:

Amortization Expense	24,000	
Accumulated Amortization		24,000

This entry shows that amortization expense results in no cash flow effects.

These reconstructed entries are reflected in the ledger accounts for both capital assets and accumulated amortization.

Capital Assets					Accumulated Amortization, Capital Assets			
Balance, Dec. 31/10	210,000						48,000	Balance, Dec. 31/10
Purchases	70,000	30,000	Sale		Sale	12,000	24,000	Amort. expense
Balance, Dec. 31/11	250,000						60,000	Balance, Dec. 31/11

In performing an actual cash flow analysis we have the entire ledger and additional information at our disposal. Here, for brevity, we are given the additional information for reconstructing accounts and verifying that our analysis of the investing-related accounts is complete.

The third step is to make the necessary disclosures on the cash flow statement. Disclosure of the two cash flow effects in the investing section of the statement appears as (also see Exhibit 19.8):

Genesis Corp.
Cash Flow Statement
For Year Ended December 31, 2011

Cash flows from investing activities:
Cash received from sale of capital assets $12,000
Cash paid for purchase of capital assets...................................... (10,000)

Note: Non-cash investing and financing activity
During the period capital assets were acquired with issuance of $60,000 of bonds.

The $60,000 portion of the purchase described in item (b) on page 942 and financed by issuance of bonds is a non-cash investing and financing activity and can be reported in a note to the statement as shown above.

We have now reconstructed these accounts by explaining how the beginning balances of both accounts are affected by purchases, sales, and amortization in yielding their ending balances.

CHECKPOINT

8. Equipment costing $80,000 with accumulated amortization of $30,000 is sold at a loss of $10,000. What is the cash receipt from the sale? In what category of the cash flow statement is it reported?

Do: QS 19-9, QS 19-10

4. Cash Flows from Financing Activities

The fourth step in preparing the cash flow statement is to calculate and report net cash flows from financing activities. We normally do this by identifying changes in all notes payable (current and non-current), non-current liabilities, and equity accounts. These accounts include Long-Term Debt, Notes Payable, Bonds Payable, Owner's Capital, Common Shares, and Retained Earnings. Changes in these accounts are then analyzed using available information to determine their effect, if any, on cash. Results of this analysis are reported in the financing activities section of the statement. *Reporting of financing activities is identical under the direct method and indirect method.*

Financing activities include those described in Exhibit 19.3. Information provided on page 942 about the transactions of Genesis reveals four transactions involving financing activities. We already analyzed one of these, the $60,000 issuance of bonds payable to purchase capital assets as a non-cash investing and financing activity. The remaining three transactions are retirement of bonds, issuance of common shares P. 739, and payment of cash dividends. We again use a three-step process in determining net cash inflows (outflows) from financing activities: (1) identify changes in financing-related accounts; (2) explain these changes using reconstruction analysis; and (3) report cash flow effects.

Bonds Payable Transactions

Comparative balance sheet information from Exhibit 19.6 for bonds payable is our starting point. The first step reveals an increase in bonds payable from $64,000 to $90,000. We need to explain this change.

The second step is to review the Bonds Payable ledger account and any additional information available. Item (e) on page 942 is relevant to bonds payable and reports that bonds with a carrying value of $34,000 are retired for $18,000 cash, resulting in a $16,000 gain. The reconstructed entry for our analysis of item (e) is:

Bonds Payable	34,000	
Gain on Retirement of Debt..		16,000
Cash		**18,000**

This entry reveals an $18,000 cash outflow for retirement of bonds. It also shows a $16,000 gain from comparing the bonds payable carrying value with the cash received. This gain does not reflect any cash inflow or outflow.

Item (b) also involves bonds payable. It reports that Genesis purchased capital assets costing $70,000 by issuing $60,000 in bonds payable to the seller and paying $10,000 in cash. We already reconstructed its entry for our analysis of investing activities. Recall it increased bonds payable by $60,000 and is reported as a non-cash investing and financing transaction. These reconstructed entries are reflected in the ledger account for bonds payable:

Bonds Payable			
		64,000	Balance, Dec. 31/10
Retired bonds	34,000	60,000	Issued bonds
		90,000	Balance, Dec. 31/11

The third step is to make the necessary disclosures on the cash flow statement. Disclosure of the cash flow effect from the bond retirement in the financing section of the statement appears as (also see Exhibit 19.8):

Genesis Corp.
Cash Flow Statement
For Year Ended December 31, 2011

Cash flows from financing activities:
Cash paid to retire bonds..   (18,000)

Common Shares Transactions

We use comparative balance sheet information from Exhibit 19.6 for the first step in analyzing the Common Shares account. This reveals an increase in common shares from $80,000 to $95,000. We need to explain this change.

Our second step is to review the Common Shares ledger account and any additional information available. Item (d) on page 942 reports that it issued 3,000 common shares for $5 per share. The reconstructed entry for our analysis of item (d) is:

Cash..	**15,000**	
Common shares		15,000

This entry reveals a $15,000 cash inflow from the issuance of shares. This reconstructed entry is reflected in the ledger account for common shares:

Common Shares		
	80,000	Balance, Dec. 31/10
	15,000	Issued shares
	95,000	Balance, Dec. 31/11

The third step is to make the necessary disclosure on the cash flow statement. Disclosure of the cash flow effect from share issuance in the financing section of the statement appears as (also see Exhibit 19.8):

Genesis Corp.
Cash Flow Statement
For Year Ended December 31, 2011

Cash flows from financing activities:
Cash received from issuing shares $15,000

Retained Earnings Transactions

The first step in analyzing the Retained Earnings account is to review comparative balance sheet information from Exhibit 19.6. We need to explain the increase in retained earnings from $88,000 to $112,000.

Our second step is to analyze the Retained Earnings account and any additional information available. Item (f) on page 942 reports that cash dividends of $14,000 were paid. The reconstructed entry for our analysis of item (f) is:

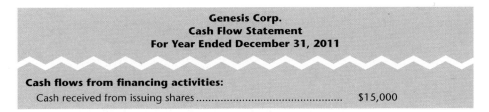

This entry reveals a $14,000 cash outflow to pay cash dividends.[5] We must also remember that retained earnings is affected by net income from the income statement. Net income was already dealt with under the operating section of the cash flow statement. This reconstruction analysis is reflected in the ledger account for retained earnings:

Retained Earnings			
		88,000	Balance, Dec. 31/10
Cash dividend	14,000	38,000	Net income
		112,000	Balance, Dec. 31/11

The third step is to make the necessary disclosure on the cash flow statement. Disclosure of the cash flow effect from the cash dividend appears in the financing section of the statement as (also see Exhibit 19.8):

Genesis Corp.
Cash Flow Statement
For Year Ended December 31, 2011

Cash flows from financing activities:
Cash paid for dividends .... (14,000)

---

[5] *Share dividends* are a non-cash financing activity.

5. Proving Cash Balances

We have now explained all of the cash inflows and outflows of Genesis, along with one non-cash investing and financing transaction. Our analysis has reconciled changes in all non-cash balance sheet accounts. The fifth and final step in preparing the statement is to report the beginning and ending cash balances and prove the net change in cash as explained by operating, investing, and financing net cash flows. This step is highlighted below for Genesis:

Genesis Corp.
Cash Flow Statement
For Year Ended December 31, 2011

Cash flows from operating activities:

Cash flows from financing activities:

Cash received from issuing shares	$15,000	
Cash paid to retire bonds	(18,000)	
Cash paid for dividends	(14,000)	
Net cash outflow from financing activities		(17,000)
Net increase in cash		$ 5,000
Cash balance at beginning of 2011		12,000
Cash balance at end of 2011		$17,000

The statement shows that the $5,000 net increase in cash from $12,000 at the beginning of the period to $17,000 at the end is reconciled by net cash flows from operating ($20,000 inflow), investing ($2,000 inflow), and financing ($17,000 outflow) activities.

9. Identify which of the following represent financing activities:

a. Paid $1,000 of interest on the bank loan.

b. Purchased $25,000 of equipment by paying cash of $25,000.

c. Issued a $75,000 bond payable.

d. Issued $50,000 of common shares in exchange for land valued at $50,000.

e. Made a $10,000 payment on the bank loan.

Do: QS 19-11, QS 19-12, QS 19-13, QS 19-14

Reporter

You are a newspaper reporter covering a workers' strike. Management grants you an interview and complains about recent losses and negative cash flows. It shows you financial numbers revealing a recent $600,000 net loss that included a $930,000 extraordinary loss. It also shows you the company's total net cash outflow of $550,000, which included net cash outflows of $850,000 for investing activities and $350,000 for financing activities. What is your initial reaction to management's complaints?

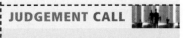

Answer—p. 956

Summary --

LO1 Explain the purpose and importance of cash flow information. The main purpose of the cash flow statement is to report the major cash receipts and cash payments for a period. This includes identifying cash flows as relating to operating, investing, or financing activities. Many business decisions involve evaluating cash flows. Users' evaluations include focusing on the transactions that cause cash inflows (outflows).

LO2 Distinguish among operating, investing, and financing activities. Operating activities include the cash effects of transactions and events that determine net income. Investing activities include: (a) purchase and sale of long-term assets, (b) purchase and sale of short-term investments other than cash equivalents, and (c) lending and collecting on loans. Financing activities include: (a) getting cash from issuing debt and repaying the amounts borrowed, and (b) getting cash from or distributing cash to owners and giving owners a return on investment.

LO3 Identify and disclose non-cash investing and financing activities. For external reporting, a company must supplement its cash flow statement with a description of its non-cash investing and financing activities. These activities are disclosed either in a note to the statement or in a separate schedule usually reported at the bottom of the statement.

LO4 Describe and prepare the cash flow statement. The cash flow statement reports cash inflows and outflows in one of three categories: operating, investing, or financing activities. Preparation of a cash flow statement involves five steps: (1) calculate the net increase or decrease in cash, (2) calculate net cash inflows (outflows) from operating activities, (3) calculate net cash inflows (outflows) from investing activities, (4) calculate net cash inflows (outflows) from financing activities; and (5) report the beginning and ending cash balances and prove the change is explained by operating, investing, and financing net cash flows. Non-cash investing and financing activities are disclosed either in a note or in a separate schedule to the statement.

LO5 Calculate cash flows from operating activities using the indirect method. The indirect method for reporting net cash inflows (outflows) from operating activities starts with net income and then adjusts it for three items: (1) changes in non-cash current assets and current liabilities related to operating activities, (2) revenues and expenses not creating cash inflows (outflows), and (3) gains and losses from investing and financing activities.

LO6 Determine cash flows from both investing and financing activities. Cash flows from both investing and financing activities are determined by identifying the cash flow effects of transactions affecting each balance sheet account related to these activities.

---

guidance answers to   **JUDGEMENT CALL**

Community Activist

There could be several explanations for an increase in net cash flows when a loss is reported. Possibilities include: (1) early recognition of expenses relative to revenues generated (research and development), (2) valuable long-term cash sales contracts not yet recognized in income, (3) issuances of debt or shares to finance expansion, (4) selling of assets, (5) delayed cash payments, and (6) prepayment on sales. Your analysis of this manufacturer needs to focus on the components of both net income and net cash flows, and their implications for future performance.

Reporter

Your initial course of action is to verify management's claims about poor performance. A $600,000 loss along with a $550,000 decrease in net cash flows seemingly supports its claim. But closer scrutiny reveals a different picture. You calculate its cash flow from operating activities at a positive $650,000, calculated as [?] − $850,000 − $350,000 = $(550,000). You note also that net income before the extraordinary loss is a positive $330,000, calculated as [?] − $930,000 = $(600,000). This is powerful information to open discussions. A serious and directed discussion is likely to reveal a far more positive picture of this company's financial performance.

guidance answers to CHECKPOINT

1. No. The cash flow statement reports changes in the sum of cash plus cash equivalents. It does not report transfers between cash and cash equivalents.

2. The three categories of cash inflows and outflows are operating activities, investing activities, and financing activities.

3. **a.** Investing

   b. Operating

   c. Financing

   d. Operating

   e. Operating

   f. Financing

4. The direct method is most informative because it separately lists each major item of operating cash receipts and each major item of operating cash payments. The indirect method is used most often.

5. $74,900 + $4,600 − $11,700 − $1,000 + $3,400 = $70,200

6. In the calculation of net income, expenses such as amortization are subtracted because these expenses do not require current cash outflows. Therefore, adding these expenses back to net income eliminates non-cash items from the net income number, converting it to a cash basis.

7. In the process of reconciling net income to net cash inflows (outflows) from operating activities, a gain on the sale of capital assets is subtracted from net income because a sale of capital assets is not an operating activity; it is an investing activity.

8. $80,000 − $30,000 − $10,000 = $40,000

   The $40,000 cash receipt is reported as an investing activity.

9. *c, e*

demonstration problem

Umlauf Inc.'s balance sheet information, income statement, and additional information follow.

Umlauf Inc. Comparative Balance Sheet Information		
	December 31	
	2011	**2010**
Cash	$ 43,050	$ 23,925
Accounts receivable	34,125	39,825
Merchandise inventory	156,000	146,475
Prepaid expenses	3,600	1,650
Equipment	135,825	146,700
Accumulated amortization	61,950	47,550
Accounts payable	31,475	33,750
Dividends payable	-0-	4,500
Bonds payable	10,000	37,500
Common shares	208,750	168,750
Retained earnings	60,425	66,525

Umlauf Inc. Income Statement For Year Ended December 31, 2011		
Sales		$380,850
Cost of goods sold	$222,300	
Other operating expenses	134,850	
Amortization expense	25,500	(382,650)
Loss on sale of equipment		(3,300)
Net loss		$ 5,100

Umlauf Inc.
Cash Flow Statement
For Year Ended December 31, 2011

Cash flows from operating activities:

Net loss	$ (5,100)	
Adjustments:		
Amortization	25,500	
Loss on sale of equipment	3,300	
Decrease in accounts receivable[1(a)]	5,700	
Increase in merchandise inventory[1(a)]	(9,525)	
Increase in prepaid expenses[1(a)]	(1,950)	
Decrease in accounts payable[1(b)]	(2,275)	
Net cash inflow from operations		$15,650
Cash flows from investing activities:		
Cash received from sale of equipment[2]	$ 6,975	
Cash paid for equipment[2]	(10,500)	
Net cash outflow from investing activities		(3,525)
Cash flows from financing activities:		
Cash paid for dividends[3]	$ (5,500)	
Cash paid to retire bonds payable[4]	(27,500)	
Cash received from issuing common shares[4]	40,000	
Net cash inflow from financing activities		7,000
Net increase in cash		$19,125
Cash balance at beginning of year		23,925
Cash balance at end of year		$43,050

[1(a)] Calculation from the solution, part 1(a)
[1(b)] Calculation from the solution, part 1(b)
[2] Calculation from the solution, part 2
[3] Calculation from the solution, part 3(b)
[4] Calculation from the solution, part 4

Note to Student: Remember that the cash flow statement explains the change in the Cash account balance from one period to the next.

Umlauf Inc.
Comparative Balance Sheet Information

	December 31	
Assets	**2011**	**2010**
Cash	$ 43,050	$ 23,925
Accounts receivable	34,125	39,825
Merchandise inventory	156,000	146,475
Prepaid expenses	3,600	1,650
Equipment	135,825	146,700
Accumulated amortization	(61,950)	(47,550)
Total assets	$310,650	$311,025
Liabilities and Shareholders' Equity		
Accounts payable	31,475	33,750
Dividends payable	-0-	4,500
Bonds payable	10,000	37,500
Common shares	208,750	168,750
Retained earnings	60,425	66,525
Total liabilities and shareholders' equity	$310,650	$311,025

Analysis component:

The 2011 cash flow statement reports a $5,500 cash outflow regarding dividends even though dividends declared in 2011 were $1,000. This is because there was a $4,500 balance in Dividends Payable representing unpaid dividends declared in the previous year. An analysis of Dividends Payable showed that the $4,500 unpaid balance from 2010 plus the $1,000 of dividends declared in 2011 were paid during 2011; this resulted in a total cash outflow of $5,500.

APPENDIX 19A

Cash Flows from Operating Activities—Direct Method

Direct Method of Reporting Operating Cash Flows

We calculate cash flows from operating activities under the direct method by adjusting accrual based income statement items to a cash basis. The usual approach is to adjust income statement accounts related to operating activities for changes in their related balance sheet accounts:

*LO7 Calculate cash flows from operating activities using the direct method.

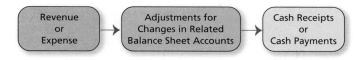

In preparing the operating section for Genesis Corp. using the direct method as highlighted in Exhibit 19A.1, we first look at its cash receipts and then its cash payments drawing on the income statement and balance sheets in Exhibit 19.6.

Genesis Corp. Cash Flow Statement For Year Ended December 31, 2011		
Cash flows from operating activities:		
Cash received from customers	$570,000	
Cash paid for merchandise	(319,000)	
Cash paid for wages and other operating expenses	(218,000)	
Cash paid for interest	(8,000)	
Cash paid for taxes	(5,000)	
Net cash inflow from operating activities		$20,000
Cash flows from investing activities:		
Cash received from sale of capital assets	$ 12,000	
Cash paid for purchase of capital assets	(10,000)	
Net cash inflow from investing activities		2,000
Cash flows from financing activities:		
Cash received from issuing shares	$ 15,000	
Cash paid to retire bonds	(18,000)	
Cash paid for dividends	(14,000)	
Net cash outflow from financing activities		(17,000)
Net increase in cash		$ 5,000
Cash balance at beginning of 2011		12,000
Cash balance at end of 2011		$17,000

Note: Non-cash investing and financing activity

During the period capital assets were acquired with issuance of $60,000 of bonds.

Exhibit 19A.1

Cash Flow Statement—Direct Method of Reporting Operating Cash Flows

Operating Cash Receipts

Exhibit 19.6 and the additional information from Genesis identify only one potential cash receipt—that of sales to customers. This section starts with sales from the income statement and adjusts it as necessary to give us cash received from customers.

Cash Received from Customers   If all sales are for cash, the amount of cash received from customers is equal to sales. But when sales are on account, we must adjust the amount of sales revenue for the change in Accounts Receivable. For example, an increase in Accounts Receivable must be deducted from sales because sales revenue relating to Accounts Receivable has been recorded for which the cash has not yet been received. This is shown in Exhibit 19A.2.

Exhibit 19A.2

Formula to Calculate Cash Received from Customers—Direct Method

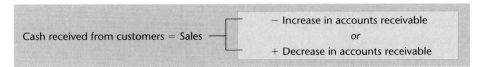

It is often helpful to use *account analysis* for this purpose. To illustrate, the T-account below reconstructs the cash receipts and payments. The balance sheet in Exhibit 19.6 shows that the beginning balance is $40,000 and the ending balance is $60,000. The income statement shows sales of $590,000.

Accounts Receivable			
Balance, Dec. 31/10	40,000		
Sales	590,000	570,000	= Collections
Balance, Dec. 31/11	60,000		

Cash receipts from customers are $570,000, calculated as $40,000 + $590,000 − [?] = $60,000. As summarized in Exhibit 19A.2, this calculation can be rearranged to express cash received as equal to sales of $590,000 less a $20,000 increase in accounts receivable.

The cash flow statement for Genesis in Exhibit 19A.1 reports the $570,000 cash received from customers as a cash inflow from operating activities.

Other Cash Receipts   While cash receipts of Genesis are limited to collections from customers, we sometimes see other types of cash receipts involving rent, interest, and dividends. We calculate cash received from these items by subtracting an increase or adding a decrease in the related receivable.

Operating Cash Payments

Exhibit 19.6 and the additional information from Genesis identify four operating expenses. We analyze each of these expenses to calculate its operating cash payment for the cash flow statement.

Cash Paid for Merchandise   We calculate cash paid for merchandise by analyzing both cost of goods sold and merchandise inventory. When the balances of Merchandise Inventory and Accounts Payable change, we must adjust cost of goods sold for changes in both of these accounts to calculate cash paid for merchandise. This adjustment has two steps. First, we use the change in the balance of Merchandise Inventory along with the amount of cost of goods sold to calculate cost of purchases for the period. An increase in inventory implies that we bought more than was sold and we add the increase in inventory to cost of goods sold to calculate cost of purchases. A decrease in inventory implies that we bought less than was sold and we subtract the decrease in inventory from cost of goods sold to calculate cost of purchases.

The second step uses the change in the balance of Accounts Payable along with the amount of cost of purchases to calculate cash paid for merchandise. A decrease in Accounts Payable implies that we paid for more goods than were acquired this period and we add the Accounts Payable change to cost of purchases to calculate cash paid for merchandise. An increase in Accounts Payable implies that we paid for less than the amount of goods acquired, and we subtract the Accounts Payable change from purchases to calculate cash paid for merchandise.

First, we use account analysis of merchandise inventory to calculate cost of purchases. We do this by reconstructing the Merchandise Inventory account:

Merchandise Inventory

Balance, Dec. 31/10	70,000		
Purchases =	314,000	300,000	Cost of goods sold
Balance, Dec. 31/11	84,000		

The beginning balance is $70,000, and its ending balance is $84,000. The income statement shows cost of goods sold is $300,000. We can then determine the cost of purchases as $314,000 (equal to cost of goods sold of $300,000 plus the $14,000 increase in inventory).

Our second step is to calculate cash paid for merchandise by adjusting purchases for the change in accounts payable. Reconstructing Accounts Payable:

Accounts Payable

		40,000	Balance, Dec. 31/10
Payments =	319,000	314,000	Purchases
		35,000	Balance, Dec. 31/11

This account shows us that its beginning balance of $40,000 plus purchases of $314,000 minus an ending balance of $35,000 gives us cash paid of $319,000 (or $40,000 + $314,000 − [?] = $35,000). Alternatively, we can express cash paid for merchandise as equal to purchases of $314,000 plus the $5,000 decrease in accounts payable.

We summarize the two-step adjustment to cost of goods sold to calculate cash paid for merchandise in Exhibit 19A.3.

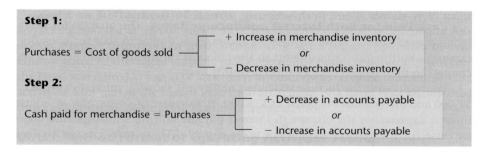

Step 1:

Purchases = Cost of goods sold —
+ Increase in merchandise inventory
or
− Decrease in merchandise inventory

Step 2:

Cash paid for merchandise = Purchases —
+ Decrease in accounts payable
or
− Increase in accounts payable

Exhibit 19A.3

Two Steps to Calculate Cash Paid for Merchandise—Direct Method

Exhibit 19A.1 shows that the $319,000 cash paid by Genesis for merchandise is reported on the cash flow statement as a cash outflow for operating activities.

Cash Paid for Wages and Operating Expenses (Excluding Amortization and Other Non-Cash Expenses)   The income statement of Genesis shows wages and other operating expenses of $216,000 (see Exhibit 19.6). To calculate cash paid for wages and other operating expenses, we adjust this amount for changes in their related balance sheet accounts.

QS 19-14
Cash flow statement preparation
(indirect method)
LO4, 5, 6

Use the following information to prepare a cash flow statement for the year ended October 31, 2011, using the indirect method.

Oma Inc. Comparative Balance Sheet Information October 31		
	2011	**2010**
Cash..	$25	$35
Accounts receivable (net)	40	45
Merchandise inventory...........................	15	6
Capital assets (net)*..............................	75	25
Accounts payable	6	2
Accrued liabilities..................................	2	5
Long-term notes payable.......................	40	50
Common shares	95	38
Retained earnings**..............................	12	16

Oma Inc. Income Statement Year ended October 31, 2011		
Sales..		$140
Operating expenses:		
Amortization expense	$ 5	
Other expenses....................................	139	
Total operating expenses		144
Net income (loss)		$ (4)

*$55 of capital assets were purchased during 2011; there were no
  sales of capital assets.
**No dividends were declared or paid during 2011.

*QS 19-15
Calculating cash paid for other
expenses (direct method)
LO7

Clendenning Ltd. had operating expenses of $968,000 during 2011. Accrued liabilities at the beginning of the year were $27,000, and were $36,000 at the end of the year. Assuming all debits and credits to accrued liabilities are related to operating expenses, what was the total cash paid for operating expenses during 2011?

*QS 19-16
Cash flows from operating activities
(direct method)
LO7

Middleton Inc. had sales revenue of $805,000 during 2011. Accounts receivable at the beginning of the year were $20,000 but were $24,000 at the end of the year. How much cash was collected from customers during 2011?

*QS 19-17
Cash flows from operating activities
(direct method)
LO7

Daum Inc. collected $737,000 cash from customers during 2011. If beginning accounts receivable were $41,000 and credit sales totalled $705,000, what was the balance in ending accounts receivable?

Use the following information to answer questions (a) through (c) below.

*QS 19-18
Calculating cash from operating activities (direct method)
LO7

Drinkwater Inc.
Comparative Balance Sheet Information

	June 30	
	2011	**2010**
Cash	$ 42,900	$17,500
Accounts receivable (net)	26,000	21,000
Inventory	43,400	48,400
Prepaid expenses............................	3,200	2,600
Furniture	55,000	60,000
Accumulated amortization	9,000	5,000
Accounts payable	8,000	11,000
Wages payable	5,000	3,000
Income taxes payable......................	1,200	1,800
Notes payable (long-term)	15,000	35,000
Common shares.............................	115,000	90,000
Retained earnings...........................	17,300	3,700

Drinkwater Inc.
Income Statement
For Year Ended June 30, 2011

Sales		$234,000
Cost of goods sold..............................		156,000
Gross profit..		$ 78,000
Operating expenses:		
Amortization expense......................	$19,300	
Other expenses	28,500	
Total operating expense		47,800
Income from operations......................		$ 30,200
Income taxes		12,300
Net income..		$ 17,900

a. How much cash was received from customers during 2011?
b. How much cash was paid for merchandise during 2011?
c. How much cash was paid for operating expenses during 2011?

Use the following information to answer questions (a) through (e) below.

*QS 19-19
Calculating cash from operating activities (direct method)
LO7

Delmar Corp.
Comparative Balance Sheet Information
November 30

	2011	**2010**
Cash...	$ 25	$ 5
Accounts receivable (net)	46	20
Inventory.....................................	80	95
Prepaid rent	30	15
Capital assets (net)	300	320
Accounts payable	40	22
Accrued liabilities.................................	35	50
Income tax payable	7	2
Common shares	100	100
Retained earnings.................................	299	281

Delmar Corp.
Income Statement
Year ended November 30, 2011

Sales..		$500
Cost of goods sold................................		190
Gross profit		$310
Operating expenses:		
Amortization expense	$ 20	
Other expenses..................................	200	
Total operating expenses		220
Income from operations		$ 90
Income tax expense		10
Net income		$ 80

a. How much cash was received from customers during 2011?
b. How much cash was paid for merchandise during 2011?
c. How much cash was paid for operating expenses during 2011?
d. How much cash was paid for income taxes during 2011?
e. Calculate the cash inflows (outflows) from operating activities using the direct method.

An asterisk (*) identifies assignment material based on Appendix 19A.

Exercises

Exercise 19-1

Classifying transactions on cash flow statement (indirect method)

LO5

The following transactions occurred during the year. Assuming that the company uses the indirect method of reporting cash provided by operating activities, indicate the proper accounting treatment for each transaction listed below by placing an X in the appropriate column.

	Cash Flow Statement			Note Describing Non-Cash Investing and Financing Activities	Not Reported on Statement or in Footnote
	Operating Activities	Investing Activities	Financing Activities		
a. Land was purchased by issuing common shares.	_____	_____	_____	_____	_____
b. Recorded amortization expense.................	_____	_____	_____	_____	_____
c. Income tax payable increased by 15% from prior year.	_____	_____	_____	_____	_____
d. Declared and paid a cash dividend.	_____	_____	_____	_____	_____
e. Paid cash to purchase merchandise inventory.	_____	_____	_____	_____	_____
f. Sold equipment at a loss.	_____	_____	_____	_____	_____
g. Accounts receivable decreased during the year.	_____	_____	_____	_____	_____

Exercise 19-2

Adjustments to derive cash flow from operations (indirect method)

LO5

	Adjust by	
	Adding	Subtracting
1. Changes in non-cash current assets:		
a. Increases..	_____	_____
b. Decreases	_____	_____
2. Changes in current liabilities		
a. Increases..	_____	_____
b. Decreases	_____	_____
3. Amortization of capital assets	_____	_____
4. Amortization of intangible assets	_____	_____
5. Interest expense:		
a. Bond premium amortized...........................	_____	_____
b. Bond discount amortized............................	_____	_____
6. Sale of non-current asset:		
a. Gain	_____	_____
b. Loss	_____	_____

Indicate by an X in the appropriate column whether an item is added or subtracted to derive cash flow from operating activities.

The account balances for the non-cash current assets and current liabilities of Jacobsen Corporation are as follows:

December 31		
	2011	2010
Accounts receivable	$ 90,000	$ 74,000
Inventory	64,000	84,000
Prepaid expenses	38,000	34,000
Totals	$192,000	$192,000
Accounts payable	$ 60,000	$ 46,000
Salaries payable	18,000	26,000
Interest payable	34,000	28,000
Totals	$112,000	$100,000

During 2011, Jacobsen Corporation reported amortization expense of $40,000. All purchases and sales are on account. Net income for 2011 was $180,000.

Required
1. Prepare the operating activities section of the cash flow statement using the indirect method.
2. Explain why cash flows from operating activities are different from net income.

Ingrid Inc.'s 2011 income statement showed the following: net income, $364,000; amortization expense, building, $45,000; amortization expense, equipment, $8,200; and gain on sale of capital assets, $7,000. An examination of the company's current assets and current liabilities showed that the following changes occurred because of operating activities: accounts receivable decreased $18,100; merchandise inventory decreased $52,000; prepaid expenses increased $3,700; accounts payable decreased $9,200; other payables increased $1,400. Use the indirect method to calculate the cash flow from operating activities.

(in thousands)	Fraser	Spern	Travis
Cash inflow (outflow) from operating activities	$ 80,000	$ 70,000	$ (34,000)
Cash inflow (outflow) from investing activities:			
Proceeds from sale of capital assets			36,000
Purchase of capital assets	(38,000)	(35,000)	
Cash inflow (outflow) from financing activities:			
Proceeds from issuance of debt			33,000
Repayment of debt	(7,000)		
Net increase (decrease) in cash	35,000	35,000	35,000
Average assets	800,000	650,000	400,000

Required
Which of the three competing corporations is in the strongest relative position as indicated by their comparative cash flow statements?

Exercise 19-3
Cash flows from operating activities (indirect method)
LO5

Check figure:
1. Net cash inflow from operating activities, $232,000

Exercise 19-4
Cash flows from operating activities (indirect method)
LO5

Check figure:
1. Net cash inflow from operating activities, $468,800

Exercise 19-5
Analyzing cash inflows and outflows
LO5, 6

Exercise 19-6
Cash flows from operating
activities (indirect method)
LO5

Use the following income statement and information about changes in non-cash current assets and current liabilities to present the cash flows from operating activities using the indirect method:

Yu Corp.
Income Statement
Year ended May 31, 2011

Sales..	$950
Cost of goods sold................................	480
Gross profit	$470
Operating expenses:	
Amortization expense .... $ 75	
Other expenses................................... 380	
Total operating expenses	455
Loss on sale of long-term investment	30
Income (loss) from operations	$ (15)
Income tax expense	-0-
Net income (loss)	$ (15)

Changes in current asset and current liability accounts during the year were as follows:

Accounts receivable	$45 decrease
Inventory	18 increase
Prepaid insurance	2 increase
Accounts payable...	10 increase
Accrued liabilities	5 decrease

Exercise 19-7
Preparation of cash flow statement
(indirect method)
LO2, 5, 6

Check figure:
Net cash inflow from operating
activities, $138,960

Required
Use the Morpurgo Ltd. information given below to prepare a cash flow statement for the year ended June 30, 2011, using the indirect method.
a. A note is retired at carrying value.
b. The only changes affecting retained earnings during 2011 are net income and cash dividends paid.
c. New equipment is acquired during 2011 for $58,600.
d. The gain on sale of equipment costing $48,600 during 2011 is $2,000.
e. Prepaid expenses and wages expense affect other expenses on the income statement.
f. All sales and purchases of merchandise were on credit.

Morpurgo Ltd.
Comparative Balance Sheet Information

	June 30	
	2011	2010
Cash	$ 75,800	$ 35,000
Accounts receivable (net).................	80,000	62,000
Inventory	66,800	96,800
Prepaid expenses	5,400	5,200
Equipment..	130,000	120,000
Accumulated amortization	28,000	10,000
Accounts payable.............................	26,000	32,000
Wages payable.................................	7,000	16,000
Income taxes payable	2,400	3,600
Notes payable (long-term)...............	40,000	70,000
Common shares...............................	230,000	180,000
Retained earnings	24,600	7,400

Morpurgo Ltd.
Income Statement
For Year Ended June 30, 2011

Sales		$655,000
Cost of goods sold................................		399,000
Gross profit..		$256,000
Operating expenses:		
Amortization expense.......................	$58,600	
Other expenses	67,000	
Total operating expenses.................		125,600
Income from operations.......................		$130,400
Gain on sale of equipment...................		2,000
Income before taxes		$132,400
Income taxes		45,640
Net income..		$ 86,760

*Exercise 19-8
Cash flows from operating
activities (direct method)
LO7

Refer to the information about Morpurgo presented in Exercise 19-7. Use the direct method and prepare a cash flow statement.

An asterisk (*) identifies assignment material based on Appendix 19A.

The following occurred during the year. Assuming that the company uses the direct method of reporting cash provided by operating activities, indicate the proper accounting treatment for each item by placing an X in the appropriate column.

*Exercise 19-9
Classifying transactions on cash flow statement (direct method)
LO7

	Cash Flow Statement			Note Describing Non-Cash Investing and Financing Activities	Not Reported on Statement‌ or in Footnote
	Operating Activities	Investing Activities	Financing Activities		
a. Long-term bonds payable were retired by issuing common shares	_____	_____	_____	_____	_____
b. Surplus merchandise inventory was sold for cash..	_____	_____	_____	_____	_____
c. Borrowed cash from the bank by signing a nine-month note payable............	_____	_____	_____	_____	_____
d. Paid cash to purchase a patent..................	_____	_____	_____	_____	_____
e. A six-month note receivable was accepted in exchange for a building that had been used in operations	_____	_____	_____	_____	_____
f. Recorded amortization expense on all capital assets	_____	_____	_____	_____	_____
g. A cash dividend that was declared in a previous period was paid in the current period	_____	_____	_____	_____	_____

In each of the following cases, use the information provided about the 2011 operations of Seghal Corp. to calculate the indicated cash flow:

*Exercise 19-10
Calculating cash flows (direct method)
LO7

Case A:	Calculate cash received from customers:	
	Sales revenue...	$255,000
	Accounts receivable, January 1	12,600
	Accounts receivable, December 31	17,400
Case B:	Calculate cash paid for insurance:	
	Insurance expense	$34,200
	Prepaid insurance, January 1	5,700
	Prepaid insurance, December 31	8,550
Case C:	Calculate cash paid for salaries:	
	Salaries expense...	$102,000
	Salaries payable, January 1..	6,300
	Salaries payable, December 31	7,500

In each of the following cases, use the information provided about the 2011 operations of Clarke Inc. to calculate the indicated cash flow:

*Exercise 19-11
Calculating cash flows (direct method)
LO7

Case A:	Calculate cash paid for rent:	
	Rent expense...	$20,400
	Rent payable, January 1	4,400
	Rent payable, December 31..	3,600
Case B:	Calculate cash received from interest:	
	Interest revenue...	$68,000
	Interest receivable, January 1	6,000
	Interest receivable, December 31...	7,200
Case C:	Calculate cash paid for merchandise:	
	Cost of goods sold	$352,000
	Merchandise inventory, January 1	106,400
	Accounts payable, January 1...	45,200
	Merchandise inventory, December 31	87,600
	Accounts payable, December 31	56,000

An asterisk (*) identifies assignment material based on Appendix 19A.

*Exercise 19-12
Cash flows from operating activities (direct and indirect methods)
LO5, 7

Use the following income statement and information about changes in non-cash current assets and current liabilities to present the cash flows from operating activities using the direct method:

Bozena Inc.
Income Statement
For Year Ended December 31, 2011

Sales		$606,000
Cost of goods sold		297,000
Gross profit from sales		$309,000
Operating expenses:		
Salaries expense	$82,845	
Amortization expense	14,400	
Rent expense	12,200	
Amortization expense, patents	1,800	
Utilities expense	6,375	
Total operating expenses		117,620
Gain on sale of equipment		2,400
Income from operations		$193,780
Income taxes		4,000
Net income		$189,780

Changes in current asset and current liability accounts during the year, all of which related to operating activities, were as follows:

Accounts receivable	$13,500 increase
Merchandise inventory	9,000 increase
Accounts payable	4,500 decrease
Salaries payable	1,500 decrease

Check figure:
Net cash inflow from operating activities, $175,080

Analysis component:
Use the information above to present the cash flows from operating activities using the indirect method. Explain the differences and similarities between the direct and indirect methods.

*Exercise 19-13
Organizing the cash flow statement and supporting footnote (direct method)
LO7

Check figure:
Net cash inflow from operating activities, $81,250

Wentzell Inc.'s records contain the following information about the 2011 cash flows.

Cash and cash equivalents balance, December 31, 2010	$ 25,000
Cash and cash equivalents balance, December 31, 2011	56,250
Cash received as interest	2,500
Cash paid for salaries	17,500
Bonds payable retired by issuing common shares (there was no gain or loss on the retirement)	187,500
Cash paid to retire long-term notes payable	61,250
Cash received from sale of equipment	25,000
Cash borrowed on six-month note payable	25,000
Land purchased and financed by long-term note payable	106,250
Cash paid for store equipment	23,750
Cash dividends paid	15,000
Cash paid for income taxes	20,000
Cash received from customers	242,500
Cash paid for merchandise	126,250
Amortization expense	72,500

Required
Prepare a cash flow statement using the direct method and a note describing non-cash investing and financing activities.

The summarized journal entries below and on page 984 show the total debits and credits to the Wong Corporation's Cash account during 2011.

Required

Use the information to prepare a cash flow statement for 2011. The cash flow from operating activities should be presented according to the direct method. In the statement, identify the entry that records each item of cash flow. Assume that the beginning balance of cash was $66,600.

Analysis component:

Consult the cash flow statement you have just prepared and answer the following questions:

a. Of the three activity sections (operating, investing, or financing), which section shows the largest cash flow for the year 2011?
b. What was the purpose of the largest investing cash outflow in 2011?
c. Were the proceeds larger from issuing debt or equity in 2011?
d. Did the corporation have a net cash inflow or outflow from borrowing activity in 2011?

*Exercise 19-14
Preparation of cash flow statement (direct method)
LO7

Check figure:
Net cash inflow from operating activities, $755,200

a.	Cash..	720,000	
	Common Shares.................................		720,000
	Issued common shares for cash.		
b.	Cash..	1,200,000	
	Notes Payable		1,200,000
	Borrowed cash with a note payable.		
c.	Merchandise Inventory	240,000	
	Cash...		240,000
	Purchased merchandise for cash.		
d.	Accounts Payable..............................	600,000	
	Cash...		600,000
	Paid for credit purchases of merchandise.		
e.	Wages Expense.................................	300,000	
	Cash...		300,000
	Paid wages to employees.		
f.	Rent Expense...................................	210,000	
	Cash...		210,000
	Paid rent for buildings.		
g.	Cash..	1,500,000	
	Sales...		1,500,000
	Made cash sales to customers.		
h.	Cash..	900,000	
	Accounts Receivable		900,000
	Collected accounts from credit customers.		
i.	Machinery...	1,068,000	
	Cash...		1,068,000
	Purchased machinery for cash.		
j.	Long-Term Investments	1,080,000	
	Cash...		1,080,000
	Purchased long-term investments for cash.		
k.	Interest Expense	108,000	
	Notes Payable..................................	192,000	
	Cash...		300,000
	Paid notes and accrued interest.		
l.	Cash..	53,200	
	Dividend Revenue		53,200
	Collected dividends from investments.		

An asterisk (*) identifies assignment material based on Appendix 19A.

m.	Cash..	105,000	
	Loss on Sale of Long-Term Investments............	15,000	
	Long-Term Investments..........................		120,000
	Sold long-term investments for cash.		
n.	Cash..	360,000	
	Accumulated Amortization, Machinery............	210,000	
	Machinery.......................................		480,000
	Gain on Sale of Machinery.....................		90,000
	Sold machinery for cash.		
o.	Common Dividend Payable.............................	255,000	
	Cash..		255,000
	Paid cash dividends to shareholders.		
p.	Income Taxes Payable.....................................	240,000	
	Cash..		240,000
	Paid income taxes owed for the year.		
q.	Common Shares...	114,000	
	Cash..		114,000
	Purchased and retired common shares for cash.		

Problems

Problem 19-1A
Cash flow statement
(indirect method)
LO5, 6

Bentley Corporation's balance sheet and income statement are as follows:

Bentley Corporation
Comparative Balance Sheet Information
December 31

Assets	2011	2010
Cash	$116,000	$ 78,000
Accounts receivable	62,000	54,000
Merchandise inventory	406,000	356,000
Equipment...	222,000	198,000
Accumulated amortization...............	(104,000)	(68,000)
Total assets	$702,000	$618,000

Liabilities and Shareholders' Equity		
Accounts payable............................	$ 46,000	$ 64,000
Income taxes payable	18,000	16,000
Common shares................................	520,000	480,000
Retained earnings	118,000	58,000
Total liabilities and shareholders' equity	$702,000	$618,000

Bentley Corporation
Income Statement
For Year Ended December 31, 2011

Sales..		$1,328,000
Cost of goods sold..........................		796,000
Gross profit.....................................		$ 532,000
Operating expenses:		
Amortization expense	$ 36,000	
Other expenses...........................	334,000	
Total operating expenses.............		370,000
Income from operations		$ 162,000
Income taxes...................................		28,000
Net income		$ 134,000

Additional information regarding Bentley Corporation's activities during 2011:
a. Equipment is purchased for $24,000 cash.
b. 16,000 common shares are issued for cash at $2.50 per share.
c. Declared and paid $74,000 of cash dividends during the year.

Check figure:
Net cash inflow from operating activities, $96,000

Required
Prepare a cash flow statement for 2011 that reports the cash inflows and outflows from operating activities according to the indirect method. Show your supporting calculations.

Analysis component:
Assume that Bentley Corporation had a net loss instead of a net income. Does a net loss mean that there will always be a cash outflow from operating activities on the cash flow statement?

Refer to the information in Problem 19-1A. Other information regarding Bentley Corporation:
a. All sales are credit sales
b. All credits to accounts receivable are receipts from customers.
c. All purchases of merchandise are on credit.
d. All debits to accounts payable result from payments for merchandise.
e. Other operating expenses are cash expenses.
f. The only decrease in income taxes payable is for payment of taxes.

*Problem 19-2A
Cash flow statement
(direct method)
LO7

Required
Prepare a cash flow statement for 2011 using the direct method to report cash inflows and outflows from operating activities.

Check figure:
Net cash outflow from financing activities: $34,000

Nissen Ltd.'s comparative balance sheet information at December 31, 2011 and 2010, and its income statement for the year ended December 31, 2011, are as follows:

Problem 19-3A
Cash flow statement
(indirect method)
LO5, 6

Nissen Ltd.
Balance Sheet Information
December 31

	2011	2010	Net Change
Cash	$ 40,000	$ 20,800	$ 19,200
Temporary investments	14,400	8,000	6,400
Accounts receivable	73,600	31,200	42,400
Inventory	95,200	69,600	25,600
Long-term investment	-0-	14,400	(14,400)
Land	64,000	64,000	-0-
Building and equipment	370,400	380,000	(9,600)
Accumulated amortization	98,400	80,800	(17,600)
Accounts payable	16,600	31,500	(14,900)
Dividends payable	1,000	500	500
Bonds payable	20,000	-0-	20,000
Preferred shares	68,000	68,000	-0-
Common shares	338,400	338,400	-0-
Retained earnings	115,200	68,800	46,400

Nissen Ltd.
Income Statement
For Year Ended December 31, 2011

Sales		$720,000
Cost of goods sold		480,000
Gross profit		$240,000
Operating expenses	$110,600	
Amortization expense	34,400	
Loss on sale of equipment	3,200	
Income taxes	15,000	
Gain on sale of long-term investment	(9,600)	153,600
Net income		$ 86,400

During 2011, the following transactions occurred:
1. Purchased equipment for $16,000 cash.
2. Sold the long-term investment on January 1, 2011, for $24,000.
3. Sold equipment for $5,600 cash that had originally cost $25,600 and had $16,800 of accumulated amortization.
4. Issued $20,000 of bonds payable at face value.

Required
1. How much cash was paid in dividends?
2. Prepare a cash flow statement for Nissen Ltd. for the year ended December 31, 2011, using the indirect method.

Check figure:
Cash inflow from operating activities, $31,500

Analysis component:
The net increase in cash during 2011 for Nissen Ltd. was $25,600. Briefly explain what caused this change using the cash flow statement prepared in part 2 above.

An asterisk (*) identifies assignment material based on Appendix 19A.

*Problem 19-4A
Cash flow statement
(direct method)
LO7

Check figure:
Cash inflow from investing
activities: $13,600

Required
Refer to the information in Problem 19-3A. Prepare a cash flow statement for 2011 using the direct method to report cash inflows and outflows from operating activities.

Other information:
a. All sales are credit sales.
b. All credits to accounts receivable in the period are receipts from customers.
c. All purchases of merchandise are on credit.
d. All debits to accounts payable in the period result from payments for merchandise.
e. Other operating expenses are cash expenses.
f. Income taxes are cash expenses.

Problem 19-5A
Cash flow statement
(indirect method)
LO5, 6

Holliday Corp.'s balance sheet information and income statement are as follows:

Holliday Corp. Comparative Balance Sheet Information December 31		
	2011	**2010**
Cash	$150,850	$214,550
Accounts receivable	182,000	138,950
Merchandise inventory	766,500	707,000
Prepaid expenses	15,050	17,500
Equipment	446,600	308,000
Accumulated amortization	96,950	123,200
Accounts payable	246,750	326,550
Short-term notes payable	28,000	17,500
Long-term notes payable	262,500	150,500
Common shares	563,500	437,500
Retained earnings	363,300	330,750

Holliday Corp. Income Statement For Year Ended December 31, 2011		
Sales		$1,389,500
Cost of goods sold		700,000
Gross profit		$ 689,500
Operating expenses:		
Amortization expense	$ 52,500	
Other expenses	382,200	
Total operating expenses		434,700
Loss on sale of equipment		14,350
Income from operations		$ 240,450
Income taxes		33,950
Net income		$ 206,500

Additional information regarding Holliday's activities during 2011:
1. Loss on sale of equipment is $14,350.
2. Paid $87,850 to reduce a long-term note payable.
3. Equipment costing $131,250, with accumulated amortization of $78,750, is sold for cash.
4. Equipment costing $269,850 is purchased by paying cash of $70,000 and signing a long-term note payable for the balance.
5. Borrowed $10,500 by signing a short-term note payable.
6. Issued 7,000 common shares for cash at $18 per share.
7. Declared and paid cash dividends of $173,950.

Check figure:
Net cash inflow from operating
activities, $93,450

Required
Prepare a cash flow statement for 2011 that reports the cash inflows and outflows from operating activities according to the indirect method. Show your supporting calculations. Also prepare a note describing non-cash investing and financing activities.

Analysis component:
Merchandise Inventory, Prepaid Expenses, Long-Term Notes Payable, and Common Shares are some of the accounts that changed during 2011. Explain what transactions likely caused each of these accounts to increase and/or decrease.

An asterisk (*) identifies assignment material based on Appendix 19A.

Required

Refer to the information in Problem 19-5A. Prepare a cash flow statement for 2011 using the direct method to report cash inflows and outflows from operating activities.

Other information:
a. All sales are credit sales.
b. All credits to accounts receivable in the period are receipts from customers.
c. Purchases of merchandise are on credit.
d. All debits to accounts payable in the period result from payments for merchandise.
e. The only decrease in income taxes payable is for payment of taxes.
f. The other expenses are paid in advance and are initially debited to Prepaid Expenses.

Seghal Corporation began operations on January 1, 2010. Its post-closing trial balance at December 31, 2010 and 2011, is shown below along with some other information.

*Problem 19-6A
Cash flow statement
(direct method)
LO7

Check figure:
Net cash outflow from investing activities: $31,850

Problem 19-7A
Cash flow statement
(indirect method)
LO5, 6

Seghal Corporation Post-Closing Trial Balance (000s)

Account	2011	2010
Cash	$3,600	$2,300
Receivables	3,500	2,600
Merchandise inventory	3,200	3,800
Property, plant and equipment	3,800	3,400
Accumulated amortization	2,400	2,300
Long-term investments	2,600	2,800
Accounts payable	2,400	1,800
Accrued liabilities	400	600
Bonds payable	2,800	3,000
Common shares	3,800	3,400
Retained earnings	4,900	3,800

Seghal Corporation Income Statement For Year Ended December 31, 2011 (000s)

Revenues:		
Sales		$4,730
Expenses:		
Cost of goods sold	$1,920	
Other expenses	1,100	
Income tax expense	360	
Amortization expense	100	
Total expenses		3,480
Net income		$1,250

Other information regarding Seghal Corporation and its activities during 2011:
1. Assume all accounts have normal balances.
2. Cash dividends were declared and paid during the year.
3. There were no sales of plant assets during the year.
4. Long-term investments were sold for cash at their original cost.

Required

Using the information provided, prepare a cash flow statement (applying the *indirect* method) for the year ended December 31, 2011.

Check figure:
Net cash outflows from investing activities, $200 (thousand)

Analysis component:
a. Seghal Corporation experienced an increase in cash during 2011. Does this necessarily represent a favourable situation? Explain why or why not.
b. Explain the causes of change in Seghal's cash situation during 2011.

An asterisk (*) identifies assignment material based on Appendix 19A.

*Problem 19-8A
Cash flow statement
(direct method)
LO7

Check figure:
Net cash inflow from operating
activities: $1,450

Required

Refer to the information in Problem 19-7A. Prepare a cash flow statement for 2011 using the direct method to report cash inflows and outflows from operating activities.

Other information:
a. All accounts payable balances result from merchandise purchases.
b. All sales are credit sales.
c. All credits to accounts receivable are receipts from customers.
d. All debits to accounts payable result from payments for merchandise.
e. All other expenses are cash expenses.

Problem 19-9A
Cash flow statement
(indirect method)
LO5, 6

S&B Ibach Inc. began operations on January 1, 2010. Its post-closing trial balance at December 31, 2010 and 2011, is shown below along with some other information.

S&B Ibach Inc. Post-Closing Trial Balance (000s)		
	December 31	
Account	**2011**	**2010**
Cash..	$1,800	$1,050
Receivables..	1,750	1,200
Merchandise inventory.........................	1,700	1,900
Property, plant and equipment.............	3,100	3,300
Accumulated amortization	1,200	1,150
Accounts payable	1,200	900
Accrued liabilities	200	300
Bonds payable....................................	1,400	1,500
Common shares..................................	2,570	1,700
Retained earnings...............................	1,780	1,900

S&B Ibach Inc. Income Statement For Year Ended December 31, 2011 (000s)		
Revenues:		
Sales..		$2,750
Expenses:		
Cost of goods sold............................	$2,100	
Other expenses..................................	550	
Amortization expense	200	
Total expenses		2,850
Net loss..		$ 100

Other information regarding S&B Ibach Inc. and its activities during 2011:
1. Assume all accounts have normal balances.
2. Cash dividends were declared and paid during the year.
3. Equipment was sold for cash equal to its book value.

Check figure:
Net cash inflows from financing
activities, $750 (thousand)

Required

Using the information provided, prepare a cash flow statement (applying the *indirect* method) for the year ended December 31, 2011.

Analysis component:
Assume that the investing activities section of the cash flow statement showed a net cash outflow of $14 thousand. What could this represent? Is a net cash outflow from investing activities necessarily favourable or unfavourable? Explain.

*Problem 19-10A
Cash flow statement
(direct method)
LO7

Check figure:
Net cash outflow from operating
activities: $50 (thousand)

Required

Refer to the information in Problem 19-9A. Prepare a cash flow statement for 2011 using the direct method to report cash inflows and outflows from operating activities.

Other information:
a. All accounts payable balances result from merchandise purchases.
b. All sales are credit sales.
c. All credits to accounts receivable are receipts from customers.
d. All debits to accounts payable result from payments for merchandise.
e. All other expenses are cash expenses.

An asterisk (*) identifies assignment material based on Appendix 19A.

Soltermann Inc. began operations on January 1, 2010. Its post-closing trial balance at December 31, 2010 and 2011, is shown below along with some other information.

Problem 19-11A
Cash flow statement
(indirect method)
LO5, 6

Soltermann Inc. Post-Closing Trial Balance		
	December 31	
Account	**2011**	**2010**
Cash	$ 78,000	$ 96,000
Receivables	52,000	38,000
Merchandise inventory......................	34,000	44,000
Property, plant and equipment	288,000	238,000
Accumulated amortization	80,000	66,000
Accounts payable.............................	62,000	78,000
Accrued liabilities	14,000	8,000
Long-term notes payable	122,000	50,000
Common shares................................	62,000	10,000
Retained earnings	112,000	204,000

Soltermann Inc. Income Statement For Year Ended December 31, 2011		
Revenues:		
Sales		$784,000
Expenses and other:		
Cost of goods sold.........................	$604,000	
Other expenses..............................	194,000	
Amortization expense	32,000	
Loss on sale of plant assets.............	26,000	
Total expenses and other		856,000
Net loss..		$ 72,000

Other information regarding Soltermann Inc. and its activities during 2011:
1. Assume all accounts have normal balances.
2. Cash dividends were declared and paid during the year.
3. Plant assets were sold during the year.
4. Plant assets worth $124,000 were purchased during the year by paying cash of $40,000 and issuing a long-term note payable for the balance.

Required
Using the information provided, prepare a cash flow statement (applying the *indirect* method) for the year ended December 31, 2011.

Check figure:
Net cash outflow from investing activities, $10,000

Analysis component:
a. The cash account balance for Soltermann Inc. decreased during 2011. Is this necessarily an unfavourable situation? Explain why or why not.
b. Explain the causes of change in Soltermann's cash situation during 2011.

Required
Refer to the information in Problem 19-11A. Prepare a cash flow statement for 2011 using the direct method to report cash inflows and outflows from operating activities.

***Problem 19-12A**
Cash flow statement
(direct method)
LO7

Check figure:
Net cash outflow from operating activities: $28,000

Other information:
a. All accounts payable balances result from merchandise purchases.
b. All sales are credit sales.
c. All credits to accounts receivable are receipts from customers.
d. All debits to accounts payable result from payments for merchandise.
e. All debits and credits to accrued liabilities result from other expenses.

Alternate Problems

Problem 19-1B
Cash flow statement
(indirect method)
LO5, 6

Clendenning Inc., a software retailer, recently completed its 2011 operations. The following information is available:

Clendenning Inc. Comparative Balance Sheet Information December 31		
	2011	**2010**
Cash	$ 75,495	$ 44,520
Accounts receivable	27,195	32,550
Merchandise inventory	245,490	195,825
Equipment..	147,630	107,100
Accumulated amortization	67,620	42,840
Accounts payable.............................	53,865	49,875
Income taxes payable	6,300	9,450
Common shares...............................	289,800	231,000
Retained earnings	78,225	46,830

Clendenning Inc. Income Statement For Year Ended December 31, 2011		
Sales..		$853,650
Cost of goods sold		390,600
Gross profit		$463,050
Operating expenses:		
Amortization expense	$ 24,780	
Other expenses..............................	251,685	
Total operating expenses		276,465
Income from operations...................		$186,585
Income taxes.....................................		62,790
Net income		$123,795

Additional information regarding Clendenning's activities during 2011:
1. Equipment was purchased for $40,530 cash.
2. Issued 4,200 common shares for cash at $14 per share.
3. Declared and paid $92,400 of cash dividends during the year.

Check figure:
Net cash inflow from operating activities, $105,105

Required
Prepare a cash flow statement for 2011 that reports the cash inflows and outflows from operating activities according to the indirect method. Show your supporting calculations.

Analysis component:
The net increase in cash during 2011 for Clendenning Inc. was $30,975. Briefly explain what caused this change using the cash flow statement prepared above.

*Problem 19-2B
Cash flow statement
(direct method)
LO7

Required
Refer to the information in Problem 19-1B. Prepare a cash flow statement for 2011 using the direct method to report cash inflows and outflows from operating activities.

Check figure:
Net cash outflow from financing activities: $33,600

Other information:
a. All sales were credit sales.
b. All credits to accounts receivable in the period were receipts from customers.
c. Purchases of merchandise were on credit.
d. All debits to accounts payable were from payments for merchandise.
e. The other operating expenses were cash expenses.
f. The decrease in income taxes payable was for payment of taxes.

Arnold Ltd.'s comparative balance sheet information at December 31, 2011 and 2010, and its income statement for the year ended December 31, 2011, are as follows:

Problem 19-3B
Cash flows (indirect method)
LO5, 6

Arnold Ltd. Comparative Balance Sheet Information December 31			
	2011	**2010**	**Net Change**
Cash	$ 70,000	$ 36,400	$ 33,600
Temporary investments........	25,200	14,000	11,200
Accounts receivable..............	128,800	54,600	74,200
Inventory	166,600	121,800	44,800
Long-term investment..........	-0-	25,200	(25,200)
Land	112,000	112,000	-0-
Building and equipment.......	648,200	665,000	(16,800)
Accumulated amortization....	172,200	141,400	(30,800)
Accounts payable..................	29,800	54,000	(24,200)
Dividends payable................	1,000	2,000	(1,000)
Bonds payable......................	35,000	-0-	35,000
Preferred shares....................	119,000	119,000	-0-
Common shares.....................	592,200	592,200	-0-
Retained earnings.................	201,600	120,400	81,200

Arnold Ltd. Income Statement Year Ended December 31, 2011		
Sales		$1,260,000
Cost of goods sold..........................		840,000
Gross profit......................................		$ 420,000
Operating expenses.........................	$194,800	
Amortization expense	60,200	
Loss on sale of equipment	5,600	
Income taxes....................................	25,000	
Gain on sale of long-term investment	(16,800)	268,800
Net income		$ 151,200

During 2011, the following transactions occurred:
1. Issued $35,000 of bonds payable at face value.
2. Sold the long-term investment on January 1, 2011, for $42,000.
3. Sold equipment for $9,800 cash that had originally cost $44,800 and had $29,400 of accumulated amortization.
4. Purchased equipment for $28,000 cash.

Required
a. How much was paid in dividends during 2011?
b. Prepare a cash flow statement for Arnold Ltd. for the year ended December 31, 2011, using the indirect method.

Check figure:
Cash inflow from operating activities, $57,000

Analysis component:
Accounts Receivable increased from $54,600 to $128,800 in 2011. What transactions cause this account to change? Accounts Payable decreased during 2011. What causes this account to change?

Required
Refer to the information in Problem 19-3B. Prepare a cash flow statement for 2011 using the direct method to report cash inflows and outflows from operating activities.

Other information:
a. All sales are credit sales.
b. All credits to accounts receivable are receipts from customers.
c. All purchases of merchandise are on credit.
d. All debits to accounts payable result from payments for merchandise.
e. Other operating expenses are cash expenses.
f. Income taxes are cash expenses.

*Problem 19-4B
Cash flow statement (direct method)
LO7

Check figure:
Cash inflow from investing activities: $23,800

Problem 19-5B
Cash flow statement
(indirect method)
LO5, 6

Yahn Inc., a sporting goods retailer, recently completed its 2011 operations. Yahn Inc.'s balance sheet information and income statement follow.

Yahn Inc. Comparative Balance Sheet Information December 31		
	2011	2010
Cash	$191,100	$100,170
Accounts receivable	103,740	127,050
Merchandise inventory	636,300	686,280
Prepaid expenses	23,940	26,880
Equipment..	389,550	302,400
Accumulated amortization	152,250	130,200
Accounts payable.............................	164,430	172,830
Short-term notes payable.................	24,150	15,750
Long-term notes payable	157,500	115,500
Common shares................................	676,200	630,000
Retained earnings	170,100	178,500

Yahn Inc. Income Statement Year Ended December 31, 2011		
Sales...		$1,516,200
Cost of goods sold...........................		819,000
Gross profit......................................		$ 697,200
Operating expenses:		
Amortization expense	$ 51,240	
Other expenses...........................	549,990	
Total operating expenses.............		601,230
Loss on sale of equipment		2,940
Income from operations		$ 93,030
Income taxes		13,230
Net income		$ 79,800

Additional information regarding Yahn's activities during 2011:
1. Loss on sale of equipment is $2,940.
2. Equipment costing $71,400 is sold for $39,270.
3. Equipment is purchased by paying cash of $53,550 and signing a long-term note payable for the balance.
4. Borrowed $8,400 by signing a short-term note payable.
5. Reduced a long-term note payable by making a payment.
6. Issued 4,200 common shares for cash at $11 per share.
7. Declared and paid cash dividends.

Check figure:
Net cash inflow from operating activities, $201,810

Required
Prepare a cash flow statement for 2011 that reports the cash inflows and outflows from operating activities according to the indirect method. Show your supporting calculations. Also prepare a note describing non-cash investing and financing activities.

Analysis component:
Using the information from the cash flow statement just prepared for Yahn Inc., identify the accrual basis net income and the cash basis net income for 2011. Explain why there is a difference between the two amounts.

*Problem 19-6B
Cash flow statement
(direct method)
LO7

Check figure:
Net cash outflow from financing activities: $96,600

Required
Refer to the information in Problem 19-5B. Prepare a cash flow statement for 2011 using the direct method to report cash inflows and outflows from operating activities.

Other information:
a. All sales were credit sales.
b. All credits to accounts receivable in the period were receipts from customers.
c. Purchases of merchandise were on credit.
d. All debits to accounts payable in the period resulted from payments for merchandise.
e. The decrease in income taxes payable was for payment of taxes.
f. The other expenses were paid in advance and were initially debited to Prepaid Expenses.

Hayes Corporation began operations on January 1, 2010. Its post-closing trial balance at December 31, 2010 and 2011, is shown below along with some other information.

Problem 19-7B
Cash flow statement
(indirect method)
LO5, 6

Hayes Corporation Post-Closing Trial Balance (millions of dollars)		
	December 31	
Account	2011	2010
Cash	$ 18	$ 43
Receivables	92	124
Merchandise inventory	136	87
Property, plant and equipment	2,300	2,992
Accumulated amortization	1,233	1,375
Long-term investments	520	103
Accounts payable	106	135
Accrued liabilities	47	39
Bonds payable	400	200
Common shares	900	700
Retained earnings	380	900

Hayes Corporation Income Statement For Year Ended December 31, 2011 (millions of dollars)		
Revenues:		
Sales		$8,900
Expenses:		
Cost of goods sold	$6,500	
Other expenses	2,350	
Amortization expense	450	
Total expenses		9,300
Net loss		$ 400

Other information regarding Hayes Corporation and its activities during 2011:
1. Assume all accounts have normal balances.
2. Cash dividends were declared and paid during the year.
3. Plant assets were sold for cash equal to book value during the year.

Required
Using the information provided, prepare a cash flow statement (applying the *indirect* method) for the year ended December 31, 2011.

Check figure:
Net cash inflow from financing
activities, $280 (million)

Analysis component:
The net decrease in cash during 2011 for Hayes Corporation was $25 million. Briefly explain what caused this change using the cash flow statement prepared above.

Required
Refer to the information in Problem 19-7B. Prepare a cash flow statement for 2011 using the direct method to report cash inflows and outflows from operating activities.

*Problem 19-8B
Cash flow statement
(direct method)
LO7

Check figure:
Net cash inflow from operating
activities: $12 (million)

Other information:
a. All accounts payable balances result from merchandise purchases.
b. All sales are credit sales.
c. All credits to accounts receivable are receipts from customers.
d. All debits to accounts payable result from payments for merchandise.
e. All other expenses are cash expenses.

An asterisk (*) identifies assignment material based on Appendix 19A.

chapter preview

This chapter shows us how to use the information in financial statements to evaluate the financial performance and condition of a company. We describe the purpose of analysis, its basic building blocks, the information available, standards for comparisons, and tools of analysis. Three major analysis tools are emphasized—horizontal analysis, vertical analysis, and ratio analysis. We illustrate the application of each of these tools using Ralco Corporation's financial statements. Understanding financial statement analysis is crucial to sound business decision making.

Basics of Analysis

Financial statement analysis is the application of analytical tools to general-purpose financial statements and related data for making business decisions. It involves transforming data into useful information. Financial statement analysis reduces our reliance on hunches, guesses, and intuition. It reduces our uncertainty in decision making. But it does not lessen the need for expert judgement. Instead, it provides us with an effective and systematic basis for asking questions, finding answers, and making business decisions. This section describes the purpose of financial statement analysis, its information sources, the use of comparisons, and some issues in calculations.

Purpose of Analysis

LO¹ Describe financial statement analysis and identify its focus, standards of comparison, and tools.

The purpose of financial statement analysis is to help users make better business decisions. These users include decision makers both internal and external to the company.

Internal users P. 9 of accounting information are those individuals involved in managing and operating the company. The purpose of financial statement analysis for these users is to provide information helpful in improving the company's efficiency or effectiveness in providing products or services.

External users P. 7 of accounting information are *not* directly involved in running the company. External users rely on financial statement analysis to make better and more informed decisions in pursuing their own goals.

We can identify many examples of how financial statement analysis is used. Shareholders and creditors assess future company prospects for investing and lending decisions. A board of directors analyzes financial statements in monitoring management's decisions. Employees and unions use financial statements in labour negotiations. Suppliers use financial statements in establishing credit terms. Customers analyze financial statements in deciding whether to establish supply relationships. Public utilities set customer rates by analyzing financial statements. Auditors use financial statements in assessing the "fair presentation" of their clients' financial statement numbers. And analyst services such as *Dun & Bradstreet*, *Moody's*, and *Standard & Poor's* use financial statements in making buy–sell recommendations and setting credit ratings.

The common goal of all these users is to evaluate company performance. This includes evaluation of (1) past and current performance, (2) current financial position, and (3) future performance and risk.

Building Blocks of Analysis

Financial statement analysis focuses on one or more elements of a company's financial condition or performance. Our analysis emphasizes four areas of inquiry

—with varying degrees of importance. These four areas are described and illustrated in this chapter and are considered the building blocks of financial statement analysis.

- *Liquidity and Efficiency*—ability to meet short-term obligations and to generate revenues efficiently.

- *Solvency*—ability to generate future revenues and meet long-term obligations.

- *Profitability*—ability to provide financial rewards sufficient to attract and retain financing.

- *Market*—ability to generate positive market expectations.

Information for Analysis

We explained how decision makers need to analyze financial statements. Some of these people, such as managers and a few regulatory agencies, are able to receive special financial reports prepared to meet their needs. But most must rely on general purpose financial statements that companies publish periodically. **General purpose financial statements** include the (1) income statement, (2) balance sheet, (3) statement of retained earnings, and (4) cash flow statement, accompanied by notes related to all four statements.

General purpose financial statements are part of **financial reporting**. Financial reporting refers to the communication of relevant financial information to decision makers. It includes financial statements, but it also involves information from filings with the securities commissions, news releases, shareholders' meetings, forecasts, management letters, auditors' reports, and analyses published in annual reports. Financial reporting broadly refers to useful information for decision makers to make investment, credit, and other decisions. It should help users assess the amounts, timing, and uncertainty of future cash inflows and outflows.

Standards for Comparisons

When calculating and interpreting analysis measures as part of our financial statement analysis, we need to decide whether these measures suggest good, bad, or average performance. To make these judgements, we need standards for comparison. Standards for comparison can include:

- *Intracompany* The company under analysis provides standards for comparisons based on prior performance and relations between its financial items.

- *Competitor (or Intercompany)* One or more direct competitors of the company under analysis can provide standards for comparison. Care must be exercised, however, in making comparisons with other firms to allow for the financial statement effects that are due to different accounting methods (i.e., different inventory costing systems or different amortization methods).

- *Industry* Industry statistics can provide standards of comparison. Published industry statistics are available from several services such as *Dun & Bradstreet, Standard & Poor's,* and *Moody's.*

- *Guidelines (Rules of Thumb)* General standards of comparison can develop from past experiences.

All of these standards of comparison are useful when properly applied. Yet analysis measures taken from a selected competitor or group of competitors are often the best standards of comparison. Also, intracompany and industry measures are important parts of all analyses. Guidelines or rules of thumb should be applied with care, and then only if they seem reasonable in light of past experience and industry norms.

CHECKPOINT

1. Who are the intended users of general purpose financial statements?

2. What statements are usually included in general purpose financial statements published by corporations?

3. Which of the following are least useful as a basis for comparison when analyzing ratios and turnovers? (a) companies operating in a different economy; (b) past experience; (c) rule-of-thumb standards; (d) averages within a trade or industry.

4. What basis of comparison for ratios is usually best?

Do: QS 20-1, QS 20-2

Tools of Analysis

There are several tools of financial statement analysis. Three of the most common tools are:

- *Horizontal Analysis* Comparison of a company's financial condition and performance across time.
- *Vertical Analysis* Comparison of a company's financial condition and performance to a base amount.
- *Ratio Analysis* Determination of key relations among financial statement items.

The remainder of this chapter describes these tools of analysis and how we apply them.

Horizontal Analysis

LO2 Explain and apply methods of horizontal analysis.

Horizontal analysis is a tool to evaluate the important relations and changes between the items in financial statements *across time*.[1] **Comparative financial statements** show financial amounts in side-by-side columns on a single statement and facilitate the comparison of amounts for two or more successive periods. For instance, WestJet's *annual report* in Appendix I has a comparative statement based on two years of financial performance.

This section explains how we calculate dollar changes and percent changes in comparative statements and illustrates their application to the financial statements of Ralco Corporation.

Calculation of Dollar Changes and Percent Changes

Comparing financial statements over relatively short time periods—two to three years—is often done by analyzing changes in line items. A change analysis usually includes an analysis of absolute dollar amount changes as well as percent changes. Both analyses are relevant since dollar changes can sometimes yield large percent changes inconsistent with their importance. For instance, a 50% change from a base figure of $100 is less important than the same percent change from a base amount of $100,000 in the same statement. Reference to dollar amounts is necessary to retain a proper perspective and for assessing the importance of changes.

---

[1] The term *horizontal analysis* arises from the left-to-right (or right-to-left) movement of our eyes as we review comparative financial statements across time.

We calculate the *dollar change* for a financial statement item as:

$$\text{Dollar change} = \text{Analysis period amount} - \text{Base period amount}$$

where *analysis period* is the point or period of time for the financial statements under analysis, and *base period* is the point or period of time for the financial statements used for comparison purposes. We commonly use the prior year as the base period.

We calculate the *percent change* by dividing the dollar change by the base period amount, and then multiplying this quantity by 100:

$$\text{Percent change} = \frac{\text{Analysis period amount} - \text{Base period amount}}{\text{Base period amount}} \times 100$$

While we can always calculate a dollar change, we must be aware of a few rules in working with percent changes. To illustrate, let's look at four separate cases in the chart below:

Case	Base Period	Analysis Period	Change Analysis Dollar	Change Analysis Percent
A	$ (4,500)	$ 1,500	$ 6,000	—
B	2,000	(1,000)	(3,000)	—
C	—	8,000	8,000	—
D	10,000	-0-	(10,000)	(100%)

When a negative amount appears in the base period and a positive amount in the analysis period (or vice versa), we cannot calculate a meaningful percent change—see cases A and B. Also, when there is no value in the base period, no percent change is identifiable—see case C. Finally, when an item has a value in the base period and is zero in the next period, the decrease is 100 percent—see case D.

We commonly round percents and ratios to one or two decimal places, but there is no uniform practice on this matter. Calculations should not be so excessively detailed that important relations are lost among a mountain of decimal points.

Comparative Balance Sheet

One of the most useful comparative statements is the comparative balance sheet. It consists of amounts from two or more balance sheet dates arranged side by side. The usefulness of comparative financial statements is often improved by also showing each item's dollar change and percent change. This type of presentation highlights large dollar and percent changes for decision makers. Exhibit 20.1 shows the comparative balance sheet for Ralco.

Exhibit 20.1

Comparative Balance Sheet

(in thousands)	2011	2010	Amount of Increase or (Decrease) in 2011	Percent of Increase or (Decrease) in 2011
Ralco Corporation **Balance Sheet** **November 30, 2011, and November 30, 2010**				
Assets				
Current assets:				
Cash and short-term investments...	$ 85,618	$ 57,000	$28,618	50.2
Accounts receivable				
Trade...	50,586	36,327	14,259	39.3
Other	2,264	2,185	79	3.6
Inventory	13,417	7,361	6,056	82.3
Prepaid expenses	1,348	812	536	66.0
Total current assets........................	$153,233	$103,685	$49,548	47.8
Capital assets (net)	38,189	28,605	9,584	33.5
Total assets	$191,422	$132,290	$59,132	44.7
Liabilities				
Current liabilities:				
Accounts payable...........................	$ 8,487	$ 5,391	$ 3,096	57.4
Accrued liabilities	10,722	6,073	4,649	76.6
Income taxes payable.....................	4,930	7,400	(2,470)	(33.4)
Total current liabilities	$ 24,139	$ 18,864	$ 5,275	28.0
Long-term debt	2,330	2,192	138	6.3
Total liabilities....................................	$ 26,469	$ 21,056	$ 5,413	25.7
Shareholders' Equity				
Common shares...........................	$ 89,732	$ 68,516	$21,216	31.0
Retained earnings..........................	75,221	42,718	32,503	76.1
Total shareholders' equity	$164,953	$111,234	$53,719	48.3
Total liabilities and shareholders' equity	$191,422	$132,290	$59,132	44.7

Our analysis of comparative financial statements begins by focusing on items that show large dollar or percent changes. We then try to identify the reasons for these changes and, if possible, determine whether they are favourable or unfavourable. We also follow up on items with small changes when we expected the changes to be large.

Regarding Ralco's comparative balance sheet, its first line item, "Cash and short-term investments" in Exhibit 20.1 stands out and shows a $28.6 million increase (50.2%). To a large extent, this increase may be explained by the increase in two other items: the $21.2 million increase in common shares and the $32.5 million increase in retained earnings.

Note that Ralco's liabilities increased by $5.4 million. In light of this, the $28.6 million increase in cash and short-term investments might appear to be an excessive investment in highly liquid assets P. 216 that usually earn a low return. However, the company's very strong and liquid financial position indicates an outstanding ability to respond to new opportunities such as the acquisition of other companies.

Comparative Income Statement

A comparative income statement is prepared similarly to the comparative balance sheet. Amounts for two or more periods are placed side-by-side, with additional columns for dollar and percent changes. Exhibit 20.2 shows Ralco's comparative income statement.

Exhibit 20.2

Comparative Income Statements

	Ralco Corporation Income Statement For Years Ended November 30, 2011 and 2010			
(in thousands)	2011	2010	Amount of Increase or (Decrease) in 2011	Percent of Increase or (Decrease) in 2011
Sales	$164,313	$105,027	$59,286	56.4
Cost of goods sold	35,940	24,310	11,630	47.8
Gross profit	$128,373	$ 80,717	$47,656	59.0
Expenses:				
Advertising	34,390	20,579	13,811	67.1
Selling, general and administrative	30,833	18,005	12,828	71.2
Research and development	10,888	6,256	4,632	74.0
Amortization	6,137	4,079	2,058	50.5
Loss (gain) on foreign exchange	1,546	(480)	2,026	—
Total expenses:	$ 83,794	$ 48,439	$35,355	73.0
Income from continuing operations	$ 44,579	$ 32,278	$12,301	38.1
Interest income	2,959	2,482	477	19.2
Less: Interest expense	98	93	5	5.4
Income from continuing operations before income taxes	$ 47,440	$ 34,667	$12,773	36.8
Income taxes	14,937	13,814	1,123	8.1
Net income	$ 32,503	$ 20,853	$11,650	55.9

All of the income statement items (except foreign exchange) reflect the company's rapid growth. Especially note the large $13.8 million or 67.1% increase in advertising. This suggests the company's leadership and strong response to competition in the software industry. Although the dollar increase in interest income was only $0.5 million, this amounted to a 19.2% increase. This is consistent with the increase in cash and short-term investments reported in the balance sheet.

Output Made Easy

Today's accounting programs and spreadsheets can produce outputs with horizontal, vertical, and ratio analyses. These analyses can include a graphical depiction of financial relations. The key is being able to use this information properly and effectively for business decision making.

DID YOU KNOW?

Trend Analysis

Trend analysis, also called *trend percent analysis* or *index number trend analysis*, is used to reveal patterns in data covering successive periods. This method of analysis is a variation on the use of percent changes for horizontal analysis. The difference is that trend analysis does not subtract the base period amount in the numerator. To calculate trend percents we need to:

1. Select a *base period* and assign each item for the base period statement a weight of 100%.
2. Express financial numbers from other periods as a percent of the base period number.

$$\text{Trend percent} = \frac{\text{Analysis period amount}}{\text{Base period amount}} \times 100$$

To illustrate trend analysis, we use selected financial data of Ralco as shown in Exhibit 20.3.

Exhibit 20.3

Revenues and Expenses

	2011	2010	2009	2008	2007
Sales..................................	$164,313	$105,027	$67,515	$52,242	$29,230
Cost of goods sold	35,940	24,310	19,459	7,735	6,015
Gross profit	$128,373	$ 80,717	$48,056	$44,507	$23,215

We select 2007 as the base period and calculate the trend percent for each year and each item by dividing each year's dollar amount by its 2007 dollar amount. For instance, the revenue trend percent for 2010 is 359.3%, calculated as $105,027 ÷ $29,230. The trend percents for the data from Exhibit 20.3 are shown in Exhibit 20.4.

Exhibit 20.4

Trend Percents of Revenues and Expenses

	2011	2010	2009	2008	2007
Sales	562.1%	359.3%	231.0%	178.7%	100%
Cost of goods sold	597.5	404.2	323.5	128.6	100
Gross profit........................	553.0	347.7	207.0	191.7	100

Exhibit 20.5

Trend Percent Lines for Revenues and Selected Expenses

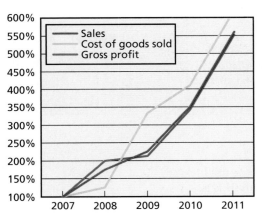

Exhibit 20.5 presents the trend percents from Exhibit 20.4 in a *line graph*. A line graph can help us identify trends and detect changes in direction or magnitude. For example, note that the gross profit line was bending upward from 2007 to 2008 but was essentially flat from 2008 to 2009. The gross profit increased at a lower rate from 2008 to 2009 but was parallel to the sales line from 2008 to 2011.

The line graph in Exhibit 20.5 also helps us understand the relationships between items. For example, the graph in Exhibit 20.5 shows that 2008 through 2011, cost of goods sold increased at a rate that was somewhat more than the increase in sales. Further, the differing trends in these two items had a clear effect on the percentage changes in gross profit. That is, gross profit increased each year at a somewhat slower rate than sales.

Trend analysis of financial statement items also can include comparisons of relations between items on different financial statements. For instance, Exhibit 20.6 shows a comparison of Ralco's total assets and revenues.

	2011	2007	Trend Percent (2011 vs 2007)
Sales	$164.3	$29.2	562.7%
Total assets (fiscal year-end)	191.4	41.9	456.8

The rate of increase in total assets was not quite as large as the increase in revenues. Is this change favourable? We cannot say for sure. It might suggest that the company is able to use assets more efficiently than in earlier years. On the other hand, it might mean that the company may realize slower growth in future years. Monitoring this relation is important to see if the company can continue to achieve high revenue growth. An important part of financial analysis is identifying questions and areas of concern such as these. Financial statement analysis often leads the analyst to ask questions, without providing one clear answer. These concerns often direct us to important factors bearing on the future of the company under analysis.

5. Analyze the following information (expressed in millions of dollars) and identify whether the trend in accounts receivable is favourable or unfavourable when compared to the trend in sales.

	2011	2010	2009
Sales	$50.0	$40.0	$39.0
Accounts receivable	13.0	8.8	7.8

Do: QS 20-3, QS 20-4

CHECKPOINT

Vertical (or Common-Size) Analysis

Vertical (or common-size) analysis is a tool to evaluate individual financial statement items or groups of items in terms of a specific base amount. We usually define a key aggregate figure as the base, and the base amount is commonly defined as 100%. For instance, an income statement's base is usually revenue and a balance sheet's base is usually total assets. This section explains vertical analysis and applies it to Ralco's statements.[2]

LO³   Describe and apply methods of vertical analysis.

Common-Size Statements

The comparative statements in Exhibits 20.1 and 20.2 show how each item has changed over time, but they do not emphasize the relative importance of each item. We use **common-size financial statements** to reveal changes in the relative importance of each financial statement item. A *common-size percent* is measured by taking each individual financial statement amount under analysis and dividing it by its base amount:

$$\text{Common-size percent} = \frac{\text{Analysis amount}}{\text{Base amount}} \times 100$$

---

[2] The term *vertical analysis* arises from the up–down (or down–up) movement of our eyes as we review common-size financial statements.

Common-Size Balance Sheet

Common-size statements express each item as a percent of a *base amount*. The base amount for a common-size balance sheet is usually total assets. It is assigned a value of 100%. This also implies that the total amount of liabilities plus shareholders' equity equals 100% since this amount equals total assets. Next, we calculate a common-size percent for each asset, liability, and shareholders' equity item where the base amount is total assets as illustrated in Exhibit 20.7.

Exhibit 20.7

Common-Size Comparative Balance Sheet

Ralco Corporation
Balance Sheet
November 30, 2011, and November 30, 2010

(in thousands)	2011	2010	Common-Size Percentages	
			2011	2010
Assets				
Current assets:				
Cash and short-term investments	$ 85,618	$ 57,000	44.7	43.1
Accounts receivable				
Trade	50,586	36,327	26.4	27.4
Other.................................	2,264	2,185	1.2	1.7
Inventory.................................	13,417	7,361	7.0	5.6
Prepaid expenses.................................	1,348	812	0.7	0.6
Total current assets.................................	$153,233	$103,685	80.0	78.4
Capital assets (net).................................	38,189	28,605	20.0	21.6
Total assets.................................	$191,422	$132,290	100.0	100.0
Liabilities				
Current liabilities:				
Accounts payable	$ 8,487	$ 5,391	4.4	4.1
Accrued liabilities.................................	10,722	6,073	5.6	4.6
Income taxes payable	4,930	7,400	2.6	5.6
Total current liabilities	$ 24,139	$ 18,864	12.6	14.3
Long-term debt	2,330	2,192	1.2	1.6
Total liabilities	$ 26,469	$ 21,056	13.8	15.9
Shareholders' Equity				
Common shares, 60,000 shares issued and outstanding.................................	$ 89,732	$ 68,516	46.9	51.8
Retained earnings.................................	75,221	42,718	39.3	32.3
Total shareholders' equity	$164,953	$111,234	86.2	84.1
Total liabilities and shareholders' equity	$191,422	$132,290	100.0	100.0

Common-Size Income Statement

Our analysis also usually benefits from an examination of a common-size income statement. The amount of revenues is the base amount and it is assigned a value of 100%. Each common-size income statement item appears as a percent of revenues.

Exhibit 20.8 shows the comparative income statement for 2011 and 2010.

Ralco Corporation Income Statement For Years Ended November 30, 2011 and 2010			Common-Size Percentages	
(in thousands)	2011	2010	2011	2010
Sales	$164,313	$105,027	100.0	100.0
Cost of goods sold	35,940	24,310	21.9	23.1
Gross profit from sales	$128,373	$ 80,717	78.1	76.9
Expenses:				
Advertising	34,390	20,579	20.9	19.6
Selling, general and administrative	30,833	18,005	18.8	17.1
Research and development	10.888	6,256	6.6	6.0
Amortization	6,137	4,079	3.7	3.9
Loss (gain) on foreign exchange	1,546	(480)	0.9	(0.5)
Total expenses	$ 83,794	$ 48,439	51.0	46.1
Income from continuing operations	44,579	32,278	27.1	30.7
Interest income	2,959	2,482	1.8	2.4
Less: Interest expense	98	93	0.1	0.1
Income from continuing operations before income taxes	$ 47,440	$ 34,667	28.8	33.0
Income taxes	14,937	13,814	9.0	13.2
Net income	$ 32,503	$ 20,853	19.8	19.8
Earnings per share	$ 0.63	$ 0.45		
Weighted-average shares outstanding	51,768	46,146		

Exhibit 20.8

Common-Size Comparative
Income Statement

One of the advantages of calculating common-size percents for successive income statements is in helping us uncover potentially important changes in a company's expenses. For Ralco, the relative size of each expense changed very little from 2010 to 2011. Evidence of no changes is also valuable information for our analysis.

Common-Size Graphics

An income statement readily lends itself to common-size graphical analysis. Revenues affect nearly every item in an income statement. It is also usually helpful for our analysis to know what portion of revenues various geographical regions take up. For example, Exhibit 20.9, based on assumed data for Ralco Corporation, uses a pie chart to highlight the contribution of each component of revenue.

Sales by Region 2010
- Other (6.6%)
- Canada (8.8%)
- Europe (47.1%)
- U.S.A. (37.6%)

Sales by Region 2011
- Canada (6.0%)
- Other (10.0%)
- Europe (37.4%)
- U.S.A. (46.6%)

Exhibit 20.9

Common-Size Graphic of Ralco's
Sales by Geographic Region

Common-size financial statements are useful in comparing different companies because the focus is changed from dollars (which can vary significantly between companies of different sizes) to percentages (which are always expressed as X out of 100, the base is constant). Common-size statements do not reflect the relative sizes of companies under analysis but a comparison of a company's common-size statements with competitors' or industry common-size statistics alerts us to differences that should be explored and explained.

6. On common-size comparative statements, which of the following is true? (a) Each item is expressed as a percent of a base amount, (b) Total assets are assigned a value of 100%, (c) Amounts from two or more successive periods are placed side-by-side, (d) All of the above are true.

7. What is the difference between the percents shown on a comparative income statement and those shown on a common-size comparative income statement?

8. Trend percents are: (a) shown on the comparative income statement and the comparative balance sheet; (b) shown on common-size comparative statements; or (c) also called index numbers.

Do: QS 20-5, QS 20-6

mid-chapter demonstration problem

Use the financial statements of Precision Inc. to satisfy the following requirements:

1. Prepare a comparative income statement showing the percent increase or decrease for 2011 over 2010.

2. Prepare a common-size comparative balance sheet for 2011 and 2010.

Precision Inc.
Income Statement
For Years Ended December 31, 2011 and 2010

	2011	2010
Sales	$2,486,000	$2,075,000
Cost of goods sold	1,523,000	1,222,000
Gross profit from sales	$ 963,000	$ 853,000
Operating expenses:		
Advertising expense	$ 145,000	$ 100,000
Sales salaries expense	240,000	280,000
Office salaries expense	165,000	200,000
Insurance expense	100,000	45,000
Supplies expense	26,000	35,000
Amortization expense	85,000	75,000
Miscellaneous expenses	17,000	15,000
Total operating expenses	$ 778,000	$ 750,000
Operating income	$ 185,000	$ 103,000
Less interest expense	44,000	46,000
Income before taxes	$ 141,000	$ 57,000
Income taxes	47,000	19,000
Net income	$ 94,000	$ 38,000
Earnings per share	$ 0.99	$ 0.40

Precision Inc.
Balance Sheet
December 31

	2011	2010
Assets		
Current assets:		
Cash	$ 79,000	$ 42,000
Short-term investment	65,000	96,000
Accounts receivable (net)	120,000	100,000
Merchandise inventory	250,000	265,000
Total current assets	$ 514,000	$ 503,000
Capital assets:		
Store equipment (net)	$ 400,000	$ 350,000
Office equipment (net)	45,000	50,000
Buildings (net)	625,000	675,000
Land	100,000	100,000
Total capital assets	$1,170,000	$1,175,000
Total assets	$1,684,000	$1,678,000
Liabilities		
Current liabilities:		
Accounts payable	$ 164,000	$ 190,000
Short-term notes payable	75,000	90,000
Taxes payable	26,000	12,000
Total current liabilities	$ 265,000	$ 292,000
Long-term liabilities:		
Notes payable (secured by mortgage on building and land)	400,000	420,000
Total liabilities	$ 665,000	$ 712,000
Shareholders' Equity		
Contributed capital:		
Common shares	$ 475,000	$ 475,000
Retained earnings	544,000	491,000
Total shareholders' equity	$1,019,000	$ 966,000
Total liabilities and shareholders' equity	$1,684,000	$1,678,000

Analysis component:

Advertising expense increased by 45%. Would you think this is acceptable given your review of the financial statements? Explain.

Planning the Solution

- Set up a four-column income statement; enter the 2011 and 2010 amounts in the first two columns and then enter the dollar change in the third column and the percent change from 2010 in the fourth column.

- Set up a four-column balance sheet; enter the 2011 and 2010 amounts in the first two columns and then calculate and enter the amount of each item as a percent of total assets.

- Answer the analysis component.

solution to *Mid-Chapter Demonstration Problem* _____

1.

Precision Inc. Income Statement For Years Ended December 31, 2011 and 2010				
			Increase (Decrease) in 2011	
	2011	**2010**	**Amount**	**Percent**
Sales..............................	$2,486,000	$2,075,000	$411,000	19.8%
Cost of goods sold	1,523,000	1,222,000	301,000	24.6
Gross profit from sales................	$ 963,000	$ 853,000	$110,000	12.9
Operating expenses:				
Advertising expense................	$ 145,000	$ 100,000	$ 45,000	45.0
Sales salaries expense..............	240,000	280,000	(40,000)	(14.3)
Office salaries expense............	165,000	200,000	(35,000)	(17.5)
Insurance expense	100,000	45,000	55,000	122.2
Supplies expense	26,000	35,000	(9,000)	(25.7)
Amortization expense	85,000	75,000	10,000	13.3
Other operating expenses.......	17,000	15,000	2,000	13.3
Total operating expenses	$ 778,000	$ 750,000	$ 28,000	3.7
Operating income......................	$ 185,000	$ 103,000	$ 82,000	79.6
Less interest expense	44,000	46,000	(2,000)	(4.3)
Income before taxes...................	$ 141,000	$ 57,000	$ 84,000	147.4
Income taxes	47,000	19,000	28,000	147.4
Net income...............................	$ 94,000	$ 38,000	$ 56,000	147.4
Earnings per share.....................	$ 0.99	$ 0.40	$ 0.59	147.5

2.

	Precision Inc. Balance Sheet December 31		Common-Size Percents	
	2011	2010	2011*	2010*
Assets				
Current assets:				
Cash	$ 79,000	$ 42,000	4.7%	2.5%
Short-term investments	65,000	96,000	3.9	5.7
Accounts receivable (net)........	120,000	100,000	7.1	6.0
Merchandise inventory	250,000	265,000	14.8	15.8
Total current assets	$ 514,000	$ 503,000	30.5	30.0
Capital assets:				
Store equipment (net)	$ 400,000	$ 350,000	23.8	20.9
Office equipment (net)	45,000	50,000	2.7	3.0
Buildings (net)	625,000	675,000	37.1	40.2
Land	100,000	100,000	5.9	6.0
Total capital assets	$1,170,000	$1,175,000	69.5	70.0
Total assets.................................	$1,684,000	$1,678,000	100.0	100.0
Liabilities				
Current liabilities:				
Accounts payable....................	$ 164,000	$ 190,000	9.7	11.3
Short-term notes payable........	75,000	90,000	4.5	5.4
Taxes payable	26,000	12,000	1.5	0.7
Total current liabilities.............	$ 265,000	$ 292,000	15.7	17.4
Long-term liabilities:				
Notes payable (secured by mortgage on building and land)................................	400,000	420,000	23.8	25.0
Total liabilities	$ 665,000	$ 712,000	39.5	42.4
Shareholders' Equity				
Contributed capital:				
Common shares	$ 475,000	$ 475,000	28.2	28.3
Retained earnings......................	544,000	491,000	32.3	29.3
Total shareholders' equity...........	$1,019,000	$ 966,000	60.5	57.6
Total liabilities and equity	$1,684,000	$1,678,000	100.0	100.0

*Columns may not add due to rounding.

Analysis component:

Assuming the advertising was effective, this appears to be reasonable given that a $45,000 increase in advertising helped increased sales by $411,000 ($9.13 of additional sales per $1 of additional advertising). However, it appears that the marginal utility of each additional advertising dollar spent is decreasing given that sales were $2,075,000 with an advertising expenditure of $100,000 ($20.75 of sales per $1 of advertising).

Ratio Analysis

Ratios are among the most popular and widely used tools of financial analysis. They provide us with clues and symptoms of underlying conditions. Ratios, properly interpreted, identify areas requiring further investigation. A ratio can help us uncover conditions and trends that are difficult to detect by inspecting individual components making up the ratio. Usefulness of ratios depends on how skillfully we interpret them, and interpretation is the most challenging aspect of **ratio analysis**.

A ratio shows a mathematical relation between two quantities. It can be expressed as a percent, a rate, or a proportion. For instance, a change in an account balance from $100 to $250 can be expressed as: (1) 250%, (2) 2.5 times, or (3) 2.5 to 1 (or 2.5:1).

This section describes an important set of financial ratios and shows how to apply them. The selected ratios are organized into the four building blocks of financial statement analysis: (1) liquidity and efficiency, (2) solvency, (3) profitability, and (4) market. Some of these ratios have been previously explained at relevant points in prior chapters.

LO⁴ | Define and apply ratio analysis.

Liquidity and Efficiency

Liquidity refers to the availability of resources to meet short-term cash requirements. A company's short-term liquidity is affected by the timing of cash inflows and outflows along with its prospects for future performance. **Efficiency** refers to how well a company uses its assets. Efficiency is usually measured relative to how much revenue is generated for a certain level of assets. Inefficient use of assets can cause liquidity problems.

Both liquidity and efficiency are important and complementary in our analysis. If a company fails to meet its current obligations, its continued existence is doubtful. Viewed in this light, all other measures of analysis are of secondary importance. While accounting measurements assume indefinite existence of the company (going concern principle P. 32), our analysis must always assess the validity of this assumption using liquidity measures.

For users, a lack of liquidity often precedes lower profitability and opportunity. It can foretell a loss of owner control or loss of investment. When the owner(s) of a proprietorship and certain partnerships possess unlimited liability P. 5, a lack of liquidity endangers their personal assets. To creditors of a company, lack of liquidity can yield delays in collecting interest and principal payments P. 533 or the loss of amounts due them. A company's customers and suppliers of goods and services are affected by short-term liquidity problems. Implications include a company's inability to execute contracts and potential damage to important customer and supplier relationships. This section describes and illustrates ratios relevant to assessing liquidity and efficiency.

Working Capital and Current Ratio

The amount of current assets P. 208 less current liabilities P. 209 is called **working capital** or *net working capital*. A company needs an adequate amount of working capital to meet current debts, carry sufficient inventories, and take advantage of cash discounts. A company that runs low on working capital is less likely to meet current obligations or continue operating.

When evaluating a company's working capital, we must look beyond the dollar amount of current assets less current liabilities. We also need to consider the relation between the amounts of current assets and current liabilities. The *current ratio* P. 216 describes a company's ability to pay its short-term obligations. The current ratio relates current assets to current liabilities as follows:

$$\text{Current ratio} = \frac{\text{Current assets}}{\text{Current liabilities}}$$

Drawing on information in Exhibit 20.1, Ralco's working capital amounts and current ratios for both 2011 and 2010 are shown in Exhibit 20.10.

Exhibit 20.10

Working Capital and Current Ratio

(in thousands)	Nov. 30, 2011	Nov. 30, 2010
Current assets..	$ 153,233	$103,685
Current liabilities	24,139	18,864
Working capital...	**$129,094**	**$ 84,821**
Current ratio:		
$153,233/$24,139	**6.35 to 1**	
$103,685/$18,864		**5.50 to 1**

A high current ratio suggests a strong liquidity position. A high ratio means a company should be able to meet its current obligations. But a company also can have a current ratio that is *too high*. An excessively high ratio means the company has invested too much in current assets compared to its current obligations. Since current assets do not normally generate much additional revenue, an excessive investment in current assets is not an efficient use of funds.

Many users apply a guideline of 2 to 1 for the current ratio in helping evaluate the debt-paying ability of a company. A company with a 2 to 1 or higher current ratio is generally thought to be a good credit risk in the short run. But this analysis is only one step in our process of assessing a company's debt-paying ability. We also need to analyze at least three additional factors:

1. Type of business.
2. Composition of current assets.
3. Turnover rate of current asset components.

Type of Business

The type of business a company operates affects our assessment of its current ratio. A service company that grants little or no credit and carries no inventories other than supplies can probably operate on a current ratio of less than 1 to 1 if its revenues generate enough cash to pay its current liabilities on time. For example, WestJet's current ratio at December 31, 2005, was 0.85 to 1 calculated as its current assets of $319,576,000 divided by its current liabilities of $376,897,000 (refer to WestJet's financial statements in Appendix I at the end of the textbook). On the other hand, a company selling high-priced clothing or furniture requires a higher ratio. This is because of difficulties in judging customer demand and other factors. For instance, if demand falls, this company's inventory may not generate as much cash as expected. A company facing these risks should maintain a current ratio of more than 2 to 1 to protect its creditors. For example, Danier Leather's current ratio at June 25, 2005, was 6.42 to 1 calculated as its current assets of $52,455,000 divided by its current liabilities of $8,170,000 (refer to Danier's financial statements in Appendix I at the end of the textbook).

The importance of the type of business to our analysis implies that an evaluation of a company's current ratio should include a comparison with ratios of other successful companies in the same industry. The industry average ratios for companies in a business similar to Ralco's are shown in Exhibit 20.11. To demonstrate how ratios might be interpreted, we will compare the ratios calculated for Ralco in the following pages against the assumed industry average ratios provided in Exhibit 20.11. In comparing the industry average current ratio of 1.6:1 to Ralco's current ratio of 6.35:1, it appears that Ralco is in a better position to meet its current obligations than its competitors are. However, recall the discussion earlier that an excessively high ratio means that Ralco may have too much invested in current assets, which are generally non-productive. Another important part of our analysis is to observe how the current ratio changes over time. We must also recognize that the current ratio is affected by a company's accounting methods, especially choice of inventory method. For instance, a company using LIFO P. 342 tends to report a smaller amount of current assets than if it uses FIFO P. 342 when costs are rising. These factors should be considered before we decide whether a given current ratio is adequate.

Exhibit 20.11

2011 Industry Average Ratios

Current ratio	1.6:1	Times interest earned	50 times
Acid-test ratio	1.1:1	Profit margin	14%
Accounts receivable turnover	16 times	Gross profit ratio	18%
Days' sales uncollected	21 days	Return on total assets	20%
Merchandise turnover	5 times	Return on common shareholders' equity	32.7%
Days' sales in inventory	70 days	Book value per common share	$8.63
Total asset turnover	2.3 times	Book value per preferred share	$15.00
Accounts payable turnover	4 times	Basic earnings per share	$1.79
Debt ratio	35%	Price–earnings per share	18.2
Equity ratio	65%	Dividend yield	$0.35
Pledged assets to secured liabilities	1.4:1		

Composition of Current Assets

The composition of a company's current assets is important to our evaluation of short-term liquidity. For instance, cash, cash equivalents, and temporary investments are more liquid than accounts and notes receivable. Also, short-term receivables normally are more liquid than merchandise inventory. We know cash can be used to pay current debts immediately. But items such as accounts receivable and merchandise inventory must be converted into cash before payments can be made. An excessive amount of receivables and inventory weakens a company's ability to pay current liabilities. One way to take account of the composition of current assets is to evaluate the acid-test ratio. We discuss this in the next section.

Banker

You are a banker, and a company calls on you for a one-year, $200,000 loan to finance an expansion. This company's current ratio is 4:1 with current assets of $160,000. Key competitors carry a current ratio of about 1.9:1. Using this information, do you approve the loan application? Does your decision change if the application is for a 10-year loan?

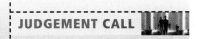

JUDGEMENT CALL

Answer—p. 1030

Acid-Test Ratio

The *acid-test ratio*, also called the *quick ratio*, is a more rigorous test of a company's ability to pay its short-term debts. This ratio focuses on current asset composition. Inventory and prepaid expenses are excluded and only quick assets P. 472 are included. Quick assets are cash, temporary investments, accounts receivable, and notes receivable. These are the most liquid types of current assets. We calculate the acid-test ratio as:

$$\text{Acid-test ratio} = \frac{\text{Cash} + \text{Temporary investments} + \text{Net current receivables}}{\text{Current liabilities}}$$

Using the information in Exhibit 20.1, we calculate Ralco's acid-test ratios as shown in Exhibit 20.12.

Exhibit 20.12

Acid-Test Ratio

(in thousands)	Nov. 30, 2011	Nov. 30, 2010
Cash and temporary investments	$ 85,618	$57,000
Accounts receivable, trade	50,586	36,327
Total quick assets	$136,204	$93,327
Current liabilities	$ 24,139	$18,864
Acid-test ratio:		
$136,204/$24,139	5.64 to 1	
$93,327/$18,864		4.95 to 1

A traditional rule of thumb for an acceptable acid-test ratio is 1 to 1. Similar to our analysis of the current ratio, we need to consider other factors. For instance, the working capital requirements of a company are affected by how frequently the company converts its current assets into cash. This implies that our analysis of the company's short-term liquidity should also include analysis of receivables and inventories. We next look at these analyses.

Accounts Receivable Turnover

We can measure how frequently a company converts its receivables into cash by calculating *accounts receivable turnover* P. 529. This is calculated as:

$$\text{Accounts receivable turnover} = \frac{\text{Net sales}}{\text{Average net accounts receivable}}$$

Accounts receivable turnover is more precise if credit sales are used for the numerator. But net sales (or revenues) are usually used by external users because information about credit sales is typically not reported.

While this ratio is called accounts receivable turnover, short-term notes receivable from customers are normally included in the denominator amount along with accounts receivable.

Average accounts receivable is estimated by averaging the beginning and the ending receivables for the period. If the beginning and ending receivables do not represent the amount normally on hand, an average of quarterly or monthly receivables may be used if available. Ending accounts receivable is sometimes substituted for the average balance in calculating accounts receivable turnover. This is acceptable if the difference between these figures is insignificant. Also, some users prefer using gross accounts receivable (before subtracting the allowance for doubtful accounts P. 508). But many balance sheets report only the net amount of accounts receivable.

Ralco's 2011 accounts receivable turnover is calculated as:

$$\frac{\$164,313}{(\$50,586 + \$36,327)/2} = 3.78 \text{ times*}$$

This can be expressed in days by dividing 365 by the turnover, e.g., 365 ÷ 3.78 = 96.56 days on average to collect accounts receivable.

If accounts receivable are collected quickly, then accounts receivable turnover is high. A high turnover is favourable because it means the company need not commit large amounts of capital to accounts receivable. An accounts receivable turnover can be too high. This can occur when credit terms are so restrictive that they negatively affect sales volume. Ralco's accounts receivable turnover of 3.78 times per year is unfavourable in comparison to the industry average of 16 times per year. The industry collects receivables more than four times faster than Ralco does.

Days' Sales Uncollected

We already described how accounts receivable turnover could be used to evaluate how frequently a company collects its accounts. Another measure of this activity is *days' sales uncollected* P. 530 defined as:

$$\text{Days' sales uncollected} = \frac{\text{Accounts receivable}}{\text{Net sales}} \times 365$$

This formula takes the usual approach of placing accounts receivable in the numerator. Any short-term notes receivable from customers are also normally included in the numerator.

We illustrate this ratio's application by using Ralco's information in Exhibits 20.1 and 20.2. The days' sales uncollected figure on November 30, 2011, is:

$$\frac{\$50,586}{\$164,313} \times 365 = 112.4 \text{ days}$$

Days' sales uncollected is more meaningful if we know the company's credit terms. A rough guideline is that days' sales uncollected should not exceed one and one-third times the days in its: (a) credit period, if discounts are not offered; or (b) discount period, if discounts are offered.

Ralco's days' sales uncollected of 112.4 days is unfavourable when compared to the industry average of 21 days. This means that Ralco has more cash tied up in receivables than its competitors do, reflecting a less efficient use of assets.

Merchandise Inventory Turnover

Working capital (current assets minus current liabilities) requirements are affected by how long a company holds merchandise inventory before selling it. One measure of this effect is the *merchandise turnover* P. 367. It provides a measure of a firm's liquidity and how quickly it can convert merchandise inventory to cash. Merchandise turnover is defined as:

$$\text{Merchandise turnover} = \frac{\text{Cost of goods sold}}{\text{Average merchandise inventory}}$$

Using the inventory and cost of goods sold information in Exhibits 20.1 and 20.2, we calculate Ralco's merchandise turnover for 2011 as:

$$\frac{\$35,940}{(\$13,417 + \$7,361)/2} = 3.46 \text{ times*}$$

This can be expressed in days by dividing 365 by the turnover, e.g., 365 ÷ 3.46 = 105.49 days on average to sell inventory.

Average inventory is estimated by averaging the beginning and the ending inventories for the period. If the beginning and ending inventories do not represent the amount normally on hand, an average of quarterly or monthly inventories may be used if available.

A company with a high turnover requires a smaller investment in inventory than one producing the same sales with a lower turnover. But merchandise turnover can be too high if a company keeps such a small inventory on hand that it restricts sales volume.

Ralco's merchandise turnover of 3.46 times is unfavourable when compared to the industry average of 5 times. This comparison indicates that Ralco sells its inventory more slowly than its competitors do.

Days' Sales in Inventory

Days' sales in inventory P. 368 is a useful measure in evaluating the liquidity of a company's inventory. Days' sales in inventory is linked to inventory in a similar manner as days' sales uncollected is linked to receivables. Days' sales in inventory is calculated as:

$$\text{Days' sales in inventory} = \frac{\text{Ending inventory}}{\text{Cost of goods sold}} \times 365$$

Applying this formula to Ralco's 2011 financial statements, we calculate days' sales in inventory as:

$$\frac{\$13,417}{\$35,940} \times 365 = 136.3 \text{ days}$$

If the products in Ralco's inventory are in demand by customers, this formula estimates that its inventory will be converted into receivables (or cash) in 136.3 days. If all of Ralco's sales are credit sales, the conversion of inventory to receivables in 136.3 days plus the conversion of receivables to cash in 112.4 days suggest that inventory will be converted to cash in about 248.7 days (= 136.3 + 112.4).

For a business selling perishables such as meat or produce, days' sales in inventory would be very low (1 or 2 days) as compared to a retailer selling slower-moving inventory such as jewellery.

Ralco's days' sales in inventory of 136.3 days is unfavourable when compared to the industry average of 70 days. This means that Ralco has more cash tied up in merchandise inventory than its competitors do.

Total Asset Turnover

Total asset turnover describes the ability of a company to use its assets to generate sales. This ratio is calculated as:

$$\text{Total asset turnover} = \frac{\text{Net sales (or revenues)}}{\text{Average total assets}}$$

In calculating Ralco's total asset turnover for 2011, we follow the usual practice of averaging total assets at the beginning and the end of the year. Taking the information from Exhibits 20.1 and 20.2, this calculation is:

$$\frac{\$164{,}313}{(\$191{,}422 + \$132{,}290)/2} = 1.015 \text{ times}$$

Ralco's total asset turnover of 1.015 times is unfavourable in comparison to the industry average of 2.3 times. This means that Ralco uses its assets less efficiently to generate sales than its competitors do.

Accounts Payable Turnover

The *accounts payable turnover* describes how much time it takes for a company to meet its obligations to its suppliers. In other words, it is a liquidity measure that shows how quickly management is paying trade credit. It is calculated as:

$$\text{Accounts payable turnover} = \frac{\text{Cost of goods sold}}{\text{Average accounts payable}}$$

In calculating Ralco's accounts payable turnover for 2011, we average accounts payable by adding the beginning and the end of the year amounts and dividing by 2. Taking the information from Exhibits 20.1 and 20.2, we calculate the ratio as:

$$\frac{\$35{,}940}{(\$8{,}487 + \$5{,}391)/2} = 5.179 \text{ times*}$$

This can expressed in days by dividing 365 by the turnover, e.g., 365 ÷ 5.18 = 70.46 days on average to pay trade creditors.

Ralco's accounts payable turnover of 5.179 times is favourable in comparison to the industry average of 4 times. It appears that Ralco manages its payments to suppliers well. However, because average accounts payable is used in this ratio, it would be possible for a company to wait until the end of the year to pay suppliers for the purpose of manipulating this ratio in its favour. Alternatively, a low accounts payable turnover may reflect an aggressive payment policy by the company; this means that payments are intentionally slowed to minimize potential borrowing and resulting interest costs.

CHECKPOINT

9. The following information is from the December 31, 2011, balance sheet of Paff Corp.: cash, $820,000; accounts receivable, $240,000; inventories, $470,000; capital assets, $910,000; accounts payable, $350,000; and income taxes payable, $180,000. Calculate the: (a) current ratio, and (b) acid-test ratio.

10. On December 31, 2010, Paff Corp. (in prior question) had accounts receivable of $290,000 and inventories of $530,000. During 2011, net sales amounted to $2,500,000 and cost of goods sold was $750,000. Calculate the: (a) accounts receivable turnover, (b) days' sales uncollected, (c) merchandise turnover, and (d) days' sales in inventory.

Do: QS 20-7 to QS 20-14 inclusive

Solvency

Solvency refers to a company's long-run financial viability and its ability to cover long-term obligations. All business activities of a company—financing, investing, and operating—affect a company's solvency. One of the most important components of solvency analysis is the composition of a company's **capital structure**. *Capital structure* refers to a company's sources of financing: shares and/or debt.

Analyzing solvency of a company is different from analyzing short-term liquidity. Analysis of solvency is long-term and uses less precise but more encompassing measures. Analysis of capital structure is one key in evaluating solvency. Capital structure ranges from relatively permanent share capital to more risky or temporary short-term financing. Assets represent secondary sources of security for lenders ranging from loans secured by specific assets to the assets available as general security to unsecured creditors. There are different risks associated with different assets and financing sources.

This section describes tools of solvency analysis. Our analysis is concerned with a company's ability to meet its obligations and provide security to its creditors *over the long run*. Indicators of this ability include *debt* and *equity* ratios, the relation between *pledged assets* and *secured liabilities*, and the company's capacity to earn sufficient income to pay *fixed interest charges*.

Debt and Equity Ratios

One element of solvency analysis is to assess the portion of a company's assets contributed by its owners and the portion contributed by creditors. This relation is reflected in the debt ratio. The *debt ratio* expresses total liabilities as a percent of total assets. The **equity ratio** provides complementary information by expressing total shareholders' equity as a percent of total assets.

Ralco's debt and equity ratios are calculated as:

	Nov. 30, 2011	Ratios	
Total liabilities...	$ 26,469	13.8%	[Debt Ratio]
Total shareholders' equity................................	164,953	86.2	[Equity Ratio]
Total liabilities and shareholders' equity...........	$191,422	100.0%	

Ralco's financial statements reflect very little debt, 13.8%, compared to the average for its competitors of 35%. The company has only one long-term liability and, at the end of 2011, its liabilities provide only 13.8% of the total assets. A company is considered less risky if its capital structure (equity and long-term debt) comprises more equity. One source of this increased risk is the required payments under debt contracts for interest and principal amounts. Another factor is the amount of financing provided by shareholders. The greater the shareholder financing, the more losses a company can absorb through its shareholders before the remaining assets become inadequate to satisfy the claims of creditors.

From the shareholders' point of view, including debt in the capital structure of a company is desirable so long as risk is not too great. If a company earns a return on borrowed capital that is higher than the cost of borrowing, the difference represents increased income to shareholders. Because debt can have the effect of increasing the return to shareholders, the inclusion of debt is sometimes described as *financial leverage*. We say that a firm is highly leveraged if a large portion of a company's assets is financed by debt.

Pledged Assets to Secured Liabilities

The ratio of pledged assets to secured liabilities is used to evaluate the risk of nonpayment faced by secured creditors. This ratio also is relevant to unsecured creditors. The ratio is calculated as:

$$\text{Pledged assets to secured liabilities} = \frac{\text{Book value of pledged assets}}{\text{Book value of secured liabilities}}$$

The information needed to calculate this ratio is not usually reported in published financial statements. This means that persons who have the ability to obtain information directly from the company (such as bankers and certain lenders) primarily use the ratio.

A generally agreed minimum value for this ratio is about 2 to 1. But the ratio needs careful interpretation because it is based on the *book value* P. 137 of pledged assets. Book values are not necessarily intended to reflect amounts to be received for assets in event of liquidation. Also, the long-term earning ability of a company with pledged assets may be more important than the value of its pledged assets. Creditors prefer that a debtor be able to pay with cash generated by operating activities rather than with cash obtained by liquidating assets.

Times Interest Earned

The *times interest earned* ratio is used to reflect the riskiness of repayments with interest to creditors. The amount of income before the deduction of interest charges and income taxes is the amount available to pay interest charges. We calculate this ratio as:

$$\text{Times interest earned} = \frac{\text{Income before interest and income taxes}}{\text{Interest expense}}$$

Ralco's times interest earned ratio for 2011 is calculated as:

$$\frac{\$44,579 + \$2,959}{\$98} = 485 \text{ times}$$

The larger this ratio, the less risky is the company for lenders. A guideline for this ratio says that creditors are reasonably safe if the company earns its fixed interest charges two or more times each year.

Ralco's times interest earned of 485 times is significantly greater than the industry average of 50 times. This means that Ralco's lenders face little or no risk in terms of collecting the interest owed to them.

> **11.** Which ratio best reflects the ability of a company to meet immediate interest payments? (a) Debt ratio; (b) Equity ratio; (c) Times interest earned; (d) Pledged assets to secured liabilities.
> **Do: QS 20-15, QS 20-16**

CHECKPOINT Read Apply Do Check

Profitability

We are especially interested in the ability of a company to use its assets efficiently to produce profits (and positive cash flows). **Profitability** refers to a company's ability to generate an adequate return on invested capital. Return is judged by assessing earnings relative to the level and sources of financing. Profitability is also relevant to solvency.

This section describes profitability measures and their importance to financial statement analysis. We also explain variations in return measures and their interpretation. We analyze the components of return on invested capital for additional insights into company performance.

Profit Margin

The operating efficiency and profitability of a company can be expressed in two components. The first is the company's *profit margin*. The profit margin reflects a company's ability to earn a net income from sales. Profit margin gives an indication of how sensitive net income is to changes in either prices or costs. It is measured by expressing net income as a percent of revenues (sales and revenues are similar terms). We can use the information in Exhibit 20.2 to calculate Ralco's 2011 profit margin as:

$$\text{Profit margin} = \frac{\text{Net income}}{\text{Net sales (or revenues)}} \times 100 = \frac{\$32,503}{\$164,313} \times 100 = 19.8\%$$

An improved profit margin could be due to more efficient operations resulting in lower cost of goods sold and reduced expenses. It could also be due to higher prices received for products sold. However, a higher profit margin is not always good. For example, a firm can reduce advertising expenses as a percentage of sales, resulting in higher net income for the current year, but perhaps also resulting in reduced future sales and profits.

To evaluate the profit margin of a company, we must consider the industry in which it operates. For instance, a publishing company might be expected to have a profit margin of between 10% and 15%, while a retail supermarket might have a normal profit margin of 1% or 2%.

Ralco's profit margin of 19.5% is favourable in comparison to the 14% industry average. This means that Ralco earns more net income per $1 of sales than its competitors.

The second component of operating efficiency is *total asset turnover*. We described this ratio earlier in this section. Both profit margin and total asset turnover make up the two basic components of operating efficiency. These ratios also reflect on management performance since managers are ultimately responsible for operating efficiency. The next section explains how we use both measures in analyzing return on total assets.

Gross Profit Ratio

Gross profit, also called **gross margin**, is the relation between sales and cost of goods sold. A merchandising company needs sufficient gross profit to cover operating expenses or it will likely fail. To help us focus on gross profit, users often calculate a gross profit ratio. The gross profit ratio, or gross margin ratio, is defined as:

$$\text{Gross profit ratio} = \frac{\text{Gross profit from sales}}{\text{Net sales}} \times 100$$

The gross profit ratios of Ralco for the years 2011 and 2010 were:

	2011	2010
Sales	$164,313	$105,027
Cost of goods sold	35,940	24,310
Gross profit from sales	$128,373	$ 80,717
Gross profit ratio	78.13%	76.85%
Calculated as	*($128,373/$164,313) × 100*	*($80,717/$105,027) × 100*

This ratio represents the gross profit in each dollar of sales. For example, the calculations above show that Ralco's gross profit ratio in 2010 was 76.85%. This means that each $1 of sales yielded 76.85¢ in gross profit to cover all other expenses. The calculations above show that Ralco's gross profit ratio increased from 2010 to 2011, reflecting a favourable trend. Ralco's gross profit ratio of 78.13% for 2011 is very favourable in comparison to the industry average gross profit ratio of 18%.

Return on Total Assets

The two basic components of operating efficiency—profit margin and total asset turnover—are used to calculate a summary measure. This summary measure is the *return on total assets* calculated as:

$$\text{Return on total assets} = \frac{\text{Net income}}{\text{Average total assets}} \times 100$$

Ralco's 2011 return on total assets is:

$$\frac{\$32,503}{(\$191,422 + \$132,290)/2} \times 100 = 20.1\%$$

Ralco's 20.1% return on total assets is marginally favourable compared to the industry average of 20%. But we need to evaluate the trend in the rate of return earned by the company in recent years and make comparisons with alternative investment opportunities before reaching a conclusion.

The following calculation shows the relation between profit margin, total asset turnover, and return on total assets:

$$\textbf{Profit margin} \times \textbf{Total asset turnover} = \textbf{Return on total assets}$$

or

$$\left(\frac{\text{Net income}}{\text{Net sales (or revenues)}} \times 100 \right) \times \frac{\text{Net sales (or revenues)}}{\text{Average total assets}} = \frac{\text{Net income}}{\text{Average total assets}} \times 100$$

Notice that both profit margin and total asset turnover contribute to overall operating efficiency, as measured by return on total assets. If we apply this formula to Ralco we get:

$$19.8\% \times 1.015 = 20.1\%$$

Return on Common Shareholders' Equity

Perhaps the most important goal in operating a company is to earn net income for its owners. The *return on common shareholders' equity* measures the success of a company in reaching this goal. We calculate this return measure as:

$$\text{Return on common shareholders' equity} = \frac{\text{Net income} - \text{Preferred dividends}}{\text{Average common shareholders' equity}} \times 100$$

Recall from Exhibit 20.1 that Ralco did not have any preferred shares P. 744 outstanding. As a result we determine Ralco's return as follows:

$$\frac{\$32,503 - \$0}{(\$164,953 + \$111,234)/2} \times 100 = 23.5\%$$

The denominator in this calculation is the book value of common shares. Book value per share was discussed in Chapter 15. In the numerator, the dividends on cumulative preferred shares must be subtracted whether they are declared or are in arrears. If preferred shares are non-cumulative, the dividends are subtracted only if declared.

Ralco's return on common shareholders' equity of 23.5% is unfavourable when compared to the industry average of 32.7%. This indicates that Ralco's competitors are earning more net income for their owners than Ralco is.

Book Value Per Share

Book value per common share and book value per preferred share were discussed in Appendix 15A. Refer to pages 760 to 762 to review these ratios.

$$\text{Book value per common share} = \frac{\text{Shareholders' equity applicable to common shares}}{\text{Number of common shares outstanding}}$$

Ralco has no preferred shares, so we calculate only book value per common share. For November 30, 2011, this ratio is calculated as:

$$\frac{\$164,953}{60,000} = \$2.75 \text{ book value per common share}$$

This reflects what each share would be worth if Ralco were to be liquidated at amounts reported on the balance sheet at November 30, 2011. The book value can be used as the starting point in share valuation methods or for merger negotiations. The main limitation in using book value is that it reflects original cost and not market value.

Basic Earnings Per Share

Earnings per share was introduced in Chapter 16. Refer to pages 797 to 802 to review this ratio.

Ralco's earnings per share figure was given in Exhibit 20.8. It was calculated as:

$$\text{Basic earnings per share} = \frac{\text{Net income} - \text{Preferred dividends}}{\text{Weighted-average common shares outstanding}}$$

$$\frac{\$32,503 - \$0}{51,768} = \$0.63 \text{ per share}$$

Ralco's earnings per share value of $0.63 is unfavourable in comparison to the industry average of $1.79. This shows that Ralco has realized less earning power per share than its competitors.

Market

Market measures are useful when analyzing corporations having publicly traded shares. These market measures use share price in their calculation. Share price reflects what the market (public) expectations are for the company. This includes both the return and risk characteristics of a company as currently perceived by the market.

Price–Earnings Ratio

The *price–earnings ratio* is the most widely quoted measure of company performance. It measures how investors judge the company's future performance and is calculated as:

$$\text{Price–earnings ratio} = \frac{\text{Market price per share}}{\text{Earnings per share}}$$

Predicted earnings per share P. 797 for the next period is often used in the denominator of this calculation. Reported earnings per share for the most recent period is also commonly used. In both cases, the ratio is an indicator of the future growth of and risk related to a company's earnings as perceived by investors who establish the market price of the shares.

The market price of Ralco's common shares during 2011 ranged from a low of $14.50 to a high of $23.25. Ralco's management reported that it did not expect 2012 revenue growth rates to be as high as those for 2011. Management also indicated that operating expenses as a percentage of revenues might increase. Nevertheless, the price–earnings ratios in 2011 are much higher than many companies'. Using Ralco's $0.63 earnings per share that was reported at the end of 2011, we calculate its price–earnings ratios using both the low and high share prices:

$$\text{Low: } \frac{\$14.50}{\$0.63} = 23.0 \qquad \text{High: } \frac{\$23.25}{\$0.63} = 36.9$$

Ralco's ratios, which are higher than the industry average of 18.2, reflect the expectation of investors that the company will continue to grow at a faster rate than its competitors.

Dividend Yield

We use *dividend yield* as a means of comparing the dividend-paying performance of different investment alternatives. Dividend yield is calculated as:

$$\text{Dividend yield} = \frac{\text{Annual dividends per share}}{\text{Market price per share}} \times 100$$

A low dividend yield is neither bad nor good by itself. Some companies decide not to declare dividends because they prefer to reinvest the cash. Ralco, for instance, does not pay cash dividends on its common shares, but its competitors pay $0.35 per common share on average.

CHECKPOINT

12. Which ratio measures the success of a company in earning net income for its owners? (a) Profit margin; (b) Return on common shareholders' equity; (c) Price–earnings ratio; (d) Dividend yield.

13. If a company has net sales of $8,500,000, net income of $945,000, and total asset turnover of 1.8 times, what is its return on total assets?

Do: QS 20-17 to QS 20-24

Summary of Ratios

This chapter has presented a variety of ratios that measure liquidity and efficiency, solvency, profitability, and market performance. One purpose of ratio analysis is to provide a standard against which actual performance can be compared. Standards of comparison were discussed earlier in the chapter and may include:

- *Ratios of other firms in the same industry.* Nortel's profit margin, for example, can be compared to Cisco's.
- *Past performance.* WestJet, for example, can compare the current year's net income in relation to sales with that of the past years.
- *Budgeted performance.* BCE can compare various ratios based on actual performance with expected ratios that were budgeted.
- *Subjective standards.* General standards of comparison can develop from past experience. Examples are a 2 to 1 level for the current ratio or 1 to 1 for the acid-test ratio. These guidelines, or rules of thumb, must be carefully applied since context is often crucial.

However all of the foregoing comparison measures involve elements of non-comparability. For example, firms in the same industry may use different accounting methods or one company may be much older than another, making it difficult to compare the costs of assets. Another limitation is that management may engage in year-end transactions that temporarily improve certain ratios. This is an unethical activity called *window dressing.*

A ratio that is significantly higher or lower than standard merely indicates that something may be wrong and should be investigated, but ratios do not provide definitive answers. Ratio analysis is based on current or past performance, but a user may be more interested in future performance. Any conclusions are therefore tentative and must be interpreted in the light of future expectations. Ratio analysis is, however, the beginning of a process of financial analysis and can help describe the financial condition of a company and help a user piece together a story about the relative strength and future potential financial health.

Exhibit 20.13 provides a summary that matches ratios with who generally uses them based on the primary interests of the users.

Exhibit 20.13

Matching Ratios to User Needs

User	Primary Interest	Key Ratios Emphasized
Short-term creditor	Assess ability of firm to meet cash commitments in the near term	Liquidity and efficiency ratios
Long-term creditor	Assess both short-term and long-term ability to meet cash commitments of interest payments and debt repayment schedules	Solvency ratios
Investor	Assess the firm's ability to make profits, pay dividends, and realize share price increases	Profitability ratios and market ratios

Extend Your Knowledge

20-1

Exhibit 20.14 presents a summary of the major financial statement analysis ratios illustrated in this chapter and throughout the book. This summary includes each ratio's title, formula, and common use.

Exhibit 20.14

Financial Statement Analysis Ratios

Ratio	Formula	Measure of:
Liquidity and Efficiency		
Current ratio	$= \dfrac{\text{Current assets}}{\text{Current liabilities}}$	Short-term debt-paying ability
Acid-test ratio	$= \dfrac{\text{Cash + Temporary investments + Net current receivables}}{\text{Current liabilities}}$	Immediate short-term debt-paying ability
Accounts receivable turnover*	$= \dfrac{\text{Net sales}}{\text{Average net accounts receivable}}$	Efficiency of collection
Days' sales uncollected	$= \dfrac{\text{Accounts receivable}}{\text{Net sales}} \times 365$	Liquidity of receivables
Merchandise turnover*	$= \dfrac{\text{Cost of goods sold}}{\text{Average merchandising inventory}}$	Efficiency of inventory
Days' sales in inventory	$= \dfrac{\text{Ending inventory}}{\text{Cost of goods sold}} \times 365$	Liquidity of inventory
Total asset turnover	$= \dfrac{\text{Net sales (or revenues)}}{\text{Average total assets}}$	Efficiency of assets in producing sales
Accounts payable turnover*	$= \dfrac{\text{Cost of goods sold}}{\text{Average accounts payable}}$	Efficiency in paying trade creditors
Solvency		
Debt ratio	$= \dfrac{\text{Total liabilities}}{\text{Total assets}} \times 100$	Creditor financing and leverage
Equity ratio	$= \dfrac{\text{Total shareholders' equity}}{\text{Total assets}} \times 100$	Owner financing
Pledged assets to secured liabilities	$= \dfrac{\text{Book value of pledged assets}}{\text{Book value of secured liabilities}}$	Protection to secured creditors
Times interest earned	$= \dfrac{\text{Income before interest and taxes}}{\text{Interest expense}}$	Protection in meeting interest payments
Profitability		
Profit margin	$= \dfrac{\text{Net income}}{\text{Net sales (or revenues)}} \times 100$	Net income in each sales dollar
Gross profit ratio	$= \dfrac{\text{Gross profit from sales}}{\text{Net sales}} \times 100$	Gross profit in each sales dollar
Return on total assets	$= \dfrac{\text{Net income}}{\text{Average total assets}} \times 100$	Overall profitability of assets
Return on common shareholders' equity	$= \dfrac{\text{Net income } - \text{ Preferred dividends}}{\text{Average common shareholders' equity}} \times 100$	Profitability of owner's investment
Book value per common share	$= \dfrac{\text{Shareholders' equity applicable to common shares}}{\text{Number of common shares outstanding}}$	Liquidation at reported amounts
Book value per preferred share	$= \dfrac{\text{Shareholders' equity applicable to preferred shares}}{\text{Number of preferred shares outstanding}}$	Liquidation at reported amounts
Basic earnings per share	$= \dfrac{\text{Net income } - \text{ Preferred dividends}}{\text{Weighted-average common shares outstanding}}$	Net income on each common share
Market		
Price–earnings ratio	$= \dfrac{\text{Market price per share}}{\text{Earnings per share}}$	Market value based on earnings
Dividend yield	$= \dfrac{\text{Annual dividends per share}}{\text{Market price per share}} \times 100$	Cash return to each share

*These ratios can also be expressed in terms of days by dividing them into 365. For example, 365 ÷ Accounts receivable turnover = How many days on average it takes to collect receivables.

Summary --

LO¹ | **Describe financial statement analysis and identify its focus, standards of comparison, and tools.** The purpose of financial statement analysis is to help users make better business decisions using the tools of horizontal, vertical, and ratio analysis to evaluate (1) past and current performance, (2) current financial position, and (3) future performance and risk. The four building blocks of analysis are: (1) liquidity and efficiency—ability to meet short-term obligations and generate revenues efficiently; (2) solvency—ability to generate future revenues and meet long-term obligations; (3) profitability—ability to provide financial rewards sufficient to attract and retain financing; and (4) market—ability to generate positive market expectations. To make conclusions from analysis we need standards for comparisons including: (1) intracompany; (2) competitor; (3) industry; and (4) guidelines (rules of thumb).

LO² | **Explain and apply methods of horizontal analysis.** Horizontal analysis is a tool to evaluate changes in financial statement data across time. Two important tools of horizontal analysis are comparative statements and trend analysis. Comparative statements show amounts for two or more successive periods, often with changes disclosed in

both absolute and percent terms. Trend analysis is used to reveal important changes occurring from one period to the next.

LO³ | **Describe and apply methods of vertical analysis.** In common-size statements, each item is expressed as a percent of a base amount. The base amount for the balance sheet is usually total assets, and the base amount for the income statement is usually net sales. Vertical analysis is a tool to evaluate each financial statement item or group of items in terms of a specific base amount. This base amount is commonly defined as 100%. Two important tools of vertical analysis are common-size statements and graphical analyses.

LO⁴ | **Define and apply ratio analysis.** Ratio analysis provides clues and symptoms of underlying conditions. Ratios, properly interpreted, identify areas requiring further investigation. A ratio expresses a mathematical relation between two quantities; examples are a percent, a rate, or a proportion. Selected ratios are organized into the building blocks of analysis: (1) liquidity and efficiency, (2) solvency, (3) profitability, and (4) market.

---

guidance answer to | **JUDGEMENT CALL**

Banker

Your decision on the loan application is positive for at least two reasons. First, the current ratio suggests a strong ability to meet short-term obligations. Second, current assets of $160,000 and a current ratio of 4:1 imply current liabilities of $40,000 (one-fourth of current assets) and a working capital excess of $120,000. This working capital excess is 60% of the loan amount. However, if the application is for a 10-year loan, our decision is less optimistic. While the current ratio and working capital suggest a good safety margin, there are indications of inefficiency in operations. In particular, a 4:1 current ratio is more than double its competitors' ratio. This is characteristic of inefficient asset use.

1. General purpose financial statements are intended for the large variety of users who are interested in receiving financial information about a business but who do not have the ability to require the company to prepare specialized financial reports designed to meet their specific interests.

2. General purpose financial statements include the income statement, balance sheet, statement of retained earnings, and cash flow statement, plus notes related to the statements.

3. *a*

4. Data from one or more direct competitors of the company under analysis are usually preferred for developing standards for comparison.

5. Accounts receivable is increasing at a faster rate than sales, which is an unfavourable trend.

	2011	%	2010	%	2009	%
Sales	$50.0	128.2	$40.0	102.6	$39.0	100
Accounts receivable...	13.0	166.7	8.8	112.8	7.8	100

6. *d*

7. Percents on a comparative income statement show the increase or decrease in each item from one period to the next. On a common-size comparative income statement, each item is shown as a percent of net sales for a specific period.

8. *c*

9. (a) $\dfrac{(\$820,000 + \$240,000 + \$470,000)}{(\$350,000 + \$180,000)} = 2.9 \text{ to } 1$

   (b) $\dfrac{(\$820,000 + \$240,000)}{(\$350,000 + \$180,000)} = 2 \text{ to } 1$

10. (a) $2,500,000/[(\$290,000 + \$240,000)/2]$
     = 9.43 times

    (b) ($240,000/$2,500,000) × 365 = 35 days

    (c) $750,000/[(\$530,000 + \$470,000)/2] = 1.5 times

    (d) ($470,000/$750,000) × 365 = 228.7 days

11. *c*

12. *b*

13. $\dfrac{\text{Profit}}{\text{margin}} \times \dfrac{\text{Total asset}}{\text{turnover}} = \dfrac{\text{Return on}}{\text{total assets}}$

    [($945,000/$8,500,000) × 100] × 1.8 = 20%

demonstration problem

Use the financial statements of Precision Inc. to calculate and identify the appropriate building block of financial statement analysis for the following ratios as of December 31, 2011:

a. Current ratio

b. Acid-test ratio

c. Accounts receivable turnover

d. Days' sales uncollected

e. Merchandise turnover

f. Debt ratio

g. Pledged assets to secured liabilities

h. Times interest earned

i. Profit margin

j. Total asset turnover

k. Return on total assets

l. Return on common shareholders' equity

Analysis component:

Indicate whether each of the ratios calculated above for Precision Inc. compares favourably (F) or unfavourably (U) to the industry average ratios in Exhibit 20.11.

Precision Inc.
Comparative Income Statement
For Years Ended December 31, 2011 and 2010

	2011	2010
Sales	$2,486,000	$2,075,000
Cost of goods sold.....................	1,523,000	1,222,000
Gross profit from sales	$ 963,000	$ 853,000
Operating expenses:		
Advertising expense	$ 145,000	$ 100,000
Sales salaries expense	240,000	280,000
Office salaries expense............	165,000	200,000
Insurance expense..................	100,000	45,000
Supplies expense....................	26,000	35,000
Amortization expense.............	85,000	75,000
Miscellaneous expenses..........	17,000	15,000
Total operating expenses........	$ 778,000	$ 750,000
Operating income	$ 185,000	$ 103,000
Less interest expense	44,000	46,000
Income before taxes	$ 141,000	$ 57,000
Income taxes	47,000	19,000
Net income	$ 94,000	$ 38,000
Earnings per share	$ 0.99	$ 0.40

Precision Inc.
Comparative Balance Sheet
December 31

	2011	2010
Assets		
Current assets:		
Cash.......................................	$ 79,000	$ 42,000
Short-term investments	65,000	96,000
Accounts receivable (net)	120,000	100,000
Merchandise inventory...........	250,000	265,000
Total current assets.................	$ 514,000	$ 503,000
Capital assets:		
Store equipment (net)............	$ 400,000	$ 350,000
Office equipment (net)...........	45,000	50,000
Buildings (net)........................	625,000	675,000
Land.......................................	100,000	100,000
Total capital assets..................	$1,170,000	$1,175,000
Total assets	$1,684,000	$1,678,000
Liabilities		
Current liabilities:		
Accounts payable	$ 164,000	$ 190,000
Short-term notes payable	75,000	90,000
Taxes payable.........................	26,000	12,000
Total current liabilities	$ 265,000	$ 292,000
Long-term liabilities:		
Notes payable (secured by mortgage on building and land)	400,000	420,000
Total liabilities	$ 665,000	$ 712,000
Shareholders' Equity		
Contributed capital:		
Common shares	$ 475,000	$ 475,000
Retained earnings	544,000	491,000
Total shareholders' equity	$1,019,000	$ 966,000
Total liabilities and shareholders' equity	$1,684,000	$1,678,000

Planning the Solution

- Calculate the given ratios using the provided numbers; be sure to calculate the average amounts where appropriate.
- Answer the analysis component.

solution to *Demonstration Problem*

Ratios for 2011:

a. Current ratio: $514,000/$265,000 = 1.9 to 1 (Liquidity and Efficiency)

b. Acid-test ratio: ($79,000 + $65,000 + $120,000)/$265,000 = 1.0 to 1 (Liquidity and Efficiency)

c. Average receivables: ($120,000 + $100,000)/2 = $110,000
Accounts receivable turnover: $2,486,000/$110,000 = 22.6 times (Liquidity and Efficiency)

d. Days' sales uncollected: ($120,000/$2,486,000) × 365 = 17.6 days (Liquidity and Efficiency)

e. Average inventory: ($250,000 + $265,000)/2 = $257,500
Merchandise turnover: $1,523,000/$257,500 = 5.9 times (Liquidity and Efficiency)

f. Debt ratio: $665,000/$1,684,000 × 100 = 39.5% (Solvency)

g. Pledged assets to secured liabilities: ($625,000 + $100,000)/$400,000 = 1.8 to 1 (Solvency)

h. Times interest earned: $185,000/$44,000 = 4.2 times (Solvency)

i. Profit margin: $94,000/$2,486,000 × 100 = 3.8% (Profitability)

j. Average total assets: ($1,684,000 + $1,678,000)/2 = $1,681,000
Total asset turnover: $2,486,000/$1,681,000 = 1.48 times (Liquidity and Efficiency)

k. Return on total assets: $94,000/$1,681,000 × 100 = 5.6%, or 3.8% × 1.48 = 5.6% (Profitability)

l. Average total equity: ($1,019,000 + $966,000)/2 = $992,500
Return on common shareholders' equity: $94,000/$992,500 × 100 = 9.5% (Profitability)

Analysis component:

	Precision Inc.	Industry Average	F/U
Current ratio	1.9:1	1.6:1	F
Acid-test ratio	1.0:1	1.1:1	U
Accounts receivable turnover	22.6 times	16 times	F
Days' sales uncollected	17.6 days	21 days	F
Merchandise turnover	5.9 times	5 times	F
Debt ratio	39.5%	35%	U
Pledged assets to secured liabilities	1.8:1	1.4:1	F
Times interest earned	4.2 times	50 times	U
Profit margin	3.8%	14%	U
Total asset turnover	1.48 times	2.3 times	U
Return on total assets	5.6%	20%	U
Return on common shareholders' equity	9.5%	32.7%	U

Glossary

Capital structure A company's source of financing: shares and/or debt. (p. 1022)

Common-size financial statement A statement in which each amount is expressed as a percent of a base amount. In the balance sheet, the amount of total assets is usually selected as the base amount and is expressed as 100%. In the income statement, revenue is usually selected as the base amount. (p. 1009)

Comparative financial statement A financial statement with data for two or more successive accounting periods placed in side-by-side columns, often with changes shown in dollar amounts and percentages. (p. 1004)

Efficiency A company's productivity in using its assets; usually measured relative to how much revenue is generated for a certain level of assets. (p. 1015)

Equity ratio The portion of total assets provided by equity, calculated as equity divided by total assets. (p. 1022)

Financial reporting The process of communicating information that is relevant to investors, creditors, and others in making investment, credit, and other decisions. (p. 1003)

Financial statement analysis The application of analytical tools to general purpose financial statements and related data for making business decisions. (p. 1002)

General purpose financial statements Statements published periodically for use by a wide variety of interested parties; include the income statement, balance sheet, statement of retained earnings, cash flow statement, and notes related to the statements. (p. 1003)

Gross margin See *gross profit*. (p. 1024)

Gross profit The relation between sales and cost of goods sold. (p. 1024)

Horizontal analysis A tool to evaluate changes in financial statement data across time. (p. 1004)

Liquidity The availability of resources to meet short-term cash requirements. (p. 1015)

Profitability A company's ability to generate an adequate return on invested capital. (p. 1023)

Ratio analysis Determination of key relations among financial statement items. (p. 1015)

Solvency A company's long-run financial viability and its ability to cover long-term obligations. (p. 1022)

Vertical analysis The analysis of each financial statement item or group of items in terms of a specific base amount; the base amount is commonly defined as 100% and is usually revenue on the income statement and total assets on the balance sheet. Also called *common-size analysis*. (p. 1009)

Working capital Current assets minus current liabilities. Also known as *net working capital*. (p. 1015)

For more study tools, quizzes, and problem material,
visit the **Student Success** *Centre* at
www.mcgrawhill.ca/studentsuccess/FAP

Questions

1. Explain the difference between financial reporting and financial statements.
2. What is the difference between comparative financial statements and common-size comparative statements?
3. Which items are usually assigned a value of 100% on a common-size comparative balance sheet and a common-size comparative income statement?
4. Why is working capital given special attention in the process of analyzing balance sheets?
5. What are three factors that would influence your decision as to whether a company's current ratio is good or bad?
6. Suggest several reasons why a 2 to 1 current ratio may not be adequate for a particular company.
7. Which assets are "quick assets" in calculating the acid-test ratio?
8. Which two short-term liquidity ratios measure how frequently a company collects its accounts?
9. Which two terms are used to describe the difference between current assets and current liabilities?
10. Which two ratios are the basic components in measuring a company's operating efficiency? Which ratio summarizes these two components?
11. What does a relatively high accounts receivable turnover indicate about a company's short-term liquidity?
12. What is the significance of the number of days' sales uncollected?
13. Why does merchandise turnover provide information about a company's short-term liquidity?
14. Why is the capital structure of a company, as measured by debt and equity ratios, of importance to financial statement analysts?
15. Why must the ratio of pledged assets to secured liabilities be interpreted with caution?
16. Why would a company's return on total assets be different from its return on common shareholders' equity?

17. What ratios would you calculate for the purpose of evaluating management performance?

18. Baker Corp. uses LIFO and Campbell Inc. uses FIFO during a period of rising prices. What differences would you expect to find with each of the following ratios: current ratio, profit margin, debt ratio, merchandise turnover, and times interest earned.

19. Refer to the financial statements in Appendix I for WestJet and calculate the percentage change in total revenues from 2004 to 2005.

20. Refer to the financial statements in Appendix I for Danier Leather and calculate the percentage change in operating expenses from 2004 to 2005.

Quick Study

Which of the following items are means of accomplishing the objective of financial reporting but are not included within general purpose financial statements? (a) Income statements, (b) company news releases, (c) balance sheets, (d) certain reports filed with the Canada Revenue Agency, (e) cash flow statements, (f) management discussions and analyses of financial performance.

QS 20-1
Financial reporting
LO¹

What are four possible bases of comparison you can use when analyzing financial statement ratios? Which of these is generally considered to be the most useful? Which one is least likely to provide a good basis for comparison?

QS 20-2
Comparing ratios
LO¹

Where possible, calculate percents of increase and decrease for the following accounts of Brewer Ltd.:

QS 20-3
Reporting percent changes
LO²

	2011	2010
Temporary investments	$203,000	$154,000
Accounts receivable	30,888	35,200
Notes payable	25,000	-0-

Calculate trend percentages for the following items using 2007 as the base year. Then, state whether the situation shown by the trends appears to be *favourable* or *unfavourable*.

QS 20-4
Calculating trend percents
LO²

	2011	2010	2009	2008	2007
Sales	$377,600	$362,400	$338,240	$314,080	$302,000
Cost of goods sold	172,720	164,560	155,040	142,800	136,000
Accounts receivable	25,400	24,400	23,200	21,600	20,000

Express the following income statement information in common-size percents and assess whether the situation is *favourable* or *unfavourable*.

QS 20-5
Common-size income statement
LO³

Waterford Corporation Income Statement For Years Ended December 31, 2011 and 2010		
	2011	2010
Sales	$1,056,000	$735,000
Cost of goods sold	633,600	382,200
Gross profit from sales	$ 422,400	$352,800
Operating expenses	237,600	148,470
Net income	$ 184,800	$204,330

QS 20-6
Common-size balance sheet
LO3

Carmon Inc.'s December 31 balance sheets included the following data:

	2011	2010	2009
Cash...	$ 51,800	$ 70,310	$ 73,600
Accounts receivable, net......................................	186,800	125,940	98,400
Merchandise inventory..	223,000	165,000	106,000
Prepaid expenses..	19,400	18,750	8,000
Plant assets, net..	555,000	510,000	459,000
Total assets..	$1,036,000	$890,000	$745,000
Accounts payable	$ 257,800	$150,500	$ 98,500
Long-term notes payable secured by mortgages on plant assets.....................................	195,000	205,000	165,000
Common shares (32,500 shares issued).............	325,000	325,000	325,000
Retained earnings...	258,200	209,500	156,500
Total liabilities and shareholders' equity.............	$1,036,000	$890,000	$745,000

Required
Express the balance sheets in common-size percents. Round calculations to two decimal places.

QS 20-7
Working capital and current ratio
LO4

Using the information below, calculate the:
a. working capital
b. current ratio using the following information (round to two decimal places)

Accounts payable..	$10,000	Long-term notes payable	$20,000
Accounts receivable	15,000	Office supplies	3,800
Buildings..	42,000	Prepaid insurance	2,500
Cash	4,000	Unearned fees..	1,000
Current portion of notes payable	7,000	Wages payable..	3,000

c. What is the difference between *working capital* and the *current ratio*?
d. Assuming this company's current ratio was 1.12:1 in the last accounting period, does the result of the calculation in part (a) above represent a favourable or unfavourable change?

QS 20-8
Acid-test ratio
LO4

a. Using the information in QS 20-7, calculate the acid-test ratio.
b. At the end of the last accounting period, this company's acid-test ratio was 0.82:1. Has the change in the acid-test ratio been favourable or unfavourable?

QS 20-9
Accounts receivable turnover
LO4

The following data are taken from the comparative balance sheets of Duncan Company. Calculate the accounts receivable turnover for 2011 and 2010 (round to two decimal places). Is the change favourable or unfavourable? Explain why. Compare Duncan's turnover to the industry average turnover for 2011 of 4.2.

	2011	2010	2009
Net sales..	$754,200	$810,600	$876,000
Accounts receivable	152,900	133,700	121,000

Calculate and interpret the days' sales uncollected for 2011 and 2010 based on the following selected information for Lumbar Cushions Company (round to two decimal places):

QS 20-10
Days' sales uncollected
LO4

	2011	2010
Accounts receivable	$ 220,000	$ 160,000
Net sales	2,380,000	1,450,000

Mamoon Company begins the year with $200,000 of goods in inventory. At year-end, the amount in inventory has increased to $230,000. Cost of goods sold for the year is $1,600,000. Calculate Mamoon's inventory turnover (round calculations to two decimal places). Assuming an industry average merchandise turnover of 4, what is your assessment of Mamoon's inventory management?

QS 20-11
Merchandise turnover
LO4

	Company A	Company B	Company C
Ending inventory	$ 20,000	$ 75,000	$ 140,000
Cost of goods sold	345,000	540,000	2,100,000

QS 20-12
Days' sales in inventory
LO4

a. Calculate the days' sales in inventory for each company (round to two decimal places).
b. Which company will take the longest to sell its current balance in inventory?

Jennifer Inc. reported the following facts in its 2011 annual report: net sales of $9,683 million for 2010 and $9,050 million for 2011; total end-of-year assets of $10,690 million for 2010 and $13,435 million for 2011. Calculate the total asset turnover for 2011 and identify whether it compares favourably or unfavourably with the industry average in Exhibit 20.11.

QS 20-13
Calculating total asset turnover
LO4

Friesens manufactures books. It buys significant quantities of supplies from various vendors in order to make its quality products. Calculate Friesens' accounts payable turnover for 2011 and 2010 and determine whether it is meeting its objective of paying trade creditors within 25 days (round calculations to two decimal places).

QS 20-14
Accounts payable turnover
LO4

	2011	2010	2009
Cost of goods sold	$10,800,000	$9,350,000	$8,100,000
Accounts payable	890,000	654,500	565,000

The following information relates to three companies that operate similar businesses:

QS 20-15
Solvency ratios
LO4

	Company A	Company B	Company C
Cash	$ 30,000	$ 65,000	$ 5,000
Accounts receivable, net	250,000	654,500	565,000
Merchandise inventory	760,000	590,000	190,000
Plant assets, net	640,000	1,850,000	985,000
Accounts payable	335,000	970,000	180,000
Long-term notes payable secured by mortgages on plant assets	590,000	1,500,000	215,000
Common shares	700,000	500,000	450,000
Retained earnings	55,000	189,500	900,000

For each company, calculate the debt ratio, equity ratio, and pledged assets to secured liabilities. Identify which company has the *least favourable* performance in each ratio and why.

QS 20-16
Times interest earned
LO4

The following information is available for Best Appliance Inc.:

Best Appliance Inc.
Income Statement
Year ended November 30, 2011

Sales...		$500
Cost of goods sold		190
Gross profit		$310
Operating expenses:		
Amortization expense	$ 20	
Other expenses.......................................	200	
Total operating expenses		220
Income from operations		$ 90
Interest expense		5
Income tax expense		10
Net income..		$ 75

Required
Calculate the times interest earned ratio for 2011 and compare it to the industry average in Exhibit 20.11. Explain why it compares favourably or unfavourably.

Use the following information to answer QS 20-17 to QS 20-22.

Delmar Corp.
Comparative Balance Sheet Information
November 30
(millions of $)

	2011	2010
Cash	$ 25	$ 5
Accounts receivable (net)........................	46	20
Inventory..	80	95
Prepaid rent..	30	15
Capital assets (net).................................	300	320
Accounts payable....................................	40	22
Accrued liabilities	35	50
Income tax payable	7	2
Preferred shares[1]	50	50
Common shares[2]	100	100
Retained earnings[3]	249	231

Delmar Corp.
Income Statement
Year ended November 30, 2011
(millions of $)

Sales...		$500
Cost of goods sold		190
Gross profit		$310
Operating expenses:		
Amortization expense	$ 20	
Other expenses.......................................	200	
Total operating expenses		220
Income from operations		$ 90
Income tax expense		10
Net income..		$ 80

[1] There were 1 million $5, non-cumulative, preferred shares issued and outstanding; no new shares were issued during 2010 or 2011.
[2] There were 25 million common shares issued and outstanding; no new shares were issued during 2010 or 2011.
[3] There are no dividends in arrears. Dividends totalling $62 million were declared and paid during 2011.

QS 20-17
Profit margin
LO4

Calculate the profit margin for 2011 and evaluate the result against the industry average in Exhibit 20.11, explaining why it compares favourably or unfavourably (round to two decimal places).

QS 20-18
Gross profit ratio
LO4

Calculate the gross profit ratio for 2011 and evaluate the result against the industry average in Exhibit 20.11, explaining why it compares favourably or unfavourably (round to two decimal places).

Calculate the return on total assets for 2011 and evaluate the result against the industry average in Exhibit 20.11, explaining why it compares favourably or unfavourably (round to two decimal places).

QS 20-19
Return on total assets
LO4

Calculate the return on common shareholders' equity for 2011 and evaluate the result against the industry average in Exhibit 20.11, explaining why it compares favourably or unfavourably (round to two decimal places).

QS 20-20
Return on common shareholders' equity
LO4

Calculate the book value per common share for 2011 and evaluate the result against the industry average in Exhibit 20.11, explaining why it compares favourably or unfavourably (round to two decimal places).

QS 20-21
Book value per common share
LO4

Calculate the basic earnings per share for 2011 and evaluate the result against the industry average in Exhibit 20.11, explaining why it compares favourably or unfavourably (round to two decimal places).

QS 20-22
Basic earnings per share
LO4

ABC Inc.'s common shares have a market value of $60 per share and its EPS is $3.50. XYZ Inc.'s common shares have a market value of $85 per share and its EPS is $4.10. You have done thorough research and are considering purchasing the shares of one of these companies.

QS 20-23
Price–earnings ratio
LO4

Required
a. Calculate the price–earnings ratio for each company (round to two decimal places).
b. Which company's shares will you purchase based on your calculations in (a) above?

ABC Inc. declared and paid an $8 per share cash dividend on its common shares during the current accounting period. The current market value of the ABC Inc. shares is $56 per share.

QS 20-24
Dividend yield
LO4

Required
a. Calculate the dividend yield (express as a percent rounded to two decimal places).
b. Would the ABC Inc. shares be classified as growth or income shares?

Exercises

Common-size and trend percentages for a company's sales, cost of goods sold, and expenses follow:

Exercise 20-1
Determining income effects from common-size and trend percents
LO2, 3

	Common-Size Percentages			Trend Percentages		
	2011	**2010**	**2009**	**2011**	**2010**	**2009**
Sales...................................	100.0%	100.0%	100.0%	106.5%	105.3%	100.0%
Cost of goods sold	64.5	63.0	60.2	104.1	102.3	100.0
Expenses	16.4	15.9	16.2	96.0	94.1	100.0

Required
Determine whether the company's net income increased, decreased, or remained unchanged during this three-year period.

Exercise 20-2
Current ratio—calculation and analysis
LO4

The following companies are competing in the same industry where the industry norm for the current ratio is 1.6.

	Current Assets	Current Liabilities	Current Ratio	Comparison to Industry Norm (F or U)
Company 1	$ 78,000	$31,000	_____	_____
Company 2	114,000	75,000	_____	_____
Company 3	60,000	99,000	_____	_____

Required
a. Complete the schedule (round to two decimal places).
b. Identify the company with the strongest liquidity position.
c. Identify the company with the weakest liquidity position.

Analysis component:
You are more closely analyzing the financial condition of Company 2 to assess its ability to meet upcoming loan payments. You calculate its current ratio. You also find that a major account receivable in the amount of $69,000 is due from one client who has not made any payments in the past 12 months. Removing this receivable from current assets changes the current ratio. What do you conclude?

Exercise 20-3
Acid-test ratio—calculation and analysis
LO4

Part of your job is to review customer requests for credit. You have three new credit applications on your desk and part of your analysis requires that the current ratios and acid-test ratios be compared.
a. Complete the following schedule (round to two decimal places).

Account	#1	#2	#3
Cash	$1,800	$1,000	$ 1,100
Short-term investments....................................	$ 0	$ 0	$ 500
Current receivables	$2,000	$ 990	$ 200
Inventory	$ 700	$1,000	$ 4,600
Prepaid expenses	$ 200	$ 600	$ 900
Land	$3,000	$4,000	$17,000
Current liabilities...	$2,200	$1,100	$ 3,650
Current ratio	_____	_____	_____
Acid-test ratio	_____	_____	_____

b. Which applications will you approve/not approve and why?

Exercise 20-4
Accounts receivable turnover—calculation and analysis
LO4

	2011	2010	2009
Net sales	$1,800,000	$1,300,000	$1,200,000
Accounts receivable..	440,000	108,000	82,000
Net income...	490,000	510,000	522,000

You review the above information for your daycare business and it reveals decreasing profits despite increasing sales. You hire an analyst who highlights several points, including that "Accounts receivable turnover is too low. Tighter credit policies are recommended along with discontinuing service to those most delayed in payments." How do you interpret these recommendations? What actions do you take? Round calculations to two decimal places.

Exercise 20-5
Days' sales uncollected—calculation and analysis
LO4

Westend Windows constructs and installs windows for new and old homes. The sales staff are having a meeting and reviewing the following information to determine how to help reduce days' sales uncollected.

	2011	2010	2009
Accounts receivable...	$ 890,000	$ 654,500	$ 565,000
Net sales..	10,800,000	9,350,000	8,100,000

Required

a. Calculate the days' sales uncollected for 2009 to 2011 and identify whether the trend is favourable or unfavourable.

b. What can a salesperson do to improve days' sales uncollected?

Exercise 20-6
Merchandise turnover—calculation and analysis
LO4

	(millions of $)							
	Computer Inc.		**Furniture Retailers**		**Freshcut Flowers Inc.**		**Furniture Unlimited**	
	2011	**2010**	**2011**	**2010**	**2011**	**2010**	**2011**	**2010**
Cost of goods sold..................	$450	$320	$980	$640	$720	$810	$730	$580
Merchandise inventory............	50	40	35	20	5	3	15	40

a. Calculate the merchandise inventory turnover for 2011 for each company (round to two decimal places).

b. Can you compare these companies? Explain.

c. Review the turnover for Freshcut Flowers Inc. Does this result appear to be logical? Explain why or why not.

Refer to the information in Exercise 20-6 and calculate the days' sales in inventory for Furniture Retailers and Furniture Unlimited for 2011 (round to two decimal places). Which company has the most favourable ratio? Explain why.

Exercise 20-7
Days' sales in inventory—calculation and analysis
LO4

Exercise 20-8
Liquidity and efficiency ratios—calculation and analysis
LO4

Fefferman Inc. Comparative Balance Sheet Information November 30 (millions of $)			
	2011	**2010**	**2009**
Cash...	$ 75	$ 15	$ 30
Accounts receivable (net)	138	60	45
Inventory......................................	240	285	234
Prepaid rent	90	45	30
Capital assets (net)	900	960	1,020
Accounts payable	120	66	54
Accrued liabilities.........................	105	150	96
Income tax payable.......................	21	6	15
Preferred shares...........................	150	150	150
Common shares	300	300	300
Retained earnings.........................	747	693	744

Fefferman Inc. Income Statement Year ended November 30, 2011 (millions of $)		
	2011	**2010**
Sales	$1,500	$1,230
Cost of goods sold........................	570	480
Gross profit.................................	$ 930	$ 750
Operating expenses:		
Amortization expense.................	$ 60	$ 60
Other expenses	600	405
Total operating expenses............	660	465
Income from operations	$ 270	$ 285
Interest expense...........................	21	9
Income tax expense.......................	30	33
Net income	$ 219	$ 243

Required

Refer to Exhibit 20.14 and calculate Fefferman's liquidity and efficiency ratios for 2011 and 2010 (round answers to two decimal places).

Analysis component:

Identify whether the change in each ratio from 2010 to 2011 was favourable (F) or unfavourable (U) and why.

Exercise 20-9
Solvency ratios—calculation
and analysis
LO4

Bhardwaj Inc. Comparative Balance Sheet Information November 30 (millions of $)		
	2011	2010
Cash	$ 10	$ 60
Accounts receivable (net)	270	160
Inventory	40	35
Capital assets (net)	1,790	1,850
Accounts payable	180	120
Long-term notes payable*	1,200	1,600
Common shares	200	200
Retained earnings	530	185

90% of the capital assets are secured by long-term notes payable.

Bhardwaj Inc. Income Statement Year ended November 30, 2011 (millions of $)		
	2011	2010
Sales	$1,800	$1,230
Cost of goods sold	630	480
Gross profit	$1,170	$ 750
Operating expenses:		
Amortization expense	$ 60	$ 60
Other expenses	500	405
Total operating expenses	560	465
Income from operations	$ 610	$ 285
Interest expense	72	96
Income tax expense	30	33
Net income	$ 508	$ 156

Required

Refer to Exhibit 20.14 and calculate Bhardwaj's solvency ratios for 2011 and 2010 (round answers to two decimal places).

Analysis component:
Identify whether the change in each ratio from 2010 to 2011 was favourable (F) or unfavourable (U) and why.

Exercise 20-10
Trend analysis, profitability ratios
LO2, 4

Bishop Corp. Comparative Balance Sheet Information November 30 (millions of $)			
	2011	2010	2009
Cash	$ 251	$ 735	$ 766
Accounts receivable (net)	343	390	164
Capital assets (net)	1,790	1,850	2,220
Accounts payable	68	164	230
Long-term notes payable	1,200	1,600	1,800
Preferred shares[1, 2]	200	200	200
Common shares[2]	800	800	800
Retained earnings	116	211	120

[1] *The preferred shares are $0.50, non-cumulative*
[2] *100 million preferred and 400 million common shares were issued and outstanding during each year.*

Bishop Corp. Income Statement Year ended November 30, 2011 (millions of $)			
	2011	2010	2009
Sales	$4,900	$7,800	$8,200
Cost of goods sold	3,430	5,460	5,740
Gross profit	$1,470	$2,340	$2,460
Operating expenses:			
Amortization expense	$ 370	$ 370	$ 370
Other expenses	490	1,560	1,804
Total operating expenses	860	1,930	2,174
Income from operations	$ 610	$ 410	$ 286
Interest expense	72	96	108
Income tax expense	183	123	80
Net income	$ 355	$ 191	$ 98

Required

Refer to Exhibit 20.14 and calculate Bishop's profitability ratios for 2011 (round calculations to two decimal places). Also identify whether each of Bishop's profitability ratios compares favourably (F) or unfavourably (U) to the industry average by referring to Exhibit 20.11.

Analysis component:
Comment on the trend in sales, accounts receivable, cost of goods sold, merchandise inventory, and accounts payable for the three years 2011, 2010, and 2009.

Use the following information to calculate the ratio of pledged assets to secured liabilities for both companies:

	Grant Inc.	Singh Inc.
Pledged assets	$541,800	$240,800
Total assets	550,000	490,000
Secured liabilities	228,200	229,300
Unsecured liabilities	266,000	390,000

Exercise 20-11
Ratio of pledged assets to secured liabilities
LO4

Check figure:
Grant Inc. = 2.37

Which company appears to have the riskier secured debt?

The following information is available from the financial statements of Rawhide Industries Inc.:

	2011	2010	2009
Total assets, December 31	$190,000	$320,000	$750,000
Net income	28,200	36,400	58,300

Exercise 20-12
Return on total assets
LO4

Check figure:
2011 = 11.1%

Calculate Rawhide's return on total assets for 2010 and 2011. (Round answers to one decimal place.) Comment whether the change in the company's efficiency in using its assets from 2010 to 2011 was favourable or unfavourable, including a comparison against the industry averages in Exhibit 20.11.

Carmon Inc.'s December 31 incomplete balance sheet information follows along with additional information:

Exercise 20-13
Evaluating profitability
LO4

	2011	2010	2009
Accounts payable	$257,800	$150,500	$ 98,500
Accounts receivable, net	186,800	125,940	98,400
Cash	51,800	70,310	73,600
Common shares*	325,000	325,000	325,000
Long-term notes payable	195,000	205,000	165,000
Merchandise inventory	223,000	165,000	106,000
Plant assets, net	555,000	510,000	459,000
Prepaid expenses	19,400	18,750	8,000
Retained earnings	?	?	?

	December 31, 2011	2010
Common shares market price	$30.00	$28.00
Annual cash dividends declared per share	0.60	0.30

32,500 shares were issued and outstanding for all three years.

Required
1. Prepare a three-year comparative balance sheet for Carmon Inc.
2. To evaluate the company's profitability, calculate the ratios for each year shown in the following schedule and determine whether the change was favourable or unfavourable.

Check figures:
1. Total assets = $1,036,000
2a. 2011 = 12.2%

	2011	2010	Favourable or Unfavourable
a. Return on common shareholders' equity			
b. Price–earnings			
c. Dividend yield			

Problems

Problem 20-1A
Calculation and analysis of trend percents

LO²

The condensed comparative statements of Glace Bay Corporation follow:

Glace Bay Corporation
Income Statement ($000)
For Years Ended December 31, 2011–2005

	2011	2010	2009	2008	2007	2006	2005
Sales	$797	$698	$635	$582	$543	$505	$420
Cost of goods sold	573	466	401	351	326	305	250
Gross profit from sales	$224	$232	$234	$231	$217	$200	$170
Operating expenses	170	133	122	90	78	77	65
Net income	$ 54	$ 99	$112	$141	$139	$123	$105

Glace Bay Corporation
Balance Sheet ($000)
December 31, 2011–2005

	2011	2010	2009	2008	2007	2006	2005
Assets							
Cash	$ 34	$ 44	$ 46	$ 47	$ 49	$ 48	$ 50
Accounts receivable, net	240	252	228	175	154	146	102
Merchandise inventory	869	632	552	466	418	355	260
Other current assets	23	21	12	22	19	19	10
Long-term investments	0	0	0	68	68	68	68
Plant and equipment, net	1,060	1,057	926	522	539	480	412
Total assets	$2,226	$2,006	$1,764	$1,300	$1,247	$1,116	$902
Liabilities and Equity							
Current liabilities	$ 560	$ 471	$ 309	$ 257	$ 223	$ 211	$136
Long-term liabilities	597	520	506	235	240	260	198
Common shares	625	625	625	510	510	400	400
Retained earnings	444	390	324	298	274	245	168
Total liabilities and equity	$2,226	$2,006	$1,764	$1,300	$1,247	$1,116	$902

Required
Calculate trend percentages for the items of the statements using 2005 as the base year.

Analysis component:
Analyze and comment on the situation shown in the statements.

The condensed statements of Crane Corp. follow:

Problem 20-2A
Calculating ratios and percents
LO2, 3, 4

Crane Corp.
Income Statement ($000)
For Years Ended December 31,

	2011	2010	2009
Sales	$148,000	$136,000	$118,000
Cost of goods sold	89,096	85,000	75,520
Gross profit from sales..........	$ 58,904	$ 51,000	$ 42,480
Selling expenses...................	$ 20,898	$ 18,768	$ 15,576
Administrative expenses.......	13,379	11,968	9,735
Total operating expenses......	$ 34,277	$ 30,736	$ 25,311
Income before taxes.............	$ 24,627	$ 20,264	$ 17,169
Income taxes........................	4,588	4,148	3,481
Net income..........................	$ 20,039	$ 16,116	$ 13,688

Crane Corp.
Balance Sheet ($000)
December 31,

	2011	2010	2009
Assets			
Current assets..........................	$24,240	$18,962	$25,324
Long-term investments	-0-	250	1,860
Plant and equipment..............	45,000	48,000	28,500
Total assets..............................	$69,240	$67,212	$55,684
Liabilities and Shareholders' Equity			
Current liabilities	$10,100	$ 9,980	$ 9,740
Common shares......................	40,500	40,500	30,000
Retained earnings...................	18,640	16,732	15,944
Total liabilities and shareholders' equity	$69,240	$67,212	$55,684

Required
1. Calculate each year's current ratio.
2. Express the income statement data in common-size percents.
3. Express the balance sheet data in trend percents with 2009 as the base year.

Analysis component:
Comment on any significant relationships revealed by the ratios and percents.

Metro Corporation began the month of March with $750,000 of current assets, a current ratio of 2.5 to 1, and an acid-test ratio of 1.1 to 1. During the month, it completed the following transactions:

Problem 20-3A
Analysis of working capital
LO4

Mar.	6	Bought $85,000 of merchandise on account. (The company uses a perpetual inventory system. P. 256)
	11	Sold merchandise that cost $68,000 for $113,000.
	15	Collected a $29,000 account receivable.
	17	Paid a $31,000 account payable.
	19	Wrote off a $13,000 bad debt against Allowance for Doubtful Accounts.
	24	Declared a $1.25 per share cash dividend on the 40,000 outstanding common shares.
	28	Paid the dividend declared on March 24.
	29	Borrowed $85,000 by giving the bank a 30-day, 10% note.
	30	Borrowed $100,000 by signing a long-term secured note.
	31	Used the $185,000 proceeds of the notes to buy additional machinery.

Required
Prepare a schedule showing Metro's current ratio, acid-test ratio, and working capital after each of the transactions. Round calculations to two decimal places.

Check figure:
March 31 working capital, $360,000

Problem 20-4A
Ratio essay
LO2, 4

Kerbey Inc. and Telcom Inc. are similar firms that operate within the same industry. The following information is available:

	Kerbey Inc.			Telcom Inc.		
	2011	2010	2009	2011	2010	2009
Current ratio...................	1.8	1.9	2.2	3.3	2.8	2.0
Acid-test ratio	1.1	1.2	1.3	2.9	2.6	1.7
Accounts receivable turnover.........................	30.5	25.2	29.2	16.4	15.2	16.0
Merchandise turnover.....	24.2	21.9	17.1	14.5	13.0	12.6
Working capital..............	$65,000	$53,000	$47,000	$126,000	$98,000	$73,000

Required
Write a brief essay comparing Kerbey and Telcom based on the preceding information. Your discussion should include their relative ability to meet current obligations and to use current assets efficiently.

Problem 20-5A
Calculation of financial statement ratios
LO4

The 2011 financial statements of Tooner Corporation follow:

Tooner Corporation	
Income Statement	
For Year Ended December 31, 2011	
Sales	$805,000
Cost of goods sold:	
Merchandise inventory, Dec. 31, 2010	$ 62,800
Purchases	500,700
Goods available for sale.........................	$563,500
Merchandise inventory, Dec. 31, 2011	49,200
Cost of goods sold	514,300
Gross profit from sales............................	$290,700
Operating expenses	227,800
Operating income..................................	$ 62,900
Interest expense....................................	9,500
Income before taxes...............................	$ 53,400
Income taxes..	15,720
Net income...	$ 37,680

Tooner Corporation	
Balance Sheet	
December 31, 2011	
Assets	
Cash...	$ 18,500
Temporary investments	20,400
Accounts receivable, net.......................................	43,400
Notes receivable...	8,800
Merchandise inventory	49,200
Prepaid expenses..	4,800
Plant assets, net...	272,100
Total assets	$417,200
Liabilities and Shareholders' Equity	
Accounts payable	$ 40,700
Accrued wages payable	5,200
Income taxes payable	5,800
Long-term note payable, secured by mortgage on plant assets...	95,000
Common shares, 160,000 shares............................	160,000
Retained earnings...	110,500
Total liabilities and shareholders' equity..................	$417,200

Assume all sales were on credit. On the December 31, 2010, balance sheet, the assets totalled $360,600, common shares were $160,000, and retained earnings were $89,700.

Check figures:

a. 2.81	g. 6.6
b. 1.76	h. 4.7
c. 19.7	i. 2.07
d. 9.2	j. 9.7
e. 34.9	k. 14.5
f. 2.86	

Required
Calculate the following: (a) current ratio, (b) acid-test ratio, (c) days' sales uncollected, (d) merchandise turnover, (e) days' sales in inventory, (f) ratio of pledged plant assets to secured liabilities, (g) times interest earned, (h) profit margin, (i) total asset turnover, (j) return on total assets, and (k) return on common shareholders' equity.

Analysis component:
Identify whether the ratios calculated above compare favourably or unfavourably to the industry averages in Exhibit 20.11.

Harpin Inc. calculated the ratios shown below for 2011 and 2010:

Problem 20-6A
Evaluating ratios
LO4

	2011	2010	Change F or U*	Comparison to Industry Average
Current ratio	1.2:1	1.1:1		
Acid-test ratio	0.98:1	0.94:1		
Accounts receivable turnover	18	21		
Days' sales uncollected	26	35		
Merchandise turnover	7	8		
Days' sales in inventory	55	42		
Total asset turnover	3.6	2.1		
Debt ratio	75	53		
Times interest earned	2.4	7.1		
Profit margin	17	21		
Gross profit ratio	19	18		

*F = Favourable; U = Unfavourable

Required
1. Identify whether the change in the ratios from 2010 to 2011 is favourable ('F') or unfavourable ('U').
2. Assess whether the 2011 ratios are favourable or unfavourable in comparison to the industry averages shown in Exhibit 20.11.

Alternate Problems

The condensed comparative statements of Dover Ltd. follow.

Problem 20-1B
Calculation and analysis of trend percentages
LO2

Required
Calculate trend percents for the items of the statements using 2005 as the base year.

Analysis component:
Analyze and comment on the situation shown in the statements.

Dover Ltd.
Income Statement ($000)
For Years Ended December 31, 2011–2005

	2011	2010	2009	2008	2007	2006	2005
Sales	$450	$470	$460	$490	$530	$520	$560
Cost of goods sold	190	197	194	208	219	212	214
Operating expenses	200	207	205	224	231	235	255
Income before taxes	$ 60	$ 66	$ 61	$ 58	$ 80	$ 73	$ 91

Dover Ltd.
Balance Sheet ($000)
December 31, 2011–2005

	2011	2010	2009	2008	2007	2006	2005
Assets							
Cash	$ 30	$ 33	$ 32	$ 36	$ 45	$ 42	$ 46
Accounts receivable, net	92	103	99	101	112	110	118
Merchandise inventory	143	149	147	156	159	169	162
Other current assets	20	21	22	24	23	26	28
Long-term investments	80	60	40	87	87	87	90
Plant and equipment, net	362	368	372	287	292	297	302
Total assets	$727	$734	$712	$691	$718	$731	$746
Liabilities and Equity							
Current liabilities	$162	$169	$152	$121	$143	$171	$216
Long-term liabilities	130	145	160	175	190	205	220
Common shares	205	205	205	205	205	205	205
Retained earnings	230	215	195	190	180	150	105
Total liabilities and capital	$727	$734	$712	$691	$718	$731	$746

Problem 20-2B
Calculating ratios and percents
LO2, 3, 4

The condensed statements of Dexter Corporation follow.

Dexter Corporation Income Statement ($000) For Years Ended December 31,			
	2011	2010	2009
Sales	$980,000	$824,000	$710,000
Cost of goods sold	545,000	433,000	338,000
Gross profit from sales..........	$435,000	$391,000	$372,000
Selling expenses...................	$131,000	$103,500	$109,000
Administrative expenses.......	98,000	104,500	95,000
Total expenses......................	$229,000	$208,000	$204,000
Income before taxes.............	$206,000	$183,000	$168,000
Income taxes........................	72,100	64,050	58,800
Net income..........................	$133,900	$118,950	$109,200

Dexter Corporation Balance Sheet ($000) December 31,			
	2011	2010	2009
Assets			
Current assets	$226,000	$125,000	$179,000
Long-term investments	-0-	7,000	27,000
Capital assets	510,000	530,000	392,000
Total assets..........................	$736,000	$662,000	$598,000
Liabilities and Shareholders' Equity			
Current liabilities	$110,000	$ 92,000	$ 77,000
Common shares....................	196,000	196,000	160,000
Retained earnings.................	430,000	374,000	361,000
Total liabilities and shareholders' equity	$736,000	$662,000	$598,000

Required
1. Calculate each year's current ratio.
2. Express the income statement data in common-size percents.
3. Express the balance sheet data in trend percents with 2009 as the base year.

Analysis component:
Comment on any significant relationships revealed by the ratios and percents.

Problem 20-3B
Analysis of working capital
LO4

Mason Corporation began the month of March with $286,000 of current assets, a current ratio of 2.2 to 1, and an acid-test ratio of 0.9 to 1. During the month, it completed the following transactions:

Mar.	3	Sold for $55,000 merchandise that cost $36,000. (The company uses a perpetual inventory system P. 266.)
	5	Collected a $35,000 account receivable.
	10	Bought $56,000 of merchandise on account.
	12	Borrowed $60,000 by giving the bank a 60-day, 12% note.
	15	Borrowed $90,000 by signing a long-term secured note.
	22	Used the $150,000 proceeds of the notes to buy additional machinery.
	24	Declared a $1.75 per share cash dividend on the 40,000 shares of outstanding common shares.
	26	Wrote off a $14,000 bad debt against Allowance for Doubtful Accounts.
	28	Paid a $45,000 account payable.
	30	Paid the dividend declared on March 24.

Required
Prepare a schedule showing the company's current ratio, acid-test ratio, and working capital after each of the transactions. Round to two decimal places.

Bower Inc. and Evans Inc. are similar firms that operate within the same industry. Evans began operations in 2009 and Bower in 2003. In 2011, both companies paid 7% interest to creditors. The following information is available:

Problem 20-4B
Ratio essay
LO2, 4

	Bower Inc.			Evans Inc.		
	2011	2010	2009	2011	2010	2009
Total asset turnover......	3.3	3.0	3.2	1.9	1.7	1.4
Return on total assets...	9.2	9.8	9.0	6.1	5.8	5.5
Profit margin...............	2.6	2.7	2.5	3.0	3.2	3.1
Sales	$800,000	$740,000	$772,000	$400,000	$320,000	$200,000

Required

Write a brief essay comparing Bower and Evans based on the preceding information. Your discussion should include their relative ability to use assets efficiently to produce profits. Also comment on their relative success in employing financial leverage in 2011.

The 2011 four-year comparative financial statements of Myers Groceries follow:

Problem 20-5B
Calculation of ratios and trends
LO2, 4

Myers Groceries
Balance Sheet
December 31

Assets	2011	2010	2009	2008
Cash	$ 41,686	$ 34,647	$ 29,084	$ 26,173
Temporary investments........................	70,000	90,000	70,000	50,000
Accounts receivable, net	150,259	62,608	39,130	21,500
Merchandise inventory	12,522	8,296	6,037	4,730
Prepaid expenses	2,003	1,096	671	430
Plant assets, net	686,000	784,000	882,000	980,000
Total assets	$962,470	$980,646	$1,026,922	$1,082,833
Liabilities and Shareholders' Equity				
Accounts payable..................................	$ 62,608	$ 41,478	$ 30,186	$ 23,650
Accrued wages payable	20,035	10,956	6,708	4,300
Income taxes payable	45,828	24,212	16,028	10,883
Long-term note payable, secured by mortgage on plant assets....................	574,000	644,000	714,000	784,000
Common shares, 180,000 shares	220,000	220,000	220,000	220,000
Retained earnings	40,000	40,000	40,000	40,000
Total liabilities and shareholders' equity	$962,470	$980,646	$1,026,922	$1,082,833

Myers Groceries
Income Statement
For Years Ended December 31

	2011	2010	2009	2008
Sales..	$1,252,160	$782,600	$559,000	$430,000
Cost of goods sold.........................	626,080	414,778	301,860	236,500
Gross profit....................................	$ 626,080	$367,822	$257,140	$193,500
Operating expenses........................	400,691	219,128	134,160	86,000
Operating income	$ 225,389	$148,694	$122,980	$107,500
Interest expense	34,440	38,640	42,840	47,040
Income before taxes	$ 190,949	$110,054	$ 80,140	$ 60,460
Income taxes..................................	45,828	24,212	16,028	10,883
Net income	$ 145,121	$ 85,842	$ 64,112	$ 49,577

Required

1. Calculate the following for 2011 and 2010 and identify whether the ratios compare favourably (F) or unfavourably (U) from 2010 to 2011: (a) acid-test ratio, (b) merchandise turnover, (c) accounts payable turnover, (d) debt ratio, (e) ratio of pledged assets to secured liabilities, (f) times interest earned, (g) profit ratio, (h) return on total assets, and (i) book value per common share.
2. Prepare a trend analysis for 2008 (the base year) through to 2011 using the income statement information.

Analysis component:
Compare and explain the trend in cost of goods sold, operating expenses, and net income to the trend in sales. Explain why retained earnings are constant over the four years.

Problem 20-6B
Evaluating ratios
LO4

Hartfiled Corporation calculated the ratios shown below for 2011 and 2010:

	2011	2010	Change F or U*	Comparison to Industry Average
Current ratio	1.3:1	1.4:1		
Acid-test ratio	1.14:1	1.12:1		
Accounts receivable turnover	12	10		
Days' sales uncollected	35	33		
Merchandise turnover	4.8	4.2		
Days' sales in inventory	72	76		
Total asset turnover	2.1	2.3		
Debt ratio	40	50		
Times interest earned	52	51		
Profit margin	13	11		
Gross profit ratio	16	18		

*F = Favourable; U = Unfavourable

Required

1. Identify whether the change in the ratios from 2010 to 2011 is favourable ('F') or unfavourable ('U').
2. Assess whether the 2011 ratios are favourable or unfavourable in comparison to the industry averages shown in Exhibit 20.11.

Analytical and Review Problems

A & R 20-1

Hope Corporation
Balance Sheet
December 31, 2011

Assets

Cash	$
Accounts receivable, net	
Merchandise inventory	
Capital assets, net	
Total assets	$

Liabilities and Shareholders' Equity

Current liabilities	$
12% bonds payable	
Common shares	
Retained earnings	
Total liabilities and shareholders' equity	$

Sales (all credit)	$450,000
Liabilities to total assets	1 to 2
Income taxes	$1,000
Net income	$36,000
Average collection period	60.83 days
Capital asset turnover	3 times
Merchandise turnover	5 times
Expenses (including taxes of 40%)	$114,000
Current ratio	3 to 1
Total asset turnover	1.5 times
Retained earnings, Jan. 1, 2011	$10,000

Required
Complete the balance sheet for Hope Corporation. Round amounts to the nearest $100.

Wild Inc. began the month of May with $200,000 of current assets, a 2 to 1 current ratio, and a **A & R 20-2**
1 to 1 acid-test (quick) ratio. During the month, the following transactions were completed
(assume a perpetual inventory system):

	Current Ratio			Acid-test Ratio		
	Increase	Decrease	No Change	Increase	Decrease	No Change
a. Bought $50,000 of merchandise on account.................						
b. Credit sales: $70,000 of merchandise costing $40,000.						
c. Collected an $8,500 account receivable.						
d. Paid a $30,000 account payable						
e. Wrote off a $2,000 bad debt against the allowance account.						
f. Declared a $1 per share cash dividend on the 20,000 common shares outstanding...........................						
g. Paid the dividend declared in (f).						
h. Borrowed $25,000 by giving the bank a 60-day, 10% note................						
i. Borrowed $100,000 by placing a 10-year mortgage on the capital assets......................................						
j. Used $50,000 of proceeds of the mortgage to buy additional machinery...						

Required

1. State the effect of each of the above transactions on the current ratio and the acid-test ratio. Give
the effect in terms of increase, decrease, or no change. Use check marks to indicate your answers.

2. For the end of May, calculate the
   i. Current ratio   **i.** Acid-test ratio   **iii.** Working capital

Both Demer Corp. and LitWel Inc. design, produce, market, and sell sports footwear and apparel. **A & R 20-3**
Key comparative figures (in thousands of dollars) from recent financial statements for these two
organizations follow:

Key figures	Demer	LitWel
Cash and equivalents	$ 445,421	$ 232,365
Accounts receivable	1,754,137	590,504
Inventory	1,338,640	544,522
Retained earnings	2,973,663	992,563
Cost of sales...	5,502,993	2,144,422
Income taxes	499,400	84,083
Net sales...	9,186,539	3,478,604
Total assets...	5,361,207	1,786,184

Required

1. Calculate common-size percents for the two companies for both years using the selected data
provided.

2. Which company incurred a higher percent of net sales as income tax expense?

3. Which company has retained a higher portion of total earnings in the company?

4. Which company has a higher gross margin on sales?

5. Which company is holding a higher percent of total assets as inventory?

A & R 20-4
Ratio analysis

Nicole Lukach always asks her advisor in-depth questions before acquiring a company's shares. Nicole is currently considering investing in Nymark Corp. Nymark's annual report contains the following summary of ratios:

	2011	2010	2009
Sales trend	128.00%	117.00%	100.00%
Selling expenses to sales	9.8%	13.7%	15.3%
Acid-test ratio	0.8 to 1	1.1 to 1	1.2 to 1
Current ratio	2.6 to 1	2.4 to 1	2.1 to 1
Inventory turnover	7.5 times	8.7 times	9.9 times
Accounts receivable turnover	6.7 times	7.4 times	8.2 times
Return on shareholders' equity	9.75%	11.50%	12.25%
Profit margin	3.3%	3.5%	3.7%
Total asset turnover	2.9 times	3.0 times	3.1 times
Return on total assets	8.8%	9.4%	10.1%
Sales to capital assets	3.8 to 1	3.5 to 1	3.3 to 1

Nicole would like answers to the following questions about the trend of events over the three-year period covered in the annual report. Nicole's questions are:

1. Is it becoming easier for Nymark to pay its current debts on time and to take advantage of cash discounts?
2. Is Nymark collecting its accounts receivable more rapidly?
3. Is Nymark's investment in accounts receivable decreasing?
4. Are dollar amounts invested in inventory increasing?
5. Is Nymark's investment in capital assets increasing?
6. Is the shareholders' investment becoming more profitable?
7. Is Nymark using its assets efficiently?
8. Did the dollar amount of selling expenses decrease during the three-year period?

Ethics Challenge

EC 20-1

In your position as controller of Tallman Inc., you are responsible for keeping the board of directors informed about the financial activities and status of the company. At the board meeting, you present the following report:

	2011	2010	2009
Sales trend	147.00	135.00	100.00
Selling expenses to net sales	10.1%	14.0%	15.6%
Sales to capital assets	3.8 to 1	3.6 to 1	3.3 to 1
Current ratio	2.9 to 1	2.7 to 1	2.4 to 1
Acid-test ratio	1.1 to 1	1.4 to 1	1.5 to 1
Merchandise turnover	7.8 times	9.0 times	10.2 times
Accounts receivable turnover	7.0 times	7.7 times	8.5 times
Total asset turnover	2.9 times	2.9 times	3.3 times
Return on total assets	9.1%	9.7%	10.4%
Return on shareholders' equity	9.75%	11.50%	12.25%
Profit margin	3.6%	3.8%	4.0%

After the meeting is over, you overhear the company's CEO holding a press conference with analysts in which she mentions the following ratios:

	2011	2010	2009
Sales trend	147.00	135.00	100.00
Selling expenses to net sales....................................	10.1%	14.0%	15.6%
Sales to capital assets	3.8 to 1	3.6 to 1	3.3 to 1
Current ratio	2.9 to 1	2.7 to 1	2.4 to 1

Required
1. Why do you think the CEO decided to report four ratios instead of the full eleven that you prepared?
2. Comment on the possible consequences of the CEO's decision.

Focus on Financial Statements

Drinkwater Inc. reported the following information: **FFS 20-1**

Drinkwater Inc. Adjusted Trial Balance March 31, (in thousands of Canadian dollars)			
	2011	**2010**	**2009**
Cash	$ 136,000	$ 98,000	$ 76,000
Accounts receivable	238,000	219,000	206,000
Allowance for doubtful accounts	2,300	2,100	2,000
Merchandise inventory.......................................	84,000	71,000	48,000
Prepaid insurance...	50	30	25
Notes receivable, due in six months	600	400	150
Property, plant and equipment assets..................	1,621,100	1,234,670	838,640
Accumulated amortization	325,000	208,000	102,000
Accounts payable...	219,000	174,000	145,000
Unearned sales..	3,100	750	315
Notes payable, due in 2016	114,000	116,200	77,950
Preferred shares; $1 non-cumulative; 20,000 shares issued and outstanding.................	100,000	100,000	100,000
Common shares; 50,000 shares issued and outstanding	250,000	250,000	250,000
Retained earnings	772,050	491,550	294,300
Sales	943,000	798,000	503,000
Sales discounts..	14,000	11,000	7,000
Cost of goods sold	424,000	335,000	196,000
Other operating expenses	141,000	103,000	50,000
Investment income	9,000	7,000	5,000
Interest expense...	5,700	6,500	8,750
Income tax expense..	73,000	69,000	49,000

Other information:
1. No shares were issued during the years ended March 31, 2011 and 2010.
2. No dividends were declared or paid during the years ended March 31, 2011 and 2010.
3. The market values per common share at March 31, 2011, and March 31, 2010, were $29 and $25 respectively.
4. Industry averages for 2011 were as provided in the chart on the following page.

Required (continued on page 1054)
1. Using the information provided for Drinkwater Inc., prepare a comparative, single-step income statement and statement of retained earnings for the years ended March 31, 2011 and 2010, as well as a comparative classified balance sheet at March 31, 2011 and 2010.

2. Complete the chart below for Drinkwater Inc. (round all ratios to two decimal places):

	Calculate the Ratio for 2011:	Calculate the Ratio for 2010:	Favourable or Unfavourable Change From Previous Year	Favourable or Unfavourable Relative to Industry Average for 2011	
				Industry Average	Favourable or Unfavourable
a. Current ratio				1.96:1	
b. Acid-test ratio				1.42:1	
c. Accounts receivable turnover				4.35	
d. Days' sales uncollected				95.12	
e. Merchandise turnover......................				5.20	
f. Days' sales in inventory...................				75.08	
g. Total asset turnover.........................				1.8	
h. Accounts payable turnover...............				8.45	
i. Debt ratio				21%	
j. Equity ratio				79%	
k. Times interest earned......................				50.16	
l. Profit margin....................................				30.14	
m. Gross profit ratio.............................				52.16	
n. Return on total assets......................				17.20%	
o. Return on common shareholders' equity.........................				31.00%	
p. Book value per commonshare..........				14.91	
q. Book value per preferred share.........				$22.00	
r. Basic earnings per share...................				$4.32	
s. Price–earnings ratio.........................				6.91	

FFS 20-2

Required

Refer to the financial statements for Danier Leather and WestJet in Appendix I at the end of the textbook. Calculate the following ratios for 2005 and 2004 for WestJet and Danier, indicating whether the change was favourable or unfavourable (round calculations to two decimal places).

1. Profit margin   **3.** Current ratio
2. Debt ratio   **4.** Can you compare Danier's ratio results to WestJet's? Explain why or why not.

Critical Thinking Mini Case

You are the new human resources manager and are reviewing the bonus policies as part of familiarizing yourself with the payroll system. The plant superintendent's bonus is calculated as the return on total assets ratio for the year times one month's salary. You have the information below and, recalling some basic accounting that you took while attending a post-secondary educational institution, you make a note to ask why double-declining balance amortization is not being used given the nature of the plant assets. Also, in speaking with one of the plant foremen, you discover that the useful life of this type of machinery is typically 12 years and its residual value is $100,000.

	December 31			
	2011	**2010**	**2009**	**2008**
Sales...	$1,252,160	$ 782,600	$ 559,000	$ 430,000
Net income (loss) before tax.......	194,844	101,469	63,146	38,714
Plant assets, net*.........................	834,000	870,500	907,000	943,500
Total assets	1,109,969	1,066,872	1,051,754	1,046,226

No plant assets have been purchased or sold since January 1, 2008; original cost $980,000; amortization is calculated using straight-line; useful life 20 years; residual value $250,000.

Required

Using the elements of critical thinking described on the inside front cover, comment.

APPENDIX I

Financial Statement Information

This appendix includes financial statement information from (a) Danier Leather Inc. and (b) WestJet Airlines Ltd. All of this information is taken from their annual reports. An **annual report** is a summary of the financial results of a company's operations for the year and its future plans. It is directed at external users of financial information, but also affects actions of internal users.

An annual report is also used by a company to showcase itself and its products. Many include attractive pictures, diagrams and illustrations related to the company. But the *financial section* is its primary objective. This section communicates much information about a company, with most data drawn from the accounting information system.

The layout of each annual report's financial section that is included in this appendix is:

- Management's Report
- Auditor's Report
- Financial Statements
- Notes to Financial Statements

This appendix is organized as follows:

- Danier: I-1 to I-16
- WestJet: I-17 to I-39

There are questions at the end of each chapter that refer to information in this appendix. We encourage readers to spend extra time with these questions as they are especially useful in reinforcing and showing the relevance and diversity of financial reporting.

More current financial information about these and other Canadian corporations can be found online at: www.sedar.com.

ANNUAL REPORT 2005

leather for living...

DANIER

MANAGEMENT'S RESPONSIBILITY FOR FINANCIAL STATEMENTS

The accompanying financial statements and other financial information contained in this annual report are the responsibility of management. The financial statements have been prepared in conformity with Canadian generally accepted accounting principles using management's best estimates and judgements based on currently available information, where appropriate. The financial information contained elsewhere in this annual report has been reviewed to ensure consistency with that in the financial statements.

Management is also responsible for a system of internal controls which is designed to provide reasonable assurance that assets are safeguarded, liabilities are recognized and that financial records are properly maintained to provide timely and accurate financial reports.

The Board of Directors is responsible for ensuring that management fulfills its responsibility in respect of financial reporting and internal control. The Audit Committee of the Board, which is comprised solely of unrelated and outside directors, meets regularly to review significant accounting and auditing matters with management and the independent auditors and to review the interim and annual financial statements.

The financial statements have been audited by PricewaterhouseCoopers LLP, the independent auditors, in accordance with generally accepted auditing standards on behalf of the shareholders. The Auditors' Report outlines the nature of their examination and their opinion on the financial statements. PricewaterhouseCoopers LLP have full and unrestricted access to the Audit Committee to discuss their audit and related findings as to the integrity of the financial reporting.

Jeffrey Wortsman
President and CEO

Bryan Tatoff, C.A.
Senior Vice-President, CFO and Secretary

AUDITORS' REPORT TO SHAREHOLDERS

To the Shareholders of Danier Leather Inc.

We have audited the consolidated balance sheets of Danier Leather Inc. as at June 25, 2005 and June 26, 2004 and the consolidated statements of earnings, retained earnings and cash flow for the years then ended. These financial statements are the responsibility of the Company's management. Our responsibility is to express an opinion on these financial statements based on our audits.

We conducted our audits in accordance with Canadian generally accepted auditing standards. Those standards require that we plan and perform an audit to obtain reasonable assurance whether the financial statements are free of material misstatement. An audit includes examining, on a test basis, evidence supporting the amounts and disclosures in the financial statements. An audit also includes assessing the accounting principles used and significant estimates made by management, as well as evaluating the overall financial statement presentation.

In our opinion, these consolidated financial statements present fairly, in all material respects, the financial position of the Company as at June 25, 2005 and June 26, 2004 and the results of its operations and its cash flow for the years then ended in accordance with Canadian generally accepted accounting principles.

PricewaterhouseCoopers LLP

Chartered Accountants
Toronto, Ontario
July 25, 2005

consolidated financial statements
For the years ended June 25, 2005 and June 26, 2004

CONSOLIDATED BALANCE SHEETS (THOUSANDS OF DOLLARS)

	June 25, 2005	June 26, 2004
ASSETS		
Current Assets		
Cash	$ 21,193	$ 22,576
Accounts receivable	594	626
Income taxes recoverable	939	-
Inventories (Note 3)	29,031	29,483
Prepaid expenses	516	903
Assets of discontinued operations (Note 2)	23	884
Future income tax asset (Note 8)	159	107
	52,455	54,579
Other Assets		
Capital assets (Note 4)	25,314	28,891
Goodwill (Note 5)	342	342
Assets of discontinued operations (Note 2)	-	1,321
Future income taxes asset (Note 9)	5,254	4,736
	$ 83,365	$ 89,869
LIABILITIES		
Current Liabilities		
Accounts payable and accrued liabilities	$ 8,170	$ 9,355
Income taxes payable	-	952
Liabilities of discontinued operations (Note 2)	-	70
	8,170	10,377
Accrued litigation provision and related expenses (Note 10)	18,000	15,450
Deferred lease inducements	1,838	2,283
Future income tax liability (Note 9)	420	472
	28,428	28,582
SHAREHOLDERS' EQUITY		
Share capital (Note 7)	22,493	24,166
Contributed surplus	230	219
Retained earnings	32,214	36,902
	54,937	61,287
	$ 83,365	$ 89,869

Approved by the Board

Edwin F. Hawken, Director   **Jeffrey Wortsman**, Director

consolidated financial statements

For the years ended June 25, 2005 and June 26, 2004

CONSOLIDATED STATEMENTS OF RETAINED EARNINGS (THOUSANDS OF DOLLARS)

	For the Year Ended	
	June 25, 2005	June 26, 2004
Retained earnings, beginning of year	$ 36,902	$ 43,999
Net loss	(185)	(7,097)
Share purchases (Note 7(c))	(2,883)	-
Dividends	(1,620)	-
Retained earnings, end of year	$ 32,214	$ 36,902

CONSOLIDATED STATEMENTS OF EARNINGS (LOSS) (THOUSANDS OF DOLLARS, EXCEPT PER SHARE AMOUNTS)

	For the Year Ended	
	June 25, 2005	June 26, 2004
Revenue	$ 166,350	$ 175,270
Cost of sales (Note 8)	82,863	88,742
Gross profit	83,487	86,528
Selling, general and administrative expenses (Note 8)	77,215	77,812
Interest (income)	(340)	(18)
Earnings before undernoted item and income taxes	6,612	8,734
Litigation provision and related expenses (Note 10)	3,098	15,450
Earnings (loss) before discontinued operations and income taxes	3,514	(6,716)
Provision for income taxes (Note 9)		
Current	1,553	3,217
Future	(622)	(4,023)
	931	(806)
Net earnings (loss) before discontinued operations	$ 2,583	$ (5,910)
Loss from discontinued operations, net of income taxes (Note 2)	(2,768)	(1,187)
Net loss	$ (185)	$ (7,097)
Net earnings (loss) per share before discontinued operations:		
Basic	$0.38	($0.85)
Diluted	$0.38	n/a
Net earnings (loss) per share:		
Basic	($0.03)	($1.03)
Diluted	n/a	n/a
Weighted average number of shares outstanding:		
Basic	6,726,658	6,920,447
Diluted	6,790,056	6,978,904

consolidated financial statements
For the years ended June 25, 2005 and June 26, 2004

CONSOLIDATED STATEMENTS OF CASH FLOW (THOUSANDS OF DOLLARS)

	For the Years Ended	
	June 25, 2005	June 26, 2004
OPERATING ACTIVITIES		
Net loss	$ (185)	$ (7,097)
Items not affecting cash:		
Amortization - continuing operations (Note 8)	6,216	5,771
Amortization - discontinued operations (Note 8)	1,330	316
Amortization of deferred lease inducements	(445)	(404)
Loss on disposal of capital assets	-	696
Stock based compensation	11	219
Accrued litigation provision and related expenses	2,550	14,241
Future income taxes	(622)	(4,023)
Net change in non-cash working capital items (Note 11)	(2,205)	8,285
Discontinued operations (Note 2)	791	(380)
Cash flows from operating activities	$ **7,441**	$ **17,624**
FINANCING ACTIVITIES		
Subordinate voting shares issued	27	171
Subordinate voting shares repurchased (Note 7)	(4,583)	-
Dividends	(1,620)	-
Proceeds from lease inducements	-	449
Cash flows from financing activities	**(6,176)**	**620**
INVESTING ACTIVITIES		
Acquisition of capital assets	(2,648)	(2,749)
Cash flows from investing activities	**(2,648)**	**(2,749)**
Increase (decrease) in cash	(1,383)	15,495
Cash, beginning of year	22,576	7,081
Cash, end of year	$ **21,193**	$ **22,576**
Supplementary cash flow information:		
Interest paid	3	223
Income taxes paid	3,846	2,376

notes to consolidated financial statements

For the years ended June 25, 2005 and June 26, 2004

NOTE 1: SIGNIFICANT ACCOUNTING POLICIES

The consolidated financial statements have been prepared in accordance with Canadian generally accepted accounting principles ("GAAP").

(a) Basis of consolidation:

The consolidated financial statements include the accounts of the Company and its wholly owned subsidiary companies. On consolidation, all intercompany transactions and balances have been eliminated.

(b) Year-end:

The fiscal year end of the Company consists of a 52 or 53 week period ending on the last Saturday in June each year. The fiscal year for the financial statements presented is the 52-week period ended June 25, 2005, and comparably the 52-week period ended June 26, 2004.

(c) Revenue recognition:

Revenue includes sales to customers through stores operated by the Company and sales to corporate customers through the Company's direct sales division. Sales to customers through stores operated by the Company are recognized at the time the transaction is entered into the point-of-sale register net of returns. Sales to corporate customers are recognized at the time of shipment.

(d) Cash:

Cash consists of cash on hand, bank balances, and money market investments with maturities of three months or less.

(e) Inventories:

Inventories are valued at the lower of cost or market. Cost is determined using the weighted average cost method. For finished goods and work-in-process, market is defined as net realizable value; for raw materials, market is defined as replacement cost.

(f) Capital assets:

Capital assets are recorded at cost and annual amortization is provided using the declining balance method as follows:

> Building 4%
> Furniture and equipment .20%
> Computer hardware and software 30%

Leasehold improvements are amortized on a straight-line basis over the term of the lease, unless the Company has decided to terminate the lease, at which time the unamortized balance is written off.

(g) Goodwill:

Goodwill represents the excess of the cost of acquisition over the fair market value of the identifiable assets acquired. Goodwill is not amortized, but is tested for impairment at least annually at year-end. If required, any impairment in the value of goodwill would be written off against earnings.

(h) Deferred lease inducements:

Deferred lease inducements represent cash benefits received from landlords pursuant to store lease agreements. These lease inducements are amortized against rent expense over the term of the lease, not exceeding 10.5 years.

NOTE 1: SIGNIFICANT ACCOUNTING POLICIES (CONTINUED)

(i) Store opening costs:

Expenditures associated with the opening of new stores, other than furniture and fixtures, equipment, and leasehold improvements are expensed as incurred.

(j) Income taxes:

Income taxes are determined using the asset and liability method of accounting. This method recognizes future tax assets and liabilities that arise from differences between the accounting basis of the Company's assets and liabilities and their corresponding tax basis. Future taxes are measured using tax rates expected to apply when the asset is realized or the liability settled.

(k) Earnings per share:

Earnings per share are calculated using the weighted average number of shares outstanding during the year (see Note 7). The treasury stock method is used to calculate diluted earnings per share. The treasury stock method computes the number of incremental shares by assuming the outstanding stock options exercisable at exercise prices below the average monthly market price are exercised during the fiscal year and then that number of incremental shares is reduced by the number of shares that could have been repurchased from the issuance proceeds, using the average monthly market price of the Company's shares during the fiscal year.

(l) Translation of foreign currencies:

Subsidiary accounts and accounts in foreign currencies are translated into Canadian dollars. Monetary balance sheet items are translated at the rates of exchange in effect at year-end and non-monetary items are translated at historical exchange rates. Revenues and expenses (other than amortization, which is translated at the same average rate as the related capital assets) are translated at the rates in effect on the transaction dates or at the average rates of exchange for the reporting period. The resulting net gain or loss is included in the statement of earnings.

(m) Financial instruments:

From time-to-time the Company utilizes derivative financial instruments in the management of its foreign currency exposure. Derivative financial instruments are not used for trading purposes. Accounting guideline (AcG13) was implemented June 29, 2003 on a prospective basis. There was no impact on the current year.

(n) Stock option plan:

The Company has a stock option plan which is described in Note 7 where options to purchase Subordinate Voting Shares are issued to directors, officers and employees.

In the year ended June 26, 2004 the Canadian Institute of Chartered Accountants (CICA) amended Handbook Section 3870 "Stock-based Compensation and Other Stock-based Payments", which provides guidance on accounting for stock-based compensation, to require the use of the fair value-based method to account for stock options. In accordance with the transitional provisions allowed under the revised accounting standard, the Company has prospectively applied the fair value-based method to all stock options granted on or after June 29, 2003. Accordingly, compensation cost is measured at fair value at the date of grant using the Black-Scholes Option Pricing Model and is recognized as an expense over the vesting period of the stock option.

The Company continues to use settlement accounting to account for stock options granted prior to June 29, 2003. In accordance with the prospective method of adoption of the new standard, no compensation expense is recognized for options granted prior to fiscal 2004. Pro forma disclosures relating to net earnings per share figures, as if the fair value method had been used for awards granted during fiscal 2003, are presented in Note 7(d).

NOTE 1: SIGNIFICANT ACCOUNTING POLICIES (CONTINUED)

(o) Restricted Share Units and Deferred Share Units:

The Company has restricted share unit ("RSU") and deferred share unit ("DSU") Plans, which are described in Note 7. RSU and DSU Plans are settled in cash and are recorded as liabilities. The measurement of the liability and compensation expense for these awards is based on the fair value of the award, and is recorded as a charge to selling, general and administrative ("SG&A") expenses over the vesting period of the award. Changes in the Company's payment obligation subsequent to vesting of the award and prior to the settlement date are recorded as a charge to SG&A expenses in the period incurred.

(p) Use of estimates:

The preparation of financial statements in conformity with Canadian generally accepted accounting principles requires management to make estimates and assumptions that affect the reported amounts of assets and liabilities and disclosure of contingent assets and liabilities at the date of the financial statements and the reported amounts of revenues and expenses during the reporting period. These estimates and assumptions are based on management's best knowledge of current events and actions that the Company may undertake in the future. Significant areas requiring the use of management estimates relate to the determination of litigation award reserves, inventory valuation, realizable value of capital assets, future tax assets, and income tax provisions. By their nature, these estimates are subject to measurement uncertainty and the impact on the consolidated financial statements of future periods could differ materially from those estimated.

(q) Comparative figures:

Certain amounts included in the June 26, 2004 comparative figures were reclassified to conform with the current year's financial statement presentation. Reclassification of these amounts had no effect on previously reported shareholders' equity or net earnings.

NOTE 2: DISCONTINUED OPERATIONS (THOUSANDS OF DOLLARS)

In March 2005 the Company announced that it would discontinue its U.S. operations which consisted of 3 shopping mall stores. On March 31, 2005, two of the U.S. shopping mall locations located on Long Island, New York were closed. The third store located in Paramus, New Jersey was closed in April 2005.

Financial results for the periods presented were restated to reflect the discontinuance of the U.S. operations. The results of discontinued operations were as follows:

	June 25, 2005	June 26, 2004
Sales	$ 2,347	$ 2,845
Operating loss	(1,288)	(1,187)
Write-down of capital assets	(1,075)	-
Lease and employee termination costs	(405)	-
Loss from discontinued operations	($2,768)	($1,187)

The net assets of discontinued operations are summarized as follows:

	June 25, 2005	June 26, 2004
Current assets	$ 23	$ 884
Capital assets	-	1,321
	23	2,205
Current liabilities	-	70
Net assets from discontinued operations	$ 23	$ 2,135

NOTE 2: DISCONTINUED OPERATIONS (CONTINUED)

Changes in current assets and liabilities of discontinued operations are summarized as follows:

	June 25, 2005	June 26, 2004
Current assets	$ 861	$ (312)
Current liabilities	(70)	(68)
	$ 791	$ (380)

NOTE 3: INVENTORIES (THOUSANDS OF DOLLARS)

	June 25, 2005	June 26, 2004
Raw materials	$ 3,456	$ 4,043
Work-in-process	634	1,363
Finished goods	24,941	24,077
	$ 29,031	$ 29,483

NOTE 4: CAPITAL ASSETS (THOUSANDS OF DOLLARS)

	June 25, 2005			June 26, 2004		
	Cost	Accumulated Amortization	Net Book Value	Cost	Accumulated Amortization	Net Book Value
Land	$ 1,000	$ -	$ 1,000	$ 1,000	$ -	$ 1,000
Building	7,064	1,319	5,745	7,066	1,080	5,986
Leasehold improvements	25,566	13,710	11,856	25,174	11,887	13,287
Furniture and equipment	9,966	5,880	4,086	12,070	7,017	5,053
Computer hardware and software	8,985	6,358	2,627	8,883	5,318	3,565
	$ 52,581	$ 27,267	$ 25,314	$ 54,193	$ 25,302	$ 28,891

NOTE 5: GOODWILL (THOUSANDS OF DOLLARS)

Goodwill of $342 (June 26, 2004 - $342) is stated at cost less accumulated amortization of $205 (June 26, 2004 - $205).

NOTE 6: BANK OVERDRAFT

As at June 25, 2005, the Company had credit facilities available to a maximum amount of $69.0 million. The credit facilities consist of an operating facility for working capital and for general corporate purposes to a maximum amount of $65 million, bearing interest at prime plus 0.25% and a $4.0 million revolving capital expenditure loan facility bearing interest at prime plus 0.75%. The maximum amount available under the revolving capital expenditure loan facility reduces by $1.0 million on each of June 30, 2005 and June 30, 2006 and by $2.0 million on June 30, 2007. The operating facility is committed until July 28, 2006 and the revolving capital expenditure loan facility matures on June 30, 2007. The Company is required to comply with covenants regarding financial performance.

Security provided includes a security interest over all personal property of the business and a mortgage over the land and building, comprising the Company's head office/distribution facility.

NOTE 7: SHARE CAPITAL (THOUSANDS OF DOLLARS, EXCEPT PER SHARE AMOUNTS)

(a) Authorized

1,224,329 Multiple Voting Shares

Unlimited Subordinate Voting Shares

Unlimited Class A and B Preference Shares

(b) Issued

Multiple Voting Shares	Number	Consideration
Balance June 28, 2003	1,224,329	Nominal
Balance June 26, 2004	1,224,329	Nominal
Balance June 25, 2005	1,224,329	Nominal

Subordinate Voting Shares	Number	Consideration
Balance June 28, 2003	5,695,225	$ 23,995
Shares issued upon exercising of stock options	25,000	171
Balance June 26, 2004	5,720,225	$ 24,166
Shares repurchased	(402,400)	(1,700)
Shares issued upon exercising of stock options	4,000	27
Balance June 25, 2005	5,321,825	$ 22,493

The Multiple Voting Shares and Subordinate Voting Shares have identical attributes except that the Multiple Voting Shares entitle the holder to ten votes per share and the Subordinate Voting Shares entitle the holder to one vote per share. Each Multiple Voting Share is convertible at any time, at the holder's option, into one fully paid and non-assessable Subordinate Voting Share. The Multiple Voting Shares are subject to provisions whereby, if a triggering event occurs then each Multiple Voting Share is converted into one fully paid and non-assessable Subordinate Voting Share. A triggering event may occur if Mr. Jeffrey Wortsman: (i) dies; (ii) ceases to be a Senior Officer of the Company; (iii) ceases to own 5% or more of the aggregate number of Multiple Voting Shares and Subordinate Voting Shares outstanding; or (iv) owns less than 918,247 Multiple Voting Shares and Subordinate Voting Shares combined.

(c) Normal course issuer bid

On February 2, 2005, the Company received approval from the Toronto Stock Exchange to renew its Normal Course Issuer Bid. The bid permits the Company to acquire up to 421,061 Subordinate Voting Shares, representing approximately 10% of the public float of the Subordinate Voting Shares, during the period from February 7, 2005 to February 6, 2006. During the year ended June 25, 2005, 402,400 Subordinate Voting Shares were purchased for cancellation at prevailing market prices for cash consideration of $4,583. The excess of $2,883 over the average paid-in value of the shares was charged to retained earnings. During the year ended June 26, 2004 no shares were repurchased under the Normal Course Issuer Bid.

(d) Stock option plan

The Company maintains a Stock Option Plan for the benefit of directors, officers and employees. As at June 25, 2005, the Company has reserved 911,275 Subordinate Voting Shares for issuance under its Stock Option Plan. The granting of options and the related vesting periods are at the discretion of the Board of Directors at exercise prices determined as the weighted average of the trading prices of the Company's Subordinate Voting Shares on The Toronto Stock Exchange for the five trading days preceding the effective date of the grant. In general, options granted under the Stock Option Plan vest over a period of one year from the grant date for options issued to directors and four years from the grant date for options issued to officers and employees and expire no later than the tenth anniversary of the date of grant.

NOTE 7: SHARE CAPITAL (CONTINUED)

A summary of the status of the Company's Stock Option Plan as of June 25, 2005 and June 26, 2004 and changes during the years ended on those dates is presented below:

| | June 25, 2005 | | June 26, 2004 | |
Stock Options	Shares	Weighted-average exercise price	Shares	Weighted-average exercise price
Outstanding at beginning of year	649,400	$ 11.21	730,400	$ 11.16
Granted	25,000	$ 10.10	44,000	$ 10.96
Exercised	(4,000)	$ 6.85	(25,000)	$ 6.85
Forfeited	(25,000)	$ 12.92	(100,000)	$ 11.80
Outstanding at end of year	645,400	$ 11.13	649,400	$ 11.21
Options exercisable at end of year	573,150	$ 10.80	523,650	$ 10.53

The following table summarizes the distribution of these options and the remaining contractual life as at June 25, 2005:

| | Options Outstanding | | | Options Exercisable | |
Exercise Prices	# Outstanding	Weighted Average Remaining Contractual Life	Weighted Average Exercise Price	# of Shares Exercisable	Weighted Average Exercise Price
$6.02	18,500	4.2 years	$6.02	18,500	$6.02
$6.85	114,400	3.0 years	$6.85	114,400	$6.85
$10.10	25,000	9.8 years	$10.10	-	-
$10.40	33,250	5.1 years	$10.40	33,250	$10.40
$10.50	15,000	5.3 years	$10.50	15,000	$10.50
$10.96	29,000	8.1 years	$10.96	25,250	$10.96
$11.20	24,000	6.1 years	$11.20	24,000	$11.20
$11.25	265,250	2.9 years	$11.25	265,250	$11.25
$15.85	101,000	7.1 years	$15.85	62,500	$15.85
$17.94	20,000	6.8 years	$17.94	15,000	$17.94
	645,400	4.5 years	$11.13	573,150	$10.80

The weighted average estimated fair values at the date of grant for options granted during the year ended June 25, 2005 was $7.18 per share (June 26, 2004 - $7.54 per share). The fair value of each option granted was estimated on the date of grant using the Black-Scholes Option Pricing Model with the following assumptions:

	June 25, 2005	June 26, 2004
Risk-free interest rate	4.11%	5.25%
Dividend yield	2.4%	0.0%
Expected volatility	58%	54%
Expected life of options	10 years	10 years

NOTE 7: SHARE CAPITAL (CONTINUED)

The Black-Scholes Option Pricing Model was developed for use in estimating the fair value of traded options, which have no vesting restrictions and are fully transferable. In addition, the Black-Scholes Option Pricing Model requires the use of subjective assumptions including the expected stock price volatility. As a result, the Company's Stock Option Plan having characteristics different from those of traded options, and because changes in the subjective assumptions can have a material effect on the fair value estimate, the Black-Scholes Option Pricing Model does not necessarily provide a reliable single measure of the fair value of options granted.

Prior to fiscal 2004, the Company used settlement accounting to account for its Stock Option Plan. No compensation cost was recorded when stock options were granted. When options were exercised, consideration paid by employees and directors was recorded in the financial statements as an increase of share capital based on the exercise price of the options.

In accordance with the transitional provisions of CICA Handbook Section 3870, the Company applied the fair value based method to account for stock options on a prospective basis. Therefore, stock options granted during the year ended June 28, 2003 continue to be accounted for using the settlement accounting method and the pro-forma effect on net earnings and earnings per share are disclosed below. Had compensation cost been determined using the fair value-based method at the grant date of the stock options awarded to employees and directors during fiscal 2003, the net earnings and earnings per share for the years ended June 25, 2005 and June 26, 2004 would have been reduced to the pro forma amounts indicated in the following table:

| | Year Ended June 25, 2005 | | Year Ended June 26, 2004 | |
	As Reported	Pro forma	As Reported	Pro forma
Net loss	($185)	($427)	($7,097)	($7,339)
Basic loss per share	($0.03)	($0.06)	($1.03)	($1.06)
Diluted loss per share	n/a	n/a	n/a	n/a

The pro forma effect on net earnings of the period is not representative of the pro forma effect on net earnings of future periods because it does not take into consideration the pro forma compensation cost related to options awarded prior to June 29, 2002.

(e) Deferred Share Unit Plan

Effective October 19, 2004, the Company established a Deferred Share Unit ("DSU") Plan for non-management directors. The DSU Plan is administered by the Human Resources and Governance Committee of the Board of Directors. Under this plan, non-management directors of the Company receive an annual grant of DSU's and can also elect to receive their annual retainers and meeting fees in DSU's. A DSU is a unit equivalent in value to one Subordinate Voting Share of the Company based on the five-day average trading price of the Company's Subordinate Voting Shares on The Toronto Stock Exchange immediately prior to the date on which the value of the DSU is determined. When dividends are paid by the Company, an equivalent number of DSU's are added to the DSU account of the non-management director based on the number of DSU's in their account and the market value of the Subordinate Voting Shares on the date the dividend is paid. After retirement from the board, a participant in the DSU Plan receives a cash payment equal to the market value of the accumulated DSU's in their account.

During the year ended June 25, 2005, each non-management director was issued 1,200 DSU's. A total of 7,317 DSU's were outstanding as at June 25, 2005 and compensation cost of $74 was included in selling, general and administrative expenses and a corresponding liability on the Company's consolidated balance sheet has been recorded. The value of the DSU liability is adjusted to reflect changes in the market value of the Company's Subordinate Voting Shares.

(f) Restricted Share Unit Plan

Effective April 20, 2005, the Company established a Restricted Share Unit ("RSU") Plan as part of its overall executive compensation plan. The RSU Plan is administered by the Human Resources and Governance Committee of the Board of Directors. Under this plan, Senior Officers of the Company are eligible to receive a grant of RSU's that vest on each anniversary of the grant in equal one-third installments over a vesting period of three years. A RSU is a unit equivalent in value to one

NOTE 7: SHARE CAPITAL (CONTINUED)

Subordinate Voting Share of the Company. When dividends are paid by the Company, an equivalent number of RSU's are added to the RSU account of the Senior Officer based on the number of RSU's in their account, the dividend paid per Subordinate Voting Share and the market value of the Subordinate Voting Shares on the date the dividend is paid. Upon the exercise of the vested RSU's, a cash payment equal to the market value of the exercised vested RSU's will be paid to the senior officer.

During year ended June 25, 2005, 5,030 RSU's were awarded and outstanding of which none were vested.

NOTE 8: AMORTIZATION (THOUSANDS OF DOLLARS)

Amortization included in cost of sales and selling, general and administrative expenses ("SG&A") is summarized as follows:

	June 25, 2005	June 26, 2004
Cost of sales	$ 842	$ 773
SG&A of continuing operations	5,374	4,998
Continuing operations	6,216	5,771
SG&A of discontinued operations	1,330	316
	$ 7,546	$ 6,087

NOTE 9: INCOME TAXES (THOUSANDS OF DOLLARS)

Future income tax asset (liability) is summarized as follows:

	June 25, 2005	June 26, 2004
Amortization	$ (420)	$ (505)
Deferred lease inducements	645	803
Litigation provision and related expenses	4,738	4,074
Other	30	(1)
	$ 4,993	$ 4,371
Future income tax asset	5,413	4,843
Future income tax liability	$ (420)	$ (472)

Furthermore, the U.S. subsidiary has unutilized non-capital loss carry forwards available to reduce future year's income taxes, the potential benefit of which have not been recognized in these financial statements. These losses can be utilized in future years up to 2020.

The Company's effective income tax rate consists of the following:

	June 25, 2005	June 26, 2004
Combined basic federal and provincial average statutory rate	35.4%	(36.1%)
Litigation provision and related expenses, manufacturing and processing deduction and other	21.7%	20.5%
Effect of foreign operating losses	67.6%	5.4%
	124.7%	(10.2%)

NOTE 10: LITIGATION PROVISION AND RELATED EXPENSES

	June 25, 2005	June 26, 2004
Provision for damages, costs and interest	$ 18,000	$ 15,000
Legal and professional fees	-	450
Accrued litigation provision and related expenses	$ 18,000	$ 15,450

In fiscal 1999, the Company and certain of its directors and officers were served with a Statement of Claim under the Class Proceedings Act (Ontario) concerning the accuracy and disclosure of certain information contained in a financial forecast issued by the Company during its initial public offering ("IPO") in 1998. The suit sought damages be paid equal to the alleged diminution in value of the shares.

In October 2001, a motion to certify the action as a class action was granted. The trial commenced in the Superior Court of Justice (Ontario) during May 2003 and was completed in January 2004. On May 7, 2004 the Judge issued a judgment in favour of the Plaintiffs and awarded damages to Canadian shareholders who purchased Subordinate Voting Shares in the IPO. The Judge concluded that at the time of pricing of the IPO, which was two weeks before the closing, the forecast was reasonable and that the Company's CEO and CFO had an honest belief at the time the IPO closed that the forecast could be achieved. The Judge further held that the forecast was, in fact, substantially achieved. Despite these findings, the Court decided that management's judgement that the forecast was still achievable at the time of closing was not reasonable. The Company has appealed this decision as discussed below.

For those shareholders who sold their shares between June 4 and 9, 1998, the Court awarded them the difference between the IPO price and the price at which they sold their shares. For those shareholders who sold or still hold those shares after June 9, 1998, the Court awarded $2.35 per share.

A hearing to determine the awarding of costs was held in April 2005. In May 2005, the Court awarded a portion of the costs claimed by the plaintiffs but referred the matter for assessment to determine the amount of costs to be paid. The quantum of the costs award will not be known until the final assessment ordered by the Court has been conducted. Based solely on the information available as of year-end, the Company estimates that this award, if unchanged on appeal, would amount to approximately $3 million to $4 million.

Based solely on the information available at year-end, if the damages award, costs and interest had been paid at the fiscal 2005 year-end, the Company estimates this amount to be about $18 million. During the fourth quarter of 2004, the Company recorded an expense and set up a provision of $15 million pursuant to this judgment. This provision was subsequently increased by $3 million to $18 million during the fourth quarter of 2005. The judgment is a joint and several responsibility of the Company and two of its Senior Officers. The Company carries directors and officers insurance and it expects that the insurance will cover the two Senior Officers' portion of the total award but the amount of insurance is not reasonably determinable at this time. The provision for recovery of income taxes related to the award is based on the entire $18 million provision and does not take account of the potential results of the appeal discussed in the next paragraph, any possible insurance recoveries or future tax adjustments. The damages award and income tax recovery is based on management's best estimate and is subject to adjustment when all facts are known and all issues are resolved. The possible adjustment could be significant.

In June 2004, a Notice of Appeal was filed by the Company and two of its Senior Officers. The appeal was heard by the Ontario Court of Appeal during June 2005. The Court reserved its decision and it is not anticipated that the Court's determination will be made before the fall of 2005. The payment of any damages and costs awarded by the trial judge is stayed pending the determination of the appeal.

NOTE 11: CHANGES IN NON-CASH OPERATING WORKING CAPITAL ITEMS (THOUSANDS OF DOLLARS)

	June 25, 2005	June 26, 2004
Accounts receivable	$ 32	$ (33)
Inventories	452	7,155
Prepaid expenses	387	(15)
Accounts payable and accrued liabilities	(1,185)	143
Income taxes recoverable/payable	(1,891)	1,035
	$ (2,205)	$ 8,285

NOTE 12: COMMITMENTS & CONTINGENCIES (THOUSANDS OF DOLLARS)

(a) Legal proceedings

In addition to the class action matter discussed in Note 10, in the course of its business, the Company from time to time becomes involved in various claims and legal proceedings. In the opinion of management, all such claims and suits are adequately covered by insurance, or if not so covered, the results are not expected to materially affect the Company's financial position.

(b) Guarantees

The Company has provided the following guarantees to third parties and no amounts have been accrued in the financial statements for these guarantees:

(i)   In the ordinary course of business, the Company has agreed to indemnify its lenders under its credit facility against certain costs or losses resulting from changes in laws and regulations or from a default in repaying a borrowing. These indemnifications extend for the term of the credit facility and do not provide any limit on the maximum potential liability. Historically, the Company has not made any indemnification payments under such agreements.

(ii)   In the ordinary course of business, the Company has provided indemnification commitments to certain counterparties in matters such as real estate leasing transactions, director and officer indemnification agreements and certain purchases of fixed assets such as computer software. These indemnification agreements generally require the Company to compensate the counterparties for costs or losses resulting from legal action brought against the counterparties related to the actions of the Company. The terms of these indemnification agreements will vary based on the contract and generally do not provide any limit on the maximum potential liability.

(iii)   The Company sublet one location during fiscal 2004 and has provided the landlord with a guarantee in the event the sub-tenant defaults on its obligation to pay rent. The term of the guarantee is approximately 3.5 years and the Company's maximum exposure is $140.

NOTE 13: COMMITMENTS (THOUSANDS OF DOLLARS)

(a) Operating leases

Minimum rentals for the next five fiscal years and thereafter, excluding rentals based upon revenue are as follows:

2006	$ 11,234
2007	$ 10,627
2008	$ 9,226
2009	$ 7,630
2010	$ 5,432
Thereafter	$ 10,579

NOTE 13: COMMITMENTS (CONTINUED)

(b) Letters of credit

The Company had outstanding letters of credit in the amount of $4,839 (June 26, 2004 - $6,804) for imports of finished goods inventories to be received.

NOTE 14: RELATED PARTY TRANSACTIONS (THOUSANDS OF DOLLARS)

During fiscal 2005, the Company expensed and paid fees of $28 to a corporation related to a director and officer of the Company. This transaction was measured at the exchange amount, which is the amount of consideration established and agreed to by the related parties.

NOTE 15: FINANCIAL INSTRUMENTS (THOUSANDS OF DOLLARS)

The carrying value of the Company's accounts receivable and accounts payable and accrued liabilities approximates their fair value.

The Company is exposed to credit risk on its accounts receivable from corporate customers through sales made by the direct sales division. Accounts receivable are net of applicable allowance for doubtful accounts, which is established based on the specific credit risks associated with each corporate customer and other relevant information.

The Company purchases a significant portion of its leather and finished goods inventory from foreign vendors with payment terms in U.S. dollars. From time-to-time the Company may enter into foreign exchange forward contracts to manage foreign exchange risk associated with these purchases. As at June 25, 2005, and as at June 26, 2004 the Company did not have any outstanding foreign exchange forward contracts to purchase U.S. dollars.

The Company is exposed to interest rate risk based on the use of the credit facilities which bears interest at floating rates. For fiscal 2005, a +/-1% change in interest rates would change interest expense by +/- $NIL (June 26, 2004 +/-$52) since the Company only incurred approximately $3 of interest expense.

NOTE 16: SEGMENTED INFORMATION

Management has determined that the Company operates in one dominant industry and geographic segment which involves the design, manufacture and retail of fashion leather and suede apparel in Canada.

2005 WESTJET ANNUAL REPORT

OWNERS'

MANUAL

MANAGEMENT'S REPORT TO THE SHAREHOLDERS

The consolidated financial statements have been prepared by management in accordance with Canadian generally accepted accounting principles. When a choice between accounting methods exists, management has chosen those it deems conservative and appropriate in the circumstances. Financial statements will necessarily include certain amounts based on estimates and judgements. Management has determined such amounts on a reasonable basis to ensure that the consolidated financial statements are presented fairly in all material respects. Financial information contained in the annual report is consistent, where appropriate, with the information and data contained in the consolidated financial statements. All information in the annual report is the responsibility of management.

Management has established systems of internal control, including disclosure controls and procedures which are designed to provide reasonable assurance that financial and non-financial information that is disclosed is timely, complete, relevant and accurate. These systems of internal control also serve to safeguard the Corporation's assets. The systems of internal control are monitored by management, and further supported by an internal audit department whose functions include reviewing internal controls and their application.

The Board of Directors is responsible for the overall stewardship and governance of the Corporation, including ensuring management fulfills its responsibility for financial reporting and internal control, and reviewing and approving the consolidated financial statements. The Board carries out this responsibility principally through its Audit Committee.

The Audit Committee of the Board of Directors, comprised of non-management Directors, meets regularly with management, the internal auditors and the external auditors, to satisfy itself that each is properly discharging its responsibilities, and to review the consolidated financial statements and MD&A. The Audit Committee reports its findings to the Board of Directors prior to the approval of such statements for issuance to the shareholders. The Audit Committee also recommends, for review by the Board of Directors and approval of shareholders, the reappointment of the external auditors. The internal and external auditors have full and free access to the Audit Committee.

The consolidated financial statements have been audited by KPMG LLP, the independent external auditors, in accordance with generally accepted auditing standards on behalf of the shareholders. The auditors' report outlines the scope of their examination and sets forth their opinion.

Clive J. Beddoe
Executive Chairman,
President and Chief Executive Officer

Alexander (Sandy) J. Campbell, FCGA
Executive Vice-President, Finance,
and Chief Financial Officer

Calgary, Alberta
February 7, 2006

AUDITORS' REPORT TO THE SHAREHOLDERS

We have audited the consolidated balance sheets of WestJet Airlines Ltd. as at December 31, 2005 and 2004 and the consolidated statements of earnings (loss) and retained earnings and cash flows for the years then ended. These financial statements are the responsibility of the Corporation's management. Our responsibility is to express an opinion on these financial statements based on our audits.

We conducted our audits in accordance with Canadian generally accepted auditing standards. Those standards require that we plan and perform an audit to obtain reasonable assurance whether the financial statements are free of material misstatement. An audit includes examining, on a test basis, evidence supporting the amounts and disclosures in the financial statements. An audit also includes assessing the accounting principles used and significant estimates made by management, as well as evaluating the overall financial statement presentation.

In our opinion, these consolidated financial statements present fairly, in all material respects, the financial position of the Corporation as at December 31, 2005 and 2004 and the results of its operations and its cash flows for the years then ended in accordance with Canadian generally accepted accounting principles.

KPMG LLP

Chartered Accountants
Calgary, Canada
February 7, 2006

CONSOLIDATED BALANCE SHEETS

WestJet Airlines Ltd.

December 31, 2005 and 2004
(Stated in Thousands of Dollars)

	2005	2004
Assets		
Current assets:		
Cash and cash equivalents	$ 259,640	$ 148,532
Accounts receivable	8,022	12,814
Income taxes recoverable	13,909	2,854
Prepaid expenses and deposits	31,746	25,493
Inventory	6,259	5,382
	319,576	195,075
Property and equipment (note 2)	1,803,497	1,601,546
Other assets (note 3)	90,019	80,733
	$ 2,213,092	$ 1,877,354
Liabilities and Shareholders' Equity		
Current liabilities:		
Accounts payable and accrued liabilities	$ 100,052	$ 91,885
Advance ticket sales	127,450	81,991
Non-refundable guest credits	32,814	26,704
Current portion of long-term debt (note 4)	114,115	97,305
Current portion of obligations under capital lease (note 6)	2,466	6,564
	376,897	304,449
Long-term debt (note 4)	1,044,719	905,631
Obligations under capital lease (note 6)	1,690	–
Other liabilities (note 5)	16,982	10,000
Future income tax (note 8)	102,651	67,382
	1,542,939	1,287,462
Shareholders' equity:		
Share capital (note 7(b))	429,613	390,469
Contributed surplus (note 7(g))	39,093	21,977
Retained earnings	201,447	177,446
	670,153	589,892
Subsequent events (note 6)		
Commitments and contingencies (notes 6 and 9)		
	$ 2,213,092	$ 1,877,354

See accompanying notes to consolidated financial statements.

On behalf of the Board:

Clive Beddoe, Director

Wilmot Matthews, Director

YOUR **OWNERS'** MANUAL

>>> **40** >>>

CONSOLIDATED STATEMENTS OF EARNINGS (LOSS) AND RETAINED EARNINGS

WestJet Airlines Ltd.

Years ended December 31, 2005 and 2004
(Stated in Thousands of Dollars, Except Per Share Amounts)

	2005	2004
Revenues:		
Guest revenues	$ 1,207,075	$ 933,407
Charter and other	181,641	119,332
Interest income	6,308	5,251
	1,395,024	1,057,990
Expenses:		
Aircraft fuel	354,065	241,473
Airport operations	219,144	173,604
Flight operations and navigational charges	183,463	148,706
Sales and marketing	124,154	85,186
Depreciation and amortization	106,624	126,338
Maintenance	75,717	78,903
General and administration	69,552	60,953
Aircraft leasing	65,647	41,239
Interest expense	55,496	44,109
Inflight	53,005	43,808
Customer service	27,322	23,570
	1,334,189	1,067,889
Earnings (loss) from operations	60,835	(9,899)
Non-operating income (expense):		
Loss on foreign exchange	(2,729)	(3,224)
Gain (loss) on disposal of property and equipment	(98)	63
	(2,827)	(3,161)
Employee profit share (note 9(b))	6,033	2,916
Earnings (loss) before income taxes	51,975	(15,976)
Income tax expense (recovery) (note 8):		
Current	(7,367)	(4,771)
Future	35,341	5,963
	27,974	1,192
Net earnings (loss)	24,001	(17,168)
Retained earnings, beginning of year	177,446	204,731
Change in accounting policy (note 1(l))	–	(10,117)
Retained earnings, end of year	$ 201,447	$ 177,446
Earnings (loss) per share (note 7(d)):		
Basic	$ 0.19	$ (0.14)
Diluted	$ 0.19	$ (0.14)

See accompanying notes to consolidated financial statements.

CONSOLIDATED STATEMENTS OF CASH FLOWS

WestJet Airlines Ltd.

Years ended December 31, 2005 and 2004
(Stated in Thousands of Dollars)

	2005	2004
Cash provided by (used in):		
Operating activities:		
Net earnings (loss)	$ 24,001	$ (17,168)
Items not involving cash:		
Depreciation and amortization	106,624	126,338
Amortization of other liabilities	(604)	–
Amortization of hedge settlements	1,391	1,391
(Gain) loss on disposal of property and equipment	98	(63)
Stock-based compensation expense	17,604	12,305
Issued from treasury stock	17,705	–
Future income tax expense	35,341	5,963
	202,160	128,766
Decrease in non-cash working capital	46,290	16,697
	248,450	**145,463**
Financing activities:		
Increase in long-term debt	256,385	429,890
Repayment of long-term debt	(100,487)	(75,819)
Increase in other liabilities	8,479	10,000
Issuance of common shares	21,094	13,949
Share issuance costs	(215)	(10)
Increase in other assets	(14,350)	(25,102)
Decrease in obligations under capital lease	(5,846)	(6,381)
	165,060	346,527
Increase in non-cash working capital	(837)	–
	164,223	**346,527**
Investing activities:		
Aircraft additions	(660,947)	(546,242)
Aircraft disposals	404,583	–
Other property and equipment additions	(46,095)	(41,545)
Other property and equipment disposals	894	2,945
	(301,565)	**(584,842)**
Increase (decrease) in cash	111,108	(92,852)
Cash, beginning of year	148,532	241,384
Cash, end of year	$ **259,640**	$ **148,532**

Cash is defined as cash and cash equivalents.

See accompanying notes to consolidated financial statements.

NOTES TO CONSOLIDATED FINANCIAL STATEMENTS

WestJet Airlines Ltd.

Years ended December 31, 2005 and 2004
(Tabular Amounts are Stated in Thousands of Dollars, Except Share and Per Share Data)

1. **Significant accounting policies:**

   (a) Basis of presentation:

   These consolidated financial statements include the accounts of WestJet Airlines Ltd. (the "Corporation") and its wholly owned subsidiaries, as well as the accounts of three special-purpose entities, which are utilized to facilitate the financing of aircraft. The Corporation has no equity ownership in the special-purpose entities; however, the Corporation is the primary beneficiary of the special-purpose entities' operations. All inter-company balances and transactions have been eliminated.

   The preparation of financial statements in conformity with accounting principles generally accepted in Canada requires management to make estimates and assumptions regarding significant items such as amounts relating to depreciation and amortization, non-refundable guest credits, lease return conditions, future income taxes, impairment assessments of property and equipment, and the valuation of derivative financial instruments that affect the amounts reported in the financial statements and accompanying notes. Actual results could differ from these estimates.

   (b) Cash and cash equivalents:

   Cash and cash equivalents are comprised of cash and all investments that are highly liquid in nature and have a maturity date of three months or less. Cash and cash equivalents includes short-term investments of $219,030,000 (2004 – $124,207,000).

   As at December 31, 2005 cash and cash equivalents include US $6,317,000 (2004 – $4,251,000) of restricted cash.

   (c) Revenue recognition:

   Guest and charter revenue is recognized when air transportation is provided. Tickets sold but not yet used are included in the consolidated balance sheet as advance ticket sales.

   The Corporation earns revenue under the tri-branded credit card agreement and is included in other revenue. Net retail sales revenue is recognized at the time the transaction occurs. Revenue related to account activations is deferred and not recognized until the credit file issued for the new activation is used or expires.

   (d) Non-refundable guest credits:

   The Corporation, under certain circumstances, may issue future travel credits which are non-refundable and which expire one year from the date of issue. The utilization of guest credits is recorded as revenue when the guest has flown or upon expiry.

   (e) Foreign currency:

   Monetary assets and liabilities, denominated in foreign currencies, are translated into Canadian dollars at rates of exchange in effect at the balance sheet date. Non-monetary assets and revenue and expense items are translated at rates prevailing when they were acquired or incurred. Foreign exchange gains and losses are included in earnings.

   (f) Inventory:

   Fuel and supplies are valued at the lower of cost and replacement value. Aircraft expendables and consumables are expensed as acquired.

NOTES TO CONSOLIDATED FINANCIAL STATEMENTS

WestJet Airlines Ltd.

Years ended December 31, 2005 and 2004
(Tabular Amounts are Stated in Thousands of Dollars, Except Share and Per Share Data)

1. **Significant accounting policies (continued):**

   (g) Deferred costs:

   Sales and marketing and customer service expenses attributed to advance ticket sales are deferred and expensed in the period the related revenue is recognized. Included in prepaid expenses and deposits are $13,236,000 (2004 - $7,400,000) of deferred costs.

   (h) Property and equipment:

   Property and equipment are recorded at cost and depreciated to their estimated residual values. Aircraft under capital lease are initially recorded at the present value of minimum lease payments at the inception of the lease.

Asset	Basis	Rate
Aircraft net of estimated residual value – Next-Generation	Cycles	Cycles flown
Live satellite television included in Aircraft – Next-Generation	Straight-line	10 years/lease term
Aircraft net of estimated residual value – 200-series	Flight hours	Hours flown
Ground property and equipment	Straight-line	5 to 25 years
Spare engines and parts net of estimated residual value – Next-Generation	Straight-line	20 years
Spare engines and parts net of estimated residual value – 200-series	Flight hours	Fleet hours flown
Aircraft under capital lease	Straight-line	Term of lease
Other assets under capital lease	Straight-line	Term of lease
Buildings	Straight-line	40 years
Leasehold improvements	Straight-line	Term of lease

   Property and equipment is reviewed for impairment whenever events or changes in circumstances indicate that the carrying amount of an asset may not be recoverable. Recoverability of assets to be held and used is measured by a comparison of the carrying amount of an asset to estimated undiscounted future cash flows expected to be generated by the asset. If the carrying amount of an asset exceeds its estimated future cash flows, an impairment charge is recognized by the amount by which the carrying amount of the asset exceeds the fair value of the asset.

   (i) Maintenance costs:

   Maintenance and repairs, including major overhauls, are charged to maintenance expense as they are incurred.

   (j) Capitalized costs:

   Costs associated with assets under development which have probable future economic benefit, which can be clearly defined and measured and are costs incurred for the development of new products or technologies, are capitalized. Interest attributable to funds used to finance property and equipment is capitalized to the related asset. Legal and financing costs for the loan facilities are capitalized to other assets on the balance sheet and amortized on a straight-line basis over the term of the related loan.

   Costs of new route development are expensed as incurred.

(k) Future income tax:

The Corporation uses the liability method of accounting for future income taxes. Under this method, current income taxes are recognized for the estimated income taxes payable for the current year. Future income tax assets and liabilities are recognized for temporary differences between the tax and accounting bases of assets and liabilities, calculated using the currently enacted or substantively enacted tax rates anticipated to apply in the period that the temporary differences are expected to reverse.

(l) Stock-based compensation plans:

On January 1, 2004, the Corporation changed its accounting policy related to stock options granted on or after January 1, 2002. Under the new policy, the Corporation determines the fair value of stock options on their grant date and records this amount as compensation expense over the period that the stock options vest, with a corresponding increase to contributed surplus. The Corporation has retroactively adopted the changes, without restatement of prior periods, on January 1, 2004 which resulted in retained earnings decreasing by $10,117,000 and an offsetting entry to contributed surplus.

As new options are granted, the fair value of these options will be expensed on a straight-line basis over the applicable vesting period, with an offsetting entry to contributed surplus. The fair value of each option grant is estimated on the date of grant using the Black-Scholes option pricing model. Upon the exercise of stock options, consideration received together with amounts previously recorded in contributed surplus is recorded as an increase in share capital.

(m) Financial instruments:

Derivative financial instruments are utilized by the Corporation from time to time in the management of its foreign currency, interest rate and fuel price exposures. The Corporation's policy is not to utilize derivative financial instruments for trading or speculative purposes.

The Corporation formally documents all relationships between hedging instruments and hedged items, as well as its risk management objective and strategy for undertaking various hedge transactions. This process includes linking all derivatives to specific assets and liabilities on the balance sheet or to specific firm commitments or anticipated transactions. The Corporation also formally assesses, both at the hedge's inception and on an ongoing basis, whether the derivatives that are used in hedging transactions are highly effective in offsetting changes in fair values or cash flows of hedged items. In the event that a derivative financial instrument is not designated for hedge accounting, does not qualify for hedge accounting or the event that the hedge is ineffective, changes in the fair value of derivative financial instruments are recorded in non-operating income or expense.

Gains or losses relating to derivatives that are designated as hedges are deferred in other assets and/or other liabilities and recognized in the same period and in the same financial category as the corresponding hedged transactions.

(n) Per share amounts:

Basic per share amounts are calculated using the weighted average number of shares outstanding during the year. Diluted per share amounts are calculated based on the treasury stock method, which assumes that any proceeds obtained on the exercise of options would be used to purchase common shares at the average price during the period. The weighted average number of shares outstanding is then adjusted by the net change.

(o) Comparative figures:

Certain prior-period balances have been reclassified to conform to current period's presentation.

NOTES TO CONSOLIDATED FINANCIAL STATEMENTS

WestJet Airlines Ltd.

Years ended December 31, 2005 and 2004
(Tabular Amounts are Stated in Thousands of Dollars, Except Share and Per Share Data)

2. **Property and equipment:**

2005	Cost	Accumulated depreciation	Net book value
Aircraft – Next-Generation	$ 1,619,850	$ 102,914	$ 1,516,936
Ground property and equipment	135,217	52,664	82,553
Spare engines and parts – Next-Generation	67,960	8,029	59,931
Buildings	39,636	3,825	35,811
Leasehold improvements	6,302	3,992	2,310
Other assets under capital lease	2,289	198	2,091
Spare engines and parts – 200-series	12,547	11,128	1,419
Aircraft – 200-series	3,892	2,861	1,031
Aircraft under capital lease	19,475	19,475	–
	1,907,168	205,086	1,702,082
Deposits on aircraft	73,493	–	73,493
Assets under development	27,922	–	27,922
	$ 2,008,583	$ 205,086	$ 1,803,497

2004	Cost	Accumulated depreciation	Net book value
Aircraft – Next-Generation	$ 1,282,308	$ 46,180	$ 1,236,128
Ground property and equipment	109,334	34,586	74,748
Spare engines and parts – Next-Generation	52,641	4,777	47,864
Buildings	39,636	2,840	36,796
Leasehold improvements	5,655	3,104	2,551
Spare engines and parts – 200-series	24,397	16,523	7,874
Aircraft – 200-series	142,657	121,182	21,475
Aircraft under capital lease	31,304	26,781	4,523
	1,687,932	255,973	1,431,959
Deposits on aircraft	156,943	–	156,943
Assets under development	12,644	–	12,644
	$ 1,857,519	$ 255,973	$ 1,601,546

In 2004, the Corporation made the decision to accelerate the retirement dates of its older Boeing 737-200 aircraft to have virtually all 200-series aircraft retired by the end of 2005 rather than in 2008 as contemplated under the previous fleet plan. As a result of the accelerated retirement dates on the 200-series aircraft, the Corporation evaluated the recoverability of the aircraft and the related rotable parts and equipment, and the 200-series flight simulator (the "200-series assets"). This analysis indicated the estimated undiscounted future cash flows generated by these 200-series assets on a specific asset by asset basis were less than their carrying values. As a result, the carrying values of the 200-series assets were reduced to fair market value which resulted in an impairment loss of $47,577,000 which was included in the depreciation and amortization expense for the year ended December 31, 2004. Management estimated fair market value using third-party appraisals and recent sales and leasing transactions with consideration made for the currently available market for 200-series assets.

During the year, property and equipment was acquired at an aggregate cost of $2,137,000 (2004 – $NIL) by means of capital leases.

During 2005, the Corporation disposed of 13 200-series aircraft to an unrelated third party and entered into an agreement to sell the remaining spare engines, parts and flight simulator. This transaction will be completed in early 2006.

During the year the Corporation capitalized $3,250,000 (2004 – $3,675,000) of interest.

Included in Aircraft – Next-Generation are estimated lease return costs for these aircraft under operating leases totaling $1,107,000 (2004 – $NIL). These amounts are amortized on the straight-line basis over the term of each lease.

3. **Other assets:**

		2005		2004
Financing fees	$	50,010	$	39,138
Security deposits on aircraft and other leaseholds		32,086		24,563
Hedge settlements		19,479		19,479
Other amounts		1,017		562
NAV Canada security deposit		–		4,500
Accumulated amortization		(12,573)		(7,509)
	$	90,019	$	80,733

Financing fees are related to the facility for the purchase of 39 Boeing Next-Generation aircraft and hedge settlements relate to certain leased Boeing Next-Generation aircraft. Amortization of financing fees totalling $3,673,000 (2004 - $2,753,000) has been included in depreciation and amortization and amortization of hedge settlements totalling $1,391,000 (2004 - $1,391,000) has been included in aircraft leasing for the year ended December 31, 2005.

NOTES TO CONSOLIDATED FINANCIAL STATEMENTS

WestJet Airlines Ltd.

Years ended December 31, 2005 and 2004
(Tabular Amounts are Stated in Thousands of Dollars, Except Share and Per Share Data)

4. Long-term debt:

	2005	2004
$1,304,197,000 in 33 individual term loans, amortized on a straight-line basis over a 12-year term, repayable in quarterly principal instalments ranging from $697,000 to $955,000, guaranteed by the Ex-Im Bank, secured by 30 700-series and three 600-series aircraft, and maturing between 2014 through 2017. 30 of these facilities include fixed rate weighted average interest at 5.39%. The remaining three facilities, totalling $104,786,000, includes weighted average floating interest at the Canadian LIBOR rate plus 0.08% (effective interest rate of 3.28% as at December 31, 2005) until after the first scheduled repayment date in January 2006, after such time the interest rate will be fixed at a weighted average rate of 4.89% for the remaining period the loans are outstanding.	$ 1,114,506	$ 954,674
$26,000,000 in two individual term loans, repayable in monthly instalments of $109,000 and $161,000 including floating interest at the bank's prime rate plus 0.88% with an effective interest rate of 5.88% at December 31, 2005, maturing in July 2008, secured by two Next-Generation flight simulators.	19,615	21,684
$12,000,000 term loan, repayable in monthly instalments of $108,000 including interest at 9.03%, maturing April 2011, secured by the Calgary hangar facility.	10,767	11,075
$12,657,000 in 18 individual term loans, amortized on a straight-line basis over a five-year term, repayable in quarterly principal instalments ranging from $29,000 to $47,000 including floating interest at the Canadian LIBOR rate plus 0.08%, with a weighted average effective interest rate of 3.39% at December 31, 2005, maturing in 2009 and 2010, guaranteed by the Ex-Im Bank and secured by certain 700-series and 600-series aircraft.	10,462	6,303
$4,550,000 term loan, repayable in monthly instalments of $50,000, including floating interest at the bank's prime rate plus 0.50%, with an effective interest rate of 5.50% as at December 31, 2005, maturing April 2013, secured by the Calgary hangar facility.	3,484	3,899
$22,073,000 in six individual term loans, repayable in monthly instalments ranging from $25,000 to $87,000 including fixed rate weighted average interest at 8.43% having matured in October 2005.	–	5,301
	1,158,834	1,002,936
Less current portion	114,115	97,305
	$ 1,044,719	$ 905,631

The net book value of the property and equipment pledged as collateral for the Corporation's secured borrowings was $1,549,107,000 as at December 31, 2005 (2004 – $1,288,497,000).

Held within the special-purpose entities, as described in note 1, are liabilities of $1,392,629,000 (2004 – $1,178,239,000) and corresponding assets of $1,393,801,000 (2004 – $1,178,342,000), which are included in the consolidated financial statements.

Future scheduled repayments of long-term debt are as follows:

2006	$ 114,115
2007	114,300
2008	127,279
2009	111,514
2010	110,660
2011 and thereafter	580,966
	$ 1,158,834

During the year, the Corporation converted US $402 million of preliminary commitments with the Export-Import Bank of the United States ("Ex-Im Bank") into a final commitment to support the acquisition of five Boeing Next-Generation 737-700 aircraft and eight Boeing Next-Generation 737-600 aircraft, their related live satellite television systems and installation of winglets on the 600-series aircraft, to be delivered between July 2005 and July 2006. As at December 31, 2005 the unutilized and uncancelled balance of the final commitment from Ex-Im Bank was US $188.8 million. In addition, Ex-Im Bank has provided a preliminary commitment of US $324 million to cover an additional 10 aircraft to be delivered between July 2006 and November 2007.

During the year, the Corporation completed financing arrangements for US $386 million supported by loan guarantees from the Ex-Im Bank on 13 aircraft as outlined above. This facility will be drawn in Canadian dollars, in separate instalments, with 12-year terms for each new aircraft. Each loan will be amortized on a straight-line basis over the 12-year term with quarterly principal instalments, and interest calculated on the outstanding balance. As at December 31, 2005 the Corporation has taken delivery of the first seven aircraft under this facility and has drawn a total of $256.4 million (US $213.2 million).

The Corporation is charged a commitment fee of 0.125% per annum on the unutilized and uncancelled balance of the Ex-Im Bank final commitment, payable at specified dates and upon delivery of an aircraft, and is charged a 3% exposure fee on the financed portion of the aircraft price, payable upon delivery of an aircraft.

The Corporation has available a facility with a Canadian chartered bank of $8,000,000 (2004 – $8,000,000) for letters of guarantee. At December 31, 2005, letters of guarantee totaling $6,830,000 (2004 – $7,977,000) have been issued under this facility. The facility is secured by a general security agreement and an assignment of insurance proceeds.

Cash interest paid during the year was $54,688,000 (2004 – $42,346,000).

NOTES TO CONSOLIDATED FINANCIAL STATEMENTS

WestJet Airlines Ltd.

Years ended December 31, 2005 and 2004
(Tabular Amounts are Stated in Thousands of Dollars, Except Share and Per Share Data)

5. Other liabilities:

Included in other liabilities is $8,000,000 (2004 - $10,000,000) of unearned revenue related to the BMO Mosaik® MasterCard®* with the AIR MILES®† Reward Option for future net retail sales and for bounty on newly activated credit cards. During the year ended December 31, 2005, the Corporation recognized $2,000,000 (2004 – $NIL) of this unearned revenue. The remaining unearned revenue balance will be recognized during the next three years with $2,000,000 earned in 2006 and $3,000,000 in each of 2007 and 2008.

At December 31, 2005, included in other liabilities are deferred gains from the sale and leaseback of aircraft in 2005 totaling $7,875,000, net of amortization, which are being deferred and amortized over the lease term with the amortization included in aircraft leasing. During the year ended December 31, 2005 the Corporation recognized amortization of $604,000.

The Corporation has also included in other liabilities $1,107,000 pertaining to the estimated lease return costs on its Next-Generation leased aircraft.

6. Leases:

The Corporation has entered into operating leases and agreements for aircraft, buildings, computer hardware and software licenses and satellite programming, as well as capital leases relating to aircraft and ground handling equipment. The obligations are as follows (see note 9 for additional commitments):

	Capital Leases	Operating Leases
2006	$ 2,622	$ 91,340
2007	411	96,821
2008	411	97,833
2009	411	94,350
2010	665	85,203
2011 and thereafter	–	373,670
Total lease payments	4,520	$ 839,217
Less imputed interest at 6.09%	(364)	
Net minimum lease payments	4,156	
Less current portion of obligations under capital lease	(2,466)	
Obligations under capital lease	$ 1,690	

The Corporation has US dollar capital lease obligations totaling $1,900,000 for 2006 which have been included at their Canadian dollar equivalent in the table above.

The US dollar amounts of operating leases which have been included at their Canadian dollar equivalent above are: 2006 – $67,468,000, 2007 – $75,507,000, 2008 – $77,276,000, 2009 – $77,264,000, 2010 – $70,636,000, 2011 and thereafter – $304,837,000.

Subsequent to December 31, 2005, the Corporation entered into an agreement with an independent third party to lease two 737-700 aircraft to be delivered during February and April 2007 for an eight-year term in US dollars. These amounts have been included at their Canadian dollar equivalent in the preceding table.

7. **Share capital:**

The non-voting common shares and the non-voting preferred shares are subject to limitations to be fixed by the Board of Directors.

(a) Authorized:

Unlimited number of common voting shares:

The common voting shares may be owned and controlled by Canadians only and shall confer the right to one vote per common voting share at all meetings of shareholders of the Corporation.

Each issued and outstanding common voting share shall be converted into one variable voting share automatically and without any further act of the Corporation or the holder, if such common voting share becomes owned or controlled by a person who is not a Canadian.

Unlimited number of variable voting shares:

The variable voting shares may be owned and controlled only by persons who are not Canadians and are entitled to one vote per variable voting share unless (i) the number of issued and outstanding variable voting shares exceed 25% of the total number of all issued and outstanding variable voting shares and common voting shares (or any greater percentage the Governor in Council may specify pursuant to the Canada Transportation Act), or (ii) the total number of votes cast by or on behalf of the holders of variable voting shares at any meeting on any matter on which a vote is to be taken exceeds 25% (or any greater percentage the Governor in Council may specify pursuant to the Canada Transportation Act) of the total number of votes that may be cast at such meeting.

If either of the above-noted thresholds are surpassed at any time, the vote attached to each variable voting share will decrease automatically without further act of formality. Under the circumstances described above, the variable voting shares as a class cannot carry more than 25% (or any greater percentage the Governor in Council may specify pursuant to the Canada Transportation Act) of the total voting rights attached to the aggregate number of issued and outstanding variable voting shares and common voting shares of the Corporation.

Under the circumstances described above, the variable voting shares as a class cannot, for a given shareholders' meeting, carry more than 25% (or any greater percentage the Governor in Council may specify pursuant to the Canada Transportation Act) of the total number of votes that may be cast at the meeting.

Each issued and outstanding variable voting share shall be automatically converted into one common voting share without any further intervention on the part of the Corporation or of the holder if (i) the variable voting share is or becomes owned and controlled by a Canadian; or if (ii) the provisions contained in the Canada Transportation Act relating to foreign ownership restrictions are repealed and not replaced with other similar provisions in applicable legislation.

Unlimited number of non-voting shares

Unlimited number of non-voting first, second and third preferred shares

NOTES TO CONSOLIDATED FINANCIAL STATEMENTS

WestJet Airlines Ltd.

Years ended December 31, 2005 and 2004
(Tabular Amounts are Stated in Thousands of Dollars, Except Share and Per Share Data)

7. **Share capital (continued):**

(b) Issued and outstanding:

On August 30, 2005, the Corporation's common shares were restructured into two classes of shares: common voting shares and variable voting shares. Each issued and outstanding common share which was not owned and controlled by a Canadian within the meaning of the Canada Transportation Act was converted into one variable voting share and the common share was cancelled. Each issued and outstanding common share which was owned and controlled by a Canadian within the meaning of the Canada Transportation Act was converted into one common voting share and the common share was cancelled.

	2005		2004	
	Number	Amount	Number	Amount
Common and variable voting shares:				
Balance, beginning of year	125,497,407	$ 390,469	123,882,490	$ 376,081
Exercise of options	1,333,791	3,389	1,611,721	13,949
Stock-based compensation expense	–	488	–	445
Issued from treasury (see note 7(e))	2,743,901	35,410	–	–
Issued on rounding of stock split	–	–	3,196	–
Share issuance costs	–	(215)	–	(10)
Tax benefit of issue costs	–	72	–	4
Balance, end of year	129,575,099	$ 429,613	125,497,407	$ 390,469

As at December 31, 2005, the number of common voting shares and variable voting shares amounted to 119,378,637 and 10,196,462 respectively.

(c) Stock Option Plan:

The Corporation has a Stock Option Plan, whereby up to a maximum of 12,683,000 common voting shares may be issued to officers and employees of the Corporation subject to the following limitations:

(i)   the number of common voting shares reserved for issuance to any one optionee will not exceed 5% of the issued and outstanding common and variable voting shares at any time;

(ii) the number of common voting shares reserved for issuance to insiders shall not exceed 10% of the issued and outstanding common and variable voting shares; and

(iii) the number of common voting shares issuable under the Stock Option Plan, which may be issued within a one-year period, shall not exceed 10% of the issued and outstanding common and variable voting shares at any time.

Stock options are granted at a price that equals the market value, have a term of four years and vest on either the first, second or third anniversary from the date of grant.

(c) Stock Option Plan (continued):

Changes in the number of options, with their weighted average exercise prices, are summarized below:

| | 2005 | | 2004 | |
	Number of options	Weighted average exercise price	Number of options	Weighted average exercise price
Stock options outstanding, beginning of year	10,682,082	$ 12.37	9,809,753	$ 10.78
Granted	4,474,184	14.46	2,927,875	15.73
Exercised	(3,506,625)	9.82	(1,959,002)	9.42
Cancelled	(147,309)	14.53	(96,544)	12.83
Repurchased	(66,724)	11.99	–	–
Expired	(6,890)	13.79	–	–
Stock options outstanding, end of year	11,428,718	$ 13.94	10,682,082	$ 12.37
Exercisable, end of year	3,920,623	$ 12.24	4,694,357	$ 10.88

The following table summarizes the options outstanding and exercisable at December 31, 2005:

| | Outstanding Options | | | Exercisable Options | |
Range of Exercise Prices	Number Outstanding	Weighted Average Remaining Life (years)	Weighted Average Exercise Price	Number Exercisable	Weighted Average Exercise Price
$9.74 - $11.81	2,749,040	1.39	$ 11.21	2,380,430	$ 11.21
$11.99 - $14.60	5,838,130	2.54	14.53	1,540,193	13.82
$14.93 - $18.41	2,841,548	2.35	15.78	–	–
	11,428,718	2.22	$ 13.94	3,920,623	$ 12.24

Under the terms of the Corporation's Stock Option Plan, a cashless settlement alternative is available whereby option holders can either (a) elect to receive shares by delivering cash to the Corporation or (b) elect to receive a number of shares equivalent to the difference between the market value of the options and the aggregate exercise price. For the year ended December 31, 2005, options holders exercised 3,151,923 (2004 – 449,635) options on a cashless settlement basis and received 979,089 (2004 – 102,354) shares.

Certain executives holding total options of 66,724, at an exercise price of $11.99, offered the Corporation an opportunity to purchase and cancel their options in consideration of payment by the Corporation in cash for a fixed price of $320,000. The agreements were accepted by the Corporation and the options were cancelled.

NOTES TO CONSOLIDATED FINANCIAL STATEMENTS

WestJet Airlines Ltd.

Years ended December 31, 2005 and 2004
(Tabular Amounts are Stated in Thousands of Dollars, Except Share and Per Share Data)

7. Share capital (continued):

(d) Per share amounts:

The following table summarizes the shares used in calculating net earnings (loss) per share:

	2005	2004
Weighted average number of shares outstanding – basic	128,031,694	125,071,208
Effect of dilutive employee stock options	392,408	–
Weighted average number of shares outstanding – diluted	128,424,102	125,071,208

For the year ended December 31, 2005, a total of 8,672,329 (2004 – 10,682,082) options were not included in the calculation of dilutive potential shares as the result would be anti-dilutive.

(e) Employee Share Purchase Plan:

The Corporation has an Employee Share Purchase Plan ("ESPP") whereby the Corporation matches every dollar contributed by each employee. Under the terms of the ESPP, employees may contribute up to a maximum of 20% of their gross pay and acquire common voting shares of the Corporation at the current fair market value of such shares.

Current market price for common shares issued from treasury is determined based on weighted average trading price of the common shares on the Toronto Stock Exchange for the five trading days preceding the issuance.

The Corporation has the option to acquire common voting shares on behalf of employees through open market purchases or to issue new shares from treasury at the current market price. For the period January to October 2005, shares under the ESPP were issued from treasury at the current market price. Subsequent to this period, the Corporation elected to purchase these shares through the open market and will continue to review this option in the future. For the year ended December 31, 2005, $17,705,000 (2004 – $NIL) of common shares were issued from treasury, representing the Corporation's matching contribution from treasury for employee contributions, for which no cash was exchanged.

Shares acquired from the ESPP are held in trust for one year. Employees may offer to sell common shares, which have not been held for at least one year, on January 1 and July 1 of each year, to the Corporation for 50% of the then current market price.

The Corporation's share of the contributions is recorded as compensation expense and amounted to $21,690,000 (2004 – $18,655,000).

(f) Stock-based compensation:

The fair value of each option grant is estimated on the date of grant using the Black-Scholes option pricing model. The following weighted average assumptions were used to determine the fair market value of options granted during the years ended December 31:

	2005	2004
Weighted average fair market value per option	$ 5.26	$ 5.83
Average risk-free interest rate	3.4%	3.7%
Average volatility	43%	45%
Expected life (years)	3.7	3.5
Dividend per share	$ 0.00	$ 0.00

Employee stock option compensation expense is included in flight operations and general and administration expenses and totaled $17,604,000 (2004 - $12,305,000), net of repurchase of $320,000 (2004 – $NIL) as noted in 7(c).

(g) Contributed surplus:

Changes to contributed surplus were as follows:

	2005	2004
Balance, beginning of year	$ 21,977	$ –
Stock-based compensation – adoption	–	10,117
Stock-based compensation expense	17,604	12,305
Stock-options exercised	(488)	(445)
Balance, end of year	$ 39,093	$ 21,977

NOTES TO CONSOLIDATED FINANCIAL STATEMENTS

WestJet Airlines Ltd.

Years ended December 31, 2005 and 2004
(Tabular Amounts are Stated in Thousands of Dollars, Except Share and Per Share Data)

8. **Income taxes:**

Income taxes vary from the amount that would be computed by applying the basic Federal and Provincial tax rate of 35.04% (2004 – 35.38%) to earnings (loss) before income taxes as follows:

	2005	2004
Expected income tax provision	$ 18,212	$ (5,652)
Add (deduct):		
Non-deductible expenses	1,219	986
Non-deductible stock-based compensation	6,208	4,329
Non-taxable portion of capital gains	(1,470)	–
Large corporation tax and capital taxes	5,009	3,721
Future tax rate reductions	(1,426)	(1,739)
Other	222	(453)
	$ 27,974	$ 1,192

The components of the net future income tax liability are as follows:

	2005	2004
Future income tax liability:		
Property and equipment	$ 148,467	$ 69,547
Future income tax asset:		
Share issue costs	(1,368)	(2,165)
Non-capital losses	(44,448)	–
Net future income tax liability	$ 102,651	$ 67,382

Cash taxes paid during the year were $10,151,000 (2004 – $7,903,000).

The Corporation has recognized a benefit on $126.3 million of non-capital losses which are available for carry forward to reduce taxable income in future years. These losses are scheduled to expire in the year 2014.

---

9. **Commitments and contingencies:**

(a) Aircraft:

The Corporation has remaining commitments to purchase 10 737-600s and nine 737-700s to be delivered over the course of 2006 through to 2008.

The Corporation has signed an agreement with Aviation Partners Boeing to install Blended Winglet Technology on certain of the Corporation's committed Boeing Next-Generation aircraft, including leased aircraft.

The Corporation has an agreement with LiveTV to install, maintain and operate live satellite television on all aircraft with the ability to cancel installing the system on future aircraft deliveries, subject to certain applicable penalties. This agreement contains an exclusivity clause which expires on July 1, 2009.

The Corporation has signed an agreement with Bell ExpressVu for a seven-year term to provide satellite programming. The agreement commenced in 2004 and can be renewed for an additional five years.

The remaining estimated amounts to be paid in deposits and purchase prices in US dollars relating to the purchases of the remaining aircraft, live satellite television systems and winglets are $368,154,000 for 2006, $143,540,000 for 2007 and $110,809,000 for 2008.

The Corporation also has an agreement to purchase a Next-Generation flight simulator, where remaining instalments for 2006 is $3,640,000.

(b) Employee profit share:

The Corporation has an employee profit sharing plan whereby eligible employees participate in the pre-tax operating income of the Corporation. The profit share ranges from a minimum of 10% to a maximum of 20% of earnings before employee profit share and income taxes. The amounts paid under the plan are subject to prior approval by the Board of Directors.

(c) Contingencies:

An Amended Fresh as Amended Statement of Claim was filed by Air Canada and ZIP Air Inc. in the Ontario Superior Court on March 11, 2005 (amending the original Statement of Claim filed on April 6, 2004) against the Corporation, two officers, two employees, two former officers, and one former employee (the "Defendants"). The principal allegations are that the Defendants unlawfully obtained confidential flight load and load factor information from Air Canada's employee travel website and, as a result, the Plaintiffs are seeking disgorgement of any incremental revenue, profits and other benefits acquired by the Defendants as a result of having access to the alleged confidential information. The Plaintiffs are claiming disgorgement, damages for the tort of spoliation and punitive damages in the aggregate amount of $220 million, but the Plaintiffs have provided no meaningful details or evidence to substantiate their claim for disgorgement and damages.

A Statement of Claim was also filed by Jetsgo Corporation in the Ontario Superior Court on October 15, 2004 against the Corporation, an officer, and a former officer (the "Defendants"). The principal allegations are that the Defendants conspired together to unlawfully obtain Jetsgo's proprietary information and to use this proprietary information to harm Jetsgo and benefit the Corporation. The Plaintiff is seeking damages in an amount to be determined plus $50 million, but the Plaintiff has provided no details or evidence to substantiate its claim. On May 13, 2005 Jetsgo Corporation

NOTES TO CONSOLIDATED FINANCIAL STATEMENTS

WestJet Airlines Ltd.

Years ended December 31, 2005 and 2004
(Tabular Amounts are Stated in Thousands of Dollars, Except Share and Per Share Data)

---

9. Commitments and contingencies (continued):

(c) Contingencies (continued):

declared Bankruptcy. As a result, this action has been stayed and no further steps can be taken in the litigation unless a court order is obtained.

Based on the results to date of (i) an internal investigation, (ii) advice from independent industry experts, and (iii) cross-examinations of witnesses in the Air Canada proceedings, and (iv) evidence filed by the Plaintiffs in support of various court applications, management believes the amounts claimed are substantially without merit. The amount of loss, if any, to the Corporation as a result of these two claims cannot be reasonably estimated. The defence and investigation of these claims are continuing.

The Corporation is party to other legal proceedings and claims that arise during the ordinary course of business. It is the opinion of management that the ultimate outcome of these matters will not have a material effect upon the Corporation's financial position, results of operations or cash flows.

10. Financial instruments and risk management:

(a) Fuel risk management:

The Corporation periodically utilizes short-term and long-term financial and physical derivative instruments to mitigate its exposure to fluctuations in jet fuel prices and accounts for these derivatives as cash flow hedges. For the year ended December 31, 2005, the Corporation recognized a net gain of $155,000 in aircraft fuel resulting from hedging transactions.

As at December 31, 2005, the Corporation has outstanding hedge contracts representing approximately 50%, 40% and 11% respectively of January, February and March anticipated fuel consumption at a rate of $0.572/litre, $0.580/litre and $0.562/litre. The total fair market value of the unsettled contracts as at December 31, 2005 is an estimated loss of $1,300,000.

(b) Foreign currency exchange risk:

The Corporation is exposed to foreign currency fluctuations as certain ongoing expenses are referenced to US dollar denominated prices. The Corporation periodically uses financial instruments, including foreign exchange forward contracts and options, to manage its exposure.

The Corporation has entered into a contract to purchase US $2.5 million per month at a forward rate of 1.22 for the payment period from March 2005 to February 2006 to hedge a portion of the Corporation's committed US dollar lease payments during the same period. The estimated fair market value of the remaining portion of the contract as at December 31, 2005 is a loss of $300,000.

Included in cash and cash equivalents at December 31, 2005 is US $35,453,000 (2004 – US $28,440,000).

(c) Interest rate risk:

The Corporation is exposed to interest rate fluctuations on variable interest rate debt (see note 4).

The Corporation has entered into forward starting interest rate agreements at rates between 4.98% and 5.00% on six future aircraft deliveries, effective from the period April 2006 and July 2006.

(d) Credit risk:

The Corporation does not believe it is subject to any significant concentration of credit risk. Most of the Corporation's receivables result from tickets sold to individual guests through the use of major credit cards and travel agents. These receivables are short-term, generally being settled shortly after the sale. The Corporation manages the credit exposure related to financial instruments by selecting counter parties based on credit ratings, limiting its exposure to any single counter party and monitoring the market position of the program and its relative market position with each counter party.

(e) Ontario Teachers' Financing Agreement:

The Corporation had an agreement with Ontario Teachers' Pension Plan Board ("Ontario Teachers") for the right to require Ontario Teachers to purchase up to $100,000,000 of common shares, which expired in 2004. The Corporation elected not to exercise the financing agreement and has included the 1% annual standby fee in general and administration expenses for the year ended December 31, 2004.

(f) Fair value of financial instruments:

The carrying amounts of financial instruments included in the balance sheet, other than long-term debt, approximate their fair value due to their short term to maturity.

At December 31, 2005, the fair value of long-term debt was approximately $1.2 billion (2004 – $1.1 billion). The fair value of long-term debt is determined by discounting the future contractual cash flows under current financing arrangements at discount rates which represent borrowing rates presently available to the Corporation for loans with similar terms and maturity.

APPENDIX II

Chart of Accounts

Assets

Current Assets

101 Cash
102 Petty Cash
103 Cash equivalents
104 Trading investments
105 Allowance to reduce temporary investments to market
106 Accounts receivable
107 Allowance for doubtful accounts
108 GST receivable
109 Interest receivable
110 Rent receivable
111 Notes receivable
119 Merchandise inventory
120 _____ inventory
124 Office supplies
125 Store supplies
126 _____ supplies
128 Prepaid insurance
129 Prepaid _____
131 Prepaid rent
132 Raw materials inventory
133 Goods in process inventory, _____
135 Finished goods inventory

Long-Term Investments

141 Investment in ____ shares
142 Investment in ____ bonds
144 Investment in _____

Property, Plant, and Equipment

151 Automobiles
152 Accumulated amortization, automobiles
153 Trucks
154 Accumulated amortization, trucks
159 Library
160 Accumulated amortization, library
161 Furniture

162 Accumulated amortization, furniture
163 Office equipment
164 Accumulated amortization, office equipment
165 Store equipment
166 Accumulated amortization, store equipment
167 _____ equipment
168 Accumulated amortization, _____ equipment
169 Machinery
170 Accumulated amortization, machinery
173 Building _____
174 Accumulated amortization, building _____
175 Land
176 Leasehold improvements
179 Land improvements, _____
180 Accumulated amortization, land improvements _____

Natural Resources

185 Mineral deposit
186 Accumulated amortization, mineral deposit

Intangible Assets

191 Patents
192 Accumulated amortization, patents
193 Leasehold
194 Accumulated amortization, leasehold
195 Franchise
196 Accumulated amortization, franchise
197 Copyright
198 Accumulated amortization, copyright
199 Organization costs
200 Accumulated amortization, organization costs
201 Goodwill
202 Accumulated amortization, _____

Liabilities

Current Liabilities

201 Accounts payable
202 Insurance payable
203 Interest payable
204 Legal fees payable
205 Short-term notes payable
206 Discount on short-term notes payable
208 Rent payable
209 Salaries payable
210 Wages payable
214 Estimated warranty liability
215 Income taxes payable
216 Common dividends payable
217 Preferred dividends payable
218 EI payable
219 CPP payable
221 Employees' medical insurance payable
222 Employees' retirement program payable
223 Employees' union dues payable
224 PST payable
225 GST payable
226 Estimated vacation pay liability

Unearned Revenues

230 Unearned consulting fees
231 Unearned legal fees
232 Unearned property management fees
233 Unearned _____

Long-Term Liabilities

251 Long-term notes payable
252 Discount on notes payable
253 Long-term lease liability
255 Bonds payable
256 Discount on bonds payable
257 Premium on bonds payable

Equity

Owner's Equity

301 _____ , capital
302 _____ , withdrawals

Corporate Contributed Capital

307 Common shares
310 Common share dividends distributable
313 Contributed capital from the retirement of common shares
315 Preferred shares

Retained Earnings

318 Retained earnings
319 Cash dividends
320 Share dividends

Revenues

401 _____ fees earned
403 _____ services revenue
405 Commission earned
406 Rent earned
407 Dividends earned
408 Earnings from investment in _____
409 Interest earned
413 Sales
414 Sales returns and allowances
415 Sales discounts

Cost of Sales

502 Cost of goods sold
503 Amortization of mine deposit
505 Purchases
506 Purchases returns and allowances
507 Purchases discounts
508 Transportation-in

Manufacturing Accounts

520 Raw materials purchases
521 Freight-in on raw materials
530 Factory payroll
531 Direct labour
540 Factory overhead
541 Indirect materials
542 Indirect labour
543 Factory insurance expired
544 Factory supervision
545 Factory supplies used
546 Factory utilities
547 Miscellaneous production costs
548 Property taxes on factory building
550 Rent on factory building
551 Repairs, factory equipment
552 Small tools written off
560 Amortization of factory equipment
561 Amortization of factory building

Standard Cost Variance Accounts

580 Direct material quantity variance
581 Direct material price variance
582 Direct labour quantity variance
583 Direct labour price variance
584 Factory overhead volume variance
585 Factory overhead controllable variance

Expenses

Amortization

602 Amortization expense, copyrights
604 Amortization expense, automobiles
605 Amortization expense, _____

Employee Related Expense

620 Office salaries expense
621 Sales salaries expense
622 Salaries expense
623 _____ wages expense
624 Employees' benefits expense

Financial Expenses

630 Brokerage fee expense
631 Cash over and short
633 Interest expense

Insurance Expenses

636 Insurance expense, building
637 Insurance expense, _____

Rental Expenses

640 Rent expense
641 Rent expense, office space
642 Rent expense, _____

Supplies Expense

650 Office supplies expense
651 _____ supplies expense

Other Expenses

655 Advertising expense
656 Bad debts expense
659 Collection expense
662 Credit card expense
663 Delivery expense
667 Equipment expense
668 Food and drinks expense
671 Gas and oil expense
673 Janitorial expense
674 Legal fees expense
676 Mileage expense
682 Postage expense
683 Property taxes expense
684 Repairs expense, _____
688 Telephone expense
689 Travel and entertaining expense
690 Utilities expense
691 Warranty expense
695 Income taxes expense
696 _____ expense

Gains and Losses

701 Gain on retirement of bonds
702 Gain on sale of machinery
703 Gain on sale of investments
705 Gain on _____
805 Loss on retirement of bonds
806 Loss on sale of investments
807 Loss on sale of machinery
809 Loss on _____
810 Unrealized holding gain
811 Unrealized holding loss

Clearing Accounts

901 Income summary
902 Manufacturing summary

Credits

Danier Leather Company logo © Danier Leather Company
WestJet Ltd. logo © WestJet Ltd.

Chapter 12
Page 589: © Creatas/PunchStock

Chapter 13
Page 652: © Steve Cole/Getty Images

Chapter 14
Page 694: © PhotoLink/Getty Images

Chapter 15
Page 734: Cover from *Love You Forever* by Robert Munsch, illustrated by Sheila McGraw, reproduced by permission of Firefly Books Ltd.

Chapter 16
Page 788: © Royalty-Free/CORBIS

Chapter 17
Page 834: © Dynamic Graphics/Jupiter Images

Chapter 18
Page 895: © Royalty-Free/CORBIS

Chapter 19
Page 936: © Royalty-Free/Getty Images

Chapter 20
Page 1001: © Mark Downey/Getty Images

Appendix I
pp. I-1 – I-16 © Danier Leather Company; pp. I-17 – I-39 © WestJet Ltd.

Index

Summary of Focus on Financial Statement Online Companies—Volume 2

Extend Your Knowledge (EYK) Index—Volume 2